W9-CLE-016

NATURAL RESOURCES
Allocation, economics and policy

NATURAL RESOURCES
Allocation, economics and policy

JUDITH REES

METHUEN
London and New York

First published in 1985 by
Methuen & Co. Ltd
11 New Fetter Lane, London EC4P 4EE

Published in the USA by
Methuen & Co.
in association with Methuen, Inc.
29 West 35th Street, New York, NY 10001

© 1985 Judith A. Rees

Photoset by Rowland Phototypesetting Ltd
and printed in Great Britain
by St Edmundsbury Press, Bury St Edmunds, Suffolk

All rights reserved. No part of this book may be reprinted or
reproduced or utilized in any form or by any electronic,
mechanical or other means, now known or hereafter invented,
including photocopying and recording, or in any information
storage or retrieval system, without permission in writing from the
publishers.

British Library Cataloguing in Publication Data

Rees, Judith
Natural resources : allocation, economics
and policy.
1. Natural resources
I. Title
333.7   HC55
ISBN 0-416-31990-4
ISBN 0-416-32000-7 Pbk

Library of Congress Cataloging in Publication Data

Rees, Judith A. (Judith Anne), 1944–
Natural resources.

Bibliography: p.
Includes index.
1. Environmental policy.   2. Natural resources—
Government policy.   I. Title.
HC79.E5R432   1985   333.7   85-13569
ISBN 0-416-31990-4
ISBN 0-416-32000-7

Contents

List of plates

List of figures

List of tables

Preface and acknowledgements

Over the last twenty-five years a plethora of natural resource crises have commanded public, political and academic attention. The problems have seemingly been highly diverse. They encompass concerns over declining environmental quality standards, the possibly irreparable damage being inflicted on global life support systems, the suffering caused by drought and desertification, the imminent physical exhaustion of mineral stocks, the economic and security threats posed by politically motivated disruptions to resource trade, and the possibility that the world economic system will collapse unless a new, more equitable, set of trading relationships can be established between the north and south. However, all these problems ultimately boil down to conflict between different social, economic and political interests over who should benefit from the exploitation of the natural resource base. The fundamental point at issue is the way natural resources, and the wealth or welfare derived from them, are distributed over space and time.

The allocative theme is central to this book. It seeks to explain the processes operating to produce current resource and welfare allocations; to evaluate the resulting outcomes; to analyse who has the power to determine the distributive patterns; and assess the role and efficacy of public policy measures to affect significant change in the allocative system.

There are, of course, no simple explanations and it is clear that effective enquiry into such issues cannot occur from any one ideological or disciplinary perspective. An attempt has, therefore, been made to consider a range of interpretations and to integrate material from various academic disciplines. However, it is inevitable that the analysis will reflect my own disciplinary training and personal prejudices. Natural resources are obviously a polyglot group, ranging from mineral substances to the services of global bio-geochemical cycles, and for the most part analysts have tended to treat mineral and environmental quality resources as two quite distinct and separate subjects of enquiry. Although there are clearly important differences in the way these resource sectors operate, I thought it important to consider both in this volume. Not only do decisions on the exploitation of stock minerals have crucial implications for the supply and quality of environmental goods and services, but also, from an allocative viewpoint, the principles and issues involved are remarkably similar for the two resource types. The economic and political forces at work to produce the spatial inequalities in mineral consumption and mineral-derived wealth also operate to influence the temporal and spatial availability of environmental quality and other renewable resource flows. The underlying problems involved in developing and implementing effective public policies are shared by the two sectors. And the same package of conceptual tools and notions are required for the study of both. However, by deciding on this width of coverage, it has proved necessary to be selective, using detailed information on specific resources or particular countries only to illustrate the basic concepts and issues.

An attempt has been made to draw on material from the broad range of *social science* disciplines which currently contribute to the analysis of natural resource issues. However, no single authored text can be truly interdisciplinary, in the sense that it treats all perspectives with equal depth and authority. Inevitably, the author's academic specialisms must dominate and, in this instance, it means that the basic disciplinary orientation is towards geography and applied economics. Although economic concepts are used throughout, these are employed only when they either aid our understanding of the allocative questions which provide the central focus of the book, or have had an important impact on resource management theory and practice. This is not, then, a text on resource economics and no previous training in the subject is assumed. The book is primarily intended for senior undergraduate and postgraduate students in planning, geography, environmental studies or specialist resource management programmes. It is, however, anticipated that students of public administration, political science, international relations and applied economics may also find it a useful reference source.

The book has had a long gestation period; the material and ideas in it have evolved over some fifteen years of research and teaching in resource management and environmental planning at the London School of Economics. Inevitably over this period I have accumulated an enormous intellectual debt to many academic colleagues, and I also owe much to generations of students, who have acted as guinea-pigs for various sections of the book and who have never failed to challenge my ideas on the subject. The people who have influenced my thinking are too numerous to mention individually, but their anonymity does not diminish the warmth of my thanks to all of them. It would be remiss of me, however, not to acknowledge the particular contributions made by Gerald Manners, who commented on a very early version of some of the material, and by Peter Odell and David Jones, who took on the unenviable task of reading and discussing the drafts of the manuscript. Their comments and encouragement were invaluable.

In addition, I am extremely grateful to all the secretarial and technical staff in the Geography Department of the LSE; all have helped in different ways to get the material into a publishable state. Special thanks are due to Nesta Herbert, Pat Farnsworth, Ann Cratchley and Jutta Muller, for typing and retyping the innumerable drafts; and to Gary Llewellyn, for transforming my hieroglyphics into maps and diagrams. It is difficult to think of a task much more tedious and time consuming than index preparation and I am most grateful to Ron Steenblik and James Judge for all the hours and effort they put into it. I would also like to acknowledge the help given by the London School of Economics not only in providing some financial assistance from the staff research fund, but also in allowing me sabbatical leave to complete the manuscript.

Finally, but by no means least, I must thank my husband. He has remained remarkably patient and supportive during the inevitably anti-social period of writing, even when his meals were always in the freezer!

The author and the publisher would like to thank the following individuals, publishers and societies for permission to reproduce copyright material:

D. K. C. Jones for plates 1, 2, 12 and 13
N. L. Cadge for plate 3
National Coal Board for plates 4 and 9
D. Brunsden for plates 5 and 14
R. T. Z. Services Ltd for plates 6, 7 and 8
United Nations Information Centre and Paul Almasy for plates 10 and 11
United Nations Information Centre and S. K. Dutt for plate 15
United Nations Information Centre and WHO for plate 16
Kogan Page Ltd, London, and P. R. Odell and K. E. Rosing for figure 2.3
Metals and Materials for figure 3.1
General Agreement on Tariffs and Trade for figure 3.11
Organisation for Economic Co-operation and Development for figure 3.12
Mining Magazine for figure 3.15
Cornell University Press for figure 4.4
Scientific American, Inc. for figure 6.1
New Scientist for figure 6.2
The Geographical Association for figures 6.3, 7.1, 7.2, 7.5 and 7.6
Pergamon Press Ltd for figure 8.1
The New Yorker Magazine, Inc. for figure 8.3
British Car Wash Association for figure 10.1

1 Introduction

ORIGINS OF CONCERN

It is hardly necessary to point out that the 1960s saw a renaissance of public and academic interest in natural resource problems. The roots of this reawakening, however, go far back in time, and it is not possible to sustain the frequently expressed view that 'widespread concern over the possibility of severe resource shortages in industrial societies in the relatively near future is a recent development' (Smith, 1975, p. vii). As Kincaid (1983) points out, most people throughout most of history have lived in penury, at the edge of scarcity; it is hardly surprising, therefore, that resource scarcity has always been a central problem in western political thought.

In Europe doom-laden warnings about shortages of material stocks, deteriorating environmental quality and even the dangers of import dependence can be found in the literature long before Malthus (1798) lent his name to such pessimistic prognostications. Even in North America fears of scarcity have reoccurred since the late nineteenth century, when the limited nature of the resource base was given visible expression through the closure of the frontier – a closure which brought to an end the myth of American exceptionalism (Pickens, 1981). In the natural resource field, as in many others, there is much validity in Whitehead's aphorism, 'Everything of importance has been said before, by someone who did not discover it' (quoted in Streeton, 1961, p. 96).

The immediate precursor of the most recent period of concern over material scarcities and environmental degradation was the rapid depletion of metallic and energy mineral reserves during the Second World War. In the United States and throughout Europe there was a wave of concern over the availability of those minerals essential for reconstruction and renewed industrial growth. Government reports predicted the imminent exhaustion of US oil reserves; world iron ore supplies were, in 1950, given only a twenty-year life; and in Europe the 'energy gap' was seen as a major threat to redevelopment efforts. However, the economic and technological response to the danger of material shortages was swift. Massive investments were made in technologies to allow the exploitation of previously subeconomic mineral deposits and to increase the efficiency in use of mineral and energy inputs. Moreover, the level of exploration activity escalated, with an upsurge of investment in previously underexploited Third World nations.

By the end of the 1950s the immediate danger of resource scarcity acting as a brake on economic development was past, but the underlying fear that physical limits must some day be reached remained. Such fears were fuelled by the rapidly rising trend of resource consumption associated with the exceptional rate of economic growth experienced in the 1950s and 1960s. In the developed market economies per capita gross national product rose by 3 per cent per annum during the 1950s and exceeded 4 per cent in the following decade; industrial output quadrupled in just twenty years, a rate of growth four times greater than that of the previous half-century. As a result, the consumption of virtually all the key metals and energy minerals escalated; at minimum a 2 per cent per annum compound consumption growth rate was experienced, and for many minerals the rates exceeded 5 per cent compound (for example, iron ore, 7 per cent; platinum, 9 per cent and aluminium, 9.8 per cent). The scene was set for the now very familiar Malthusian models, which compared these exponential consumption trends with an assumed fixed resource base and then predicted imminent economic catastrophe.

Reinforcing the concern over potential material scarcities was the growing realization that physical laws on the conservation of matter dictate that resource materials do not conveniently vanish after processing and use. Rather a residual mass, broadly equal to that initially extracted, must eventually be discharged – albeit in a transformed state – to accumulate somewhere in the global ecosphere. Environmental change was, therefore, increasingly seen as the inevitable consequence of mineral exploitation. Moreover, the progressive pressure to use ever more low-grade and inaccessible deposits would not only increase the proportion of waste materials generated, but also necessitate greater inputs of energy and push exploitation into more environmentally sensitive regions. Fears over the capacity of the environment to absorb waste were thus added to the already growing concern over the physical limits to material supply. There was a growing realization that the natural environment was a virtually closed system, with its dimensions essentially fixed in terms of mass–energy and assimilative–regenerative capacity (d'Arge, 1972). To many, therefore, there was a basic incompatibility between the growth oriented nature of established economic and political institutions and the fixed limits of 'spaceship earth'.

These fears for the sustainability of human life erupted with a messianic fervour during the late 1960s (Cotgrove, 1982). The ecological challenge to economic growth met with a receptive audience, particularly in North America, among the already disaffected young involved in the civil rights and anti-Vietnam movements. As Chisholm (1972, p. xi) puts it, 'during the autumn of 1969, ecology caught on like a new religion among the young on college campuses across the country'. The environmental movement appeared to offer a new philosophy of life to those already questioning the rationality of consumerism and choosing to opt out of the economic rat race. It also found sympathy among a much wider public, concerned with the declining quality of their local environments under pressure from all forms of economic development.

THE NATURE OF RESOURCE CONCERNS

There are always dangers in attempting to categorize the extremely hetero-geneous range of resource problems which have been analysed over the last twenty-five years. However, generalizing very broadly, it is possible to divide the new era of resource concern into two, by no means distinct, phases.

Environmental limits

During the first phase the focus was largely on the physical environment, its limits and deteriorating quality. The basic resource problems tended to be defined in physical terms, with attention being centred around four types of scarcity:

(1) the exhaustion of essential metallic and energy minerals;
(2) the danger that pollution and biological simplification would so disrupt the crucial global bio-geochemical cycles that the capacity of the ecosphere to sustain life would be severely restricted or even totally ruined;
(3) the depletion of naturally renewable 'productive' resources, such as aquifer water, soils, forests and fish;
(4) the loss and increasing scarcity of those environmental quality resources which were of recreational, amenity and aesthetic value to some at least of the population.

The last three issues had pollution and renewable resource depletion as the central problems, but in the latter two cases these were not viewed as global threats, rather attention was focused at the local and regional spatial scales.

Before the emergence of the environmental movement as a political force, the level of interest among social scientists in resource and environmental questions was extremely limited. Even as late as 1980 Schnaiberg could correctly point to a dearth of material treating environmental issues from a distinctive social perspec-tive. Similarly, geographers who at one time would have defined their subject as the study of man–environment relationships had, by the 1960s, become pre-occupied by the quantitative revolution and the search for spatial order; the physical environment vanished behind neat rules for the spacing of urban settlements and the development of transport networks. Undoubtedly, the dominant social science contribution to natural resource issues came from economics, although even here the number of analysts undertaking applied research in the area was extremely small. Working very much within a conven-tional welfare economic framework, renewable resource depletion and environ-mental degradation were treated as products of market failure and the existence of unpriced externalities. To promote a rational, efficient use of all natural resource products and environmental services it was necessary to ensure that they were priced (valued) and fully incorporated into the market system. Throughout it was assumed that the legitimate objective of any resource management programme was to maximize the economic welfare derived from resource use. In other words, the paradigm of growth was accepted, and little attention was paid to the possible ecological constraints imposed by the limited physical system.

Overall social scientists were ill-prepared to play a distinctive role in the first phase of concern over resource scarcity. They reacted to the problems as posed by others, but did little to redefine the central questions from their own disciplinary perspective.

Predictably most reaction was generated by the visions of global Armageddon, which emerged from the work of Ehrlich (1970a), Forrester (1970), Commoner (1972b), Goldsmith *et al.* (1972), Meadows *et al.* (1972) and scores of others. The idea that scarcity of material stocks must act as an absolute and imminent barrier to economic expansion was strongly refuted. Such refutations correctly stressed the cultural, dynamic nature of resources, and emphasized the role of technology and socioeconomic change in countering physical shortages of particular minerals. The solutions proposed by the ecocatastrophists were also challenged. Those who demanded an end to population growth, technological change and economic development were regarded as élitist, callous and immoral. The price they were prepared to pay for ecological integrity and a sustainable future for the few would involve the certain death of millions. Social scientists began to analyse the socioeconomic consequences and the political feasibility of the various no-growth scenarios and, as they did so, the seeds were sown for the second phase of the new era of resource concern.

Socioeconomic and political concerns

What marked this second phase was a redefinition of the central resource problems and a shift of attention from physical scarcity and environmental change *per se* to a broader investigation of the social, economic and political dimensions of resource use. By 1975 models predicting stock resource depletion had largely been discredited and overtaken by events; the key issues were now geopolitical scarcity and global redistributive equity.

There were many who viewed the 1973 oil crisis as the dawn of a new international economic order. The literature was full of statements such as, 'October 1973 was a turning point in the history of international relations . . . the point when the Third World countries became aware, not of their rights, but of their power' (Amin, 1979, p. 65). In similar vein Gardner *et al.* (1977, p. 57) saw OPEC as having 'detonated an explosion in north–south economic relations that has been building up for years', while Cohen (1978, p. 276) was arguing that what had occurred was 'nothing short of a fundamental shift in the international economic power configuration'. With the advantages of hindsight, these claims look just as exaggerated – and as naïve in conception – as the neo-Malthusian scarcity models had been shown to be. They were, in some cases, based on wishful thinking and always on a false perception of the fragility of extant socioeconomic and political institutions. However, the attention paid to the geopolitical aspects of resource exploitation and international trade relations was a valuable stimulus to research, mainly in economics, international relations, politics and law, which has considerably enhanced our understanding of the international mineral system.

The study of environmental change and renewable resource depletion problems had also broadened markedly by the mid-1970s. No one pretended that these were not real issues, although more sober scientific judgements had shown the claims of the 'eco- gloom-and-doom' school to be exaggerated and based on dubious data. There were numerous foci of attention. The rise of the environmental movement was studied as a social phenomenon; alternative management strategies were analysed in terms of their economic efficiency, efficacy, political feasibility and distributive consequences; assessments were made of the power of environmental interests to influence resource policy and management decisions; and the way resource policy was established and implemented was scrutinized.

It was quickly realized that environmental pollution and renewable resource depletion had no absolute meaning common to all people in all countries. As Holdgate (1979, p. ix) correctly says, 'because the world is environmentally and economically diverse, problems are rarely universal . . . societies will rightly differ in the detail of their priorities'. This point was made abundantly clear at the United Nations conference on the human environment in 1971 (Stockholm Conference), where the developing countries showed their deep-seated suspicion that the environmental movement was yet another ploy to rob them of a chance to achieve material prosperity. Moreover, it also became clear that strategies and techniques to control pollution, or reduce the depletion of resource flows, could not simply be transferred from one country to another; their performance critically depended on the socioeconomic, legal and political context in which they were applied.

Even within individual nations there is no consensus over the objectives of renewable resource management and pollution control policies; nor is there agreement over the methods to be used to achieve these objectives. There are no simple solutions which can be found by 'value-free' scientific assessments. The fact that pollution occurs, landscapes are changed, fish stocks are depleted and biotic species are lost does not automatically mean that measures *should* be taken to avoid such environmental alterations. All forms of renewable resource degradation impose economic and welfare losses on some groups in society, but the avoidance of depletion and pollution damage is not a costless procedure. Someone has to pay the costs involved, and the type of avoidance mechanisms chosen will crucially affect who this will be. Ultimately choices have to be made about which environmental goods and services to provide, who should receive them and who pays; inevitably these are subjective, political, social and moral choices. They will not, and cannot, be made by rational analysis.

Just as some commentators regarded the oil crisis as marking a sea change in international economic relations, so the environmental movement was seen by many as a turning-point in the history of economic development. It was thought to represent the start of a new post-material era, in which there was a shift away from material values. However, once again such interpretations appear more the product of hope than reality. While more and more people are demanding environmental goods and services, it seems doubtful whether the struggle for material wealth will lessen as a result; as Miewald and Welch (1983, p. 10) argue, 'the attainment of affluence leads to an increased demand for material prosperity to be delivered in prettier packages'.

VOLUME OBJECTIVES

The above very brief review of the nature of resource concerns has, I hope, shown that the range of issues is extremely wide and that there are various perspectives from which these issues can be viewed. It is clearly not feasible in any one volume to attempt to provide an encyclopaedic coverage of the subject area. Certainly, it is not the intention here to discuss the location, economics and policy problems of each individual resource or set of resources in turn. The concern is with principles and concepts which have general application throughout the natural resource sector, although of course these will be illustrated by reference to particular minerals or flow resources.

The book has four basic objectives. First, it aims to explain the processes or forces operating to produce three sets of distributions:

(1) the spatial distribution of resource availability, development and consumption;
(2) the distribution of these resources – and more important, the wealth and welfare they generate – between nations, interest and social groups, and individuals;
(3) the allocation of resource products and services over time – clearly, this involves a consideration of potential future scarcities.

This concentration on distributions stems from the belief that all resource problems basically arise from conflict over the way resources, or rather the welfare derived from them, are allocated between groups over time and space. The explanations are not simple and must involve an understanding of physical systems, economic processes, social organizations, legal and administrative structures, and political institutions. In this search for explanations it is necessary to abandon the idea that any one model, theory, or disciplinary perspective can provide all the answers. Any attempt to explain and improve our understanding of these distributive patterns is, of course, a challenging and worthy academic exercise in its own right. However, unless we are prepared to merely accept the distributive outcomes, explanations are not an end in themselves, but are a crucial input into policy formulation. It is impossible to correct any perceived defects in the current resource development and use process without an understanding of how the process works.

The other aims of the book are concerned, in different ways, with the development and implementation of natural resources policy. The second objective is to assess how far the allocation of resources satisfies important, but often conflicting, public policy objectives. It is assumed that no resources have intrinsic value; their worth lies in their contribution to human welfare. Most people will not object to this assumption while the discussion is confined to inanimates, such as iron ore or coal, but it will undoubtedly offend all those who argue that every form of life on earth has inherent value quite separate from its use or aesthetic importance to humans. However, resources are by definition an aid or means of support to the human species; they cannot be assessed other than through the meanings or values which people attribute to them.

All efforts to evaluate the performance of resource management systems in terms of their contribution to human welfare have to confront the problem that there is no one welfare measure. Therefore, even assuming public policy was actually concerned with welfare, there is no single resource policy objective. It is necessary to look at a range of performance criteria, and the ones chosen here are economic efficiency, distributive equity, economic growth and employment generation, resource security/stability, and the maintenance of 'acceptable' environmental quality standards. However, it is recognized that in the real world less worthy objectives, such as keeping a particular political party in power or making certain individuals wealthy, also play a vital role in the development of the natural resources sector.

The third objective of the study is to analyse the range of policy measures which have been, or could be, used to correct perceived deficiencies in current resource allocations. As was said earlier, the various types of correction mechanism used can have vastly different distributive consequences. Moreover, given the interrelated nature of socioeconomic, political and environmental systems, a measure designed to allow one policy objective to be fulfilled may make the achievement of the others even more difficult. Finally, but by no means least, an attempt will be made to analyse how policies are formed, who forms them and to whose advantage they operate.

This is by no means a book in the 'resource doom' school, of which there are already far too many littering library shelves. However, its conclusions will be regarded as pessimistic by all those who feel disadvantaged by the established resource allocation system. From the analysis of effective resource policy it is difficult to see much challenge to the status quo; the forces preventing significant change are deeply entrenched within our socioeconomic and political structures.

VOLUME ORGANIZATION

In organizing the material contained in the book it was decided to retain the conventional division of the subject into stock and renewable resources, with the latter including environmental quality resources. It must be stressed, however, that the basic distributional problems and the difficulties involved in devising effective policy responses are common to both resource sectors. Moreover, the physical distinction between them is somewhat artificial. Only the energy minerals can clearly be labelled as fixed stocks. The element minerals are all, theoretically at least, recyclable and are, therefore, renewable as a result of human investment. Similarly, only water, air and the energies derived from the sun are always naturally renewable, although in the first two cases human intervention may change the availability of their quality. All other of the so-called renewables can be transferred by overuse into the stock category, and then their renewability will also depend on human investment.

The main reason for treating the two resource sets separately, apart from convenience and ease of exposition, is that by custom most stock resources (but not all) are subject to ownership by a single firm (public or private). Decisions on the way resources, their products and derived wealth are distributed are made by these firms working to fulfil their own objectives within, of course, the constraints set by the economic and political system. Many renewable resources, on the other hand, cannot be individually owned for all their end-purposes. An important function of public policy is, therefore, to devise systems capable of allocating usage rights and controlling use, and deciding which resource products and services should be made available, in what quantities and when.

The sequence of the chapters has been designed gradually to introduce the reader to different perspectives and increasingly more complex issues. It starts with a straightforward discussion on the nature and scarcity of resources, considering both mineral stocks and the renewables. From there it moves on to discuss the mineral sector. Chapter 3 attempts to explain the patterns of resource development and trade; it employs only very basic economic models and is heavily, but not exclusively, focused on decisions within the private sector and on the factors which influence them. Although the chapter is about minerals, many of the basic principles apply equally to renewable resources which provide productive inputs for industry. The behaviour of, and influences on, timber and tin producers are little affected by the type of resource they happen to market.

Chapter 4 contains an evaluation of the performance of the minerals sector. In the process of this evaluation the notion of economic efficiency will be introduced; the assumptions it is based on are then discussed and its limitations analysed. Although this concept will be illustrated exclusively by reference to minerals, the efficiency notion is a crucial one, which will be widely employed in the discussion on renewables. The chapter also introduces the critical issue (and one which is central to this book) of distributive equity, considering it at both the international and national scales. In a minerals context it is impossible to divorce equity from the potential role of resources in generating economic growth and employment; therefore, all these performance criteria will be discussed in tandem. Chapter 4 ends with an evaluation of the emotive issue of national security and of the extent to which LDC producers can and have exercised their resource power to achieve a more equitable distribution of wealth. Chapter 5, the last dealing with minerals, begins the consideration of public policy formulation. It includes a brief introduction to the nature of policy and to the severe constraints faced by policy-makers in ensuring that public bureaucracies and private corporations operate to meet public, rather than their own, objectives. However, because these subjects are extremely complex, the full development of the arguments will not occur until Chapter 9; instead attention is focused on the different measures employed by governments to alter some aspect of the performance of the minerals sector.

The remaining chapters of the book, except for Chapter 10, are concerned with renewable resources. They begin with a discussion of the diversity of perspectives on the nature of flow resource problems, their causes and the objectives of management. Most analysts agree that the performance of the renewables sector is defective; depletion and degradation are undoubtedly occurring and scarcities of some of the most basic resources, such as water, are already affecting the lives of millions. But there the accord ends; there is no consensus over why it is defective, nor over what should be done about it.

Chapters 7 and 8 use an economic perspective as a starting-point from which to analyse two key policy questions. First, how should available resource supplies be allocated between competing users, and what allocative mechanisms should be used? And second, what investment should take place to provide additional supplies for the future? These questions clearly have an economic dimension, but the economic perspective cannot provide any necessarily 'correct' solutions to what are essentially moral, social and political issues. Most of the examples used in these chapters are taken from environmental quality resources (i.e. the pollution control question), water and fisheries; the concepts and principles, however, apply equally throughout the renewable sector.

Up to this point in the book it is, for the most part, assumed that the development of resources policy is a relatively rational process. This assumption is dropped in Chapter 9, where once again the theme of effective policy formulation and implementation is taken up. Policy is dynamic; there is no standing policy target against which the performance of resource management systems can be judged. Effective policy is formed by myriad individual decisions (including the decision to do nothing), taken at all levels from central government down to the individual resource user. It is important, therefore, to gain some understanding of the way decisions are made and what factors determine (or influence) choice. These are subjects which have generated considerable dispute, with an enormous ideological divide between those who see decisions as outcomes of pluralist bargaining processes and those who regard them as products of the structure of capitalist society.

Before moving on into the substance of the book, it is probably necessary to make two minor points. First, not all natural resources are covered in equal depth and some have hardly been mentioned. No doubt, there will be those who will lament the lack of attention paid to renewable energies, gold or even sand and gravel. But it is hoped that a full enough range of examples has been considered, from a broad enough spectrum of countries, to illustrate effectively the key issues, principles and paradigms. It was necessary to be selective and, inevitably, ignorance played a role in the selection process. However, there are some deliberate omissions; food, for example, is frequently included in resource texts but has been excluded here along with other 'manufactured' goods. Clearly, its supply is critically dependent on a whole range of natural resources but is itself, *sensu stricto*, no longer a 'natural' product. This distinction cannot be pushed very far since most resources conventionally classified as natural are manmade, at least by the time they have any use value; there was, however, the need to draw the line somewhere.

Second, but in somewhat similar vein, while considerable efforts have been made to draw on material from the various academic disciplines which have contributed to our understanding of resource problems, it is impossible to pretend that all disciplinary perspectives have been covered with equal depth and authority. Dolman makes the point clearly when he says:

> The analyst is usually the prisoner of his own background and he carries the intellectual baggage of his own professional discipline. However much he

advocates the need for trans-disciplinary approaches to the study of complex phenomena, he inevitably wears monodisciplinary spectacles which condition his view, not only of how problems should be tackled, but also, and more importantly, of which problems should be tackled. (Dolman, 1980, p. 4)

Regrettably, female analysts have no more perfect vision.

2 Natural resources: their nature and scarcity

RESOURCES DEFINED

Resources are defined by man, not nature. As Ciriacy-Wantrup (1952, p. 28) puts it, 'the concept "resource" presupposes that a "planning agent" is appraising the usefulness of his environment for the purpose of obtaining a certain end'. Human beings are continually surveying the physical environment and assessing the value of particular organic and inorganic elements within it. Before any element can be classified as a resource, two basic preconditions must be satisfied: first, the knowledge and technical skills must exist to allow its extraction and utilization; and, second, there must be a demand for the materials or services produced. If either of these conditions is not satisfied, then the physical substances remain 'neutral stuff' (Zimmermann, 1951). It is, therefore, human ability and need which create resource value, not mere physical presence.

Dynamism in the resource definition

Ideas on what constitutes resources have altered dramatically over time, in response to increased knowledge, technical improvements and cultural developments which have changed perceived needs. Even though the total physical endowment of the earth is essentially fixed, resources are dynamic with no known or fixed limits. The history of resource use to date has been one of continuous discovery, with an ever widening definition of the resource base. Palaeolithic man perceived few resources. Naturally available plants and animals, water, wood and stone were the basic resource armoury. The Neolithic revolution, which transformed primitive food gatherers into farmers and the subsequent introduction of metal-based technologies in Sumeria, Egypt and China began a cumulative process of change in the structure and organization of society. Each stage in this process brought a new set of demands for goods and services, which in turn stimulated technological innovation and led to a reappraisal of the usefulness of components within the physical environment. These technical and economic changes then affected the structure of society and so the cycle continued.

The development of spatially distinct cultural groups meant that, even at any one period of time, there was no single definition of the resource base; a substance with a high resource value in one society could be 'neutral stuff' in others. Even today there are spatial variations in the way resources are appraised.

However, modern systems of communication and the increased interdependence of all nations within the world economic system have considerably narrowed the range of definitions for the metallic and energy minerals; these resources are now largely defined in terms of the technology and demands of the developed nations. Internationally determined assessments of resource value occur much less frequently for environmental quality resources such as landscape and natural ecosystems. It is now well recognized that the cultural significance of elements within the natural environment varies markedly between societies, and that the value or priority given to resources which satisfy aesthetic needs is related to a country's material wealth.

The dynamism in the definition of mineral resources is easy to illustrate. Throughout time technological innovations have suddenly created resources from previously unvalued and unused physical substances. Bauxite, for example, owes its resource status to the invention, in 1886, of the Hall–Heroult electrolytic refining process, which made possible the commercial extraction of aluminium (Warren, 1973). More recently the development of nuclear power, both for military purposes and electricity generation, has created the resource value of uranium ores. However, it cannot be stressed too strongly that knowledge and technical skills only create opportunities; they have no deterministic powers. Whether such opportunities are actually taken will depend, first, on the strength of demand for the end-products; second on the way the economic system is organized; and third on the vested interests at work to maintain established technologies. For example, the existence of techniques to produce usable energy from renewable sources (the tides, wind, or the sun) in no way ensures that they will be employed.

Environmental quality resources are equally dynamic in nature, varying *not directly* with technology and economic conditions, but in response to changes in human values, aspirations and lifestyles. Here the words 'not directly' are chosen advisedly since the growth of 'environmentalist' ideals has been, in major part, a reaction to the perceived 'ills' of industrialization – whether these were seen in terms of the divorce of man from communion with nature, the disruption of life support systems, or the breakdown of traditional social structures. It appears that environmental values have not been static, but have risen and fallen episodically in response – as Lowe and Goyder (1983) have claimed – to fluctuations in the world business cycle. Towards the end of periods of sustained growth (in the 1890s, late 1920s, late 1950s and early 1970s) the effects of new technologies and the pace of industrial expansion brought greater awareness of the costs involved. Moreover, with their increased relative affluence, people were able to afford to turn their attention to non-materialist values.[1]

Although within individual societies there will be some widely held notions about the importance of nature preservation, landscapes, or river and air quality, there is not necessarily a consensus valuation of specific environmental components. What may be a resource of great intrinsic value to one person can be a costly hinderance or an irrelevance to others. For example, a waterlogged stretch of marshy ground may be regarded as a crucial nature conservancy area by the ecologist or bird watcher, a nuisance which lowers agricultural productivity by the farmer, and may not be regarded at all by the unemployed urban dweller. It is these differences in valuation that lie at the heart of so many of the current conflicts over the use and allocation of environmental resources, which are discussed in Chapters 6–9.

RESOURCE TYPES

Resources are commonly divided into two major types, stock or non-renewable and flow or renewable (Figure 2.1). The essential difference between them lies in the timescales over which they develop. Since all resources are products of natural cycles, all are, strictly speaking, renewable but at very different rates.

Stock resources

Stock resources – all minerals and land – are substances which have taken millions of years to form and so from a human perspective are now fixed in supply. There must, therefore, be a limit to the quantity which can ultimately be used, although we neither know where this limit lies nor whether the substance will still be regarded as a resource if this limit is approached. The stock resource class is not, however, a homogeneous one; an important distinction arises between those which are 'consumed by use' and those which can be recycled.

In the case of the 'consumed by use' set, which includes all the fossil fuels, current rates of consumption must affect future availability. Therefore, a key management question is what is the optimal rate of use over time? This issue has been much debated in the literature and is not amenable to simple unequivocal answers. It is only in the idealized world of a perfectly working, competitive

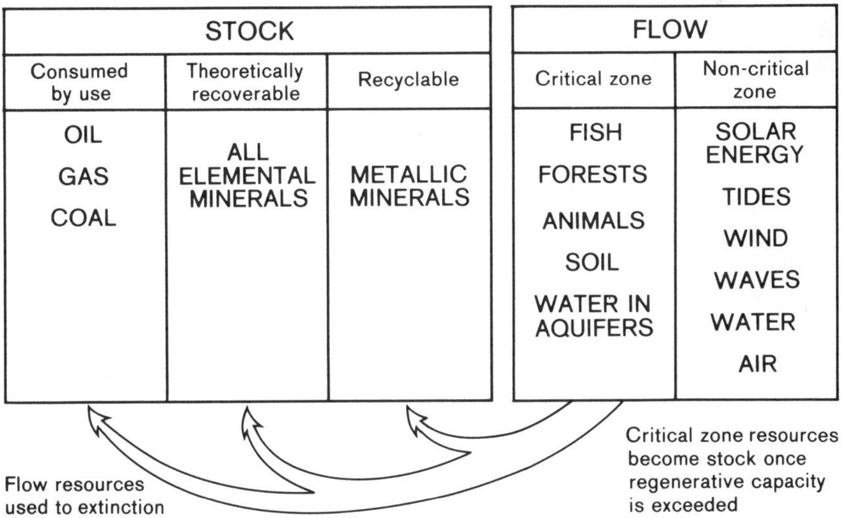

STOCK			FLOW	
Consumed by use	Theoretically recoverable	Recyclable	Critical zone	Non-critical zone
OIL	ALL ELEMENTAL MINERALS	METALLIC MINERALS	FISH	SOLAR ENERGY
GAS			FORESTS	TIDES
COAL			ANIMALS	WIND
			SOIL	WAVES
			WATER IN AQUIFERS	WATER
				AIR

Flow resources used to extinction

Critical zone resources become stock once regenerative capacity is exceeded

Figure 2.1 A classification of resource types

market system that it is possible to set out the conditions under which an optimal depletion path can be achieved for any individual resource stock (Fisher, 1981). As shown in Chapter 4, this theoretical approach not only has to be adapted to take account of the so-called imperfections in the market system, but in addition the whole notion of an optimal rundown rate rests on the way optimality is defined and on the assumption that resource managers will actually aim to achieve it. In the more blurred and complex world of reality there is no one optimal rate of depletion; nor can there be given the diverse perspectives, needs and objectives of resource owners, developers and users.

The technology exists to allow most metals to be reused many times over with little loss of quality. In principle, then, the total stock must remain constant over time, taking account of both the metal remaining in the earth's crust and that temporarily stored in products. This notionally also applies for all non-metallic elemental minerals, such as potash, but in this case even an optimist with faith in the technological ingenuity of man would admit that the prospects for significant recovery of all such minerals are slight. Even for the metals the idea of complete recycling is likely to remain a theoretical one. As early as 1955 Price pointed out that the thermodynamic law of entropy indicates that unavailability (chaos) is an ultimate tendency of the utilization of specific materials; in other words, minerals may eventually become too dispersed and mixed with impurities during use to be recoverable. Furthermore, reuse is an energy-intensive activity relying heavily, at least at present, on 'consumed by use' resources (Pearce and Walter, 1977).

Flow resources

Flow resources are defined as those which are naturally renewed within a sufficiently short timespan to be of relevance to human beings; they include water, air, animal and plant life, solar radiation, wind power and tidal energy. It is necessary, however, to make a distinction between those flows which do not appear to be dependent on human activity and those which are only indefinitely renewable if use remains at or below their capacity to reproduce or regenerate.

All the so-called *critical zone* resources can be exploited to exhaustion. If the rate of use exceeds the rate of natural replenishment, such resources effectively can be mined like any mineral stock. At some point – the critical zone – the depletion process may be so far advanced that natural recovery of the supply flows fails to take place, even when all exploitation has ceased. Resources which depend on biological reproduction for their renewal most obviously come into this category. When plant, animal and bird populations become small and dispersed, they may not only fail to reproduce, but also may become more vulnerable to predation. It is well known that overfishing, hunting, pollution and the destruction of habitats has already drastically reduced the renewal capacity of many species, and numerous examples can be given where exploitation has been pursued to its ultimate conclusion – extinction. Tivy and O'Hare (1981) have pointed out, for example, that by 1968 the known global loss of 36 species of mammals and 94 species of birds had been recorded, with a further 311 species being classified as severely endangered.

In addition to these biological resources, it is possible that some soils and aquifers may also have critical zones. Once land has been so overused and misused that it becomes degraded by soil erosion, salinization and desertification, it is by no means certain that recovery can take place, either naturally or through planned remedial programmes, within timescales of relevance to human activity. The recent admission by the United Nations that its intensive Desertification Programme had failed to control the degradation process or to recover significant areas of damaged land is a clear indication that soils can effectively be transformed by human use from a flow resource into a short-lived stock. Similarly, when aquifers (such as those underlying the Sahel) are relic features, products of past climate regimes, they too may be exploited to exhaustion, with no hope of recovery for hundreds of years.

Non-critical zone resources remain renewable irrespective of human activity, although some can be depleted temporarily by overuse. River flows can be reduced by overpumping, the capacity of water bodies to degrade waste products can be ruined by too high levels of effluent and sewage discharge, and the quality of local air resources can fall due to polluting emissions. In all such cases flow and quality levels are naturally and speedily restored once the rate of exploitation is controlled within the regenerative or assimilative capacity.[2] It was once thought that the size of the energy flows produced by the sun, tides, wind and waves was unaffected by human beings, although the usable energy derived from them was a function of human decision and investment. However, during the 1970s considerable scientific and political debate arose over whether incoming and outgoing radiation flows could be affected inadvertently by the use of the atmosphere for the disposal of waste products. The ozone layer is a significant absorber of solar radiation and, as such, is a major control of world climate; any pollutants which reduced ozone concentrations could result in a marked increase in incoming radiation. It has been postulated that nitrogen oxides from aircraft exhausts and chlorofluorocarbons – used as refrigerants and spray-can propellants – could have this effect (Hare, 1984). Similarly, it has been hypothesized that increasing concentrations of carbon dioxide (CO_2) in the atmosphere, produced largely by fossil-fuel consumption, could have the so-called 'greenhouse' warming effect. The escape of radiated energy back to space could be impeded, so increasing planetary surface temperatures (Holdgate, 1979). Although as yet there is little or no observational proof that either of these two effects are actually occurring, most scientific evidence supports the view that CO_2 generated temperature rises will be experienced in the next century (Kellogg and Schware, 1981). If this is the case, then no renewable resource flows will be beyond the influence of human activity.

MEASURES OF RESOURCE AVAILABILITY: STOCK RESOURCES

Once a substance has been defined as a resource, the question inevitably arises as to how much is available for use by man. Many attempts have been made to estimate the ultimate use limits, resulting in a confusing array of vastly different estimates. While some of this variation is due to the different assessment techniques employed and to the varying assumptions made about the future potential for technological and economic change, it also arises simply because the various studies are not always considering the same resource category. To unravel the web of conflicting evidence it is, first, essential to identify the different ways in which the term resource and its various subdivisions have been used.

The resource base

The most comprehensive view of potential availability arises when the concept of the *resource base* is employed. This is defined as the total quantity of a substance or property within the geosystem. While this is a conceptually simple notion when applied to stock resources, it is much more difficult to use for the renewables since, by definition, their availability is not static. In the case of solar energy, for example, it is possible to calculate the maximum inflow in any one period but the total amount available over time is for all practical purposes infinite.

Some attempts have been made to calculate the resource base for particular non-fuel minerals by multiplying their elemental abundance measured in grams per metric ton by the total weight of the earth's crust, or more usually the weight of the crust to a depth of 1 kilometre or 1 mile (Lee and Yao, 1970). As Table 2.1 shows, calculated in this way available resources are vast, and if annual consumption levels remain static at those of 1972–4, all of these minerals would last millions of years. However, even at a 2 per cent per annum compound rate of growth in consumption, resource life falls dramatically, and at a 10 per cent growth rate all minerals would be exhausted in under 260 years.

Such life expectancy calculations are based on the assumption that technological developments will occur to allow all available elements to be exploited at costs low enough to maintain demand levels. This is clearly a difficult assumption to justify. It has been argued that only a fraction of the 'element' base will ever be exploitable in practice, in which case the life expectancy figures derived from it will be grossly optimistic. However, the element approach contains another fundamental flaw which leads to the contrary suggestion that the life expectancies are in fact unduly pessimistic. With the exception of uranium used in nuclear fission, elemental minerals are not destroyed by use; theoretically they are available for reuse and the total stock is, therefore, constant.

In reality the concept of being able to calculate an ultimate resource base, even for the element minerals, remains an elusive one. When concentrations in the crustal rocks or in used mineral products becomes very low, it is not known whether technological developments will allow continued recovery, at least at cost levels which would maintain any demand for the products at all. Moreover, it is also uncertain that the energy needs of recovery can be met, or that society would be willing or indeed able to sustain the levels of environmental degradation produced by such intense extraction efforts.

The ultimate resource base for each of the hydrocarbon energy minerals is an even more hypothetical notion. While it is obvious that there must be one, there is no way of obtaining availability estimates independent of current knowledge and

Table 2.1 The elemental resource base and life expectancy estimates for selected minerals

Mineral	Resource base (metric tons)*	Life expectancy in years with different consumption growth rates†				Average annual growth, 1947–74 (%)
		0%	2%	5%	10%	
Aluminium	2.0×10^{18}	166×10^9	1107	468	247	9.8
Cadmium	3.6×10^{12}	210×10^6	771	332	177	4.7
Chromium‡	2.6×10^{15}	1.3×10^9	861	368	196	5.3
Cobalt	600×10^{12}	23.8×10^9	1009	428	227	5.8
Copper	1.5×10^{15}	216×10^6	772	332	177	4.8
Gold	84×10^9	62.8×10^6	709	307	164	2.4
Iron	1.4×10^{18}	2.6×10^9	898	383	203	7.0
Lead	290×10^{12}	83.5×10^6	724	313	167	3.8
Magnesium	672×10^{15}	131.5×10^9	1095	463	244	7.7
Manganese§	31.2×10^{15}	3.1×10^9	906	386	205	6.5
Mercury	2.1×10^{12}	223.5×10^6	773	333	178	2.0
Nickel	2.1×10^{12}	3.2×10^6	559	246	133	6.9
Phosphorus	28.8×10^{15}	1.9×10^9	881	376	200	7.3
Potassium	408×10^{15}	22.1×10^9	1005	427	226	9.0
Platinum	1.1×10^{12}	6.7×10^9	944	402	213	9.7
Silver	1.8×10^{12}	194.2×10^6	766	330	176	2.2
Sulphur	9.6×10^{15}	205.3×10^6	769	331	177	6.7
Tin	40.8×10^{12}	172.2×10^6	760	327	175	2.7
Tungsten	26.4×10^{12}	677.2×10^6	829	355	189	3.8
Zinc	2.2×10^{15}	398.6×10^9	1151	486	256	4.7

* The resource base is calculated by multiplying its elemental abundance measured in grams per metric ton times the total weight (24×10^{18}) in metric tons of the earth's crust.

† Life expectancies were calculated based on the average annual production figures for 1972–4 and these were taken from US Bureau of Mines, *Commodity Data Summaries*, 1972–6; and US Bureau of Mines, *Minerals Yearbook*, 1974.

‡ Production figures assume that concentrates are 46 per cent chromium.

§ Production figures assume that concentrates are 46 per cent manganese.

Source: Tilton, 1977, pp. 12–13.

technology. All judgements about possible future discoveries are conditioned by past development trends and will change not only with improvements in survey and extraction technologies, but also with altered economic and political circumstances. In this case attempts to calculate future availabilities normally do not employ the resource base concept, but rather use the notions of *reserves*, *hypothetical resources* and *speculative resources*.

All of these categories are dynamic subsets of the fixed resource base and as knowledge changes over time they can be envisaged as expanding to cover a greater proportion of the resource base (Figure 2.2). To date the growth in

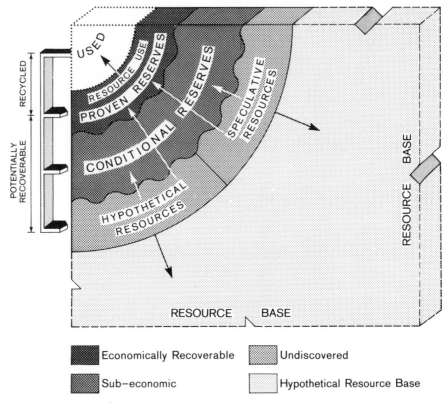

Figure 2.2   The stock resource base and its subdivisions

reserves and in estimated undiscovered resources has more than kept up with the loss to the system through exploitation and use. Inevitably at some point in time this process must stop for each individual stock. Whether this will occur because the outer physical limit of the base is reached or because production cost increases act to destroy the substances' resource value remains unknown. Some who take an optimistic view about human ingenuity would argue that economic exhaustion will always precede physical exhaustion; others doubt that economic and political institutions can act fast enough to prevent consumption from hitting the physical barrier to availability (see p. 44).

Proven reserves

Proven reserves are defined as deposits already discovered and known to be economically extractable under current demand, price and technological conditions. It may sound from this definition that at any point in time there is one agreed figure for the proven reserves within any specific deposit or country. This is not so. What is economically extractable depends upon the judgements and profit requirements of producers, and there can be major disagreements between private extraction companies and producer governments about reserve levels.

As will be seen in Chapter 3, if a company only regards as economically viable a deposit which yields a 15 or even a 20 per cent net return on investment, then this limits the number of proven reserve sites. A lower return requirement would increase proven reserves even if demand, price and technology were held constant. Moreover, required private rates of return vary from country to country, being largely dependent on the producers' assessment of the risks to their investments. Thus, what is regarded as a proven reserve in the United States or South Africa, for example, would not necessarily be so regarded if the deposit happened to occur in Zambia or Botswana (see Chapter 3, p. 105). Since governments usually do not have the same production objectives as private companies, proven reserve evaluations can change markedly if mineral exploitation is taken into public hands or if the private sector is 'encouraged' to take the wider state objectives into account. Objectives such as employment generation and import reduction may allow deposits to attain, or retain, a proven reserve status, which they would not have achieved if the market system had operated freely. In other words, there is no one objectively derived figure for the proven reserves of any resource.

When proven reserves – however determined – are used to forecast resource life, the implicit assumption is made that there will be no new discoveries, no technological change, no revision of production objectives and no price changes. Reserves are only proved after considerable sums of money have been spent on surveys and test borings. Mining companies, whether private or government owned, are unlikely to invest heavily in exploration when they hold enough reserves to meet projected demands for the next twenty to thirty years. Thus, for most minerals, proven reserves simply reflect current consumption levels and the search policies of the companies and say little about the potential size of the total resource stock. In fact some companies have a direct economic incentive to limit the size of their proven reserves because they are taxed on them as company assets (Tanzer, 1980, p. 33).

At any point in time proven reserve levels depend on five major and related factors:

(1) The availability of *technological knowledge and skills*.
(2) *Demand levels*; these will in turn depend on a whole range of variables including population numbers, income levels, consumer tastes, government policies and the relative prices of competitive or complementary goods.
(3) *Production and processing costs*; in part these are determined by the physical nature of the deposits and their location, but also crucial are the costs of all factors of production (land, labour, capital equipment and investment funds) and the level of government taxation. In addition, this cost category must include the risks to the fixed assets from political disorder or expropriation.
(4) *The price of the resource product*; price will inevitably reflect both the level of demand and the supply costs, but it will also be affected by the pricing policies of producers and by government intervention.

(5) *The availability and price of substitutes*; this includes the cost of recycled products.

All of these are highly dynamic factors and as they change they can have dramatic effects on proven reserves. For example, mineral oil has been known and used by man for centuries, but until 1859 the only proven reserves were deposits which seeped to the surface or could be trapped at shallow diggings. However, the nineteenth-century spread of mechanization vastly increased the demand for, and the price of, lubricating oils. This provided an incentive to develop subsurface extraction techniques. Drake's discovery that simple cable-drilling methods could be used set in motion a cycle of technical, supply, price and demand changes which has revolutionized our views of proven reserves. Following this technical breakthrough, increasing supplies and falling prices stimulated further technological changes to expand the range of uses to which oil could be put, demand was thus increased and the cumulative process of change continued. It is now possible commercially to exploit deposits lying at depths and in areas unheard of twenty years ago. Moreover, it is also feasible to extract a much higher proportion of the oil trapped within an oil-bearing structure. In the 1940s somewhat less than a 25 per cent recovery rate was achieved, but the introduction of secondary and tertiary extraction techniques, whereby natural gas or water are pumped into the rock structure to force oil out under pressure, allows recovery of up to 60 per cent (Odell and Rosing, 1980). A producer's assessment of the proven reserves in any one structure will critically depend on commercial judgements about whether – and to what extent – such extraction methods will be employed.

These same five variables also affect the location of proven reserves. Not only do the price and demand conditions vary from market area to market area, but also total production costs, the availability of technology and the cost and availability of capital all show marked spatial variations. Deposits with similar physical characteristics will not, therefore, all be classified as reserves in every country of the world. In the Soviet Union, for example, the mineral self-sufficiency objective means that sources of such resources as tin or bauxite are regarded as reserves under occurrence and production-cost conditions which would not be acceptable in most market economies. It must also be remembered that proven reserves are the result of exploration.

As will be shown in Chapter 3, the pattern of mineral search has been heavily skewed to the advanced countries; therefore, the present reserve position in many LDCs may bear very little relationship to the real resource endowment. One example will suffice to illustrate this point. Jamaica, at present crippled by the cost of its essential oil imports, is thought to have enough indigenous deposits to meet 50 per cent of its requirements (Barnet, 1980). The demand is there, but the country itself has neither the capital nor technological expertise to undertake the exploration drilling necessary to prove the existence of reserves recoverable on the basis of its own viability criteria. The oil majors which have the finance and technology are working on entirely different criteria of economic recoverability. They are, in the main, interested in developing deposits large enough to provide for an export market and must include in their viability calculations the risk of political unrest and asset expropriation.

Conditional reserves

Conditional reserves are, like proven reserves, deposits which have already been discovered, but they are not economic to work at present-day price levels with currently available extraction and production technologies. There is, of course, nothing static about this reserve category; the history of resource development is littered with examples of deposits crossing the economic viability boundary and not in only one direction. Moreover, as has just been seen, the relationship between economic and uneconomic deposits is a complex one, being critically dependent on political and market forces. Although technological innovation plays a key role in changing the viability boundary, it normally only does so under the stimulus of rising demands and prices, or of the perceived need to develop diversified supply sources in what are regarded as secure, stable and politically friendly countries.

The changing fortunes of copper ore deposits provide a good illustration of the way the division between proven and conditional reserves can vary both over time and space. At the beginning of this century copper ores with less than a 10 per cent metal content could not be used in most smelters and were, therefore, virtually valueless. Forty years later technological changes, coupled with major demand increases, had allowed deposits with only 1 per cent metal to be defined as proven reserves (Warren, 1973). Today ores with as little as 0.4 per cent copper may be economically exploitable *if* the deposits are favoured by a combination of key cost or risk-reducing factors. They would need to be large to allow economies of scale in production, near enough to the surface to permit highly mechanized, open-cast mining, and located in a country with a well-developed infrastructure and stable government. Similar-grade ores with less favourable physical characteristics or requiring massive infrastructure investments will, however, continue to be classified as conditional. As we shall see, ore grades normally must be much higher in LDCs to counterbalance both the additional infrastructure costs and, most important, the perception of private producers of the stability and political complexion of the host government (see p. 73).

Even within these two known and already identified resource categories there are marked differences in the degree of certainty that can be assigned to any reserve figures. Where a deposit has been intensively surveyed to establish its dimensions, quality and geological characteristics, the reserve is said to be 'measured', and the availability estimates lay within a margin of error of less than 20 per cent. Less intensively surveyed deposits have 'indicated' reserves derived in part from survey data and in part from reasonable geological projections. Finally, where deposits have been located but remain unexplored the reserve figures are only 'inferred'; such reserves are, therefore, guestimates derived from the likely geological conditions in the area.

Hypothetical resources

Unlike the reserve categories, *hypothetical resources* are not known deposits, but are those which we may expect to find in the future, in areas which today have been only partially surveyed and developed. The North Sea already produces significant quantities of oil and natural gas but by no means all the potentially oil-bearing strata have been test-drilled; it is, therefore, an area in which hypothetical resources should exist. A common method used to estimate the extent of these hypothetical resources is to extrapolate from past rates of growth in production and proved reserves, or from the past discovery rate per foot of drilling (see, for example, Hubbert, 1969, 1974). Inevitably such extrapolations assume that all the variables (political, economic and technical) which have affected past discovery and production rates will continue to operate as they have done in the past. As prices and technological innovations are highly unstable variables, estimates can vary widely depending on the time period over which such projections are made. For example, hypothetical oil resources calculated from pre-1973 price levels will be considerably lower than those which only use post-1973 price data.

Some attempts to get over the problems of mechanical extrapolation have been made by asking panels of experts to forecast likely discoveries and then taking the mean of their range of estimates (Exxon, 1978). This approach has obvious limitations, in that the estimates will be based on unstated assumptions about future technology and economic conditions, which reflect the innate optimism or caution of the experts. Oil company experts in particular have been accused of being very conservative in their estimates (Odell, 1977; Wall *et al.*, 1977; Odell and Rosing, 1977). It has been argued that companies have a vested interest in making conservative estimates in order to paint a picture of scarcity and thus maintain high prices and profits (Tanzer, 1980; Barnet, 1980).

Speculative resources

If hypothetical resources are difficult to estimate with any degree of certainty, *speculative resources* present even greater problems. These are deposits which could be found in hitherto unexplored or little-explored areas where reasonably favourable geological conditions are thought to exist. In the world there are, for example, some 600 sedimentary basins where oil and gas could exist but very little exploratory drilling has as yet taken place in one-third of them (Exxon, 1978). Compared with the USA, very few exploration and development wells have been drilled in other potentially petroliferous areas; China, South-east Asia, Africa and Latin America remain relatively untouched, as Figure 2.3 shows (Odell and Rosing, 1983). Once drilling does occur in unexplored areas, their resource potential status may change markedly. Twenty-five years ago the North Sea was an area where only speculative resources might exist; today it is assumed to have hypothetical resources, which will be located in time. On the other hand, when extensive drilling fails to establish the presence of hydrocarbons, areas may lose even their speculative status.

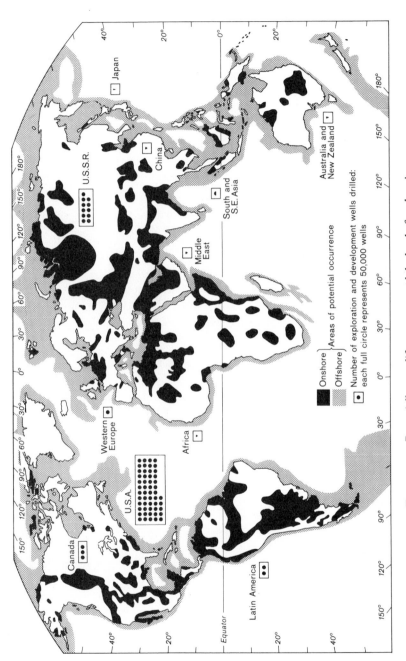

Figure 2.3   Potentially petroliferous areas and the level of exploration
Source: Odell and Rosing, 1983, pp. 27, 33

While some attempts have been made to estimate speculative resources by extrapolating from past discovery patterns in explored areas, this approach involves the assumption that the currently unexploited areas will be as physically productive and financially rewarding as those developed in the past. However, a number of commentators have argued that this is extremely unlikely. There is every possibility that the largest, most geologically favourable and accessible structures are being tapped already. If this proves to be the case, then the financial returns on capital *may* fall as exploration is pushed into more physically and politically difficult areas; the level of investment would fall and with it the rate of oil and gas discovery.

Ultimately recoverable resources

Given the estimation problems involved and the uncertainty about future technologies, market factors and political circumstances, it is hardly surprising that widely different estimates have been made of ultimately available resource stocks. Although marked disagreements have emerged over the future of all minerals, controversy has been particularly acute in the oil case. Today most oil industry estimates suggest that between 1700 and 2200 thousand million (10^9) barrels are likely to be recoverable from conventional sources, not including tar sands or oil shales (Warman, 1972; Lichtblau and Frank, 1978). However, in the 1940s a similar consensus of opinion put ultimately recoverable resources at only 500×10^9 barrels; but 'proven reserves' alone now exceed this figure. Although estimated ultimate resources have increased fourfold in the last forty years, Warman (1972, p. 293) argues that 'our knowledge has increased to a point where future continued expansion on the same scale seems unlikely'. This value judgement has been hotly contested. Odell and Rosing (1980) have argued that the 2000×10^9 figure tells us more about the oil companies' judgements of future politicoeconomic conditions than about the ultimate resources. While Barnet (1980) claims that all estimates made from within the industry rise and fall, depending on what it is in the companies' interests to disclose. Areas in which the companies are not able, or willing, to invest are estimated to have low resource potential. For example, the ultimate resources of Latin America, an area generally politically hostile to the companies, have been placed at only $150-230 \times 10^9$ barrels, a figure which other forecasters say is likely to be achieved by Mexico alone (Odell and Rosing, 1980). Even within the oil industry a few experts are now beginning to talk about world resources of 3000 or even 4000×10^9 barrels (Institut Français du Pétrole, 1978) and recent Russian estimates are even higher at $11,000 \times 10^9$ barrels (Styrikovich, 1977). The validity of all these estimates will only be tested by time. It is, however, important to remember that none includes the vast potential of oil shales and tar sands, which could contribute a further $30,000 \times 10^9$ barrels (US National Academy of Sciences, 1975).

In addition, the development of economically attractive alternative energy forms could make the whole question of ultimate oil resources redundant. This possibility may well have been hastened by events since 1973. Oligopolistic pricing policies have kept oil prices well above supply costs, so encouraging the development of alternative energy sources and promoting energy economy. At the same time, continued political upheavals in the major exporting states have not only weakened consumer confidence in oil, but have also, according to Rosing and Odell (1983), sapped the confidence of the oil industry in its ability to cope with a changing global political environment. As a result, intra-industry projections of future recoverable resources have fallen over the last five years and 'the industry . . . will . . . have been so weakened by contemporary difficulties as to render it incapable of ever utilizing the world's oil resources' (Rosing and Odell, 1983, p. 19).

MEASURES OF RESOURCE AVAILABILITY: RENEWABLE RESOURCES

Maximum resource potential

Anthropocentric attempts to estimate the future availability of renewable resources are usually based on the notion of resource capacity or potential to produce useful products or services in a set period of time. Estimates of the physical maximum energy potentials have been made for various renewable energy resources such as solar, tidal or wind power. The availability figures produced by such exercises paint highly comforting pictures; the total energy received from the sun, for instance, could theoretically provide for world energy consumptions about 10 million times greater than those of today. However, they are of little practical relevance; in reality, availability will be determined by human ability to convert these potentials into actual energy resources and by people's willingness to bear the costs involved, including those of environmental degradation.

Similar estimation exercises have been conducted to calculate the total biological capacity of the land and sea. These suggest that 'run' to its maximum capacity, the earth could produce about 40 tons of food per person per annum at current population levels. This is some 100 times greater than needs and does not include the possibilities of chemically synthesizing food from carbon dioxide, water and nitrogen which, while technically feasible, require massive inputs of energy. Such estimation exercises must be regarded as essentially trivial and of no value in the practical planning for future renewable resource developments. What is important is not some notional physical capacity, but the potential for human beings to make the required investments, as well as the enormous social, attitudinal, organizational and economic changes, which would be involved. The very notion of running the earth's biological system as though it were a machine, solely devoted to providing the needs of one species, man, is untenable, to some at least, on moral grounds. Moreover, ecologists have argued that, in any case, it would be a disastrous strategy since it would involve a massive simplification of the world's ecosystem and result in major disruptions to the natural biological cycles.

Both the energy and biological potential estimates are based on the physical output of natural systems, neglecting the constraints imposed by the capacity of human economic and social systems. However, another way of approaching the renewable resource potential question is to extrapolate from the most developed to the under- or undeveloped parts of the globe. This approach has been most popular in attempts to calculate the area of land potentially available for agriculture. By assuming that the proportion of the land, in each specific soil category, under agriculture in the most farmed areas could be made to apply in the least agriculturally developed economies, it has been estimated that the world's cultivated land could be extended to between 3.2 and 3.6 billion hectares, compared with the existing level of 1.4 billion hectares (Gerasimov, 1983). Clearly, this approach is limited by the assumption that the factors which have produced the existing land allocations will hold over time and space, but it does at least acknowledge some human constraints. It produces availability estimates considerably below the figure of 6.6. billion hectares obtained by simply finding the total land area which is physically capable of cultivation using existing technologies (US President's Science Advisory Committee, 1967).

Sustainable capacity

When the physical potential of a renewable resource is tempered by the requirement that its use must be allocated over time to give equality of opportunity to future generations, then the concept of *sustainable capacity* or *yield* is employed. In the case of a fishery it is theoretically possible to maintain a set yield of fish over time by controlling the level of exploitation effort. At any point along the sustainable yield curve, shown in Figure 2.4, the annual output is compatible

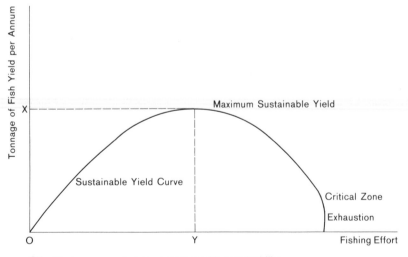

OX= Maximum annual yield consistent with sustainability
OY= Annual effort required to maximize sustainable yield

Figure 2.4   The sustainable yield curve

with maintaining the fish stock at a level which can produce that same output in future years. When fishing commences, the sustainable yield at first rises as some of the competition for food is reduced, allowing the rate of growth in the fish population and its biological productivity to increase. However, if the fishing effort exceeds X, the sustainable yield will start to fall until the critical point is reached when the population becomes too depleted to reproduce itself.

Similar sustainable yield notions have been employed for aquifers, with the recommendation that the pumping rate should not exceed the annual average rate of replenishment. Such a management rule may be acceptable for aquifers, such as those in Britain, which have relatively short recharge periods, but there are major difficulties with its application to those which are 'relic' products of past climatic regimes. People critically dependent on the Saharan artesian basins for their survival are not, for instance, likely to be willing to sacrifice their livelihood to maintain the water stock intact for future generations. It is often accepted as axiomatic that renewable resource use should be controlled within sustainable capacity (IUCN, 1980). However, this particular, albeit extreme, example serves to show that the adoption of such a policy is dependent on value judgements and priorities.

As economists such as Scott (1955a) have pointed out, the maintenance of sustainable yields is not a costless strategy since it implies the reduction of current consumption. This forgone consumption can be regarded as a form of investment for the future, the merits of which must be evaluated alongside other potential investments (see p. 71 and Chapter 8). It is quite possible for the conservation of a particular renewable resource to occur at the expense of other investments, in which case the composition of the endowment available for future generations may be changed but the total endowment will not increase and may even fall. In other words, to return to the artesian-well example, if the regulation of use to sustainable yield levels results – as it inevitably would – in a decline in economic development in the area, then any future generations may have plentiful water stocks but considerably less of everything else which growth could have produced. The idea that there *may* conceivably be circumstances in which the mining of a renewable to the point of extinction is an acceptable policy is, of course, anathema to those who see man as having a moral obligation to husband 'God's bounty' for the future. It is also regarded as a short-sighted strategy by ecologists, who regard the loss of genetic and species diversity as a major long-term threat to man's own life support systems (Eagles, 1984).

Absorptive capacity

A further capacity concept which also crucially depends upon value judgements is that of absorptive or assimilative capacity. This is employed where environmental media (water, land or air) are used either consciously or inadvertently for the disposal of the waste products from human activity. As long as the wastes are subject to the natural biological processes of decomposition all environmental systems have some capacity to absorb them without ecological or aesthetic changes occurring. However, if the rates of discharge exceed the breakdown capacity, or if the materials are non-biodegradable or degrade only over long time periods, then environmental change is inevitable.

The absorptive capacity of any environmental medium is not fixed; it not only varies naturally in response to climatic changes, but it can also be altered by man. For example, the capacity of a stream to degrade sewage or effluent discharges can be increased by augmenting either the stream flows or the levels of available oxygen. On the other hand, capacity reductions occur when water abstractions restrict the flow; when channel straightening, deepening or concrete lining decrease oxygen uptake; or when the available oxygen is already being used to decompose previously discharged pollutants. Taken to an extreme, the whole process of decomposition can be stopped completely when bacteria are starved of the oxygen they require to function. A policy based on controlling waste disposal to the limits of absorptive capacity involves the assumption that renewable resources should be maintained in their 'natural' state. As such a policy involves economic costs to society, there is by no means a consensus over whether these costs are outweighed by the damage and risks involved in environmental change.

Carrying capacity

A final measure of renewable resource availability which is in common use is the notion of *carrying capacity*. This concept, borrowed from agriculture, is analogous to those of absorptive and sustainable capacity, in that it too is based on the assumption that resource use should be limited to levels where no appreciable environmental changes occur or where resource productivity is sustained over time. McHarg (1969) and Odum (1971), for example, have employed the idea in attempts to establish the limits to human settlements within regions, while numerous studies have been conducted to calculate the capacity of recreation areas. In the latter case the limits to recreational activity are not only established by physical damage criteria, but also by the perceptions of the visitors (Stankey and Lime, 1973). In all its applications it is impossible to establish one simple, single and absolute value for carrying capacity; any estimates are critically dependent on the objectives of management, the specific way resources are used and on the standards of living or space which are assumed to be required by the user.

THE POLARIZED SCARCITY DEBATE

In the late 1960s and 1970s it was a widely held, much expressed belief that there was an imbalance between the availability of essential resources and future demands for them. A series of books were published presenting an apocalyptic vision of the future of mankind (Forrester, 1970; Goldsmith *et al.*, 1972; Meadows *et al.*, 1972, are but three well-known examples). Stock resource scarcity was viewed at best as a major barrier to continued economic development, with the depressing implications which this has for the economies of the Third World, and at worst it was predicted that complete exhaustion of essential mineral stocks would cause the total collapse of society during the early part of the twenty-first century. The concern kindled by such publications was then fanned by the 1973 oil crisis, which followed the Arab-Israeli war, and by the success of OPEC[3] in cutting oil supplies and achieving a massive rise in real oil prices (Figure 2.5). Scarcity became a political issue; the possibility that producer countries could and would exercise political and economic power through withholding supplies of essential minerals appeared as a major threat to the developed countries who, throughout the 1960s, had increased their dependence on imports from the less developed world.

Such fears of scarcity were by no means new, as the essay written by Malthus in 1798 on the 'Principle of population' so amply testifies. He argued that there was an immutable and universal law governing the relationship between population and resources. Given limited and fixed resources and the tendency for population to increase exponentially, it was inevitable that per capita incomes must fall over time until starvation and disease restored the balance between resources and population numbers. Malthus was in fact concerned with agricultural products which could be renewed using the fixed stock of land; his law became even more alarming when applied to mineral resource stocks, which decline with use. However, Malthus – perhaps understandably given the period in which he was writing – neglected the roles of technology and capital in increasing productivity. Engels, writing some forty years later, took a different view. He argued that if population grew exponentially, then so too did the labour power to produce food (Sandbach, 1980). By stressing labour productivity and the ability of man to

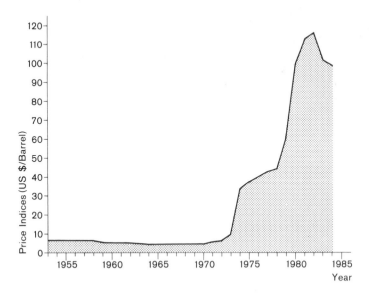

Figure 2.5   Oil price index, 1953–84 (100 = 1979)
Source: Compiled from data in International Monetary Fund, *International Financial Statistics Yearbook*, Washington, DC, IMF, 1983; and *International Financial Statistics* (IMF), XXXVII (7), 1984

utilize science and technology to provide for his needs, Engels saw nothing immutable in the Malthusian law. To date at least it is Engels who has been proved correct. Technological and economic changes have not only prevented the exhaustion of resource stocks, but have done so despite massive increases in population and per capita consumption levels.

It is even difficult to find cases where the pre-physical exhaustion stage in the resource development process has been reached. According to Ricardo (1817), the 'best' or least-cost resource deposits would be used first, in which case increases in consumption could only be met by exploiting progressively inferior elements in the total stock. Productivity must, therefore, fall as increasing inputs of labour or capital are required to produce each additional unit of output. Before absolute physical exhaustion occurs, there ought then to be a stage when the marginal physical product starts to fall and diminishing returns (or output) per labour unit set in (Figure 2.6). In other words, resource exploitation costs should rise in *real terms* when measured by the quantity of factor inputs required to maintain output. Although it is indisputable that lower-grade ores and deposits occurring at greater depths and in areas less accessible to markets are now being utilized, diminishing returns to labour and capital do not appear to have arisen (Barnett *et al.*, 1984). Technological innovation appears to have been able to postpone the appearance of diminishing returns. The curve representing the marginal physical product of the labour used in mineral exploitation has, as shown in Figure 2.6, been shifted upwards and outwards over time from T to T^2.

However, if it is accepted that Ricardo's underlying law remains in force, then two major questions face resource analysts. First, to what extent can such shifts continue to occur in the future? And, second, if declining returns do set in for one particular mineral, then will technological, economic and social change act to

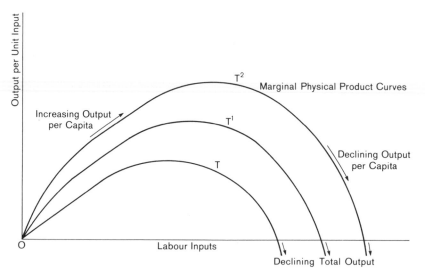

Figure 2.6   Diminishing returns and marginal physical product curves

reduce its resource significance? Different judgements about the answers to these two questions largely account for the highly polarized debate over resource scarcity which occurred in the early 1970s. While the pessimistic school concentrated on the limits inherent in a closed, fixed physical system, the optimists argued that the market system, purposeful technological innovation and social change would act together to solve all scarcity problems.

The pessimistic school

By far the most pessimistic and crude measures of stock resource life occur when current proven reserves are taken as the limit of resource availability. As we have already seen, 'statistics on reserves are no more than an expression of the mining industry's inventory of useable resources' (Manners 1977, p. 387). Their use implicitly involves the assumptions that no successful investment in exploration will take place and that no technological, political, or economic changes will occur to transform conditional reserves into economically recoverable resources. The life of each mineral can then be crudely calculated by dividing current reserves by the present annual consumption to give the so-called *static life index*. On this basis most of the major mineral resources would be exhausted within forty years, although coal would apparently last for 2000 years and iron ore would have about a 200-year life.

Much more alarming results arise if it is assumed that annual consumptions will not remain constant at current levels, but will increase as they have done in the past. As Figure 2.7 shows, at static levels of consumption bauxite reserves would last for approximately 100 years – but will run out within twenty-five years if consumption rises at the average annual rate of 9.8 per cent, which it did between 1947 and 1974. This type of estimation exercise inevitably produced the conclusion that 'present reserves of all but a few metals will be exhausted within fifty years' (Goldsmith *et al.*, 1972, p. 4). Oil and gas would vanish within thirty years and even coal would have only a 100-year life. Although the economic recession of the late 1970s and early 1980s has seen falling rates of increase in mineral consumption and in some cases absolute decline, any resource life estimates based on proven reserves must lead to the conclusion that the whole process of economic development will grind to a halt sometime in the next century.

It is easy to show how misleading in the past forecasts based on proven reserves have been. In 1939, for example, the US Department of the Interior predicted that indigenous oil stocks would be exhausted within thirteen years. However, since then additions to reserves have matched the increasing rate of annual production. Although US proven reserves have fluctuated in response to major new finds, they have remained between nine and fifteen times greater than production for the last forty years. In the same way, predictions made in 1950 that world iron ore reserves would be exhausted by 1970 have proved to be wildly inaccurate; in fact by that date enough reserves had been established to last a further 240 years at the then current level of consumption.

The simple truth is that, for most minerals, the rate at which new discoveries

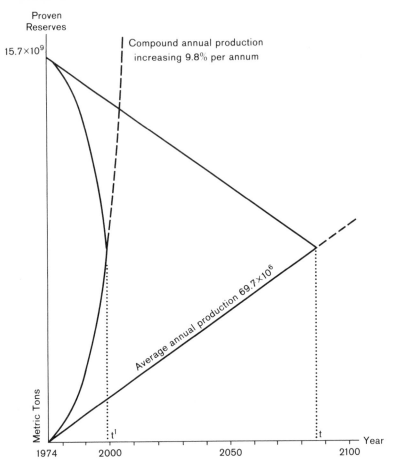

Proven
Reserves

15.7×10⁹

Compound annual production
increasing 9.8% per annum

Average annual production 69.7×10⁶

Metric Tons

t¹

t

Year

1974   2000   2050   2100

Proven reserves are only those containing 52% or more aluminium

Figure 2.7 The life of bauxite reserves using static and exponential life indices; the trend lines are calculated by extrapolating 1950–74 data

and technological and economic changes have added to proven reserves has exceeded, or at least kept pace with, increases in consumption. Table 2.2 clearly shows that this has been the case for virtually all the commonly used non-fuel minerals, and it applies equally to oil and natural gas. World oil consumption is now over seven times greater than it was in the 1940s but the ratio of proven reserves to annual consumption has not fallen. Rather the reverse, for whereas in 1940 the ratio suggested that world supplies would be exhausted in barely fifteen years at the then consumption level, today something over thirty years of life remain. Odell and Rosing (1983) have argued that even assuming no new discoveries, oil reserves would in fact last much longer than the reserves –consumption ratio would suggest. This view arises from the fact that the

Table 2.2 Cumulative production and addition to known reserves for selected minerals, 1950–74 (in metric tons)

Mineral	1950 reserves	1974 reserves	1950–74 cumulative production	1950–74 addition to reserves*
Asbestos	3.9×10^7	8.7×10^7	6.2×10^7	1.1×10^8
Bauxite	1.4×10^9	1.6×10^{10}	8.5×10^8	1.5×10^{10}
Chromium	1.0×10^8	1.7×10^9	9.6×10^7	1.7×10^9
Cobalt	7.9×10^5	2.4×10^6	4.4×10^5	2.2×10^6
Copper	1.0×10^8	3.9×10^8	1.1×10^8	4.0×10^8
Gold	3.1×10^4	4.0×10^4	2.9×10^4	3.7×10^4
Iron	1.9×10^{10}	8.8×10^{10}	7.3×10^9	7.6×10^{10}
Lead	4.0×10^7	1.5×10^8	6.3×10^7	1.7×10^8
Manganese	5.0×10^8	1.9×10^9	1.6×10^8	1.6×10^9
Mercury†	1.3×10^5	1.8×10^5	1.9×10^5	2.5×10^5
Nickel†	1.4×10^7	4.4×10^7	9.4×10^6	3.9×10^7
Phosphates	2.6×10^9	1.3×10^{10}	1.3×10^9	1.2×10^{10}
Platinum	7.8×10^2	1.9×10^4	1.7×10^3	2.0×10^4
Potash	5.0×10^9	8.1×10^{10}	3.0×10^8	7.6×10^{10}
Silver	1.6×10^5	1.9×10^5	2.0×10^5	2.3×10^5
Sulphur	4.0×10^8	2.0×10^9	6.1×10^8	2.2×10^9
Tin	6.0×10^6	1.0×10^7	4.6×10^6	8.6×10^6
Tungsten	2.4×10^6	1.6×10^6	7.6×10^5	-4.3×10^4
Zinc	7.0×10^7	1.2×10^8	9.7×10^7	1.5×10^8

* Calculated by adding cumulative production to 1974 reserves and subtracting 1950 reserves.
† Data on reserves for communist countries incomplete.

Source: Tilton, 1977, p. 10.

declared proven reserves in any field at the time of discovery are highly conservative estimates and are almost invariably revised upwards when production actually gets underway. The process of *reserve appreciation* means that declared reserves in any one year may understate the true position by more than a factor of three. Data published by British Petroleum (1979), for example, suggests that the declared reserves in 1950 for all non-communist countries of 100×10^9 barrels have subsequently been appreciated to 350×10^9 barrels. Clearly, this revision process crucially affects the reserves to production ratios and life expectancy estimates, as Table 2.3 shows.

Some forecasters have attempted to compensate for the obvious fact that proven reserves will continue to increase for at least some time to come by assuming that ultimately known reserves will be some arbitrary factor of the current level, five times being a popular figure. Alternatively, an equally arbitrary ultimate limit can be derived from current levels of consumption. Meadows's 'World III' model, for example, contains the unjustified and unjustifiable assumption

Table 2.3   The reserve appreciation process for proven oil reserves, 1950–81

Year	A Reserve life based on declared reserves (years)	B Reserve life based on appreciated reserves (years) (1978 calculations)	C Reserve life based on appreciated reserves assuming increasing annual use	% annual increase in consumption
1950	24.7	95	19.2	5.41
1951	23.8	91	17.6	6.50
1952	25.9	90	18.9	6.74
1953	27.8	84	20.3	6.76
1954	31.3	84	22.7	6.97
1955	33.5	75	23.4	7.77
1956	37.6	75	25.6	8.28
1957	40.4	73	27.7	8.13
1958	41.6	75	30.2	6.95
1959	41.0	71	28.7	7.71
1960	38.9	66*	27.6	7.38
1961	38.0	64*	28.1	6.55
1962	35.3	63*	25.5	7.08
1963	34.7	58*	25.0	7.08
1964	33.0	55*	23.3	7.51
1965	32.0	53*	23.2	6.94
1966	32.0	51*	23.3	6.88
1967	31.7	53*	23.0	6.98
1968	30.6	46*	20.7	8.37
1969	34.0	46*	23.8	9.75
1970	32.4	45*	22.4	7.96
1981	32.8	Will not be known until 2001	31.6	0.04†

* The full appreciation process for these years is unlikely to be completed yet.
† Average annual increase in consumption, 1973–81.

Source: Odell and Rosing, 1983, p. 43
Note: Columns A and B give the reserve to production ratios assuming that consumption remains at the then annual level; column C gives the ratio taking into account the average percentage increase in the rate of oil consumption over the previous ten years.

that 250 times the 1970 consumption is 'an order of magnitude estimate of world resources' (Meadows, 1974). Whatever figure is used, there is the implicit assumption that the process of reserve discovery and redefinition will not act in the future as it has in the past.

An ultimate resource base five times greater than the current level of proven reserves may appear to be generous but in just twenty years, from 1950 to 1970, increases of or above that order of magnitude were experienced for iron, chromite, bauxite, oil, potash, phosphates and many other of our most widely used minerals. Similarly, the use of the 250 times consumption figure may seem optimistic but the fact is that the cumulative reserves of several key minerals have already shown this level of increase in the post Second World War period. For example, by 1974 cumulative iron reserves had reached 76×10^9 tons, or over 260 times the 1950 iron ore production figure. It is clear that in the past, if consumption has increased exponentially, so too have known reserves, and often at a faster rate. The proven world reserves of oil have increased since the 1950s almost 2 per cent per annum faster than consumption. Any models containing assumptions that the ultimate resource base is a factor of current proven reserves or consumptions must also be making the assumption that the process of reserve discovery and redefinition is slowing down. Although it is axiomatic that for each individual resource stock there must be a limit, we neither have the information to say what this is nor any certainty that the substance will still be regarded as a resource when its physical limit is neared. If a model contains the conditions that a substance is essential to economic development, that it is not substitutable and must meet exponentially growing consumptions, then it must reach the same conclusion irrespective of the magnitude of the fixed resource limit upon which it is based. Different reserve estimates may change the date at which physical exhaustion will halt production, but will only do so marginally given the nature of exponential consumption growth. In other words, all models, however complicated, which give a static physical dimension to the dynamic resource concept are 'programmed to catastrophe by Malthusian reasoning' (O'Riordan, 1976, p. 60).

All physically deterministic models fail to take account of the fact that resources are culturally determined, a product of social choice, technology and the workings of the economic system. Man is not a blind automaton programmed to push stock resource consumption to catastrophic limits. Lifestyles do not have to be dependent on particular resource stocks. In theory, at least, we have the capability of controlling consumption, through conservation and recycling, and of developing the potential of renewable resources. The way the resource pessimists ignored both human response mechanisms and the cultural nature of resources has brought them under severe criticism. Forrester's and Meadow's work has been variously described as 'a significant retrogression in scientific technique' (Nordhaus, quoted in Kay and Mirrlees 1975, p. 141), 'essentially trivial' (Graham and Herrick, 1973, p. 415) and 'naïve in conception, amateurish in construction', with 'negligible – and warped – use of empirical data' (Kay and Mirrlees, 1975, p. 147). Leaving aside for the moment the fundamental question of whether economic growth is in fact desirable on social or environmental grounds (pp. 240–3), the question still remains whether our political, social and economic institutions could in practice act fast enough to prevent stock resource scarcity from becoming a barrier to continued economic development. Whereas the pessimists, by constructing their models in the manner they did, were in effect assuming that response mechanisms did not exist or would act too slowly, the optimistic school argue that the market system would respond automatically to prevent severe exhaustion problems (Beckerman, 1972b, 1974).

The market optimists

THE MARKET RESPONSE MODEL

In a perfectly working market economy the price of any resource commodity which was becoming scarce would inevitably rise. The increased production costs associated with diminishing returns would mean that producers would be willing to supply less to the market at existing price levels – prices would, therefore, rise until supply and demand were again in balance. Such price rises would immediately set in train a whole series of demand, technological and supply responses (Figure 2.8). First, demands decrease as users turn to cheaper substitutes, or introduce economy and conservation measures. In the case of metals, demand for the primary resource also falls as recycling becomes more economically viable and scrap becomes more valuable and worth collecting. Second, both the price rise and fears of scarcity provide an incentive for innovation. The resulting technological changes are likely to increase the availability and decrease the cost of substitutes, and improve conservation methods. These changes will then feedback through the price mechanism to curb demands and so reduce pressure on the originally scarce commodity. Third, the price rise will make it economic to exploit hitherto unviable deposits, encourage the search for new supply sources and promote development of new extraction

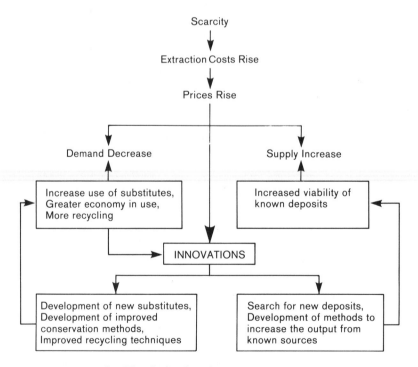

Figure 2.8   The idealized market response to resource scarcity

technologies to increase effective yields from known deposits. It is, of course, recognized that this last adaptation mechanism cannot continue indefinitely for any single stock resource material.

If this scenario about the working of the economic system is accepted, consumption will not continue to increase until it hits some physical ceiling when it collapses, but it will tail off relatively gently as prices rise. Meadows's 'World III' model assumes that supply costs will increase twenty times by the time 90 per cent of the resource stocks have gone.[4] It is untenable to assume that such major cost increases will fail to have any impact on the demand curve for the resources. Although the responsiveness of demand to price changes is not known with any certainty, particularly over the longer term, it is believed that for most non-fuel minerals demand will fall by between 6 and 20 per cent for each 10 per cent increase in price (US Congress, 1974; Tilton, 1977). Oil demands have also been shown to be price responsive, as the reduction in world consumption since 1973 demonstrates (p. 89). Moreover, the rapid fall in US demands following the deregulation of prices in 1979 suggests that a significant response can occur over very short time periods (p. 172).

THE ROLE OF SUBSTITUTION

The optimistic stance does not stop with the argument that falling demands will slow down the rate of exhaustion, but it also states that such decreases *need not* automatically imply reduced living standards or declining rates of economic growth. Although some of the initial demand reduction following a price rise will occur because consumers can no longer afford to buy as much of the more costly mineral products, in time substitution will become the key demand adaptation mechanism. It has to be remembered that by definition resources have no intrinsic worth, but derive value from the useful services or products they yield. Therefore, as long as other methods can be found to fulfil these same functions at no extra *real* cost, then real incomes and growth rates need not be affected. This whole line of argument is, of course, based on the assumption that no individual stock resource commodity is absolutely essential; substitutes exist or will be found to replace it.

Substitution can take a whole variety of forms. In the first place, *direct substitution* can and does occur, when one resource commodity takes over the role of another. The same mineral can normally be obtained from different types of geological source and in a variety of chemical combinations with other elements. When the traditionally used source material becomes scarce, efforts may be made to develop technologies to allow extraction from alternative sources. For example, fears for the future availability of bauxite supplies have encouraged research into techniques for extracting aluminium from non-bauxite ores such as kaolin clays, carbonaceous shales, nemeline and nephelite (see Chapter 3, p. 75). In this case the fears are not the result of any potential physical scarcity, but arise from the dependence of the major consumer nations on bauxite imports and the perceived threat that supply embargoes or price 'hikes' could pose to their economies.

Similarly, one mineral could be directly replaced by other materials in at least some of its end-uses. For instance, aluminium, stainless steel and plastics are all substitutes for copper; aluminium has already widely taken over the high-voltage transmission line market and, together with stainless steel, has largely ousted copper pans from the kitchen. Plastic piping has similarly replaced copper for many household plumbing purposes, although the increased cost of oil has slowed the penetration of plastics into traditional metal end-use markets. Going through the list of stock resources, it is difficult to find ones which have no substitutes at all, although there are cases where the technical problems and the costs involved in substitution are great (pp. 168–9). This applies, for example, in attempts to curb the use of manganese in steelmaking, which currently accounts for 90 per cent of all production of the higher-grade manganese ores (Klass *et al.*, 1980).

It is the potential for direct substitution plus the diversity of elements available in the earth's crust which has led commentators such as Manners to argue that scarcity in an absolute physical sense is a non-issue:

> There can not possibly be doubts about the prospective physical adequacy of most mineral supplies, since there exist within the surface of the earth more than enough mineable materials for the longer term needs of mankind . . . a recognition of the composition of the earth's crust denies practical meaning to the notion of mineral exhaustion in a purely physical sense. The entire planet is composed of minerals, and man can hardly mine himself out. (Manners, 1977, p. 388)

Another rather different form of substitution occurs when the need for specific resource products or services is reduced by the substitution of technology and capital for the resource. To take the copper example once again, the need for undersea transmission cables, a hitherto major copper end-use, has significantly declined with the development of microwave technologies and communication satellites (Mikesell, 1979). Measures to improve the efficiency with which a specific resource is used have also had marked effects on consumption. It is well known that the coke needed to produce 1 ton of pig-iron has fallen dramatically, from over 8 tons in the mid-eighteenth century, to 3 tons in 1900 and under half a ton today. In exactly the same way households can reduce their energy consumption by investing in double-glazing and other forms of insulation. All these cases illustrate that demand reductions can be achieved without declining living standards or reduced growth rates. The resource optimists argue that technological change is now a planned cumulative process which under the stimulus of the market system can be expected to minimize the impact of the depletion of any one specific stock resource.

A third form of substitution involves the increased use of 'secondhand' materials at the expense of the freshly mined product. For a number of metals, recycled old scrap[5] already serves a significant proportion of the final market but many commentators have argued that relatively minor new ore price rises could make much greater levels of recycling economically possible. It has been calculated that in the USA some 30 per cent of redundant copper products are already collected for reprocessing but this could rise to 50 or 60 per cent by the year 2000 (US Bureau of Mines, 1974). Even the notion that entropy may operate to limit reuse appears of dubious relevance in the foreseeable future since only about 1 per cent of the copper unrecovered over the period 1961–70 is dissipated beyond recovery (Mikesell, 1979). In fact, the use of solid waste disposal sites, which act as sinks for many metal products, may serve to concentrate rather than to disperse used metals and could provide the mines of the future. The potential for copper recycling is by no means atypical of that for other metals, and reuse need not be confined to the metallic minerals; considerable quantities of chemical materials and non-metallic element minerals are already collected and reused – in part for cost reasons, but also as a pollution control measure.

Finally, substitution – in a rather different sense – occurs when lifestyle or demand changes alter the mix of final goods and services. The process of changing from an economy based on heavy industry and primary production to one which is much less resource intensive is already well advanced in the western world. As Ridker (1972) has shown, changes in the economic mix, with the greater importance of complex secondary processing, tertiary activities and leisure, can produce marked reductions in stock resource need. While the economic system left to itself can be expected to produce some lifestyle changes, it should also be remembered that individuals and governments have choices about how they live and what stock resources they consume; although whether they will be willing or able to exercise their choice is quite another matter.

The fact that these forms of substitution have occurred in the past is incontrovertible, and there is no reason to assume that they will suddenly cease to operate in the future. Kay and Mirrlees (1975) have shown quite clearly that Meadows's 'World III' model can be made to yield startlingly different results if demands are allowed to fall in response to price increases and capital is substituted for resources. On high, but not necessarily unreasonable, assumptions about the potential for substitution, the model can be made to allow productive output to increase 40,000 times with only an eightfold growth in resource use, which is within the proven reserves of virtually all resources! The authors stress that their efforts at manipulation should not be regarded as serious attempts to predict future economic activity and resource use. However, their work amply demonstrates the deficiencies in models which implicitly assume that negligible response to impending scarcity is feasible.

CHALLENGES TO OPTIMISM

Any predictions of demand changes, technological innovation and social adaptations are subject to great uncertainty and are likely to become more and more inaccurate the further they are pushed into the future. Ridker and Watson express this clearly when they say,

> It is not possible to make many useful predictions about the long-term future in any absolute sense. The future will be determined by new discoveries and inventions, new ideological movements and institutional arrangements, and

perhaps at times by the decisions of wilful, impetuous individuals who happen to be strategically placed. Such discontinuities in human history have never been amenable to prediction. (Ridker and Watson, 1980, pp. 11–12)

While books, such as that by Herman Kahn *et al.* (1976), which look at the next 200 years or so may be regarded as interesting pieces of imaginative fiction, most serious forecasters are now confining their attention to the resource picture in the next twenty-five to fifty years. Almost without exception current work has concluded that over this timescale the physical scarcity of stock resources will not cause any serious losses in economic welfare. Notions that absolute physical scarcity will produce the imminent, catastrophic collapse of society may therefore be dismissed. However, there are many reasons for challenging as absurdly optimistic the view that all scarcity problems will automatically be solved by market processes.

There are three key bases upon which the challenges to optimism have been founded: first, the market system is manifestly imperfect; second, the results of market operations may not conform to the social, economic and political objectives of society; and third, the market cannot cope with – in fact it creates – some forms of natural resource scarcity.

Market imperfections

To produce the demand, technological and supply responses necessary to allocate resources optimally between competing users over space and time, the market would need to be perfectly competitive, comprised of firms acting in a pre-scribedly rational way to maximize profits and peopled by managers endowed with omniscient powers to predict future resource demands and price levels. Moreover, the system would need to be free from intervention by governments. It is axiomatic that such conditions do not apply in the real world, and so the question is raised whether 'imperfections' could in fact produce physical scarcity problems in the relatively short-term future.

The fact that stock resource output tends to be controlled by a few relatively large private corporations or nationalized industries has led some commentators to argue that scarcity becomes less not more likely. Imperfectly competitive firms, by definition, are large enough to affect the final market price for their product.[6] To maximize profits over time they will restrict current output to maintain price levels, and such output restrictions may continue over long periods if there are barriers which inhibit the entry of new firms into the industry. In other words, less resources are produced and consumed than there would have been under perfect market conditions. Therefore, more must be available for future use. It has even been suggested that this means that resources are currently being *underexploited*, with a 'real danger that the world's resources are being used too slowly', and that 'the interests of future generations will be better-served if we leave them production equipment rather than minerals in the ground' (Kay and Mirrlees, 1975, p. 171).

THE EFFECTS OF RISK AND UNCERTAINTY

However, the existence of other market imperfections leads to the opposite, and more generally accepted, suggestion that resources are being exploited too rapidly to maximize the long-term benefits from their use. For an imperfect competitor to make an optimal choice about how much product to withhold now in favour of future returns, he would need to know how demand, supply and price conditions will alter over time. He would, therefore, have to be able to predict the future state of the world economy, technological innovations, the actions of other suppliers and changes in consumer tastes or lifestyles. Nor can he reduce the uncertainty surrounding future returns by selling his expected output now in long-term futures markets (Heal, 1975; Dasgupta and Heal, 1979). In the absence of forward markets it is likely that risk and uncertainty will push producers to accelerate the rate of development of known deposits.

Not only have the prices for some resource products been extremely volatile, but over time the terms of trade have tended to move against raw materials – their prices having risen more slowly than those of manufactured goods. In these circumstances producers can reduce their uncertainty about future incomes by increasing current output at known price levels and investing the proceeds in commodities for which the terms of trade are more favourable. Particularly when resources have substitutes which are already economically viable, or are likely to become so in the near future, there is little incentive to conservation. The tendency to exploit known resources as rapidly as possible is reinforced for private companies by the risk of expropriation of their assets. Given the political instability and strength of feeling against multinational corporations in many producer states, companies are likely to exploit the deposits rapidly and secure their investments in as short a time period as possible. Available evidence suggests that the major private mineral companies are indeed highly averse to risk and uncertainty. They are 'discounting'[7] their potential future income from resource developments – especially in less developed countries – at very high rates, which not only reduces the number of 'proven reserve' sites, but also implies rapid exploitation levels. In addition, it is known that a number of the major mineral multinationals are diversifying their interests into other sectors of the economy (see Chapter 3, p. 75).

Although these factors may result in the over-rapid exhaustion of known reserves, they may also create even more important long-term difficulties by stifling exploration and the development of new supply sources. Tilton (1977, p. 24) suggests that lack of investment in providing and exploiting new deposits 'poses a serious threat – more serious than depletion – to mineral supplies over the next decade or two'. His view mirrors those of many other commentators. For example, in 1975, a tripartite report by fifteen economists from Japan, the EEC and North America stated that 'a more realistic constraint on mineral supplies than resource depletion could be insufficient investment – the factor which transforms mineral occurrences into marketable supplies' (Brookings Institution, 1975, p. 17). Even in developed countries extremely large amounts of capital are required to find a viable deposit and to develop the necessary extraction, processing and transport facilities; moreover, a major part of the investment capital must be committed well ahead of any returns. Volatile prices, the declining real value of raw materials, and the risk of nationalization, increased taxation or export restrictions could all act to reduce the incentive to commit investment capital on the scale and over the time period needed to secure future supplies.

Nor are matters necessarily improved if stock resource development is taken out of private hands and into public control. In the first place, governments may have little incentive to save output from known sources for the future. The need to seek re-election in democratic societies tends to enhance the perceived short-term income and trade advantages of rapid exploitation. If economic growth and improved living standards are critically dependent on the income derived from resource exports, then there are even greater development pressures.

At the present time it is clear that many less developed countries have extremely limited capabilities of curbing resource exports to allow for potential future domestic use since export income is desperately required to pay for essential imports and to service foreign debts. The political future of most governments, even authoritarian regimes, is usually dependent on the achievement of observable short-term economic gains for the present population; the potential needs of unborn generations inevitably become a secondary consideration. In addition, state ownership may in itself act to curb exploration activity. The inflow of foreign private venture capital is likely to be reduced (indeed it may be discouraged), but only rarely will indigenous capital sources, private or those of the government, be available at the levels needed to undertake major resource exploration activities (see Chapter 3, pp. 68–9).

Resource security

Even if we make the assumption that despite the imperfections the market will still act to avoid worldwide physical scarcity problems, difficulties may still arise because of the uneven spatial distribution of resource consumption, production and reserves (see pp. 78–93). The market system will not necessarily ensure that consumer demands are met in each individual country by the development of indigenous resources. In planned economies, closed to world markets, a minerals self-sufficiency policy could create the demand and technological adaptations necessary to ensure that all needs are met from internal resources. This is, of course, subject to the presumption that the physical base is diverse enough to generate substances capable of producing a full range of essential goods and services. However, outside such closed systems, producers would develop, all other things being equal, the least-cost mineral sources irrespective of their location *vis-à-vis* national boundaries. This raises the possibility that individual countries will experience physical shortages because they are unable to import the required materials. Third World nations may lack the financial resources to do so, while the developed nations could be affected by political upheavals in their supply areas or by trade embargoes.

Particularly since the early 1970s the western bloc of advanced nations has reacted with alarm to the possibility that Third World governments could attempt to use their mineral resources as political weapons. The formation of producer cartels for tin, copper, bauxite, iron ore, mercury and tungsten makes it conceivable that attempts will be made to emulate OPEC, with the use of output restrictions and price fixing to increase their share of the wealth created by mineral developments. Moreover, as the 1973 oil embargo so dramatically illustrated, the producer states could use trade restrictions to further their political objectives.[8] Fears over import dependence have been further fuelled by the notion that, given the long history of resource exploration and exploitation in western countries, a high proportion of future discoveries will be made in the relatively underexplored Soviet bloc, or in those LDCs already or potentially within the Soviet sphere of influence. If this proves to be the case, a dramatic shift in the power balance could occur which, at least in the eyes of the US National Commission on Materials (1973), would impair 'the long run security and economic growth of this and other free nations' and affect the 'dynamic nature of capitalism'.

It will be argued in Chapter 4 that it is highly unlikely that other producers will be able to achieve OPEC's market power and if they did it would not have the same impact on the developed economies of the west. However, it would be unwise to discount the possibilities of at least temporary shortages, arising from trade restrictions or war. Whether the security fears are real or imaginary, they have already affected both the resource use policies of consumer countries and the investment behaviour of private corporations. The United States has for many years carried large strategic stockpiles and most western nations have now adopted a similar policy. For example, in 1975 the French allocated funds for stockpiling, and in early 1976 the Japanese government decided to stockpile copper, aluminium, lead and zinc (Tilton, 1977). Attempts have been made to form consumer nation associations to agree on demand control strategies. Planning restrictions have been eased on the exploitation of indigenous resources and incentives given to increase the level of exploration. In addition, greater attention is now being paid to the development of substitutes and improved conservation techniques. All these reactions may in the long term have damaging effects on the underdeveloped resource exporters, and may further widen the wealth gap between the west and the Third World. Existing income disparities are already the subject of great concern, and many have argued that a new international economic order (NIEO) must be created to ensure the harmonious growth of the world economic system and the promotion of a more equitable distribution of available resources (Brandt Commission, 1980; Dolman, 1980).

A Catch-22 situation has arisen. The way the world market system operates, with all its imperfections, fails to satisfy either the income and political control objectives of Third World producers or the security objectives of the developed importing countries. Attempts by host governments to change the way the profits from resource exploitation are allocated, then, both discourages private invest-ment in new exploration ventures within their national borders and causes consumer governments to attempt to reduce their perceived vulnerability. These reactions in turn raise the possibility that the level of investment needed to establish new proven reserves will not occur, thereby creating physical shortages even in the short run. On the other hand, if a combination of private enterprise and consumer government responses redirect the investment, without decreasing the total, then physical scarcities could be prevented; but at the expense of creating still further international wealth disparities and all the attendant political and economic difficulties.

Economic exhaustion

Further problems arise because there is nothing in the market system which can prevent the exhaustion of specific mineral deposits, or the economic and social disruption which this would cause in any nation or region dependent upon them. In fact market forces are likely to accelerate the onset of exhaustion since deposits are almost inevitably economically exhausted long before they are physically worked out. The coalmines closed in Britain since the 1960s, and scheduled for closure today, still contain coal but given current market conditions (and political circumstances) it can only be sold at prices below production costs. The role of market forces in determining when any particular mineral deposit reaches the point of exhaustion can be illustrated by reference to Figure 2.9. As the deposit

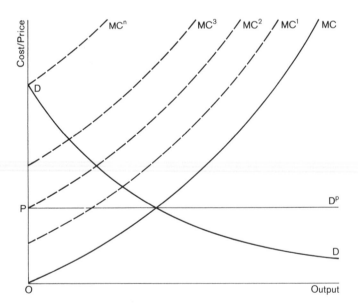

MC – MCⁿ Marginal Cost/Supply Curves at different points in time
D–D Total Market Demand Curve
P–Dᵖ Demand Curve faced by perfectly competitive firm

Figure 2.9   The onset of economic exhaustion

becomes more physically difficult to mine supply costs rise and, over time, the marginal cost supply curves (MC–MC'') will shift upwards.[9]

The producer will, therefore, need to receive progressively higher prices for each unit of output in order to cover the production costs. But as prices rise, so fewer and fewer consumers will be willing or able to purchase the mineral. If the deposit accounted for *all* supplies reaching the market, the producer is faced by the market demand curve (D–D) and some production will still be sold until, at MC'' cost levels, no output can be produced at prices consumers are prepared to pay. However, if the deposit is only a minor contributor to total supply, the relevant demand curve faced by the producer is represented by the line P–D^p, and output can only be sold at the market price. In these circumstances economic exhaustion occurs much more rapidly, and by the time the supply costs have shifted to MC^2 there is no demand for the mineral. The argument here greatly simplifies the forces at work in the complex, imperfectly competitive market system of the real world but does demonstrate that the economic factors, which may prevent the worldwide physical exhaustion of resources, do nothing to prevent local economic exhaustion. It is this fact which explains why so many governments intervene in the minerals markets to subsidize indigenous producers or restrict competition from foreign producers.

The effects of depletion at the local, regional, or national scale will depend on the extent to which other self-sustainable activities have been generated. While the economic base remains dependent on the exploitation of a single stock resource, major social and economic problems must result from its economic exhaustion. Private resource ownership may exacerbate these problems since the rate of rundown which optimizes producer profits is unlikely to be the one which minimizes social and economic disruption. By and large, developed nations have highly diversified economies able to withstand the depletion of a single resource stock without major declines in the national gross domestic product or significantly increased rates of total unemployment. However, even in these countries regional rundown and unemployment problems have by no means been trivial; the difficulties involved in generating employment to replace that lost in the coal industries of Europe and Canada are well known (Donald, 1966). Moreover, the rundown of an indigenous resource may further exacerbate fears over national security.

Undoubtedly, the resource exporting countries in the Third World face even more critical depletion problems. Many of them are highly dependent on the export of a single – or a group of related – mineral products. As Table 3.7 (p. 95) shows, in some cases well over 50 per cent of all export earnings can be derived from raw materials. With relatively few exceptions, in the LDCs the exploitation of resources has not generated the sort of mixed industrial and service base which could sustain the collapse of a major industry; all too often much of the growth associated with mineral developments has been exported to the advanced countries of the world. In these circumstances the possibility that a crucial mineral could become economically exhausted poses a major threat to the entire national economy. And of course, this could arise not through any increases in production costs, but because technological, demand or price changes wipe out the market for the product. It is not very difficult to envisage the situation in which new copper produced outside the advanced economies loses much of its resource value, nor to imagine what effects this would have on the already hard-pressed economies of Zaire, Zambia or Peru.

Environmental change

A final set of issues or challenges which must be raised here relates to what sort of society would be produced if market processes were indeed able to prevent the physical exhaustion of stock resources and were allowed to do so unchecked by government activity. We have already seen that the geopolitical threats to resource availability may be overcome at the expense of multiplying the already considerable economic and social problems of Third World nations. Many commentators have further argued that it could take place at the ultimate expense of all human life, by ruining the environment as the 'sustenance base' of society.

Snyder (1971, p. ix), for example, has claimed that 'few people alive now will survive the next three decades'. Rather less lurid warnings have also been given, among many others, by Ehrlich (1970a), Schaeffer (1970), Commoner (1972b) and Ward and Dubos (1972). Still others have taken a less extreme view, concentrating on the quality of life which the surviving population would enjoy or endure, and arguing that although market forces may protect material interests, real standards of human welfare would decline (Barnett and Morse, 1963; Mishan, 1967). One of the key bases for these ideas is the observable fact that the exploitation of industrial raw materials also involves the exploitation of environmental resources. It is a characteristic of resources such as water and air quality, plant and animal life, and landscape value that they have traditionally been treated as *free goods*, with little or no market value. Decisions on stock resource production and consumption have, therefore, been made without considering the related use of the non-market environmental resources. (These issues will be considered in more detail in later chapters.)

At each stage in the stock resource development and use process the services of various environmental resources are required. Extraction involves disruption to soils, vegetation and drainage patterns, produces significant levels of water and air pollution, reduces landscape values, and may also result in major economic and social losses being incurred by the workforce and by others in the community. Damage to health, materials and buildings, reduced agricultural productivity and increased water supply costs, may all be costs which must be added to the *real* price of minerals. Moreover, particularly in the energy sector, accidents during extraction can cause major environmental damage and loss of life. In 1969, for example, over 78,000 barrels of oil leaked from a well in Santa Barbara, California, causing damage at an estimated \$16.4 million (Garvey, 1972).

For most minerals, the degree of environmental damage escalates as lower-grade deposits are worked, the scale of operations increases and modern 'mass-mining' technologies are employed. Furthermore, the pushing of mineral exploitation into untapped, undeveloped areas, remote from market areas may

1   Vein mineral working within the Peak District National Park; a very small part-time operation but nevertheless having a severe impact on the local environment.

2   Dramatic alterations to land surface characteristics as a result of limestone extraction, lime burning and the disposal of waste products, near Buxton, Derbyshire.

3   Ridge and vale topography produced by ironstone mining in Northamptonshire.

4   Giant walking dragline working on the open-cast coal site at Maesgwyn Gap, Glyn Neath, South Wales.

not only destroy (or at least drastically alter) the ecology of the few remaining natural environments, but also have a profound impact on the culture and lifestyles of the indigenous populations. These effects were major issues in the dispute over the development of the Alaskan oilfields and are still a major source of controversy in Australia, where uranium and iron ore are mined on aboriginal lands. In other words, many of the processes that have delayed the appearance of diminishing returns to stock resource production have accelerated environmental and social change. Inevitably, this exacerbates conflict between those who place a high value on mineral products and those who wish to use land and other environmental resources to produce different goods and services.

Nor do the effects of stock resource utilization stop with their extraction; at the smelting, refining, transportation and processing stages waste products are discharged into the air and water bodies or are tipped on to land. Not only does this reduce the quality of these environmental media, but it is clear that it can have serious feedback effects on human health. One of the best-documented examples is the Miniamata mercury poisoning episode in Japan, where the water-borne wastes from copper refining contained methyl mercury. This accumulated in fish and shellfish, which when eaten by people caused severe foetal abnormalities; the miscarriage rate increased and deaf, blind and heavily spastic children were born to mothers who themselves appeared unaffected by mercury poisoning (Holdgate, 1979).

Major accidents serve to draw public and press attention to the costs and risks involved in mineral use. The explosion in 1979 which killed fifty people during the unloading of the tanker *Betelgeuse* at Bantry Bay, in Ireland, highlighted the risks associated with oil and gas transportation. Questions were raised about the safety of workers and residents in areas such as Canvey Island or the port of Rotterdam where unloading facilities and storage tanks are concentrated. Similarly, the grounding of the *Torrey Canyon* (1967) and the *Amoco-Cadiz* (1978) provided spectacular illustrations of the costs involved in oil-spills, including not only the damage to marine ecosystems, but also the clean-up costs and economic losses suffered by local fishing and tourist industries. Potentially even more worrying incidents, such as the near disaster at the Three Mile Island nuclear power plant in March 1979, show the risks involved in relying on nuclear technology to replace fossil fuels. However, while these events are dramatic, most environmental changes occur in a much more humdrum manner through the everyday use of the environment to dispose of waste products during the extraction, processing and consumption of resources.

These incremental changes lower the amenity and recreation value of environmental resources and thus reduce social welfare levels. Even more crucially, ecologists and other scientists have argued that man cannot continue to use the environment as a waste dump without destroying the bio-geochemical cycles on which life itself depends (Commoner, 1972b). It is known, for instance, that the burning of fossil fuels is changing the carbon cycle by adding carbon dioxide to the atmosphere, a process made more injurious by the widespread removal of forests which act to absorb CO_2. What proportion of the additional CO_2 is building up in the atmosphere and is it affecting the transfer of solar radiation? Could it cause major adverse climatic change? Is the sea acting to absorb more CO_2 and can it continue to take up the concentrations? What will be the long-term effects on marine ecosystems? The answers to these sorts of key question are badly needed before it is known whether man is destroying his life support systems. While concerns for the survival of the human species may be greatly exaggerated, the prudence of unthinkingly allowing the process of change to continue unabated must be questioned (Holdgate, 1979).

It is just possible that the technological changes and other forms of adaptation generated by the market to avert stock resource scarcity will prove compatible with the maintenance of the critical bio-geochemical cycles, but it would be an act of supreme faith (or extreme folly) to rely on such a happy coincidence of interests. Some adaptations, such as changing lifestyles, economy in use and the greater use of renewables, could reduce the environmental and social costs involved in stock resource use. However, the development of synthetic substances to replace naturally occurring mineral elements may increase ecological risks, and a number of writers have asserted that modern technologies are increasingly damaging to the environment (Commoner, 1972a; Schnaiberg, 1980). Although the evidence to support such claims is open to question (see p. 240), there seems little doubt that the failure of the market system to incorporate the services of the environment into the mineral production and use cost calculations makes it more likely that adaptations to circumvent stock scarcities will occur at the expense of increasing the scarcity of environmental resources.

The interrelationships between the industrial minerals sector and the life support and aesthetic services of the environment raise two key questions. First, to what extent should governments intervene to ensure that the social and environmental costs, including risk, are incorporated into economic decisions? And second, what effects will such intervention have on the processes of adaptation to physical stock resource depletion? Some people may regard the risks and costs as acceptable payments for the material benefits which resource development can bring. Others, preoccupied by short-term economic gains or ignorant of the long-term risks involved, may never have questioned the desirability of continuing current exploitation practices. Undoubtedly, for many LDCs the uncertain long-term effects of pollution become an irrelevance besides the known economic and social consequences of any major restrictions on resource production. Even in the major industrial nations where the environmental movement of the late 1960s and early 1970s placed environmental values in a key position on the political agenda, it is now clear that economic recession and unemployment have shifted the balance of power back to those who place a high priority on material growth (see Chapter 9).

Claims that the activities of environmental pressure groups, the delays involved in obtaining planning consents and the costs of meeting pollution control regulations were stifling investment in resource exploration and exploitation were commonplace in the 1970s (Tilton, 1977). Without doubt, opposition to oil developments in the United States did hold up the construction of the trans-Alaskan pipeline and curbed production in the continental shelf area of the south-eastern USA (Manners, 1981a). Similarly, pollution control regulations have clearly imposed additional costs on resource producers, particularly in the United States and Japan, and widespread opposition to nuclear power programmes has been one factor slowing down the expansion of nuclear-generating capacity. However, fears that major scarcity problems would occur because of lack of investment in proving new reserves and in developing technologies to allow substitution appear unfounded, given the preoccupation of governments with economic growth.

Environmental interest groups may succeed in imposing some curbs on stock resource producers in periods when growth is buoyant and no availability difficulties appear imminent, but as soon as problems of economic revival, rising unemployment and import dependence occur, then almost invariably these economic problems take precedence over environmental issues. In the United States, for example, the powers of the Environmental Protection Agency have been reduced by the Reagan government, the clean air regulations have been relaxed, federal lands have begun to be opened up to mining and incentives have been given for domestic oil and gas exploration (p. 210). While stock resource development is perceived to be a vital input into the economic growth process, and while national security fears place a premium on safe indigenous supply sources, it is extremely doubtful that environmental controls will pose any significant barriers to continued investment in mineral exploitation. On the other hand, this implies that more pressures will be placed on the absorptive capacity of the environment and, therefore, on the availability of environmental quality resources.

FLOW RESOURCE SCARCITY

The overuse and misuse of flow resources will be discussed in depth in later chapters. At this stage it is only necessary to outline briefly the reasons for believing that flow resource scarcity and degradation may paradoxically be more pressing problems than stock resource exhaustion.

It seems clear that technological progress and market forces have not acted to reduce pressures on renewable resources as they have in the stock resource case; rather the reverse is true (Johnson, 1975; Dasgupta, 1982). In the advanced economies higher real consumer incomes have not only increased demands for a better quality of life and a cleaner environment but, coupled with rising levels of personal mobility, have intensified pressures on amenity landscapes and other recreational resources. At the same time, the sheer size of modern industrial output, the rapidity of technological developments and the continued pressure for more material growth have all combined to increase the rate of environmental change. In Britain, for example, changes in agriculture designed to increase farm output, such as the use of pesticides and fertilizers, removal of hedgerows, drainage of wetlands and the ploughing up of moorlands, have all affected landscape quality and reduced the diversity of flora and fauna. In some cases they have also destroyed the natural structure of the soils and caused soil erosion (Shoard, 1980; Green, 1981). All of these changes in the rural environment stem from the pressure to intensify production – a pressure which would have been understandable in an LDC where food shortages were endemic, but highly questionable in an economy where obesity and agricultural surpluses are recurrent problems.

If anything, the failure of technology and market forces to ensure the continued availability of renewable resources is even more marked in the Third World. The widespread existence of malnutrition and starvation provides ample testimony that attempts to increase ecosystem productivity have failed in many countries to provide for the food needs of the poorest groups in society. Optimism that the 'green revolution' and other technological approaches to world food production would solve all scarcity problems crumbled during the early 1970s, under a complex combination of climatic, economic, social and political circumstances. Drought highlighted the fragility of those semi-arid and arid environments which came under pressure to support increased pastoral and arable production. As agriculture was pushed into the more marginal areas, so their natural resistance to climatic variation was weakened, and this carried with it the danger that the destruction of vegetation and soil would sharply reduce potential productivity in both biological and economic terms.

This danger has been widely realized not only in the much-publicized case of the desertification of the Sahel, but also in South America, particularly in northern Chile and Argentina, the Middle East and in the more mountainous parts of Asia. Attempts to intensify output from established agricultural areas, through irrigation, mechanization, increased fertilization and the use of chemical pesticides, have likewise often failed to produce the expected productivity gains. Salinization and waterlogging of irrigated land are widespread threats to the

5   Accelerated erosion; the end-result of population pressure, deforestation and the spread of agriculture on to marginal land. This scene near Kathmandu, Nepal, is typical of the situation in many mountain areas.

maintenance of yields, and technologies designed for temperate soil and climatic conditions have often speeded the degradation of tropical, semi-tropical and semi-arid ecosystems.

To such problems must be added the increased vulnerability of these 'advanced' agricultural systems to world economic and political events, a vulnerability brought about by their dependence on imported equipment, investment capital, chemical fertilizers and pesticides. Many commentators (for example, Feder, 1976; Dasgupta, 1977) have now shown that far from alleviating the food problems of the very poorest groups, technological change, when coupled with economic forces, has served to exacerbate social inequalities in the LDCs. Small farmers unable to afford to make use of the new technologies have been forced off their land, so causing a proliferation of landless workers and even greater pressures for the extension of agriculture into more and more marginal areas. Soil productivity is not, of course, the only renewable resource that has failed to keep pace with human needs; deforestation and the resulting fuel wood shortages, critical scarcity of water and the rapid deterioration of water and air quality resources must all be added to the resource availability problems of the Third World.

As will be seen, the reasons behind the continued pressure on renewable resources are complex. Simple explanations and simple solutions will not be found for problems which require an understanding of physical systems, socioeconomic relations, political forces and the institutional barriers to acceptable remedial action. It is, however, relevant at this point to say that many of the problems of flow resource depletion and degradation are exacerbated because they are often *common property* or a *common pool*. This simply means that they cannot be owned exclusively by any one person or private company. They have traditionally been regarded as inexhaustible, freely available for use by all. Individuals have no incentive to take conservation or pollution reduction actions, and technological changes have taken place which assume their continued free availability. Resources such as fish, wildfowl, water and air extend indivisibly over very large areas; as a result, no single user can regulate the supply, control the number of other users or the quantity they take. Therefore, it is common for overproduction or overuse to occur in the short run, with the danger of long-run depletion (see pp. 247–53).

CONCLUSION

In this chapter it has been shown that resources cannot be defined in physical terms, nor can scarcity be regarded as a problem in any narrowly physical sense. It is now largely accepted that in the foreseeable future economic development will not be brought to a catastrophic halt as it hits the stock resource availability barrier. Nor does it appear likely that market imperfections, geopolitical problems or environmental controls will create any really significant mineral scarcity problems *for the now advanced nations*. However, it is not possible to be so sanguine either about the future for countries in the Third World or about the continued availability in all societies of environmental resources. The economic system, with its imperative of continued consumption and production, does not contain mechanisms which can ensure an equitable distribution of resource goods and services, or prevent the scarcity of common property resource flows. Government intervention is then necessary to ensure that resource exploitation and consumption processes can meet the social, material and environmental demands placed upon them. But, while such statements are very easy to make, there are formidable barriers inhibiting the formulation of acceptable resource policies at all governmental scales – local, national and international. Not the least of these is the lack of agreement over the legitimate objectives of resource exploitation and allocation policies. It is such barriers which provide the focus for the following chapters of the book. Although the stock and flow resource sectors are interrelated through the operation of economic, political and environmental systems, in order to understand the processes at work behind the current patterns of exploitation and the problems these create it is necessary to consider the two sectors separately. Chapters 3–5 are concerned with the mineral stock resources, while in the later part of the book the problems of renewable resource management are addressed.

NOTES

1 For a useful synopsis of the growing body of literature on the growth of environmental values see O'Riordan and Turner, 1983, pp. 1–62.
2 There are, however, some pollutants that biodegrade only very slowly; these remain in the environment for considerable periods of time after their production has ceased (see p. 269). For such pollutants, therefore, the assimilative capacity of the environment is only renewed over long time periods.
3 Organization of Petroleum Exporting Countries.
4 This relationship between supply costs and stocks is unproven and unprovable given past cost trends. Work by Barnett and Morse, 1963, and Nordhaus, 1974, among others, has shown that the average cost of resources has actually fallen markedly in *real* terms over time. Although in the early 1970s it appeared that this trend would not continue, it has in fact done so. Measured both in terms of the cost of labour input and against the costs of manufactured goods resources are now cheaper than in 1975 (Barnett *et al.*, 1984).
5 A distinction is drawn between 'old' scrap, which has actually been used in products, and new scrap, which arises in resource processing and is usually reprocessed 'in house'.
6 The behaviour of imperfectly competitive firms and their impact on the allocation of resources will be considered in more detail in Chapter 3, pp. 74–6; 108–14; and in Chapter 4, pp. 121–33.
7 The discounting procedures used by private companies to assess their resource investments are discussed in Chapter 3, p. 71.
8 It should be pointed out that neither mineral price manipulation nor politically motivated trade embargoes are anything new. International private corporations, in the oil, aluminium and nickel industries, for example, have for years formed trading cartels to divide up markets, control production and maintain prices. Moreover, the embargo weapon has been used widely to rebuke such politically 'wayward' governments as Cuba, the Soviet Union, South Africa and Rhodesia (Zimbabwe).
9 The economic concepts introduced here are further explained in Chapter 3.

3 Minerals: distribution, production and economics

INTRODUCTION

Few would deny that mineral exploitation has played an important role in generating industrial development and economic growth. This is not, however, to suggest that the existence of minerals *per se* has any deterministic power over the scale or the location of economic development. To suggest as much ignores the crucial role that man and his demands, technology and institutions play in imparting resource value to 'neutral stuff'. Before minerals can attain any value or generate any growth, they have to be located, extracted and converted into usable products for which a demand exists, and delivered to consumers in the required quantities and qualities at the needed times and locations. By the time they are usable most must be regarded as manmade products, marketable only after the investment of considerable amounts of capital, energy and labour.

Patterns of mineral exploration, exploitation, refining and trade cannot be explained simplistically in terms of the physical endowments of various countries, but require study of the way resource investment decisions are made and of the factors influencing the decision-making process. Who makes such investment decisions? What are their objectives? And how far are they subject to political pressures? These are all important questions which must be addressed during any meaningful attempt to understand mineral developments, their location and scale. The operations of mining corporations, international financial institutions, mineral purchasing companies and governments are critical factors explaining the spatial pattern of mineral production. In the same way, study of the role of natural resources as a generator of economic development must go far beyond the outlining of patterns of ownership and trade. There is a need to assess the way in which market structure, corporate and institutional behaviour and government policies influence not only the value of individual mineral deposits, but also the proportion of the generated wealth and growth which accrues to the producer states.

In this chapter attention will be focused on the identification and analysis of the complex set of physical, economic and political variables which affect both the search for valued minerals and the extent to which any known mineral source is then exploited. The variables involved are many and interrelated – their relative importance varies not only from mineral to mineral, but also over time and space. Current patterns of exploitation are a palimpsest, with the variables of importance today operating from the base created by layers of past actions. Therefore, while simple models of producer behaviour can help isolate some of the explanatory variables, they can never provide a satisfactory explanation of current patterns of resource development and use. The understanding of present spatial patterns and of the forces which have created them may be regarded as worthy academic exercises in their own right. However, unless we are going passively to accept whatever resource availabilities and allocations these forces create, it is necessary to go beyond the description of variables into the realm of policy. Chapter 4 will, therefore, address the key question of the extent to which the minerals industry operates in line with such important public policy objectives as economic efficiency, distributive equity, the generation of economic growth, supply security and the maintenance of environmental quality. This will be followed, in Chapter 5, by a consideration of the range of policy measures available to governments seeking to change current patterns of mineral production, trade and consumption, or to alter the distribution of wealth and development which results from them.

The search for valued minerals

SPATIAL BIAS IN EXPLORATION ACTIVITY

Investment in the search for minerals has never taken place (and still does not) uniformly over all the potentially mineraliferous areas of the world.

In Chapter 2 it was shown that the pattern of exploration drilling for oil and gas had been heavily skewed to North America (see Figure 2.3, p. 23). By the early 1960s over 1,987,000 exploration wells had been drilled in the United States – which stood in marked contrast, for example, to the level of activity in Australia. Despite the fact that Australia has a broadly comparable area of land which is geologically promising for oil discoveries, by 1963 a mere 600 wells had ever been drilled there (Hedberg *et al.*, 1964). During the 1960s there was a comparative lack of interest in exploration in the United States; the long-term decline in real oil prices, uncertainties surrounding federal import and price control policies and diminishing drilling success rates all reduced the incentive to invest. Even so, over 10,000[1] new wells were still drilled each year, and, after the 1973 oil crisis and the subsequent revision of federal energy policies, the rate of exploration drilling escalated. According to the American Petroleum Institute, over 80,000 exploration wells were drilled in the United States in 1981 alone.

The enormous size of US exploration activity can be readily appreciated by comparing it with the rate of drilling elsewhere in the world. In Australia exploration peaked in 1978, when at a total cost of over $A116 million a record fifty-three exploration wells were drilled (*Australian Year Book*, 1981). Similarly, although drilling in the Norwegian, Dutch and Danish sectors of the North Sea reached record levels in 1982, in total only 100 exploration wells were drilled. To these must be added a further ninety in the British offshore sector and twenty-seven in onshore locations (*Petroleum Economist*, April 1983). If the level of exploration activity is minor in these areas when judged by North American standards, it fades to insignificant proportions in Third World nations, which lack the indigenous resources to mount major exploration efforts and are regarded as politically unfavourable for western investment.

This type of exploration bias is by no means unique to oil, in fact it is typical of the pattern which emerges for virtually all minerals. In the case of coal where the location of deposits is somewhat simplified by the continuity of seams – often forming layers extending over hundreds of square kilometres – drilling and testing work must still be undertaken to establish the size and quality of reserves. Historically the detailed appraisal of coal reserves has been heavily skewed to the traditional coal-using economies of Europe, but even so major new fields, such as the Belvoir field in north-east Leicestershire, are still being proved. It was not until 1974 that the National Coal Board undertook the survey work needed to establish that the long-known deposits were commercially viable and would add some 1400 million tonnes to the country's proven reserves.

Elsewhere, even in a technologically advanced country like Canada, knowledge of potential reserves is often rudimentary. Coal deposits are known to exist in the inhospitable land north of 60° latitude, but detailed drilling to prove reserves has not occurred to provide even a broad estimate of stocks. In fact only 8.5 per cent of Canada's estimated 109×10^9 tonnes of reserves has been test-drilled and the field extent measured; 42 per cent is 'indicated'; and a further 49 per cent is only 'inferred' from information on geological structure (UN Economic Commission for Europe, 1978). By and large, the southern hemisphere remains poorly surveyed for coal. The extent of Australian reserves is only now becoming clear. With the exception of South Africa, the coal potential of Africa remains largely unknown. Botswana, for example, may have extensive resources of low-sulphur steam coal; but given the limited internal markets, capital shortages and the difficulty in exporting any mineral from a land-locked country, with at best tenuous transport links to suitable ports and located in a politically sensitive area, there has been little incentive to invest in proving the existence of reserves (see pp. 105–7).

In the case of metaliferous deposits, the presence of most of which depends upon relatively localized geological conditions, a systematic and detailed analysis of the subsurface geology is necessary before the existence, extent and quality of deposits can be established. There remain vast tracts of potentially metaliferous land where such detailed, systematic analyses have yet to be carried out. Obviously geological considerations impose constraints on the areas of exploration but within such constraints the general picture emerges of an exploration investment pattern highly biased to the technologically advanced nations of the world. The bias is even more marked in the case of relatively low-value, bulky non-metallic minerals, where the costs of transport have kept production tied closely to market areas. It is not, for example, a fortunate geological accident which makes the United States the largest producer of gypsum or barytes, but the level of internal demand.

The distribution of exploration investment

Published data on the level and location of capital investment in mineral exploration are sketchy and global figures are non-existent. However, it is clear that the expenditure historically has been concentrated in the already developed countries, and certainly such a spatial bias in investment patterns is very evident today. In the years following the Second World War the traditional patterns of exploration appeared to break down as the demands imposed by the reconstruction boom, fears for the depletion of indigenous resources and improved transport facilities encouraged European and North American companies to direct more of their search investments to the relatively unexploited countries of the Third World. It has been estimated, for example, that by 1961 the European group of mining companies were investing 57 per cent of their exploration budget in LDCs (Manners, 1979).

From surveys of US overseas investments it also appears that by 1960 the LDCs were receiving 53 per cent of total foreign investment in the mining and minerals sector (Table 3.1). However, these data do not separate out exploration expenditure and, of course, give no indication of the scale of internal US investment.

Table 3.1 Value of US foreign direct investment in mining and smelting (in millions of dollars, 1976 constant prices)

	Developing countries	Developed countries	% in developing countries	Total
1960	1600	1411	53	3011
1965	1814	1971	48	3785
1970	2522	3646	41	6168
1975	2150	4398	33	6548
1976	2309	4749	33	7058
1977	2164*	4507†	32	7066
1978	2303‡	4331§	33	6990
1979	2241‖	4495‖	31	7185

* Excluding Chile and Venezuela.
† Excluding the UK, South Africa and New Zealand.
‡ Excluding Chile, Venezuela and Peru.
§ Excluding the UK, South Africa and New Zealand.
¶ Excluding Venezuela.
‖ Excluding South Africa and New Zealand.

Source: Mikesell, 1979, p. 249; and US Department of the Interior, Mineral Yearbook, for 1977–9.
Note: In the 1977–9 figures data on investments in certain countries have been withheld to avoid disclosing company proprietory information. This means that the developed plus developing country investments do not add to the total. Data for the 1980s do not allow disaggregation into individual countries.

This shift in the historic investment pattern was to prove short-lived. Using data collected by Rio Tinto Zinc, Crowson (1981) has shown that the proportion of exploration expenditure by European companies directed to the LDCs fell markedly in the 1960s and 1970s (Figure 3.1). By 1975 it was only 15 per cent of total exploration investment, and although interest in the Third World revived somewhat towards the end of the 1970s, they still attracted only about 20 per cent of European private exploration expenditure. Similarly, a 1976 survey of eighteen US and Canadian companies showed that over 90 per cent of their exploration expenditure went to developed countries. Some indication of the relative decline in US total mineral development activity in the LDCs can also be obtained by considering the data on foreign direct investment shown in Table 3.1. There is little doubt that the European and American figures are typical of the worldwide pattern. Tanzer, for example, asserts that

> since the early 1970s nearly 85 per cent of world mineral exploration expenditures (excluding oil) have been channelled into the developed countries, with about 80 per cent going to the four 'safe' countries – the United States, Canada, Australia and South Africa. (Tanzer, 1980, p. 50)

Historic reasons for the exploration bias

Historically it is easy to understand why a skewed pattern of exploration activity should have occurred. We have already seen that resources are cultural appraisals, their value being determined by technology and by socioeconomic conditions. In view of this it is natural that exploration should have occurred first,

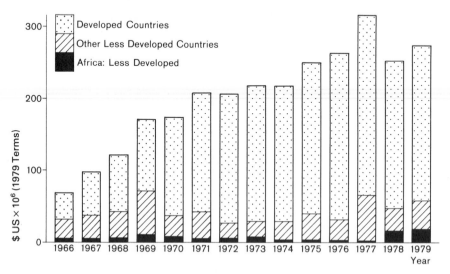

Figure 3.1   The distribution of exploration investment by European companies
Source: Crowson, 1981, p. 51

and been most intense, in the industrialized nations. It is, however, too simplistic to attribute the present dominance of advanced nations solely to their technical knowledge of how to develop and use resources. People of European descent had no monopoly over metalworking skills. The richness of the art and metal artifacts produced by early civilizations in South America, India and China is well known and the sophistication of metalworking in Africa long before the arrival of Europeans is now increasingly recognized. Archaeological evidence puts the beginning of mining in Swaziland at around 43,000 BC; the copper mines of Katanaga were extensively worked by indigenous peoples before colonialization and the quality of Mozambique's iron products was noted by Livingstone (Lanning and Mueller, 1979). What was crucial was not the knowledge of how to mine and use metals, but the scale of demands and the economic system which fuelled such demands and provided the necessary development capital.

SPECULATIVE PROSPECTORS

As nations industrialized, so the increased demands for all forms of minerals provided the impetus for highly speculative exploration ventures. Even in the late nineteenth century exploration was still typically undertaken by individual prospectors, mostly of European origin, working with extremely limited resources. The more individualistic of their number relied heavily on their own geological knowledge and interpretative skills; they concentrated their activities in areas with which they were familiar, at sites which were thought to have been exploited by indigenous peoples, and in those areas where geological maps or survey data were available and showed promising conditions. The vast majority, however, followed the herd to recent finds, so fuelling exploration search in relatively limited areas.

Mineral exploration is popularly associated with the famous gold and diamond rushes where prospectors in their thousands were attracted into inhospitable and inaccessible areas. Remoteness from markets, lack of bulk transport facilities and other forms of infrastructure presented few barriers to prospecting activity when such high-value minerals were concerned. But this was not typical. For the majority of minerals, exploration followed in the wake of agricultural settlement and its range was constrained by the economic fact that deposits were valueless unless the extraction, processing and transport costs were low enough to allow their product to be priced competitively in the market centres. Outside the industrialized countries themselves the pattern of exploration activity was closely allied to the establishment of colonies, the development of regular transport routes and the incorporation of colonies into the market economies of the developed nations.

ACCIDENTAL DISCOVERIES

It must not be forgotten that many mineral finds were accidental, discovered by chance because of other activities in the area. In Australia the spread of pastoral farming was crucial to the first discoveries of minerals; the copper ores at Burra (1845) and Moonta (1860), both in South Australia, and the silver and lead deposits at Broken Hill (1883), were all chance discoveries by stockmen. The famous Kimberley diamond area (South Africa) was stumbled across when the children of Dutch settlers found a glittering stone while playing on the banks of the Vaal River. Similarly, the Sudbury mineral deposits were found by accident when the excavation of a cutting for the Canadian Pacific Railway exposed the ore body; while the copper mines of Sederholm, in Finland, owe their discovery to the excavation of a minor canal. There are also numerous examples of minerals being discovered during drilling for water or oil.

Once exploration had begun in an area for one mineral, geological knowledge was improved and so the possibilities for other finds were revealed. The famous Mount Isa copper mines in Australia owe their discovery to a double dose of chance. Lead and zinc ores had been found by stockmen, and it was during drilling to prove the extent of these ore bodies that the copper was found. Since the copper ores occur at least 600 feet below the surface and trend very steeply downwards, so having a very limited vertical extent, chance was crucial to their discovery; no company would have been prepared to drill the prospect with sufficient intensity to have any hope of intersecting the copper lode as part of a deliberate exploration effort (Raggatt, 1964).

GEOLOGICAL SURVEY DATA

Another important element influencing the location of exploration was the availability and quality of geological information. The existence of basic top-ographical and geological maps allowed the identification of potentially mineral-iferous zones. Following the formation of the Geological Survey of Great Britain in 1832, more and more governments recognized the advantages of establishing a systematic survey of their territories. By the end of the nineteenth century survey organizations had been established in most European countries, the Soviet Union, Canada and the United States; moreover, the British, Belgian and Dutch surveys were extending their activities to provide basic geological and geomorphological data for the colonies.

Although the first established survey agencies were not intended to be government mineral prospectors, finds were made during routine survey work, and the quality, extent of coverage and the scale of the maps influenced private sector investment decisions. There were, in addition, individual government geologists who became so convinced of the presence of minerals from their analysis of geological data that they deliberately set out to prospect; the Marampa iron ore deposits in Sierra Leone owe their discovery, for example, to the prospecting zeal of N. R. Junner, a survey geologist from the neighbouring Gold Coast. The survey agencies have also played an important role in refining knowledge about mineral occurrences and in improving exploration techniques. The Blind River area, west of Sudbury in Canada, had been rejected as a potential uranium source as old mine tailings had too low a uranium content to be of interest. However, when work by the US Geological Survey revealed that uranium was leached out by the sulphuric acid produced by oxidization in the mine wastes, the area was reappraised and large economically viable deposits were found.

Until the 1940s the survey methods used by both government and private sector teams were basic: individual geologists had literally to cover the ground, identify and delimit outcrop rocks, test-drill to establish the nature of the solid geology and its structure and take material samples for analysis. The sheer size of many countries affected the completeness of cover, as did the climate, the physical nature of the terrain, the depth of accumulated superficial deposits and the availability of transport facilities. Even in relatively affluent countries, such as Canada and Australia, the scale of the survey task and vast inhospitable tracts of land were major barriers to the provision of complete geological coverage. By 1963, despite the fact that the Canadian Geological Survey had been at work for 120 years, one-quarter of the country had not been geologically mapped even at scales of 1:500,000 or 1:250,000. Similarly, a complete 1:250,000 cover of Australia was only finished in 1980. In both countries large areas remain to be mapped at the scale most useful for mineral exploration – namely, 1:100,000.

Since the Second World War the use of various forms of remote sensing imagery has revolutionized the task of providing basic topographical and geological maps. Although these techniques can rarely establish the presence of specific minerals,[2] they have removed a major barrier to exploration by allowing more detailed survey work to be directed to areas with high potential. However, as we have already seen, this has not as yet prompted an exploration investment boom in the previously undersurveyed Third World, although it has accelerated the pace of survey in Australia, Canada, South Africa and, to a lesser extent, Brazil. In order to explain current patterns of investment we need to look at the different forms of mineral search, the different agencies and organizations involved and at the factors which influence their decisions.

TYPES OF MINERAL SEARCH

The discussion so far has focused on exploration for new deposits of already valued minerals. However, this is only one form which the search for minerals can take; equally important is the development of new technologies to allow the commercial exploitation of known but uneconomic deposits and the production of minerals from widely available but non-conventional sources. Although exploration and research into new technologies occur simultaneously, they are to some extent substitutes and are in competition for scarce investment funds. The emphasis placed on each varies over time and has a significant effect on the location of mineral search activities. There is some evidence to suggest that over the past fifteen years an increasing proportion of total search expenditure has been devoted to technological change to allow the commercial utilization of subeconomic deposits or source materials, which are already known to exist in the economically advanced consumer nations (see pp. 75–6).

Exploration itself is not just one activity but takes a variety of forms or phases. First, *preliminary investigations* involve the analysis of basic topographical and geological maps (giving the broad physical characteristics of a whole country or region) along with any other survey and past mining data to identify 'target' zones for more detailed study. The second phase involves the *identification* of potential prospects by mapping target zones to determine their small-scale structure and geology, and by testing superficial materials for trace elements. In phase three, *deposit evaluation*, these prospects are drilled and analysed using a variety of geochemical and geophysical techniques.

If this work proves the existence of a suitable mineral concentration, the basic exploration task is over; but the deposit has still to be *appraised* to establish its commercial viability. The ore body or mineral-bearing structure has then to be delimited, its structural characteristics assessed, its quality and the presence of impurities established. In addition, investigations must move outside the physical analysis of the mineral source to test the political, economic and legal environments. Planning regulations, the leasing conditions, government restrictions on capital, foreign ownership and trade and the likely infrastructure costs must all be assessed before any mineral find can be classified as a proven workable reserve. Finally, it must be noted that this appraisal work does not stop when production starts; individual sites are frequently reassessed in the light of new physical data, technological innovations or changing market conditions.

THE ACTORS IN THE MINERAL SEARCH PROCESS

There are essentially four types of investor currently involved in mineral search: national governments; private companies operating solely within one producer country; multinational corporations; and international financial or aid agencies. It cannot be assumed that these different groups have the same goals or objectives or even that any one type of investor will have a single and consistent goal.

Economic models which attempt to explain or to predict 'optimal' investment behaviour normally assume that we are dealing with rational 'economic man', whose objective is to maximize profits.[3] This may be a reasonable approximation to reality for some firms in the private sector, although it is well known that other business aims, such as 'satisfactory profits', a quiet life, income stability, risk minimization or maintenance of market share are also important. For the public sector it is common for there to be multiple objectives, the priority given to each of which may change markedly over time. Maximization of the direct financial returns from any investment may be one aim but other considerations will also play a role. These include income redistribution, employment generation, inflation control, avoidance of trade deficits, reduction of foreign debt, promotion of national security, avoidance of environmental damage, maintenance of political power and national prestige. Conflicts inevitably arise between these objectives; an investment strategy which, for example, creates employment need not produce maximum financial returns, or allow inflation control. Final decisions, therefore, involve trade-offs, which reflect current (often short-term) political or economic preoccupations.

The role of government in the planned economies

In the socialist planned economies the government is the major, and frequently the only, investor in mineral search, although technical and financial aid may be obtained from other governments or even from the private international mineral corporations. For example, the Chinese are now encouraging the multinational oil companies to participate in exploration, particularly in offshore ventures where advanced drilling technologies and experience are crucial. It is impossible to divorce socialist mineral policies from the political ideology of the state, the kind of economy which is being built and from the role which the country is trying to play in international politics. The search for minerals becomes part of a planned process designed to meet the wider economic, social and political goals of that society. As these goals vary between countries and over time, so too will the patterns of search activity and of subsequent mineral exploitation.

THE SOVIET EXAMPLE

In the Soviet Union, for example, the priority given to search for different resource types, the scale of expenditure and its spatial distribution cannot be explained without considering four basic policy tenets, which have shaped the economy ever since the Bolshevik revolution. First, rapid industrial growth was to be the priority in order to close the development gap between the capitalist nations and the new communist state. This was to be achieved through an emphasis on large-scale and basic heavy industry. The output of consumer goods was to be restricted to allow a higher proportion of the country's resources to be devoted to the production of physical capital and infrastructure. Inevitably this was a mineral- and energy-intensive growth strategy and required massive investments in the mineral sector. The second basic policy aim, to make the country secure militarily, acted to reinforce this investment pattern. Military intervention by Britain, France and the United States in support of the White Russian cause fanned the fears of 'capitalist' aggression, so setting in train the almost paranoid emphasis on heavy arms production and on the steel industry upon which it depended.

The third basic policy objective was to spread economic development across the country; while this did not affect the scale of mineral exploration or the type of mineral given priority, it clearly was a crucial influence on the spatial distribution of activity. This goal in part stemmed from the desire to reduce regional inequalities, and Warren has argued that it has its roots in Marxist ideology, occurring in both the 1848 *Communist Manifesto* and in the writings of Engels. To support this view he quotes from a passage in Engels's work, *Anti-Duhring*:

> only a society which harmoniously combines its productive forces in accordance with a single overall plan can permit industries to be distributed throughout the country in a way most favourable to their own development and to the preservation and development of the remaining elements of production. (Warren, 1973, p. 174)

However, the desire to disperse productive capacity was also bound up with state security. It not only reduced the country's vulnerability to attack from the west, but it could also help prevent internal dissent by spreading prosperity and by binding the various republics which make up the Soviet Union into a closer economic and social relationship.

The fourth key policy objective was to make the country self-sufficient in essential minerals, agricultural produce and manufactured goods. Once again security was a major and understandable motive. Capitalist governments and companies, which controlled the international trade and banking systems, were opposed to the Soviet regime ideologically and were – not unreasonably – aggrieved by the expropriation of their Russian investments. The country's vulnerability had been illustrated by the 1920 trade and credit embargo and self-sufficiency became the obvious answer. It also had the advantage of allowing industrial growth to be more closely planned. Freed from the need to compete in international markets, the goods produced and the factors of production used could be decided by government, not by market demands and world price levels. This meant that minerals could be derived from deposits or unconventional source materials which could not have been exploited economically within the international system of development and trade.

Before 1920, it was recognized that, in terms of its broad geological patterns, the Soviet Union was potentially mineral-rich, but the vast bulk of the country had never been systematically surveyed. The harsh climate, the sheer size of the territory, lack of internal markets and the distance from the major industrial centres of western Europe and North America all inhibited exploration. This neglect had to be rectified if the new regime was to have any hope of achieving its policy objectives. In the 1920s and 1930s a massive geological survey programme was undertaken, under which expenditure increased from the mere 200,000 roubles spent in 1906, to 10 million roubles in 1927–8 and 141 million roubles in 1932 (see Warren, 1973). Before the Second World War, expenditure on geological surveys in the Soviet Union was some twenty times greater than that of the US government, although it is difficult to make direct comparisons since the level of private investment within the United States is largely unknown. While the choice of areas surveyed was naturally influenced by existing geological knowledge, the policy of spreading production was clear in the emphasis given to areas east of the Urals. Moreover, the self-sufficiency objective meant that mineral search was not solely devoted to exploration; technological change to allow the use of known low-grade ores, indigenous energy sources and available but unconventional source materials were also essential. The classic examples here are the work done to enable peat to be used in electricity generation, and the development of processes to extract alumina from nepheline concentrate and alunite ores, rather than from bauxite.

As a result of this search activity, the entire mineral geography of the country has been dramatically altered. Whereas in the 1920s some 60 per cent of mineral needs were imported, today the country is virtually self-sufficient in minerals and in fact exports about 20 per cent of its production, mainly in the form of oil and gas. This is, of course, a remarkable achievement, particularly given the massive growth in domestic industrial production over the period. But it must be emphasized that self-sufficiency was much easier to achieve in an economy insulated from international competition and where personal consumption levels were held down. Since the 1960s the decision to allow living standards to improve and to place greater emphasis on the production of private consumer goods, particularly cars, has started to break down the country's isolation from the world economic system. There is some evidence to suggest that Soviet mineral planners have now become caught in a Catch-22 situation. In order to exploit the resource potential of Siberia at the speed needed to supply internal demands, provide for exports and to pay for imported food and equipment, more western capital goods, technological expertise and financial credit are required. This in turn increases the need to exploit still further the country's mineral wealth to provide the necessary hard currency. And so the wheel turns on.

Governments in the mixed economies

DIRECT GOVERNMENT ROLE

The relative importance of government and private investment varies greatly from country to country. There are those, including Australia, Canada, South Africa and the United States, where, officially at least, the government role is confined to providing basic geological survey data, developing mineral law to allocate clear and secure ownership rights and generally to create a milieu which encourages 'free enterprise'. However, even in that archetype capitalist country, the United States, the government has been directly involved in detailed prospecting for specific strategic minerals. In 1956, for example, over 600 federal government geologists were employed to search for uranium; militarily it was regarded as crucial that indigenous sources of this nuclear feedstock were found. Moreover, all governments have attempted to direct private search activities – to alter the scale of exploration, its location and the type of mineral involved – in order to further various national economic, military and political policy objectives.

GOVERNMENT INFLUENCES ON PRIVATE INVESTMENT

In most cases the emphasis has been on securing indigenous supply sources, in order to promote economic growth, improve the balance of payments, or reduce the country's vulnerability to trade embargoes or attempts to force up mineral prices. To do this, a variety of tools have been used: direct subsidies, tax concessions, favourable royalty or leasing conditions and the imposition of import taxes or quota restrictions are all long-established methods (see Chapter 5, pp. 186–216). Subsidies and a plethora of tax concessions have been used both to stimulate search for selected strategic minerals and to generate an overall increase in exploration activity. In the first case military considerations have often been important, as in the 1934 German oil subsidy programme or the US uranium prospecting bonus. Whereas a more general subsidy on all forms of exploration has usually been justified on balance-of-payments or overall supply security grounds. For example, balance-of-payments savings prompted the British government in 1971 to devote £50 million to encouraging domestic exploration.

In the main, governments have been concerned with the scale of indigenous exploration, but there are cases where speed has been a crucial consideration. A classic illustration of this is British policy for the development of North Sea oil and gas; a major objective here was 'to secure that exploration continues as fast as reasonably practicable' to allow 'the attainment as early as practicable of net self sufficiency in oil' (UK Government, 1978). To achieve this, three measures in particular were important. First, companies had to return for reallocation 50 per cent of their licence areas at the end of a six-year period. It was assumed that this would speed up the initial survey work as no company would want to risk handing back blocks with a high find probability. Second, licence areas were not auctioned, but firms in effect had to compete for the most favoured blocks by submitting work programmes. And, finally, the price fixed in the first contract for delivered gas was generous, which many commentators saw as a deliberate ploy to encourage other companies who assumed, wrongly as it happened, that such favourable terms would also apply to them.

Although most attempts by advanced nation governments to influence private exploration activity have been concerned to stimulate indigenous resource development, tax incentives have, on occasion, been employed particularly in the 1950s and 1960s to encourage investment overseas. In part the motive was concern over the rapid depletion of domestic reserves and fears of shortage, but the maintenance and spread of political influence was undoubtedly also an important consideration. For example, the US and European governments allowed oil companies to offset tax paid to overseas governments against their domestic profits (Hartshorn, 1962). Moreover, in the US case a further 14 per cent allowance was given for operations in South America and Canada, while the French gave special concessions for exploration in the 'franc zone' (Devaux Charbonne, 1964).

While measures to influence private investment have undoubtedly had an impact on exploration, they in no way guarantee that search activity will occur in line with national economic and political objectives. Inevitably it is most difficult to ensure that private actions support government goals when foreign firms are the predominant source of investment capital. Such difficulties have certainly contributed to the trend in mixed economies for the state to take direct responsibility for exploration, at least for strategic minerals, and to exclude or limit the activities of foreign companies. While this is particularly a characteristic of less developed countries, it is by no means confined to them. Sweden, for example, banned foreign citizens and companies from taking out mining claims as early as 1916. While in Britain, France and Finland, among many others, nationalized mineral industries now have a direct exploration role.

CAPITAL CONSTRAINTS IN THE LDCS

In the LDCs governments are severely handicapped in any attempt to undertake significant levels of exploration on their own behalf, although some have done so. Mexico for example, which nationalized the oil industry in 1938, can point to an impressive past record of finds but capital shortages and foreign debt problems are now causing considerable difficulties. Capital shortages act as a major constraint on government exploration activity. Internal sources are limited, and

> international loan sources are usually not available for these purposes, partly because of the risk involved and partly because international institutions such

as the World Bank, have taken the position that since capital for the extractive industries is available from private sources, the international institutions should employ their own limited loan funds for transportation, power and other industries for which private capital is not ordinarily available. (Mikesell, 1971, p. 61)

Moreover, in recent years the already high levels of debt and the difficulties experienced in repayment impose a further limit on borrowing. Other constraints arise from the tendency for a relatively few large international companies to have acquired something of a monopoly over the necessary technologies and expertise and, even more important, to dominate the major mineral markets. Such companies may have budgets which far exceed that of an LDC government, and have the advantage of being able to spread the risks of exploration over different countries. These limits on independent exploration activity mean that most Third World governments must either rely heavily on the foreign private sector or enter into joint ventures. Exploration for copper in Chile, Mexico, Peru, Zaire and Zambia is, for instance, carried out jointly by multinationals and the respective governments.

The role of international organizations

A number of commentators, including Mikesell (1971) and Tanzer (1980), have argued that the World Bank (International Bank for Reconstruction and Development) and its related organizations, such as the Asian Bank, have played a minor role in funding exploration investment. It has been particularly difficult to get the international banks to fund broad-scale surveys to identify potential prospect areas. In part this may be due – as is argued by Tanzer – to the World Bank's goal of promoting private foreign investment and its tendency to protect American interests. However, it also arises because of the nature of banking activity; bank loans have to be repaid and whereas once a mineral deposit has been found there is a reasonable chance that the investment will yield a return, the earlier exploration phases are inevitably highly speculative. Whatever the reasons behind it, this loan policy is clearly a major source of difficulty for those undersurveyed LDCs, which are now receiving only a small proportion of total foreign private exploration expenditure.

To some extent the operations of the United Nations have helped to improve the LDC position. The rather limited UN Special Fund provided some aid by supporting the intensive investigation of limited specific areas where occurrences of economically useful minerals had already been revealed or were strongly presumed to exist (Schwob, 1964). However, the fund did not support geological or geophysical reconnaissance operations or related topographic mapping, nor would it finance any form of petroleum exploration. Moreover, the total sums of money involved were minor. Between 1959 and 1963 only $88 million were spent on survey work and this was shared between resource and industrial surveys.

The deficiences in the Special Fund provisions were officially recognized by the United Nations in 1961 when, under the auspices of the Development

Programme (UNDP), it launched a scheme designed to stimulate geological and mineral surveys. It was argued that whereas there was an ample supply of capital to develop minerals once found, lack of basic survey data hindered the whole exploration process. By 1978 it was estimated that this programme had revealed deposits worth at least $13,000 million (Lanning and Mueller, 1979). However, while the programme has provided valuable base survey material in countries such as Zambia, Liberia, Niger, Swaziland, Mexico, Chile and Malaysia, UNDP officials have themselves pointed out the inadequacy of the efforts in relation to the total needs. Between May 1959[4] and June 1976 the total expenditure was $139 million, which can be put into perspective by comparing it with the $15,000 million spent annually by the oil majors on exploration. The United Nations simply did not receive enough contributions from its member governments to fill the survey gaps.

In 1974 a further attempt was made to increase available resources by establishing a Revolving Fund for Natural Resources Exploration. The aim here was to require countries which had received funds to pay a share of the proceeds from successful ventures into a pool which could then be reallocated. Inevitably it will take some time for such a fund to be self-sustaining, and its success will critically depend on the initial voluntary contributions needed to start the ball rolling. By 1978 the fund stood at $10 million, a sum hardly sufficient to survey even one potential copper prospect!

The role of the private sector

THE COSTS OF SEARCH

Outside the communist bloc private search expenditure still dwarfs that of governments. Mineral search, whatever form it takes, is a costly venture and is subject to considerable risk and uncertainty. For example, it was estimated that in the early 1970s over $10 million had to be invested to give a 50 per cent chance of finding just one economic deposit of a major non-ferrous metal such as copper or tin. This figure only gives a very broad and generalized idea of the actual costs and is based on the assumption that prospecting would occur only in areas known to be promising geologically (Freyman, 1974).

However, exploration costs pale into insignificance besides the expenditure then required to bring a new find into production. On average, exploration will account for only about 5 per cent of the total capital investment needed for a non-fuel mineral. In deciding the location of search investment the companies take account of the fact that expected total pre-production expenditures will vary markedly over space, being greatest in inhospitable areas, lacking any basic infrastructure. The potential difficulties involved in having to commit major sums in advance of any returns can be illustrated by the Dome Petroleum case in Canada. By 1981 it had already invested over $Can.500 million in the Beaufort Sea concession in the Arctic, and needed to spend as much again, over a two- to three-year period, before the deposit could be put on-stream. However, in September 1982 the company was unable to pay the interest due on its borrowings; only the eventual agreement of the banks, under some pressure from the Canadian government, to renegotiate the loans and extend further credit prevented liquidation.

AN ELEMENTARY ECONOMIC MODEL

It is obviously a complex task to try to understand the myriad private decisions that together make up the total investment pattern; much generalization and simplification must be introduced and inevitably an element of theoretical abstraction. As a starting-point it is useful to consider the standard treatment of investment decisions in elementary economic theory not because it provides a good description of the way decisions are made in practice by individual firms, but because it helps isolate some of the key decision variables. Let us take a hypothetical, and quite unrealistic, situation in which an economically rational producer has perfect knowledge about:

(1) the probability of successful search, including technical change, for all potential mineral sources;
(2) both the initial capital expenditures and the running costs involved in extracting, processing and marketing the mineral;
(3) the levels of future demand for and the price commanded by each mineral and, therefore, of the stream of revenue which each deposit will yield.

Armed with such perfect information, the producer would be able to rank all potential mineral search investments according to their expected net returns. However, this necessitates comparing streams of costs incurred and revenues received at different time periods, a large proportion of the costs occurring before any revenue is generated. To allow comparison it is, therefore, essential to adjust all the values to a constant time period. This is usually done by converting future costs and revenues into *present values* by discounting them by the relevant rate of interest.[5] By deducting the present value of the costs from the present value of the revenue, an expected net return can be calculated for each project. A rational producer would, first, undertake projects with the highest net returns, and then would continue down the list as long as positive returns were made. In any time period available investment funds are limited and mineral projects must compete for these with opportunities in all other sectors of the economy. Capital will only be attracted into minerals if the expected rate of return on investment at least equals the prevailing rate obtainable on other forms of investment. Therefore, if a mineral development will only yield a positive return if the interest rate is below, say, 5 per cent, but a factory producing microcomputers would remain profitable at a 10 per cent rate, then clearly a profit-maximizer would not invest in minerals. The market rate of interest is relevant even if the firm already has the necessary capital and does not need to borrow since the option is there to lend it to others.

Ignoring for the moment the many heroic assumptions contained in this simple economic treatment, the model identifies three sets of crucial variables affecting the decision to invest in mineral search. First, the costs involved; second, the expected revenue; and, third, the net yields from investments in other sectors of the economy. In reality, none of these key elements can be known with any degree of certainty, particularly considering the time taken for any search investment to yield marketable resource products. But the producer has some past experience on which to base his assessments and can take a variety of actions to reduce both the risks and uncertainties involved.

The costs of search will obviously critically depend on the time taken to find an economic deposit or to develop technologies which allow the economic exploitation of conditional reserves or of unconventional mineral source materials. Costs, in the exploration case, are also affected by the location of the search area, its physical character and the availability of equipment, trained personnel and infrastructure. In remote areas, particularly in LDCs, it may well be necessary to import all the equipment and survey teams, along with a significant proportion of their food and other home comforts, to build housing and test laboratories from scratch, and to contend with the access problems caused by the poor or non-existent road network. But in choosing to focus search in particular areas a producer will look beyond the search costs *per se* to analyse the expenditures involved in getting any find into production and in running the mining operations. A crucial factor will be the amount of basic infrastructure required before production can start and how much of this must be paid for by the company rather than a government body. Once production is under way the running costs involved will vary with: the quality of the mineral; the size of the deposit; the physical characteristics of the site and mineral-bearing structures; the costs of labour, power and transport to market; and the taxes, rents and royalties paid to local and national governments.

When all these costs are taken into account, it is not always the areas with potentially the most favourable geological conditions or the highest-quality minerals which will be chosen for search. Crowson (1981) has shown that for copper the least *total* cost locations are not necessarily those with the highest ore grades. As Table 3.2 illustrates, Zambia has ore grades almost 2.5 times higher than the western world average and yet it shares, with the United States, the position of the most expensive producer country. On the other hand, South Africa, which has poor average grades, has by far the lowest break-even costs. With all other factors being equal, market forces will tend to favour further search in low-cost countries and, within them, in areas where mines and their associated infrastructure are already located: 'the existing geographical pattern of mineral development is likely to be perpetuated as long as expansion possibilities exist at operating mines' (Crowson, 1981, p. 50).

If we assume for the moment that free and perfect markets exist and that capital is perfectly mobile, then the other two key decision variables in the simple economic model, revenue and interest rates, will affect the overall *scale* of investment in search but not its spatial distribution. Revenue will be determined by output levels and the market price for the mineral, both of which are dependent on the strength of overall demand, the amount of the mineral put on the market by other producers and the price of substitute materials. Clearly, search activity will tend to be most buoyant in periods when mineral demands are growing, and when potential scarcity increases expected price levels. In the same way, low interest rates will stimulate search since more projects will appear

Table 3.2 Comparative production costs for copper, 1978

	Share of total western world production (%)	Average ore grade	Mining and milling cost	Break-even cash cost, mining, milling, administration, taxes and marketing
Australia	3.6	204	253	59
Canada	10.6	74	112	78
South Africa	3.4	55	142	7
United States	22.3	65	73	132
Chile	17.0	118	83	78
Papua New Guinea	3.3	65	53	66
Peru	6.0	119	87	100
Philippines	4.3	51	39	103
Zaire	7.0	493	173	89
Zambia	10.6	244	166	132

Source: Crowson, 1981, p. 50.
Note: The figures presented in columns 2–4 show the relative costs and ore grades on an index basis, with 100 being the western world average.

profitable with positive net returns in the investment appraisal calculations. Since the mid-1970s the world economic recession and the resultant dramatic declines in both prices and consumption of raw materials, coupled with sharp increases in interest rates, have resulted in a decline in exploration activity, with the notable exceptions of uranium and non-OPEC oil sources.

RISK AND UNCERTAINTY

While some of the features of the current search pattern can be explained using the basic economic investment model, it can by no means provide a complete picture. Firms clearly want profits, but to obtain any they must survive in business. Therefore, attempts must be made to protect the value of fixed capital assets and to maintain a stable income flow large enough to keep the firm running. There is little point in undertaking a profit-maximizing investment which yields returns only after the firm has been liquidated because it has failed to meet its running costs or service its debt. Firms not only vary in their willingness to take investment risks, but also differ markedly in their ability to do so. Small firms normally have neither the financial reserves nor sufficient access to credit to enable them to embark upon potentially highly profitable but high-risk ventures.

The investor in mineral search faces four basic types of risk:

(1) the intrinsic risk that an economically viable find or new exploitation technology will not result;

(2) the risk that production costs will rise significantly;
(3) risks involved in changing market conditions (price falls, increasing interest rates, the development of substitutes or cheaper alternative supply sources);
(4) a whole set of political risks, ranging from war and political instability, nationalization of assets and new demands for royalties or taxes, to the imposition of exchange, trade or planning controls.

While these risks can never be avoided entirely, a number of methods can be employed to reduce them, or at least to reduce their significance. The range of risk-reducing strategies open to individual companies varies markedly, however, depending on their size, product structures and the spatial scale of their operations. To some extent, all companies can minimize intrinsic risk by searching in areas where there is historical evidence of mineral presence, where good base maps and survey data are available and where successful discoveries have already been made. Production and market risks can be lessened by restricting search to those areas and minerals in which the company has proven expertise. Finally, all firms operating outside their country of origin can, whatever their size, reduce political risks by eschewing any involvement in politically unstable countries or ones with a bad past record of government restrictions on private enterprise.

The large multinational mineral corporations are particularly well placed to extend this range of risk-reducing methods. They have the economic resources to adopt four additional strategies. First, intrinsic risk can be virtually eliminated by acquiring already explored deposits or by taking over or merging with companies known to hold significant proven reserves. Some companies, such as Newmont, Noranda and Rio Tinto, have traditionally preferred to purchase into deposits which have at least been partially explored – and in recent years many more firms are employing this acquisition option. The economic depression has pushed a number of companies into cash flow problems, so forcing down dividends and relative share prices. If such firms have good reserve assets, their acquisition can be an attractive, relatively cheap and much lower risk method of obtaining reserves. The oil majors have been particularly active in recent take-over attempts, using them not only to acquire oil reserves in 'safe' areas, but also to diversify their investments.

Diversification, the second important risk-reducing strategy, involves both spreading investment sites over as many different countries as possible and producing a wide range of mineral and non-mineral products. Many of the multinationals traditionally have been highly spatially diversified; in 1970 the Anglo-American Corporation was prospecting in thirty countries, in six continents. But international political uncertainties have undoubtedly increased the vulnerability of firms heavily committed to one LDC or one mineral product and, therefore, have acted to promote diversification as a desirable production objective. This has been most evident in the case of oil. Exploration had already started to shift from the Middle East before the OPEC states nationalized company assets and all exploration rights. Most attention had been focused on the offshore waters of western Europe and North America despite the fact that the investment costs per daily barrel of output were some five times greater than in the Middle East (Auty, 1983).

More recently, during the 1970s, the oil majors bought considerable non-oil assets. They not only moved into coal, metallic minerals and nuclear energy, but also into a range of manufacturing and retailing activities. British Petroleum had the stated aim of reducing the proportion of its assets in oil from 80 per cent in 1980 to 50 per cent by 1990. Its US subsidiary, Sohio (purchased to obtain access to the Alaskan oilfields and US markets), bought out Kennecott (copper) in 1981 and also paid about $760 million for the bulk of US Steel's coal interests (*Mining Annual Review*, 1982). Similarly, Gulf Oil invested heavily to build up its US steam coal operations; in 1981 it acquired Kemmerer Coal for $325 million and Republic Steel's North River coal property for a further $155 million. Although some of the enthusiasm for functional diversification has been dampened by the poor performance of a significant number of the ventures (Shell's excursion into nuclear power and Mobil's venture into retailing for instance), it still remains an important long-term strategy (Ross, 1985).

The third risk-reducing strategy is the substitution of technological innovation for exploration in order to make use of deposits or substances already known to exist in 'safe' areas. As a US Academy of Sciences report puts it,

> Because of political uncertainties in many areas the mineral industry will be forced to give more attention to the development of domestic deposits. The mining of these deposits ... will require the development of improved technology if mining operations are to remain viable. (US National Academy of Sciences, 1978, p. 3)

However, it would be an oversimplification to see this as solely a political risk-avoidance strategy. The development of low-grade minerals, which are found close to areas with an established mining infrastructure, involves significantly lower capital expenditures, and possibly lower administration and marketing costs.

Particularly in the United States experiments are being conducted to allow the recovery of valuable metals from small or low-grade ore deposits by using '*in situ* leaching' and borehole mining techniques.[6] Similarly, as was seen in Chapter 2, technologies are being developed to allow aluminium to be extracted from various non-bauxite ores. Pechiney is already building a commercial-scale plant to produce alumina from shales, while Alcoa has investigated the possibility of using anorthosite and coal tailings. This activity is taking place despite the fact that the cost of producing alumina from US domestic non-bauxite ores is about 80 per cent more expensive per ton than imports (Klass *et al.*, 1980). Technological innovation has also played a role in the diversification policies of the oil companies, with investments being made both in non-conventional oil sources and renewable forms of energy. British Petroleum has, for example, funded experiments in renewable energies, been active in attempts to produce oil commercially from shales and tar sands, and played a role in developing technologies to obtain oil and chemical feedstocks from coal. However, while such investments looked attractive when oil was between $34 and $39 a barrel, they appear much less so in 1985 with prices hovering around $28. One further example of search by technological innovation is provided by the considerable investments which have taken place to allow the commercial extraction of manganese nodules from the ocean floor, conveniently beyond the grasp of 'hostile' governments.

Finally, risks can be reduced by pooling them. It is now common for new mineral sources to be developed not by one company alone, but by consortia. Apart from reducing risks by decreasing each company's capital commitment to one location and mineral, Cobbe (1979) has suggested that it may also reduce the likelihood of 'hostile' government actions. If the constituent companies come from different countries, then the host state may be reluctant to disturb relationships with several foreign governments at the same time. Moreover, it is common for one of the involved companies to be a local firm, which may again offer a measure of protection. Even if pooling fails to influence producer government behaviour, it still markedly reduces an individual company's exposure to risk and could encourage more exploration investment in those LDCs where production costs are relatively low, but where the risks are too great for any one company to bear.

NON-OPTIMIZING BEHAVIOUR

To understand the complex patterns of mineral search activity it is necessary to drop the assumption that all firms attempt to maximize profits, albeit with a risk constraint. Many – if not most – firms simply do not behave in the optimal, rational way prescribed by economic theory. All companies or corporations are collections of interests and search decisions may reflect the power of different divisional managers within the corporate structure; given a set total exploration budget, the ability of the head of any regional exploration division to present a case could be crucial. In the same way, a set level of exploration may be maintained to keep together a highly trained group of surveyors, geologists and geophysicists, or to keep expensive equipment, such as offshore drilling platforms, working to capacity. Moreover, companies may allocate funds to exploration using rule-of-thumb procedures rather than any notions of optimality. For example, a fixed percentage of net annual sales, or a fixed percentage of the capital budget, may be set aside each year for exploration or for research and development.

Some companies will invest in mineral search to maintain or increase their volume of sales or their market share in particular minerals. For all vertically integrated firms (i.e. the same company mines, transports, refines, produces and markets final mineral products) exploration activity is closely related to their internal reserves/production situation. In 1971, for instance, Anaconda had over one-half of its copper ore reserves nationalized by Chile, and in order to ensure that its brass and wire mills could be kept supplied it needed to build up another reserves base. Its annual exploration expenditure virtually doubled and, naturally enough, this was concentrated in relatively safe countries, the United States, Canada and Australia. In the same way, Auty (1983) has shown that Texaco and Gulf, the two oil majors with the worst reserves–production ratios, have given the highest priority to exploration investment, devoting three-quarters of their entire 1980 investment budgets to the search for additional reserves. Businesses which aim to maximize their volume of sales or their market shares do not necessarily also aim to maximize profits. But it is possible that a firm could make more profit by exercising the control over prices which a large market share can give rather than by attempting to optimize investment returns in the first place.

IMPERFECTIONS IN THE CAPITAL MARKET

Finally in this discussion of investment in mineral search, the theoretical notion that capital markets are perfect must be dropped. Capital is neither fully mobile nor does it command the same price (interest rate) everywhere. A relatively small firm may only be able to get investment funds in an area where it has a good reputation, or for ventures in which it has a proven track record. Major international companies are not so constrained, and traditionally most have financed the bulk of their exploration and capital programmes out of reinvested earnings. However, these companies critically affect the availability and the effective price of capital in different countries of the world by their judgements on the relative risks involved. The interest rates they employ in exploration investment appraisals will differ markedly between countries. In the 1960s the US oil majors were using a 10–12 per cent figure for domestic and Canadian investments, at least 15 per cent for projects in less developed countries and up to 25 per cent in particularly high-risk areas. Inevitably this practice limits LDC exploration ventures since the higher the interest rate used, the fewer the number of investments which are likely to achieve positive net returns.

Mining, mineral consumption and world trade

Mining can obviously only occur where successful search has established the presence of deposits, and in that respect the spatial pattern of mining must reflect the past distribution of search activities. Moreover, as we have already seen, search does not stop when mining begins in an area; known but uneconomic reserves are reassessed as market, political and technical conditions change, and investment in exploration or technological adaptation is often attracted to established mining centres. However, there is no deterministic relationship between the known presence of mineral deposits and mining activity.

By no means all known deposits are classified as proven reserves at any one point in time, and not all proven reserves are worked with equal intensity; from a bank of potentially viable deposits producers *decide* which to develop and at what speed. Furthermore, once mining commences the full productive capacity is not necessarily used. Not only will the proportion of unutilized capacity reflect changes in total economic activity and the demands for raw materials, but it also depends upon specific economic and political factors operating within individual countries. For example, in 1976 about 67 per cent of Libya's oil production capacity was unused, while at the present time output in Iran and Iraq is well below capacity for obvious reasons.

SPATIAL DISTRIBUTIONS

It is beyond the scope of this book to describe in any detail the worldwide spatial patterns of mineral production, consumption and trade for the myriad currently used minerals. However, in order to understand present concerns over the way the minerals sector operates, and the public policy measures adopted in response to them, it is essential to have an outline picture of the basic distributions. It is also important briefly to put present-day spatial patterns in their historic context.

The first obvious locational fact is the dominant position of the currently advanced nations[7] in both the production and consumption of minerals. The striking imbalance in levels of consumption between the developed and developing worlds is well known and well documented (see, for example, the Brandt Commission, 1980). In the period immediately after the Second World War the United States alone consumed some 66 per cent of world oil output, over 90 per cent of natural gas, 99 per cent of uranium, over 60 per cent of all aluminium, copper, tin and nickel, and some 50 per cent of the world's production of zinc, lead and iron ore. Since then the degree of consumption concentration has declined markedly, the relative[8] US position having been eroded by rapid economic growth in Japan, the Soviet Union and, to a lesser extent, Western and Eastern Europe.

Although mineral consumption in the LDCs has risen absolutely, in relative terms they still account for only a small proportion of total world consumption. Over the last forty years the predominant position of the United States has merely been replaced by a more general advanced nation dominance. This can be exemplified by the 1980 energy consumption data shown in Figures 3.2 and 3.3. The differences between the advanced and developing world were still enormous, particularly when measured in per capita terms, despite the fact that over the previous decade Third World consumption rose 80 per cent, while developed

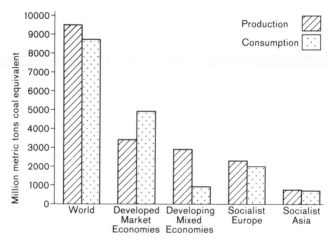

Figure 3.2   The distribution of global energy production and consumption, 1980
Source: Compiled from data contained in UNCTAD, 1982a

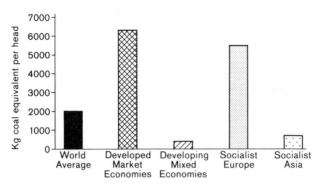

Figure 3.3   Per capita energy consumption, 1980
Source: As Figure 3.2

country use increased by only 18.8 per cent. The bias in energy consumption is typical of that for all other minerals. In 1981 the developed countries consumed over 80 per cent of world slab zinc, 85.3 per cent of primary aluminium and over 87 per cent of primary tin (ABMS, 1982), and similar percentages are repeated for virtually all other minerals. Figures 3.4–3.10 show the current world patterns of production and consumption for the most widely traded metallic minerals; in all cases they reveal the relatively minor contribution of the Third World to total mineral consumption.

The myth of reliance on LDC exports

It is a common piece of mythology that the bulk of advanced nation consumption is only made possible by mass imports from the Third World. The literature abounds with such phrases as 'Third World resources became available as a means of fulfilling the industrialized world's growing demand' (Tanzer, 1980, p. 44) or, more extremely, 'Having exhausted or destroyed the resources of our own lands we have turned once more to plunder of the lands whose

Table 3.3   Annual growth rates of mineral production (LDCs and developed nations) (in percentages)

Developed capitalist countries (all extractive industries)		Third World countries (non-fuel minerals)	
1948–52	3.5	1948–52	7
1953–8	1.9	1953–7	8
1959–65	2.6	1958–70	6
1966–72	2.1		

Source: Tanzer, 1980, p. 45.

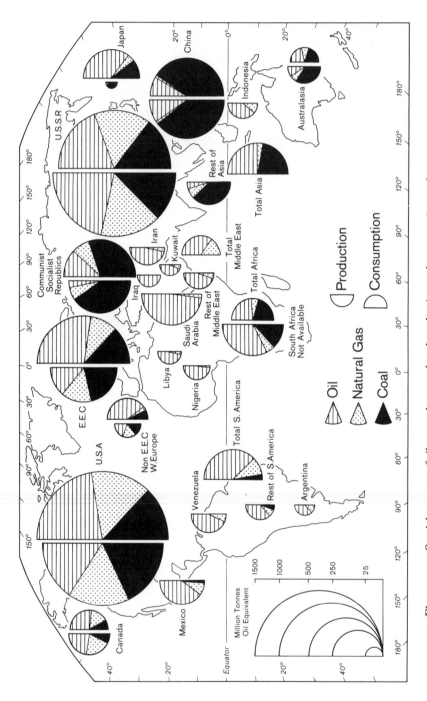

Figure 3.4   Spatial patterns of oil, natural gas, and coal production and consumption, 1981
Source: Compiled from data contained in British Petroleum, *Statistical Review of World Energy* London, BP, 1982

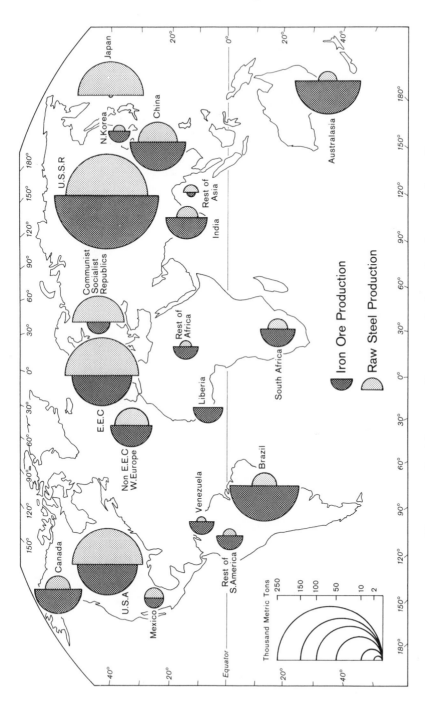

Figure 3.5   Spatial patterns of iron ore production and steel consumption, 1980–1
Source: Compiled from data contained in *Metal Bulletin Handbook,* 1982

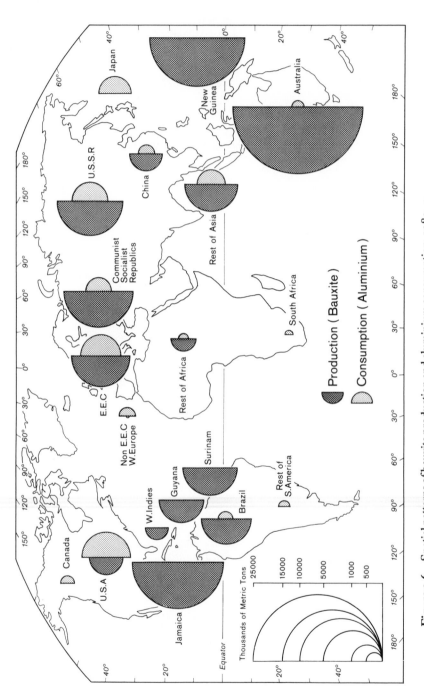

Figure 3.6   Spatial patterns of bauxite production and aluminium consumption, 1980–1
Source: Compiled from data contained in American Bureau of Mining Statistics, *Non-Ferrous Metal Data*, 1982

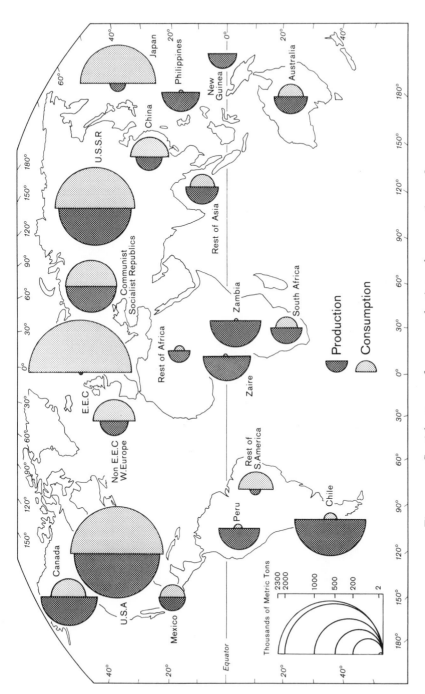

Figure 3.7   Spatial patterns of copper production and consumption, 1980–1
Source: As Figure 3.6

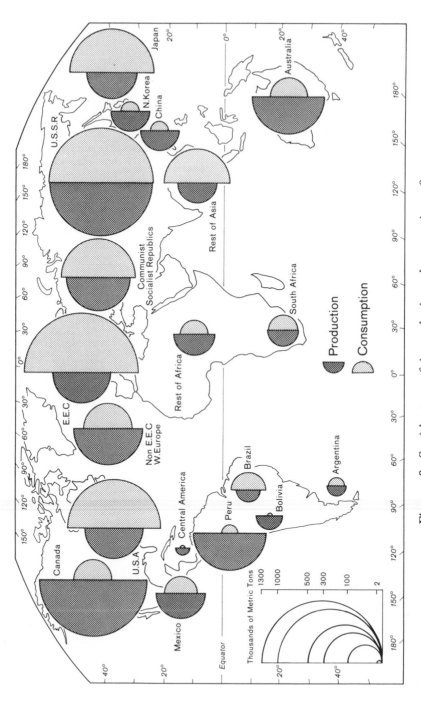

Figure 3.8   Spatial patterns of zinc production and consumption, 1980–1
Source: As Figure 3.6

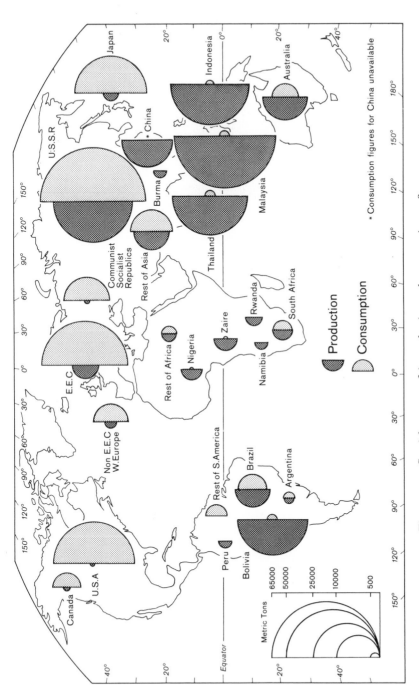

Figure 3.9   Spatial patterns of tin production and consumption, 1980–1
Source: As Figure 3.6; and for Soviet data, British Geological Survey, 1984

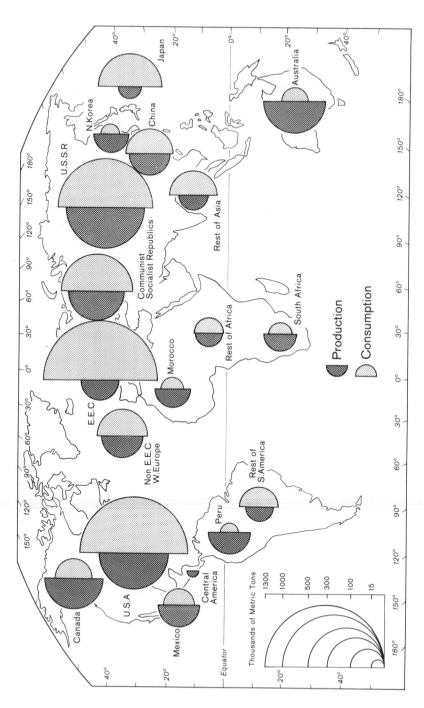

Figure 3.10   Spatial patterns of lead production and consumption, 1980–1
Source: As Figure 3.6

development was for long held back by colonial rule' (Barratt-Brown, 1976, pp. 5–6) or again 'It is now the Third World that supplies most of the capitalist world's raw materials' (Michael Meacher, 1976, p. 43). Such assertions may even be backed up by spurious data. For example, Tanzer has claimed that the figures given in Table 3.3 '[show] quite vividly the intensity of the mining company's post war movement towards the Third World' (Tanzer, 1980, p. 44). Such claims, based on percentage growth figures, ignore the fact that the LDCs were starting from a very much smaller base; a 20 per cent rise in output on a base of only 1000 tonnes is minor in real terms compared with a 2 per cent increase on a 1 million tonne production figure.

While in no way disputing that Third World countries do export significant quantities of raw materials, the fact remains that the developed nations are themselves the chief mineral producers and the chief source of their own mineral consumption. In other words, Meacher's statement is simply factually incorrect. Even in the energy sector, where the importance of OPEC oil to total world production is well established, the developed capitalist economies produced 69.2 per cent of their own energy requirements (measured in tonnes of coal equivalent) in 1980, the developed socialist nations were more than self-sufficient, and the mixed and planned economy LDCs (including OPEC) together produced only 33 per cent of total world energy output (UNCTAD, 1982a) (see Figure 3.2). Moreover, it is clear that since the 1973 oil crisis the contribution of OPEC to world oil production has fallen markedly (Table 3.4). Hostilities in the Middle East and the deliberate action of OPEC to use output constraints to push up world oil prices were the initial forces behind this shift, although the increased emphasis in the socialist states on the production of consumer goods and their greater needs for hard foreign currency were also of relevance (see pp. 65–7). At the present time the artificially high oil prices[9], coupled with the success of western efforts to reduce their dependence on oil imports (Figure 3.11), are continuing to erode OPEC's production dominance. As Figure 3.12 shows, total oil imports into the OECD countries have tumbled since 1979, in major part reflecting the reduction in oil consumption, but also affected by the increase in indigenous oil and gas production.

Table 3.4 Distribution of World crude oil production, 1973 and 1981 (in billions of tonnes)

	1973		1981	
World Total	2.87		2.86	
OPEC	1.52	(53%)	1.12	(39%)
Other less developed nations	0.08	(3%)	0.18	(6%)
Developed market economies	0.60	(21%)	0.67	(23%)
Socialist States	0.50	(17%)	0.73	(33%)

Source: UNCTAD, 1982a.

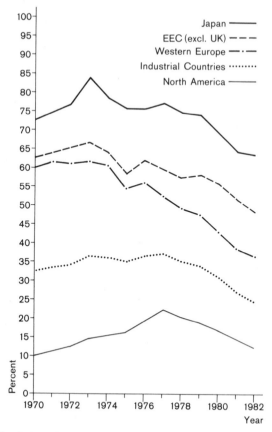

Figure 3.11   Declining oil import dependence of industrial countries, 1970–82
Source: General Agreement on Tariffs and Trade, *International Trade, 1982–3*, Geneva, GATT, 1983, p. 75

In the case of non-fuel minerals the proportion of total world production contributed by the advanced nations is even higher than for the energy minerals. In 1980 the less developed nations produced well under one-third of the world total of many important metals (27 per cent iron ore; 26 per cent chromite; 22 per cent lead; 26 per cent manganese; 23 per cent zinc; 26 per cent tungsten; and 32 per cent nickel). Only in the case of tin does the Third World attain production dominance, contributing over 68 per cent to the total. In addition, LDCs now produce less than 42 per cent of world bauxite and only 46 per cent of world copper, although in both cases they had been responsible for over one-half of world output at the beginning of the 1970s (US Department of Interior, 1982; Metal Bulletin, 1982). Similarly, the LDCs' role in non-metallic mineral production is relatively minor, except for phosphates, where they contribute about 33 per cent; they produce just over 9 per cent of world asbestos and sulphur but less than 3 per cent of total potash output.

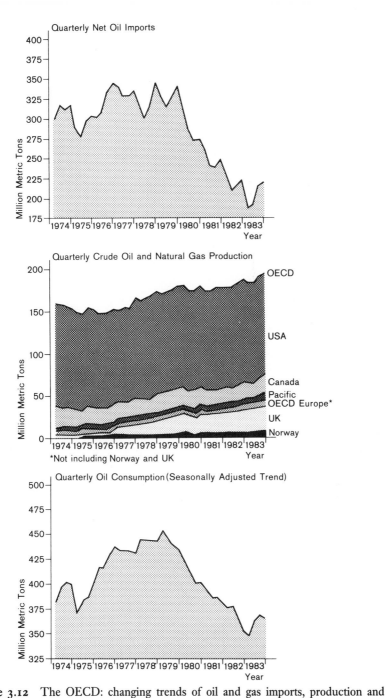

Figure 3.12 The OECD: changing trends of oil and gas imports, production and consumption, 1974–83
Source: OECD, *Quarterly Oil and Gas Statistics of OECD Countries, Fourth Quarter 1983*, Paris, International Energy Agency, 1984, pp. xxv, xxvi

Table 3.5 Trade as a percentage of apparent mineral consumption in the EEC, North America and Japan, 1974/5 and 1978/9 (in current prices)

Product group	Column A EEC		Column B United States/Canada		Column C Japan		Column D Total	
	1974/5	1978	1974/5	1978	1974/5	1978	1974/5	1978
Primary products								
1 Coal, petroleum, natural gas								
$ million apparent consumption	59,955	84,894	60,534	183,781	24,132	29,793	144,063	297,834
Trade as % of consumption (all external imports)	76.2	59.8	29.7	19.7	97.3	94.9	58.3	37.7
LDC imports as % of consumption	70.2	53.6	29.1	18.6	80.7	80.8	55.0	34.8
2 Other mining and quarrying crude products								
$ million apparent consumption	12,053	17,720	12,372	28,985	6,029	6,601	30,334	52,963
Trade as % of consumption (all external imports)	75.3	74.7	19.8	14.9	88.0	85.5	45.63	36.4
LDC imports as % of consumption	24.4	21.8	10.8	6.9	41.0	39.2	22.24	16.0
Manufactured and semi-processed mineral products								
$ million apparent consumption	182,660	251,902	200,851	295,792	85,628	141,709	468,141	687,926
Trade as % of consumption (all external imports)	8.0	7.6	7.45	6.9	5.15	4.7	5.05	4.9
LDC imports as % of consumption	2.3	2.0	3.5	3.1	2.8	2.9	2.9	2.7

Source: UNCTAD, 1982a, pp. 424–31.
Notes: Product groups – coal, petroleum and natural gas = standard industrial classification (SIT) categories 321, 331 and 341; other mining and quarrying = SIT categories 27, 281, 283, 285, 286 and 667; manufactured and semi-processed = SIT categories 332, 661–6, 282, 284, 67 and 68.
External imports – in the case of Japan, this is the same as total imports; for the EEC and USA/Canada it means trade from outside but not between the countries themselves; in the total column, trade between Japan, the EEC, USA/Canada is omitted.

It is meaningless to attempt to obtain aggregate output figures for the non-fuel minerals since there is no common physical unit of account; comparisons must, therefore, be made in money value terms.[10] Table 3.5 gives some idea of the importance of LDC exports to consumption in the EEC, the USA and Canada, and Japan. In 1978 the less developed nations accounted for 34.8 per cent by value of all the coal, petroleum and natural gas consumed in these three major demand centres (column D), but only 16 per cent of other crude minerals. The table also shows that since 1974/5 the relative contribution of LDC exports to total consumption has fallen markedly at least in money terms. It is clear that the EEC and Japan rely much more heavily on Third World sources than do the United States and Canada, and particularly so for their energy needs. But as a whole the EEC imported less than 22 per cent of its total consumption of metallic ores and other crude non-fuel minerals from the LDCs, while Japan imported under 40 per cent. Moving to the processed mineral sectors (e.g. refined petroleum, refined or smelted ores), the LDCs clearly make only a very marginal contribution to advanced nation consumption.

It must be remembered that a considerable proportion of mineral production never enters world trade – it is produced and consumed in the same country. Even for a major traded mineral such as iron ore only approximately 32 per cent is put on the international market. Similarly, in the copper case less than 20 per cent of crude ores and concentrates are exported, while only approximately 38 per cent of smelted and refined copper (including that derived from scrap) is traded internationally (Metal Bulletin, 1982). Although there are minerals where a high percentage of total production is for export – at least 60 per cent of antimony, for example – these are the exception and not the rule.

By analysing world mineral trade figures it becomes clear that the major exporters are advanced, not Third World, countries. In 1973 the developing countries exported only a little over one-third of all ores and minerals entering international trade, the developed socialist states exported a further 12 per cent, and a small group of advanced western economies accounted for 50 per cent (Fried, 1976). Since 1973 this position has not changed. As the United Nations development reports have shown, there has been a virtual stagnation in the volume of LDC exports to the developed countries (UNCTAD, 1982b). In fact available evidence strongly suggests that Third World nations are playing a declining role as sources of raw materials for advanced nation markets. The EEC, United States, Canada and Japan have all reduced the contribution of LDC imports as a percentage of their total consumptions (Table 3.5), although to what extent this is a long-term change rather than a temporary consequence of the economic recession is not known with any certainty.

The same trend of declining LDC contributions emerges from study of the origin and destination of all crude non-fuel minerals entering international trade. As Table 3.6 shows, in 1975 the less developed nations contributed 32 per cent of total world trade and 34 per cent of the imports into the developed market economies. However, in both cases the percentage had been reduced to 29 per cent just four years later. At no time in the decade did the developed countries take less than 60 per cent of their total imports from other advanced

Table 3.6 Network of exports of crude non-fuel minerals

		Destination	Millions US dollars (FOB)			
Origin	Year	World	Developed market economies	Developing market economies	Advanced socialist states	Less developed socialist states
		(%)	(%)			
World	1970	10,460 (100)	8,721 (100)	546	1,053	42
	1975	20,595 (100)	15,864 (100)	1,556	2,565	97
	1979	33,033 (100)	25,619 (100)	3,176	3,914	175
Developed Market economies	1970	6,084 (58)	5,590 (64)	312	87	5
	1975	11,265 (55)	9,484 (60)	961	315	41
	1979	19,650 (59.5)	16,929 (66)	1,924	617	106
Developing market economies	1970	3,251 (31)	2,766 (32)	207	241	29
	1975	6,617 (32)	5,375 (34)	535	623	42
	1979	9,466 (29)	7,600 (29)	1,133	607	54
Advanced socialist states	1970	1,031 (10)	300 (3)	25	700	6
	1975	2,477 (12)	896 (6)	45	1,516	15
	1979	3,395 (10)	858 (3)	83	2,438	16
Less developed socialist states	1970	92 (1)	64 (<1)	2	26	n.a.
	1975	235 (1)	110 (<1)	15	110	n.a.
	1979	457 (1)	181 (<1)	41	232	n.a.

Source: UNCTAD, 1982a, annex A, pp. 458–500.
Note: Non-fuel minerals include crude fertilizers, non-metallic minerals, metalliferous ores (not including precious metals) and metal scrap.

western nations, and by 1979 this proportion had increased to 66 per cent.

These production and trade facts are important in order to keep in perspective the widely held view that the advanced market economies are dependent on imports from 'hostile' Third World nations. Although the EEC is 100 per cent dependent on imports for its consumption of a metal such as nickel, the proportion taken from LDC sources is minor: 80 per cent of matte nickel (48 per cent metal content) comes from Canada, while 77 per cent of refined nickel is imported from Canada, South Africa, Australia, Norway and Finland. Similarly, 66 per cent of EEC bauxite imports, 60 per cent of manganese ores, 65 per cent of lead, 61 per cent of zinc ores, concentrates and metal, 83 per cent of molybdenum ore and 95 per cent of titanium ores are all taken from a small group of advanced nations, with the United States, Canada, Australia and South Africa predominating (Crowson, 1977).

It is, of course, possible to find specific minerals where the LDC contributions to both total world trade and advanced nation imports are substantial. These are primarily in five commodity groups, crude fertilizers, petroleum, non-ferrous ores, concentrates and metals, iron ore, and uranium and thorium ores (Figure 3.13). In all these groups LDC exports represented over 40 per cent or more of the total world trade, although this does not necessarily mean that they account for such a high percentage of advanced nation consumption. In the uranium case, for instance, by far the largest producers are the United States, South Africa, Canada and probably the Soviet Union, although data for the last are too poor to allow reliable output estimates. In all, LDC producers account for less than 21 per cent of total market economy mineral output, but virtually all of this goes for export (ABMS, 1982).

Apart from the well-known concern over petroleum, it is the non-ferrous group of metals that provides most cases of high advanced nation dependence on Third World imports. Tin production, for example, is heavily biased to the less developed nations, which together in 1981 produced 82 per cent of capitalist world output. In fact just four countries, Malaysia, Thailand, Indonesia and Bolivia were responsible for 77 per cent (ABMS, 1982). Similarly, over 54 per cent of the bauxite, 46 per cent of copper ore and 27 per cent of the zinc produced in the non-socialist world comes from LDC sources. Of course, it does not follow that the dominant position of Third World nations as producers of particular minerals necessarily implies high risks for the advanced countries. The likelihood of future supply restrictions also depends on the availability of substitutes, the degree to which output and reserves are concentrated in just a few countries and on the ability or willingness of producers to form supply cartels (see Chapter 4, pp. 165–74).

LDC export dependence

Mineral dependence is clearly a double-edged sword. Many LDCs are critically dependent on their exports of a single mineral, or a few closely related minerals, to obtain the foreign exchange needed not only to pay for essential imports, but

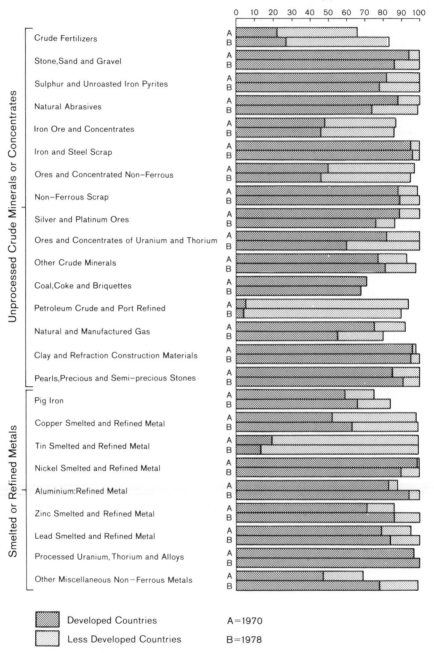

Figure 3.13 The contribution of the less developed countries to world trade in selected minerals and mineral products

Source: Compiled from data contained in UNCTAD, 1982a

also to service their overseas debts. As Table 3.7 shows, a number of countries obtain well over 50 per cent of their total export earnings from fuels or other mineral products. The healthy positive trade balances experienced by most OPEC states during the 1970s have evaporated in the 1980s, and many of the metal exporters are in an even worse trade deficit position. Bolivia already had an overall deficit of $110 million by 1980, with 45 per cent of its total export earnings needed to repay outstanding loans and pay the interest on the debt. If anything, Chile and Peru were in an even more difficult debt situation, needing 59 and 52 per cent respectively of their export earnings for loan and interest payments. All such countries are highly vulnerable to changes in international mineral markets

Table 3.7   The value of mineral exports as a percentage of all exports from selected Third World countries

Country	Year	Fuels (%)	Ores/Metals (%)
Algeria*	1979	97.7	
Bahrain*	1979	85.6	
Bolivia	1977		66.5 (tin and other non-ferrous ores)
Brunei	1979	99.9	
Chile	1978		62.7 (mainly copper ores and concentrates)
Gabon	1977	81.07	
Indonesia	1980	71.9	
Kiribati	1979		84.65 (crude fertilizers)
Kuwait*	1978	88.5	
Liberia	1978		62.7 (iron ore and related materials)
Libya*	1979	99.57	
Mauritania	1975		90.1 (iron ore 70% plus non-ferrous metals)
New Caledonia	1980		94.8 (pig-iron, nickel and other non-ferrous ores)
Niger	1978		78.3 (uranium and thorium ores)
Nigeria*	1978	90.27	
Papua New Guinea	1976		59.9 (mainly copper ores and concentrates)
Peru	1977		53.3 (mainly copper ores and concentrates)
Togo	1977		49.4 (crude fertilizers)
Zaire	1979		73.1 (mainly copper ores and concentrates)
Zambia	1978		95.8 (mainly copper ores and concentrates)

* These high proportions are typical of those recorded in other OPEC states.

Source: UNCTAD, 1982a, pp. 106–29.

which reduce the volume and/or value of their sales. Between 1980 and 1982 alone the dollar market price for non-fuel minerals fell by 12.5 per cent per annum, and the situation was further worsened by declining export volumes and by the rise in prices for imported manufactured goods. Despite much discussion about solutions to the international debt crisis, little has occurred to lower real interest rates or to increase real mineral export prices, without which there is little hope of improving the financial position of the export-dependent LDCs.

The location of mineral processing

It was shown in Table 3.5 that the major market centres imported only a minor proportion of their processed mineral needs from the LDCs. This category of commodities is a large one, including smelted and refined metals, metal alloys, scrap, bars, ingots, plates, tubes and other forms of basically processed metals, as well as petroleum products, cement, glass and other processed construction materials. For the construction minerals the minor role played by the LDCs simply reflects the fact that very little international trade occurs in them since they are widely available and are normally too low value and bulky to stand the cost of long-distance transport. However, the minimal LDC contribution to trade in processed metals and oil products arises because of a traditional split in the location of the different stages in the mineral production process. While the concentration and benefication of low metal content ores had traditionally been located close to the mines to avoid the unnecessary costs of transporting vast quantities of waste material, further processing has tended to be located either at the market or in advanced nations with a low-cost energy source, particularly hydroelectric power or natural gas. Bauxite provides a classic example of such a split in the production process (Table 3.8).

In 1968 less developed countries in Central and South America alone produced 42.2 per cent of world bauxite, and other Third World nations contributed a further 12.6 per cent. But alumina production and aluminium refining were heavily concentrated in the developed world, particularly on the Gulf Coast of the United States, and near Canadian and Norwegian hydroelectric power sites. Since alumina has a market value per metal content tonne almost three times that of bauxite, LDC producer country revenues could increase markedly if this processing stage were located at the mines. However, despite considerable producer pressure, the only major bauxite producer to process a significant proportion of its ore is Australia. In part this reflects the availability of cheap hydroelectric power and coal, but even more crucially it results from the political complexion and stability of the country and the government's relatively lenient treatment of foreign private investors. These same factors have also played a vital role in turning Australia from an insignificant producer in 1960 to the world's largest just twenty years later, with an output equal to that of the next two most important producers, Guinea and Jamaica, taken together.

Whenever minerals are traded internationally between the LDCs and the developed nations, the production process typically shows this type of locational split, even though the Third World countries have been anxious to retain a higher

Table 3.8 Distribution of world bauxite, alumina and aluminium production, 1980 (in thousands of short tons and percentages)

Country/area	Bauxite	Alumina	Aluminium
United States and Canada	1,638 (1.7%)	8,707 (21.8%)	6,178 (35.7%)
Jamaica	12,864 (13.0%)	2,811 (7.0%)	—
Other Central and South America	12,655 (12.8%)	2,184 (5.5%)	873 (5.0%)
Europe	5,947 (6.0%)	4,724 (11.8%)	3,908 (22.6%)
Guinea	15,000 (15.2%)	747 (1.9%)	—
Rest of Africa	1,000 (1.0%)	— —	508 (2.9%)
Total Asia (including China)	6,675 (6.7%)	3,062 (7.7%)	1,870 (10.8%) of which oil states 271 (1.6%) Japan 849 (4.9%)
Australia and New Zealand	28,154 (28.5%)	7,812 (19.5%)	591 (3.4%)
Soviet Union and East European socialist states	14,884 (15.1%)	6,757 (16.9%)	3,383 (19.5%)

Source: ABMS, 1982

proportion of the value added in the processing of their minerals. It takes, however, very strong economic forces to overcome both the inertia of traditional production patterns and the reduced risks involved in market or other advanced nation locations. Only for one of the major metals, copper, have such forces proved strong enough to break down established location patterns. The extremely low metal content of the ores, coupled with the cost advantages of integrating refining, smelting and concentration in one plant, has now acted to pull all stages of the production process to the source of the raw materials, especially where relatively cheap energy sources are also available. Major ore producers, such as Chile, Zaire and Zambia, now smelt and refine about 60 per cent of their ore (Metal Bulletin, 1982).

PRODUCTION DECISIONS IN THE PRIVATE SECTOR

The role of government in determining the distribution of mineral production has increased markedly since the 1940s not only through the nationalization of mineral operations and by increasing tax and royalty payments, but also through controls on trade and prices and through planning and pollution control regulations (see Chapter 5). Increased government activity is by no means a phenomenon confined to the less developed mineral-exporting countries, but occurs just as widely in the mixed advanced economy nations. Nevertheless, private investment decisions are still the most crucial determinants of patterns of mineral production, except in the planned economies of course.

A simplified economic model

In order to try to understand the complex set of factors which influence private sector decisions it is useful, as a starting-point, to consider the basic economic theory of demand and supply. Although it is based on several key and totally unrealistic assumptions, it nevertheless allows us to isolate a number of important decision variables.

If we assume that the market for minerals is perfectly competitive, completely free from government intervention and staffed by perfectly rational profit-maximizers, then the *scale* of mineral production will be determined by the level of consumer demands and the cost of getting the mineral to them. The demand curve for each individual mineral at any point in time will be determined by the technological level and scale of economic activity in an economy, by the number of consumers, their tastes and affluence and by the price of substitute products. For most goods the demand curve will slope downwards as *DD* in Figure 3.14. The higher the price, the smaller the quantity which consumers are willing or able to purchase. If real income levels rise over time, the curve may shift outwards

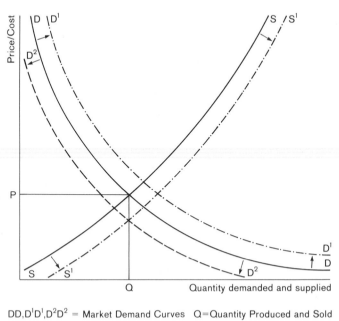

DD,D¹D¹,D²D² = Market Demand Curves   Q=Quantity Produced and Sold

SS,S¹S¹   = Market Supply Curves   P=Market Price

Figure 3.14   Market demand and supply curves

(D^1D^1), as consumers would be able to afford to take more of the mineral at all price levels. Alternatively, the development of a new low-priced substitute could cause consumers to switch their use, in which case the demand curve would shift markedly downwards (D^2D^2).

At the same point in time producers have a supply quantity which they are willing and able to put on to the market at different price levels. In a perfectly competitive situation this would be determined by the costs of production, including normal entrepreneurial profits and the market return on invested capital, and by the costs of transporting the mineral to the market. As prices rise, so higher-cost producers could provide supplies and it becomes possible to transport the resource from more and more remote production centres; hence the shape of the supply curve SS. Just as the demand curve can shift over time, so shifts in the supply curve could occur. If technological innovation reduced the cost of mining, processing, or transporting the material, then more could be supplied at all price levels (S^1S^1). Conversely, increases in the market price of capital, freight rates, or energy costs could all act to shift the curve upwards, making less available at all price levels.

In this highly simplified world the quantity Q and the mineral price P will be determined by the point at which the supply and demand curves intersect. The market price would then determine the location of production; fixing the mines, smelters and refineries from which the required quantity could be provided profitably. If more was supplied than was demanded at a given price level, the market price would fall and the highest-cost producers would be forced to cut or stop production. Even though the behavioural and competitive assumptions of the model are highly unrealistic, it does identify three key variables which play a considerable role in influencing patterns of production. These are, first, the location, size, composition and affluence of different market centres; second, the costs of production (including the provision of essential infrastructure); and third, the costs of transporting the mineral to market.

The market factor

MARKET LOCATION

As market centres have changed in their relative importance, so too has the location of the least-cost mineral production sites. The growth over the last forty years in the number of mineral producers throughout the world and the changes in their relative importance in part, at least, reflect the reduced concentration of mineral consumption. Iron ore mining provides a good illustration of this. In 1950 the United States dominated world steel consumption, taking over 47 per cent of total supply, but its market share has since plunged to barely 16 per cent in 1981 – compared with the Soviet Union, 21 per cent; Japan, 14 per cent; and Europe, including the socialist planned economies, 31 per cent. Moreover, although the advanced nations still dominate world steel consumption, accounting for 83 per cent in 1981, the beginnings of industrialization in many parts of the Third World have further broadened the range of potential ore markets. As a consequence, the United States has declined in relative importance as an ore producer, and a wide range of new ore sources have found profitable market outlets. Countries such as Australia, India, China, South Korea, Brazil, Angola, Liberia, Venezuela and South Africa, which were either small or non-producers in the 1940s, are today major supply sources. For example, the massive growth in Australian production, now some 95 million metric tons per annum compared with under 4 million metric tons in 1950, owes much to the rapid expansion of the Japanese market.

A broadening of aluminium markets has likewise had an impact on the location of bauxite mining. In 1941 only fourteen countries had any refining capacity; there was none at all in Africa, Latin America, Australasia or Asia, outside the then Japanese Empire (Warren, 1973). Today refining occurs in over forty countries, spread throughout the world. Although the United States is still the largest single aluminium market, its share has declined from 45 to 28 per cent, whereas Japanese and West European demands have each risen from under 1 per cent to 7 and 22 per cent respectively, while the socialist economies have also increased their market share from 17 to 22 per cent. In the Third World some of the traditional bauxite exporters, such as Surinam, now have a small refining capability. But most capacity developments have occurred either in countries such as Bahrain, where low-cost energy supplies are available, or in those LDCs which are industrializing most rapidly, Korea, Taiwan, India and Brazil being typical examples. Once again the widening of markets has helped increase the number of bauxite-producing areas and has also contributed to shift the balance of advantage between producers. Although the relative, and in recent years the absolute, decline of Central and South American output has clearly been influenced by government attitudes and fears over political stability, the reduced relative importance of the US market has not been an insignificant factor.

The general widening of markets has a long-term impact on the broad spatial distribution of production, but over a shorter timescale the stability and relative vigour of the different markets will also have feedback effects on output levels in the various established mining centres. In recent years the economic depression has been much more pronounced in Europe and North America than in Japan. Declining European vehicle sales – the major market for sheet steel – and reduced demands for constructional steels have both had a major impact on indigenous iron ore output. Ore production in the ECSC[11] plunged by a massive 52.5 per cent between 1976 and 1981, whereas the 1981 world output was the same as that of 1976. While the prices for most iron ores marketed in Europe remained unchanged in 1980–1, which means they declined in *real* terms, the Japanese price rose by 7–8 per cent. Established Japanese ore suppliers, such as Australia, Brazil, India, South Africa and Chile, have therefore been relatively protected from the world recession.

MARKET COMPOSITION

The *composition* of market demand can also have important effects on the location of production. In the first place, producers of crude minerals or concentrates are to some extent in competition with the producers of smelted and refined products to serve the demand in specific market areas. In any particular market-place final consumption can be supported by importing varying proportions of each type of commodity. This point can be clarified by looking at the Japanese aluminium market.

Although aluminium consumption only declined by 2 per cent per annum between 1978 and 1981, internal production of the refined metal fell by 30 per cent over the same period; and smelter capacity was reduced by 31 per cent, with the remaining capacity operating at less than 50 per cent of its full rate. The rise in oil prices had increased the production costs at Japan's oil-based refineries and smelters at a time when the world market price for refined aluminium had been declining steadily. As a result, by 1981 imported metal cost $600 per ton less than home produced, and imports were 52 per cent higher than in 1978. Inevitably this has affected established bauxite and alumina suppliers, such as Australia and Guyana, and has encouraged Japanese companies to extend their interests in overseas refinery capacity, a trend further stimulated by the government's decision to allow them to import metal from their associated plants duty-free.

A second market composition effect arises when the type of final mineral product demanded influences the quality of the raw material which can be used in its production. For example, over the last twenty years most of the advanced nations have increased their use of very high-quality steel, which has reduced their demand for ores containing silica and similar impurities. In the same way, increasingly stringent pollution control regulations in North America, Europe and Japan have limited the demand for, and cut the price of, oils containing a high content of sulphur. Whereas the 1981 Rotterdam price for refined oil with 0.5 per cent sulphur content was $273 per tonne, a 1 per cent sulphur oil only fetched $194.

Another aspect of market composition is the price and availability of substitutes in each market centre. Very few minerals have no substitutes. For many purposes energy needs could be met from coal, gas, oil, nuclear fuels, hydropower plants or a variety of non-conventional renewable sources. In the short run a country may be fixed into two or three of these because of past investment in capacity, but over time marked energy mix changes occur. Different markets exhibit varying degrees of flexibility in their choice of energy sources. The United States with its range of indigenous resources has, for example, more room for manoeuvre than Japan. In the metals case, competition not only exists between metals but also arises through the use of synthetics and recycled materials. Any factors which change the relative competitiveness of a mineral *vis-à-vis* its substitutes inevitably must feed back and affect production levels.

THE INTERDEPENDENCE BETWEEN DEMAND AND SUPPLY

In the previously discussed simple economic model the demand and supply curves were separately and exogenously determined.[12] However, in one crucial respect market demand does affect the supply curve. If a producer is tied into one particular market, its size will help determine whether it is possible to obtain economies of scale in production and transportation. The production of minerals is a highly capital-intensive activity; the greater the output over which the capital costs can be spread, the lower the unit production cost. The larger the output, the greater the use of expensive – but cost-reducing – bulk production and transportation technologies. A small producer, constrained by a limited local market, may then be forced out of business by his failure to compete with larger concerns serving several markets, who have achieved much lower unit production costs. This has certainly been one factor which has favoured the large multinational companies against small indigenous producers.

The production cost factor

PHYSICAL DEPOSIT AND SITE CHARACTERISTICS

As has already been seen, the physical characteristics of a particular mineral source are only one set among the many variables which affect the overall production costs at each site (pp. 72–3). Nevertheless, all other things being equal, the facts of geology and physical geography do have a role to play in helping to determine which supply sources will be developed and at what speed. In the first place, the size of the deposit will affect the possible production scale, with large deposits allowing scale economies to be achieved. Secondly, the quality of the mineral and the possibility of producing co-products or by-products from the same source will inevitably influence per unit production costs. Low metal content ores normally will be more expensive to mine, since a high proportion of the extracted material will be waste, and even more important, such ores will involve much higher processing costs. Any ores which are concentrated, smelted, or refined using oil have been adversely affected by rising oil prices and this is particularly so for those with low metal contents. For example, US copper producers, who exploit ores well below the average world metal content (see pp. 72–3), have been hard-hit by a combination of rising energy costs and falling copper prices. The 1981 delivered[13] copper price of $0.84 per pound was 48 per cent below its 1974 peak; in 1982 the price fell to $0.65 per pound and is now below 65 cents. As most US producers have a range of break-even costs between $0.75 and $1.00 per pound, a whole series of mine closures or production cutbacks have occurred. Anaconda has closed its Carr Fork mine in Utah; Newmont has indefinitely suspended operations at Magma, Arizona; and Phelps Dodge has stopped – again for an indefinite period – all copper production in its US mines (*Mining Annual Review*, 1982). Although low ore content is not the sole factor, it does partially explain the relatively high per unit costs in the United States and the difficulties experienced during periods when copper demands and prices are low.[14]

The third physical factor affecting production costs is the structure of the deposit and the nature of its surroundings. Offshore oil and gas production is normally over four times more costly than an onshore operation, and drilling costs increase markedly with depth, mainly because of the extra costs of the rig. In the case of non-drilled minerals extraction costs will depend upon the nature and the thickness of overburden and the degree to which the mineral-bearing rocks are faulted and folded. Where the site characteristics allow surface mining techniques to be used, mining costs tend to be much lower; the capital and labour costs involved in draining and ventilating the mine, supporting overlying rocks and providing underground transport systems are all avoided (Figure 3.15).

CAPITAL COSTS

Given the large number of exploited minerals and the wide range of conditions under which each is produced, it is extremely difficult to generalize about which factors of production (land or materials, labour and capital) are the most vital components in the total cost structure. Moreover, within the limits set by available technology, companies are able to change the combination of factors used in production, in response to spatial and temporal variations in factor costs. However, at least for recent mine and processing developments it is clear that fixed costs – the expenditure on constructing the plant and associated infrastructure plus the rate of interest on the invested capital – are the most important element in total costs.[15]

Available evidence suggests that these fixed costs *normally* now far outweigh the variable costs (wages, materials and parts, energy, output taxes and administrative expenses) of operating the plant. There are, however, some important exceptions to this; the wage component is, for instance, a significant cost element in deep-mined coal, particularly in the advanced economies.

In an earlier section it was pointed out that the costs of infrastructure (power plants, water, schools, hospitals, housing, recreation facilities and transport) can

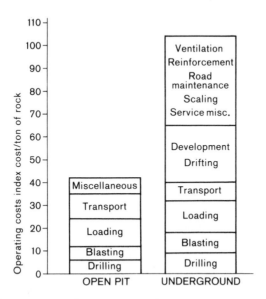

Figure 3.15   A comparison of the unit costs of operation between surface and underground mining
Source: Hedberg, 1981, p. 179

dwarf the capital cost of the mine or plant itself. This is particularly so for completely new ventures in areas not already established as production centres. For example, it has been estimated that the 1960s iron ore, coal and nickel developments in Australia involved expenditures on infrastructure of about $1.8 million for every $1 million spent on the mines (Van Rensburg and Bambrick, 1978). Significant cost advantages, therefore, accrue to sites where the mining companies can plug into existing services, and particularly favoured are those projects which involve the expansion of production at existing mining or processing centres. Even before infrastructure costs are taken into account, green field developments will normally be at least 70 per cent more expensive than onsite expansions. If a company has to pay for all the infrastructure, then the mineral deposit would need to be very large, so that the capital costs could be spread over enough units of output to allow them to be competitively priced.

When it comes to deciding which of several potential sites to exploit, companies will naturally be influenced by the willingness of local and national governments to at least part-finance the infrastructure needs. Coal production in the Australian states of New South Wales and Queensland has undoubtedly been increased by their willingness to spend millions of dollars on coal loading facilities at ports to assist in the development of the coal export trade. Governments in LDCs rarely have sufficient capital to finance significant infrastructure projects and major mining projects, such as the development of the rich Borni Hills iron deposits in Liberia, can be delayed for years until aid or loan funds are made available.

Capital costs are not only important as an influence on the location of production, but may also affect output levels once production is under way. In the simple economic model firms would cut output as prices fell, and high-cost producers could shut down completely. However, since the capital costs are fixed and do not vary with output, firms may well maintain output levels as long as the variable costs are covered and at least some contribution is being made to fixed costs. Some companies may be able to maintain loss-making output levels for years – and may find this preferable to abandoning the plant and losing all the fixed assets. This tends to mean that production levels need not be responsive to price fall, supplies continue to exceed demands and prices are driven still lower. Such supply inflexibility is one factor contributing to the massive price fluctuations which are characteristic of a number of metals (see Figure 4.2, p. 127).

LABOUR COSTS

Several writers have suggested that mining companies have been attracted to less developed countries and to South Africa because of the enormous differential between their wage rates and those in advanced countries. Tanzer (1980) has calculated that the average wage per employee in South Africa was only $900 per annum in 1972, and in Brazil it was only marginally higher at $1000, whereas in the United States and Australia the rates were $10,800 and $8200 respectively. He goes on to claim that this 'enormous exploitation of labour' has laid the basis for the profitability of multinational company operations in the Third World (ibid., pp. 46, 174). In the South African case low wage rates undoubtedly help to keep down per unit production costs, but it is oversimplistic to attribute the profitability of operations solely to labour costs.

As we have already seen, capital costs normally exceed net operating costs, and within the variable costs energy and output taxes are frequently more significant elements than labour. There is in fact little evidence to suggest that average operating costs are lower in the LDCs. For example, in 1975 primary copper producers in Africa were operating at a cost of 48.5 cents per pound of metal, which equalled that in the United States and exceeded cost levels in Canada, Europe and Australia. Moreover, comparison of wage rates may give a misleading impression about the real cost of labour, which will be affected by productivity and by the range of facilities which must be provided for the workforce. In the developed nations where the workers may live in established communities, the considerable costs involved in building an entire workers' town can be avoided.

The transportation factor

In the simple market model the ruling commodity price minus the costs of transferring it from the production point will determine the revenue received for each unit of output. This in turn will determine whether the output at any particular site can be profitably marketed. This approach involves many unrealistic assumptions (see pp. 111–13), but nevertheless the availability of transport facilities and transfer costs have had a major impact on the location of mineral production and on patterns of trade.

TRANSPORT AVAILABILITY

It is axiomatic that, except for precious metals, no minerals can be exploited until a bulk transport network has been created. Warren (1973) provides a whole series of examples of the role of rail–port complexes in the development of such currently key mining areas as Pilbara (Western Australia), Kedia d'Idjil (Mauritania), and the Wabush Lake area in Canada.

It also goes without saying that companies are more likely to pursue the development of deposits in countries where transport systems are already well developed, and in which their transport infrastructure costs are much reduced. As Figure 3.16 clearly shows, the dense railway network and deep-water port facilities of South Africa stand in marked contrast to the situation in Botswana and other land-locked states in the region. The very existence of such a good transport system acts as a catalyst to further mineral exploitation. Although coal exports provided the motive and revenue for the construction of the eastern Transvaal–Richards Bay railway–port complex, this has stimulated the production of phosphates, chromium and a variety of other minerals, all of which only need bear the cost of small branch-line construction or road transport to the railhead (Van Rensburg and Bambrick, 1978). In stark contrast the known mineral deposits of Botswana, which include manganese, copper, nickel and coal, remain relatively undeveloped and are likely to remain so until the $800 million trans-Kalahari railway project to link the country with the Namibian port of Walvis Bay becomes more than a paper plan. Political conflict in Namibia, the

Figure 3.16 The availability of bulk transport facilities in Southern Africa, 1983

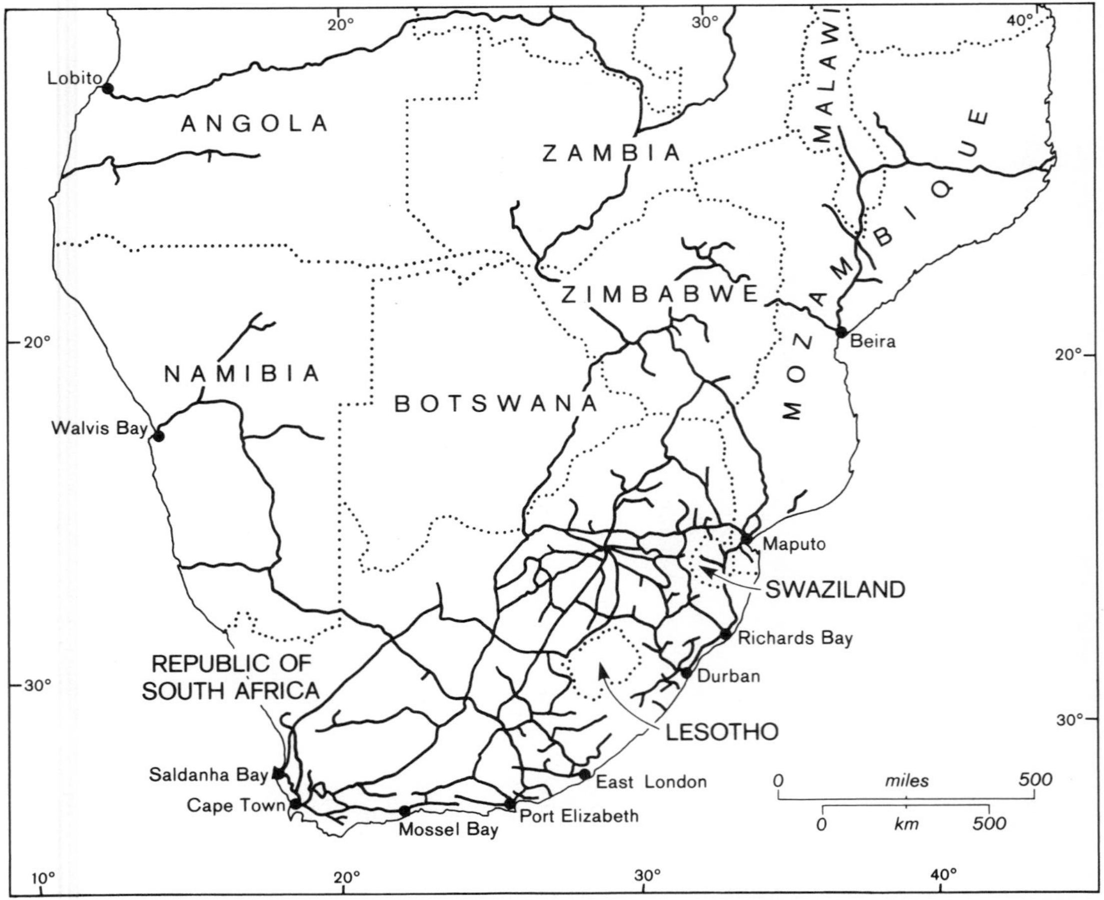

Source: Compiled from data on 1:2,500,000 (1979), 4th edn, Pretoria, Government Printer, 1979; updated from Cartactual, various dates

activities of anti-government forces in Mozambique, the notorious delays and bottlenecks at the ports of Beira and Maputo, and continuing concern over the stability of Zimbabwe, all make it unlikely that Botswana's transport problems will be solved in the foreseeable future, despite the commissioning in 1983 of yet another feasibility study.

TRANSFER COSTS

Little information on the total costs of transferring minerals from centres of production to markets can be obtained by simply considering the distances involved. In fact for some minerals distance *per se* may have only a minimal impact on the costs incurred; Mikesell (1979, p. 26) has shown that in the copper case 'transportation costs as reflected by distance have not had a significant effect on the pattern of refined copper trade'. Minerals transfer costs comprise two distinct components. Handling charges (loading and unloading, port fees, insurance and similar charges) can be a considerable cost element, particularly if the mineral has to be transferred between transport modes at a number of points along the route; such charges remain broadly constant irrespective of the distance travelled. The second component, the freight rate per kilometre tonne, is however distance dependent, but only partially so.

If transport operators always set their rates to reflect the costs involved in providing the service, rates would vary between transport modes, sea transport being normally considerably cheaper than overland movement. In addition, whatever the mode, rates would decline both with the distance involved and the amount of traffic handled since the fixed costs of the network and equipment can be spread over more units of transport.

The cost picture is further complicated by the fact that freight rates may not actually be set to cover the costs of particular movements. Operators cross-subsidize between routes to maintain traffic on high-cost lines, and give special rates to large users and to those willing to transport their commodities at off-peak periods or in directions counter to the dominant trade flows. A classic example of this are the back-haul rates used to attract cargo into ships which would otherwise have to travel back from the market ports in ballast. Alternatively, they may simply charge what they consider the traffic will bear, reducing charges where the materials are of low value or when a competitive alternative form of transport exists. Furthermore, many of the vertically integrated mineral operators run their own transport system, or at least part of it, in which case the freight charges become a matter of internal accounting.

It is, then, very difficult to generalize about the overall contribution of transfer costs to the determination of patterns of mineral production. What is clear, however, is that the progressive lowering of costs, with the development of larger-scale and more efficient transport and handling systems, has considerably widened the spread of locations from which any particular market can be served. Low-value non-metallic and non-fuel minerals still have highly restricted supply areas, but once a mining area has access to a bulk transport network, transport costs raise few barriers to world trade in the major metals and fuels.

Decisions in an imperfectly competitive world

Although variations in market demands, production and transport costs help influence production decisions they by no means tell the whole story. In the minerals sector perfectly competitive conditions rarely exist. Most – although by no means all – mineral industries exhibit high levels of *supply concentration*, which means that a large proportion of the demand in a particular market is supplied by a small percentage of firms. Moreover, it is not unusual for just one or two consumers to constitute an entire market. A further source of imperfection arises through the widespread existence of vertically integrated companies, in which case there is no market in the accepted sense: both producer and consumer are part of the same enterprise. In these circumstances firms are not blind automatons reacting to exogenously determined market prices. They have varying degrees of power over the market and an element of choice about their output scale, the location of production and product prices. How they exercise such choice will depend upon their business objectives and their willingness or ability to accept risk.

THE DEGREE OF SUPPLY CONCENTRATION

Supply concentration, perhaps predictably, tends to be higher at the individual-country level than at a world scale. For example, the four largest private copper producers have a majority ownership interest in less than 19 per cent of the non-socialist world's mine output, and the leading ten companies together only have a 35 per cent output share. In marked contrast, production in the United States is still highly concentrated, with just three companies – Anaconda, Kennecott (now largely owned by British Petroleum) and Phelps Dodge – alone accounting for 55 per cent of output, and the leading eight companies producing 88 per cent of the total (Mikesell, 1979). However, even at the world market level the production and trade of many internationally important minerals are dominated by a handful of vertically integrated firms.

In the past the leading firms were almost entirely privately owned, and although they still control a high proportion of non-socialist smelting and refining capacity, it is increasingly common for government organizations to be among the dominant producers in the mining sector. To take the copper case once again, in 1980 the four largest ore producers, with 42 per cent of world output, were the state-owned companies of the Soviet Union, Zambia, Chile and Zaire. The rise of such government bodies may increase the degree of concentration, but does not necessarily do so if supply sources are scattered. However, it does mean that both business objectives and the mechanisms through which potential market power is exercised are significantly altered, and together these can have marked effects on spatial patterns of production and trade. An obvious example here is the international oil industry. Until the 1960s it was controlled by a tight oligopoly of seven[16] firms which owned 55 per cent of non-socialist crude oil sources and 60 per cent of refinery capacity. The industry is even more concentrated since the rise of OPEC, but the power over crude oil production is now split between two powerful interest groups with quite different objectives. The struggle between them over the distribution of the monopoly rent from oil production has not only altered the geography of energy production and use but has, of course, affected the entire world economic system.

Today the mineral commodities most tightly controlled by private firms are bauxite and aluminium; six companies, Alcoa, Reynolds, Kaiser, Alcan, Péchiney and Alusuisse, own wholly or in part over 70 per cent of non-socialist mining and smelting capacity. However, even such a basic mineral product as steel, which has traditionally been the keystone of industrialization and is now produced in most countries of the world, is still dominated by a small number of firms. In 1981 according to data published by Metal Bulletin, just twenty firms, most of them privately owned, produced over 52 per cent of non-socialist world output, and eight alone were responsible for 29 per cent. The level of concentration would have been even greater if the Soviet Union's state industry had been included since it alone produces over 21 per cent of total world output.

In general, the degree of supply concentration at a world scale appears to have declined over the last thirty years, in part reflecting the widening of markets and the rise in nationalized producer country companies. However, it also results from the strategies used by the major metal and oil companies to reduce risk (see pp. 75–6). As was noted earlier, it is now common for production consortia to involve several companies and, in addition, the majors have diversified over a range of minerals. These strategies have produced a highly complex pattern of ownership and reduced apparent power concentration, while still allowing a small group of multinational conglomerates to retain a considerable influence over international mineral markets. As in other parts of the economic system the trend for a small percentage of firms to control an even greater percentage of total productive output is present in the mineral sector, but disguised by diversification, multiple-owned subsidiaries and shareholdings in nominally independent companies.

The sheer size of the mineral majors can be readily appreciated by comparing the value of their sales with the gross national products (GNPs) of entire advanced countries. Dickens and Lloyd (1981) have shown that in 1973 Nippon Steel, the first-ranked world steel producer, had sales in excess of the gross national products of Ireland or Israel, while the much bigger oil majors, such as Exxon and Royal Dutch Shell, had sales greatly above the GNPs of Greece, Hungary, New Zealand and Portugal. Almost inevitably such firms can command financial resources far in excess of most of the LDCs in which they operate, which gives them considerable bargaining strength.

THE REASONS FOR CONCENTRATION

There are many factors which have acted to produce such large concerns, and to maintain their position once established. The first of these is the existence of scale economies, particularly relevant in the highly capital-intensive mineral sector. As J. S. Bain (1954) has shown, a firm may have to serve a significant proportion of the market before it achieves its *minimum operating scale* – the scale at which unit production costs are minimized. A US steel producer, for instance, would need to serve about 5 per cent of the domestic market. Another form of scale economy, *economies of integration*, has pushed companies into vertical integration which inevitably increases their size still further. By bringing together ore concentration, smelting and refining operations at one plant, considerable energy savings can be made since the need to reheat the metal is avoided. Even when the operating stages remain spatially split, the advantages of owning raw material resources, primary processing plants and final manufacturing concerns can be considerable. Not only can output at the various stages be carefully orchestrated, but also risks can be reduced and prices internally manipulated to serve the interests of the company as a whole. For instance, a multinational with its production stages split between countries has an opportunity to minimize its total tax liability by adjusting internal prices, and therefore the profits made at each stage, so that a high proportion of total company profits is apparently made in countries with the most favourable tax regimes (Cobbe, 1979).

Another factor which allows large companies to maintain their market position is the sheer size of the venture capital now required to search for and produce minerals. There is, in other words, a major cost barrier to the entry of new firms into the industry. By and large, the firms best able to surmount this cost barrier are either already large corporations wishing to diversify their interests or companies established by governments.

Established firms also tend to have their position reinforced by control over technical knowledge and expertise. In a field where technological change is rapid, large 'insider' companies have a clear economic advantage and can afford to support research and development programmes to maintain their technological superiority. A company monopoly over a technology can also be sustained by patent laws. In the late 1880s the Pittsburgh Reduction Co. (the predecessor of Alcoa) acquired the US patent over Hall's electrolytic process for refining aluminium, while in Europe patents over Heroult's discovery of the same process were acquired by the progenitors of Alusuisse and Péchiney. It was not until the Second World War that the possibility of using the patented technology was opened to new companies by which time these three companies had a firmly entrenched position.

Finally, once a company, or a small group of companies, achieves a dominant market position, it can then act to exclude competitors. The classic historic example of this is the aggressive way the Rockefeller Standard Oil monopoly squeezed out small refining companies by manipulating the freight charges they had to pay on its transportation network, and by lowering product prices in their traditional market areas. It would be naïve to believe that anti-trust restrictive practice legislation had abolished entirely the use of such exclusion tactics today (Evely and Little, 1960).

THE EFFECTS OF CONCENTRATION

Industrial concentration – however produced and maintained – has marked effects both on product prices and output levels. It is a characteristic of large imperfectly competitive firms that they produce such a high proportion of total output that the volume they offer for sale will affect the market price. This contrasts with the position of a perfectly competitive firm whose individual output is far too small to have any impact on total market supplies or prices. Unless the demand curve shifts, a large imperfect competitor can only increase the quantity produced, in any one time period, by decreasing the price at which the output is sold. Therefore, an extra unit of production involves sacrificing some of the revenue which potentially could have been earned by the already produced units. The extra, or marginal, revenue curve must then lie below the demand curve and must fall more sharply than that curve.[17]

COPING WITH THE DECLINING MARGINAL REVENUE CURVE

In this situation a firm can adopt three strategies to increase profit levels. First, it can attempt to force up the market price by restricting output. This is particularly effective if the demand curve for the product is inelastic,[18] in which case consumers do not, or cannot, cut their consumption markedly in response to price rises. In 1973, for example, the short-run elasticity of demand for oil was extremely low; electricity-generating capacity could not be switched overnight to other fuels, diesel trains still had to run and the private motorist was unwilling to forgo using his car. Therefore, OPEC was able to achieve a fourfold increase in price by relatively small output cuts. However, as was seen earlier (see pp. 87–9), in the medium term, demands have proved much more flexible and OPEC has now been forced to cut output to approximately 40 per cent below capacity in an attempt to maintain price levels against the substitution trend away from its oil. This serves to show that producers can rarely hope to maintain artificially high price levels if substitutes for their product are made available. It also helps to explain the second profit maintenance strategy – the attempt to reduce the importance of substitution by gaining control over the production of the substitutes or by tying consumers to one technology. The already discussed moves by the oil majors to invest in coal and other energy sources are not unrelated to this strategy and a number of examples are given later in Chapter 4 (see pp. 124–5) of measures which restrict consumer product choice.

The third possible profit-increasing strategy is to split the total market into segments, so that output for one segment cannot affect the price received for the product in the others. To clarify this point take the case of a firm which needs to produce a set quantity of output in order to achieve maximum economies of scale. This cannot all be sold in the market which it dominates without pushing down the price so much that unit production costs are no longer covered. To avoid spoiling the market the firm simply unloads some of the output in another, institutionally distinct, market area. There are numerous well-known examples of this strategy in operation; the EEC's famous 'butter mountain' is unloaded in the Soviet Union, while some European steel producers have dumped their excess production on the US market. The oil industry provides another classic example. During periods of crude oil surplus the oil producers have maintained prices in markets which they dominate but have given large 'discounts' to consumers elsewhere; this strategy was widely employed in the 1960s by the 'seven sisters' and at the present time OPEC countries are heavily discounting prices on non-tied sales. All these profit maintenance strategies must affect the spatial patterns of mineral production and consumption.

PRICING POLICIES

Large imperfectly competitive firms have an element of choice over which markets they will attempt to serve and over what prices individual consumers will be asked to pay. A crucial factor here is the method used to price the mineral commodities; a variety of pricing systems may be adopted which in effect discriminate between consumers. One of the most common is 'contract' pricing, where a reduced price is given to large consumers, particularly those willing to make a long-term commitment to take set amounts of the mineral commodity. This has obvious advantages not only in reducing the risks involved in market price variations, but also in helping to ensure that production is maintained at the level required to achieve scale economies.

In addition, a pricing system known as CIF (cost, insurance and freight) can be, and in fact is, widely used (Chisholm, 1966). Under this system all consumers within a specified region pay the same price for the product irrespective of the transport costs involved in supplying them. It has the effect of discriminating between consumers located at different distances (measured in transport cost terms) from the production centres; consumers located near the producer pay part of the transport costs incurred by those in more remote locations. There are several reasons why firms should adopt CIF. In the first place, it has the advantage of administrative simplicity, obviating the need to calculate the transfer costs on each transaction; moreover, the greater simplicity will reduce the administrative costs involved. Second, if the producer wishes to sell a given volume of output or maintain a specific market share, it may be necessary to keep prices down in a distant market. Finally, when a firm operates a number of plants in different locations it is unlikely that they will all have the same unit costs of production; a CIF system can be designed to allow low-cost centres to subsidize the higher-cost plants.

The common existence of this pricing strategy has important locational implications. This notion, so frequently encountered in basic industrial location theory, that producers of manufactured goods can be pulled to locate near their raw material source in order to reduce transport costs, becomes untenable if, in reality, the raw material is priced CIF. As Warren (1966) has pointed out, attempts to generate employment in depressed regions by using a basic industry, such as iron and steel, as a magnet to attract associated manufacturing are doomed to failure if the steel producer then decides to sell at the same price to all consumers in the country, irrespective of the transport costs involved. Since British Steel has chosen to price its sheet steel CIF, the hope that plants like Llanwern and Ravenscraig would attract the intended new manufacturing employment was always a vain one.

COLLUSION

The existence of just a few dominant firms in an industry raises the possibility of collusion to restrict output, fix prices and allocate specific markets or market shares to each company. Examples of open collusion by private companies have to be taken from the past because of widespread monopoly control legislation. The two much-quoted classic cases are the International Oil cartel and the US Iron and Steel cartel. As Stocking (1954) has clearly shown, by the use of the Pittsburgh plus basing-point pricing system (whereby all steel was priced as though it had been manufactured in and transported from Pittsburgh) the iron and steel cartel was able to maintain production levels in the Pittsburgh area and severely curb output growth in the Birmingham (Alabama) region.

The International Oil cartel operated a similar basing-point pricing system. In the interwar period all oil was priced as though it had been produced in the Gulf Coast area of the United States, and as though it had been transported from there. Inevitably this slowed down the growth of the Middle East as a centre of production, and lowered consumption in Europe. This single base-point system broke down during the Second World War, mainly because the British and later the American governments were less than happy to find that the price they paid to refuel ships in the Middle Eastern ports was the US price plus a massive transport cost element. The companies solved this problem by adopting a system under which US cost price levels were retained but the Middle East became a base for the transport cost calculations. Only after 1945, under pressure from the Marshall Plan administration, were the much lower Middle Eastern production costs introduced into a multiple base-point system.

Today collusion, in the private sector at least, is much more covert. Firms may follow the market leader, possibly by agreement or more likely to avoid the risks of cut-throat price competition. But it is difficult to believe that more active collusion does not occur when, for example, the price of refined aluminium is analysed. The 'producer prices'[19] used by the six dominant companies for their tied outlet and contract sales have not only been remarkably stable, but are common to all companies.

PRODUCTION FLEXIBILITY

The existence of large international companies is also important in the determination of mineral production patterns because they are able to choose which of their possible sites to develop at particular times and at what speed. We have already seen that companies are exploring in areas where production costs are relatively high but, in their view, risks are low; inevitably the same risk assessments will also affect output levels. Diversification of potential output centres gives the firms considerable flexibility to respond to changing economic conditions or to restrict output from countries where the governments are attempting to regulate their activities or to increase the state share of mining profits.

To give one example: as Table 3.9 shows, British Petroleum switched its crude oil supply sources markedly in just six years. Moving out of Nigeria after the nationalization of its assets and decreasing the role of other OPEC states, it increased output from the North Sea and the United States as well as from other small non-OPEC producers. Such flexibility is one factor limiting the extent to which producer states can ensure that the private companies will develop and use the resource in line with national objectives (see Chapter 4, pp. 170–3 and Chapter 5, pp. 186–201, 217–21).

Table 3.9   British Petroleum: crude oil sources, 1974 and 1980

Country	1974		1980	
	(mbd)	(%)	(mbd)	(%)
Iran	2.02	44.9	0.04	1.7
Kuwait	1.04	23.1	0.25	10.5
Nigeria	0.69	15.3	—	—
Abu Dhabi	0.35	7.8	0.15	6.3
Iraq	0.24	5.3	0.04	1.7
North Sea	—	—	0.51	21.3
United States	—	—	0.71	29.7
Other	0.16	3.6	0.69	28.9
TOTAL	4.5		2.39	

Source: Auty, 1983, p. 6.

CONSTRAINTS ON MARKET POWER

The mere fact that mineral production is concentrated in the hands of just a few large firms does not, of course, automatically give them a high degree of control over their markets. In the first place, mineral producers can only work within the limits set by the affluence or tastes of the final consumers of the end-products. Furthermore, crude mineral producers may be constrained by concentrated consumer power. For example, the ability of the state-owned copper-mining companies to fix prices is limited by the fact that they have to sell much of their metal to a few refining and manufacturing companies which still dominate the key market areas. In the same way, iron ore producers attempting to export to the United Kingdom are faced by the British Steel monopoly. Moreover, the smaller so-called fringe producers may be influential enough to limit the freedom of choice of the dominant companies, particularly in periods when overall market demand is weak. A further limit arises because virtually all minerals have substitutes, at least for some of their end-uses. Primary copper producers, for instance, are constrained not only by aluminium and plastic prices, but also by the price and availability of scrap, which can account for a high proportion of final copper consumption. In the United States some 46 per cent of estimated total consumption was met from scrap in 1974 (Mikesell, 1979). Finally, the activities of all mineral producers are restricted, and increasingly so, by the actions of governments, local and national, and by intergovernmental agencies.

INTRODUCING THE ROLE OF GOVERNMENT

As will be shown in Chapter 5, the concept of free mineral markets must be abandoned in any attempt to seek realistic explanations for the spatial patterns of output, consumption and trade. This is self-evidently the case for the planned economies and is also true for the western capitalist countries. Governments not only intervene by directly taking over production, but also by imposing myriad regulations, which restrict trade, set wage rates and employment conditions, curtail take-overs and mergers, fix prices, or impose planning and pollution controls. The imposition of various forms of tax and the payment of production subsidies can likewise have a marked impact on mineral output. Moreover, governments inevitably have an indirect influence on the mineral industries through their general management of the economy and through their political complexion and stability.

Purposeful intervention by governments in the minerals sector must imply that it is failing to perform in line with public policy objectives. It is this failure which provides the focus for the discussion in Chapter 4.

NOTES

1 This figure is taken from official statistics *US Energy: A Summary Review*, Washington, DC, Department of the Interior, 1972. Other writers, for example, H. D. Hedburg, Vice-President for Exploration of the Gulf Oil Corporation, have put the figure as high as 40,000.

2 There are exceptions to this. For example, the presence of copper in rock outcrops produces a distinctive coloration on certain types of computer-enhanced Landsat imagery. However, field analysis is still necessary to establish the size and ore content of the deposit.

3 This assumption has been widely criticized for over forty years; see, for example, Simon, 1947.

4 This includes the Special Fund expenditure on resource exploration.

5 The rationale for this procedure is a simple one which reflects the different time value of money. To take a very simple example, if an individual put a capital sum in a building society today, at the end of ten years he would expect to receive back not this same sum, but his initial principal plus all the interest compounded over the period. By the same token, for it to be worth his while putting his capital into the construction of a mine or factory, the future revenue from production must be at least equal to the principal *plus* the forgone building society interest. Unless we assume that the interest rate is zero, the only way to compare future revenue with costs incurred now is to discount it back to present values using the relevant rate of interest over the expected life of the project.

6 These methods involve the use of chemicals to separate the metal from the ore, or high-pressure jets to force ore slurries to the surface (US National Academy of Sciences, 1978).

7 Throughout this discussion the advanced nations are taken to be the United States, Canada, South Africa, Australia, New Zealand and Western Europe, plus the planned economies of Eastern Europe and the Soviet Union.

8 It must be remembered that these changes in relative position have taken place within the context of a massive increase in total mineral use.

9 It is estimated that in the absence of the OPEC cartel, free market oil prices would be somewhere between $3–$11 a barrel.

10 This is not ideal partly because of fluctuating prices and exchange rates, and partly because it involves the assumption that the price paid is a true measure of the

product's importance in the production process and is unaffected by government intervention or monopoly price fixing.

11   European Coal and Steel Community.

12   This means they were determined by factors outside the model, and do not affect each other.

13   Price for copper delivered to the customer, including therefore the transport costs.

14   The problems of the US domestic copper producers have been compounded by the strength of the dollar. World copper demand has revived since 1983, and London Metal exchange prices have risen, but such rises have been nullified by falling sterling values.

15   This may not be the case for long-established operations, where the capital sum and the interest have already been repaid out of past revenue.

16   The so-called 'seven sisters' are Exxon, Texaco, Standard Oil of California, Mobil, Gulf, British Petroleum and Royal Dutch Shell.

17   If a producer can sell y units at $100 each, but $y + 1$ at only $98 each, then clearly the sale of $y + 1$ gives him an extra revenue of $98 *minus* $y \times$ $2.

18   The elasticity of demand is a measure of the responsiveness of demand to price changes, and is defined as

$$\frac{\% \text{ change in quantity demanded}}{\% \text{ change in price}}$$

A demand curve is said to be inelastic if a percentage change in price produces a lower percentage change in the quantity demanded.

19   Producer prices are not the same as those on the London Metal Exchange which deals in only a tiny percentage of total production.

4 The performance of the mineral production process

INTRODUCTION: EVALUATION CRITERIA

Just as minerals have no intrinsic worth outside the human system which creates their resource value, so the mineral production and consumption process can only be judged in terms of its implications for human welfare. In other words, the mineral sector must be evaluated by its performance, by the extent to which it fulfils the wider economic, social, environmental and political objectives of society. No such evaluations can be free of value judgements; the chosen performance criteria and the relative weight given to each will not only depend upon the ideology of the analyst, but vary over time and space reflecting the different (and changing) value systems of the societies in which the mineral industry operates.

Although by no means an exhaustive list, there are five major and commonly employed objectives, or criteria, against which the results of the mineral production system can be evaluated: economic efficiency; distributive equity; economic growth and employment generation; supply security; and the maintenance of environmental quality. The first four of these will be the subject of concern in this chapter, while environmental quality objectives will be considered later.

The patterns of mineral production, consumption and derived wealth which fulfil any one of these objectives may, and probably will, be incompatible with the achievement of the others. An economically efficient mineral production system is unlikely to produce an allocation of products, welfare or growth which conforms to most accepted notions of distributive equity. The most secure pattern of supplies may result in major efficiency losses and could involve increased environmental degradation. Similarly, the development pattern which minimizes environmental damage is unlikely to be one which allows economic growth to be maximized. Almost inevitably, therefore, any attempts to make the mineral industry perform more closely in line with any particular societal objective involves trade-offs against the others.

The economic efficiency objective

THE EFFICIENCY CONCEPT

The notion of economic efficiency is basic to neo-classical economics, and provides one of the key rationales for the free market system. Governments have tended to assume that private enterprise has a predisposition towards efficiency, albeit with some recognized imperfections which can be corrected. Furthermore, it is common to require public sector industries to work to the same objective, and to do so by adopting more 'commercial' attitudes. In Britain formal government statements on the nationalized industries and other public sector enterprises are liberally peppered with exhortations on the need for efficiency, and rules of conduct have been laid down which theoretically should allow this to be achieved. The two White Papers produced in the 1960s, on *The Financial and Economic Obligations of the Nationalized Industries* (Cmnd 1337 and 3437, UK Government, 1961, 1967) show clearly the importance of the efficiency objective in government thinking at that time, and it has since become an even more dominant tenet of faith.

Economic efficiency as a concept contains three distinct, although related, elements: *technological, product-choice* and *allocative efficiency*. If a given level of output is produced using least-cost methods of production, then the industry is said to be technologically efficient. It is assumed that competitive private firms will automatically seek to achieve this since inefficient producers would fail to be profitable and would not survive. In the same way, it is regarded as axiomatic that the goods and services produced must reflect consumer preferences if the firm is to remain in business. The notion is that the consumer is sovereign; preferences for goods are established exogenously and producers merely respond to consumer requirements. However, in the real world it is clear that producers can and do manipulate consumer demands by advertising, and by what products they choose to place on the market.

Consumer choice is constrained by what is made available (*availability constraints*) and by what consumer durables or capital equipment have already been purchased (*contingent preference constraints*). The packaging around products is taken whether it is required or not; goods with short lives, with obsolescence built into them, have to be purchased if more robust products are not marketed; and householders cannot easily switch to alternative energy sources if expensive space heating systems are already installed.

Allocative efficiency is concerned with the entire distribution of factors of production and goods or services within an economy. Various definitions of this form of efficiency have been devised, but the most widely used and known is the 'Pareto' criterion. Resource allocations are said to be efficient if it is impossible to reallocate them so as potentially to make some consumers better off (in their own estimation) without simultaneously making others worse off. To put it the other way round, a situation is inefficient if it is possible to move a unit of labour or capital, or a unit of a good or service, between different users or uses and in doing so make someone better off without making someone else worse off. This sounds a worthy objective, but in reality it applies to too few situations to be generally useful. Outside the basic textbook examples of two men swapping their cars, or exchanging apples for eggs, most decisions of any significance in the real world do in fact cause some people to gain at the expense of others. As Butlin (1981, p. 4) has said, 'no policy change worthy of the name would have a universally neutral or beneficial effect'. For this reason variants of the Paretian criterion have been devised which involve the use of the so-called *compensation rule* (Kaldor, 1939; Hicks, 1939).

The compensation problem

Under the Kaldor–Hicks formulations it was recognized that most resource reallocations would make someone worse off, but it was argued that this was not a barrier to efficiency. If the gains made by some people are great enough to allow them to compensate the losers, then the new distribution of factors of production, goods and services is regarded as more allocatively efficient. The basis for the compensation rule can be shown very simply in diagrammatic form. Figure 4.1 shows the demand (marginal utility) curves of two consumers for a single product. Let us assume that we start from a situation in which consumer B has OX units of the product and consumer A has nothing. The value B places on an extra unit of the product has shrunk to zero, but to A it is worth much more (OZ). If just one unit was taken from B and given to A, B's loss would be minimal (see black area) and A could easily afford to make up this loss out of his gains (shaded area) and still be markedly better off. This process of reallocation and possible compensation could go on until XY units have been transferred from B to A, and the value of the product is now equal for both consumers (EE); no further compensation payments are feasible and an optimal allocation of the product has been achieved. Under this modification of the Pareto definition allocative efficiency basically means the maximization of net benefits in the economy.

Although under the Hicks compensation scheme a Pareto optimal situation was one in which nobody was worse off and at least some people were better off *after* the gainers had compensated the losers, in the Kaldor version it did not matter whether compensation *was* actually paid, merely that it *could* be paid. In

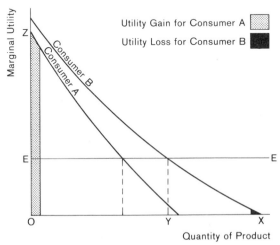

Figure 4.1   Marginal utility curves and the compensation rule

practice, it is the Kaldor rule which is most commonly applied, as cases where compensation is paid are comparatively rare. This clearly has implications for distributive equity. It is crucial to realize that in all the definitions of allocative efficiency the resulting distribution of income, goods and services in the economy is irrelevant. A situation can be efficient if 1 per cent of the population owns 90 per cent of the wealth, and a project or policy could be efficient if all the gains go to this 1 per cent. There is, therefore, nothing necessarily equitable about economic efficiency.

Efficiency and perfect market conditions

Under certain conditions it is possible to show that the market system would automatically operate to allow all those forms of efficiency to be achieved. The most important of these conditions are:

(1) Consumers are economically rational beings, with the ability to maximize their utility functions not only at the present time, but also in the future.
(2) Producers are also 'economic men', rationally aiming – and with the omniscient ability – to maximize their profits over time.
(3) All parts of the economy are perfectly competitive, including the capital and labour markets.
(4) All factors of production are perfectly mobile.
(5) All goods and services are within the market system; there are, in other words, no unpriced public goods or environmental resources.
(6) The economy is free from government intervention.

It will be readily appreciated that these conditions simply do not apply in the real world.

Economists attempting to model part of the economic system may justify assuming that some, or even all, of these conditions do in fact hold. As with all model-building exercises, it is necessary to simplify reality in order to gain some understanding of how one or two variables operate. Dasgupta and Heal (1979, p. 9), for example, begin their well-known book on *Economic Theory and Exhaustible Resources* by stating their 'belief . . . that for the purposes of developing a deep and intuitive understanding of the complexities of an economic system, it is best to abstract dramatically and consider only a skeletal representation of the key factors and their interactions'.

However, it can be argued that the existence of such abstract models has allowed the perpetuation of two common myths. First, that the market system, as it actually exists, can produce even an approximation to technological efficiency and an efficient allocation of resources in the economy. And second, that observable sources of inefficiency can be corrected. The notion that there are specific market failures, which legislation, administrative change or price regulation can correct, so restoring 'efficiency', is a common one. It provides the rationale for much government intervention in the minerals sector and, as will be shown later, also serves as the basis for economic remedies to common property resource and pollution problems. However, the whole idea of correction becomes untenable when the entire system is made up of inefficient conditions; when inefficiency is not the exception but the rule. Imperfectly competitive firms, imperfect labour and capital markets, non-rational behaviour, the immobility of factors of production, government activity, unpriced public goods, common property and environmental resources are everywhere: how, then, is it even possible to conceive of a meaningful programme of correction?

In addition to these two myths, the abstract models lead to a further danger, that they will be (as indeed they have been) used to devise rules of conduct for public sector enterprises to ensure that they are economically efficient. The advocacy of a marginal cost pricing system for public utilities and the use of cost–benefit analysis to evaluate public sector investments are both based on Paretian notions of allocative efficiency and on the highly abstract model of the economy needed to allow efficiency to be achieved by market mechanisms. It is now well established that such pricing and investment rules will fail to produce an optimal allocation of national resources if inefficient conditions prevail in other sectors of the economy. Therefore, it has been necessary to devise 'second-' or even 'third-best' strategies,[1] under which public enterprises must adjust their behaviour to take account of all the inaccurate resource cost and demand information coming from the inefficient 'deviant' sectors of the economy. To undertake all the required adjustments a massive data collection exercise would be needed to establish the 'inaccuracies' in the prices of all factor inputs, complementary products and substitutes. Not surprisingly, second-best notions have been received with a singular lack of sympathy by those responsible for management as a practical rather than a paper exercise.

TECHNOLOGICAL EFFICIENCY IN PRACTICE

It is clear that the minerals sector does not conform to any of the conditions needed to ensure that market forces will create economic efficiency. As Randell (1975, p. 805) has said, 'It would be an arduous task to compile an unabridged compendium of the ways in which the essential conditions are violated in the real world'. Just the fact that much of the mineral production and consumption process is characterized by imperfect competition suggests that technological and product choice efficiency is highly unlikely to occur. Moreover, since techno-logical efficiency is a prerequisite of allocative efficiency, the latter cannot possibly be achieved either. Inevitably if a mineral producer could use less labour and capital to produce a given output, the resulting resource allocation could not be optimal since theoretically the excess factors of production could be used elsewhere in the economy without penalizing mineral users.

Whereas in a perfectly competitive situation it may be assumed that individual manufacturers would have to operate at minimum cost levels in order to stay in business, no such assumption can be made about private firms with enough market power to, at least partially, determine their own price and output levels. The existence of monopoly, cartels, vertically integrated concerns, long-term supply contracts, price fixing or tacit price leadership agreements removes the efficiency imperative. In theory, in the longer term the entry of new firms into the industry, plus the competition from substitutes, would eventually force the industry to produce using least-cost methods. However, in practice there are three factors which suggest that non-minimum-cost operations can be maintained over very considerable periods of time. First, there are natural, technical and artificial barriers to the entry of new competitive firms. Second, multinational conglomerates may now control the output of a whole range of substitute materials. And third, firms maintain output at relatively high-cost centres to reduce risk, and the need to do this is unlikely to diminish over time. Similarly, state-run mineral industries cannot be assumed to be technologically efficient. Not only do they face limited competition, but they are usually operated for a variety of non-profit-maximizing objectives.

In Chapter 3 several cases were discussed where technological efficiency could not possibly occur and in fact where it would have been against company interests to even aim to achieve it. For instance, it is difficult to find a period in the history of the world oil industry when total output has been produced at least cost (Penrose, 1968; Sampson, 1975).[2] The whole basis of the 'Gulf plus' pricing system was to maintain the output and profitability of company operations in areas which were relatively high-cost, so retarding the development of least-cost production sites (see p. 113). In the late 1960s it was estimated that the long-run marginal costs of production in the Middle East were only $0.05–$0.25 per barrel compared with the approximate $3 figure for US production (Cobbe, 1979). The companies had enough control over the markets to maintain output from their traditional sources, retain a diversity of supply sources and earn huge abnormal profits on their Middle Eastern operations. The rise to power of OPEC has done nothing to increase technological efficiency; not only do its pricing and output-control policies allow the higher-cost producers in the cartel to serve their set negotiated market share, but also the oil majors and consumer governments are developing output in areas, such as the North Sea and Arctic Canada, which are acknowledged not to be least-cost, but which have security and control advantages. Although the oil industry represents an extreme example, it is merely an exaggerated case of the situation which applies for most of the major traded minerals.

Throughout the minerals sector multisite and multiplant enterprises are common. By adjusting their pricing and costing arrangements to cross-subsidize between plants, total production costs may be increased, but risks are considerably reduced by maintaining a diversity of production centres and, moreover, sales or market share targets may be achieved. The importance of risk avoidance as a business aim makes it highly unlikely that any multinational company would aim to be a least-cost producer, *sensu stricto*, at any point in time. Each of the major aluminium firms, for example, maintains bauxite production in a variety of countries under markedly different cost conditions. The possibility of supply interruptions is, therefore, minimized as all are unlikely to fail together (Girvan, 1970, 1973).

In the case of vertically integrated concerns the products from, and the services of, their own companies will be employed at the secondary production stages whether or not these are the least-cost inputs. North American steel corporations will not necessarily use the lowest-priced coal given their backward integration into the mining industry. The common existence of long-term supply contracts for raw or semi-processed minerals also means that, even without ownership links, many companies are not free to seek out least-cost inputs over periods as long as twenty or even thirty years. Taken together the existence of integration and contracts can tie up a considerable proportion of the total supply of many minerals. On a world scale, 40 per cent of traded iron ore is captive through ownership ties and a further 40 per cent is tied under twenty-year contracts (Bosson and Varon, 1977); inevitably this implies that the bulk of steel producers need not be utilizing least-cost inputs. It is worth pointing out that by the norms for the mineral sector as a whole, world iron ore production is highly competitive, but continuity of supply is too important to iron and steel producers to allow them to take much advantage of this competitive situation. It is clear that, within limits, the benefits of supply security, control and administrative ease outweigh any cost advantages from being free to use whichever supply source is cheapest at different points in time.

The public sector mineral industries likewise provide a whole host of examples where technological efficiency is explicitly or implicitly sacrificed to other objectives, such as achieving favourable trade balances, securing indigenous supply sources, and reducing the social, economic and political costs of unemployment. In Britain the maintenance of production at high-cost coalmines, cross-subsidization between pits and the subsidization of the electricity industry to retain coal-burning power stations must mean that neither the coal nor electricity industries are producing at least cost. Therefore they are not achieving either technological or allocative efficiency.

All the cases discussed so far involve situations where imperfect competition gives producers sufficient market power to allow them to choose their supply sources, pricing and output strategies. Their decisions to adopt practices which are technologically inefficient may, of course, be perfectly rational given their production objectives, and may even result in long-term profit maximization if their judgements about risk prove to be correct. However, even perfectly competitive mineral producers need not, and probably will not, adopt least-cost production strategies. If satisfactory profits or a quiet life are the real-world business aims, if there are major information barriers and if firms are tied to particular factor inputs or raw materials by previously purchased capital equipment or by labour agreements, then technological efficiency cannot be assumed. Moreover, both perfectly and imperfectly competitive firms are faced by major imperfections in capital, land and labour markets, which introduce further technological inefficiencies into the system. Of particular importance are inefficiencies in the allocation of financial capital, which make capital imperfectly mobile, particularly between countries, and the rigidities which past capital investments introduce into the system. Firms cannot easily adopt current least-cost methods when this involves discarding existing plant or machinery, and entrenched labour practices may also inhibit adaptation.

PRODUCT CHOICE EFFICIENCY IN PRACTICE

The idea that product choice efficiency will automatically occur must also be abandoned in the minerals sector, as it must for most parts of the economy. As the demand for many minerals is derived from the demand for final consumer goods, it could be argued that primary producers are remote from consumers and are not, therefore, in a position to influence consumer choice. While this argument holds for, say, the small-scale tin producers in Malaysia, or the smaller independent copper producers, it is by no means always the case. Many minerals are characteristically produced by vertically integrated firms and one of the attractions of forward integration into the final stages of manufacture, or even into the service sector, is to gain greater control over markets.

The energy sector is the most clearly imperfect in product terms. The large advertising budgets of the oil companies – Esso alone spends some $8 million per annum – allow considerable scope for the manipulation of consumer preferences. The capital investments required to convert most fuels to usable energy impose clear contingent preference constraints, and there are numerous availability constraints. Users have to 'demand' nuclear energy as they have no mechanism for refusing the electricity generated in nuclear stations and mixed with power from other sources. British motorists are forced to consume lead, as lead-free petrol brands are still not marketed and the limited number of filling stations offering gas (liquefied petroleum gas) as an alternative to petrol imposes further product choice constraints.

Barnet (1980) has argued that producers deliberately constrain consumer choice by gaining control over, and then destroying, enterprises providing substitute goods and services. He cites cases where oil companies have combined with motor vehicle and tyre manufactures to buy out concerns providing urban mass transport services, so ensuring that the motor vehicle reigns supreme. A consortia made up of General Motors, Esso and Goodyear bought the San Francisco trolley bus company and promptly converted it to petrol-driven buses, and 'General Motors, Firestone and Standard Oil of California ripped up the Los Angeles inter-urban train system. In all, 100 electric railway systems in forty-five cities were destroyed as a result of similar conspiracies' (ibid., p. 23). By no means everyone would subscribe to Barnet's notions on conspiracy, but there is little doubt that private economic decisions to market only specific goods and services act as a major availability constraint on consumer product choice.

Whenever firms produce a range of substitute products, their decisions on what to market, where and at what price are based on internal economic considerations and may neglect the broader social costs and benefits involved. A classic example of this has arisen in the development of 'wet' or associated natural gas, which is found in conjunction with oil and often produced by companies whose primary interest is the oil. Some companies have been loath to incur the expenditure necessary to transport the gas to market centres where it would compete with oil; considerable quantities have, therefore, been flared or vented to the atmosphere. Despite opposition from several governments, such wastage still occurs even in areas where established gas markets exist in relatively close proximity to the centres of production. In the

British North Sea, for instance, companies have argued that it is neither economic for them to make it available to consumers at current price levels, nor viable to invest in reinjection equipment, which could allow its use in the future. The economic viability calculations are, of course, done solely in terms of private costs and returns, and these are influenced by the fact that gas is a major competitive fuel, which is sold in the final market at prices largely beyond the control of the oil companies. It remains to be seen whether the recently announced plans to privatize British Gas will allow the oil companies to exert a greater influence over gas prices.

ALLOCATIVE EFFICIENCY IN PRACTICE

Allocative efficiency is, as has already been established, dependent on the prior existence of technological and product efficiency. However, even if it is assumed that this necessary condition is in fact met, there are many factors suggesting that allocative efficiency would still not occur in the minerals sector. There are two major allocative issues that must be considered: first, the current distribution of available mineral supplies between users; and, second, the distribution of supplies over time or between generations. This last is of obvious importance when an exhaustible mineral is being considered since the level of current consumption must affect future rates of use.

For a mineral resource to be distributed between present-day consumers in a Pareto-efficient manner two pricing conditions must be fulfilled. First, each class of consumer must pay the marginal costs incurred in supplying them, and second, within each supply cost category, the unit price must be set equal for all consumers (the rationale for this last rule was illustrated in Figure 4.1). By instituting both these pricing rules, every consumer should, theoretically at least, use the mineral until its value to them equals the cost of supply and it would be impossible to increase the total benefits derived from the supply available at a given point in time by reallocating it between consumers. Even assuming that firms could unequivocally calculate what their marginal production costs are,[3] there are many reasons why it would not necessarily be in their interest to employ these as a basis for product pricing. A number of these reasons have in fact already been discussed, albeit in a somewhat different context, in Chapter 3 (see p. 112).

Discriminatory pricing practices

Large imperfectly competitive firms risk spoiling their major markets by increasing available supplies and yet they need to maintain output levels to achieve scale economies, to spread the high fixed capital cost element over a large number of product units and also to allow any sales volume or market share objectives to be met. In these circumstances it frequently pays them to adopt discriminatory pricing practices, so violating the Paretian pricing rules. To avoid having to reduce prices on all sales in order to achieve the required output scale, customers are split, wherever possible, into discrete markets. Vertically integrated firms can implement this strategy by discriminating *against* their own tied outlets in markets which they dominate, and unloading any excess production outside the ring fence. The desire to achieve set output or market share targets or to retain a diversity of operating sites may also lead to discrimination between consumers located at different distances from the production centres. To be allocatively optimal each consumer should pay the production cost plus the cost of transporting the product to them. Such a system (normally known as free-on-board, or FOB) would, however, restrict a firm's market area.[4] Therefore, CIF and rule-of-thumb pricing, or price setting at levels the traffic will bear, become common practices (see p. 112).

A further form of price discrimination occurs when vertically integrated corporations attempt to give a competitive advantage to their own subsidiary companies by setting internal transfer prices below market rates. This occurs most commonly when the markets for finished products are more competitive than the mining and primary processing stages, as is the case for copper which faces competition from scrap and substitute metals. The motives behind this practice are mixed. In part it may serve to increase the corporations' market control and allow market share objectives to be met. In addition, it may be used in an attempt to ensure that the turnover of the subsidiary is relatively stable; this not only makes it easier to integrate and plan production at all previous processing stages, but also reduces the need to sell surplus raw and semi-finished metal on the more risky open, or auction, markets. However, not all vertically integrated concerns will adopt the same discriminatory practices. As Labys (1980, p. 67) has pointed out, 'since firms can assign whatever prices they like to transactions within their domain, any of the traditional explanations of pricing cease to be valid'. Firms will adjust the cross-subsidy flows between different stages in the production process over time to reflect changes in economic conditions, tax levels, or risk assessments.

To some extent the common practice of giving favourable terms to large, long-established or contract customers may also be seen as a form of price discrimination, but they can normally be supplied at much lower unit costs and, therefore, constitute a distinct supply cost category (Meyer, 1975). In any industry where fixed capital dominates the cost structure, the maintenance of high load (or throughput) factors becomes an important objective of pricing policy since unit production costs rise markedly if a large proportion of available capacity lies idle. This is particularly relevant for many mineral producers since they tend to be faced by marked demand fluctuations. In the energy case these are seasonal and diurnal, while for many metals demands vary in response to changes in the overall level of economic activity. Producer problems are compounded when it is difficult or extremely costly to store significant quantities of their output for use at peak periods. Therefore, in all industrial countries the gas and electricity authorities offer considerable 'discounts' to attract large industrial consumers, whose use is normally much more stable than the highly weather-sensitive demands of the domestic and commercial sectors.

PRICE VOLATILITY

The demand for, and price of, many metallic minerals are characteristically highly volatile, fluctuations being most extreme for copper (Figure 4.2), tin and

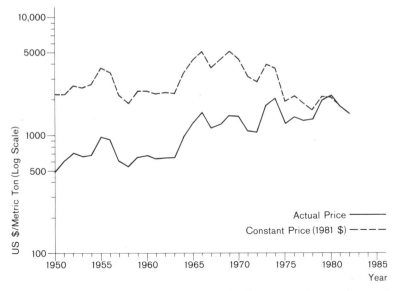

Figure 4.2   Fluctuations in copper prices in actual and constant price terms, 1950–82/3
Source: Compiled from data contained in International Bank for Reconstruction and Development, *Commodity Trade and Price Trends*, 1982–3, p. 115

gold. In the idealized world of perfect competition and perfect factor mobility a demand change would affect price levels, and this would immediately cause the quantity supplied to change in response. Therefore, shortages and gluts (and the associated price fluctuations) should be short-lived features. However, there are four major imperfections in the operation of the minerals sector which combine to inhibit a quick market response and act to compound the problems of the cyclical volatility of prices. It should not be assumed that those minerals markets with relatively stable price trends are less imperfect and conform more closely to the idealized, perfectly competitive market model; in fact rather the reverse is true. The stability of producer prices for aluminium, for example, reflects the tight and controlled oligopoly which dominates all stages of production.

First, since it normally takes at least four years to bring new supply capacity on-stream, shortages can persist, resulting in major price rises. Second, once capacity exists and fixed costs have been incurred, producers are reluctant to curb output as long as some contribution is being made to overheads. Surpluses, therefore, also persist over time, and, if anything, these are exacerbated when national governments, dependent on mineral exports for their revenue, take over production. Third, price variations are magnified by the nature of demand for some minerals. The major end-uses for a number of metals are the construction industry and the production of machinery, commercial vehicles and other intermediate goods, all of which are more profoundly affected by recession than other sectors of the economy. During periods when consumer demand for final goods is falling or static, manufacturers of these products will have sufficient capacity to meet demands and, therefore, have little incentive to expand their production facilities. Moreover, their financial ability to pay for capacity extensions will also be cut. Inevitably, then, the effects of recession will be magnified for the producers of intermediate goods; in their case the recession will not only be deeper, but also more prolonged, since consumer demand has to pick up before new orders for plant and machinery are made. However, in periods when the economy is buoyant the fact that metallic minerals normally contribute only a small proportion of the total costs of final goods means that there is little response to metal price rises in the short run. For example, it has been estimated that bauxite costs are responsible for only 35 per cent of aluminium rod and sheet prices, while the aluminium itself is a minimal contributor to the construction cost of a new factory or office block. In the short run manufacturers tend to be tied into existing production arrangements and will only incur the costs of substitution if high prices are persistent and are regarded as a long-term market feature.

The fourth important factor creating cyclical volatility is the nature of many of the open or auction markets for minerals. In most cases these are strictly marginal, that is they deal with only a fraction of total production and sales. As has already been seen, less than 20 per cent of iron ore is available for open market sale, and only 5–10 per cent of world copper trade goes through the London Metal Exchange (LME) and still less is exchanged in the other major market, the Commodity Exchange of New York (COMEX) (Labys, 1980). The open market for aluminium is even more restricted; there is no real 'spot' price at all – producers either transfer supplies internally or make long-term contracts. Although there is now a small market at the LME for aluminium futures, this was only established in 1978 after considerable opposition from the major companies and has little relevance as a price-fixing mechanism. At the time of the 1973 oil crisis, the spot market accounted for only 2.3 per cent of all crude oil transactions, which helps explain why scarcity fears had such a dramatic effect on spot prices. Since then, in part due to the crude oil surplus, the proportion of total trade going through the spot market has increased markedly, but it still accounts for less than 30 per cent of all transactions.

THE EFFECTS OF SPECULATION

Inevitably when the open markets are dealing with relatively small quantities, fairly minor demand or supply changes can have a marked impact on prices. Moreover, it is possible for producers and consumer governments to manipulate the prices and for speculators to operate in the market. Most analysts have shown that speculation tends to accentuate, very severely at times, the already endemic fluctuations in price (Cooper and Lawrence, 1975; Prain, 1975; Tilton, 1977). If the system worked as predicted by economic theory, then speculation should stabilize the market since purchases would be made when prices were low and selling would occur when prices were high. However, many of those dealing in the exchanges are metal fabricators. During a recession such firms will not be able to afford to hold large metal stocks and will, therefore, tend to reduce their holdings, so driving prices down still further. However, when trade improves, they will have the financial capability of buying in more stocks, so fuelling the metal price rise. Moreover, independent speculators (with no production or consumption interest in the metal) tend to reinforce this trend; when prices are falling they delay buying in the hope that further falls will occur, and vice versa when prices rise. If enough speculators behave in this way, they in effect ensure that their expectations are fulfilled. When consumer governments enlarge or dispose of their security stockpiles, the quantities involved are frequently large enough to have a destabilizing effect on the markets. It is worth noting that when the markets deal in a small proportion of total supply, consumer governments and major private companies will normally hold sufficient stockpiles to be able to manipulate prices. This has important implications for any producer nation attempting to circumvent the mineral conglomerates by selling directly to consumers (see pp. 160–1).

The very fact that markets are unstable introduces yet other imperfections into the system. Not only does it reinforce the tendency for companies to go for vertical integration, so allowing them to reduce their vulnerability to price and demand fluctuations, but it also makes tied long-term contract sales much more attractive to consumers. In addition, it is one factor behind producer, and sometimes consumer, government attempts to form price- and output-fixing cartels (see pp. 170–3).

Allocative efficiency over time

Overall it is inconceivable that the current distribution of inputs and products in the minerals sector bears even a fleeting resemblance to the optima, as defined by welfare economic theory. Nor does it seem likely that the highly imperfect system will be any more efficient in allocating available mineral reserves between generations. However, it is difficult to state categorically that the current mineral development process is too fast or too slow to optimize resource use over time. Enormous uncertainties exist about ultimate resource stocks, the pace and nature of technological change, the vulnerability of natural bio-geochemical cycles and future social preferences. Analysts will not only make quite different judgements about these key factors, but in addition their ideas on what constitutes the 'best' depletion path will depend critically upon the way they define – and on the priority they attribute to – intergenerational equity.

THE EFFICIENT DEPLETION PATH

The most common economic definition of an optimal, or efficient, depletion path is one which maximizes the sum of the net benefits from resource use accruing to the present and all future generations, measured in present value terms.[5]

This approach, usually referred to as *utilitarianism*, is based on Paretian efficiency rules as modified by Kaldor–Hicks, and it provides the underpinning for the simple investment appraisal model discussed in Chapter 3, as well as for all conventional cost–benefit analyses. If we assume that the market is working under the perfect conditions of economic nirvana, then the profit-maximizing depletion rate chosen by individual private firms will automatically produce the socially optimal allocation of resources over time. The firm will consider future cost and demand patterns; will discount future net revenue at the rate determined by consumer time preferences; and will strike the optimal balance between consumption and conservation. Ignoring the fact that these idealized conditions never occur, it is instructive to consider the value judgements which underpin this approach.

The whole resource utilization question is viewed from the present; the rate of time preference for money, income and consumption is determined by the current generation. Clearly, the yet unborn cannot be consulted on the matter. Most people observably value income now more highly than income in the future (if they were indifferent, the real rates of interest, adjusted for inflation, on borrowed capital would be zero), and this preference is built into the depletion calculations. Inevitably, then, there is a bias towards present consumption, while the benefits which future generations may receive from resource use are devalued. If the resource-use pattern derived from current preferences 'calls for extinction of certain fish stocks, exhaustion of certain mineral deposits, decline in environmental quality, and the eventual self-destruction of the human race, *nil desperandum*: in a Pareto world, all that matters is maximum economic efficiency' (Butlin, 1981, p. 6).

Economists argue that their approach is ethically neutral; they do not choose the social discount rate which is determined by prevailing value systems. If market mechanisms produce intertemporal allocations which contravene accepted notions of morality and social justice, then it must be a matter for political decision. In theory, it would be possible to conceive of governments deciding to introduce negative discount rates, which would positively discriminate in favour of resource conservation, but in practice the growth-oriented nature of our economic, social and political systems makes the probability of this actually happening infinitesimally small.

The ethical basis of allowing present-day preferences to determine resource availabilities in the future has been questioned since the 1920s. Pigou (1932), perhaps the best known of early critics, argued that individual preference decisions were myopic, limited by the human lifespan and a weakness of imagination. Although people may be concerned over the welfare of their grandchildren, the human mind fails to conceptualize future needs in a manner that has any significant effect on current usage behaviour. Most people fail, or prefer not to see, that their consumption of minerals and environmental resources *may* have profound implications for future generations. In fact, given the high discount rates prevailing since the 1960s, people are in effect disregarding their own future needs, never mind those of their children.

People's preferences for conservation or consumption are not formed independently of the economic system in which they live. Persuasion to consume is part of the market growth generation process. Nor have the major companies stood aside when conservation and zero-growth strategies have been suggested to minimize import dependence and long-term scarcity problems. Mobil, for example, ran a massive two-page message in the *New York Times* to persuade people that new energy supply developments must go ahead immediately and that 'conservation alone cannot do it all'. Phrases abound which equate cutbacks in energy supplies with 'breadlines' and human suffering, and which stress that reduced economic growth 'means a general lowering of living standards' (*New York Times*, 26 January 1975).

It has, however, been commonly argued that the bias towards present consumption is both rational and ethically justifiable since, in the future, people will be better off and will command much-improved technologies. Just as it would have been ridiculous for our nineteenth-century ancestors to have cut their coal consumption and living standards to allow us the chance to utilize it, so too, it is argued, it would be silly for us to deprive ourselves on the off-chance that this will benefit future generations. A recent expression of this view can be found in O'Toole and Walton (1982, pp. 64–5), who argue that 'saving fossil fuels may not benefit future generations even in terms of their own preferences'. They justify their opinion on three basic grounds. First, technological changes will probably occur which would significantly reduce the value of stocks of fossil fuels. Second, if we use least-cost energy sources now, our economy will be more efficient and this will allow the diversion of resources to the development of scientific knowledge.[6] There is, in other words, a trade-off between leaving future generations with some fossil fuels or with knowledge of alternative production processes, which could ultimately be of greater value to them. And third, by using least-cost energy, more productive growth will occur in the economy, so increasing future national output and per capita consumption opportunities. Therefore, is it reasonable to ask the current generation 'to forgo some of its income by using more expensive renewable energy resources to further increase posterity's wealth'? (ibid., p. 65).

However, the future is uncertain. If the coming generations are not more prosperous, if technological change does not alleviate stock resource scarcity, if any life-threatening pollution problems are not solved, and if the future generations happen to have strong social preferences for landscapes, artesian water sources, forests or animal species that have long since vanished, then the efficient depletion path cannot be equated with any generally accepted notions of equity. Moreover, when the imperfections in the market allocation system are taken into account, there are strong reasons for suggesting that the *actual* output pattern will be even more pollution and primary-resource intensive than the efficient one.

DEPLETION PATHS IN AN IMPERFECTLY COMPETITIVE WORLD

In Chapter 2 the view was discussed that the existence of monopoly and imperfect competition in the stock resource sector should, in theory, act to promote conservation and slow down depletion to below the efficient rate (see p. 40). There are isolated examples where this has occurred in practice – the post-1973 behaviour of OPEC is an obvious case – but these are the exceptions not the rule. There is little or no evidence that the extractive industries in general have conserved known reserves to avoid spoiling present-day markets (Page, 1981). Many of the already described characteristics of mineral producers explain their apparently non-rational, non-profit-maximizing behaviour. In the first place, most firms are risk-averse. Not only does this greatly accelerate the depletion path of reserves located in areas judged to be politically unstable or hostile, but it also biases the whole production process against the future. Even in countries where political problems are minimal, any postponement of sales carries with it the risk that mineral prices will fall, a risk made even more acute by the continued real decline in primary-product prices. Second, firms need not greatly restrict current output to maintain price and profit levels if they have the power to manipulate market demand. When consumers are so tied into particular products that they become essential, then very small output cuts can push up price levels. Moreover, if firms succeed in persuading consumers to change their preference patterns to consume more oil or tin cans, then the whole demand curve is shifted outwards and output cuts may be unnecessary. Furthermore, many companies split their market into discrete entities explicitly to avoid having to lower prices or cut production.

Third, as the bulk of mineral producers are large capital-intensive enterprises, they need to maintain output to achieve scale economies. The costs involved in restricting production may, therefore, far outweigh any potential price advantages which may result. Over time the introduction of mass-production technologies and the size of the fixed capital needed to start production in remote or physically inhospitable locations have probably acted to accelerate depletion. Fourth, in many firms sale volume, market share and output stability objectives may override profit maximization as the dominant business aim. Where ownership is divorced from control – as long as satisfactory profit levels are achieved – management status, security and success are all likely to be related to business size; more output means more employees, more equipment and plant, and bigger budgets. Even in owner-managed concerns growth may represent a more tangible, obvious measure of success, and a more 'worthy' objective than increasing already acceptable profit levels.

Finally, all companies, whether private or government run, have to survive now in order to produce in the future. They must, then, generate enough present-day income to maintain plant, equipment and a labourforce before potentially higher profits over time become a relevant concern. Small private companies will not have the reserves to allow them to withhold output for any significant length of time in the hope that higher prices will reign in the future. Executives in multinationals have to maintain enough output and development activity to protect the technostructure of the corporation. Moreover, they are not likely to be sacked for failing to maintain a depletion path which maximizes profits for their successors, but may be if present growth and profits are judged to be inadequate. The pressure for rapid depletion is even greater when the financial needs of LDCs have to be met in large measure from mineral exports. As the terms of trade continue to move against primary products and as the problems of servicing past debts become ever more acute, so many nations see their only option as increasing output to maintain their total revenue. Thus the plunge in copper prices since 1974 has been exacerbated by the needs of Zambia, Zaire, Peru and Chile to earn foreign exchange. In just four years world prices were halved but copper continued to be pushed out on to the highly depressed market. Short-term needs had to take precedence over potential long-term profits.

When uncertainty, market manipulation and non-profit-maximizing objectives are taken into account, the imperfectly competitive nature of the mineral sector no longer appears as a major force promoting conservation and an efficient allocation of available resources over time. Moreover, virtually all the other 'imperfections' in the system tend to reinforce the bias towards present consumption. The fact that long-term forward markets and adequate risk insurance markets rarely exist pushes firms still further to produce now at known returns. The failure of the market to incorporate the full costs of environmental change into production decisions diverts industries into a more resource- and pollution-intensive output pattern (see pp. 244–6). Furthermore, many government taxes and regulations also tend to accelerate the speed of development, emphasizing growth and volume of output at the expense of conservation (see Chapter 5).

THE EFFICIENCY ILLUSION

Overall it is difficult to argue that the minerals industry achieves even an approximation to economic efficiency, despite the fact that efficiency is so often used as a justification for the free market system. The scale of the imperfections are such that technological, product-choice and allocative efficiency cannot be the assumed attributes of the system, and any policy of meaningful correction would imply massive state intervention.

However, there is still a powerful body of thought that denies the all-pervasive nature of market 'failures' and argues that governmental attempts to correct the occasional imperfection must avoid any deep intrusions into the working of the market mechanism. Typical of such views are those expressed by W. P. Tavoulareas (president of Mobii, and director of Bankers' Trust New York and General Foods), who states that the government's role is to 'establish a climate favourable for development of additional energy sources, in a clear and orderly way which avoids conflicting bureaucratic procedures and organizations that hinder timely and efficient production' (Tavoulareas and Kaysen, 1977, p. 17). The market system and technological change will, it is claimed, provide for future energy needs as long as governments eschew 'inappropriate and counterproductive measures', such as 'overly severe environmental restrictions' and conservation through reduced consumption. 'A policy that focuses disproportionately on reducing consumption is essentially a policy of despair' and 'is not necessary in a country with the resources and technology of the US' (ibid., p. 8).

Nor are oil company presidents alone in their faith in the market. Anders *et al.* argue that

> [the] real danger is that we may foolishly restrict the exploitation of current resources, forego investment opportunities and allow conserved resources to be obsolete. Only if we eliminate market incentives for innovation and investment must we face a real, long-term resource crisis. (Anders *et al.*, 1980, p. 263)

This time the authors include a senior policy adviser to the Ontario Ministry of Natural Resources, a member of the US House of Representatives and economic consultants to the Canadian and American governments on energy and resource conservation. It is, of course, possible that such writers may be correct in assuming that market mechanisms may operate to avoid long-term stock scarcities, but what happens if they in fact prove to be wrong? Moreover, the claim that this has anything to do with efficiency is of dubious validity: there is enough evidence to suggest that the private mineral industries are not marvellously efficient engines of global economic growth and prosperity.

Distributive equity and economic development

DEFINING EQUITY

Since in theory an economically efficient industry, operating within a perfect market, would maximize the net benefits from mineral development, such an industry would also create the greatest potential for economic growth. However, neither the equity with which the benefits from production are allocated between people over space and time nor the spatial location of any associated growth and development are matters of concern in the efficiency model. But these closely related issues are rarely matters of indifference to governments, which are concerned both with the proportion of income, employment and growth accruing to their own particular countries and with the distribution of these over the national territory and between distinct social groups.

Any discussion of distributive equity is plagued by the very different definitions which have been employed. To some equity means equality with equal shares for all, to others it means allocating shares according to need. Still others regard it as equitable to give the greatest share to those who have made the greatest contribution, giving rewards to the industrious, those willing to take risks and those with greater skill or knowledge. A further group argues that it is equitable to allocate shares according to people's willingness to pay for them.

This last is the equity concept embedded in the notion of consumer sovereignty. As Young (1980, p. 125) has pointed out, basically it boils down to: 'to each according to the contribution of the resources in his possession.' 'This means that those possessing large initial resource endowments will receive proportionately large shares of the system's output and vice versa.' Although few would openly argue that a system was equitable if it served to make the rich still richer, it is the concept implicitly held by all those supporting an untrammelled market system (Friedman, 1962). It is common for the 'willingness to pay' and 'reward the greatest contribution' concepts to be seen as interrelated. If the most affluent groups in an economy are those who contribute most to the value of current productive output, then there should be a broad identity between the two ideas. However, this breaks down completely when resource endowments are the result of historic legacy, as in large measure they inevitably are.

All the above equity concepts are concerned with outcomes, with who gets what from a productive system. However, there is an alternative notion which stresses the process involved rather than the end-results. This is the idea that there should be equality of opportunity, or equality of access to the decision-making process. Within the international minerals sector this has been a commonly used notion. The LDC producers have long argued that the system of international exchange is unequal and inequitable since it fails to allow them to be full and equal partners within the interdependent world economy. They have not been able independently to pursue the mineral development strategies most suited to their individual needs, but have to follow those dictated by the capitalistic system of exchange.

The use of such vastly different equity concepts in part reflects genuine ideological differences between analysts, and helps explain the highly polarized debate over the equity of the mineral production process. There is little meeting of minds between those who argue that equity involves the imperative that all receive an equal share of the world's productive resources, and those who claim that the market system will produce an equitable distribution of income by ensuring that everyone receives in proportion to the value of their contribution to production.

The arguments over equity are complicated even further by the fact that it is by no means unusual for governments and individuals to appeal simultaneously to quite different equity notions when it is in their interest to do so. Equity can be used as a means of legitimizing decisions made on quite different grounds, or to justify demands and actions which are in reality motivated by self-interest. An additional difficulty arises because there is often a lack of conformity between the dominant conventional wisdom, or rhetoric, on equity and the accepted economic system within a society. Coates *et al.* (1977) argue that in the western world there is an overwhelming consensus in moral or social thought which identifies equity with equality. Perhaps so; but there is also a widespread belief in the efficacy of the market system, despite the fact that this implies acceptance of quite a different equity concept.

EQUITY AND DEVELOPMENT IN THE INTERNATIONAL MINERAL ECONOMY

Distributive equity and growth are quite distinct issues conceptually. In a no-growth economy the equity with which the now fixed national product was distributed would still be a relevant concern. However, in practice it is impossible to dissociate the two issues when considering the mineral industry at an international scale. For many of the Third World producer states both their pace of economic development and their national incomes are highly dependent upon the way the revenue from mining, and the industrial growth associated with mining, is distributed between nations.

Equity and free trade

It is difficult to believe from the perspectives of today that the question of equitable trade relations has only been an issue since the Second World War. While it is true that Marx argued that the colonies would be plundered for low-cost resources to allow the process of capital accumulation to continue (*Capital*, vol. 2, p. 7), by the end of the nineteenth century the dominant economic philosophy was *laissez-faire*. It was assumed that private enterprise, in pursuing its own interests within a system of free trade, would provide benefits for all. Notions of comparative advantage held sway; each country should specialize in the products which they could produce most efficiently and, in the process, the entire world economy would gain from economies of scale and specialization. By becoming integrated into the international economy, each country would benefit from reduced production costs, and national incomes would rise since the best use was being made of a given resource endowment.

In practice, this normally meant that LDCs would export unprocessed minerals and agricultural raw materials, leaving processing and manufacturing industry in the hands of the developed nations, who had built up a considerable initial advantage in these forms of economic activity. Few expressed concern that such an international division of labour was in any sense inequitable. While it was accepted that it would not produce equal consumption and income levels, the spatial disparities would reflect differences in productivity and would, therefore, be broadly 'fair'. It was commonly assumed that the market contained equilibrating mechanisms which would eventually act to reduce spatial inequalities. Capital would be attracted away from the advanced nations, with their high-cost labour, and into the LDCs, so providing employment and bidding up wage rates. Only when the real cost of labour, measured in output terms, was equal in all countries would the process of international capital redistribution stop.

Faith in the market mechanism and free trade as growth-generating forces is by no means dead. Indeed it has had something of a resurrection since the 1970s. Bauer (1972), for long the voice of dissent in development economics, has been joined by the neo-Friedmanites in arguing that market forces will produce the most productive use of resources and the greatest impetus for growth in the Third World (Little *et al.*, 1970). Burenstam-Linder typifies the views of this school of thought when, after outlining the theoretical advantages of free trade, he concludes:

> It is good theory. It has proven to be so again and again in practice. Trade, as an engine of growth and a support for political stability, has advanced the countries that have engaged in it to ever increasing income levels. (Burenstam-Linder, 1982, p. 227)

This is not the view of the international trade system held by most governments in the Third World. Nor has it gone unchallenged by academic analysts.

Unequal exchange

Over the last few decades most LDC governments have argued that the system of exchange developed during the *laissez-faire* period, and essentially perpetuated since then, was inherently unequal. In 1974 the adoption by the UN General Assembly of the Declaration and Programme of Action on the Establishment of a New International Economic Order suggests, on the surface at least, a widespread recognition of the force of these arguments. The trade system was regarded as inequitable in two senses. First, it had conspicuously failed to narrow the income gap between rich and poor nations (Brandt, 1980); and, second, it consigned the LDCs to a position of economic dependence. In fact dependence was often regarded as the root cause of inequality. The LDC governments tended to ascribe their countries' poverty and lack of growth to their dependence rather than any failure of domestic economic policy. This view has been supported by many development theorists working from various ideological standpoints.

In the 1950s and 1960s analysts such as Nurkse (1953), Myrdal (1957) and Prebish (1961) all argued that free trade would neither produce the employment or rates of economic growth necessary to raise living standards in the Third World, nor act to reduce global inequalities. Myrdal very persuasively showed that the already developed industrial core, with its mass market, offered the greatest returns on investment capital; *backwash effects* would, therefore, operate to deprive peripheral areas of their locally generated capital and their skilled and most enterprising workers, so increasing spatial disparities. Most recently the dependency and uneven development schools of theorists – many, but by no means all, working from a neo-Marxist perspective – have argued that unequal trade relations and inequalities in income levels are the logical consequences of the exploitive capitalist system (Frank, 1967, 1978; Sunkel, 1972; Cardoso, 1972; Amin, 1976). The development and unequal trade debate is clearly much wider than the minerals sector. But for most LDCs any discussion of international welfare disparities must involve consideration of the way the mineral industries have operated, and more particularly, must assess the crucial role played by the multinational corporations. The international minerals sector is relevant not only to those countries dependent on mineral exports, but also to all those newly industrializing nations dependent on mineral imports, most notably oil.

The role of the multinational corporations

By the 1950s virtually every significant extractive enterprise in the Third World was owned by a foreign firm and the products were destined for export. Although many such industries had been developed from scratch by the foreign companies, this was by no means universally true. In Chile indigenous producers had developed an active copper trade, supplying 60 per cent of world copper in the 1870s. But during the first half of the twentieth century these were gradually taken over, mostly by corporations of American origin (Frank, 1967). With the rise in nationalist feelings, the very fact of foreign ownership of key national assets was politically unacceptable in a number of countries, where the view was strongly held that natural resources should be owned by and developed for the benefit of the indigenous peoples. Moreover, it was also argued that the manner in which the multinationals operated ensured that the host countries received less than an equitable share of the financial and economic growth returns from their resource stock. Therefore, without strict controls over company operations, natural resource exploitation and trade would perpetuate, indeed exacerbate, international welfare inequalities. Analysts have varied in their detailed case against the multinationals, but it is possible to identify five common themes.

REPATRIATION OF RESOURCE RENTS

In the first place, it was argued that the companies took and repatriated a disproportionately high amount of the direct profits or economic rent from extraction. A much-quoted illustration of this is the proportion of the revenue from Middle Eastern crude oil production which was remitted abroad in the pre-OPEC period. As Table 4.1 shows, over 45 per cent of the gross receipts were directly transferred abroad, chiefly to the United States and Europe, and this understates the total level of money transfers since a major proportion of the cost of operations would have been used to pay for imports, or would have been remitted home by foreign employees.

Similar figures have emerged from a whole series of studies of the copper industry. Moran (1975) has shown that in the 1920s the Chilean government's tax on the international copper producers amounted to a mere 12 per cent, at a time when Kennecott was earning 20–40 per cent per annum on its investments. Girvan (1974) has estimated that between 1935 and 1969 91 per cent of all the profits made on Chilean copper were transferred out of the country, leaving only 9 per cent for internal reinvestment. Taking a longer timespan, 1910–70, Frank and Diaz (1974) calculated that US companies transferred a total of $10,800 million out of the country, despite the fact that their total input of investment funds over the period amounted to less than $104 million. High levels of repatriation also apparently occurred from Peru:

> According to official sources American mining companies repatriated $790 million of profits out of Peru between 1950 and 1970 – $669 m in the last decade. Net investment amounted to $284 m. (Mezger, 1980, pp. 151–2)

If anything, still less of the profit from copper mining remained in what is now Zambia. In the ten years before independence the two copper-mining corporations, Rhodesia Selection Trust and Anglo-American, sent £260 million out of the country and, even after 1964, they still repatriated some £25 million per

Table 4.1   Financial results of oil operations in the Middle East (from start of production to formation of OPEC, 1960)

	1000 million US$	%
Gross receipts of oil companies	32.1	100
Cost of operations	5.9	18.1
Royalties, rents and taxes	9.9	30.8
Reinvestment in producer states	1.7	5.3
Transferred abroad	14.6	45.5

Source: Issawi and Yeganeh, 1962, p. 108.

annum. Nor were the mining companies the only foreign organizations to gain from the Zambian copper trade. According to Lanning and Mueller (1979), the British Treasury took £40 million in taxes between 1923 and 1964, and yet spent only £5 million on development. In addition, even the royalties from mining went to a foreign company; the British South Africa Co. received more than £160 million gross in the thirty years before independence.

Although such figures have not gone undisputed, few would doubt that approximately 40 per cent of the net profits from working mines were typically remitted overseas by the multinational companies, at least until the late 1960s. What is in dispute is whether this was inequitable exploitation, rather than a 'just' payment for the work done in developing the resource. The companies have argued that it was their risk capital, equipment, technical knowledge and marketing arrangements which gave the resource its value, whereas the countries involved were merely sitting back and collecting the unearned economic rent created by their geologically fortunate inheritance. Moreover, they have correctly pointed out that figures which merely cite the profit take on viable working mines are extremely misleading and overstate the real total profit position; they ignore the losses made on exploration and development efforts which do not yield workable finds.

Individual LDC governments were rarely sympathetic to the profits from their domestic operations being employed to offset losses incurred in other countries. From their perspective all profit remission represented a loss of development capital. It was a frequently expressed view that the host states would be better off if they left their minerals in the ground. Then at least they would have a capital stock available for future use. Current exploitation merely depleted this stock and transferred the bulk of its capital value abroad. Girvan (1970, 1976), for example, has argued that exports should be gradually phased out since every ton of an exhaustible resource taken from the national system represents a loss of productive input into the domestic growth process. However, the difficulty with this argument is that a stock resource has no value either as a source of capital or a factor of production until it is exploited. There is no certainty that future patterns of demand and technologies will give the mineral the same value as it has today.

PRICE MANIPULATION

A second common complaint against the multinationals was that they exerted a considerable degree of control over the price of the raw mineral because of their dominance in the markets. Prices could, therefore, be manipulated to suit company interests or even to meet the needs of consumer governments. Girvan (1976) has claimed that during the Second World War the US copper multinationals concluded an agreement with the US government to freeze prices well below the market rate, an arrangement that cost Chile some $500 million that it could ill-afford. The vertically integrated nature of many mining conglomerates also raised the possibility that the nominal prices paid for the mineral by downstream companies could be set to minimize payment of producer profit taxes and royalties. Moreover, if the internally determined transfer price was low, then the producer states also lost foreign exchange earnings on their exports.

Both Peru and Chile regarded the copper companies' practice of selling to the United States in the 1950s and 1960s at prices below those ruling on the London Metal Exchange as a measure designed to rob them of tax and exchange earnings. However, the companies concerned have pointed out that lower and more stable prices were necessary to minimize the already rapid penetration of the traditional copper markets by aluminium and plastics. Any slight loss on each unit of sales was more than compensated by the maintenance of export volume. In the same way, the lowering in 1959 and 1960 of the posted price of crude oil was necessary, in the eyes of the oil majors, to maintain output levels and avoid a glut, but was viewed by the producer states as a major threat to their revenues since the ruling posted price was used as the basis for tax and royalty calculations.

Since the 1960s most LDC governments have acted to control the companies' use of internal transfer pricing, and, with nationalization and the establishment of producer cartels, are in a stronger position to bargain over mineral prices. But with the notable exception of oil, they have had relatively little success in bidding up real export prices. One of the major reasons for this is that the multinationals still control downstream processing activities and, therefore, the markets for the raw minerals. The more tightly integrated the industry, the more difficult it is for an LDC producer to circumvent the companies and sell direct to the final consumer. This is particularly so in the case of bauxite, where transnational companies own a very high proportion of 'western' alumina and aluminium production capacity and where other market outlets are highly constrained. After nationalizing its bauxite industry in 1971, Guyana found an outlet in Eastern Europe, but the opportunities for other producers to adopt this strategy are limited. The Soviet bloc has restricted requirements for bauxite, is short of hard currency and is reluctant to abandon the mineral self-sufficiency policy.

CONTROL OVER TECHNOLOGY

A third common case against the multinational mineral companies was that they were employing inappropriate technologies. Capital-intensive, large-scale production techniques developed to suit the factor endowments of advanced nations restricted the remunerative employment opportunities which could have been created by mineral extraction. It was also frequently asserted that such investment practices have distorted the whole employment structure in the LDCs, making them incapable of adequately employing their populations (Schervish, 1979).

A 1973 United Nations report on *Multinational Corporations in World Development* showed that, in 1970, the total stock of foreign investment capital in Third World nations amounted to some $40,000 million, but it provided employment for only 2 million workers, less than 3 per cent of the labourforce, which means that the capital cost per job was $20,000 (Streeton, 1979).[7] It is probable that for most mineral developments the investment required per job is now much higher than this; Mezger (1980) has estimated that for copper extraction the figure is approximately $250,000. From such data it seems clear, given current technologies, that investment in the extractive enterprises cannot make a significant *direct* contribution to LDC employment problems. Moreover, the current trend towards massive open-cast operations is reducing employment opportunities still further.

Although capital-intensive technologies do require some highly skilled labour, this has normally been imported or, particularly in Africa, provided by the expatriate white community. The bulk of jobs available to indigenous workers were unskilled and therefore lowly paid, with few opportunities for acquiring useful skills which could be transferred to other sectors of the economy. For example, in Zambia before independence, black Africans were effectively excluded from skilled positions by a colour bar enforced by the strongly organized white unions (Berger, 1974).

A further issue concerning technology is that of technological dependence. A number of writers, primarily those working in the neo-Marxist tradition, have claimed that technological innovation is a mechanism used by international capitalism (both individual companies and capitalist governments) to maintain control over production and to consign the LDCs to a position of permanent dependence on imported technical skills. Tanzer (1980, p. 200) has argued that 'for the United States, the leading mineral-using country, control over technology is seen as the key to enhancing its power, and every effort will be used to maintain that control as long as possible'. While Sutcliffe writes that

> technology has always been the basis of metropolitan monopoly. The underdeveloped areas have been unable to establish a complete industrial structure because they have been unable to establish the industries possessing at the same time the most complex and advanced technology. (Sutcliffe, 1972, p. 190)

In the specific context of minerals there are three important aspects of these dependency arguments. First, complex mining, smelting and refining technologies almost inevitably require the import of the necessary technical skills and capital goods into the LDC. Indigenous firms cannot provide the required goods and services since they lack the needed engineering skills, and it is common for foreign engineering companies to be subsidiaries of – or associated through ownership links with – the multinational mineral corporations (Mezger, 1980). If the technologies are constantly being refined and made more complex, the LDCs cannot realistically ever hope to be in a position to take over from foreign engineering companies. Second, the more sophisticated the technology the greater the required input of capital. If this is imported by the multinationals, then part of the economic rent from exploitation will be remitted overseas. However, the alternatives of attempting to raise the investment capital internally, or by borrowing from the international financial institutions, bring opportunity cost and indebtedness problems. It is, therefore, argued that technological dependence also brings capital dependence, and that these forms of dependence remain even when the multinationals are no longer allowed to own the mining industry itself.

Finally, technological change can be and has been used by the multinationals to maintain their control over supply sources, so weakening the bargaining strength of LDC producers. The risk avoidance strategy of developing tech-

6 and 7   The large-scale, capital-intensive nature of modern mineral extraction is clearly illustrated by the copper operations at Bougainville, in Papua New Guinea. Plate 6 shows open-pit mining of low-grade copper ores containing approximately 0.5 per cent copper per tonne. Plate 7 illustrates the sophistication of the equipment – a scene from the control room of the ore-crushing section.

niques to allow the extraction of marginal deposits or entirely new mineral sources, in 'safe' areas of the world, has been seen as part of a 'conspiracy' to ensure that LDC producer states toe the company line. However, there is no need to ascribe to any grand theory of international capitalist conspiracy to realize that behaviour which is quite rational from the company viewpoint must serve to limit an LDC's freedom of action. Basically, nations have to work within an exchange system substantially dominated by the multinationals, or operate outside it, by retreating into self-sufficiency or joining the Soviet trading bloc. Neither of these alternatives will necessarily help fulfil LDC growth objectives.

DISTORTION OF THE INDIGENOUS ECONOMY

A fourth commonly cited reason why foreign companies cannot generate the required economic development in the Third World is that their very existence reduces local savings, investment and entrepreneurial initiatives. Nurkse (1953), for instance, has suggested that there is a consumption demonstration effect. The relatively affluent members of the indigenous community attempt to emulate European or American consumption patterns; this reduces their propensity to save and so restricts still further the amount of locally available investment capital. Moreover, since many of the desired consumer goods are imported, the increased rate of consumption fails to generate internal markets and investment opportunities. Further, Hirschman (1971), among others, has argued that the inflow of foreign capital and management skills in itself stunts local development by depressing the supply of entrepreneurs, managers and appropriate technological innovation.

Perhaps of even more importance is the argument that the presence of powerful foreign companies, with their production geared to export sales, seriously circumscribes the planning power of the local government:

> In most countries where the multinationals have an important measure of control they become planners by default. Major social decisions about communications, consumption patterns, the growth of cities, transportation, and the like are made as by-products of private profit maximizing strategies. (Barnet, 1979, p. 155)

In particular, the communications and other infrastructure networks are geared towards the requirements of the companies, and as these are outward-looking the resulting pattern is not necessarily that best suited to internal development needs. As Brown (1975) has argued, for many LDCs the spatial distribution and pace of development, employment creation and trade levels are more likely to be determined by boardroom decisions in New York, London and Osaka than by the national government.

EXPORTED DEVELOPMENT

The final, but in many ways the most crucial, reason for suggesting that the international mineral production system is inequitable, is that it 'exports' from the area of extraction much of the associated spin-off development in servicing and processing industries. This argument in fact incorporates most of the other complaints against the multinationals. Ideally, the mineral industry would not only act as a source of capital and foreign exchange but would also provide a catalyst for other activities. The agricultural sector would be stimulated by the demands of the mining community and the construction industry would expand, as would all those providing maintenance and infrastructure services. Money pumped into the economy through payments for these goods and services, the wages of mineworkers and the mine profits would stimulate the development of internal markets, thus creating new profitable investment opportunities. Moreover, if metal processing and manufacturing industries were also established within the country, then significantly higher levels of spin-off activity should be generated since the value added in production is much greater than in mining itself. With minerals as the initial motive force, the economy should, theoretically, pass through a set of development stages until it has enough momentum to survive the inevitable exhaustion of the mineral itself. (See, for example, Perloff and Wingo, 1960).

In order for this *multiplier process* to actually stimulate domestic economic growth the leakages of money capital from the national system must be small. This has characteristically not been the case for mining ventures in the Third

World. The bulk of the plant, equipment, construction materials and spare parts have been imported, as have the most skilled and highly paid elements in the workforce. A high proportion of mine profits has been remitted abroad and not reinvested; moreover, capital assets would normally be depreciated against profits as rapidly as possible to minimize losses in the event of any 'hostile' government action. Furthermore, only a small proportion of the mineral itself would be processed within the producer countries. In other words, the multiplier-effects of mining were siphoned away to the major market centres of the world.

Although host governments have introduced measures to stem the outflow of capital and mineral-related economic activities, their efforts have been constrained by their dependence on the companies for investment capital, technology and markets. The impotence of producer states to control their mineral economies comes out clearly in Girvan's *cri de coeur*:

> the Caribbean bauxite industry is a classic case of economic imperialism. It is entirely owned and operated by a small number of vertically integrated North American transnational aluminium companies. . . . These companies also control the bulk of world production and reserves of bauxite and they dominate the world aluminium market. Capital and technology for the Caribbean bauxite industry come from the transnational aluminium companies. There is no 'market' for its output other than the plants of the companies. Prices are fixed by the companies according to their convenience. Levels of production and the rates of investment and expansion are matters of company policy, determined by the global economies of the transnational firm. Only a part of the value of the industry's 'sales' actually accrue to the Caribbean economies; and only an infinitesimal fraction of the value of the end products flows back to Caribbean people. Thus, the Caribbean bauxite industry is entirely subject to the needs, policies, and authority of corporate monopoly capital based in North America. (Girvan, 1976, pp. 99–100)

The fact that much of the capital invested in LDC mineral ventures was 'foreign' clearly in part explains why the leakages from the multiplier process were so high, but it by no means provides the full explanation. As early as 1957 Myrdal argued that with the low levels of income and effective demand in the Third World economies, there were relatively few profitable investment opportunities. The forces at work in the capital market would lead to capital export not internal reinvestment, and these forces would still operate even if the original source of the investment finance had been internal.

The price commanded by unprocessed minerals is inevitably much lower than that of finished or semi-finished metal goods. Aluminium products, for example, are forty times more valuable than the bauxite that went to produce them. Therefore, all other things being equal, a mineral deposit should become much more valuable to an LDC, both as a source of investment capital and foreign exchange and as a generator of growth and employment, if it is processed internally and sold as finished or semi-finished products.

However, this critically depends on the cost and availability of all the factor inputs required for processing and on the presence of markets open to the products. In practice, the benefits accruing to the LDCs can be severely limited by the need to import some factors of production, particularly investment capital and energy, and by the trade barriers erected against imported finished goods by the consumer states. But unless primary producers can break into the production of high-value manufactured goods, international income disparities must continue to increase. The whole economic trend is towards the production of more and more complex finished goods; as this happens the basic mineral inputs decline in relative value and, therefore, the relative growth rates must be lower in those parts of the economic system which specialize in primary production. Moreover, in the longer term any country relying solely on the export of a stock mineral cannot hope to maintain its income; inevitably at some time in the future economic exhaustion must occur.

It is, however, neither in the interests of the major mining corporations nor the consumer states to allow a significant proportion of processing activity to be redistributed to LDC mining centres. From the company viewpoint, even if the producer country was relatively stable politically, it would still be a rational risk minimization strategy to spread, rather than concentrate, their investments. If, for example, a new low-cost supply source were found, it would be more difficult to take advantage of it when the processing plants were tied to existing sources. By retaining most of their processing capacity in the market areas, companies can take raw materials from a range of supply sources which can be adjusted in line with any political, economic, or technological changes which may occur. It is also likely that such a policy serves to keep supply prices relatively low, at least during periods of surplus when producer countries are competing against one another for sales.

Additionally, it is much easier for the companies to respond quickly to customer requirements and to maintain technical quality standards when the processing plant is located in a developed consumer country. Even further incentives for market location occur when consumer governments act, for balance-of-payments, security, or employment reasons, to discourage the import of processed minerals. As will be seen in Chapter 5, production subsidies and a variety of differential tariffs and import embargoes have all been used to encourage the development, or retention, of processing capacity.

Appropriate policy responses

Given the way the minerals industry has operated in the past, it is difficult to deny that it has not been able to generate the growth and employment needed in the Third World; nor has it served to reduce the income and welfare disparities between north and south. However, what is in dispute is whether it could do so if 'adjustments' were made to the system. In this debate there are three major distinct and opposing schools of thought.

Free trade economists argue that the only necessary adjustments are for governments, both producer and consumer, to stop intervening in the operation of the market. But this view involves two key assumptions: first, that the existing market system is operating efficiently; and, second, that equity is served when each country is rewarded in proportion to its contribution to the world's productive output. The first of these has already been shown to be invalid for the minerals sector, and the second is fraught with difficulties. Apart from the fact that not everyone accepts the 'rewards for contribution' concept of equity, the major problem is that the value of a country's productive contribution is defined in terms of the income levels and consumption patterns of the major market centres. In other words, the 'rewards' from production are allocated according to ability to pay. There is no absolute measure of value. If the distribution of income is changed, so too is the apparent 'value' of each country's output. The parameters of comparative advantage, and the division of labour which it implies, are determined by the requirements of the already advanced economies. While current comparative advantages are partially a function of the intrinsic physical differences between countries (climate, soil fertility and resource stocks), of much greater importance are differences in accumulated wealth and capital. It is precisely because the Third World nations are not prepared to accept existing patterns of comparative advantage as given, that free trade is not a feasible strategy.

The second school of thought acknowledges that the market system has a role to play, but argues that its operation must be regulated by government action at the national and international scales. Markets are recognized to be imperfect; they are not necessarily self-regulating, do not automatically ensure full employment of all factors of production and do not afford protection to the weak and the poor. For decades now the northern industrialized countries have deemed it 'inequitable' to allow the completely free play of market forces within their domestic economies and have redistributed real income to the disadvantaged sectors. What is now required, it is argued, is 'the natural evolution of the welfare state philosophy which is already accepted at the national level' into the international arena (Tinbergen, 1976; Kitamura, 1982).

Third World governments would need to actively manage their own internal economies, but, even more crucially, intergovernmental action would be necessary to create a 'New International Economic Order (Brandt, 1980; Behrman, 1974; Bhagwati, 1977). To produce more equal international trade relations four basic changes are needed:

(1) the prices of primary commodities must be maintained *vis-à-vis* manu-factured goods;
(2) the violent fluctuations in mineral prices must be controlled to give the producer states a stable income;
(3) the north must open its markets to the primary and manufactured products from the south;
(4) funds must be made available to allow the producer states to develop their processing industries and develop their manufacturing potential.

The emphasis throughout the so-called north–south dialogue has been on trade, export opportunities and the rapid recycling of the returns from past investment into new development projects. However, such an export-led de-velopment strategy is rejected completely by the third school of thought. Amin

(1976, 1977), among many others, has argued that it is a chimera which can do nothing to reduce international income and welfare disparities. The basic reasoning underlying such a view is simple. The level of export income is determined by the level of demand from the advanced nations and, therefore, an export-dependent economy must always *follow* the growth in the importing economies, and can only hope to capture a proportion of the extra income generated by such growth. Moreover, to support the extension of a modern export sector resources must be diverted from other parts of the national economy, and imports invariably escalate. The economy, therefore, enters a dependency treadmill; the export sector has to grow to sustain itself, to avoid bankruptcy, retain international credit, meet the interest on overseas debt and pay for imports. Amin (1977) has concluded that the whole process of development based on exports is a 'dead end', with no possibility of transition to a 'self-centred' system based on the production of mass consumption and capital goods (Bienefeld and Godfrey, 1982). The development experience in South Korea and Singapore appears to suggest that Amin's pessimistic assessment may not apply to all LDC export economies. Nevertheless, the horrendous debt problems now faced by countries such as Brazil and Mexico serve as a reminder of the vulnerability of export economies.

Empirical evidence clearly suggests that a country derives benefits from international trade roughly in proportion to its position on the scale of economic development (Thoman and Conkling, 1967). If trade occurs between partners of broadly similar economic standing then it would be expected to result in a reasonably equal distribution of advantage between them. But as Kitamura (1982, p. 347) has pointed out, market forces 'make inequality more marked where it is an all-pervasive condition'.

EQUITY AND MINERAL DEVELOPMENT WITHIN LDCs

Economic dualism

The orthodox approach to the role of minerals in the internal development of a country suggests that investment in their exploitation can act to spread growth and prosperity both across space and down to the poorest groups in society. First, it can do this directly through the operation of the economic multiplier; and, second, it can generate capital, which could be employed to invest in developing other sectors of the economy. However, in the Third World, leakages from the system have severely limited the capacity of the multiplier, and, moreover, the export sector has itself absorbed much of its generated capital surplus. Mining has typically been associated with the creation of a *dual economy*, the export-oriented extractive sector remaining as a modern enclave with few linkages into the traditional predominantly subsistence economy. In the most extreme cases the mining activities are developed in isolated self-contained communities, spatially as well as culturally detached from the rest of the country.

Neither the fact that the mineral is destined for export nor the use of imported capital are in themselves sufficient explanations of dualism. There are cases

8   An aerial view of Arandis, a modern workers' town built for employees of Rössing
Uranium, Namibia. The standard of housing and infrastructure services stand in marked
contrast to conditions elsewhere in the country. It provides a classic illustration of enclave
development, spatially and culturally isolated from most of the indigenous economy.

where the multiplier from a large-scale mining venture has led to cumulative
regional growth and has spread development on through the economy. Undoubtedly, the large deposits of low-grade copper and magnetite ores found in
the Phalaborwa area on the edge of the Kruger National Park, in north-eastern
Transvaal, have provided a focus for the industrial development of that region
and have had an impact on growth in other parts of South Africa. Out of an initial
investment of £37 million (1967 prices), all but £8.5 million came from overseas
sources:

> Yet the money was in the main spent in South Africa, whose firms provided
> most of the equipment and the 24,000 tons of cement and 20,000 tons
> of structural steel. Through these industries the multiplier effect of the
> development of the open pit and smelter went rippling outwards through the
> economy of the country. (Warren, 1973, p. 214)

But in this case the country already had well-developed steel and construction
industries, the necessary engineering skills, a government with the capital to

invest in associated infrastructure services and willing to do so as part of its regional development strategy, and a political system which provided a relatively secure home for foreign investments. In countries lacking a steel industry, mine machinery manufacturers and skilled engineering companies the spin-off developments from the construction and operation of mines are severely limited. These are normally confined to the mining area itself, the port and to a narrow strip along the transport link between the two.

There are numerous illustrations of dualism, but perhaps the classic example is Zambia (Figure 4.3). At the time of independence in 1964, despite some forty years of large-scale copper mining, the country remained predominantly a peasant economy:

> Almost no schools, hospitals, or even tarmac roads were constructed away from the narrow strip along the line of rail. Scattered, sparsely settled peasant holdings, cultivated with hoes, axes and cutlasses as of old, produced scarcely enough to provide a bare subsistence for the three-fourths of the population remaining in the more remote rural areas. (Siedman, quoted in Cobbe, 1979, p. 230)

Those black Africans working within the market economy received less than 20 per cent of the European wage, and since fewer than 1000 Zambian children had ever completed secondary education, few could hope to move into more highly paid employment.

Since independence the government has markedly increased its share of the returns from mineral exports, but this has had little impact on the living conditions of the poor. In fact the cleavages between different groups within the society have widened. Real income levels within the copper-dependent 'market' sector of the economy have escalated, while those in the traditional subsistence areas have barely changed. Moreover, within the market sector itself, major income disparities have emerged, with the top 10 per cent of employees now receiving 45 per cent of all wages and salaries. The élites working within the copper industry and the civil service form the hard core of the ruling party's (United National Independence Party) urban support, and as such have been well rewarded (Lanning and Mueller, 1979). These groups have acquired the consumption patterns of an advanced industrial society, demanding goods which cannot be produced internally, and thus limiting the operation of the economic multiplier in spreading development to other sectors of the economy.

Similarly, in Liberia a major study of the economy showed that in the mid-1960s approximately one-half of the country's national income accrued directly to foreign households and firms, one-quarter went to 97 per cent of the population and the remaining quarter was reserved for a tiny political élite. This élite was comprised of households in which one or more members held political office or salaried positions in government (Clower et al., 1966), and political solidarity was cemented by family ties (Liebenow, 1969). As Figure 4.4 shows, virtually all the major positions in the country were held in 1967–8 by people with some sort of family link back to President Tubman. Although the Zambian and Liberian cases are extreme, the pattern of increasing welfare disparities within

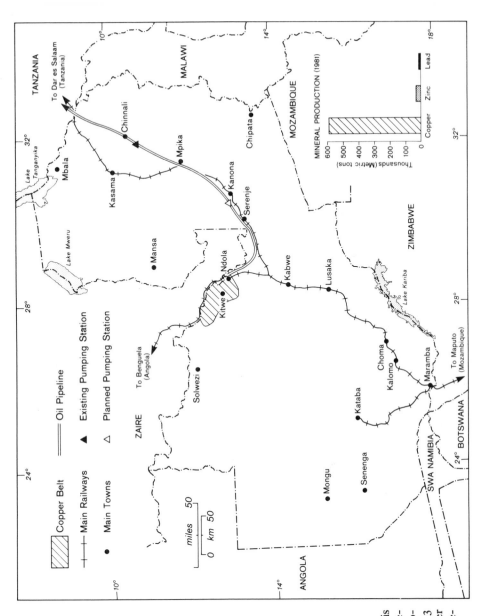

Figure 4.3 Zambia: the basis of a dual economy; urban settlement and economic development in the country was in 1983 still concentrated in the copper belt and along the railways developed to export the ore

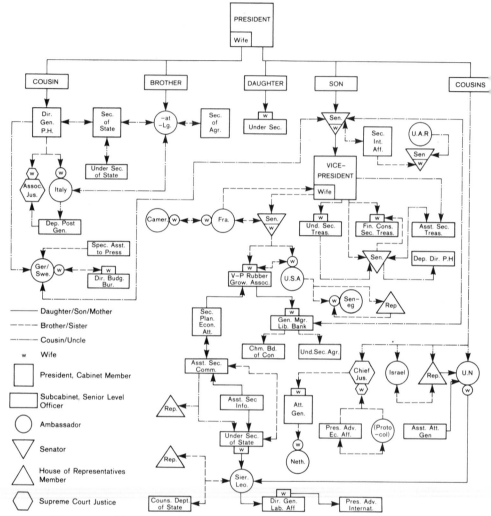

Figure 4.4 Nepotism in Liberia (positions of power held by a small political élite and their kinship ties)

Source: Adapted from Liebenow, 1969, p. 272. Copyright © 1969 Cornell University

the national economy is by no means atypical of other Third World mineral producers.

DUALISM AS A TEMPORARY CONDITION

Extrapolating from the experience of the now industrialized nations, some analysts view such widening income disparities as a temporary phenomenon, associated with the first stages of economic growth. Eventually the equilibrating mechanisms of the market will break down the dual economy and spread growth throughout the national system (Perloff *et al.*, 1960; Williamson, 1965; Richardson, 1969).

Others go one step further and regard greater inequality as a *necessary* condition for an economy struggling to take off into sustainable growth. Under the Harrod–Domar growth model the rate of capital formation is the most critical factor determining the rate of economic development (Little *et al.*, 1970; Heilleiner, 1973). An explicit choice has to be made between satisfying consumption needs now and reinvesting the sectoral surplus to enable higher consumption in the future. To maximize growth rates an LDC would need to ensure that the highest possible returns were achieved from the available factor endowment. This virtually precludes the possibility of investing in projects designed to meet the needs of the poor since their low effective incomes would limit the rate of return on the investments. Moreover, the poor groups in society would inevitably have a high propensity to consume; any measures which increased their incomes would yield little savings and, therefore, little reinvestable capital (Lewis, 1955). On the other hand, the modern capital goods sector of the economy, including mining, characteristically has high reinvestment ratios. Therefore, any attempts to redistribute the income surplus from this sector would inevitably reduce the rate of growth.

In other words, an income distribution which is equitable, in the sense of giving those in greatest need a share of the returns from mineral and associated export-based developments, would conflict with growth and the ultimate long-term welfare interests of all. Only when the process of investment concentration has created self-sustained growth could the government afford to take measures to redistribute income. By this time market forces would, in any case, have begun to equalize the returns to labour and capital throughout the economy and the rewards from development would have begun to spread spatially and to *trickle down* to the poor.

With the current resurgence of market orthodoxy, this growth strategy is in fact being forced on the capital-dependent nations of the Third World through the operations of private banking corporations and such multinational financial institutions as the International Monetary Fund. The conditions for new loans or, more usually today, the restructuring of old ones, have commonly required budget changes to curb consumption, welfare programmes and imports. The IMF's 'new assertiveness in monitoring the economic policies of its members' to ensure that they adopt 'responsible' economic policies, means that more of the countries' resources are pushed into the most 'productive' sectors of the economy. Thus the already considerable trends towards internal inequality are further reinforced.

CAN THE MINERALS SECTOR BE A DEVELOPMENT POLE?

There are, however, considerable doubts about the efficacy of the minerals sector as a development pole from which growth can spread and trickle down throughout the economy, given the socioeconomic and political conditions characteristic of many LDCs. Inevitably all those analysts who reject the idea that export-led development strategies can eventually reduce international welfare disparities also reject the idea that market forces will act to promote income convergence *within* each LDC. Inequality is regarded as an inevitable product of the capitalist system; the forces at work to keep Third World producers at the periphery of the international economic system also operate at the national scale to perpetuate the dual economy. In Tanzer's words,

> Within the capitalist world, not only is there vast inequality of wealth and income, but basic mechanisms exist to ensure that the gap between needs and resources, between poverty and opulence, both within and among countries, will not be bridged. Only a genuine social revolution within each country can make the rational use of its own resources possible. (Tanzer, 1980, p. 245)

The whole 'concentrated' investment strategy presupposes that the sectoral surplus is actually reinvested within the national economy to increase the rate of capital formation. As has been seen, there are undoubtedly economic processes operating within the international system, which can leak a significant proportion of the returns from investments in the mineral sector out of the producer states. But it is simplistic to attribute the continued lack of broadly based growth and widening welfare disparities solely to such processes. The conspicuous consumption of the new political élites, increased imports of western consumer goods and military equipment, funds siphoned off into safe overseas bank accounts and expenditure on prestigious, but low-yield, projects are all factors limiting the spread effects from the economic multiplier in many LDCs. As the case of Nigeria's dissipated oil revenues demonstrates clearly, economic mismanagement and the power of vested interests within nations can be as important in maintaining the dual economy as the operation of international capitalism *per se*.

EQUITY ISSUES IN THE ADVANCED ECONOMIES

The distributional effects of production and consumption decisions

Virtually all significant decisions in the minerals sector involve trade-offs between different interest groups and raise questions of distributive equity. There are four sets or divisions of the population over which the distribution of welfare can be an important political issue; class groups; distinct ethnic or cultural communities; those adhering to different value systems; and those located in different parts of the country. These sets are clearly interrelated; the most disadvantaged class groups may well be locationally concentrated, tend to belong to the same ethnic group and broadly adhere to one value system. But there is no absolute correspondence between them and particular problems arise when attempts to reduce inequalities within one of the sets merely act to increase disparities within another.

Decisions on *rates* of *mineral consumption* may involve conflict between, on the one hand, groups with strong economic interests in development and anxious to maintain levels of material growth, and on the other, those concerned with current levels of environmental pollution or with sustainable future lifestyles and intergenerational equity (see pp. 301–5). The choice of *production methods* may likewise affect environmental interests and can bring conflict between those whose prime aim is to achieve high rates of return on capital and those concerned to maintain employment levels. Conflict also arises over the *location* of production activity. Regions (or in a federal system the constituent states or provinces) frequently compete for development opportunities; in Australia, for instance, New South Wales and Queensland are both bidding to increase their share of the coal export market. Within regions, clashes of interest occur between individuals protecting their own particular localities from unsightly or polluting extractive industry (see pp. 380–2).

Similarly, decisions on the *mix* of energy or metals used to meet final demand inevitably involve a complex web of trade-offs between economic, environmental and regional interest groups. The price paid to ensure that the cheapest mineral sources are employed may well include increasing spatial inequalities as unemployment rises in traditional production centres. Increased levels of local unemployment may also result from attempts to reduce environmental pollution by accelerating the rate of investment in renewable energy, recycled minerals or conservation.

On the other hand, measures to reduce spatial inequalities by protecting established mineral producers from competition, or efforts to maintain environmental quality standards, could serve to exacerbate inequalities between class groups. This is particularly likely to be the case when such measures increase energy costs within an economy. It is now well established that expenditure on energy represents a much higher proportion of the total income of the poor than of the rich (see Table 4.2). Therefore, any moves which raise energy prices are 'akin to taxing a commodity which appears prominently in the budgets of the poor' (Webb and Ricketts, 1980, p. 4).

Table 4.2 United States: expenditure on energy by income group, 1972–3

Income status	Average income	Average annual consumption	Annual income spent on energy
	($)	(Million BTU*)	(%)
Poor	2,500	207	15.2
Lower middle	8,000	294	7.2
Upper middle	14,000	403	5.9
Well-off	24,500	478	4.1

* British Thermal Units, a measure of the heat value of fuels.

Source: Ford Foundation, 1974, Table 2b, p. 118, as given in Webb and Ricketts, 1980, p. 4.

The distribution of resource rents

Just as the allocation of the *economic rent* from mineral exploitation is a major international issue, so too it can be a matter of considerable controversy intranationally. Those living within producer regions frequently assert their right to the wealth generated by development. In addition to claims made in stark ownership terms, two basic equity arguments are employed to justify producer area demands. First, since minerals are exhaustible assets, it is only 'fair' that resource revenues should accrue to the level of government which will incur the socioeconomic burdens of depletion. And, second, equity is served when those bearing the costs of exploitation, in terms of infrastructure provision and environmental damage, receive the benefits. While national governments may concede that such arguments have some force, they normally appeal to the equality notion of equity and demand that the benefits accrue to all citizens.

Numerous examples of conflict over the allocation of resource rents could be cited. Scottish demands for a greater share of the oil revenues from developments in the northern part of the North Sea, featured strongly in the mid-1970s debate over the devolution of power to an Edinburgh-based Assembly, and were prominent in the national party's campaign for independence. In Australia the rival claims of state and central governments to sovereignty over offshore resources were the subject of a 1975 Supreme Court case, which eventually found in favour of the Australian government. Canada has, however, been the scene for some of the most protracted, politically contentious and constitutionally complex sets of disputes, involving both on- and offshore resources (Scott, 1975).

CONFLICT OVER RENT ALLOCATIONS: THE CANADIAN EXAMPLE

The individual Canadian provinces have undisputed jurisdiction over onshore resources and have clear rights to the revenue from royalties and provincial income or land taxes.[8] As oil royalties paid to Alberta and Saskatchewan escalated, particularly after the 1973 world oil price rise, so the widening gap between the revenues available to the individual provinces became a major political issue. One of the underlying principles of federation was the redistribution of income to ensure that all the member provinces could provide the same levels of basic services to their population. But the central exchequer found it increasingly difficult to fund, from its normal tax income, the programme of equalization grants designed to bring the revenue of the 'have-not' provinces up towards national average levels. The subsequent attempts to boost the national share of oil rents by taxing exports, and to maintain oil prices throughout Canada at below world levels, were seen as threats to the incomes and jurisdictional integrity of the oil-rich provinces. Although compromise financial and price arrangements have since been made, the fundamental and underlying battle over the allocation of oil rents remains unresolved (pp. 204–5).

Still further acrimonious conflicts have emerged over offshore mineral developments, where the division of jurisdictional responsibility between the two tiers of government has been far from clear. Canadian government claims to 'own', under international law, all mineral rights on the continental shelf have been vigorously disputed by the Maritime provinces. Negotiations over jurisdiction and the distribution of royalties have been going on since 1967, when the petroliferous potential of the Maritime offshore zone was widely recognized, and it seems likely that the disputes have delayed the exploration and exploitation of the area.

Only in 1977 did New Brunswick, Nova Scotia and Prince Edward Island eventually agree with the federal government to set aside their 'jurisdictional differences' and to share the royalties, 25 per cent going to the central exchequer and the rest to the provinces (Harrison, 1978). However, Newfoundland refused to sign the agreement and Nova Scotia withdrew its consent in 1978. Both provinces argued that as their equalization grants would be cut in line with any royalty payments they received, they would derive little or no direct benefits from offshore developments. Nova Scotia has since negotiated to receive a 100 per cent share of all royalties, until its revenue reaches national average levels, but in return it has surrendered its 'ownership' claims over offshore resources. Newfoundland refused to make a similar compromise arrangement, but the Supreme Court has recently upheld the Canadian government's jurisdictional claims. However, the conflict over the allocation of revenue continues. Politically it would be extremely difficult for the central government to deprive a 'have-not' province of a share of the royalty payments, when much wealthier areas were gaining considerable benefits from mineral exploitation.

Equity and pricing practices

Mineral pricing arrangements also raise questions of distributive equity, which deserve brief attention in this section of the chapter. Pricing equity has been relevant particularly for those energy resources which provide final consumer products. In the UK equity notions have been employed in the debate over electricity, gas and coal prices; in the United States gas prices have been regulated to ensure that they are 'just', 'reasonable' and 'non-discriminatory'; and in Canada, as in many other countries, it has been held to be 'unfair' to allow marked interregional variations in oil prices. Different pricing strategies can produce quite marked variations in the effective distribution of real income between consumer groups, but it is by no means unusual for the various elements in the tariff structure of a single industry to be justified using quite different equity concepts. Moreover, there are also conflicts between economically efficient pricing rules and widely held notions of equity.

Allocative efficiency requires that all consumers pay the marginal costs incurred in providing their supplies (see p. 125). This implies that there should be no cross-subsidy flows between consumers, although in practice this rule has to be relaxed to avoid the administrative burden involved in calculating all the individual cost contributions. To some, efficient prices would also be equitable since no one would be paying towards someone else's consumption. However, it is also commonly thought to be equitable if every user pays the same price for the same service or for the same amount of a good. As supply costs vary markedly between consumers, tariff structures based on the equal payment notion can involve major cross-subsidy flows and are, therefore, inefficient. However, prices set on either of these criteria would not necessarily allow low-income households to purchase the supplies they require, thus the idea that equity is served when consumers pay according to their ability is introduced into the 'appropriate' pricing policy debate.

Although the charging structures of public sector energy industries vary considerably from country to country, no (known) system within the advanced western economies adheres consistently to one pricing rule. Typically, tariff arrangements have evolved in a series of *ad hoc* adjustments to meet the equity demands of particular groups at particular periods of time, and different elements in the price structures are based, explicitly or implicitly, on all three criteria. Consumers taking supplies in bulk or at offpeak periods are normally charged lower per unit prices, on the ground that the provision costs are lower. However, it is commonly regarded as inequitable to levy differential charges on consumers living in different locations within large supply regions. As supply costs to dispersed rural settlements are almost invariably higher than those incurred by households living in densely populated urban areas, equal standard unit prices involve considerable cross-subsidy flows. Some of these may well result in the regressive redistribution of real income from the urban poor to the relatively affluent, living in low-density suburban developments or rural areas. On the other hand, in some countries attempts have been made to effect a progressive income redistribution, by adjusting the prices paid by low-income or small consumers. In most cases such arrangements have been introduced to ensure that the poorest groups in society can afford to heat their homes to tolerable levels.

In Eire, for instance, old-age pensioners in receipt of social security benefits have been exempted from standing electricity charges since 1967 and have also been given a free allowance to ensure that their basic heating requirements are met. By 1975 12 per cent of consumers were receiving benefits and the cost of over £2.5 million was recouped from other electricity users (Webb and Ricketts, 1980). Rather similar systems are used in Japan and California, where so-called *inverted* or *lifeline tariffs* were introduced in 1974 and 1975 respectively. No standing charges are levied and the unit price increases with consumption; therefore, the large user will normally subsidize the small. However, whether this achieves progressive income redistribution will depend on how closely consumption is related to income and wealth. It is certainly conceivable that a low-income family with young children, or any poor person living in a badly insulated house, could end up subsidizing a relatively well-off working couple who do not need to heat the house during the day.

The introduction of such systems in the United Kingdom has generally been resisted, primarily on the ground that it is inefficient to employ utility prices to achieve redistributive objectives; these are best met by direct transfers through taxation and welfare payments. In theory, at least, those in need can obtain additional supplementary benefits to pay for essential heating; but in 1982 it was estimated that less than one-half of those entitled to claim were actually doing so.

Moreover, it is somewhat inconsistent to reject the use of energy prices as tools for the progressive redistribution of welfare, when current charging arrangements already produce major cross-subsidy flows. It has to be recognized that every pricing structure produces different real income distributions, although remarkably little work has been done to trace the actual effects of alternative systems (Rees, 1981a).

National security objectives

THE HISTORY OF SECURITY CONCERNS

Concern over the security of essential raw material supplies is not a new phenomenon. The history of international trade is littered with examples of government interventions in the name of national security. Long before the Industrial Revolution the trading nations of Europe engaged in military and diplomatic activity to secure vital trade routes, and the whole process of colonial expansion was at least partially motivated by the economic advantages of ensuring access to plentiful, low-cost primary products. Throughout, security has been as much concerned with ensuring economic prosperity and protecting national economic interests as it has been with minimizing military or political threats. In fact there was such a close relationship between a country's economic strength and its military status that the two interests were assumed to be identical. It is significant, for example, that the prime instigator of the British government's pre First World War purchase of a majority interest in the Anglo-Persian Oil Co. (now BP) was Winston Churchill, then First Lord of the Admiralty. As Hartshorn (1962, p. 233) puts it, this 'represented the first open manifestation of the vital interest to the government of a country lacking indigenous oil supplies of securing a source of supply that it recognized as strategically vital'.

For the countries of western Europe security was seen to require the maintenance of free access to low-cost overseas supplies and the protection of trade routes. On the other hand, the Soviet government reacted to its security problem in quite a different way. After the trade and financial boycott of Russia which followed the revolution, the security of the country – and of communism itself – came to mean avoiding dependence on foreign imports and foreign markets; mineral self-sufficiency became, and has since remained, a central tenet of Soviet minerals policy (see pp. 65–7). Both of these 'security' strategies involved costs. The Soviets lost flexibility and the advantages of being able to utilize whichever supply source was least cost at different periods of time, while European reliance on imports involved both the risk of trade disruption and exposed the economy to the notoriously unstable prices which characterized the markets of many of the internationally traded minerals. Only the United States was in the enviable position, until the 1940s, of not having to trade off the economic gains from imports against the disadvantages of greater vulnerability. It was a relatively low-cost producer, virtually self-sufficient in the then essential minerals, and with no import significant enough for supply restrictions or price rises to have an appreciable impact on the economy (Ridker and Watson, 1980).

TRADE DISRUPTIONS AND APPROPRIATE RESPONSES

Inevitably countries relying on imports to meet their mineral requirements are vulnerable to all sorts of trade disruptions. Strikes by seamen and dockers, civil disturbance or miners' strikes in the production centres, closure of key trade routes, civil and international wars and the nationalization of supply sources – all could create potential shortage problems. It is worth pointing out that nationalization need not, of itself, disrupt trade flows if acceptable bargains are struck over compensation payments, service contracts, tax and price levels. For example, the government take-over of a 51 per cent interest in the Zambian copper mines in 1969 did not affect supplies; in fact the foreign companies kept effective control over production. However, for many consumer states national security is not solely a question of maintaining a fairly stable flow of imports, but also involves control over the supply source and the maintenance of low raw material prices. Therefore, nationalization is often interpreted as a security threat, as are LDC attempts to increase export taxes, form producer cartels, or withhold supplies to force up prices. In order to unravel some of the often confused debate over security it is useful to consider potential shortage risks in terms of distinct time horizons.

Short-term disruptions and stockpiling

First, there is the problem of *short-term* trade disruptions lasting a few weeks or months. These have normally been circumvented by maintaining stockpiles, and on occasion, particularly for the energy minerals, by curbing consumer demands.[9]

Governments in the major industrial nations have for long held emergency reserves of strategic minerals. In the United States stockpiles were established under the 1946 *Strategic and Materials Stockpiling Act*; these could not be run down past a target figure, except in times of military emergency. However, any stocks above this baseline could be used to cope with peacetime disruptions and, as Klass *et al.* (1980, p. 14) very tactfully put it, 'at times surplus strategic stocks have been disposed of in a manner which seems at least partly motivated by a drive to stabilize prices'. In addition, as part of normal business practice, private and public sector industries will hold inventories of the minerals essential to their own production process, and the multinational mineral corporations also normally carry considerable stocks of the minerals in which they trade. Since the 1950s most consumer nations have held stockpiles to cover between six and twelve months' consumption, and from 1976 the US government alone (excluding private stocks) has aimed to hold stocks of ninety-three strategic materials against a three-year military emergency (see ibid.).

Stockpiling is not, of course, a costless activity. The administrative and storage expenses are considerable, but they are dwarfed by the opportunity cost of the tied-up capital; the market value of the US government stocks exceeded $9000 million in 1978. It does, however, mean that any attempts by producers to deliberately withhold supplies has to be extremely long-lasting before the effects begin to bite. Moreover, the very existence of such substantial stocks may well deter the use of the embargo strategy. A further advantage is that governments have been able to use their stock purchases and sales to manipulate – or from another viewpoint bring stability to – mineral markets.

Medium-term disruptions and source diversification

If an economy becomes dependent on one particular supply source there is a danger of medium-term trade disruptions since it could take a number of years to develop replacement supply sources or substitute materials or alternative consumption patterns. In the meantime essential needs would have to be purchased on the open market, at probably much-inflated price levels. The economic effects would vary markedly from case to case, being most severe when demands for the affected mineral were already outstripping output capacity, when few supplies in excess of contract or tied commitments were available and when the dependent economy's demands were large relative to the world total.

One such emergency occurred in 1951 when the Mossadegh government of Iran nationalized the Anglo-Iranian Oil Co. (later BP), in which the British government was a majority shareholder. The loss of crude and, even more crucially, the Abadan refinery meant that Britain experienced a 75 per cent supply cut overnight, at a time when fuel was still in short supply. This shortfall could only be made good at a price and, significantly, this price had now to be paid in US dollars rather than sterling, so adding £300 million a year to the import bill, with major consequences for the trade balance and the domestic cost of living. The immediate reaction to the crisis was to use every means possible to restore the company to its former position, short of taking direct military action which carried the danger of Soviet intervention. Iranian exports were boycotted by virtually all the oil companies,[10] the tanker fleet was withdrawn and intense diplomatic pressure was exerted on any government likely to purchase Iranian oil; and eventually, according to Wise and Ross (1964, p. 110), 'the CIA organized and directed the 1953 coup that overthrew Premier Mohammed Mossadegh'. After the demise of Mossadegh, the shah 'invited' the foreign oil firms back, with all the major companies taking shares in a new Iranian production corporation.

This attempt to stem the rising tide of nationalism in the less developed producer states and to maintain the status quo against their demands for more control over, and a greater share of the returns from, their mineral deposits was by no means the last. However, as an effective response to security problems it was much less significant than the second reaction to the Iranian crisis, which was to begin in earnest the process of supply source diversification. The oil multinationals widened the spatial spread of their exploration activity, attempted to reduce the proportion of crude derived from any one country and, very important, shifted the location of refining capacity away from the producer states. Likewise the metal corporations became increasingly concerned to minimize the risks to their capital investments and the costs of disruption to their downstream processing activities. Eventually, as we have seen, continued political unrest and the rise of 'hostile' governments throughout the Third World pushed a much larger proportion of available investment capital into the safer advanced industrial economies.

Source diversification meant that the security risks involved in import dependence became relatively minor for the consumer nations. Import patterns could be rearranged with comparative ease, temporary shortages of supply could be covered by stockpiles and the price effects of trade disruptions tended to be short-lived. Even in 1967 when the oil-importing countries were hit by a double crisis, the Nigerian civil war and the six-day Arab-Israeli war, it was possible to avoid significant supply shortages. In June 1967 Britain was taking 70 per cent of its oil from Arab states and a further 10 per cent from Nigeria. Just two months later Iran, which had previously contributed less than 5 per cent, was supplying 62 per cent and the United States (previously 1 per cent) a further 19 per cent. Demand constraints never become necessary and shortages on the spot market only produced a price hiccup.

As long as the producers remained isolated from one another and were willing indeed eager to fill the gap created by the loss of one source, and were critically dependent on mineral exports as sources of capital and foreign exchange, then medium-term trade disruptions did not occur. This position was perceived to have changed dramatically in 1973.

Longer-term security threats

However, there is a third mineral security problem, which involves a much longer-term time horizon. In fact there are two quite distinct concerns here: first, the fear that at least some minerals will become scarce on a world scale in an absolute physical sense; and second, that the balance of known reserves is shifting away from the advanced capitalist nations of the west towards the Soviet bloc and the Third World countries. Neither of these is a new problem, although they clearly achieved much greater salience in the debate over appropriate mineral policies during the early 1970s. It is important that the two issues are kept distinct since they imply quite different policy strategies.

If worldwide physical exhaustion is the perceived problem, then a solution could involve reducing consumption by conservation, following a no-growth development strategy and changing lifestyles, investing heavily in renewable resources and encouraging technological innovation to allow previously un- or underutilized materials to become substitute inputs into production. On the other hand, if the problem is not exhaustion but the distribution of low-cost supplies or reserves in the world economy, then it has been common to regard it as essential for the advanced capitalist nations to retain their economic and military strength by ensuring access to and control over foreign supply sources. Frequently this last view has been linked with the conservation of domestic reserves to ensure their future availability. In other words, the idea boils down to 'let's keep our own resources intact and use other people's while we can'!

Security and economic interests

When discussing arguments over mineral security, it is impossible to divorce people's positions on national security from their economic and political interests (Odell, 1970; Tanzer, 1969). Like equity, security has been used to justify and legitimate actions and demands which in reality stem from quite different motivations. One set of economic interests is clearly served by a strategy which maintains the import of low-cost minerals. Manufacturers concerned with the competitiveness of their products, shipping companies and road hauliers, and the mineral multinationals themselves, all combine with those genuinely seeking to reduce domestic living costs. Another set of interests associates security with import dependence and demands protection and subsidies for home producers; domestic oil firms and both employers and workers in the coal, nuclear power and steel industries clearly come into this category. Further economic interest groups benefit from investments in conservation measures, technological innovation and renewable resources.

Exactly which of the conflicting long-term security strategies becomes accepted government policy at different points in time depends on a complex set of factors. Among them, the balance of power between interest groups and prevailing political or socioeconomic circumstances are at least as important as – indeed probably much more important than – the real mineral trade and reserves position. Immediately after the Second World War, minerals were generally in short supply, domestic producers were little affected by overseas competition and the emphasis was on securing access to foreign supply sources. On balance this emphasis remained the dominant one in virtually all the advanced economies, at least until the early 1970s. As Odell (1970, p. 176) has argued in the case of oil, 'strategic concern over oil quickly tends to evaporate because of the substantial economic gains to be made from keeping the oil flowing'. What he means by this is that dependency fears are eclipsed by the economic interests favouring trade. But the strategic arguments are much wider than dependency.

From one viewpoint it is in a country's strategic interest to expand foreign investments not only to gain control over low-cost material supplies, but also to maintain a strong economic presence in politically sensitive areas. In the United States, in particular, a strong body of opinion regarded it as crucial economically to expand into key LDC economies, to contain the spread of communism and limit the Soviet sphere of influence. In other words, 'keeping the oil flowing' from the Arab states and Iran to the west was not only important for economic prosperity, but was also vital politically in order to deny the Soviets access to the oil and foil their expansionist tendencies. It is this apparent symbiosis between political and economic interests which has been so crucial. The view that the security interests of the United States were identical to those of the US oil companies was clearly expressed in a statement made in 1965 by Andrew Ensor, the then director of the Office of Fuels and Energy in the State Department: 'a healthy oil industry overseas is as vital to the United States security as a sound domestic industry' (quoted in Tanzer, 1969, p. 54).

This is not to say that the interest groups which see import dependence as a strategic concern and favour the protection of domestic production have not been without influence. In the United States, for example, oil imports exceeded exports for the first time in 1948 and low-cost Middle Eastern oil started to make considerable inroads into the domestic market. The influential home producers' lobby was quick to raise the spectre of import dependence and eventually succeeded in getting voluntary and then, in 1959, mandatory quotas imposed on imports (Odell, 1970). This action was taken at a time when crude was in surplus, and when the producer states were divided and critically dependent on their export earnings. Realistically, then, imports presented few security threats. Similarly, in Western Europe a whole range of measures have been introduced to restrict imports, protect indigenous coal and nuclear industries, encourage the exploration of new domestic mineral sources and subsidize the development of domestic refinery capacity. National security and the need to avoid import dependence was invariably one of the arguments used in favour of their introduction. To give one example: Britain banned Soviet oil imports in 1962, a major justification for this being that oil could be used as a political weapon to create dependence and undermine the economies of Western Europe. However, the measure was not unrelated to the financial interests of Shell and British Petroleum, or the need at that time to avoid further unemployment in the coalmining regions.

SECURITY ISSUES AND THE 1973 OIL CRISIS

In the early 1970s several events conspired to bring the whole question of mineral security to the forefront of political attention. First, in 1971 the United States moved once again into oil deficit and oil imports began to rise sharply. Second, Libya and then the other OPEC countries achieved a 50 per cent increase in world oil prices between 1970 and 1972. Third, beginning in late 1972, both agricultural and mineral prices started to rise rapidly, so that most had increased over 200 per cent by mid-1974. Finally, but of greatest importance, in retaliation for the resupplying of Israel with arms during the October 1973 war, the Arab producers cut output by 25 per cent, and placed an embargo on sales to the United States and other 'unfriendly nations', including Japan, Britain and France. It was recognized that such an embargo was largely unenforceable, given the international character of the oil business, and the panic it created on the 'marginal' spot markets exceeded all Arab expectations. The panic-buying clearly demonstrated that the consumers would bear much higher price levels and the rest of OPEC followed Iran in, first, doubling prices, and then doubling them again three months later. Together these events led to the common belief that a drastic change in the balance of power had occurred between the industrial nations and the Third World.

The success of OPEC was regarded by many as merely the beginning. It was feared that similar demands from other mineral producers, acting unilaterally or in collusive cartels, would follow (Bergsten, 1974). Such views appeared vindicated by the price increases announced by the Moroccan government's phosphate agency,[11] which totalled 400 per cent over the nine months prior to July

1974, and by Jamaica's fivefold increase in bauxite taxes in June 1974. The fears raised by the situation inevitably brought a crop of hardline proposals such as military invasion of the oilfields (Tucker, 1975), or 'breaking' OPEC and similar cartels by placing embargoes on food and manufactured goods. But the most commonly suggested solution was to retreat as rapidly as possible from import dependence.

For almost a decade US government thinking was pervaded by the view that 'oil imports must be reduced though aggressive conservation efforts and realistic energy prices . . . domestic energy resources must be developed and used to the fullest extent possible' (Sawhill, 1981, p. xvi, Deputy Secretary of the US Department of Energy). President Nixon's Project Independence aimed to eliminate oil imports by 1980; President Carter's ill-fated 1977 Energy Plan was somewhat less ambitious, seeking to reduce 1985 imports to 6 million barrels per day (mbd) from the then current 8.6 mbd and well below the 16 mbd forecast level. Likewise, the deregulation of energy prices has been an important element in the fall in US oil demands and imports since 1980.

Similar ideas were also present in Japan's ambitious programme of investments in nuclear and renewable energy sources, including Project Sunshine, which emphasized the development of solar, geothermal and coal conversion technologies; and in Britain's plans for nuclear and coal to replace oil when indigenous sources are depleted. It was recognized that all such measures would take time to implement. In the meantime short-term embargoes were to be covered by increased stockpiles and 'unreasonable market pressures and supply interruptions' were to be countered by, on the one hand, a 'dialogue' with the producer states,[12] and on the other, by the development of collective contingency plans by the major consuming nations.

Inevitably the bulk of the policy prescriptions focused on the energy question, but it was commonly argued that similar measures would be required to reduce dependence on other minerals. Recently the notion that the Soviet Union is conducting an undeclared 'resource war' against the west has been added to the perceived threat from Third World producers. Soviet moves to increase their purchases of critical metallic minerals, together with their 1980 decision to stop the export of titanium, have been used as evidence to support the claim that deliberate efforts are being made to jeopardize western supplies of the minerals needed for high-technology products such as computers and military aircraft. These claims have been employed by US politicians and officials, including the then Interior Secretary, Mr James Watt, to justify the opening up of federal lands for exploration by mining companies (*Nature*, 11 June 1981, p. 444).

THE REALITY OF SECURITY THREATS

Before considering in Chapter 5 the adequacy of actual policy responses to short-, medium- and long-term scarcity issues, it is important to attempt to penetrate beneath the fears, and the rhetoric of vested interests, to investigate the real extent to which the security of the advanced economies is threatened. Insecurity cannot be proven merely by showing that a significant proportion of current supplies is imported. It is true that international trade, by its very nature, increases the probability of short-term disruptions simply because the range of potential problems is greater. But self-sufficiency is no guarantee of freedom from disruption, as the effects in Britain of the 1972–4 coalminers' strikes and overtime bans amply testify. Since short-duration trade cuts can be – and in the advanced world are – met by stockpiles, actual security problems arise only from medium- and long-term shortages and from significant real price rises. The probability of these occurring is dependent on the extent to which producer states can achieve market power and are then willing and able to use it.

In all, seven key factors determine the potential acquisition and use of market power, among which import dependence is but one. The others are:

(1) the extent to which current production and reserves are spatially concentrated in just a few countries;
(2) the political affiliation of the major suppliers, or of their political élites, and their dependence on the political and military support of the advanced capitalist nations;
(3) the dependence of the producers on mineral exports as a source of capital and foreign exchange;
(4) the dependence of producers on the capital, technology, or manufactures of the consumer states;
(5) the cost and availability of substitute materials, which will affect the price elasticity of demand for the affected mineral;
(6) the 'essentiality' of a particular mineral product to the economy of the consumer states (see Arad *et al.*, 1979).[13]

In the very long run scarcity of some mineral stocks will inevitably occur but import controls and the concentration on home production are, at best, only a partial solution to these problems. In fact they could merely serve to accelerate domestic depletion rates, unless accompanied by reductions in growth and consumption levels and by technological change to allow renewable resource use.

The effective power of individual non-fuel mineral producers

The potential for an *individual* mineral-producing country to gain significant power in a dependent market is relatively small. Table 4.3 lists the non-fuel minerals in which the United States, Western Europe and Japan are import dependent to a substantial degree; clearly, the United States is dependent on a much smaller number of minerals than are the European or Japanese economies. For five of these minerals, bauxite, copper, iron ore, tin and tungsten, the spread of producers means that supply security problems would only occur if an effective cartel was formed (see pp. 170–2). In the tungsten case, however, there could possibly be a long-term (beyond the year 2010) supply risk since nearly 70 per cent of known reserves are thought to be in communist countries (Ridker and Watson, 1980). For a further four metals, lead, nickel, uranium and zinc, a high proportion of production and reserves is concentrated in the United States, Canada and Australia. Although Canada and Australia have both supported actions designed to raise mineral prices, the probability is slight that they will

Table 4.3 Import dependence and the supply security risk: the USA, Western Europe and Japan

	Four major producing countries, 1982	% of world output contribution by countries, 1982	Difficulty of substitution ‡	Economic importance ‡
Bauxite	Australia, Guinea, Jamaica, USSR	63.7 (Australia 29.5)	6	6
Chromium	USSR, South Africa, Albania, Turkey	78.3	6	1
Cobalt	Zaire, USSR, Zambia, Cuba	76.5 (Zaire 55)	5	1
Copper*	Chile, USA, USSR, Canada	52.6	5	6
Iron ore*	USSR, Brazil, Australia, China	64.1 (USSR 31.2)	8	10
Lead*	USSR, USA, Australia, Canada	52.9	5	1
Manganese	USSR, South Africa, Brazil, China	75.7 (USSR 39.2)	7	1
Mercury	USSR, Spain, USA, China	76.1	2	1
Nickel	USSR, Australia, Canada, New Caledonia	66.3	4	2
Phosphates*	USA, USSR, Morocco, China	75.6	4	3
Platinum	USSR, South Africa, Canada (others minor)	98.7 (USSR and South Africa 94.4)	8	1
Tin	Malaysia, Indonesia, Thailand, USSR	62.4 (Malaysia 21.6)	3	1
Tungsten	China, USSR, Canada, Australia	58.7 (China 27.2)	7	1
Uranium†	USA, Canada, South Africa, Australia	70.5	2	1
Zinc*	Canada, USSR, Australia, USA	34.5	2	1

* Minerals in which Western Europe and Japan are import-dependent but the United States is not.

† Excludes data for Soviet Union.

‡ These are crude scales 1–10, 10 being the most difficult to substitute, or of the most economic importance. The economic importance refers to a combination of the essential nature of the mineral end-uses and the effect of any major price rises on the economy.

Sources: ABMS, 1983; UK Iron and Steel Statistics Bureau, 1983; BGS, 1984; Klass *et al.*, 1980; Arad *et al.*, 1979.

either deliberately withhold supplies or demand such massive price rises that their actions will affect significantly the other advanced capitalist nations. Their economies are simply too intertwined with those of the import-dependent countries. This does not mean that occasional supply restrictions will not occur; the 1969 nickel-miners' strike in Canada did cause shortages in the United States, but such events can be covered by stockpiles and cannot be regarded as major security risks.

That leaves six minerals in which the independent action of a single producer could potentially affect import supplies and prices. However, effective monopoly power requires that there are no close substitutes in the major end-uses and that demand is price-inelastic. If these conditions do not hold, the producer would not gain from aggressive supply restrictions or price rises. This would appear to rule out both mercury and phosphates as major risks. Mercury demand is already on a declining trend, and

> acceptable alternatives are now known for all major uses of mercury, except possibly for high performance electric batteries. . . . For minor uses, such as pharmaceuticals or laboratory uses, which amount to less than 1 to 5 percent each of the total, alternatives have not been sought very seriously because the amount of mercury is small. We can hardly imagine society collapsing or even being impeded . . . if we have to do without mercurial pharmaceuticals or mercury batteries. (Goeller and Weinburg, 1976, quoted in Ridker and Watson, 1980, p. 152)

There are also substitutes for phosphates, 80 per cent of which are used in fertilizers. Although decreased supplies and increased prices would have important knock-on effects in agriculture, the freedom of action of the major producer, Morocco, is circumscribed by what the market will bear. Demands appear elastic and certainly fell dramatically after the 1974 price hike.

The platinum/palladium group of metals present an unusual case. Imports are heavily dependent on South Africa and the Soviet Union, an unholy alliance which appears to tacitly collude over the supply and price of the metals, as it also does over gold and diamonds. Platinum is important in industry, particularly in catalytic and electrical uses, but these involve small quantities and demand in most other end-uses appears moderately price-elastic. Moreover, its high value makes it virtually 100 per cent recyclable, and old metal stocks would be more than adequate to meet essential needs. However, it is also a *speculation* mineral, which raises the possibility that considerable price rises could be achieved if it acquired still greater scarcity value. On the other hand, the attempt by the Soviet Union to double the selling price of palladium in 1974 merely resulted in large sales from inventories which depressed prices (Klass *et al.*, 1980). Overall most commentators conclude that dependence on South Africa and the Soviet Union is a risk but that supply restrictions or major price rises would not materially affect the industrial prosperity of the major consumers.

Manganese is an essential input into steelmaking and the demand is highly price-inelastic. However, it cannot be regarded as a security risk mineral for three main reasons. First, manganese contributes less than 0.4 per cent to the cost of finished steel, therefore very large price increases would have an imperceptible effect on the price of final consumer goods. Second, any major price rise would give resource value to the ores containing less than 35 per cent metal, which currently do not count in reserve calculations. The United States alone has known deposits of these low-grade ores to cover the current level of demand for sixty years, and other known supplies are widely distributed throughout the world. Finally, deep-sea manganese nodules could provide a massive new supply source in the long run. Few events would resolve the international disputes over the allocation of sea-bed exploitation rights more quickly than the loss of South African supplies to the world market.[14] The possibility of supply disruptions affecting output before these alternatives could be developed is covered by the size of existing stockpiles. In the United States government stocks alone cover two and a half years' consumption at current rates.

The dominant position of Zaire as a producer of cobalt – it contributes nearly 70 per cent to non-communist world supplies – suggests that this may be a major risk mineral. A deliberate supply embargo seems highly unlikely, given the dependence of the country on its export income, but there is a clear danger that political events could stop production. However, cobalt is crucial to few industrial processes, reasonable substitutes are already available for most end-uses and deposits of subeconomic ores are known to be widespread, including those in ocean nodules (Klass *et al.*, 1980; Ridker and Watson, 1980). Stockpiles already exist to cover between one to three years' consumption but medium-term shortages could occur if new supply source development and substitution cannot take place in this time. Overall it is difficult to envisage that these possible medium-term shortages could have a profound effect on the economies of the industrialized nations.

The final mineral for which supplies from one country are sufficiently high to cause potential problems is chromium. Current imports are predominantly derived from the Soviet Union, South Africa and Zimbabwe, with known reserves seemingly concentrated in the last two countries. The economic consequences from the loss of Zimbabwe's output alone would not be severe, as the admittedly rather ineffective United Nations embargo at the time of UDI shows. Problems could arise, however, if the Soviet Union, or the two African countries together, withdrew from the world market. The metal is widely employed as a stainless-steel alloy and for some end-uses there are no adequate substitutes. Short-term shortages are highly unlikely because the risks of import dependence have long been recognized and relatively large stockpiles accumulated. Approximately four years' supply is held in the United States, and in most other industrial nations stocks normally cover at least two years' consumption. Medium-term scarcity is, however, a distinct possibility. Whether this constitutes a significant economic threat is doubtful since demand appears sufficiently flexible to release the supplies needed for essential purposes. It has been suggested that the risks are great enough to warrant immediate attempts to convert to the use of substitutes, but in a major report for the US Department of Commerce, Charles River Associates concluded that 'a more efficient policy would be to ensure more post-disruption adjustment time by means of a larger stockpile, and to begin converting to substitutes only after a serious disruption in chromium supply develops' (Klass *et al.*, 1980, p. 164).

Producer cartels: is OPEC the model?

We return now to those non-fuel minerals for which import dependence is only a risk if effective cartels can be formed. The key question is whether the OPEC experience provides a generally applicable model of what may be expected. With some reservations (see Tilton, 1977), most serious analysts have concluded that the probability is slight that other producer cartels could either achieve the same market power as OPEC or create anything like the economic impact if they did. There are four major reasons for this view.

First, there are too many producers, with far too heterogeneous political and economic interests, for agreements on prices and market shares to be concluded and, even more crucially, maintained over time. Certainly, this appears to be the case for iron ore, where the sheer number of countries with known reserves is a major barrier to effective action. The Iron Ore Exporters' Association (IOEA),[15] formed in 1975, omitted such major producers as Canada, the United States, Brazil and Liberia. Therefore, its ability to push up, or even stabilize, prices critically depended on the reaction of these 'outsiders'. Although outsider companies frequently follow a cartel-induced price rise in order to obtain a short-term revenue advantage, such prices cannot hold unless output restrictions maintain the balance between supply and demand. The capital-intensive nature of mining means that output cuts produce few cost savings; therefore, at times of surplus capacity there is always an incentive to maintain production levels. In these circumstances the IOEA has considerable difficulty in controlling the sales even of its own members, and no hope at all of stopping existing or new non-cartel producers from entering the export markets.

This also clearly applies in the bauxite case. Brazil, a relatively small producer in 1974, remained outside the International Bauxite Association and subsequently became by far the fastest-growing centre of production. In just five years, 1976–81, output rose from 83.2 to 559.5 thousand metric tons per month, to make the country the fourth largest producer after Australia, Guinea and Jamaica, and well ahead of Guyana and Surinam, who saw their output fall absolutely over the same period. It is also significant that the market share of the copper producers' cartel, CIPEC, has actually fallen since its formation, as investment has been concentrated in less 'hostile' countries (Mezger, 1980).

Even when an emerging producer is rapidly incorporated within the cartel, the internal cohesion is considerably weakened by the difficulty involved in reconciling the demands of the established producers to maintain the existing status quo, with the needs of countries with newly developed capacity to actually achieve a reasonable market share.

Some commentators have stressed the role of differences in political ideology as a major factor in weakening producer cartels. But this point cannot be pressed too far. As Tilton (1977, pp. 85–6) has pointed out, the Soviet Union and South Africa do co-operate when their mutual economic interests are involved: 'Similarly, despite its ideological commitment to free markets, the United States under the Webb–Pomerene Act allows its mineral producers to participate in cartels as long as only foreign markets are affected.' It does, however, seem likely that advanced capitalist countries may act as a moderating force within a cartel; certainly, Australia is usually thought to act in this way within the International Bauxite Association.

The second common reason for doubting whether effective cartels can be formed for the non-fuel minerals is the dependence of the LDC producers. Their need for investment capital and foreign exchange limits their potential to sustain sales cuts for significant periods of time. Even if per unit export prices were raised by output restrictions, the economic advantages of cheating the cartel and selling more at the increased prices may be irresistible. The long established International Tin Council has had problems with members openly disregarding their export quotas, and in preventing smuggling from member states. For example, Burma, a non-ITC country, has frequently had annual export sales up to five times higher than its total production! The only explanation for this is large-scale smuggling from Thailand to circumvent its export quota.

Dependence on the western advanced economies for technology, aid, investment capital or manufactured goods may also constrain the willingness of LDC producers to agree to aggressive price or supply control measures since they are exceptionally vulnerable to any retaliatory actions taken by consumer governments or the mineral multinationals. A further element in the dependency argument is that the political élites in some LDCs rely on the economic and military support of the west to maintain their internal power base. The shah's position in pre-revolutionary Iran, Mobutu's regime in Zaire and the Pinochet junta in Chile are but three illustrations of this. To retain the necessary foreign support such regimes cannot, it is argued, afford to go against the interests of international capital. According to Mezger (1980, p. 212), describing Chile under Pinochet, their economies become 'a model of national expropriation to the benefit of foreign capital . . . which is supported by a section of the local bourgeoisie and made possible by the internal state of siege'. However, this point should not be pushed too far; it is worth remembering that the first government to demand the over-400 per cent oil price rise in 1973 was in fact Iran under the shah.

The third reason why non-fuel cartels seem unlikely to gain much effective power is the nature of metal markets. Although short-run demand elasticity is slight, in the medium and longer term it is considerable. New metal not only faces competition from secondary sources, but there are few major metal end-uses for which there are no adequate, already available, substitutes. Copper and tin producers have already seen major penetration into their traditional markets; price increases, therefore, have to be broadly in line with those of the substitute to avoid further losses. In the same way, the embryo tungsten cartel is faced by a wide range of substitutes in virtually all its end-uses.

Finally, the effectiveness of non-fuel mineral cartels is now limited by the measures already taken to curtail their power. As shown in Chapter 3, the multinationals have acted to spread their risks; have focused their investments in safe areas; and have embarked on technological research to allow the use of subeconomic deposits and new widely available materials. Moreover, they have seemingly been prepared to counter cartel attempts to increase prices by direct manipulation of market prices. The fact that metal prices actually fell in 1974 following CIPEC's announcement of a 10 per cent export cut appears to indicate that the companies, and/or possibly the US government, released stocks as a countermeasure. This ability to manipulate prices partly arises from the marginal nature of many markets, and is also helped by the comparative ease with which ores can be stored.

Overall there is little evidence to suggest that the import of non-fuel minerals represents a threat to the economic security of the advanced capitalist nations, or that there has been a shift of commodity power towards Third World producer states. Rather the reverse appears true. Continued LDC dependence on the resource trade makes them extremely vulnerable to changes in the international economy, as the effects of the 1980s economic recession amply demonstrate. Moreover, the private risk avoidance strategies employed by the mineral corporations appear to be ensuring that resource power remains firmly in the hands of the north.

OIL SECURITY

The oil problem stands in a category of its own. Despite over a decade of adjustments to reduce import dependence, most countries of the world – advanced and LDC alike – are still vulnerable to OPEC's supply and pricing decisions and to political upheavals in the Persian Gulf. However, many analysts now take the view that conditions in the 1980s' world oil market are such that policies designed to further decrease imports are of questionable value, at least for the advanced nations.

One school of thought argues that the trend away from oil as an energy source has become firmly entrenched in the economic system. Therefore, when the world finally moves out of recession the real demand trend, adjusted for increased industrial output, will continue downwards. Support for this view is taken from the major slump in oil demand which has occurred, particularly since 1980. World demand fell by 17 per cent between 1980 and 1982 and, despite falling dollar oil prices[16], has subsequently failed to revive. Even more significantly US imports, which were some 8.5 mbd in 1980, have plunged to just over 3 mbd in early 1984. Rosing and Odell (1983, p. 27) further argue that the established moves towards conservation and oil substitution will continue to be reinforced by the maintenance of oil prices above competitive levels: 'The interests of so many powerful nations and other groups are now so tied up with present oil prices that prices seem almost certain to be higher in the short to medium term than they need be.' It is thus projected that oil's contribution to world energy supplies will fall from 46 per cent in 1980 to about 37.5 per cent by 2010 (assuming an overall energy demand growth of 2.2 per cent per annum in the 1980s, increasing to 2.5 per cent after the year 2000) (ibid., p. 33).

Another group of commentators base the argument that import dependence is a declining threat on the belief that OPEC's resource power is crumbling, in which case it will not be able to maintain cartel cohesion in the future (Brown, 1981; Singer and Stamas, 1982; Goldstein, 1983). Certainly, by early 1982 it became clear that the continued demand falls were reducing OPEC's ability to maintain official prices. Both Nigeria and Iran were openly selling at $1 and $4 respectively below agreed price levels, and Iran was reported to have concluded a covert deal with a West German company at $25 a barrel, a 25 per cent discount on official prices (*Sunday Times* 28 February 1982). Oil prices have fallen from the 1981 peak of $34 to under $29 in late 1984, and a number of serious commentators are predicting further falls in 1985 to $20 a barrel. Moreover, Nigeria had switched from being a net lender to the international banks of $2200 million in 1981 to a net borrower of $2300 million only a year later, and OPEC as a whole has since moved into a balance-of-payments deficit. It has become the conventional wisdom that the need for foreign exchange and capital will make it difficult for the cartel to maintain its production ceilings; the individual members have too great an incentive to make short-run revenue gains by exceeding their export quotas.

Even if OPEC can maintain cohesion, there seems little doubt that its effective power to control oil markets has declined. Its relative contribution to world production has fallen markedly (see Table 3.4, p. 87), and the output of new non-OPEC producers, such as Britain, Mexico and Norway, now exceeds that of cartel members. Consumers would increasingly switch to these sources unless OPEC moderated its demands. Odell has gone so far as predicting that changing patterns of energy demand, coupled with the growth of new supply sources, threaten to cut away the markets for Persian Gulf oil by 1990. He suggested that new regional groups like Western Europe and North Africa, and eastern and south-eastern Asia, would club together to form energy self-sufficient zones, leaving oil surplus areas such as the Gulf on the outside, serving only to meet fluctuating marginal needs (*Observer*, 4 August 1982).

It is, therefore, no longer in OPEC's interest to take aggressive measures against the major consumers. Rather, the reverse appears to be the case. Not only will the returns made on the now considerable Arab investments overseas depend upon the economic health of the advanced western nations, but oil revenues will depend on restored consumer confidence in oil generally, and in OPEC oil in particular. The Gulf Arab states, led by Saudi Arabia, have clearly shown that their economic (and political) interests are best served by ensuring the stability of the oil export trade and by keeping their prices competitive. During the protracted Iran–Iraq war attempts have been made to keep open the Strait of Hormuz; Saudi Arabia has built up a floating crude oil stockpile to limit the effects of any closure or damage to oil installations; and all the Gulf states have agreed to compensate buyers of oil shipped from their ports for any oil lost in attacks on tankers. This last move follows the sharp increase in insurance rates for tankers entering the war zone, which has increased the effective price of Gulf oil (*Financial Times*, 12 June 1984). All these measures suggest that OPEC's economic interests are now largely thought to coincide with the consumer nations' interest in supply security.

Only time will tell whether these changes in world oil markets will in fact prevent a repetition of the 1973 and 1979 crises. There must always be short- and even medium-term security risks while the notoriously politically unstable Persian Gulf area remains an important exporting centre. Yet another Arab-Israeli war or revolution in Saudi Arabia could once again produce tumult in the oil markets.

CONCLUSION

In this chapter an attempt has been made to establish the extent to which the minerals sector operates in line with four possible public policy objectives: economic efficiency, economic growth, distributive equity and supply security. There seems little doubt that the conditions under which the current production and exchange system operates do not even approximate to those required for the efficient allocation of resources over space and time. Likewise when its performance is judged against most widely accepted notions of equity, the minerals sector does not provide for an equitable distribution of resource consumption, economic development or generated wealth. Even within the advanced capitalist nations important equity issues are raised by the operations of the mineral industries, but it is at the global and intra-LDC scales that the most serious problems of distributive equity arise. The minerals development and exchange process has conspicuously failed to help reduce spatial welfare inequalities, and many would argue that it has played a key role in exacerbating them. Since in large measure the equity aspirations of the LDCs are seen to conflict with the supply security objectives of the advanced capitalist economies, it is perhaps not surprising that the minerals sector performs best when judged against this last policy objective.

There is nothing immutable about the current patterns of mineral exploitation and consumption, nor about the present distribution of the economic growth, income and social welfare derived from minerals. If the minerals sector fails to perform in line with public policy objectives, it is conceptually possible to devise a whole range of policy measures to 'correct' the perceived deficiencies. However, in market economies which are deeply embroiled in the international capitalist system this task of correction is by no means a trivial one. The forces at work to produce the present development and distributive patterns are complex and the resulting system is highly interrelated; changes in any one part of the system have ramifications and feedback effects. As no single national government can control more than a small part of the whole international production system, the range of effective policy options is seriously limited.

Even if we assume that a government has just one overriding objective for its mineral sector, the fact of its incorporation within the complex international web of trade and finance may constitute a major barrier to achievement. However, in practice few governments will be in a position unequivocally to assign priority to one objective, or devise measures that lead the industry in one consistent direction. At some periods of time efficiency will be sacrificed to equity and security; at others the pressure to maximize the net returns from investments in minerals will override all other objectives. Moreover, throughout this trade-off process the need to maintain the power of the state or of particular political élites will be as important as any socioeconomic considerations.

The measures available to governments to intervene in the minerals sector and the difficulties involved in developing coherent minerals policies are discussed in Chapter 5.

NOTES

1 The terminology used gives an interesting insight into the way these key problems are regarded.

2 This does not mean that firms do not attempt to minimize production costs at individual sites.

3 In practice, ambiguity in the definition of marginal cost arises particularly in industries where major capital indivisibilities exist. When demand can be met from already developed mineral sources, the marginal cost of producing an extra unit of supply will be relatively small, being confined to the additional operating and transport costs. But as soon as a new mine is needed to meet demands, the marginal costs escalate since the costs of the capacity extension must now be covered. If firms strictly adhered to marginal cost pricing, prices would clearly have to fluctuate wildly. In addition, in any industry where long-run economies of scale are achieved, and long-run average production costs are falling, then the marginal cost must be below the average and the firms using it to set prices would make a loss. This last problem has been encountered in establishing optimal pricing strategies for the electricity industry in Britain.

4 This feature is the basis for Loschs's famous theoretical delimitation of market areas around manufacturing plants.

5 For simple treatments of the economic approach to intertemporal resource allocations see Fisher, 1981, and MacInerney, 1981.

6 The validity of this assertion is questionable. By having to employ renewables or conservation, society could generate more knowledge than if it continues to utilize conventional energy sources. Moreover, any efficiency gains may simply be used to increase consumption and need not go into education or basic research.

7 These data relate to *all* multinational company investments; the capital cost per job is likely to be much higher for the minerals sector taken alone.

8 These are not the total economic rent; the producer companies and the national government also take a share, in the latter case through normal corporation taxes.

9 In some cases demand restrictions, or threats of restriction, appear to have been used to enhance public awareness of and backing for the government's position.

10 In the years between the take-over and the restoration of the companies only three independents – one Japanese and two Italian – purchased significant amounts of Iranian oil, so producing a major financial crisis in the country.

11 The Office Cherifien des Phosphates, a state-owned monopoly which supplied Western Europe with almost one-half of its imports.

12 It was this proposal which brought together the south's demands for equity with the north's need for security in the debate over the new International Economic Order.

13 This admittedly clumsy term is used to indicate how vital specific mineral end-uses are to the industrial base of a country. If, for example, the sole use of a mineral was in the manufacture of jewellery, cosmetics, or billiard cues, the supply loss would hardly be a matter of economic life and death.

14 The speed with which the dispute over the division of the North Sea was settled after the hydrocarbon potential had been established is a clear illustration of the way points of principle vanish when economic interests are at stake.

15 The original members were Algeria, Australia, Chile, India, Mauritania, Peru, Sweden, Tunisia and Venezuela.

16 It should be noted that in many countries actual oil prices have *risen*, not *fallen*, since mid-1983; this is because of the greatly increased value of the dollar in foreign exchange markets against most other currencies.

5 Public intervention in the minerals sector

THE HISTORICAL ANTECEDENTS OF CONTEMPORARY INTERVENTION

There has been a tendency to regard both government intervention in private sector activities and directly state-run enterprises as relatively recent phenomena, only having achieved major economic significance in the second half of the twentieth century. Estall and Buchanan (1980, p. 132), for instance, write: 'Government activity has assumed great significance in the economic and social affairs of all nations in recent decades', the implication being that it had not done so in the past. Within economic geography it was not until the 1960s that the role of government started to emerge from its position of obscurity among a ragbag of 'other' influences on the location of economic activity, considered after the traditional factors (raw materials, labour, transport, markets and so forth) had been studied. Similarly, public sector analysis was not generally recognized as a distinct field of economic enquiry until the late 1950s; the earlier emphasis was firmly on private choices, with some attention paid to taxation as an influence on these (Haveman and Margolis, 1970). However, while widespread interest among spatial and economic analysts may be comparatively recent, the fact of government activity is certainly not.

Interventions in trade to encourage or protect domestic commercial, mining and industrial interests have a long history and, in some cases at least, were probably as significant to the economy of the period as they are now. Certainly, the eighteenth-century development of the British export trade owed much to protectionist measures. The Navigation Acts,[1] for example, ensured that the growing market in the American colonies was virtually monopolized by British firms; both foreign competition and colonial industrial development was restricted (Davis, 1969).

In the history of international exchange, periods of relatively free trade have been the exception, not the norm. Even the non-protectionist era in the mid-nineteenth century was short-lived. By the 1880s the United States and the continental European countries had reverted to high tariffs and Germany, among others, was heavily subsidizing industries of national or strategic importance. Only Britain retained faith in free trade up to the First World War. Virtually all the countries which industrialized after Britain accepted that domestic producers needed to be isolated from competition from firms with a well-established initial advantage. Therefore, most countries undergoing Rostow's first stage of economic growth adopted rigid protectionist policies.

In the same way, state trading and industrial companies and state expenditure were frequently vitally important in the early economic development of a number of the now advanced nations. Japan is the classic example here. During the Meiji period (1868–1912), which saw the take-off of the economy into economic growth, the government invested heavily in infrastructure and such basic industries as iron and steel. Rosovsky estimated that approximately 40 per cent of physical capital investment during the period was public not private, and this proportion rose markedly if military capital equipment is included in the calculations (Bronfenbrenner, 1982). These sorts of figures are not dissimilar to the present percentage government contributions in Britain and other modern capitalist states. In the same way, government investment and publically owned enterprises played a vital role in Napoleonic France, and in Bismarck's Germany.

Finally, it should be pointed out that the principle that governments should control private sector firms for social, national economic and environmental reasons was well established long before the beginning of this century. In 1870 Cairns was declaring that 'the maxim of laissez-faire has no scientific basis whatever', and a few years later Jevons argued in the House of Commons that 'the State was justified . . . in doing any single act which in its ulterior consequences adds to the sum of human happiness' (both quoted in Allen, 1961). The late nineteenth century saw a plethora of legislation dealing with conditions of work in factories and mines, conciliation by the state in trade disputes, controls over monopoly, pollution abatement and so on.

Even a cursory glance at the early history of trade and development in the now advanced capitalist nations suggests that protection and encouragement of indigenous private firms, and (outside Britain) major state capital investment programmes, did play an important role in the generation of economic activity. Moreover, it was recognized quite early in the development process that private enterprise would have to be controlled to prevent it abusing its power, and imposing unacceptable costs on other groups within the economy. This in no way implies that the adoption of similar measures by contemporary Third World governments will allow them to move into self-sustained growth. The forces operating both within the nations concerned and within the world economy are too dissimilar from those at work in nineteenth- and early-twentieth-century Europe, North America and Japan to allow meaningful comparison. However, there would seem to be a need to exercise some caution before accepting the currently fashionable view that LDCs' growth depends upon them reverting from an interventionist–protectionist approach to adopt market liberalization policies.

It is not the intention here to deny that the overall level of government intervention in the minerals sector has increased markedly over the last few decades. This is indisputable and has occurred at all geographical scales, from local government to the international agencies. The increase has taken place in part as a result of changing philosophies about the role of the state, but also reflects the much greater volume and spatial diversity of the international minerals trade and the increased number of independent national governments. However, this growth in the level of state intervention should not be allowed to obscure the fact that, historically, few governments have been content to let private interests entirely determine the development of a sector so vital to the health of the whole economy.

PUBLIC INTERVENTION AND THE PUBLIC INTEREST

It cannot be taken as axiomatic that government regulation or ownership will, in itself, ensure that mineral industries operate in a manner consistent with the welfare interests of the public at large. Assuming for the moment that government policy reflects general public interest, there are two basic reasons why attempts to intervene in the minerals sector commonly fail to bring its performance more in line with the economic efficiency, distributive equity, environmental quality and other socioeconomic or political objectives of the state. These are, first, the nature of bureaucracy, and, second, the constraints imposed by the incorporation of an economy within the international capitalist system. In the following section of this chapter the nature of the policy-making process will be discussed briefly, in order to establish how far the assumed identity between public policy and public interest holds true in practice.

Bureaucracy in the nationalized mineral industries

It is normally assumed that public sector enterprises operate in ways which diverge significantly from private practice. However, while there clearly will be some differences in operating behaviour between the two sectors, there is little evidence to suggest that the bureaucracies controlling investment, production and sales decisions within private and public firms work to markedly different rules or objectives. Sales levels, market shares, satisfactory profits or returns on capital, and survival of the individual managers and the internal technostructure of the industry are important considerations in both. It is true that what is defined as 'satisfactory profits' or returns *may* be less stringent in the public sector and that the penalties for failure to achieve these may also be reduced.[2] But neither of these factors need alter the general operating strategies of the industries. In most countries the dominant philosophy has been that the nationalized sector should be commercial. Investments should be justified on the same basis of return as in the private sector, using broadly similar interest rates and pricing practices.

There is a marked tendency for *both* public and private mineral industries to operate to an internal and commercially oriented logic, in which the net contribution to public welfare becomes, at best, a secondary consideration. Of course, it is argued that public welfare is maximized if the industry is efficient and competitive. But as we have seen, firms with market power need not be economically efficient, and efficiency itself is only in the public interest if equity is ignored. The commercial orientation of public enterprise can be seen in the behaviour of the British electricity and gas industries, which not only compete with oil and coal for sales, but have engaged in aggressive advertising campaigns against each other. Advertising by the Electricity Council alone rose from £5 million in 1979 to £20 million in 1982, while the counterblast from gas now costs

£15 million per annum (*The Times*, 18 October 1983). While some of this expenditure may be justified as in the public interest since it provides information, it is doubtful whether actual public requirements have much real relevance. What matters is the achievement of bureaucratically determined sales or market share goals.

Once an internal bureaucracy is established in a set developmental or operating pattern, successive governments may have little real power to alter its direction, particularly when the industry has a monopoly over recognized technical competence. For instance, the vested interests in large-scale electricity generation, including nuclear, have largely prevailed over those who have argued that public interest in environmental quality or conservation would be better served by small-scale combined heat and power stations and by an increased emphasis on renewable energy sources.

Government difficulties in controlling the bureaucracy of the state enterprises are not, of course, confined to the advanced western economies. In fact they probably apply with more force in the less developed world, where there are even fewer people outside the industry with the technical expertise to challenge the inside experts. As the role of state-owned companies increased in the mineral-dependent LDCs during the late 1960s and early 1970s it was vital that such firms at least yielded some tangible returns. However, as Gillis (1982, p. 628) has pointed out, 'experience thus far, from countries as diverse as Bolivia, Indonesia, Zambia, Zaire, Turkey and Brazil does not strongly suggest that state-owned minerals enterprises will always act as responsible taxpayers, much less act in the public interest at large'. One of the classic illustrations of this is the conduct of the Indonesian state oil company, Pertamina. Between 1971 and 1976 it accumulated over $10,000 million in debt by attempting to grow rapidly and extend its influence into other sectors of the economy such as insurance, tourism and steel.

The constraints of the capitalist system

Even in economies where governments are willing and able to control their public industries, incorporation within the world economic system places limits on the extent to which a state enterprise *can* be run to achieve non-commercial objectives. Unless a society aims to be self-sufficient and largely remains isolated from the world economy, the public sector producers (or their indigenous customers) have to remain broadly competitive. It is, therefore, counterproductive to push an industry to fulfil equity or security objectives to the point where it fails to maintain the sales necessary to allow it to contribute much to the economy at all. The more dependent the country is on the production of the nationalized industry in question, the greater the dilemma facing a government wishing to introduce non-commercial operating objectives. This clearly applies to LDCs, who could not afford either to lose exchange earnings or to subsidize a loss-making mineral industry for significant periods of time. Even if the industry's product, say, coal or electric power, was destined for home consumption, the 'opportunity costs' on the capital involved in non-profitable operations would be considerable.

However, the problem is not confined to LDCs. Wherever the nationalized sector provides basic inputs to manufacturing, its health affects the profitability and export competitiveness of all secondary producers. Moreover, where the nationalized sector is a significant contributor to GNP, its performance affects the achievement of economic growth objectives, which still dominate economic policy in virtually all countries, planned or capitalist. In Britain, for example, during the 1970s government investment amounted to 50 per cent of all industrial investments, and approximately one-half of this was in the energy and minerals sectors;[3] therefore, any reduction in the earnings on this capital had a marked effect on growth, on exchequer revenue and, therefore, on tax levels.

As was seen in Chapter 4, the way the market system operates also limits the ability of governments to regulate private enterprise to fulfil socioeconomic or political objectives. Regulations are only possible while they allow firms working within them to achieve their private business goals. Inevitably this severely constrains the achievement of any public welfare objectives, which do not support the continued growth of material output and the accumulation of capital.

THE NATURE OF PUBLIC POLICY

Policy as a trade-off process

Any government's ability to develop effective minerals policies is severely affected by its invariable desire to achieve several, possibly incompatible, objectives at the same time. It is by no means unusual for the state simultaneously to want producers to operate in a manner consistent with efficiency, security, equity, growth and environmental quality, plus a whole host of other economic and political objectives, such as increasing national prestige, rewarding a political élite, maintaining a particular party in power, curbing inflation, or avoiding balance-of-trade deficits. The fact that some of these may be recognized to conflict makes them no less desirable as policy objectives. In these circumstances public policy frequently consists of a series of *ad hoc* measures taken against a shifting background of social attitudes, political pressures, economic realities and the distribution of effective power within society.

The development of government policy is a bargaining or trade-off process in two distinct senses. First, trade-offs will have to be made between objectives to meet, often short-term, economic, social or political exigencies. And, second, the favoured prime objective, at any point of time, will be determined by the balance of power between groups having different economic interests and holding to different value systems. As Schumpeter (1950) has put it,

> Only in a very special sense can we speak of a nation's policy or policies. In general, declared policies are nothing but verbalizations of group interests and attitudes that assert themselves in the struggle of parties for points in the political game, though every group exalts the policies that suit it into eternal principles of a 'common good' that is to be safeguarded by an imaginary kind

of state. Nobody has attained political maturity who does not understand that policy is politics. (Quoted in Cobbe, 1979, p. 74)

Policy and the interests of capital

Within a Marxist framework of analysis such trade-off problems become a non-issue; Schumpeter's statement would be amended to read 'policy is politics and politics is economics'. Given the Marxist emphasis on the fusion of political and economic power, the interests of the capital-owning class inevitably dominate those of all other groups and the whole apparatus of government functions in support of capital (Milliband, 1973, p. 17). There is little doubt that many of the *outcomes* of the mineral production system do conform to those 'predicted' by such an interpretation of events, particularly when viewed over the long term. But this form of 'economic determinism' presents a highly simplified picture of the processes involved in establishing the patterns of development and consumption and in the formulation of public policies. It is in fact dubious whether any single theoretical construct can adequately explain the complexity of real-world forces, processes and events. As Saunders (1980, p. 14) has said, 'no single body of theory and no one paradigm can be expected to provide all the answers to questions'. In order to achieve even an approximation to real understanding it is necessary to adopt 'a degree of theoretical pluralism and epistemological tolerance'.

FRACTIONS OF CAPITAL

One obvious difficulty with the classic Marxist interpretation of policy is that neither capital nor labour are single, cohesive groups with consistent and opposing objectives. Competition occurs between companies and, clearly, the interests of owners of competitive fuels or metals may conflict. In addition, policies which support the interests of indigenous companies will not necessarily aid the owners of multinational corporations. The potential for conflict between fractions of capital was seen in Chapter 4, in the discussions on equity (pp. 154–5) and security (pp. 163–4).

Furthermore, it is not realistic to ignore the fact that in the minerals sector, as in all parts of the economy, the owners of capital do not necessarily control the companies. With the twentieth-century rise in joint-stock companies, ownership has become increasingly divorced from control. Why, then, should managers take decisions to maximize profits for the benefit of a largely unknown set of shareholders? As Stretton (1976, p. 264) has pointed out, 'The profit motive has become less *directly* important in a good deal of big businesses where the operative motives have become more like those which motivate managers and bureaucrats in any big organization'. Alternative objectives to profit are acknowledged to be important: these include long-run survival of the corporation and its management team; increased company size, which tends to enhance the power, prestige and probably the money income of managers; avoidance of risk or losses which can destroy the technostructure of the corporation; and management ease, which favours working to set decision rules rather than making myriad conscious choices about investment, pricing, marketing and so on. In other words, corporate interests are not necessarily synonymous with the interests of capital. Moreover, corporations are best regarded as collections of interests or as 'coalitions'. Actual decisions represent compromises between the various groups within the corporation and will vary over time to reflect personality changes and all those other internal and external forces which affect relative bargaining power.

FRACTIONS OF LABOUR

In the same way, the tendency to reduce individuals and their interests to their labour function is an oversimplification. Any person is at one and the same time a consumer, worker, taxpayer and increasingly also an owner of capital.[4] It is, of course, possible to argue that all these functions are determined by class position; however, in advanced capitalist economies there is no longer any simple or direct relationship between class, values, income and occupation. Inevitably individuals experience a confusion of objectives and the way they strike a balance between conflicting aims will change over time, not only with altered family stage and status, but also with external political and socioeconomic circumstances. To take a very simplistic example: a miner may want to protect his job in a high-cost pit and obtain a higher price for his wage labour, but as a consumer he may demand cheap electric power and reduced air pollution, while as a taxpayer he will not want the coal industry as a burden on the exchequer; as an owner of property he may well resist the location of a coal gasification plant in his neighbourhood, which could depress property values, and as the holder of pension rights and insurance policies he may well desire capital accumulation. Even if the potential conflicts between these various wants or interests are explicitly recognized, which they by no means always are, the relative importance attached to each will vary over time and between individuals.

Both traditional welfare economists and Marxist analysts see individual preferences or interests as objective reality. The first group assume that all individuals have an ordered, consistent structure of preferences, objective utility functions which they attempt to maximize. Commonly it is further assumed that these preferences are 'revealed' by actions, which basically means that they are revealed by the goods and services purchased. These notions have been widely criticized. Joan Robinson (1981, p. 48), for instance, refers to utility as a 'concept of impregnable circularity, utility is the quality in commodities that makes individuals want to buy them, and the fact that individuals want to buy commodities shows that they have utility'. Apart from such challenges to the logic of the concept itself, other critics have argued that it is behaviourally inaccurate, ignoring both the irrational, inconsistent, subjective and changing way preferences are formed and the manner in which preferences are constrained and manipulated.

In Marxist interpretations objective preferences are not revealed by actions, nor indeed are they necessarily even recognized by the individual, but they are determined by class position (Balbus, 1971). However, the reduction of the question of conflicting interests to class divisions neither helps to determine what these interests are (Plamanetz, 1954), nor gives much guidance in situations where the conflicts are internal to one class (or indeed to one individual) or where coalitions of interest transcend traditional class barriers. Neither the economic approach, which neglects both the constraints imposed by the uneven distribution of income and wealth and the fact of market manipulation, nor the notion of class-bound interests can provide full explanations of real-world situations. Both approaches can, however, give useful insights into the problems involved with the present operations of the mineral sector and into the formulation and outcomes of public policies.

FRACTIONS OF GOVERNMENT

Just as mineral companies and individuals are coalitions of interest, so a government cannot meaningfully be seen as one entity. In both neo-classical economic and Marxist analyses the state tends to be seen as a purposive actor attempting to maximize some reasonably well-defined goal, be it economic efficiency or the interests of one particular social class. However, as Young (1981, p. 182) has argued, 'it [i.e. the state] is more appropriately conceptualised as an institutional framework or arena within which social choice processes take place on a continuous basis'. This conceptualization in no way implies that the choice process is a 'fair' one, allowing equal access and weight to all interest groups.

The various branches, departments and levels within the apparatus of the state operate with different prime objectives, which are again not static but respond to changing political, social and economic conditions. For example, in a British context little understanding of energy policy can be achieved without recognizing that the Treasury, Department of Energy, Central Electricity Generating Board, British Gas Corporation, Coal Board, local government authorities, and so on, are all working to different targets. Final policies whether explicitly formed or derived by practice and by non-decisions are normally compromises.[5] As Higgins (1978, p. 166) says, 'decisions are therefore mostly reached by committee, resulting in half-baked compromises which reflect bureaucratic horse-trading as much as objective needs'. Given the nature of compromise and the multiplicity of objectives and interests, it is not surprising that mineral and energy policies rarely lead in any clear, much less coherent, direction.

The notion that the state inevitably operates in support of capital must also be regarded as too much of a simplification, not the least because different segments of capital have quite distinct, and possibly conflicting, interests. Some commentators have seen the introduction in 1959 of mandatory oil import quotas by the United States as a clear example of the state upholding the interests of capital (Tanzer, 1969). The measure clearly did support the powerful indigenous oil producers' lobby, and also protected all other primary-fuel producers. But manufacturers and oil-importing companies clearly suffered financial losses, as did the regional economies of areas, such as New England, which lost access to a cheap energy source. Virtually any significant government measure inevitably benefits some fraction or other of capital. What is crucial is which fraction manages to sway opinion in which branches of government at particular points in time. Policy outcomes will depend not only on the relative intrinsic power of the various actors but also on exogenous political and socioeconomic circumstances.

Voices in the policy process

Even the most stubbornly free market economies have introduced price regulations, planning and pollution controls, labour laws and anti-monopoly or trust measures, all of them in opposition to the direct interests of capital (see pp. 201–13). Other interests do obtain a voice in the social choice process, although the struggle for attention can never be an equal affair. Large mineral corporations invariably enjoy highly privileged access to, and influence over, many branches of the state, and this 'typically serve[s] to restrict or channel the substantive content of the outcomes flowing from social choice processes' (Young, 1981, p. 182). There also appears to be examples where the allegiance of politicians has been bought; Barnet (1980), for instance, has argued that the Nixon presidential campaigns were heavily supported by oil money.[6] He goes on to quote Franklin D. Roosevelt as lamenting that: 'The trouble with this country is that you can't win an election without the oil bloc and you can't govern with it' (ibid., p. 24). More usually, however, the political power of the mineral corporations lies less in who their money can buy than in their success in convincing governments, and many of the public, that specific measures which serve their interests are vital to economic efficiency, growth, employment generation, healthy trade balances or security – and that these particular societal objectives must take precedence over the rest.

Policy formulation is inevitably a complex process. At a purely descriptive level it may be reasonable to accept the *pluralist* notion of a large number of interest groups, each with overlapping memberships and all attempting to influence policy (Polsby, 1963). But the highly uneven distribution of effective bargaining power inevitably means that there is an inbuilt bias in the system favouring some objectives or interest groups against the others. The final results, however, are probabalistic, not deterministic. It is rare for governments to have an overall stated policy for the development and use of non-fuel minerals, and energy policy statements have only become common in the last fifteen years. Where formal policies do exist, they may diverge markedly from what is actually happening in practice.

INTERVENTIONIST MEASURES

Each government has a perceived set of 'tools' or 'mechanisms' which it can employ to intervene in the mineral production and consumption process. Effective policy in any country will be determined by three factors. First, whether the government chooses to intervene; in many cases the decision to allow private and public firms to develop and allocate resources in their own interests becomes policy by default. Second, which interventionist measures are adopted. And, third, how these are implemented in practice. The fact that a particular measure is encapsulated in legislation or official statements does not necessarily mean that it becomes part of effective policy. The way it is actually interpreted and then enforced is the critical element (see Chapter 9, pp. 339–49). In the rest of this chapter attention will be focused on the key measures which have been employed by governments to alter some aspect of the performance of the minerals sector, and on the impact these have had on the mineral production and consumption process. In Chapter 9 the more complex question of policy formulation and the influence of powerful economic interest groups on policy-making will be considered in more detail.

Literally hundreds of government actions exert some influence on the minerals and energy industries, but the concern here will be limited to those that are purposeful, designed specifically to alter some aspect of the sectors' performance. Measures which apply equally to all types of economic activity, such as controls over working hours, child labour, health and safety at work, or anti-trust regulations will not be considered, neither will the indirect effects of policies designed to regulate the whole economy. Their omission does not imply that they are unimportant. Spatial variations in minimum wage rates have some influence over the location of mining and processing activity (see p. 104), while controls over the competitive structure and behaviour of producers can also have an impact on pricing policies, sales levels and the location of production (see p. 112). However, consideration of the whole gamut of government's incidental influence is simply beyond the scope of this volume.

Although the methods or tools of purposeful intervention overlap considerably, for ease of presentation they can be divided into six major categories:

(1) trade regulation;
(2) taxation;
(3) price fixing;
(4) planning and environmental regulations;
(5) subsidies;
(6) government ownership.

Theoretically each of these could be used by all levels of government, although in practice at the regional (or local) and international scales the range of effective measures is somewhat more restricted.

Trade regulation

In virtually all countries regulation of trade flows over an international boundary is the prerogative of the national government. Even where regional governments have constitutional jurisdiction over mineral development itself, as in Australia and Canada, international trade remains a central government function. However, it is increasingly common for some national powers to be partially delegated to multinational agencies, through the creation of trading blocs, producer cartels and international institutions charged with regularizing and stabilizing trade relations.

Historically, the bulk of government intervention in trade has had a negative effect on flows, and this is generally true today. In theory, a more open trade system has now been constructed through the international General Agreement on Tariffs and Trade (GATT). This works on the premiss that governments should, in concert, set the general rules of trade but allow the free interplay of supply and demand to settle the outcomes (Zysman and Cohen, 1983). While

GATT undoubtedly has been influential in reducing the formal barriers to trade and in liberalizing tariffs, informal trade barriers and state intervention to alter the way market forces operate have become increasingly prevalent. In the 1960s and early 1970s the development of producer cartels illustrates this move towards intervention, while over the last decade advanced nation measures to subsidize and protect their own producers from competition in a period of worldwide recession have further reinforced the trend. More and more trade is now being conducted outside the GATT rules, and the whole system has proved incapable of coming to terms with the growth of non-tariff barriers (Muldoon, 1983).

EXPORT TARIFFS

In the past the imposition of import or export tariffs was the most common form of government intervention. Export tariffs, although rarely imposed by the advanced consumer states,[7] have been widely used by LDC mineral producers both as a revenue-raising measure and to encourage the establishment of domestic processing industries. Until the 1960s LDCs employed a relatively small and unsophisticated array of tax and royalty devices to capture some of the economic rent from natural resource developments. The literature is full of cases where the lack of bargaining skills and knowledge of fiscal management techniques placed host governments at a marked disadvantage in dealing with the mineral multinationals (see, for example, Smith and Wells, 1975).

Specific export taxes were common. These were a fixed amount per unit weight; while they had the advantage of providing the governments with a relatively stable income, they meant that the companies enjoyed all the 'windfall' profits made when commodity prices were high. This was particularly important for metals, such as copper, where marked price fluctuations characterized the markets. *Ad valorum* tariffs, or royalties set as a percentage of export value, did allow the capture of some windfall profits, particularly if the percentage take varied with the export price. After 1966, for example, Zambia imposed an extra 40 per cent export tax on sales of ores at prices above a set baseline figure. However, such taxes involved the difficulty of ensuring that the companies did not minimize their tax liability by setting nominal prices for transfers between affiliates. The potential for tax understatement was great since the bulk of trade was intracorporation in nature. Even as late as 1977 95 per cent of the total exports by the oil majors and 78 per cent by the metal conglomerates went to affiliated companies (Gillis, 1982).

Where export tariffs were used as a revenue-raising measure, their level had to be kept relatively low. Any host government imposing taxes out of line with other producing countries ran the risk that revenue would fall, since their exports would become uncompetitive and the companies would shift production to areas with more favourable tax regimes. Over the last twenty years export tariffs and royalties have declined markedly in importance as a revenue source for most producer states. Although a few countries such as Bolivia, Jamaica and New Caledonia do still rely heavily on them, by and large they have been displaced by a complex set of profits and windfall taxes and by government equity sharing agreements. Some countries, such as Chile, Ghana, Guinea and Zambia, no longer impose any export taxes at all (Mikesell, 1983). Moreover, where they do still operate, the scope for tax understatement has been cut considerably by linking them to some readily observable market quotation, such as those ruling on the London Metal Exchange. If there is no independent market valuation other than that fixed by the mineral companies, the price of processed materials has been taken as a surrogate. For example, since 1974 Jamaica has overcome the lack of a market price for bauxite by using aluminium-ingot prices for tax assessment purposes.

When tariffs have been used in an attempt to encourage the establishment of processing industries, high rates were imposed on crude minerals and low or no taxes were levied on processed commodities. However, there was no guarantee that private companies would respond in the desired way to such differential tariff structures, and in most cases the measure was counterproductive, resulting in falling mine output and little or no processing activity. Today, therefore, their use is rare, except among hardwood exporters (Gillis, 1982). In their stead governments have tended to adopt the much more direct tactic of attempting to make the construction of processing facilities a condition of the mining contract. However, over the last few years there is evidence that many governments are increasingly wary of pushing for local processing unless the project is an economically viable proposition. Past experience of such developments as tin smelting in Bolivia, petrochemicals in Colombia and an integrated steelmill in Indonesia have shown that uneconomic projects can involve the government in massive subsidy and protection programmes and can require costly imports of fuel, equipment and spare parts.

IMPORT TARIFFS

Import duties, premiums or tariffs are still in widespread use; many are revenue-raising devices and rates tend to be low unless the products have a highly inelastic demand schedule. In Britain, for instance, the 1961 duty on fuel oils was primarily designed to benefit the Exchequer, although its retention subsequently came to be justified by the need to protect coal. Much higher tariff barriers are needed when the whole objective of the exercise is to reduce demand and imports. Governments have for long used duties (and exchange controls) as part of the general management of the balance of payments, and in recent years these have tended to become much stricter in the LDCs as attempts are made to cope with mounting debt problems.

There are also numerous cases where selective protective tariffs have been designed specifically to encourage the development of new domestic mineral sources and related industries, to promote conservation and mineral security and to insulate established domestic producers from foreign competition. Most European governments have, for instance, employed differential tariffs to favour domestic oil refining and to protect indigenous steel or coal interests. The EEC import tariff system is as a whole designed to increase the degree of material processing; zinc concentrates are, for example, imported into the community duty-free, but *ad valorem* tariffs of 3.5 and 8 per cent are imposed on unwrought and wrought zinc respectively. Manners (1979) has pointed out that this amounts to protection of 21 per cent on zinc sheet, with even higher levels (32 per cent) operating for copper sheet. Similarly, LDC producers have imposed duties on the construction materials, machinery and spare parts required by the mining sector in an attempt to build up domestic production capability. However, as with differential export taxes, this measure frequently has been counterproductive and today it is employed selectively to ensure that domestic companies are used only when they have the technical capability of producing goods comparable in price and quality with imports. Chile and Indonesia, for instance, use a duty exemption system to allow duty-free imports of materials and equipment not available from within the national economy (Mikesell, 1983).

The use of import tariffs raises several problems. They cannot alone guarantee that private producers and consumers will react in the desired way. Where the demand for the affected goods proves inelastic, imports may not fall markedly; the tariff will merely be passed on in increased prices. In the industrialized countries the short-run demand elasticities for most metals and oil are known to be low,[8] therefore duties tend to be inflationary. This not only runs contrary to the key economic objective of reducing inflation, but also can affect the competitiveness of exported manufactured goods. Moreover, tariffs on fuels tend to act to regressively redistribute effective incomes. Similarly, in the LDCs duties on construction materials, industrial energy sources and equipment have often served to reduce investment in the minerals sector as projects appeared less commercially viable. Duties on oil, while seemingly essential after 1973 to reduce the growing trade deficits, often made indigenous refining, smelting and manufacturing industries still less competitive.

Even when tariffs initially had the desired effect, levels have to be monitored carefully and adjusted regularly in line with inflation, fluctuating exchange rates, prices changes and patterns of demand. Particularly in those countries with rapid rates of inflation, it has proved difficult to maintain tariffs as an effective protective measure. A further problem, which applies to all forms of protection, is that it may encourage and maintain inefficient domestic enterprises, which can only survive if continually insulated from foreign competition or heavily subsidized.

NON-TARIFF BARRIERS

Physical constraints on trade take many forms including import and export quotas, 'voluntary' export restraints, total import bans, export embargoes, import and export licences and import regulations. These last include the detailed specification of the product's quality, such as the sulphur content in oil or the impurities allowable in metals. The sudden imposition of *quotas* or *embargoes* can have a major impact on patterns of resource trade and consumption, as the 1959 US oil import quota and OPEC's 1973 trade embargo clearly demonstrate. But while these events were indeed dramatic, they merely represent the tip of an iceberg of trade constraints; in fact it is difficult to find one mineral for which free trade conditions apply.

Virtually all the consumer nations favour the import of crude minerals and the establishment of domestic processing industries. In Japan, MITI (Ministry of

Trade and Industry) licences have been used to curb the import of refined oil and metals; although in recent years the fuel costs involved in domestic metal smelting and refining have resulted in a policy change with licences to import already refined metals much more freely obtainable (see p. 101). Similarly, crude oil and oil products can only move into France under government licence; these are used to encourage the development of indigenous refining capacity, and to ensure that the two national companies maintain their market share (Deese and Nye, 1981). Refusal of import licences, open import bans or quota limits have all been employed from time to time to protect domestic mineral industries; Britain has, for example, refused licences for US coal, while the United States has periodically imposed quota restrictions on oil, lead, copper, steel and zinc imports.

Since the 1973 oil crisis there have been moves to introduce import quotas as part of a co-ordinated strategy by the major consumer nations. The International Energy Agency was formed in late 1974, and at first agreement could not be reached on ceiling import levels, although a scheme for sharing oil supplies during emergencies was devised. However, in 1979 it was agreed to limit overall imports to 26 mbd by 1985, and each country was set an import ceiling. Japan, for example, was given a target of 6.3–6.9 mbd, which represented a 17–28 per cent increase over 1979 levels. This agreement has subsequently been overtaken by the rapid demand falls experienced after 1980, and it is just possible that quotas established solely by the IEA will be superseded by informal co-operative arrangements between producers and consumers. Some evidence that moves in this direction are occurring comes from the proposals of OPEC's long-term strategy committee. In October 1983 it advocated a system whereby prices and output levels would be fixed according to a flexible formula, taking account of inflation and allowing for increases in production in line with economic growth (*Observer*, 16 October 1983).

As would be expected, among the advanced capitalist nations physical measures to control *exports* have not been particularly common, but they have occasionally been used both for economic and political reasons. Australia restricted iron ore exports until 1960, primarily to promote the development of indigenous industry, and has periodically considered controlling the export of uranium, mainly because of pressure from the anti-nuclear lobby. Similarly, the United States has from time to time limited the export of strategic minerals, controlled metal scrap exports when indigenous refiners feared shortages and banned sales to communist regimes. There has also been a ban on the export of Alaskan oil, which is still operating despite pressure from the Alaskans and from the oil producers for the government to rescind the measure.

For many LDC producer countries export controls have come to be regarded as a key policy measure. In the past some governments, such as Venezuela, have unilaterally imposed restrictions either in a vain attempt to force price increases or as a conservation measure. A slower rate of resource depletion would, it was argued, act to spread revenue receipts over time and reserve some of the mineral for possible future domestic needs. However, output controls are now much more commonly adopted in a package of measures introduced by producer cartels to curb supply surpluses, bring greater stability into markets and push up the price of their minerals. As was seen in Chapter 4, in practice agreements on market shares and commitment to respect established output quotas have been extremely difficult to achieve. Smith and Wells (1975, p. 183) have argued that commodity agreements all have the same Achilles' heel: 'If the incentive for a member to break the agreement is not counterbalanced by an equally strong penalty and enforcement mechanism, the life of the agreement is likely to be short.' In most cases export controls alone are unlikely to be effective. Once excess capacity exists, production costs do not increase markedly with output, and the short-run advantages of increasing sales by undercutting the official price may be an overwhelming temptation.

Where demand and prices are notoriously unstable, output quotas need to be accompanied by an agreement to introduce *buffer-stocks*. Without this, the quotas would have to be constantly readjusted, making it impossible for members to plan production effectively. The efforts of the Tin Producers' Association, now incorporated within the International Tin Council, provide a classic illustration of the problems involved in managing an export-quota, buffer-stock scheme. In 1931 producers responsible for nearly 90 per cent of the world's tin, including Bolivia, Malaya, Siam and the Dutch East Indies, agreed to restrict output to support prices and between 1934 and 1938 they also operated a buffer-stockpile. Their efforts had minimal effect; they could neither halt the decline in price which occurred during the Great Depression, nor could they combat the price escalation which accompanied the arms build-up before the Second World War.

Since 1956 there have been six international tin agreements between producer and consumer nations in an attempt to bring greater stability to the industry. It was agreed to contain prices within a narrow band, buying into stock when prices looked like falling below a floor price and releasing these again when the ceiling price was neared. The first three of these agreements had little chance of success since neither the Soviet Union nor the United States were party to them. During the first agreement the Soviet Union increased its exports at the same time as the US government stopped purchasing tin for its strategic stockpile. The British and Dutch governments restricted Soviet tin imports, but during the 1958 downturn in world economic activity the Tin Council rapidly ran out of funds and prices tumbled. Just three years later the buffer system broke down again – this time stocks were insufficient to meet increased demand. The suggestion that the United States could release some of its strategic stockpile was violently opposed by the LDC producers, who had everything to gain, at least in the short run from the high price levels. Both the second (1961–6) and third (1966–71) agreements similarly crumbled when the buffer-stock management ran short of either capital or tin reserves. The Soviet Union joined the tin agreement system in 1971, and the United States at last became a member in 1976.

During the 1970s the agreements undoubtedly did bring greater output and price stability, and producer output restrictions have had some success in pushing up price levels. In 1974 prices in real terms were 50 per cent higher than the general level in the 1960s, but even during periods of economic growth the consumption trend has been downwards. By 1980 it was clear that economic recession and falling prices were again placing great strains on the system. The

United States was apparently compounding the problems of a weak market by selling the metal surplus to its strategic stock requirements. It proved impossible to obtain a new international agreement and producers stormed out of a Tin Council meeting in 1980, when the United States refused to allow a substantial upward revision of the buffer-stock price range. A year later the ASEAN producers, Malaysia, Thailand and Indonesia, issued a communiqué which stated that 'narrow and short-term national interests of some developed consuming countries were restricting the implementation of the integrated programme for commodities and undermining the spirit of international cooperation in commodity agreements' (*Financial Times*, 2 June 1981).

TRADE PROMOTION MEASURES

National governments have periodically instituted measures to stimulate trade. Promotion drives, favourable loan conditions, direct trade subsidies, tied aid and government underwriting of private sector risk have all been used by the advanced nations to increase exports. The motives behind such measures are nearly always mixed: humanitarian concern being leavened by economic and political advantage. This can be illustrated clearly by the way US trade subsidies are operated. Under the terms of the US Trade Act 1974, which allows various subsidies for trade with Latin and South America, countries like Venezuela and Ecuador are rendered ineligible because of their membership of OPEC (Deese and Nye, 1981). Likewise, the Soviet Union has given aid, developed barter schemes and provided soft loans in an attempt not only to expand its oil exports, but also to achieve political objectives. Similarly, mixed motives lie behind the now considerable aid programmes developed by OPEC members. In part they reflect a genuine desire to help other nations, particularly fellow Muslim states, but they also act to enhance national prestige and, more important, serve to keep exports flowing by allowing oil-dependent LDCs to continue importing.

Another increasingly important trade promotion measure has been the growth in countertrade[9] deals. These take a variety of forms. Some are pure barter, where goods are exchanged without the use of money; for instance, the US government has imported Jamaican bauxite for its strategic stockpile, in return for various surplus dairy products (Vogt, 1983). Similarly, the Iranian and New Zealand governments have reputedly swopped oil for lamb. More commonly, money remains the medium of exchange, and *counterpurchase*, *buy back* or *offset* agreements are concluded. A major vehicle manufacturer, for example, has agreed to act as a trader for an African country's zinc, on the understanding that half of the foreign exchange earnings would be made available to its local subsidiary to allow it to import knocked-down vehicle kits and spare parts. Similarly, China has now conducted a number of deals with suppliers of capital equipment, where the suppliers agree to buy back the products produced with their plant and equipment; thus Japanese coalmining equipment is paid for by subsequent coal sales. Alternatively, imported capital goods may only be accepted if the supplier agrees to purchase indigenously made components, invest in local production facilities or otherwise put back into the local economy the value of the imported goods.

Historically, the Comecon bloc of countries have been most active in counter-trade, using it to ease shortages of hard currency and to extend their economic and political spheres of influence. However, in recent years, the recession in international trade, mounting debt problems and critical foreign exchange shortages have pushed a number of LDCs into this unconventional form of trade. Highly indebted countries employ it to finance the import of vital commodities and equipment when normal sources of credit are no longer available. They may also use it to avoid making international debt repayments; by receiving goods not currency for their exports they are still not in a position to repay IMF or other loan agencies. Other nations see countertrade as a means of extending the market for their products; while still others have used it to unload surplus production at periods of slack demand. Evidence suggests that some OPEC members have used countertrade deals to 'sell' oil at considerable discounts on official price levels.

Good data on the extent of countertrade do not exist: recent estimates have varied enormously from as little as 1 per cent to over 40 per cent of total world trade (EIU, 1984). But the likelihood is that it is now approaching 20 per cent of all trade and its significance is known to have increased markedly over the last five years (Zysman and Cohen, 1983). In the minerals sector most agreements appear to follow the typical north–south trade pattern, with bulk raw materials ex-changed for capital goods, including military equipment. To a considerable extent such deals replace conventional trade rather than generating new trade flows, and their importance may be expected to decline as the international economy moves out of recession. However, agreements between LDCs, particu-larly the Asian countries, are increasingly common and in the longer term these could have a significant impact on patterns and levels of trade.

In recent years mineral-exporting nations have further sought to increase exports, or at least to develop more control over the markets, by buying into processing ventures in consumer areas. This has particularly occurred in the oil industry; the Iranian national oil company has participated in an Indian refinery development and the Indonesian oil company, Pertamina, has negotiated a joint distribution venture with Japan. The Canadian government has made somewhat similar moves to gain control over the sales of its natural resources. The Canada Development Corporation – a government-created investment company – man-aged in 1973 to acquire a 35 per cent controlling interest in Texasgulf Inc. despite legal attempts to block the purchase. About two-thirds of Texasgulf's profits were derived from zinc and silver deposits in Ontario. Canada has been increasingly concerned to reduce US foreign investment, which in 1971 accounted for nearly 90 per cent of all investment in the country's oil and gas industries, and over 80 per cent in its metals (*Sunday Times*, 9 September 1973). By purchasing directly into US companies, or by using grants to 'persuade' them to take on Canadian private company partners, the government had managed to cut foreign ownership in oil to 74 per cent in 1979, and to 66 per cent by the end of 1982 (*Petroleum Economist*, October 1983, p. 381).

Periodically consumer governments have acted to increase, or at least safe-guard, their raw material imports by adopting a wide range of measures, from political pressure and cheque-book diplomacy to giving tax incentives to stimulate private overseas investment. The US government, according to Tanzer (1969), Engler (1961) and others, has used its political power to ensure the access of US oil companies to important supply sources. The French have been remarkably successful in retaining for French companies the rights to raw materials in the ex-colonies: 'It is notable that every major mining project in Gabon and Mauritania includes at least one French firm as a shareholder' (Smith and Wells, 1975, p. 195). The Japanese government has likewise been active in securing its supply sources, using both diplomatic and economic methods. In 1973 when it was classified as an 'unfriendly' nation by the Arabs and included in the oil embargo, the political reaction was swift. A cautiously worded statement was issued endorsing Palestinian rights and indicating that it might 'reconsider its policy towards Israel'. This along with diplomatic activity and promises of aid earned Japan a transfer to the Arabs' friendly-nation list (Juster, 1977; Nye, 1981).

Taxation

In most countries the national government is the prime taxing body, but in federal systems the picture can be much more complex, with both the central and regional administrations attempting to gain a share of the revenue cake. Garnaut and Clunies Ross's description of the situation in Australia is not atypical of other countries where provincial governments have jurisdiction over the minerals found within their territories:

> The fiscal system within which the Australian mining industry operates has been developed with little co-operation or even communication between the various states or between the two tiers of government. The result has been a complex, unstable, and distorting system. (Garnaut and Clunies Ross, 1983, p. 245)

Which level of government is more successful in the conflict over revenue shares varies considerably between countries. In Canada, as we have seen, the provinces have managed to capture a significant proportion of the economic rent, but the more usual situation is for the central authority to receive the bulk of the revenue.

When the regional tier of government has the right to tax extractive industry, tax levels can vary considerably over the country. For example, in the US, Montana levies a 30 per cent of value tax on surface strip-mined coal, which compares with 2 per cent in Idaho, 4.5 per cent in both Kentucky and South Dakota and 8.5 per cent in Wyoming. In 1974 the Montana government fixed this high rate deliberately in view of the environmental damage caused by open-cast operations, and although it was contested in the courts, a final Supreme Court ruling in 1981 upheld Montana's right to assess rates of this magnitude (Richardson and Scott, 1983). In the United States matters are further complicated by the existence, within individual states, of major resource developments on public land 'owned' by the federal government in its own right or as a custodian of Indian land rights.

There are basically three types of tax which can be levied on mineral producers: output taxes, profit taxes and property or capital value taxes.

OUTPUT TAXES

This form of taxation – often also called *royalties* or *severance taxes* – can either be a specific levy per unit output or a percentage of the value of production. Therefore, they are analogous to export tariffs and indeed in LDCs they can effectively become tariffs if virtually all the mineral production is destined for export. Until the 1950s they accounted for a very high proportion of the total revenue which Third World governments received from the exploitation of their minerals; in the oil case, for example, most of the early concession agreements simply required the producing companies to pay a specific levy per barrel of output. However, although taxes on output are still widely employed, they have normally been displaced as the chief revenue source by profit taxes or by profit shares (see p. 196).

Today most governments levy relatively low percentage of value royalties to give themselves at least a basic income in years when the mining venture fails to make a profit on its sales. These can be as low as 1 per cent (in Papua New Guinea and Liberia, for instance) but are more normally in the 4–10 per cent range for metals and 10–20 per cent for oil and gas. Over the last few years some countries have also introduced *windfall royalties*, taking a higher percentage when prices exceed some base figure established by the government. Both Peru and Malaysia use this system for oil, and Malaysia again employs it for tin. In some federal systems, such as Malaysia and the United States, output taxes have tended to remain the revenue source for the regional level of government, with most profit and corporation taxes going to the central Exchequer.

The principal difficulty with any taxation of output is that it directly affects average and marginal costs of extraction. At each market price the producing company is willing to sell less of the product and marginally viable fields may be shut down entirely. If the government wants to slow down the rate of depletion of its known indigenous reserves as a conservation measure, such an effect may be desirable. However, even this is somewhat doubtful, since it will also serve to reduce investment in exploration and may also cause previously proven reserves to be redefined as uneconomic. Unless demands are controlled, it could also result in increasing imports, which brings the possibility of conflicts with mineral security objectives. In general, if the government's major concern is to obtain revenue, then royalty levels must be kept relatively low to stop output falling.

Theoretical analyses have shown that the potential revenue take with this form of tax is small when there are many other producing areas. Moreover, even where a country or region is the sole supplier to a specific isolated market, revenues decrease when a monopolistic producer is exploiting the source. Richardson and Scott (1983) have sought to verify these notions empirically by analysing the occurrence of state severance taxes within the United States. Taking six resources – sand/gravel, sawn timber, coal, oil, natural gas and nickel – they first plot the spatial patterns of output and calculate the production concentration ratios for the four leading producer states. In the case of nickel one state only,

Oregon, produces all the mined nickel in the country,[10] but for the other resources the four-state concentration ratio varies from 28.6 per cent for sand and gravel to 76.2 per cent for oil and 85.3 per cent for natural gas. As expected from theory, the states have very little power to levy output taxes on sand and gravel firms; only six states out of fifty with some production even attempt to do so, and only in Kentucky are they at all significant. In 1980 Kentucky introduced a new law which levies a 4.5 per cent of value tax on all natural resources, except oil and coal, but this could have the longer-term effect of driving a significant proportion of the sand and gravel industry into surrounding states. Conversely, where the concentration ratios are high, the number of producer states imposing taxes increases markedly and the tax take of the top producers is quite high; Louisiana, for instance, imposes a 12.5 per cent levy on oil, while Alaska's rate is still higher at 15 per cent. It might be expected that Oregon as the sole output centre would be able to tax its nickel mining, but this is not so since competition from by-product nickel and imports already makes production marginally viable.

Although Richardson and Scott's work was concerned with the situation within one country, the approach clearly has relevance at the international scale. An LDC's effective power to use output taxes is constrained by the number and output capacity of alternative production centres. As was shown in Chapter 3, there are relatively few minerals for which Third World production represents a high proportion of the world total, and still fewer where a limited number of producing countries have achieved monopoly power. Moreover, still further limitations are imposed on those host governments which are faced by companies who have themselves achieved market power. In this case quite high output cuts could occur, with revenue losses for the host government.

PROFIT TAXES

According to basic economic theory, taxes on net *incomes* or *profits* should have the advantage for a revenue-concerned government of not affecting output levels. They neither affect average or marginal production costs, nor do they change demand. Let us assume that an imperfectly competitive firm, acting to maximize profits, is producing OX units of output (Figure 5.1). To sell this output a price OP would be charged to consumers. As long as average costs include all the normal returns to investment capital and enterprise, a price in excess of OQ produces pure profit. In this case PQ profit is made on each unit of sale and the firm's total profit is represented by the rectangle $QYZP$. The government could cream off a significant proportion, indeed in theory all of it, without affecting output levels at all.

However, as Cobbe (1979, p. 105) has pointed out, 'unfortunately this is one of the situations in which the elegance of formal models produces, as a result of necessary simplification, conclusions at variance with common sense and experience'. Apart from the fact that the firm need not be adopting a profit-maximizing strategy (carefully producing at the point where the marginal revenue and cost curves intersect), the difficulty is that for many minerals we are dealing with firms with several supply sources in different countries. If the corporation as a whole has excess capacity in relation to demand, then it is only sensible to conclude that

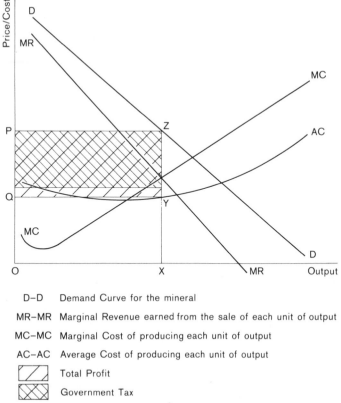

D–D	Demand Curve for the mineral
MR–MR	Marginal Revenue earned from the sale of each unit of output
MC–MC	Marginal Cost of producing each unit of output
AC–AC	Average Cost of producing each unit of output
	Total Profit
	Government Tax

Figure 5.1   The theoretical advantages of profit taxes

output will be taken from the country with the lowest profit tax levels, all other things being equal. Moreover, in the longer term, the decision to invest in new capacity will inevitably be affected by the tax regime. Therefore, in practice, governments find it necessary to maintain the profit take at broadly comparable levels to competing suppliers. The word 'broadly' is used advisedly here. Very low-cost producers can afford to impose a somewhat higher tax; and companies may be prepared to accept lower profits if the tax regime and the country are particularly stable, or if generous levels of expenses are allowed before net profits are calculated. A further complication arises when a company is allowed to write off taxes paid to a host government against any tax liabilities incurred in the parent country; this is the case for the United States and most West European based multinationals.

For metals basic profit taxes tend to be in the 35–50 per cent range, although for the remaining non-nationalized oil ventures they can be considerably higher than this. However, since about 1970 many producers have introduced extra windfall profits or excess profit taxes to further increase their take in periods of abnormally high profits or on particular projects which prove to be especially profitable. The companies have strongly opposed their imposition, arguing, first, that above-average profits are necessary to cover risky ventures and the costs of unproductive exploration, and, second, that the governments do not directly bear losses when they occur. Despite this opposition, the practice has been widely adopted by such countries as Zambia in 1970; Papua New Guinea, 1974; Canada, (Saskatchewan) 1976; Colombia, 1976; and Indonesia, 1977. In some cases the excess taxes are a fixed percentage on returns above a set normal profit level; for instance, on Bougainville copper (Papua New Guinea) all profits above a 15 per cent rate of return on capital are subject to a 70 per cent tax (Mikesell, 1983). Other governments have adopted a progressive rate system; the Saskatchewan uranium tax is a fairly typical illustration of this method. It is based on the ratio of operating profit to capital investment and is set at zero below 15 per cent profit, rises to 15 per cent on profits between 25 and 45 per cent, and then escalates to 50 per cent on profits above 45 per cent (Webb and Ricketts, 1980).

Gillis (1982) has argued that these excess tax schemes, coupled with government reluctance to give tax holidays or similar concessions and the moves to reduce the scope of transfer pricing abuses, had, by 1980, considerably increased the profit share of the host nations. This was particularly evident in the oil case. Malaysia had managed to obtain a 98.5 per cent share in total profits, Colombia captured 70 per cent and other countries still operating with private sector involvement commonly had shares of between 75 and 85 per cent (ibid., p. 629). In metals the shares were typically less impressive but usually exceeded 60 per cent.

However, over the last four years there have been clear signs that events are becoming less favourable for producers. In 1980 Chile lowered its tax rates on new copper investments to just under 50 per cent, and Britain has recently under the provisions of the Finance Act 1983 reduced the average rate of tax on future North Sea oilfields from 70 to 60 per cent, and is proposing the abolition of royalties. Canada, employing a different device but with the same aim in mind, has cut the border price for gas sales to the United States from $4.94 to $4.40 per million BTU (*Petroleum Economist*, October 1983). Moreover, a high profit share is only meaningful when profits are actually being made. The early 1980s have seen major real price falls for minerals, and over a much longer timescale the rate of investment in politically unstable, high-tax regimes has fallen markedly. This suggests that the short-term revenue gains made in the 1970s may have been counterproductive in the longer run.

CAPITAL VALUE TAXES

The final, and rather different, type of tax is predominantly to be found in the advanced industrial economies, as part of the general package of company taxes which has been built up over time. It involves taxing the value of the property owned by a company rather than the production or profits. There are, in fact, two forms of this value tax, both of which can affect the rate of mineral extraction and exploration. If an *annual* tax is levied on the value of proven reserves held by a company, then the rate of depletion of existing reserves should increase and the level of exploration to prove new deposits should fall. The reason for this is fairly simple: no company is going to hold on to deposits, or spend money trying to find new ones, if it already has sufficient reserves to meet expected sales levels for the next few years. To do so would merely add to the tax burden.

The effects of the second type of value tax, *capital gains* taxes, are more difficult to judge. Where these are in operation, a company becomes liable for taxation on the sale of an asset which has increased in value, after making allowance for all expenditure incurred on it, during the period of ownership. It is just possible that this will deter investment in mineral deposits if there are other assets which are exempt from capital gains. However, as it is operated in practice, particularly in the United States, it may be a force for conservation (McDonald, 1967). This arises because the effective rate of capital gains tax, after all the allowable expenses, is considerably less than the tax on the profits from mineral sales. Moreover, companies may obtain considerable financial advantages, such as greater ease of loan raising, if they can increase their apparent wealth or capital value by holding deposits.

TAX CONCESSIONS

The whole question of assessing the impact of all forms of tax is made even more complex by the numerous tax concessions which are normally available to different types of firms. Until the 1970s many LDC producers gave extremely liberal incentives to attract foreign investment. *Tax holidays* for three to ten years following production start-up were commonplace to allow the investors to recoup their capital more rapidly. On top of these holidays the rate of tax take was normally low in the first years of production. The practice of *free depreciation* was also widespread; this allowed companies to write off their capital assets against their tax liability in whatever way was most beneficial to them. Similarly, in some countries firms were allowed to 'expense' (write off) certain durable assets against tax as though they were operating costs, or they could claim a tax credit (in addition to depreciation) for a proportion of the cost of investment. In still other cases any losses could be carried forward against future tax liabilities.

Undoubtedly, these incentives did allow companies to achieve exceptionally high rates of return from some ventures. One of the classic examples is Rio Tinto Zinc's investment in Bougainville copper. The initial contract gave a three-year tax holiday; a write-off of all capital investment at an accelerated rate, which in effect extended the tax-free period for another two to four years; low initial tax rates of 25 per cent, increasing to 50 per cent after four tax years and remaining fixed at that level until the twenty-sixth year; and throughout income tax was to be applied on only 80 per cent of actual net income. In the first year the company earned a massive 40 per cent on its investment, which predictably brought protests from the newly independent government of Papua New Guinea and, in 1974, the contract was 'renegotiated'.

It is easy to see why producer governments regard such high rates of return as 'exploitation' and attempt to renege on the contract which allowed them. But there is also much validity in the view that:

> any tax regime which is reasonable and encourages a company to undertake the massive mining and infrastructure costs associated with a new risk venture will appear quite unreasonable during periods of very high metal prices. And even if governments were willing to take the longer term view . . . few opposition leaders are! (*Mining Magazine*, April 1975)

It is difficult to avoid the conclusion that the arbitrary removal of tax incentives and imposition of new tax burdens did proceed too far in the 1970s. Certainly, in most recent agreements the companies have managed to obtain guarantees of tax stability and freedom from windfall taxes during the period of capital recovery, and sometimes for a few years after this. The new Chilean model foreign investment agreement, for example, guarantees stability for ten years from start-up (Mikesell, 1983). It remains to be seen whether such agreements will withstand a major change in the political complexion of the government.

Controversy over tax incentives or allowances is by no means confined to LDC producers. There is a vast literature on the practice of 'expensing' and percentage depletion allowances in the United States, both of which act in favour of indigenous oil and gas producers. It is usually argued that by giving the expensing privilege to the oil industry but not to manufacturing concerns, too much investment will occur in the mineral sector, producing an inefficient allocation of resources in the economy as a whole.

A similar effect could also result from the use of depletion allowances. In the United States most mineral producers were allowed to deduct 22 per cent of their gross income from sales as an allowance for the fact that theirs was a wasting asset. In 1955 it was estimated that this measure increased investment in the affected industries by over 36 per cent (Harberger, 1955), although it became conventional economic wisdom in the 1960s to dispute this level of impact when price expectations and the effects of other forms of tax were taken into account (McDonald, 1961). However, it was generally agreed that the rate of investment in minerals and the rate of depletion of domestic resources was accelerated by the allowances. This was contrary to the economic efficiency objective but, in the short term at least, reduced the need for imports and thereby increased mineral security. Ironically the percentage depletion allowance for integrated oil and gas producers was abolished by the US Tax Reduction Act 1975, at precisely the time when security anxieties were high! It was retained, however, for some other minerals such as uranium.

Finally, it is worth pointing out that some LDC governments have got themselves into difficulties over the taxation of their own companies, both state-owned and private. They have not thought it 'proper' to subject indigenous enterprises to all, or sometimes any, of the taxes and fiscal levies imposed on foreign firms. Gillis (1982) has argued that the major benefits that host countries derive from the highly capital-intensive investment in extractive industries is government tax revenue, since the employment and multiplier-effects are minimal. This observation is likely to apply as much to domestic as to foreign investment; therefore, it could be argued that greater benefits to the whole economy would accrue if the mineral was left in foreign hands. While the Arab oil producers have not left anything more than a small fraction of the surpluses from oil exports in the hands of the state oil firms, this has by no means been the case elsewhere. Indonesia, Colombia, Bolivia and Ghana provide just a few examples of nationalized enterprises operating to their own internal logic, largely in their own interests, with minimal reference to the investment needs of the economy as a whole.

Price regulation

According to simple economic models, mineral or energy prices are established by the forces of supply and demand; in reality, however, the situation is often very different. The pricing practices of producer cartels, both intergovernmental and those comprising private companies, have already been discussed, so in this section attention will be focused on the regulation of prices by consumer nation governments. During periods of general price restraint to combat inflation all mineral producers will be affected by government price objectives, but direct regulation of non-fuel mineral prices is comparatively rare. Metal prices have been controlled during wars, and the price of construction minerals has been regulated in postwar reconstruction periods, but most cases of intervention come from the energy sector.

THE REGULATION OF DOMESTIC ENERGY PRICES

Virtually every major consumer government has taken some steps to regulate domestic energy prices, although the degree of control, the methods used and the objectives have varied considerably, both between countries and within one country at different periods of time. Generalizing greatly, there have been three major justifications for regulation. First, to protect consumers and the competitive position of manufacturing exports, prices have been held *below* 'free' market rates. This has occurred widely since the 1930s and was originally directed against indigenous energy-producing monopolies or oligopolies. However, in countries such as the United States, Canada and Australia it has been employed more recently to combat the price-fixing operations of OPEC. In other words, the existence of 'imperfections' within the market have bred further imperfections through government regulation.

Inevitably the imposition of price controls affects the profitability of domestic producers. If they are imposed too strictly on private concerns, they eventually become self-defeating since exploration and development activity decline, supplies are constrained and prices will need to increase to restore the demand and supply balance. However, if imposed on nationalized concerns, an immediate conflict arises between the consumer protection objective and the desire to maintain rates of return on capital and levels of employment in the controlled industry. Moreover, the 'low' prices inflate demands which can bring conflict with conservation and, where supplies are imported, with balance-of-payments requirements. This last dilemma is clearly reflected in the shifting policy responses of Japan to the post-1973 oil price rises; MITI, using its powers over oil-refining licences, introduced formal restrictions on the prices of refined products in 1973 as an anti-inflation measure, but two years later these were largely abolished to promote reductions in demand. Similarly, despite protests from consumer groups, controls over electricity prices were eased, and then rates were increased by a massive 50 per cent in 1979–80 to encourage conservation and reduce the need for oil-based power generation.

Both the second and third justifications for government price regulation act to maintain price levels *above* market rates; these are the need to protect indigenous energy producers (and their employees) from low-priced foreign competition, and the desire to promote energy conservation, usually for balance-of-payments and supply security reasons. Inevitably there is always the difficulty of reconciling any measures (import taxes, quotas or bans, value added taxes and so on) which increase price with consumer protection and manufacturing competitiveness. Such problems help explain the *ad hoc* shifts in the direction of government intervention in energy prices, which has typified events in most West European countries, particularly those with large domestic coal industries.

During the immediate postwar period the pressure was intense to keep energy prices – in large measure this meant coal prices – low in order to promote economic recovery. However, this conflicted with the need both to modernize the coal industry and avoid the cost of imports to the balance of payments. From about 1957 to the mid-1960s the dominant political preoccupation was protection for coal and the employment dependent upon it. But towards the end of the 1960s periodic price restraint to combat inflation became more common, and in the Netherlands, Norway and Britain the picture was further complicated by the development of the Groningen and later the North Sea energy sources.

In Britain, where all the energy industries except oil are nationalized, ministerial intervention in price determination has been virtually an annual event. In theory, the government sets the overall ground rules for public sector operations but does not intervene in day-to-day management decisions. However, under a gentleman's agreement, all proposed price increases are submitted in advance to the minister for approval. In practice, price decisions have come to reflect the policy preoccupation of the moment, be it inflation control, reducing nationalized industry losses, unemployment, the balance of payments or economic efficiency. The system has tended to become highly politicized. As Coombes (1971, p. 108) argues, 'political judgment based on electoral advantage, party ideology, patronage or bargaining' becomes the basis for price fixing.

PRICE REGULATION IN THE UNITED STATES

It could perhaps be assumed that energy markets would be 'freer' in countries where the energy industries have traditionally been private sector, but as this brief discussion of policy in the United States and Canada shows, this is far from being the case.

In the United States significant central government controls over energy prices have been exercised since the mid-1930s. With the enactment of the *Federal Power Act* 1935 and the *Natural Gas Act* 1938, the Federal Power Commission's (FPC) duties were extended to include the regulation of the rates and services of electricity and natural gas utilities when interstate transactions were involved.

Within each state regulatory commissions were also developed and these acquired the power to determine the maximum rate of return on investment which could be earned by their intrastate energy utilities; they also decided on the level and type of expense which could legitimately be charged against revenue before net returns were calculated. In effect, both electricity and gas prices came to be established administratively, not by market forces (Glaeser, 1957).

The regulatory agencies were established to protect the public from the local monopoly power inevitably enjoyed by the utilities but they became increasingly 'politicized' over time. After 1960 the FPC began to directly impose ceiling prices on producers of natural gas selling in the interstate market, maintaining prices below those for oil and coal in energy value terms. This allowed gas to significantly increase its market share. However, by the early 1970s it had created a major imbalance between demand and supplies, as evidenced by the long waiting-lists of potential customers, increasingly frequent supply interruptions and the need to impose physical rationing measures. In 1976 the regulated well-head price of natural gas in interstate commerce was only 25 per cent of the price for imported crude oil of the same calorific value (Webb and Rickets, 1980). Not surprisingly demands escalated but producers had little incentive to explore for new supply sources. Moreover, the artificially low price meant that many known deposits, particularly the smaller ones, were classified as uneconomic. As a result, the proven reserves to annual consumption ratio fell dramatically from 26:1 in 1950 to 11:1 in 1970. Where new fields were brought into production, normally those found 'accidentally' as a by-product of oil exploration, they were largely devoted to use within the producer states. From 1973 to 1977, for instance, less than 20 per cent of additional gas production was committed to the interstate market.

By the mid-1970s oil prices were also being established by government bureaucratic choice. In 1970 the quotas on oil imports, first introduced in 1959, started to be eliminated, imports escalated and production by the no longer protected domestic industry began to decline absolutely. As a response to the oil crisis of 1973 the government created a new regulatory agency, the Federal Energy Administration. Under its so-called *entitlements programme* this agency established an average price for domestically produced oil, and required the producers to buy an entitlement to refine it, at a then cost of about $2 a barrel. Importers of crude oil also had to have a refining entitlement ticket, but this time they were given a subsidy worth $3 per barrel. The exact payments under this tax and subsidy system varied from year to year with the changing average price of domestic and imported oil. In the winter of 1975 the government, worried about low stocks of distillate fuel oils, added another import subsidy specific to this quality of oil, of an extra $5 per barrel. This was administered through the same entitlement system and further reduced domestic price levels. In the event, this additional subsidy proved short-lived; the other western consuming nations objected strongly to what they regarded as a 'beggar-thy-neighbour' policy and, in June of the next year, at the Tokyo Summit, agreement was reached not to employ similar import subsidies in the future (Deese and Nye, 1981). However, the basic entitlements programme remained and, by January 1980, imported oil was effectively being subsidized by $5.28 per barrel, and US prices were $11 below world levels.

In these circumstances it is hardly surprising that the rhetoric about conservation and security was not matched by any reduction in US imports, in fact they rose from 3.5 mbd in 1970 to 8.5 mbd in 1980. The tax on domestic production slowed down exploration and investment, while the relatively low prices did not provide a significant incentive to conservation. Moreover, it must be remembered that artificially low oil and gas prices affected the level of investment in alternative fuel or energy sources, and so the apparent viability of coal, nuclear and renewable energy projects was reduced.

President Carter's ambitious National Energy Plan of 1977 clearly recognized the contradictions inherent in previous policy measures. The plan throughout laid great stress on the role of the price mechanism in promoting conservation, new energy source development and import reduction; it, therefore, proposed to raise effective oil and gas prices by the imposition of taxes. But concerns over the economic and social costs of rapidly increasing prices led to the proposal that change must be gradual, and the principle that internal oil prices should be set as high as world levels was not accepted in full. On equity grounds gas would be sold everywhere in the country at the same price as domestic oil (in energy value terms).

However, when the plan emerged – in a highly mangled form – from Congress in the autumn of 1978, many of the key price increase measures had vanished; there was to be no tax on crude oil or on petrol, nor on the electricity utilities which used oil and gas as the generating power. Some deregulation of gas prices was agreed, but only of new gas and then only by 1985, and federal price controls over interstate movements were to be extended to intrastate sales. This last may have made prices more equal and equitable, but it was hardly a stimulus to conservation. Only after the 1979 oil crisis and the advent of the Reagan administration, with its commitment to efficiency and security, did the process of oil and gas price deregulation begin in earnest.

PRICE REGULATION IN CANADA

There has also been a long history of price regulation in Canada. In the 1950s the concern was over the viability of domestic coal producers in Nova Scotia (Donald, 1966), but by the 1970s oil was the focus of most attention. Before 1973, the country was effectively divided into two oil price zones. Consumers living west of the Ottawa Valley were supplied with domestically produced oil, at prices above international levels and largely determined by the taxation and depletion policies of the Albertan provincial government. Eastern refiners, however, used imported oil at world prices and were clearly hard-hit by the 1973 price rise. As a result, the federal government established an Oil Import Compensation Programme, setting one regulated price over the whole country.

At first, this programme, which effectively subsidizes East Coast provinces, was mainly funded from oil export taxes (see p. 222, n. 7). But following the 1979 world price hike, the cost of the compensation payments rose to more than

$ Can. 4000 million per year, well in excess of the government's revenue from the oil export tax and the excise duty on petrol. One solution to this problem was to increase domestic prices, so reducing the need to make compensation payments. However, this strategy had two snags. First, it would provide the already wealthy oil-producing provinces with a major 'windfall' increase in their tax revenues, and this would immediately mean that the federal government would have to increase its 'equalization' subsidies to the poorer provinces. And second, oil price rises were politically unpopular; the short-lived Conservative government of 1979–80 owed its election defeat in considerable part to its energy price and conservation policy.

In September 1981 the Ottawa and Edmonton governments managed to agree on a compromise National Energy Programme, and an artificially low 'made in Canada' oil price became enshrined in official policy; prices have been kept at 45 to 30 per cent below international levels. Since then domestic demand has slumped. Exploration drilling in the western provinces has fallen sharply as producers have moved their rigs south to take advantage of the opportunities arising from US price deregulation. And exports of both oil and gas have declined markedly, in part at least because the controlled trade prices established by the federal government exceeded those operative in the United States.

The Canadian example provides an excellent illustration of the *ad hoc* political nature of energy policies, and of the difficulties involved in establishing a coherent, consistent policy direction in the face of rapidly changing events within the international energy economy.

Planning and environmental regulations

The plethora of regulatory tools used in an attempt to protect environmental quality are largely common to all sectors of the economy, and will be considered in detail in later chapters. However, it is appropriate to outline briefly the development of planning controls over minerals and to discuss the measures which are distinctively applied to mining, while considering their economic implications.

THE EVOLUTION OF CONTROLS

Forty years ago there were few controls over the location, development or operating practices of mineral industries anywhere in the world. The emphasis in legislation and the licensing of mine operators was on giving the producer clear and secure title to the mineral rights, with relatively little interest in what was then done in the exercise of such property rights. For instance, in the United States the General Mining Law 1872 provided that operators could establish rights to mineral deposits merely by discovery, without prior administrative approval. Even public lands could be appropriated, with companies acquiring title to the land under a mineral claim by federal patent (Henning, 1974).

The major exception to this lack of concern about the way the industries operated was the nineteenth- and early-twentieth-century legislation designed to improve the health and safety of mineworkers, who generally were employed in appalling and hazardous conditions for long hours at minimal wage rates.[11] In Britain, for example, the Mines and Collieries Act 1842 prohibited the employment of women and girls underground and raised the age limit for boys to 10. There was also the occasional early addition to the statute-book concerned with the impact of mining on adjacent or overlying property; the Brine Pumping (Compensation for Subsidence) Act 1891 provides an early British example (Roberts and Shaw, 1982). But in the main those suffering damage had to seek redress through Common Law, a notoriously cumbersome and costly procedure, which primarily afforded protection to property and not people (Sandbach, 1980).

In general, it was accepted that the economic advantages from mineral exploitation justified most of the associated environmental and social costs. According to Atwood (1979, p. 59) until the 1950s in the United States 'most surface mines in the west . . . operated according to the unwritten principle that mined land would be treated as a sacrifice area', and as late as 1974, Henning, in discussing mining on public lands, was asserting that 'the present minerals policy (particularly under the Mining Act of 1872) permits too many unnecessary and avoidable abuses of the environment through unwise selection and exploitation of locations with little concern for such tangible and intangible effects as pollution' (Henning, 1974, p. 93). It is not without relevance to note that mining interests were strongly represented on the US Public Land Law Review Commission, which recommended that 'mineral exploration and development should have preference over some or all other uses on much of our public lands. . . . Also, development of a productive mineral deposit is ordinarily the highest economic use of land' (ibid., p. 92). Similarly, in 1971 MacNeill could write of the Canadian mineral industry that 'it was, and still is, accepted practice to mine as cheaply as possible . . . such practices have left behind a legacy of scenic devastation and acid-laden waters' (MacNeill, 1971, p. 124).

The minimal control situation started to change significantly in Britain with the passage of the Town and Country Planning Act 1947, the National Parks Act 1949, the Minerals Working Act 1951, and the Open Cast Coal Act 1958. However, in most of the economically advanced countries the peak years for the development of planning and environmental controls over the mineral and energy industries were from about 1960 to 1975. Although environmental controls are generally much less stringent in the LDCs, from approximately 1970 environmental provisions started to creep into mining and smelting agreements. Mikesell (1983) shows that some countries are now insisting on detailed environmental impact studies (EIS) before allowing mine developments. In the agreement between the government of Papua New Guinea and a consortium brought together by the Broken Hill Pty Co. to develop the Ok Tedi copper ores the subject-matter for inclusion in the EIS extended over seven pages. It not only included the disposal of overburden and tailings and the effects of run-off on the biochemistry of local streams, but also required study of the effects of the mine, the infrastructure, townships and workforce on the farming, tribal life and the general sociology of the region (ibid., p. 22).

AD HOC REGULATORY RESPONSES

Much of the control legislation was enacted in response to specific pressures or crises, in the absence of a coherent, comprehensive ideological policy for the environment (see pp. 337–9). New regulatory agencies were created to tackle particular problems (this was the typical US model), or new environmental functions were tacked on to the duties of existing agencies (the prevalent British strategy). As a result, the administrative arrangements for environmental planning, as they affect the minerals sector, are normally highly fragmented both spatially and functionally.

In the United Kingdom, as Figure 5.2 clearly illustrates, the picture is one of some considerable complexity. Different types of mineral, classified by their end-use not on any clear physical criteria,[12] come under the jurisdiction of separate central government departments. The various environmental media which could suffer damage are protected under different legislation and controlled by separate agencies. A variety of levels of government are involved and range from district councils to central ministries, including several semi-autonomous inspectorates and regional bodies. Moreover, the government has tended to regard the administrative systems for planning and pollution control as quite distinct entities; the planning system functions to allocate land between competing uses, whereas the pollution control authorities subsequently regulate the operations of the land user (Miller and Wood, 1983).

However, the UK structure begins to look simple when compared with those operating in federal government systems, where the state or provincial tier of authority also plays a key role. In such cases the legislation is by no means uniform across the country, and there is often considerable jurisdictional uncertainty, causing problems of lack of integration, inconsistency and overlapping powers. Regional governments frequently compete for economic development, and in this struggle concessions over formal planning or environmental conditions are common. The competition among the east coast states of Australia to attract companies involved in coal export and aluminium smelting is just one example of this. In all countries where a single piece of control legislation is implemented by separate regional or local government bodies, considerable variations appear in the way it is interpreted and enforced in practice, reflecting differences in economic circumstances and the relative political strength of interest groups within the local economy (see p. 339). Moreover, even for a single regulatory agency the stringency of enforcement will vary over time in response to changing economic, social and political pressures. Considerable care has to be taken, therefore, in assessing the real impact on the mineral and energy industries of the upsurge during the 1960s and 1970s in formal control agencies and legislation.

THE EFFECTS OF CONTROL

Given that few countries are now prepared to merely accept the environmental costs associated with mining activities, there are basically two choices – stop production or reduce the damage by reclamation and preventative measures.

In practice, the first of these is rarely exercised, except for such ubiquitous minerals as sand and gravel. Where there is a wide range of alternative production

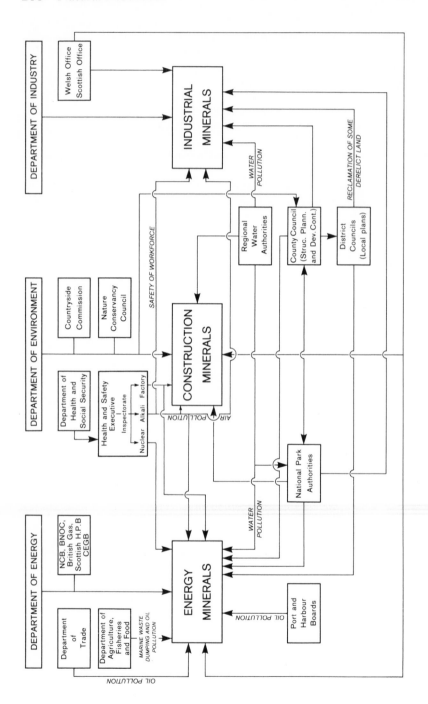

Figure 5.2 Administrative complexity: fragmentation of control over UK mineral developments

sites, it is conceptually possible to envisage a nationwide development programme to minimize total damage costs by utilizing the sources in the least
environmentally sensitive areas. The idea that planning should be based on the
'best environmental option' is a popular one in the academic literature but has
limited practical relevance (see pp. 265–6). It not only presupposes that the
country has an administrative system and Constitution which allow the allocation
of development rights in such a comprehensive and coherent manner,[13] but also
assumes that the information base exists to calculate damage costs in any broadly
objective fashion. The tendency is for output to be pushed into areas where
ignorance about potential environmental damage is greatest, or where there are
few powerful interest groups demanding protection from development. This can
be illustrated by the marked increase in the quantity of marine dredged sand and
gravel going to supply the large market for aggregates in south-eastern England.
Plans to extend production on land invariably raise powerful political emotions
and a number of the more affluent counties effectively have a presumption
against new workings written into their structure plans and development control
procedures. However, few pressure groups are concerned to defend the sea-bed
and there is little data on the effects of dredging on marine or coastal ecosystems
or on coastal erosion processes.

There are various planning and environmental control procedures (planning
applications, public inquiries, environmental impact assessments and the use of
the courts), which superficially suggest that the 'stop production' option is real for
less widely available minerals. This is rarely so. Mineral use is regarded as
essential for the continued economic vitality of the economy and indigenous
production is seen as crucial for security, balance-of-payments and employment
creation reasons. A typical expression of this view comes from Edwin Arnold, a
well-known mining correspondent:

> Import savings ... can only make our economy that much richer and
> stronger. And without financial strength, the total quality of our national life
> must decline in the long run. No country, in my view, is so rich that it can
> afford to ignore the potential of its mineral resources. (Quoted in Smith,
> 1975, p. 97)

Not surprisingly, there are few examples where environmental interests have
succeeded in halting economically attractive developments at least over the
longer term, although determined opposition can markedly delay the process.
The furore, for instance, over Shell's plans to test-drill for oil in the New Forest
was enough to divert drilling activity, for the time being at least, to less
well-defended areas of southern England. Claims are sometimes made that
pressure group activity forced Rio Tinto Zinc to abandon its plans in 1973 to
mine gold and copper in the Snowdonia National Park, but it is fairly clear that at
best the projects were marginally viable, at the current price levels. As the
MacEwens (1982, p. 234) put it, 'the issue has been deferred only until the
progressive exhaustion of richer ore bodies makes it profitable'. Undoubtedly, in
Britain environmental conservation interests have little effective power to stop
developments when there are strong market forces at work favouring mining.

Normal planning controls do not apply for exploration work, and once the presence of a valuable mineral has been established, it would be a very unusual government indeed that was prepared to forgo the economic benefits from production.

In the United States where environmental groups have generally been much more influential than in Britain, the late 1960s and early 1970s saw some spectacular victories for conservation and pollution control interests. One highly controversial case was the refusal in 1970 to allow the West German firm BASF to establish a major petrochemical complex near the Hilton Head Island resort area of South Carolina (Gladwin, 1977). However, the environmental case was considerably aided by the fact that domestic petrochemical interests were actively opposed to this attempt by a foreign company to make inroads into their traditional markets (Faith, 1972). Similarly, Shell had to abandon a $200 million oil refinery project in Delaware and relocate across the estuary in more sympathetic New Jersey, and it is well known that opposition to the trans-Alaska pipeline delayed major developments in the Alaskan oilfields for about five years. Bitter battles also took place against oil, oil shale and open-cast mining schemes on federal and Indian lands; they certainly slowed down exploitation but in no way halted it. As Davis *et al.* (1983) have shown, royalties, lease sales and rents are a major income source for the states, the Indian tribes and the federal government, and play a vital role in maintaining social programmes. When these interests are coupled with the economic benefits to the mineral companies, environmental groups may obtain pollution control and reclamation concessions but rarely stop extraction.

Since the advent of the Reagan administration the position of the environmental lobby has been significantly weakened. Federal land areas, previously under protective orders, have now been opened up for mineral development, and such key agencies as the Environmental Protection Agency have been 'requested' to change their 'mistaken' interpretations of their duties and of environmental laws (Wilson, 1981; Mosher, 1981, 1982). Similarly, the Department of the Interior has rewritten the coalmining regulatory programme to make it 'less burdensome' for coal companies and has considerably weakened enforcement by reducing the number of Office of Surface Mining field inspectors by two-thirds (Lovell, 1983). Actions against coal operators for contravening the Surface Mining Control and Reclamation Act, which was only passed in 1977, have decreased by over 30 per cent in the last two years. In addition, the administration's policy of decentralization has also acted to reduce environmental protection. More environmental control functions have been devolved to the states but federal money allocated to them for enforcement and monitoring has declined by 20 per cent for the 1983 fiscal year, and further cuts were expected in 1984 and 1985 (Jubak, 1982). It seems unlikely that many states will be willing or able to continue enforcement activities at anything like past levels of stringency. Some will feel unable to meet the financial burden of control, and others will be unwilling to impose costs on to companies threatening to move to another less restrictive state.

Whenever reclamation or damage prevention measures are a condition for allowing mineral developments, the question is inevitably raised of who pays. Although the idea that the polluter should pay for the damage caused has a neat intuitive appeal, this need not be an equitable, politically acceptable or even feasible proposition. While most people would consider it broadly fair that Union Oil, Texaco, Gulf Oil and Mobil should pay some $13.5 million in compensation for the massive damage done by the Santa Barbara oil-spill of 1969, it is rare for the case to be so relatively clear-cut. In this instance the damage was obviously imposed by the companies albeit accidently. The companies were financially able to bear the costs, were unlikely to merely pass them on to consumers as price increases and, even if they did, it would not have an observable effect on price levels; furthermore, there was no question of the firms closing down production and causing local revenue and employment losses. When this rather special set of conditions does not apply, the question of who should pay becomes much more controversial.

In the first place, it is often unclear who causes damage to whom (Coase, 1960). It is common for long-established mining enterprises to be confronted with demands that they undertake major reclamation, pollution abatement and screening exercises. Bartlett (1980) has traced one such case in his book *The Reserve Mining Controversy*. When the Reserve Mining Co. first began the benefication of low-grade taconite ores on the shores of Lake Superior in 1956, it was hailed as the saviour of the area. The extraction of low-grade iron ores suddenly became a commercially viable proposition, and ore bodies previously thought to be exhausted were given new economic life. But as Bartlett puts it, the company 'with no change whatever in its policies or behaviour, found itself being transformed from a benefactor of economic progress to a malefactor of environmental degradation' (ibid., p. 4). Initially on aesthetic grounds, but later because of a potential but unproven health hazard, the company's practice of dumping 67,000 tons of taconite tailings into the lake each day came under fire. Eventually after eight years of litigation, the company was forced to construct an on-land dump at a cost of $470 million (1977 prices). If it had refused or not been financially able to comply, 3000 people would have immediately been put out of work, the local and state governments' revenue budgets would have been in chaos and US imports would have had to rise to cover the 15 per cent of total ore use which the Reserve Mining Co. produced. It is cases like this which raise doubts about who is the damaged party.

Another problematic 'who pays' issue arises when the polluter is a publicly owned concern. The land reclamation and pollution control measures introduced by the UK National Coal Board are in effect paid for by the taxpayer, as the Board has consistently failed to be profitable. In some situations, such as the removal of dangerous tip heaps in South Wales following the 1966 Aberfan disaster, when 147 people, including 116 young children, died, the consensus view would undoubtedly regard the costs as justifiable. But much more difficult equity choices arise in the case of the Belvoir coalfield, in Leicestershire. Should

9   At this open-cast coalmining site, Shilo South in Derbyshire, the viaduct – part of the disused Nottingham–Derby railway – is a listed structure of 'special architectural or historic interest'. It has, therefore, to be protected during the operations, which not only sterilize the coal beneath it, but also increase production costs.

the taxpayer be asked to pay for backpacking or extensive spoil heap reclamation when the major beneficiaries are the relatively affluent interest groups concerned to protect the landscape quality and property values in the area? Similarly, whenever pollution control costs are passed on to final consumers in increased prices, there is a possibility that regressive redistributions of real income will occur (see p. 155). Therefore, although environmentalists are undoubtedly correct in highlighting the damage caused by the mineral industries and the benefits from conservation, the issue still remains of whether it is equitable to ask the relatively poor to pay a proportionately higher amount of the control costs. In the real world when the costs of pollution abatement are actually paid through unemployment, reduced income for already disadvantaged groups or severe balance-of-payments difficulties then 'the polluter pays' principle becomes at least questionable.

Subsidization

To many economists government subsidies (to allow the installation of pollution abatement equipment), the maintenance of employment in uneconomic industries and the provision of low-priced goods and services are all sources of 'inefficiency' within the market system. They distort product prices, supplies and consumer demand and result in a misallocation of national resources. However, standing in marked contrast to the theoretical rejection of the practice is the frequency with which it is actually employed. A number of indirect subsidies have in fact already been discussed: tariff protection and tax incentives are both extremely common forms of effective subsidy for mineral and energy industries. Subsidies as a pollution control measure will be considered separately in Chapter 7. It is only necessary here to refer briefly to the role of government subsidy in boosting domestic mineral production.

Declining mineral industries, exploration programmes, conservation[14] and the development of indigenous refining and processing capacity have all received widespread support. As with most policy measures, the motives behind it are mixed: security, employment generation or unemployment reduction, balance-of-payments considerations, national prestige and the protection of vested economic interests being the most common. In some cases the support may also be a token gesture to diffuse public controversy; many would argue that Britain's energy conservation programmes have been an example of such tokenism (Davidson and MacEwen, 1983). To support the home production objective governments have basically employed three types of subsidy:

(1) direct grants and low-interest loans to private producers and consumers to encourage them to take specific measures;
(2) direct and indirect transfers from general tax revenues to mineral producers. These include tax concessions, rent and royalty rebates, and the write-off of accumulated debt;
(3) cross-subsidy flows from other consumer or producer groups.

EXPLORATION SUBSIDIES

Many of the industrialized countries have used grant aid, preferential rate loans and deferred loan repayment schemes to encourage domestic mineral exploration. The federal government of Canada has provided considerable assistance for the exploratory drilling for oil in frontier regions, such as the Beaufort Sea, the Arctic Islands and the East Coast continental shelf. Although the difficult physical conditions occurring in such areas are used to justify the aid, in reality it is impossible to divorce the government's interest in their development from its constitutional battle with the provinces over jurisdiction (see pp. 156–7).

The northern part of the country is a territory administered directly by the central government, which would therefore receive the bulk of the tax revenue from any oil finds. The UK government has also attempted to stimulate domestic exploration. In 1972, for example, it introduced an incentive scheme whereby 35 per cent of the costs of prospecting and assessing the viability of any discovered deposits could be reclaimed through a grant-in-aid. More recently the Petroleum Royalties (Relief) Bill, introduced in Parliament in October 1983, was intended to stimulate further developments in the North Sea by ending royalty payments on new fields in the northern sector.

CONSERVATION SUBSIDIES

Direct grants have been widely used throughout Europe to promote energy conservation. In Britain's case a £453 million expenditure programme was introduced in December 1977 to run until 1981 (Harns and Davis, 1981). Nearly one-half of this money was to go to improve insulation in domestic properties; most householders were able to claim 60 per cent of the cost of roof insulation up to a £65 limit, although pensioners could obtain 90 per cent of the cost up to a maximum of £90.[15] Another £153 million was to be spent on improving insulation within public sector buildings (this was basically a transfer payment within government) and a relatively minor subsidy scheme was introduced for industrial and commercial properties. More recently, the Department of Industry has operated a grant system to provide up to 25 per cent of the capital cost of new energy-saving equipment for some firms, and the Department of Energy is helping fund a Neighbourhood Energy Action Scheme, under which local voluntary groups insulate and draughtproof the homes of low-income families.

Although more than half a million households have taken up these grants, the conservation effort in Britain is lamentably small when compared with other European countries, particularly Sweden. It is also dwarfed by the level of expenditure being pumped into developing new energy sources. The government appears now to have recognized the paucity of past policy; Mr Peter Walker, the Energy Secretary, has confirmed that over the last decade the energy-saving campaigns had produced at most a 5 per cent saving (*Guardian*, 1 November 1983). But the mere creation of an Energy Efficiency office and yet another £3 million publicity campaign will do little to get at the underlying factors inhibiting conservation. First, the energy industries are geared to promote energy use and sell their product; second, domestic gas prices have been held down, in part due to the embarrassingly high profits made by a nationalized industry; and, third, minor grants paid after the installation of one form of insulation do not go anywhere near solving the difficulties faced by some households in finding the necessary capital sums to undertake energy-efficient home renovation measures.

In 1982 the House of Commons Select Committee on Energy put the whole conservation effort into perspective when it pointed out that a 20 per cent reduction in domestic consumption alone would save energy valued at more than £1000 million a year, and a countrywide 20 per cent consumption fall could cut £7000 million a year from the national fuel bill. But at present only £149 million per annum is invested by government in energy conservation, while £800 million is spent annually on allowances to enable people to afford to consume energy (Davidson and MacEwen, 1983) and £35 million is spent by the gas and electricity industries on advertisements designed to increase demand!

OUTPUT SUBSIDIES

A variety of effective subsidies have been and are still employed to maintain European coal production and, to a somewhat lesser extent, to accelerate the development of nuclear power generation.

In the United Kingdom the NCB has been subsidized directly by major write-offs of accumulated debt to the Exchequer; in 1965, for example, £400 million out of the £960 million debt was removed from the account and a further £1000 million was wiped off in 1972. Further payments have been made as social cost grants, paid when the government required the Board to maintain operations at high-cost pits to avoid exacerbating already severe unemployment problems in the depressed areas. Additional support has been received in the form of low-interest loans. Not only has the Treasury borrowing rate normally been below private sector interest rates, but in recent years the Board has been able to take advantage of the EEC Commission's policy of encouraging coal production to reduce reliance on imported oil. Between 1974 and 1979 it was able to attract over £300 million in 'soft' loans from the European Coal and Steel Community (Manners, 1981b). Furthermore, under the Coal Industry Act 1980 the NCB is able to defer interest payments on major capital projects until these start to show a return. Finally, a rather different method of subsidization arises through the policy of maintaining a compulsory level of coal burn in electricity generating stations.[16] In theory, major capital expenditure programmes to modernize established pits and bring new efficient mines into production were meant to leave the industry in a good competitive position, able to break even in 1983/4 except for social grants. Many commentators (see, for example, ibid.) have expressed considerable doubts about whether this was ever a realistic objective (even without the activities of the National Union of Mineworkers), given demand trends and the level of investment in other energy sources.

Although the coal industry is the classic illustration of the impact of government subsidy programmes, there are many other cases where the level of production and the location of processing industries can only be explained by considering the role of government.

Aluminium smelting and refining was largely attracted into the United Kingdom through government investment grants and other forms of support. In all, three smelters were built between 1968 and 1972 at a total cost of £150 million, of which £60 million was grant aid and a further £62 million was provided as soft loans (Warren, 1973). The location of the smelters was highly dependent upon regional policy and regional politics, going in the end to Anglesey in Wales, Invergordon in Scotland and Blyth in Northumberland. The aluminium case also provides a good example of the way the energy industries compete for custom, a practice which results in complex cross-subsidy flows between consumers. The Invergordon smelter received extremely cheap-rate hydroelectric power; it made no contribution to the capital cost of the integrated generating and distribution system, so effectively raising the contribution needed to cover these from other consumers. The unwillingness or inability of the Scottish Hydroelectric Board to continue providing subsidized supplies was the major reason given by the company for the plant's closure in December 1981. Similarly, Alcan's smelter at Lynemouth, near Blyth, benefited greatly from the competition between the CEGB and the NCB to supply the power. In the end coal won and was provided at what the CEGB called 'unrealistically low' prices, to which both other coal users and the taxpayer have made a contribution.

GOVERNMENT OWNERSHIP

The historical development of public ownership

Public ownership of gas and electricity utilities was well established in Britain and continental Europe in the nineteenth century (Robson, 1937). Even in the United States municipalities frequently owned the local town gas industry; the ones established in Philadelphia (1841) and Richmond, Virginia (1852), are but two early examples. From the 1880s publicly owned electricity utilities were vital in providing power, particularly to smaller communities, where the potential for private profit was limited. In Canada the 1906 establishment of a provincially owned hydroelectric commission in Ontario became the prototype for similar developments in the rest of Canada and the United States (Glaeser, 1957).

However, the spread of government's direct involvement in production was relatively slow in the western capitalist economies until first the 1930s depression and then the Second World War brought a major extension of public ownership. In the United States Roosevelt's New Deal resulted in a rapid increase in local, state and regional power schemes, including the creation of the Tennessee Valley Authority, while in Europe major non-utility industries such as coal, iron and steel were widely brought under government control (Baum, 1958; Lister, 1960). In Britain, for example, the postwar Labour government established the National Coal Board in January 1947, the British Electricity Authority in April 1948, and the Gas Council in May 1949.[17] The Swedish government likewise took a major direct role in its metal and power industries, while in France and Italy national oil companies were created.

By the end of the 1950s the upsurge of public ownership in the mineral and energy industries of the economically advanced countries tailed off. Nationalization of established ventures became unusual, although the creation of national enterprises continued to occur to develop new supply sources – the creation of the state-owned oil company Petro Canada, the Dutch government's partnership in the development of the natural gas fields, the establishment of the British National Oil Corporation, the widespread development of state-owned nuclear industries and the Australian government's participation in uranium and coal-mining are just a few of the many examples which could be cited.

LDC nationalization programmes

These brief historical details are designed to put into comparative context the major extension of public ownership which has taken place in the less developed mineral-exporting countries. Neither the fact that governments should wish to take direct control of vital industries, nor the view that profit-seeking private enterprise would fail to operate in the wider interests of the community, should have been surprising. Such issues had been well aired in the public v. private debate which had been conducted in Europe and North America for over a century. Hostility to LDC nationalization programmes was less concerned with opposition to public ownership *per se*, which was after all already well established in the western capitalist countries, than with loss of economic and political power and with the effects on the capital investments of the multinational companies.

The peak period for LDC government moves to bring their mineral-exporting industries under state ownership occurred in the decade from the mid-1960s to the mid-1970s. Long before this, direct state participation in production had become widely accepted, particularly in Latin America where in Argentina, Chile and Bolivia nationally owned firms date back as far as the 1920s. Chile, for instance, created a state monopoly over oil exploration and production as long ago as 1927 (Odell, 1970). But in the main such public companies were concerned with developing minerals to serve domestic needs and had no effect on international markets.

However, there were also a few very early expropriations of foreign capital, which provoked immediate and hostile reactions, both from the multinationals and from their home governments. The 1951 Iranian episode has already been discussed (p. 161), but an even earlier example was the take-over by Mexico in 1938 of all its oil interests. Reaction by the oil majors was swift; the country immediately lost its entire export trade, which had accounted for approximately 10 per cent of all internationally traded oil. Until the government agreed to compensate the companies by paying them the book value of their assets over a period of twenty-five years, the companies threatened legal action and supply boycotts on anyone who purchased oil from the new Petroleos Mexicanos (PEMEX). The national company survived to provide for the rapidly expanding domestic market and only in 1975 did Mexico re-enter the export trade on any significant scale. Major new finds in the south-eastern part of the country, the redefinition of subeconomic deposits after the oil price rise, the ever more desperate need for foreign exchange to pay for imports and service international debt and the country's position outside OPEC have all contributed to its new importance as an oil exporter.[18]

Other early moves towards state ownership occurred in Bolivia in 1952, when three 'exploitive' tin-mining groups, Patino, Hochschild and Aramayo, were taken over, but approximately 50 per cent of the industry remained in private hands. Similarly, in Indonesia a wide range of industries were nationalized and foreign capital investment was rejected from the early 1950s to 1966, when an abrupt policy reversal occurred. However, none of these moves had much lasting impact except, of course, on the producing country which lost revenue, foreign exchange' and development capital. Only after 1964 did what appeared to be a major shift in commodity power start to occur.

Through a series of nationalizations, in Chile (partial in 1964 and complete in 1971), Peru (partial 1972), Zambia (1969) and Zaire (1967) the multinationals lost full ownership of most of their major LDC copper sources, which had together contributed approximately 55 per cent of internationally traded copper. In 1968 Peru expropriated the La Brea y Parinas oil complex, the property of the US-owned International Petroleum Co. Iraq followed in 1972, taking over the holdings of all the western oil majors and, by 1975, most major oil-producing countries had established national companies with a monopoly over exploration and oil development. This did not mean that the international oil companies were excluded entirely; management contracts, service or work contracts or production-sharing agreements were all reached to ensure that the technical skills and the marketing networks of the majors could still be employed.

Similar moves were also made in other minerals; traditional concession agreements were widely renegotiated to give the producer state a greater share of the economic rent from its mineral resource base. This frequently, but not always, involved the government taking a majority share of the equity in the production companies; a common pattern was for a national company to be formed, which worked in partnership with the mining multinationals. Some of these new national companies are now among the 500 largest enterprises operating outside the United States; these include Petrobas of Brazil, Gecamines of Zaire, Codeko of Chile and Pertamina of Indonesia. As these state-owned enterprises have developed, they have not only played a key role within their home country, but some have moved into neighbouring states, providing the capital and technical skills for mineral exploration and development. The Brazilian firms have, for example, been active in exploration for coal, oil and uranium in Colombia and other Latin American countries.

During this period of nationalization and the development of state-owned enterprises most attention was paid to the highly acrimonious battles which took place when take-over was achieved unilaterally by government fiat. Two of the most well-documented cases were Peru's oil nationalization and its refusal to pay compensation, and the Allende government's expropriation of the Chilean assets of the Kennecott and Anaconda copper companies. Kennecott, under an agreement with the earlier Frei government, had already sold 51 per cent of its copper operations to the state, but Anaconda had refused all moves towards 'Chileanization'. In July 1971 both companies were nationalized completely, and compensation was withheld on the ground that they had made and transferred abroad 'excessive' levels of profit. The government was not challenging the principle of compensation itself. It did in fact make payments to owners of smaller mines which had also been nationalized.[19] But for both Anaconda and Kennecott it was determined that the excess profits exceeded any appropriate compensation. Predictably the companies disputed this on the ground that the proposed 'book value' level of recompense used in government calculations failed to consider the loss of potential earnings and the replacement cost of establishing operations elsewhere. They had difficulty in denying that the profits on their Chilean operations were well above the average earned on their worldwide assets since this emerged all to clearly in the official consolidated accounts of the companies (Mezger, 1980). This dispute was not resolved until Allende was toppled in 1974 and the new military junta agreed compensation terms as part of a wider international financial agreement rescheduling Chile's $1000 million external debt.

While other cases of unilateral take-over have occurred, these were usually followed fairly quickly by a compensation settlement and the conclusion of marketing, management and equity-sharing agreements with the companies. Public ownership, therefore, became part of the package of items which were negotiated in deals between producer states and foreign international capital. When a government was seeking to control an industry which could be viable serving domestic markets, it could afford a complete take-over, buying in independent foreign expertise as necessary. However, if the resource had to be sold on international markets, then some accommodation had to be reached with those companies controlling the markets. Peru, for example, felt able to nationalize the International Petroleum company as Peruvian consumers absorbed most of its output. But when new deposits were found which could only be exploited with foreign capital and serving overseas markets, the international oil companies were invited back on a partnership basis (Smith and Wells, 1975). A government's freedom to gain effective control of its mineral production is critically determined by the need to market the products. This basic fact of life within the international economic system was expressed clearly by Sheikh Yamani, 'Nationalization does not guarantee the State concerned the means to market its crude' (Mikdashi, 1974, p. 159).

For an exporting producer to gain significant advantages from unilateral nationalization one of three conditions must apply. First, the mineral already has to be in scarce supply, with no surplus developed capacity, or with artificial scarcity created by export restrictions or wars in other producing centres. Second, the producer country has to control enough of world supply to produce scarcity by withholding supplies and has then to have the financial reserves to sustain the loss of export income long enough to exhaust security stockpiles. Or, third, a buyer from outside the traditional market centres has to be willing and able to take the output. The first two of these conditions clearly applied during the period when oil production came under state ownership, and the third occurred when the Soviet Union took bauxite from Guyana's national company.

However, such cases are the exception not the rule and, as the OPEC case shows, the advantages gained may be short-lived when new source developments remove the supply scarcity. Copper is another clear illustration of this. Despite the fact that high-grade copper was thought to be a scarce commodity, the effective control which nationalization has brought to the host governments is strictly limited. During the Allende period in Chile copper sales plummeted; exports to the United States and Canada were minimal and sales to France and Germany fell by 65 and 35 per cent respectively as both a French company, Penarroya, and the German-based Metallgesellschaft were also affected by the policies of the new regime. The financial strains caused by the loss of export revenue, coupled with the refusal of the international banking institutions to reschedule the country's foreign debt, were major factors in the fall of Allende and the establishment of a right-wing government more sympathetic to the interests of foreign investment capital.

In both Zaire and Zambia the governments recognized that they had neither the capital nor the indigenous management and technical skills to run the copper industry alone. They, therefore, chose to go for partnership with the mineral multinationals. In Zaire's case the Belgian firm, Union Minière, basically retained its management and marketing functions under an agreement with the state-owned company, Gecamines, and the terms of the deal were generally thought to be generous to the Belgian firm (Mezger, 1980). Zambia took a 51 per cent share of all productive capacity in 1969 and created a state monopoly over future exploration, but the two major mining conglomerates, Anglo-American and Roan Selection Trust, are still responsible for day-to-day management, and have the right to veto expansion plans or appropriations for capital, exploration or prospecting expenditures. In addition, the foreign companies still market the bulk of the copper sent for export.

It is by no means clear that public ownership *per se* need improve the financial position of producer governments, although it may bring important internal political advantages. Smith and Wells (1975) have shown that in a number of the early participation or equity-sharing agreements the government's revenue take actually fell. They, for example, describe the Liberian National Iron Ore Co. deal with Bethlehem Steel as 'so disadvantageous to the government that the most charitable interpretation must be that the issue was not clearly understood by government negotiators' (ibid., p. 39). Most analysts have not been so charitable and put the agreement terms down to bribery and corruption. It seems likely that a number of early agreements were biased towards the multinational companies by the lack of experience and negotiating skills of government officials; it is clear that this no longer applies. Mikesell (1983, p. 7) argues that 'the existence of state mining enterprises and of mining ministries well staffed with geologists, mining engineers, and financial experts has tended to equalize the bargaining capabilities of the negotiators'. But that does not mean that bargaining power is also equal.

By and large, it does not matter to the mineral multinationals whether a government chooses to take its profit share as dividends or as income tax; what is important at the end of the day is how much the company can make under the arrangement. They have, therefore, been quite prepared to accept the principle of equity sharing, and a number of agreements contain clauses transferring the entire ownership of the production company over to the state after fifteen to twenty-five years; in other words, after the company has taken its return on the investment. Hanna's agreement with the government of Colombia, for example, included provision for the reversion of the nickel-mining operations to the state after twenty-five years (Smith and Wells, 1975). Ultimately the terms of any mining agreement will depend on how badly a mineral conglomerate needs a particular deposit, on the availability of alternative sources of capital, technological expertise and market outlets, and on the degree to which the producing country is dependent on export revenue. Undoubtedly, the 1970s saw conditions shift in favour of the producer states and their share of mining profits has risen markedly. But unless entirely new markets can be established for mineral products, the multinationals still hold the key bargaining card.

CONCLUSION

It is clear that the level and variety of government interventions in the operations of the minerals sector has increased significantly over time. Undoubtedly, this has affected the location of production and consumption, the scale and configuration of trade patterns, the relative level of use of different substitutable minerals, and the allocation of the wealth and economic growth associated with mineral exploitation. However, care must be taken not to overemphasize the direct power of governments. Within advanced western societies a large proportion of effective policy decisions are still in practice made by the private sector, while at the international scale private objectives and interests still dominate trade and consumption patterns and continue to have a critical impact on the location of production for export. Some of the most important changes in the distribution and scale of resource developments have resulted not directly from government activity, but from the response of the international mineral industries to it. And this response has frequently been antipathetical to the original objectives of the government. State intervention to make the minerals sector operate more in line with societal efficiency, equity, employment or environmental quality goals can only be successful within the constraints set by the market system.

In addition, it cannot be assumed that government regulation or even state ownership will mean that the mineral industries will operate more closely in line with the general 'public interest'. It is never clear what public interest means; in practice it tends to be a concept manipulated for private gain by the plethora of vested interests attempting to shift the direction of policy. In the complex process of public decision-making, conflict between objectives and between interest groups typically means that change occurs through a series of *ad hoc* measures, introduced to meet particular 'crises' or pressures. The end-results may fail to improve significantly the performance of the minerals sector and on some criteria may actually reduce it.

As will be seen, the problems involved in developing and implementing effective minerals policy are by no means confined to this type of resource; they apply with just as much force for the renewables sector. In many respects failure to take appropriate public measures is even more serious for environmental quality and depletable flow resources since the market system contains few mechanisms to ensure their continued availability.

NOTES

1 It is worth noting that these Acts were not an insignificant factor underlying the American War of Independence.
2 In Britain, for example, some of the nationalized mineral enterprises, such as the Coal

Board, have been given financial objectives much less stringent than those tolerated in the private sector, and have frequently failed to achieve even these (the coal industry has rarely met its break-even target). However, the financial targets set for electricity and gas have, theoretically at least, been broadly based on private sector rate of return criteria. Further, it has recently been argued that the Thatcher government is requiring the water industry to generate returns on capital which *exceed* private sector requirements.

3   These proportions are likely to decline in the 1980s if the current privatization programme of the Thatcher government continues.

4   This last is true in most modern advanced capitalist economies. It does not hold for much of the Third World, where there has been an increase in the non-capital-owning, landless class.

5   The concepts of 'policy as practice' and non-decisions will be discussed in Chapter 9.

6   Gulf Oil alone is reported to have dispensed $10 million between 1967 and 1972, through secret funds to political campaigns.

7   There are some exceptions to this, most commonly in federal systems, where the national governments do not receive royalties from indigenous mineral producers (see p. 194). Canada introduced in 1975 an oil export tax to curb the outflow of domestically produced oil from the western provinces at a time when eastern refineries were increasingly reliant on higher-priced and less secure Middle Eastern imports. Similarly, the Australian government imposes a specific duty on coal exports; when introduced in 1975, it was motivated by a desire to claim as taxation some of the windfall profits accruing to the coal exporters following the oil crisis (Garnaut and Clunies Ross, 1983).

8   As has already been seen, this is not true in the medium and longer terms.

9   There is no universally accepted definition of countertrade. Its key feature, however, is that it involves an element of reciprocity. An exporter takes goods and services produced in the importing country in full or part payment for the imports.

10   It is, however, produced elsewhere in the country as a by-product in other production processes, and two-thirds of all supplies are imported.

11   A particularly vivid impression of the working and living conditions endured by miners and their families in the French coalfields between 1860 and about 1890 can be gained from Emile Zola's classic novel *Germinal*.

12   Limestone from the same pit could be used as an industrial mineral (chemicals) or as a construction mineral (aggregates).

13   In the United States, for example, any nationalization of the right to develop privately owned land would be regarded as a 'taking' of property and would, therefore, be unconstitutional. If regulation proceeds too far, it is also recognized as 'taking'. Although zoning is allowable, it must leave some element of profitability in the hands of the private owner, which clearly raises problems in attempting to use zoning to stop a mining development in favour of, say, wildlife protection: see Garner, 1980.

14   It may seem odd to include conservation as a means of increasing home production, but it does of course raise domestic self-sufficiency; energy conservation is now commonly termed the 'fifth fuel'.

15   These grants are still available but have been reduced to £50, or £70 for pensioners.

16   This is not just a UK measure, but is also practised in Belgium, Holland and Germany: see UN Economic Commission for Europe, 1978.

17   The iron and steel industry was also taken into public ownership at this time, but was denationalized in 1951, to be nationalized again in 1967.

18   In 1974 total proven reserves stood at 5.8×10^9 barrels, enough for domestic

requirements but with little export surplus. By 1980 they were 60.1×10^9. Oil exports rose from zero in 1973 to over 900,000 barrels a day in 1981.

19 It had been a long-established principle in international law that compensation was due. In 1962 the UN General Assembly Resolution on Permanent Sovereignty over Natural Resources called for 'appropriate compensation' – but left open the meaning of 'appropriate'.

6 Renewable resources: the diversity of perspectives

THE CONCEPT OF RENEWABILITY

The term 'renewable resource' has been used extremely widely in the literature, becoming almost a catch-all expression to encompass the highly diverse 'products' of physical environmental systems which are not classified as mineral stocks. The central characteristic of renewable resources is that they are thought to be capable of *natural* regeneration into useful 'products' within a timespan relevant to man. This distinguishes them from fossil fuels, which are transformed by use into forms of matter which cannot provide usable energy, and from the element minerals, which need to be reprocessed by man before they are available for reuse. However, the dividing-line between stock and flow resources is very fine and owes more to conventional patterns of thought than physical realities (see Figure 2.1, p. 13).

The strains in the definition are immediately evident in the case of land, which is, to all intents and purposes, a fixed stock, although it has a renewable capacity to support all forms of biological life. The fertility of the soil regenerates naturally when the land is not used intensively, but under all forms of modern agriculture it has to be managed and renewed artificially by man. Moreover, the effective supply of land available for this reproductive purpose can be decreased by urban-related developments and by agricultural practices which induce erosion and desertification. In reality, therefore, the continued flow of usable land is as much dependent on human decision and investment as is the rate of recycling of metallic minerals.

Similarly, in the case of water, modern societies are rarely prepared to accept the limits imposed on population numbers, agricultural productivity or industrial activity by reliance on natural flows. Even in temperate areas, such as Britain, massive capital investment is required to augment natural availability by storage, recycling and the development of transfer networks. In this situation the concept of natural regeneration becomes redundant; availability is now a function of investment, and scarcity occurs not because of any absolute physical flow limitations but because of the lack of capital. The perceived need for flow augmentation and the costs involved will inevitably vary spatially; in part this is a result of the natural variability in precipitation, evapotranspiration and run-off regimes, but to a very large extent it reflects different socioeconomic circumstances, public policy objectives and institutional arrangements.

For most flow resources the whole idea of natural renewability is only meaningful in terms of the level or intensity of use; it is a relative not absolute concept.[1]

This is most clearly seen for *critical zone* resources, which remain naturally reproducible at rates of use at or below their regenerative capacity but can only sustain any greater levels of use if management takes place to increase the flows 'artificially'. It is, therefore, useful to abandon the notion that stock and renewable resources are two quite distinct types, rather they are on a continuum. At one extreme lie the fossil fuels where the current rates of use massively exceed regeneration, and at the other there are water and air resources for which, on a global scale at least, the demands are still relatively minor both in relation to the total stock and to the environment's capacity to make reprocessed units available.

Within this continuum individual resources do not necessarily occupy one set position common to all time periods and spatial divisions. For instance, hardwood forests regenerate only slowly on a human timescale but they remain naturally renewable in some parts of the world where local timber demands are low and the forests have not been penetrated by the timber exporters or come under pressure from agricultural interests. However, on a worldwide basis hardwood is now a depleting mined resource, and further decreases in the stock can only be prevented by major curbs on use or by replanting. When timber is obtained from artificially regenerated areas it ceases to be a natural resource, *sensu stricto*, but becomes a plantation crop.

It is clear from the timber example that the concept of natural regeneration cannot be divorced from the spatial scale of concern. For many resources it is not the notional overall availability and renewability within the global physical system which are relevant, but the balance between supply and the rate of use within a defined unit of territory. Most usually these territorial units are not natural divisions but are determined by administrative and political decision. This can be illustrated by reference to water, where for all practical purposes there is a physically unlimited recyclable supply. Storage and transport can adjust spatial and temporal imbalances between primary water supply and use, the natural cleansing cycle can be accelerated by waste-water renovation and the option exists to tap the massive stores held in the oceans. The fact that use exceeds natural flow is an area-specific problem, the significance of which will vary enormously, reflecting differences in the political, institutional, economic, environmental and energy availability constraints on flow augmentation and re-use.[2]

When we discard the idea that all flow resources have some special distinctive regeneration capacity which is determined by nature not man, and instead see effective flows as functions of the intensity of use and human investment, it no longer seems surprising that scarcity, depletion and degradation should occur. It is not, of course, disputed that there is a natural regenerative process at work. But as has been shown, for critical zone resources management of demands or artificial flow augmentation are needed to maintain this process, while for non-critical zone resources (water, solar or wind energy) investment is required to translate the flow potential into actual supplies. In other words, the availability of renewable resources is dependent on the political, institutional and socioeconomic systems which manage demand and supply, and which determine the allocation of available flows over time and space. Just as the mineral production and allocation system fails to perform in line with some social objectives, so too the renewable resource management system is unlikely to be able to fulfil the often conflicting objectives of different groups within society.

THE NATURE OF THE FLOW RESOURCE PROBLEM

In a book of this type it is clearly impossible to attempt to describe the spatial patterns of flow resource availability and use, or to detail the many changes in supply and quality which have undoubtedly occurred over time. It will be taken as beyond question that scarcity, depletion and degradation problems already exist, and that the ecological, energy and bio-geochemical cycles which sustain all forms of life are being altered (Holdgate *et al.*, 1982). The prime concern here will be to explain why these have occurred and to analyse the appropriateness of alternative policy responses. No attempt will be made to look at physical cause–effect relationships, rather explanations will be sought within the socioeconomic, institutional and political arenas.

As is well known, the 1960s and 1970s witnessed an avalanche of literature identifying a vast range of individual resource depletion problems and environmental threats; the work of Carson (1962), Nicholson (1970), Wilson (1970), Ward and Dubos (1972) and Ward (1979) are among the best-known and readily accessible material. Many of the books were polemics focusing attention on a particular issue from one narrow social perspective, while others were detailed technical reports showing that specific physical changes or damage were being induced in some part of the environmental system. Commonly such reports contained the implicit assumption that change was bad and, therefore, regulation was automatically justified. It was rare for the socioeconomic consequences of regulation to be assessed or for the political, legal or administrative feasibility of control measures to be analysed. All too often the treatment of the issues was highly simplistic, with a clear tendency to assume that the myriad concerns broadly classified as 'environmental' were all aspects of one fundamental problem, were all traceable to one fundamental cause or related group of causes, and all demanded a set policy response. However, the renewables are a polyglot group of resources utilized under a wide range of socioeconomic and political circumstances to fulfil a variety of policy objectives. It is both analytically misleading and practically unhelpful in the search for implementable solutions to aggregate flow resource concerns into one package.

While recognizing the interdependence of world economic and environmental systems, Ahmed has pointed out,

> the pressing priorities of the developing world constitute a very different set of environmental problems from those encountered in the developed countries. . . . In general – and at the cost of some oversimplification – it may be said that developed country environmental problems are caused by an overindulgent and wasteful pattern of consumption (and production) without

considering environmental spillover, while developing country environmental problems are the result of poverty and underdevelopment. (Ahmed, 1976, pp. 226–7)

This same point is made by Hardoy and Satterthwaite (1984, p. 308), who argue that in the Third World the concerns are not so much with 'what are conventionally understood in the West as "environmental" problems', but with 'the problem of poverty . . . and the refusal (or inability) of . . . governments to tackle poverty's underlying causes'. The problems caused by what Mabogunje (1984) so graphically calls the 'pollution of poverty' are unlikely to require the same means of correction as those arising from the 'pollution of affluence'. Although still a gross generalization and simplification, it is useful conceptually to distinguish four major classes of problem: scarcity, uncertainty, welfare distribution and depletion. As we shall see, none of these is a discrete entity and a specific resource concern may encompass all four types of problem. But they do enable us to identify the central points at issue in most conflicts over renewable resource use and allocation.

Baseline scarcity

Scarcity is first used here in a restricted sense to refer to the situation where supplies of essential flow resources are insufficient to enable human beings to survive at 'baseline' standards of living. Baseline levels of supply are culturally determined. The notion is simply and very generally used to exclude shortages of environmental 'quality' resources, which, although important to individuals, can hardly be classed as basic human needs. Defined in this way, scarcity is at present primarily a Third World problem, although conceivably a breakdown of the global life support systems would make it applicable everywhere. There can be no doubt that severe shortages of several vital flow resources are already affecting the basic existence of millions of people. Soil erosion and desertification are now widespread phenomena, resulting in marked reductions in agricultural productivity, particularly (but not exclusively) in semi-arid areas.[3]

Endemic water shortages affect nearly 50 per cent of the world's population, and not only act directly to reduce human health and welfare standards, but also exacerbate the difficulties faced in improving agricultural yields. In addition, deforestation has already created critical local scarcities of firewood, still the most important fuel source in many LDCs, and is also a factor contributing to the pace of soil erosion.

LACK OF EFFECTIVE DEMAND

These types of scarcity are created by a complex of economic, social, demographic, institutional and political conditions, and they are not amenable to simple solution. Food, water and timber have clear use value and have for long been potentially marketable products, with a recognized price even in the poorest areas of the world. But the mere existence of a use value or price cannot ensure their adequate supply. In part the problems are ones of international and regional

10 and 11 Water scarcity is a fact of life for nearly 50 per cent of the world's population, including those in countries such as Peru which have relatively high precipitation levels; the scarcity problems are not physical but arise from inadequate investment. In this suburb of 25,000 inhabitants drinking water is available three times a week, each time for about three hours. With only three supply outlets, the queue of cans forms early, and then there is the long trek home.

12 and **13** Nepalese women must now trek considerable distances to collect vital firewood and fodder for their animals due to deforestation around the rural settlements. The deforestation also speeds erosion in this deeply dissected area.

distributive equity, and they are directly analogous to those which arise in the allocation of mineral resources. Just as many LDC consumers lack the effective demand to justify investment in minerals or manufactured products to serve domestic markets, so too they are unable to articulate, within the existing economic, political and financial systems, their needs for the augmentation of renewable resource flows.

Moreover, baseline scarcities cannot simply be solved by investments in water supply provision, irrigation and other technical means of increasing the availability of resource products. The history of the 'green revolution' provides ample evidence that technological and financial aid packages have to be accompanied by socioeconomic, political and institutional change. As Feder (1976), Dasgupta (1977), Stewart (1977) and many others have pointed out, the advantages from improved agricultural productivity all too often became concentrated in the hands of a relatively small indigenous élite and the poorest social groups were 'marginalized' still further, both in economic and spatial terms. This process, whereby indigenous income disparities are increased by 'development', is of course paralleled in the stock resource field by the way the material gains from mineral exploitation have benefited an urban political élite and have had relatively little impact on the living conditions of the mass of the population.

UNMARKETED RESOURCE PRODUCTS

Scarcity problems also arise for renewable resources which traditionally have not been marketed, or by their nature cannot be marketed; the capacity of the

14   The over-use of the regenerative capacity of the soil is not just an LDC problem as this illustration of Castle Hill Basin, New Zealand, shows. Deforestation, overgrazing and fire have left the area denuded of vegetation and prone to accelerated erosion.

15 The dangers to health are clear: waste water is in contact with supplies used for drinking and washing, so providing ideal conditions for the spread of diarrhoeal diseases.

16 Once again the conditions depicted here constitute a clear health hazard; runoff contaminated by sewage and other waste products flows uncovered down the street.

environment to receive wastes (solid, liquid and gaseous) without loosing the ability to provide other essential services clearly comes into this category. Although undoubtedly such problems can arise in advanced nations, by and large they do not endanger the ability of human beings to survive at 'baseline' standards of living or indeed to survive at all.[4]

In the LDCs the picture tends to be very different. Water pollution, for example, is threatening the livelihood of millions of fisherman (Agarwal, 1983; Smil, 1984) and the health of millions of others. Although some of the contaminants are products of industry, the bulk of the difficulties arise through the deliberate discharge of untreated sewage and from run-off contaminated by sewage and other waste products. Hardoy and Satterthwaite (1984) cite the case of the River Bogota, flowing through the capital of Colombia, and receiving the untreated effluents from a city of 5 million inhabitants. At a distance 120 km downstream from Bogota the river still had an average faecal bacteria coliform count of 7.3 million, against the 100 normally considered safe for drinking water sources! Lack of basic infrastructure services for the removal and disposal of all forms of human waste create urban environmental conditions unthinkable in a developed country context. Such problems not only require the investment of scarce capital, but also major changes in administrative systems, patterns of urban and economic growth and in political attitudes.

Economic scarcity

To the economist scarcity arises when the quantity demanded is higher than that being supplied *at the going price*. If price is increased, the quantity demanded will decline, and the quantity supplied will rise until equilibrium is regained and no economic shortages occur. In a sense the basic flow resource scarcities in Third World nations are economic since the price people can and do pay is insufficient to provide an incentive to maintain supplies. But in such cases price rises will only remove the appearance of scarcity within the market, leaving untouched – in fact exacerbating – the fundamental problem of the gap between supply and baseline needs.

When consumption is not essential for survival, any supply shortages which arise can be tackled either by increasing supply or controlling demand, and price rises are one possible method of control. In Chapter 5 it was shown that regulation had held US gas prices below the level required to achieve a demand–supply equilibrium; economic scarcities resulted, which became more marked over time as the incentive to invest in new supply sources was reduced. This form of scarcity also occurs widely for public water supplies, particularly to the domestic and irrigation sectors. When supply authorities maintain unit prices well below the long-run cost of supply, shortages tend to arise *unless* physical rationing devices are introduced or massive capacity extensions undertaken, subsidized either by other water users or by taxpayers (Hirschleifer *et al.*, 1960; Rees, 1976, 1982). It should, of course, be noted that price changes can solve this created scarcity but can only satisfactorily resolve the problem of allocating supplies between competing users if it is accepted that ability to pay is the correct distributive criterion.

Risk and uncertainty

The second category of problem, *uncertainty*, is of a fundamentally different nature. It is critically bound up with lack of knowledge, with largely unquantifiable risks, and with our highly imperfect institutional and economic mechanisms for dealing with *risk*.

GLOBAL RISK

For many years now scientists have argued that human activity has reduced biological diversity and changed the global energy budget and critical biogeochemical cycles. From an anthropocentric viewpoint change in itself is not the problem. There is nothing intrinsically good about a particular environmental state – natural systems alter markedly over time quite independently of human activity. Kellogg and Schware (1981, 1982), for example, have demonstrated quite clearly that the 'natural' climate has an ever changing character. Some 18,000 years ago much of Canada and north-western Europe was covered by ice sheets – in fact such glacial episodes and the kind of interglacial period we are now experiencing have alternated at approximately 100,000-year intervals for at least the last two million years. These natural changes in global heat and water balances dwarf any changes as yet induced by man, who had minimal impact until about fifty years ago. What is now at issue is whether the human contribution to change is compatible with the long-term survival of the species. As O'Riordan (1983a, p. 407) has put it, 'it seems that we really have no idea what we are doing to ecological, energy and biochemical-cycles which interact in a complex way and may mutually degenerate if gyroscopic restraining forces are broken and thresholds of tolerance transgressed'.

At the height of the 1970s environmental movement pseudo-scientific predictions of the imminent collapse of life support systems were commonplace, often based on extremely dubious extrapolations and guesswork about natural regulatory or adjustment mechanisms. Today most scientists see the global system as rather more robust, and the likelihood of total failure to be remote, although it is generally accepted that man-induced environmental change could have profound socioeconomic implications. Increasing levels of atmospheric CO_2 (Figure 6.1) could, for example, act to improve plant productivity at least in the short term, but more important, could so alter the global water budget that major shifts in world climatic patterns occurred.

The currently most favoured scenario suggests that large areas of the Middle East, Africa, India and China might cease to be water-deficient areas, whereas much drier conditions could occur over much of North America and the Soviet Union (Figure 6.2). It is ironic to think that such inadvertent alterations to regional water balances could actually serve to reduce international spatial inequalities, a measure which the political and economic systems have been manifestly unable to achieve.

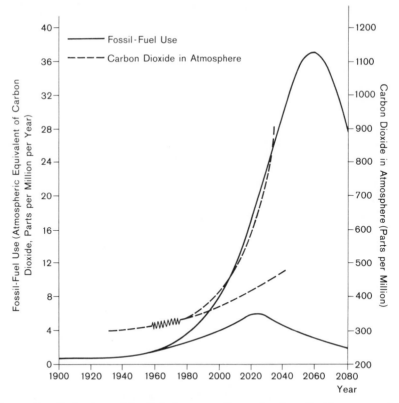

Figure 6.1   Projections of fossil-fuel consumption and carbon dioxide content of the atmosphere: minimum and maximum plausible rates of increase
Source: George M. Woodwell, 'The carbon dioxide question', *Scientific American*, 238 (1), January 1978, p. 40. Copyright © 1978 by Scientific American, Inc. All rights reserved

However, that is idle speculation. What is relevant here is that solutions to this category of problem will depend on how they are perceived in relation to the mass of other – usually more immediate – economic, political and social 'crises' within the world economy, and on the political will to intervene. It also necessitates the creation of international machinery capable of making decisions about the use of environmental systems and then enforcing them.

LOCAL RISK

At a less all-encompassing scale, uncertainty is a hallmark of many conflicts over environmental pollution.[5] Quite fundamental disagreements occur, even

Figure 6.2   Predicted northern hemisphere temperature changes if the carbon dioxide warming continues (top), and corresponding changes in rainfall (bottom)
Source: *New Scientist*, 3 January 1980, p. 16

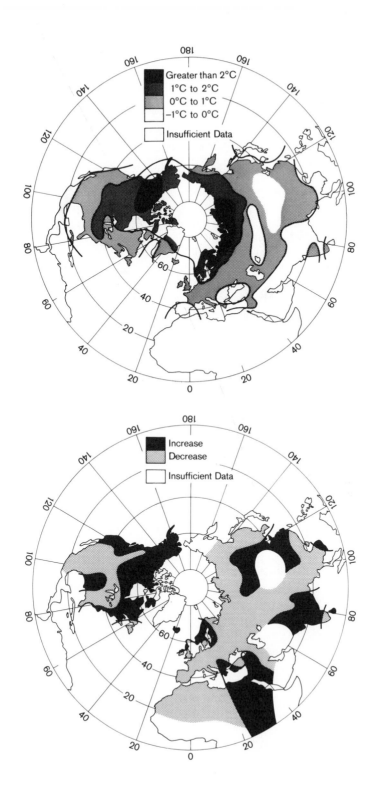

between scientific experts, over the risks associated with hazardous installations (including nuclear power plants), the use of artificial fertilizers and pesticides and the disposal of potentially harmful waste products. Most of these risks are public in nature, with individuals having few effective risk-spreading or averting strategies at their disposal.

Economists have long been occupied by the question of how to add risk into the accounting procedures used to evaluate whether a potentially hazardous activity should be allowed (see Haveman, 1977, for a brief summary). But such efforts to view the issue 'objectively' always come up against the hurdle that most environmental risks are subjective assessments. The scientist views risk in terms of probability estimates, the period of time or interval to which the probability applies and the consequences as assessed in terms of deaths, injuries or damage (Burton and Pushchak, 1984). But as the literature on natural hazards has shown, the public perceive risk subjectively and rarely evaluate it rationally; differences in risk perceptions are crucial to an understanding of human response (Burton *et al.*, 1978; Schwing and Albers, 1980; Whyte and Burton, 1982). Even in cases such as flooding or drought, where records often exist to give a reasonably accurate idea of the probability of occurrence, an individual's perception may differ markedly from the actual likelihood and will vary with experience, education and so on.

In welfare economics, following the consumer sovereignty line of reasoning, it has been customary to assume that individual tastes and beliefs, aggregated in some suitable way, should be the basis for decision-making (Dasgupta, 1982). This raises three problems relevant to environmental risks.

First, when public beliefs about risk are based on imperfect knowledge or an imperfect understanding of probability, should these be taken into account? This is particularly difficult for low-probability risks such as the failure of a nuclear generating plant. Not only do most people find it difficult to conceptualize a risk of, say, 1 in 10,000, but also risk perceptions tend to be less 'accurate' if the individual has no experience of the event. However, if public beliefs are too inaccurate to be taken into account, is it reasonable to rely solely on 'expert' opinion? Dasgupta has argued 'that in many cases (most especially where public health is at issue) environmental protection is rather like a *merit good*, and so there is a case for the government to base its policies on only the most informed opinions' (ibid., p. 70). Such a view is somewhat difficult to justify when the polluter has a monopoly over accepted expertise. This is a key dilemma in the nuclear power case, where the bulk of the experts have economic interests in ensuring that developments take place and their jobs are safeguarded.

Second, if public assessments on risk acceptability are to form the basis for decision-making, who constitutes the relevant public? Except when we are talking about risks to life support systems, the probability of an individual being affected by a pollution hazard not only varies spatially, but is also a function of lifestyle, type of employment and physiological characteristics. For example, airborne lead represents a hazard to young children, whereas smogs particularly affect those with existing chest or heart complaints. Given this variation in potential effect, should those at greatest risk have the greatest say, or should everyone in the country have equal access to the decision-making process? Inevitably those groups who have to live with the fear of a hazard (i.e. they bear the costs of uncertainty) will tend to have lower risk acceptability thresholds than those not directly affected who can take a more 'neutral' stance. People may well argue that the risks from nuclear reactor failure or from the disposal of radioactive wastes are more than offset by the benefits from cheap and secure electric power – until, that is, the plant or storage site seems likely to become a neighbour.

Finally, since individuals vary in their perception of and aversion to risk, how can their views be aggregated? There have been some ingenious attempts to develop aggregation techniques, including efforts to show that if risks are pooled over large numbers of people, society as a whole may be risk-neutral (Arrow and Lind, 1970; Arrow, 1971). This conveniently allows the costs of uncertainty to be ignored in the assessments. But this whole supposedly objective aggregation approach has little practical significance to the political decision-making process which in reality determines the acceptability and spatial distribution of pollution risk (see pp. 375–90).

Once a risk has been identified there are three decisions that have to be made. First, are the risks outweighed by the benefits derived from the polluting activity? Second, how far is it worth investing in risk reduction? And, third, who is going to have to bear the remaining costs of uncertainty and any losses if the risk event should actually occur? In countries lacking pollution control or planning agencies the judgements of producers will in effect determine the risks which are acceptable and who will bear them. Where there are established regulatory agencies, most of the decisions will take the form of bargains between the controlled and controllers, in which public tastes and beliefs will play a minimal role (see p. 361). It is really only in cases where pollution risk becomes a visible political issue that individual views on acceptability will be incorporated into the decisions. All three acceptability and distribution choices involve trade-offs between different interest groups, and the outcomes will in no sense be 'objective', but will reflect prevailing social attitudes and the balance of effective power in society. In practice, therefore, most of the environmental risk issues become indistinguishable from those relating to the allocation of wealth and welfare.

Welfare distribution

This conveniently takes us to our third problem category, welfare distribution. Renewable resource degradation in all its forms clearly imposes real economic and welfare losses. These include damage to human health; the reduction of agricultural, fish or forest yields; increased water treatment costs; accelerated depreciation of buildings or other materials; and the declining value of particular environments as aesthetic or recreational resources. On the other hand, damage avoidance or abatement are rarely costless procedures (see pp. 261–2). Ulti- mately, then, the basic question is how are these various costs and losses to be distributed spatially and temporally between different groups within society? In other words, the underlying concern is with the effective allocation of income, wealth and welfare.

For some types of pollution, the costs involved are obvious transfers from one group of people to another; solid household wastes taken miles away to a land dump do not affect the polluter. In other cases the damage flows are much more complex, with polluters, to a greater or lesser degree, sharing the damage and risks. Industrialists discharging waste into the air or local watercourses feel the effects, but usually in their separate persona as householders, yachtsmen, fishermen or bird watchers. Likewise, car owners living in high-density traffic zones contribute to the level of atmospheric lead, which may affect their own children's health. Pollution cost flows not only involve effective wealth transfers between people, but also change the composition of the package of environmental goods and services available to each individual. Similarly, the way the costs and benefits of pollution abatement are distributed may alter relative income levels and affect the set of goods received by different households.

Our knowledge of the extent of damage and its allocation between people is still poor, and even less is known about the distribution of abatement costs and of the benefits from pollution control or amenity resource provision (Berry, 1977; Dorfman, 1977; Pearce, 1980). What evidence there is does suggest that the distribution of physical pollution is essentially regressive, but this does not necessarily mean that expenditure on control will have progressive effects on the allocation of real income. Much depends upon the value attached to a cleaner environment by different groups within society, and on who bears the control costs.

Whereas the fact that pollution losses are being incurred is undeniable, it is still a matter of dispute whether they are significant enough to warrant the costs of control. In such disputes there can be no single manifestly correct solution, which can be found by employing comprehensive, objective and supposedly value-free scientific assessments. In the end the issues are judgemental and the perceived correct solution will vary from individual to individual reflecting their different values and interests. It is easy to imbue pollution control and landscape or wildlife protection with an air of moral virtue, but it is by no means axiomatic that they *should* occur if the results imply a regressive redistribution of real income. (This issue will be treated in more detail when environmental pressure group activity is discussed in Chapter 9). In practice, as both Sandbach (1980) and Schnaiberg (1980) have pointed out, it is impossible to divorce questions of environmental quality and renewable resource conservation from the more wide-ranging issue of equity in the distribution of social welfare.

Resource depletion

The final problem category is resource depletion. This issue is in part subsumed in the previous problem categories but is treated separately to highlight the fact that, from an anthropocentric viewpoint, there is *no* necessary identity between depletion and scarcity. In some cases, such as aquifer water, forests, or soil fertility for example, depletion does produce crucial supply shortages. But scarcity is a cultural concept and implies the need for specific goods and services; if alternatives exist, depletion, or even the total exhaustion of a flow resource need not mean scarcity. To take an extreme example: the extinction of wolves in Britain is hardly perceived as a scarcity issue since, apart from some conservationists, few people would regard them as a valuable resource. Just as the exhaustion of natural gas stocks need not matter if alternative energy sources are readily available, so the exhaustion of cod stocks need not be significant if adequate alternative food supplies are assured. This raises the possibility that depletion could be a rational strategy *if* new sources were expected to replace the flow resource in question as a provider of goods and services. Such a line of reasoning is, of course, total anathema to the ecologists, who see the diversity of natural physical systems as crucial for the long-term survival of the human species. It is also rejected by all those who regard birds, fish or animals as having intrinsic value, and by the bioethics school of writers who argue that all animate beings have rights to life.

THE CAUSES OF RENEWABLE RESOURCE PROBLEMS

In the environmental literature of the 1960s and early 1970s writers working from different analytical perspectives suggested various fundamental problem causes, of which five were particularly popular: population pressure, technological change, economic growth, market failure and ethical beliefs. Typically one of these was selected as the prime cause, and this led axiomatically to a set of solutions given an assumed single-policy objective.

Population

Many writers viewed population pressure as the basic issue, and called for 'zero population growth' or even more draconially 'the one-child family' (Ehrlich and Ehrlich, 1970). Birth control and liberalization of abortion were, therefore, seen as the obvious answers. Apart from the fact that these need not be politically or morally acceptable as solutions, it is clear that population numbers, as such, are only one dimension in the level of demand for flow resource goods and services. A static or even declining population will not prevent depletion, scarcity and environmental degradation if those remaining experience an increase in their material prosperity. This is clearly illustrated by reference to Western Europe, where population stability or low growth rates have been characteristic for the last twenty years, but this has neither stopped depletion of North Sea fish stocks nor prevented pollution.

One of the primary objectives of LDC population control programmes is to increase, or at least maintain, living standards; how, then, can this be consistent with the use of the same mechanism to reduce the pressure of demand on resources (Schnaiberg, 1980)? If households merely increase their per capita food, wood or water consumption to take up the products effectively released by a forgone child, then there will be no change in the resource use position. Moreover, it is quite possible that with increased material prosperity people may start to demand goods and services which place even more strain on natural systems; for example, a change in diet from cereal to animal proteins would imply an increased need to enhance land productivity. While few[6] would deny that population control programmes may be desirable or even essential for the solution of LDC scarcity and depletion problems it is difficult to see them as more than an adjunct to other social and economic policies. Moreover, a reduction in population growth rates offers little help in overcoming the problems of uncertainty and welfare distribution.

Technological change

Another group of analysts ascribe all renewable resource problems to the pace and environmentally unsympathetic nature of *technological change*. It is commonly argued that new techniques of production are inherently more disruptive and polluting than the technologies they displace (Commoner, 1972a, 1972b). There is little doubt that mass-production techniques, increased levels of packaging, the production of more complex processed goods, energy-intensive techniques and the development of synthetic 'unnatural' substances have all added to the demands placed on the natural system. But it must be remembered that traditional production techniques can also cause depletion and pollution. Soil erosion, desertification, water scarcity and deforestation do not require sophisticated production methods, just the most basic traditional techniques applied at a scale incompatible with natural regenerative cycles.

All forms of production involve some use of environmental resources; whether depletion and damage result will depend on how intensively they are used. In part the question of whether modern methods are judged to be more environmentally damaging than past techniques depends upon which segment of the natural system is the subject of prime concern. It is at least debatable that the overall damage[7] to all environmental media, per unit of energy consumed, is no greater when oil or gas are used in preference to the older sources, coal or timber. In the same way, it is often claimed that new technologies involve greater risk and uncertainty than those used in the past. This is, however, a matter of subjective judgement. The nature of risk has undoubtedly changed. Technological developments have created risks that are generally less likely to occur but with consequences that are potentially more damaging and widespread in effect (Burton and Pushchak, 1984). In terms of loss of life and the quality of the working environment nuclear power production could be regarded as less risky than coalmining. There are also technologies which are unequivocally less damaging than the ones they replace; health risks and pollution are clearly reduced when sewerage and sewage treatment displace the direct discharge of wastes into streams, cesspools and septic tanks. Technological change exacerbates some flow resource problems – but it will continue to offer solutions to others.

Economic growth

It is not, however, meaningful to view technology as an autonomous 'cause' separate from the economic growth which powers it, and is in turn powered by it. Growth and new investment stimulate technological change, which in turn produces new market opportunities which then fuel the growth process (Rosenberg, 1976; Layton, 1977). This brings us to the third popular cause of environmental problems, the pace of *economic growth* and its measurement in materialistic terms. The solutions commonly advocated are to stop growth or at least redefine it to include 'quality-of-life' variables (Mishan, 1967; Tsuru, 1972).

This cause has three clear, related strands. First, it is argued that economic growth is incompatible with the essentially closed and limited physical system of the earth (Daly, 1973; see also Chapter 8, pp. 302–5). Second, the view is taken that politicians and economists are preoccupied by economic growth in the short run. This distorts the whole process of production towards maximizing the net present value of physical output as defined by current tastes and income levels, to the detriment of spatial and temporal distributive equity. Not only are the requirements of future generations ignored but present-day consumers are denied non-marketable quality-of-life goods and services. In the longer term it is argued that the continued pursuit of material growth will serve to reduce *not* increase real social welfare.

GNP AND SOCIAL WELFARE

The third strand in the argument concerns the use of GNP as a measure of economic welfare. Gross national product is the market value of all goods and services produced in an economy, and as a concept it is predicated on the exchange of goods within the market system. Any non-market products and services (unpaid housework, voluntary services, home-produced vegetables and so on) are all excluded, as are such undesirable but unpriced environmental and social costs as pollution, habitat loss, crime, overcrowding or mental stress. Ironically increases in some of these disbenefits can actually serve to increase GNP: more crime necessitates a larger police force, increased pollution may raise 'demands' for medical care or cleansing agents and so on.

To equate growth in GNP with growth in human welfare requires three basic and heroic assumptions. First, virtually all goods and services, including disbenefits, must be priced and included within the market exchange system. This clearly does not hold, and is particularly relevant in the renewable resource sector, where few environmental 'services' are marketed. Second, the consumer must be sovereign, determining the value of all goods free from manipulation by producers; the problems inherent in this concept have already been discussed (see pp. 124–5). Since it is difficult to avoid concluding that in modern industrial societies the 'producers have the greater power and influence' (Scitovsky, 1976, p. 5), market valuations, and the collection of goods and services placed on the market, are at best only weakly related to consumer preferences.

Finally, there must be a direct relationship between the physical output produced by an individual, his wealth and the use value of things to him. Once again this does not hold; earned income and wealth are not the same thing and what a person is *able* to pay may not be a correct reflection of use value. As Marx has stated, as soon as human labor, in its immediate form, has ceased to be the great source of wealth, labor time will cease, and must of necessity cease to be the measure of wealth, and the exchange value must of necessity cease to be the measure of use value. (quoted in Tsuru, 1972, p. 12)

Whenever willingness to pay is used to assess the real benefits derived from products and services, there is always the problem of inability to pay.

An enormous literature now exists on the deficiencies of GNP and similar market price measures of economic welfare, and many attempts have been made to devise more meaningful 'real' welfare indicators. However, these have had negligible impact on the way GNP growth is calculated in practice, or on its central role as a perceived policy objective. One difficulty is that it is far easier to show that market values are inappropriate than to devise a system of measuring real welfare, including such disbenefits as noise pollution, landscape change or the loss of particular plant and animal species (see p. 318).

THE IMPLICATIONS OF 'NO GROWTH'

To some analysts economic growth *per se* is the fundamental cause of all resource problems since, however it is measured, it still implies increasing consumption and therefore greater demands on the earth's resource base and its life support systems. But the implied 'no growth' solution has little practical relevance or moral justification when applied to countries in the Third World. In the first place, some growth would have to occur to allow those living at bare subsistence levels to continue to live at all; unless, that is, population growth was also cut to zero. No growth would simply consign millions of people to levels of material existence, which few would seriously suggest are acceptable. Moreover, it can do nothing to solve the problems which already exist when present use intensities exceed the natural regenerative capacity of the environment.

Neo-Malthusian writers working from the assumption that 'spaceship earth' cannot support on a sustained basis even the current population at present levels of consumption have argued that attempts to produce growth in LDCs should be halted. Ehrlich (1970b, p. 64), for instance, has consistently taken the view that 'we will have to recognize the fact that most countries can never industrialize and that giving them industrialization aid is wasteful'. Rather he sees an ideal state of 'semi-development':

Kenya and Tanzania . . . and some other African nations, can supply the world with a priceless asset: a window on the past when vast herds of non-human animals roamed the face of the Earth. They could also provide one of the many living stockpiles of organic diversity, stockpiles which may prove of immense value as mankind attempts to replenish the deteriorated ecosystems of the planet. These and similar areas could serve as rest-and-rehabilitation centers for people from the more frantic industrialized parts of the planet. They would also serve as guarantors of cultural diversity, as areas specifically reserved to permit peoples to maintain their traditional ways of life. (Ehrlich and Ehrlich, 1970, p. 313)

This type of argument is based on a highly romantic notion of what conditions are actually like in many traditional societies and ignores the fact that the people concerned may have quite a different vision of their own fate. As Sachs (1972, p. 128) says, it 'manipulates the concepts of cultural pluralism in such a way as to propose an international division of labour closely resembling [the] relationship between public and animals in a zoo'. To maintain what is assumed to be the correct balance between population and resources in such ecological and cultural game parks the numbers of people currently living there would have to plunge, presumably by allowing, in Malthusian fashion, starvation and disease to act as 'natural' control mechanisms. Certainly, this morally repugnant strategy is proposed by the Paddocks (1967), who argue that the medical notion of 'triage' should be employed. No help would be given to the hopeless cases, who would be allowed to die, in order to concentrate resources where the chances of success are greatest.

The arguments of Mishan (1967), Hodson (1972), Daly (1973), Schumacher (1973) and many others who see growth mania, material acquisitiveness and conspicuous consumption as reflections of misplaced moral values have greater intuitive appeal when applied to affluent industrial societies. It is easy to dismiss the need for growth when it results in the production of computer games, animal beauty parlours and elaborate restaurant meals. But needs are a relative not absolute concept. Although income and wealth disparities are less marked in the developed nations, and welfare programmes go some way to alleviating abject poverty, the relatively poor still perceive their disadvantage. Unless no-growth policies are accompanied by a mass redistribution of wealth at both national and international scales, it seems inevitable that most people will demand the chance to enjoy the affluence demonstrated by the wealthy. The notion that a no-growth situation will result in greater 'real' social welfare contains value judgements about what welfare actually means to individuals, not just at the present time but also in the future (Abrams, 1974; Cotgrove, 1976). Not only will individuals make different judgements, which raises the problem of interpersonal comparison, but also all valuations are dependent on current social, economic and political relations.

It can hardly be denied that greater levels of consumption will inevitably place increased pressures on the resource base. Moreover, these pressures will not necessarily be reduced if consumption growth occurs through services rather than material possessions. There is a currently rather fashionable view that resource problems will decrease in 'post-industrial' societies, as material consumption hits some satiation plateau. But the evidence for this is rather slender; as Schnaiberg (1980) has pointed out, the new service requirements tend merely to be *added* to the older material consumption. Furthermore, many new service demands are intensive users of environmental quality resources; this most clearly applies to outdoor recreation, overseas travel and landscape or wildlife protection. While most people would accept that growth is one factor contributing to current resource depletion and degradation, such recognition is far removed from the acceptance of no growth as a morally, politically or economically feasible policy option.

Defects in the market system

When the growth issue is seen as a GNP calculation problem, the desirability of continued growth is not challenged, rather it must be redirected to ensure that it actually produces real improvements in human welfare. This line of reasoning in effect takes us to the fourth popularly invoked cause of environmental problems, the imperfect, incomplete operation of the market system.

THE EXTERNALITY CONCEPT

The notion of *externalities* is central to the conventional economic treatment of renewable resource depletion and degradation issues. Externalities (or external costs and benefits) are simply the uncompensated side-effects of any economic or social activity which are not considered by individuals when making private decisions. The word 'uncompensated' is important as it serves to exclude all the external costs and benefits that arise in the course of normal market transactions. For example, if two families compete to purchase a particular house, the gain of that property by the eventual purchasers will have the side-effect of causing a loss to the other family, but, in theory at least, the latter is compensated by the retention of the purchase price. Externalities only occur in extra-market situations when the by-products of an activity result in costs or benefits to other people, which go uncompensated by an exchange of money or goods. Whenever producers or consumers make usage decisions on the basis of their own private costs and benefits and are allowed to neglect the external effects of their actions,[8] the usage patterns are likely to deviate markedly from those that are socially optimal or desirable.

Within any social system externalities are a commonplace feature of everyday life: smoking in crowded rooms, talking in libraries or practising the trumpet at 3 a.m. are all obvious cases where external costs are incurred. Many such externalities are too minor or expensive to correct, although planning controls, zoning of buildings or trains into smoking and no-smoking areas, and banning the use of car horns at night are just a few examples where some efforts have been made to reduce the social costs of individual actions.

When the externality concept was first applied to the analysis of economic relations, there was a tendency to assume that most goods and services were incorporated into the market system of exchange and that uncompensated external costs were the exception, not the rule. However, it was quickly recognized that in the renewable resource sector externalities were all-pervasive, an inevitable consequence of the way our economic system deals with the cycle of production, consumption and disposal of goods. Only those environmental goods and services which were directly used in production and consumption were priced and incorporated into the market. The reverse flow of unwanted products back to the environment was systematically ignored. No value was placed on the limited capacity of the environment to absorb and renovate waste products.

Recognition of the importance of the reverse waste flows owes much to the now classic essay of Boulding (1966), who argued that consumption was not the 'final act' of the economic system; this position was taken in fact by waste disposal.

According to the first law of thermodynamics, matter is neither created nor destroyed, it merely changes form with use. Therefore, at every stage in the material production and consumption process matter is returned to the environmental system (Figure 6.3). In other words, by adding in the return (residual) flows, the economic system becomes closed and to be sustainable must maintain a *materials balance* (Ayres and Kneese, 1969; Ayres, 1972). The idea of a materials balance not only brings home the ubiquity of waste production and externality problems, but also suggests that attention must be shifted from waste removal to waste reduction and reuse. In addition, water, air, sea or land pollution cannot meaningfully be regarded as separate issues. If, for example, attempts are made to curb effluent discharges to rivers the same total of waste may simply be transferred elsewhere in the environmental system.

CORRECTING MARKET FAILURE

When the failure of the market to account for externalities is viewed as the 'cause' of renewable resource problems, the solution appears simple. By ensuring that all resource products and services, including the environment's capacity to assimilate waste and provide a habitat for all species of life, were priced and incorporated into the market system of exchange, all resources (stock and flow) would be allocated to maximize their net value in use. The conceptual difficulties with this market efficiency approach have already been discussed in Chapter 4, and will be dealt with in more detail when economic strategies for controlling pollution and flow resource depletion are assessed in Chapters 7 and 8. At this stage it is only necessary to point out that the neat theoretical simplicity of correcting market failure belies several crucial political, social, practical and ethical limitations – limitations which go far to explain why there is a major discrepancy between the way most economists have viewed flow resource and environmental problems,

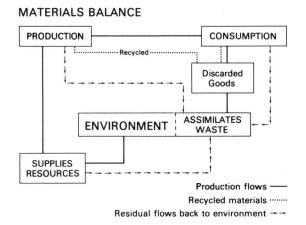

Figure 6.3   The materials balance
Source: Rees, 1977, p. 314

and the approach taken by virtually everybody else, including those responsible for practical management decisions.

There is little doubt that the failure of our economic system to incorporate all the social costs involved in resource use has contributed to the depletion and degradation of environmental systems. But the economic policy prescriptions which appear to follow from this type of analysis can do nothing to resolve the fundamental problems which arise from the conflicting aspirations and values of different interest groups. Nor, in practice, can they resolve the dilemmas over intergenerational equity and the attainment of sustainable patterns of development.

Ethical beliefs

The final commonly identified cause of renewable resource degradation concerns man's fundamental ethical beliefs. There are numerous strands to this argument but basically two interrelated points are made. First, the dominant religious and political philosophies in 'advanced' cultures envisage man as separate from and above nature (Tuan, 1974; Cotgrove, 1982). This does not occur in many 'traditional' societies where nature, man and God are interdependent and neither is man separate from nature nor nature from God. In 'man above nature' philosophies the environment becomes a collection of goods and services provided for human satisfaction, irrespective of the rights of other species. Moreover, it is a widely held belief that nature can be tamed, subjugated to serve immediate human needs, with insufficient attention paid to the longer-term effects on complex and interrelated life support systems. Second, man is inherently 'myopic', with an inbuilt preference for the known present over the uncertain future (Ramsey, 1928; Pigou, 1932). This means that social, political and economic decisions are inevitably biased towards the needs of the present generation with the consequent disregard for the potential requirements of future generations.

These sorts of arguments have been advanced by a highly diverse set of analysts. Ecologists have tended to stress that man is just one element in the global ecosystem, while economists have for long concentrated on the problems of myopic preferences. In both cases the arguments have been essentially man-centred, attitude changes being necessary to allow the survival of the human species or to give future generations an equitable share of the earth's resources. However, other writers such as Pedlar (1979) and Lovelock (1979) have argued that plants, animals and even rocks have rights to life, quite separate from the human desire to ensure that they survive because they provide, or may provide, some service or aesthetic satisfaction to man. It is extremely difficult to pursue this line of reasoning very far since it is a human concept, a product of moral judgements and reasoning. As Fleischman (1969, p. 26) pointed out, nature is not concerned with bioethics: 'Nature will not miss whooping cranes or condors ... Conservation is based on human value systems. Its validation lies in the human situation and the human heart'.

In practice, the supporters of the 'change in philosophy' school are merely another group with interests in using scarce environmental resources, in this case for the conservation of nature. Moreover, calls for attitude change based on abstractions about our anti-ecological culture are of little relevance in the search for implementable solutions to resource depletion and environmental quality problems (Schnaiberg, 1980).

While all these five approaches yield some insights into the problems, it seems clear that *there is no one simple cause or any universal panacea*. Nor should we expect there to be.

THE COMMON PROPERTY ISSUE

In addition to the five popular problem causes discussed above, many analysts have gone on to suggest that these produce particularly acute and intransigent difficulties for renewable resources because of their common property characteristics (p. 54).

International common property resources

At a global scale the ecosystem itself, and all the ecological, energy and bio-geochemical cycles which are encompassed within it, represent the most clear common property resource of all. Uncontrolled free access need not matter while usage remains within the system's natural absorptive or adjustment capacity. But once this has been exceeded, continued use will impose damage costs on everyone, irrespective of any personal contribution to such costs. Unless we retreat into science fiction and imagine an all-powerful world government assuming effective ownership over the life support systems of the globe and controlling every aspect of the human–environmental interaction, they will remain common property. Private usage decisions will continue to neglect the full social costs involved and degradation problems will occur.

In the same way international agreement is also necessary for subsystems within the whole, such as air, oceans, migratory birds and fish, which extend over large areas with total disregard for man's artificial boundaries to sovereignty. As the seven-year wrangle over the EEC's common fisheries policy and the even longer-running dispute over international whaling illustrate, agreement is never easy to achieve. Although each country may agree in principle that access restrictions and output controls are necessary, they inevitably attempt to minimize their own share of the associated costs. Even where share agreements have been signed, there are critical problems of enforcement.

In the case of marine fisheries an alternative approach to international common property problems can be adopted, whereby individual states assert and defend, by force if necessary, exclusive national access rights.[9] Iceland, for example, has claimed a 200-mile exclusive economic zone (EEZ), within which foreign fishing vessels are banned and domestic fish catches are controlled. Similarly, under the Fishery Conservation and Management Act 1976 the

United States asserted exclusive authority to manage fisheries within its EEZ and imposed on all fishermen, national and foreign, an array of regulations on catch tonnage, fishing seasons, permitted gear, net mesh size and so on. As Young (1981) shows, the costs (some $20 million a year) and the problems involved in enforcing these regulations are formidable, but even greater difficulties arise for LDCs with limited coastguard and air-patrol capacity. It has recently been reported, for instance, that despite Mauritanian efforts to control fishing in its EEZ, 'the organized pillage of its maritime resources continues virtually un-abated by ultra-modern fishing vessels from Europe and Asia in connivance with Mauritanian businessmen and Government officials' (*Guardian Third World Review*, June 1984). The short-term profits from continued exploitation far outweigh the minimal chance of being caught illegally fishing and the minor resultant fines; moreover, they provide a powerful incentive for the corruption of officials.

When share agreements or the unilateral assertion of jurisdiction occurs, in one sense the resource is no longer common property, it is now subject to a rather imperfect form of ownership and control. However, at the level of the individual user it is still common property; there is still competition for the available flow and the incentive to conservation will be determined by the appropriateness of the control regulations and the effectiveness of enforcement. As numerous writers have shown (Holt, 1975; Young, 1981; Mitchell and King, 1984), the record of past regulation attempts is not an impressive one.

Another, rather different, form of international common property resource occurs when specific species or habitats found only within one or two countries are given a high value by the international conservation community. The unique wilderness area of south-western Tasmania, giant pandas and the East African game species would all come into this category. This raises two related issues. First, should the valuation placed on the resource by international conservation interests have precedence over possibly different national or local values? And, second, if conservation is to occur, who should bear the opportunity and control costs involved?

In the controversy over the Tasmanian Hydroelectric Commission's plan to dam the Gordon River, the state government took the view that the employment and industrial growth benefits from the project exceeded the conservation value of the wilderness resource.[10] This view was not shared by the Australian national government or world conservation interests. Such divergences in values and interests raise important equity issues. Should one of the least affluent of the Australian states be expected to forgo potential development in order to satisfy the interests of others? Similar and even more obvious equity problems arise over the conservation of African wildlife. Not only does conservation imply that areas must be kept out of agricultural use, but also the costs of policing the reserves to stop poaching are high. It is at least debatable that international wildlife in-terests should bear these costs, not the governments of already disadvantaged nations.

Intranational common property resources

When we turn to flow resources that are spatially confined within national boundaries, common property characteristics in part arise from convention rather than from the physical nature of the resource itself. This occurs when the system of property rights developed over time allows many users freedom of access. For example, under the British common law system, rights to use water for supply purposes or for the discharge of wastes were obtained by owning property adjacent to, or above, a particular watercourse, while historic grazing rights to common land were acquired by residence within a particular community. Similarly, access to public lands in the United States has been determined by government fiat and has usually been restricted to particular user categories; in the national parks, for instance, passive forms of recreation are allowed but other users are normally excluded. It should be noted that access to most intranational common property resources is not, and never was, *free to all*, but is restricted to specific classes of user by custom, common law or legislation.

Multipurpose resources present a rather different common property case. Although a specific landowner may have an absolute property right, he may not be the only person with interests in the way the land is managed. An area under forest not only provides the owner with potential timber output, but is also valuable to others as a visual amenity, a recreational resource, a wildlife habitat, a barrier to soil erosion or a regulator of water flows. Difficulties arise since the owner normally has a developmental interest (agricultural or timber production or speculative building, for example) which others wish him to forgo, in whole or part, in order for the resource to retain its value to them.

Further externality problems arise over time when ownership is divorced from use. If tenancy arrangements only give usage rights for a limited period of time, then it is likely that attempts will be made to maximize current yields, ignoring the long-term productivity of the soil or the forest. In other words, tenants will be concerned with their own private costs and benefits over the period of the usage right and will ignore the longer-term social costs of their actions.

Common property problems in the minerals sector

Although it is usual to assume that common property problems only arise for the traditionally more plentiful, and generally less commercially valuable, flow resources, this is not so. In a number of countries the legal system also failed to provide for exclusive private ownership of particular stock mineral deposits. For instance, where extraction rights were obtained through landownership, there was a tendency for many firms to buy small parcels of land and then compete to capture as much of the mineral for themselves as possible; the early development of the oil and natural gas industries in the United States is a classic illustration of this. Under such conditions few producers made much profit from their activities, the chief beneficiary being the original landowner, who gained considerable unearned economic rent[11] on the land sales. The problems created by non-exclusive extraction rights were sometimes solved when one company, sometimes a publicly owned enterprise, effectively bought out all the competition, or when the advantages of co-operation were so evident that binding production agreements were signed; this last was much easier to achieve when only a few firms were involved. In other cases governments have sought to impose co-operation. For example, most state governments in the United States have established regulatory agencies, while in the British sector of the North Sea, oil companies were required, under the conditions of their licence, to exploit each distinct oil-bearing structure on a joint basis.

A major and still unresolved common property problem occurs over the extraction of manganese nodules from the sea-bed. Each company would need exclusive rights over large areas to make the venture commercially viable, but outside territorial waters this requires international agreement over an appropriate rights allocation system. If companies were allowed to peg out a claim on a 'first come, first served' basis, then the returns from exploitation would inevitably accrue solely to the technologically advanced nations. The same would broadly be true if claims were to be guaranteed by military might, with home governments policing the areas being exploited by their own companies. A further option of dividing up the sea-bed among the coastal states, as the continental shelf areas have been, is clearly unacceptable to land-locked countries and those with relatively short coastlines bordering potentially productive oceans.

An alternative proposal that an international agency issues exclusive extraction licences solves nothing; it still leaves the underlying difficulty of devising an allocative system which is regarded as equitable by all countries. Inevitably only the advanced countries have the technology to actually extract the nodules, and ultimately there are three quite distinct questions which have to be answered. First, how will those with the technical capability be guaranteed development rights? Second, how much of the economic rent from exploitation will they be prepared to give up? And, third, on what basis will any released rent payments be distributed among non-producing nations? Until these questions are answered, potentially valuable resources could remain largely unexploited. International agreement appeared to move a step nearer in April 1982, when the eleventh session of the Third United Nations Conference on the Law of the Sea finally adopted a draft convention. This would have established an international licensing agency which would use its fees and royalties to provide aid to the Third World. But Comecon and six member states of the EEC abstained (which effectively debars the whole community since a majority of members must adhere to the convention to ensure EEC participation) and the United States voted against the convention (Johnson, 1983). This means that the whole system has little chance of being workable since the bulk of the countries with the technology and capital to undertake exploitation are not party to the agreement.

EXTERNALITY PROBLEMS

The existence of common property and multiple-purpose resources produces three related forms of externality problem. The first arises because of the existence of *external benefits*. On the surface the possibility that private actions could create welfare gains for others would seem to be a good thing. But in practice it means that individuals may have little incentive to invest in flow augmentation programmes or in the provision of environmental services if the private costs exceed any private gains. The fact that the total social benefits exceed the costs involved is not a relevant concern to the individual decision-maker, who is unable to ensure that the external beneficiaries contribute to the provision expenditure.

External benefit problems basically arise whenever goods and services flow to people whether they want them or not, and when the person providing the facility cannot prevent this flow. They occur in a wide range of situations. For example, farmers or foresters may be unwilling to forgo losses in productive output in order to retain trees, hedgerows or marshland which have conservation value to others. The fact that the benefits, in terms of landscape amenity, preservation of wildlife habitats and decreased rates of run-off, may exceed the productive loss plays little or no role in the decision-making process. In the same way, the private gains from flood control, wildlife sanctuaries or recreation areas may be too small to encourage their provision. Similarly, individual users of an aquifer or commercial fishery have no incentive to invest in any artificial recharge or replenishment schemes, unless they have some means of preventing others from reaping the rewards of the investment. Moreover, even private collective action may be debarred if enough individuals decide that they will be able to share the benefits without sharing the costs. In order to prevent such 'cheating' a community needs to have strong social institutions which instil a sense of collective responsibility. Such 'moral' checks to selfish actions were common in small-scale traditional societies but appear to have declined markedly in advanced industrialized economies.

Both the second and third form of externality problem involve spillover costs, which can be neglected by the individual decision-maker. The dividing-line between them is somewhat blurred but, nevertheless, it is worth distinguishing *reciprocal* from *transfer* externalities.

In the reciprocal case all users of a common property resource impose costs on all, including themselves. For instance, if a number of firms and farmers are competitively pumping an aquifer at a rate which exceeds natural replenishment, every extra litre pumped will increase everyone's pumping costs. However, individuals will only control usage when it costs them personally more to pump than the extra water is worth. All users may be perfectly aware that they are using a depleting asset, but unless everyone agrees to take the same conservation measures the individual bears all the costs of pumping restrictions, while any benefits will be shared by all users. Moreover, there is no guarantee that benefits will actually accrue if others take advantage of the situation and simply increase their usage. Reciprocal externalities similarly occur in the exploitation of common land, fisheries and wildlife. In all these cases individual users can ignore the effects of their use on the rate of resource depletion, and can do nothing to augment supplies or control the actions of others.[12] Unless some usage controls are imposed, resources tend to be overused in the short term, and in the longer term the total flow could be exhausted.

The tragedy of the commons

This is the sort of depletion problem, which Hardin (1968) had in mind in his well-known, if in part rather ill-conceived, essay on the 'Tragedy of the commons'. The focus of this article was the growth of population within a finite world. To show that 'our present policy of laissez-faire in reproduction' will lead to disaster the analogy of the use of common land by herdsmen is employed: 'Picture a pasture open to all. It is to be expected that each herdsman will try to keep as many cattle as possible on the commons. As a rational being each herdsman seeks to maximize his gain.' Even when the carrying capacity of the common land is exceeded, each rational herdsman will continue to add stock because he receives all the gains from the sale of the additional animals but only shares a fraction of the costs of the resulting overgrazing: 'Therein is the tragedy. Each man is locked into a system that compels him to increase his herd without limit – in a world that is limited. . . . Freedom in a commons brings ruin to all' (ibid., p. 1244).

There is, of course, no dispute that Hardin's basic notion that uncontrolled free access to a resource in finite supply is likely to result in overuse and degradation.[13] But there are certain limitations in his analysis of the commons issue and in its use as an analogy for human population growth. The assertion that an individual would be compelled to increase the herd without limit is inaccurate. As was seen in the aquifer case, there is a private limit to pumping when the extra pumping costs equal the value of the water. In the same way, as Dasgupta (1982, p. 14) has pointed out: 'Animals are not costless, even to the herdsmen who own them. And such private costs set limits on the number of animals each herdsman finds most profitable to introduce.' This applies even more strongly in the case of population growth; it is clearly wrong to assume that extra children are costless. Certainly, in advanced economies the opportunity costs of extra children, both in material and effort terms, appear to have been a powerful private incentive to birth control.

It must also be remembered, in the common land case, that private incentives to curb use tend to increase as the herd grows. The sale value of the cattle will decline not only because the increased supply of animals will tend to reduce market prices, but also because overgrazing will reduce their quality. When private costs exceed the benefits, producers will leave the industry; this has clearly occurred in the case of commercial whaling, where the major firms have long since moved on to more profitable activities. In these circumstances total exhaustion of the resource flow is not inevitable.

Hardin's assumption that common land was open to all is also misleading. It was in fact only open to those within specific communities, governed by strict rules of social conduct and collective responsibility. In other words, social institutions existed when private economic control incentives were not strong enough to prevent serious external losses. It is worth pointing out that as early as 1938 Ciriacy-Wantrup was stressing the historic importance of social controls over common property resource use: 'Common property of natural resources in itself is no more a tragedy in terms of environmental depletion than private property. It all depends on what social institutions . . . are guiding resource use' (quoted in Clawson, 1974, p. 61). As Stillman (1982) argues, Hardin in fact artificially creates a set of conditions which makes the destruction of the commons inevitable. In practice, social institutions are adaptable and have tended to change once the effects of depletion become evident. Common land, overtaxed aquifers and depleting fisheries frequently have either become subject to some form of government regulation or been expropriated into private ownership.

In theory, if one firm was able to acquire all the usage rights to a previously commonly exploited resource the externality problems would be solved. All the costs and benefits of use would be taken into account by the producer when making decisions about usage rates. However, while the resource may be exploited more efficiently, the privatization solution may well exacerbate social inequalities. Moreover, it should be noted that the internalization of usage decisions in no way guarantees that depletion will not occur; the owners may still run down the resource if the benefits of current usage outweigh, in their estimation, the costs associated with depletion.

Transfer externalities

Whereas in the reciprocal externality situation all affected individuals share the damage they create, in the *transfer* or *unidirectional* case, the costs are imposed by one economic unit on other users of the same resource.[14] This classically arises when firms or households discharge waste products into the environment. When, for instance, a manufacturer uses a watercourse for effluent disposal, the private costs of waste removal are minor. But the external costs could include loss of fish yields, increased water-treatment costs, declining recreational and amenity value of the stream, and the losses involved if the water quality precludes its subsequent use for spray irrigation or domestic supplies. All these costs are ignored when the producer chooses a location, the plant design, output levels, production techniques or the type of raw material inputs. As a result, too few productive resources are devoted to waste disposal, too little research is conducted into improving waste reduction or removal techniques and too much waste is produced in relation to the damage it causes. Moreover, as unintended subsidies flow to manufacturers using high waste-producing technologies, the relative prices of goods and services within the economy are distorted. The price of highly polluting products will be too low and they will be sold in too large quantities.

The distinction between reciprocal and unidirectional externalities is less clear when waste disposal occurs to the air. Some of the damage costs will be transferred to downwind locations, as the acid rain problems of Scandinavia and Canada amply demonstrate. However, there are conditions in which dispersal is much more limited, and a major part of the damage falls on the polluters themselves. All users of vehicles within urban areas share a proportion of the damage costs they create.

When transfer externalities are created and incurred by only a few concerns, it is conceivable that the affected parties, if left to themselves, will negotiate a voluntary agreement (or set of bribes) to achieve a more 'optimal' resource allocation (Coase, 1960; Turvey, 1963a). However, the number of situations in which such voluntary solutions to externality problems could occur is limited. Normally there are too many affected concerns, most of whom will be imperfectly aware of the costs they impose or incur, to make full negotiation between all the parties involved a realistic option. Baumol and Oates (1975) report an interesting case where bargaining did take place between the company owning a polluting oil refinery in Göteborg (Sweden) and a neighbouring vehicle manufacturer, but where the large number of local inhabitants from the area were excluded from the decision-making process. When low quality petroleum was being refined and the prevailing wind direction carried airborne residuals towards the car plant, there was a marked increase in the level of corrosion of the metal and paint of recently produced vehicles. After negotiation the oil company agreed to restrict its low quality refining operations to periods when the corrosive elements were borne away from the vehicle plant but *towards the residential area*. In money terms it is possible that this agreement did reduce the net external damage costs if the value of the reduced vehicle corrosion exceeded the value of the extra damage experienced collectively by the local residents. But it is equally possible that total damage costs remained constant, or were even greater, after the agreement than they were before. In this case no efficiency gains would have been achieved, only the redistribution of effective income or welfare from private citizens in Göteborg to the vehicle company and its customers. To be reasonably effective, voluntary bargaining would need to include all affected parties, and to be broadly equitable would require that they all had similar bargaining power, measured in terms of financial resources, information and political influence. Therefore, in the vast majority of cases, solutions to transfer externality problems require some form of government intervention.

While there is little doubt that resources exploited in common tend to be misused and depleted, the notion that these problems can be solved simply by taking the resources into single ownership, private or public, denies the conflicts of interest that underpin the allocation of all goods and services within an economy. Private ownership does nothing to resolve problems of distributional equity over space and time, nor to reduce uncertainty, and it may still result in depletion and scarcity. Public ownership merely 'internalizes' resource use conflicts, but can do little to resolve them.

ENVIRONMENTAL MANAGEMENT OBJECTIVES

The literature on environmental management is further confused by lack of a consensus over objectives. Most analysts agree that present patterns and rates of renewable resource use are defective in some way, but there the accord ends. The perceived defects and the conceptualization of the problems are crucially dependent on the ideological perspective of the writer. Similarly, the proposed solutions are contingent on value judgements about what constitutes an ideal state in both the natural and human worlds. The ideological gap between different schools of thought is enormous; as Cotgrove and Duff (1980, p. 349) put it, 'the debate about environmental issues becomes a dialogue of the blind talking to the deaf'. It is possible to crudely divide the protagonists into three categories, two proposing the total restructuring of society and one prepared (or even happy) to work within the existing social, economic and political systems.[15]

The first of the groups advocating radical change are the *eco-revolutionaries*, whose starting-point is nature, the limits, needs and rights of elements within the ecosystem. Some among their number see the aim of management as restoring the environment to its 'natural' condition. Others doubt that such an objective has any meaning, arguing that there is no one naturally correct environmental state, and proposing instead that physical systems must be 'sustainable'. This immediately raises the question of the sustainability of what for whom? Very different levels and types of use are implied if it is accepted that all species have equal rights to life, rather than if the sole concern is the sustainability of humans. While members of this group differ in detail, the emphasis is on the total transformation of society, to produce lifestyles which allow man to live within natural limits as part of the integrated ecosystem.

This whole approach of putting the requirements of nature first is disputed by the second group advocating revolutionary change, the *social radicals*. Some regard environmental concern as a non-issue or a false issue, arguing that it diverts attention from more fundamental political, economic and social problems. They fear that conservation and pollution control will favour the already affluent, swallowing up resources which could be better used in a general war against poverty. However, others view environmental quality as a relevant issue since the poor tend to occupy the most polluted and degraded environments. All writers from this perspective recognize that key flow resource scarcity problems (water shortages, desertification and so on) are occurring but reject solutions which call for an end to economic growth, industrialization and technological change. Such solutions, it is argued, do nothing to address the real problem of spatial and social inequalities and would fail to allow everyone a decent quality of life (Marwell, 1970). Revolution is required not to create a system more in accord with the limits of nature but to provide for the needs of all human beings.

As is to be expected, the writers who work within existing socioeconomic and political structures are a polyglot group, blurring into the more radical schools of thought, but taking the pragmatic view that in the absence of revolution current institutions must be made more sensitive to environmental or social needs. Within this very broad church there is no consensus about the ultimate objective of management; most talk in terms of improving social or economic welfare but fail to agree on what these terms actually mean. Some take the economic efficiency line, arguing for changes in the market system to allow resources to be developed and allocated to maximize their net value in use. Others see equality in the distribution of effective incomes as the ultimate societal goal, while still others argue in effect for equality of opportunity.

This last group emphasize the need for change in administrative systems to allow equal access to the decision-making process and assume that acceptable compromises over the distribution of environmental goods and services will then be achieved (see, for example, O'Riordan and Turner, 1982, p. 10). However, political scientists, in particular, have disputed that calls for public participation, or the incorporation of protesters into consultative processes, can achieve real equality of opportunity. Not only is there some evidence that when protest groups become part of the official bargaining process they are co-opted by government and big business, and are thereby rendered ineffective as radical forces (Sandbach, 1980; Lowe and Goyder, 1983), but in addition equality of access to decision-making must remain a theoretical notion unless people have equal resources and influence. Finally, it should be mentioned that there is a large and influential body of opinion which sees little wrong with existing flow resource management strategies and advocates 'business as usual'. This group, referred to by O'Riordan (1977) as the technocentric cornucopians, rely on the dynamism of economic and technological change to solve any resource depletion or degradation problems.

The confusion over objectives is further exacerbated by the fact that it is often difficult to separate ideology from self-interest. It is common for concepts with a high moral flavour, such as equity, conservation or environmental quality, to be used to justify demands for a greater share of environmental goods. Conservation can be used to protect property values, or to choke off demands for 'positional' goods. This term was employed by Hirsch (1977) to denote commodities which are socially scarce, the value of which declines as more people have access to them (peaceful rural scenery, or village community life are, for example, both 'ruined' when no longer the preserve of the few). In some cases self-interest is fulfilled not by the acquisition of material benefits, but through aesthetic satisfaction. As Maslow (1954) argued, once individuals have satisfied their material needs, a set of goals related to intellectual and aesthetic satisfaction take on central importance (self-actualization needs). A number of writers, such as Ingelhart (1977) and Cotgrove and Duff (1980), have followed this line of reasoning to argue that there is a close correlation between 'post-materialistic' values, including environmental quality, and socioeconomic status. Those that have sufficient income and are not directly dependent for their livelihood on the productive sectors of the economy are in the forefront of demands for environmental services which cannot be evaluated in money terms (Marsh, 1981; Cotgrove, 1982). It goes without saying that the satisfaction of such aesthetic goals are deemed to be secondary, or indeed an irrelevance, by those whose material needs are not satisfied.

CONCLUSION

It is clear that there can be no value-free solutions to flow resource problems. The approach taken here will be to regard the environment as a set of resources, available for use, within limits, by man. Viewed in this anthropocentric way there are three central questions. First, how are these resources currently allocated between competing uses and users over time and space? Second, how far does the resulting distribution satisfy the basic objectives of society, maximization of economic welfare, social equity and security (stability)? And, third, what public policy measures can be adopted to correct any perceived resource misallocation problems? These questions will provide the focus for Chapters 7–9. It is recognized that this analytical framework will immediately be rejected by the eco-revolutionaries since it places nature in the service of man, rather than accepting that there is an integrity of natural ecosystems which man must respect. However, humans are separate from nature in the sense that they alone appear to have conscious choice and the power of reason. They can, therefore, hardly escape from judging their environment and using it to satisfy needs. It could, of course, be the case that the resulting choices will be misguided, products of misplaced values and short-term material advantage, and will in the longer term prove to be unsustainable. As Pearce (1977, p. 365) puts it, 'Mankind has already entered a "Faustian bargain" with Nature, trading evident and desirable increases in material standards of living for unknown and unforeseen costs'.

NOTES

1   This is not true for solar, tidal and wind energy, which are derived from forces outside the 'fixed earth'. These flows continue unaffected by levels of use.
2   Water transfers and storage have implications for the availability and quality of other flow resources (such as flora and fauna) which may impose limits on artificial augmentation programmes. In addition, both desalination and waste-water renovation are energy-intensive activities, and this could further constrain supply augmentation possibilities if fossil fuels remain the primary energy source. However, it is much more likely that supply limits will be imposed by costs, not by any physical constraints.
3   The overuse of the natural regenerative capacity of soil resources is not, of course, confined to LDCs (Jacks and Whyte, 1955), but it is a problem of quite a different order when it occurs in advanced industrial economies. In the first place, they are not dependent on food production from such areas and, in addition, they can employ a range of amelioration options which are only rudimentarily present in LDCs. They can seek to reduce use intensity, employ capital and technology to invest in artificial regeneration and, up to a point, renovate eroded land and import water to desertified areas. This is not, of course, to suggest that such options will necessarily be taken up. Much will depend upon whether the costs of land renovation measures are justified by the value of the resultant agricultural or amenity outputs.
4   The exception to this, of course, arises when pollution causes or exacerbates 'killer' diseases, such as cancer.
5   Krutilla, 1967, drew attention to a further source of uncertainty when he argued that the loss of biotic species could impose major opportunity costs by depriving man of potentially valuable drugs or the gene base for more resistant and productive crops.
6   There are some writers such as Simon, 1977, 1981, who doubt that population growth has serious ill-effects and, therefore, find population control of dubious value.
7   The notion of overall damage is an extremely difficult one to put into meaningful quantitative terms. We have no value-free method of comparing, for instance, forest depletion with smoke pollution (see pp. 318–23, 330–1).
8   Private costs (benefits) plus Externalities = Social costs (benefits).
9   This practice clearly raises important questions of international distributive equity and is strongly opposed by land-locked nations and those with short coastlines. The universal adoption of a 200-mile EEZ would appropriate about 90 per cent of the world's current marine harvest to national control: see Cooper, 1977.

10   Davis, 1979, 1980, has strongly argued that the 'need' for additional electric power and the supposed developmental benefits have been grossly exaggerated.

11   The extra value of the land (or other resource) over and above its next most profitable use.

12   When the rate of depletion is relatively slow, the user can pass on the problem of possible total exhaustion to future generations, therefore the difficulties tend to become even more intractable. In these cases *intertemporal* or *intergenerational* externalities occur.

13   Contemporary desertification problems in the Sahel and similar semi-arid areas testify that Hardin's thesis does have some validity.

14   Unidirectional transfers can also occur over time, when damage costs are passed to future generations.

15   There have been various attempts to categorize groups within the environmental movement. See, for example, O'Riordan, 1977; Cotgrove, 1982; O'Riordan and Turner, 1983; and for a totally different view, Sachs, 1972.

7 The allocation of renewable resource flows – economic perspectives and mechanisms

THE NEED FOR AN ECONOMIC PERSPECTIVE

In this and the next chapter an economic perspective will be taken as a *starting point* from which to analyse the flow resource sector and to evaluate alternative public policy measures. This viewpoint has no monopoly over the truth. Being firmly grounded on the notions of efficiency, consumer sovereignty and utility maximization, the conventional economic approach to renewable resource management raises all the methodological problems already discussed in the chapters on resource stocks. It is now well recognized, by economists themselves, that their treatment of the problems will not necessarily yield solutions which are acceptable politically, conform to widely held views on distributive and intergenerational equity or satisfy demands for long-term security (sustainability or ecological stability). As a result there is now a vast literature attempting to incorporate alternative social values and political objectives into the traditional assessments of market processes and investment procedures (Little and Mirrlees, 1974; Squire and Van der Tak, 1975; Helmers, 1979). It has also been clearly acknowledged that market exchange is only one form of social control over resources, and that other social choice processes have an important role to play (Dasgupta, 1982).

It became somewhat fashionable in the 1970s to reject the whole package of established economic concepts and analytical techniques, arguing that environmental resource issues raise such distinct and complex problems that 'the conventional framework and tools of economic theory are ill-adapted and are irrelevant for the analysis of the phenomena under discussion' (Kapp, 1970, p. 839). Today there has been some revision of attitudes. Few now pretend that conventional economic approaches based on economic efficiency criteria can provide absolute and objective solutions to problems which must involve essentially subjective political, social and moral choices. But they do provide valuable insights into why flow resource scarcity, depletion and degradation are characteristic in capitalist economies, both those operating under private and state capitalism. For example, the whole concept of externality was developed by economists, and although there are well-known problems involved in calculating the full range of external costs and benefits, it still remains a key and powerful analytical tool (Beckerman, 1972a). Moreover, economic assessments do suggest alternative management strategies which could play a role in the implementation of environmental and renewable resource policies.

As Sandbach (1980) has stressed, resource problems cannot adequately be understood without reference to the social, economic and political organization of the societies within which they arise. Economic organizations play a key role since neither social nor political institutions can be divorced from the way the economic system operates to direct production and allocate rewards. We cannot simply ignore market processes and economic choice mechanisms in the analysis of flow resource problems and in the development of appropriate policy responses. To do so ignores the basic, if at times unpalatable, fact that any changes in traditional resource use practices impose costs on some sections of the community.

Given existing economic, political and social systems, most renewable resource problems in practice boil down to the distribution of available goods and services over space and time. Not all these goods and services are material and incorporated within the traditional system of market exchange. But the basic questions at issue are, what package of products – including environmental quality and conservation – should be produced; who gets what, and when? Inevitably these involve economic choices. It was argued earlier that all public policy measures worthy of the name affect the allocation of effective income between people, and changes in flow resource management strategies are no exception. Although economic analysis cannot determine what the final distribution of welfare *should* be, it does help identify the nature, extent and direction of income change.

As was seen in Chapter 6, most economists have viewed renewable resource problems as products of common property rights and the neglect of the full social costs and benefits of resource use. The vast majority of these problems would require some form of government intervention to effect their solution. State ownership or regulation does not, however, in itself solve anything. It has to be accompanied by mechanisms to *allocate* available supplies or usage rights between competing demands and to *provide* neglected environmental services, including investments to augment natural resource flows.

Not surprisingly, the conventional economic approach has been to suggest that market mechanisms and evaluation criteria should be adopted for these purposes. Assuming that existing renewable resources are to be managed to maximize their net value in use, allocation decisions should be left to the sovereign consumer, to individual revealed preferences for specific environmental goods and services. For this to happen, prices (or preference measures) must be established for all those resource products hitherto unvalued by the market. The decision to undertake investment to increase the level of renewable resource flows available in the future (this includes conservation) should also, in theory, be based on consumer preferences and should be taken on broadly the same appraisal criteria as apply in the private sector. However, this appraisal task is made much more complex by the need to include a wide set of social costs and benefits in the analysis. Although decisions on how to allocate existing resource flows between competing users and on investment in new supplies are closely interrelated, the issues, problems and appropriate economic tools are rather different in the two cases. Therefore, attention, in this chapter, will be focused on the allocation question, while Chapter 8 will be concerned with conservation and investment decisions.

Most theoretical economists suggest that the principles governing the management of available resource flows are the same for all types of renewable resource. As Dasgupta (1982, p. 201) puts it, 'the conceptual apparatus that is needed to study the economics of pollution control is the same as are required for fisheries, ground water basins, forestry and so on'. It is not, therefore, necessary to discuss the vast range of individual renewable resources which now have been subject to economic analysis.[1] Instead, the approach, its limitations and use in practice will be assessed using pollution control as the type example. However, some reference will also be made to the fisheries and water supply cases, where these help to bring out specific conceptual, political or practical problems.

THE POLLUTION CONTROL CASE: ESTABLISHING OPTIMAL USE LEVELS

Theoretical simplicity

To manage a given existing supply of any multipurpose renewable resource in an economically efficient manner it is first essential to determine how much should be allocated to each competing use. In the conventional economic treatment of pollution control this involves establishing a balance between the use of the environment for waste disposal and its use for all other purposes. The solution is not to ban all waste discharges, but to find the position where the benefits – or damage reduction advantages – of control equal the costs involved in curbing the level of disposals (see Figure 7.1).

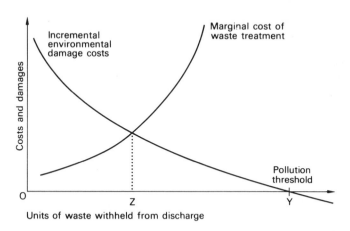

O–Z   Optimal level of waste reduction

Y   Point at which level of waste disposal is low enough to cause no environmental damage

Figure 7.1   Optimal level of pollution abatement
Source: Rees, 1977, p. 315

It is always possible to withhold waste *from any one environmental medium* at a cost. In most industries quite major reductions can be achieved by changing the amount of waste generated per unit output: this can, and has been, done by modifying the production process itself, altering the nature and quantity of raw materials or fuels used and by changing product type or design.[2] Once generated, the quantity of residuals actually discharged to the environment can be curbed by the installation of recycling or by-product recovery technologies and by treatment facilities. An individual firm can also reduce its apparent discharge by paying contractors to remove it. Unless the waste is then used for refabrication, this does not cut the total emissions to the environmental system, but may serve to reduce the resulting damage (see p. 265). Finally, although an extreme option, residual discharges can be cut by output reductions or plant closure.

Normally the costs involved in introducing these control measures rise as more and more waste units are withheld from discharge (Martindale, 1979). Kneese and Schultze (1975, p. 19) have argued: 'As a virtually universal phenomenon, the greater the percentage of pollutants already removed from an industrial process, the higher will be the cost of removing an additional amount'. They go on to cite the example of a typical large meat-processing plant discharging waste in water. When 30 per cent of the residuals, measured in terms of their biological oxygen demand (BOD), have been removed, the unit cost of further waste reduction is 6 cents per pound weight. But once 90 per cent of the BOD is removed, another pound reduction costs 60 cents and above 95 per cent the cost rises to 90 cents. The cost pattern will vary considerably between firms but by and large it is clear that the marginal cost of pollution control will rise as levels of discharge are cut (Figure 7.1).

On the other hand, as the quantity of residuals emitted to the environmental system is reduced, or as their quality is improved, so the amount of damage created will fall. Eventually the *pollution threshold* will be reached. At this point discharges are within the natural absorptive capacity of the environment and no damage costs are imposed on society. However, for most pollutants the marginal costs of control will have exceeded the benefits from further reductions in waste discharge levels long before this zero-pollution point is reached, although there are some possible exceptions where the polluting substances are highly toxic and are not biodegradable, or only degrade over exceptionally long time periods. From an economic perspective the optimal use of the environment for the removal of waste products would occur at point Z; pollution continues to be caused by ZY waste units, but it would be inefficient to pursue the waste reduction effort further since the costs involved would exceed the benefits.

The practical problems

CALCULATING THE DAMAGE FUNCTION

The idea of attempting to balance abatement costs against the benefits from waste reduction is intuitively appealing, although the problems involved in actually calculating the equilibrium point are legion. An important group of difficulties arise over establishing the nature of the damage function. In the first place, the damage associated with a set amount of discharge at one particular location is not fixed, but varies markedly over time. When watercourses are used as the disposal media, damage costs fluctuate in response to seven major variables:

(1) stream velocity and flow volume;
(2) climatic conditions, particularly ambient air temperatures and wind speed, both of which affect the level of natural oxygen within the river;
(3) channel characteristics – most notably bed irregularities which affect turbulence, and the ratio between surface area and water volume; both of these influence natural reoxygenation rates;
(4) the time period over which the waste disposal occurs – less damage will be created if disposal takes place gradually and if levels are adjusted in response to natural variations in the absorptive capacity of the stream;
(5) the number, size and location of other pollution sources in the area; as Figure 7.2 shows, if firms A, B and C use a stream to remove their effluents, no damage results as the load is within the regenerative capacity of the watercourse; but as soon as firms D and E discharge into the same stretch of water, the pollution threshold is reached and damage is caused; in this situation it is not clear which disposal actually causes the pollution;
(6) the nature of other polluting substances in the stream – pollution damage can be exacerbated if synergism occurs (the combined action of two or more pollutants increases the level of damage above the summation of the damage created by each individually); thus if copper and cadmium occur together, they are more than twice as toxic to fish as either one of them acting alone (Sandbach, 1982);
(7) the number, location and type of other stream users – damage will obviously

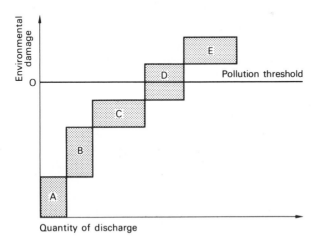

A, B, C, D, E Firms discharging waste into a stream

Figure 7.2   Effluent discharges and the pollution threshold
Source: Rees, 1977, p. 318

be much greater if water supply intake points, spray irrigators, or favoured recreation areas are located immediately downstream from the discharge pipe.

Of these variables only the timespan of disposal is controllable by the polluters themselves. In many cases the apparent damage created by a firm increases without any change in discharge practices because other water users alter their behaviour. Stream flows may be reduced if upstream abstractors increase their consumption or if flood control or hydroelectric power agencies decide to install regulating reservoirs. Similarly, the activities of drainage or navigation authorities can increase pollution damage by removing obstacles in the stream-bed or by straightening and canalizing the channel, thus reducing the natural rate of reoxygenation. Increases in downstream recreation demands, public water supply needs or the acreage under irrigation can likewise result in higher levels of pollution damage. In all these situations it is no longer clear who imposes damage upon whom (Coase, 1960).

Exactly the same type of problems arise in the air pollution case. Here damage will vary markedly with wind speed and direction, sunshine levels, the intensity, duration and distribution of rainfall and the temperature variations with height. It is also crucially dependent upon the quantity and type of other pollutants present. Photochemical smogs, for instance, are produced by complex synergistic (photolytic) reactions between nitrogen oxides, hydrocarbons and ultraviolet solar radiation. When damage is the result of such complex combinations of substances or chemical processes, it becomes extremely difficult to calculate the individual contribution attributable to any one pollution source (Bach, 1972; Gilpin, 1978).

A second crucial problem in estimating the damage function arises because many of the costs are not easily, or even meaningfully, translated into money terms. An enormous amount of research has been undertaken to estimate monetary pollution damage costs, but as Pearce (1976, p. 81) says, 'the state of play cannot be considered such as to inspire sufficient confidence in the orders of magnitude obtained to suggest that they be used in actual . . . policy decisions'. The problems involved in such forms of cost–benefit assessment will be considered in Chapter 8. At this stage it is merely necessary to point out that considerable difficulties arise in calculating the costs involved, even where physical damage occurs to land or property.

But these pale into insignificance beside the problems of putting monetary measures on reduced human health or premature deaths and on losses in aesthetic or recreational value. The damage from noise, smell, visually intrusive developments and hazardous installations are all essentially subjective, varying enormously from person to person, which makes objective assessment difficult, and some would claim impossible (Kapp, 1970, 1972; Adams, 1974a, 1974b). However, unless translation into money occurs, it is not only impossible to aggregate all the disparate types of damage into one function,[3] but also there is no means of comparing the benefits and costs of pollution control.

A further estimation problem results from our limited knowledge at any point in time. Clearly, the damage function can only include currently known costs. But as we saw in Chapter 6, one important set of environmental problems arise because of uncertainty over the effects of change on natural systems. In practice, therefore, it is not known with any certainty whether the current economically efficient equilibrium position is compatible with ecological sustainability. At a less all-embracing scale ignorance of pollution damage on human health, and on flora and fauna, is very common (Saunders, 1976). For instance, some 70,000 different chemicals are currently produced commercially in the United States, only a fraction of which have been adequately studied to assess their persistence and long-term biological effects (Sandbach, 1982).

ENVIRONMENTAL INTERDEPENDENCE

In addition to these calculation problems, there are also major conceptual difficulties in the economic equilibrium approach. In the first place, it is essentially static and is only really capable of dealing with clear, spatially confined types of pollution damage. But one of the basic characteristics of environmental systems is their interdependence. Pollution effects in one part of the system can set up widespread chain reactions: 'These interdependencies and the causal chain which give rise to environmental disruption differ in kind and complexity from those with which economists have traditionally been concerned' (Kapp, 1970, p. 835).

Although Kapp is correct to point out the complex nature of physical systems, it is debatable whether the interdependency problems actually differ markedly in degree from those which exist within the economic system and which *have* been subject to economic analysis. What makes damage assessment so difficult is that interrelationships in both the environmental and economic systems have to be taken into account.

When damage costs are calculated it becomes necessary to break into both sets of causal chain reactions somewhere and the point chosen will be essentially arbitrary. Figure 7.3 shows in a highly simplified form the sort of difficulties involved in attempting to trace the damage from emissions to the air by fossil-fuel-based electricity generating stations. What spatial scale is relevant in the damage assessment? Clearly, apparent damage costs will be much lower if transnational pollution effects are ignored. What is the appropriate cut-off point along any of the damage chains? Once again the costs will appear to be much lower if only the first-order effects are considered, ignoring secondary and all subsequent impacts.

CROSS-MEDIA TRANSFERS AND THE BEST ENVIRONMENTAL OPTION

Further difficulties arise because the damage function is dependent on the type of pollution abatement measures which are employed. The two curves shown in Figure 7.1 are thus not capable of independent assessment. As we have already seen, matter is neither created nor destroyed and waste products must go somewhere within the total environmental system, unless complete recycling occurs. Therefore, the form of the residuals, the receiving media and damage levels all change as different abatement techniques are used. By ensuring that final disposal occurs at the least environmentally sensitive sites, or into media

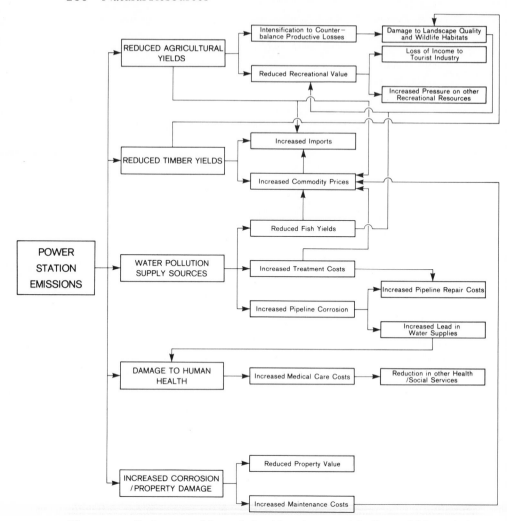

Figure 7.3 Environmental interrelationships: the potential effects of SO_2 emissions from power stations

which have surplus absorptive or regenerative capacity, the damage created by a given discharge level can be minimized. In other words, we are dealing with a multidimensional problem which cannot adequately be expressed in just two dimensions – damage and control costs. The data required to optimize the use of the total environmental system would be prodigious. Information would be necessary on the marginal damage costs incurred in *all* alternative environmental media at *all* feasible disposal sites, *and* on the abatement costs associated with each of these alternatives. Moreover, in practice, it would be necessary to have an administrative system capable of ensuring that the full range of disposal options is taken into account.

ABATEMENT METHODS

Both the damage and abatement cost curves can also be shifted if government pollution control agencies decide not to leave damage reduction solely to the polluters and undertake collective abatement measures. This could result in a more efficient solution, in the sense that a given environmental improvement could be achieved at a lower total cost. In areas where polluting units are concentrated, it may well be cheaper for the wastes to be treated collectively rather than for each firm to invest in control technologies. If scale economies can be achieved, then the abatement cost curve would be shifted outwards and downwards. Moreover, public pollution control authorities are able to employ a much wider range of damage reduction techniques than the individual firm.

In the water case, for instance, the absorptive capacity of the environment could be increased by raising stream flows or reoxygenation rates. Alternatively, zoning techniques could be used, separating the polluters from those liable to damage; some streams could be reserved for amenity and recreation, allowing others to carry the waste loads (Kneese, 1964; Kneese and Bower, 1968; OECD, 1977). Similarly, the damage created by air pollution could be reduced by adopting a variety of urban planning measures, including land zoning, the use of green 'filter' belts to lower levels of airborne impurities, improved highway design, the exclusion of motor vehicles from shopping centres and so on (see Bach, 1972). If any of these are employed, the incremental damage curve is shifted downwards. Under these circumstances the search for *one* optimal solution is a highly complex undertaking, and the problem may well prove insoluble as too many variables have to be taken into account.

IDEOLOGICAL PROBLEMS

Finally, it is necessary to refer briefly to the ideological basis of the economic efficiency approach and its assumption that individual preferences, weighted by wealth, *should* determine the optimal usage pattern for environmental resources. This subject has already been discussed, in Chapter 4, in the context of stock resource allocations but the principles involved are no different for the renewables case. It is only important here to stress four points.

First, individual revealed preferences are subject to manipulation, both by interest groups intent on minimizing their own abatement costs and by pressure groups which place high value on specific environmental quality resources (see Chapter 9, pp. 377–84). Second, individual preferences are often based on myopically short time horizons and on ignorance. Third, preferences will shift, often quite rapidly, to reflect changing economic and political circumstances or simply in response to reports in the media. This means that the apparent damage curve will also shift, making it extremely difficult to use it as a basis for a consistent pollution abatement strategy. Finally, use of monetary assessment involves the difficulty that the resulting policies will be biased towards the preferences of those with high incomes. The damage curve cannot, therefore, be envisaged as a fixed, objective entity. Unless it can be assumed that all income groups have identical preference sets, which hardly seems likely, the damage function will shift in response to changes in the distribution of wealth and income.

It is now well recognized that the notion of an 'optimal' level of waste reduction, based upon the objective assessment of the costs and benefits involved, has to be abandoned. Rather the required levels of abatement have to be established through 'bargained' environmental quality standards or objectives. This does not mean that the idea of attempting to achieve a balanced use of environmental resources should be rejected, or that efforts to calculate damage levels and the distribution of damage costs should be ignored. It is, in fact, essential to have as much cost data as possible as an input into the bargaining process. Without it, there is a clear danger that pollution control priorities will continue to be set by the most vocal and powerful vested interests. While the benefits from abatement remain ill-defined, the already considerable bias in pollution policy formulation towards economic interests will inevitably be reinforced. Data on damage costs is crucial as a counterbalance to industrial and farming lobbies, which can point to identifiable control costs when opposing moves for environmental improvements or demanding cost subsidies.

INTERTEMPORAL DEPENDENCE AND THE AVAILABILITY OF RESOURCE SUPPLIES

The conventional economic treatment of pollution externalities is essentially static, atemporal in nature. In effect, it is assumed that the potentially usable regenerative capacity of the environment and the damage inflicted by pollutants in any time period are unaffected by previous waste disposals and that current discharge decisions will not affect future absorptive capacity or damage levels. Each time period is treated as a distinct entity and the difficulties created by temporal interdependence are omitted from consideration. Such an approach may be reasonable in cases where the pollutants are quickly degraded into harmless substances and where the rate of complete resource replacement is rapid. For instance, although over short timespans particular stretches of river flowing through heavily industrialized and urbanized areas can be completely denuded of all regenerative capability, it would broadly be valid to assume that for most contaminants the load discharged in one year will not affect the assimilative capacity available in the next. However, even in this case, while the renewal of the water quality resource itself may be independent of previous pollution levels, the same is not true of the river's aquatic life; once spawning grounds have been damaged, it could take many years for the fish population to regenerate naturally.

Examples of intertemporal dependence in the pollution case

There are, however, numerous situations where it is inappropriate to approach the analysis of optimal pollution abatement strategies in a temporally discrete manner. Whenever the average rate of residuals discharge exceeds the rates of resource renewal and the breakdown of the polluting substances, the effects are cumulative. In lakes or land-locked seas, where natural water replacement occurs relatively slowly, any contaminants not completely degraded in one time period will reduce the absorptive capacity available in the next. If disposal continues to exceed resource renewal, the water body will be mined of its natural ability to degrade pollutants in much the same way as overfishing can exhaust a fishery.

Problems of temporal interdependence are greatly magnified when the discharged contaminants, or a proportion of them, are only biodegradable over relatively long time periods. For the so-called stock pollutants – some forms of radioactive waste, cadmium or mercury – the natural breakdown and fixing processes may operate too slowly to have much relevance to man (Nobbs and Pearce, 1976; Pearce, 1976). In extreme cases it may be more appropriate to envisage the capacity of the environment to receive such pollutants as an essentially fixed stock, with each disposal reducing the quantity which can be safely discharged in the future. However, there is great uncertainty over where to draw the safety limits, particularly as not all of the discharged stock pollutants will accumulate in areas or environmental media where they can be harmful. For instance, although element minerals, such as mercury, are virtually indestructible they only create damage problems while they remain 'free', unfixed by the processes of deposition in the sediments which will eventually form mineral-bearing rocks. It is not, therefore, easy to establish a direct relationship between levels of discharge and the accumulated pollutant stock. Much depends upon the spatially and temporally variable rates of deposition.

What is clear for all the long-lived pollutants is that the harmful effects arising from a given level of discharge are critically dependent on the quantity already present in the affected ecosystem. This certainly applies to DDT, with its half-life of around thirty years, and to mercury (Holdgate, 1979). The problems created by both these contaminants are exacerbated by their tendency to be concentrated up food chains. Similarly, the health costs imposed on individuals by lead pollution are not just related to current dose levels, but are also a function of past exposure, since much of the lead inhaled or ingested in previous time periods remains trapped in body tissue. Even noise pollution can be cumulative in effect. Although noise itself does not accumulate as a stock, damage to hearing can occur through prolonged exposure. Therefore, in a sense, the effective capacity of a particular environment, such as a factory or airport, to absorb noise may decline over time, assuming of course that the population of affected individuals remains fairly constant.

Intertemporal dependence and other flow resources

These few examples are merely illustrative of the numerous situations where it is essential to drop the assumption that there is always a constant, exogenously determined flow of environmental quality available for allocation in each time period.[4] In many cases availability cannot be treated as an independent variable but must be seen as some function of past rates of use. The biodegradable capacity of the environment is thus no different from any other flow resource which is dependent on biological processes of regeneration. For such resources economic analysts have long recognized that attempts to establish optimal levels of use must include consideration of the relationship between available supplies and consumption levels. The earliest and most elementary treatment of this subject was developed in the context of marine fisheries but has since been applied to a wide range of other resource flows.

THE FISHERIES EXAMPLE:
A SIMPLIFIED STATIC MODEL

In the fisheries case the problems of use-availability dependence were first tackled by envisaging a *sustainable yield curve* (see pp. 26–7) and by restricting the optimization task to finding the point on this curve where the net returns from fishing were maximized. Thus the analysis was considerably simplified and made essentially static by assuming that the optimal harvest per time period was compatible with the replenishment of the remaining stock (Gordon, 1954; Scott, 1955b; Schaefer, 1957; Copes, 1981). The possibility that it might be socially optimal to run the fishery down to the point of exhaustion was not included in this elementary model. It should be pointed out that although it is easy to draw a sustainable yield curve on paper, it is no minor task to calculate its real world dimensions. The maximum carrying capacity of the fishery, the size of the existing fish population and its natural rate of regeneration can rarely be known accurately. Stochastic modelling may, therefore, be necessary – a process made even more complex if other factors, such as pollution, are also acting to change the basic parameters.

To many non-economists a rational management strategy would involve controlling the fishing effort in order to *maximize* the sustainable fish yield per annum. But to the economist the objective is not to maximize the weight of fish which can be landed, but rather to maximize the difference between the costs of fishing and the revenue derived from selling the catch. The concern is not with food production *per se*, but with profit.

In Figure 7.4 the sustainable yield curve is converted into a sustainable revenue curve by the expedient of assuming that the price of fish is constant – by multiplying the tonnage yield by this price, the curve now shows the sale value of each year's harvest. By then assuming that each unit of fishing effort involves the same unit costs, costs become proportionate to effort and a straight-line cost curve can be drawn through the origin.[5] In an uncontrolled fishery the vessels would continue to operate until OA units of effort were expended, assuming of course that the fishermen are 'economically rational' beings. Up to this effort point further fishing is warranted since the revenue from the catch would exceed the harvesting costs, which are assumed to include normal returns to the employed labour and capital. However, no rational fisherman would operate beyond this point since the costs would exceed sustainable returns.

It is easy to see that OA cannot be an economically efficient use of labour and capital since the same revenue yield could have been achieved at much lower cost and with only OB effort units. But OB itself is not the optimal effort level, this occurs at OC where the value of the harvest exceeds the fishing costs by the largest possible amount. The net returns (or rent) from the fishery are now maximized.

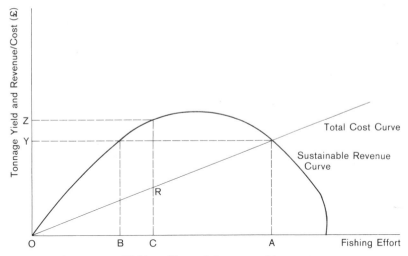

Figure 7.4   Fishing effort and the sustainable revenue curve

From this type of analysis it is evident that common property fisheries will not be exploited in an economically optimal fashion unless some management agency can remove BA vessel days from the industry.

THE PROBLEMS IN PRACTICE

The economic approach outlined here is admittedly much simplified and justice is hardly done even to the comparative static models which have now been developed, to say nothing of the much more complex dynamic treatments which have become a feature of the literature since the early 1970s (Clark, 1976; Munro, 1981). However, it does allow the identification of three key areas where the optimization prescriptions may run counter to the objectives and political realities of fisheries management in practice.

In the first place, major problems arise over the fate of the labour and capital made redundant by any effort control measures. Theoretically the excess factors of production could be put to more productive use elsewhere in the economy, but this presupposes that the men and vessels are mobile and that alternative employment possibilities exist. Fishermen rarely have the range of skills which allow their easy transfer into other occupations, a problem exacerbated by the relative remoteness of many fishing communities from major industrial and urban centres. Similarly, there are limited opportunities to redeploy the capital already locked up in existing fishing vessels, although clearly the investment capital which would have gone to produce new boats is more mobile. A reduction in fishing effort could, therefore, optimize the use of the marine resource and reduce the external costs of overexploitation but there is a real possibility that this will merely produce other forms of social cost. The effects of unemployment, the run-down of local fishing communities and the wastage of the fixed capital invested not only in the vessels, but also in the infrastructure of the affected communities, must all be considered in the formulation of politically acceptable fisheries management strategies.

Both the social impact and the political significance of a run-down in fishing effort will be greater when unemployment or underemployment are already endemic in the national economy. If open access exploitation of the fishery is compatible with yield sustainability (as it is in Figure 7.4), then the social costs of further employment losses may exceed the economic benefits from 'optimizing' fishing effort. However, this would not be true of a fishery where uncontrolled access could rapidly exhaust the entire fish stock and, therefore, deprive all fishermen of their livelihood. Rapid exhaustion is most likely to occur in a so-called 'gauntlet' fishery, where the fish move *en masse* along a few known and easily blocked tracks to spawning grounds. Salmon affords an obvious example; simple and very low-cost harvesting techniques can wipe out an entire race of fish (Pearse, 1972). In such cases it may well be necessary to accept the social costs of some unemployment now in order to avoid the much larger costs associated with complete resource exhaustion.

The second problem area concerns the redistributive consequences of optimization. If the fishermen who are allowed to remain in the industry keep the increased net returns (or newly created resource rent), then income is effectively redistributed from the displaced labour to those still employed. Since the optimal management strategy would result in higher total returns, in theory the advantaged men could afford to pay compensation to all those displaced and still be better off. The new situation affords a potential welfare improvement according to Paretian criteria (see pp. 118–19) but, in practice, compensation actually may well not be paid. Open-access fisheries are often characterized by low income levels and, therefore, one of the most common management objectives is to secure higher incomes for fishermen. This conveniently can be achieved by allowing them to retain the newly generated rent, but inevitably difficulties arise in deciding who should benefit. These are particularly acute when vessels from several nations have traditionally exploited the now controlled fishery; few governments will willingly accept cross-national redistribution of real income.

Most economists have argued that the price mechanism should be utilized to decide which individuals (or nations) should provide the effort retained in the optimally managed fishery. By imposing taxes on each unit of catch, or by auctioning the remaining fishing rights, the most efficient producers would continue to operate but high-cost inefficient vessels would be forced to leave the industry. Such allocative mechanisms imply that the newly generated rent would accrue to the management agency and thus to the public exchequer. It would then be a matter of political decision if the revenue was redistributed as compensation payments to the excluded units of labour and capital. Many conventional economic assessments of optimal fisheries management have ignored these key distributive issues (Eckert, 1979), but they are rarely far from the centre of concern when implementable and politically acceptable control strategies are being developed.

The final important problem with the whole optimization approach is one which has already been encountered in the discussion of minerals – namely, that it rests on the assumption that the price paid for a commodity reflects the true value to consumers. In the fish case this may be broadly reasonable for advanced countries where food scarcities rarely occur and where health problems are more likely to be caused by overeating than undernourishment. However, it has extremely dubious validity when applied to those less developed nations, where food, and particularly protein, deficiencies are commonplace. In such situations it may well be socially optimal to manage the fish resources to maximize sustainable yields rather than economic rents.

There is no one objective method of establishing the ideal level of use for any flow resource. Economic efficiency provides one criterion for assessment, but it is rarely the only one considered by managers and political decision-makers. Employment needs and the distribution of real income play vital roles in the establishment of acceptable levels, as indeed do the desire to minimize acrimonious public debate and the need to 'reward' vocal or politically important interest groups. Economically suboptimal usage patterns may have to be accepted to avoid other forms of social cost or as an expedient to get any agreement to implement some control measures.

THE ALLOCATION OF AVAILABLE RESOURCE SUPPLIES: THE POLLUTION CASE

Control use or increase capacity?

If we now assume that the objective of pollution control is to reach some specific environmental quality standard (or even just to reduce waste discharges below present levels), the question arises of which management tool to adopt to achieve this. Overall there are two very broad, distinct but not mutually exclusive options. First, the absorptive capacity of the environment could be increased; and second, the waste load could be reduced. Exactly the same two options are present for such resources as water supply, forests, fish, soils or wildlife. In such cases supplies could be increased by investment in storage capacity, replanting, the creation of artificial fish hatcheries, animal breeding programmes and so on. Alternatively, demands could be managed within an arbitrarily determined 'natural' limit.

Customary modes of thought and traditional practices determine which of these options is normally employed. It will be shown that in the water supply case engineering capacity extension (supply-fix) programmes have been historically regarded as the most appropriate solution, with a considerable neglect of demand management techniques. On the other hand, when it comes to pollution, it is normally assumed that controls on the level of waste discharged are the most appropriate policy measures.[6] The emphasis on controlling pollutants reflects the fact that in all countries environmental policy has been reactive, geared to rectifying specific pollution problems after damage has become an obvious fact. Once the polluting discharges already exist, the management task becomes a fire-fighting exercise and is understandably defined in terms of finding methods to cut discharge loads or to treat them post generation. Although it has been widely advocated that environmental policy shifts from ex-post correction to ex-ante preventive planning (Simonis, 1984), at present the option of changing the assimilative capacity of the environment is rarely exercised. The conventional economic treatment of pollution has followed the bias of practice and has concentrated almost exclusively on the demand reduction option. This is somewhat surprising in view of the central importance of supply increases in all other sectors of the economy.

Within the waste load reduction option, there are six alternative control methods which may be employed: (1) pricing all environmental resources (i.e. making a charge for the use of the absorptive capacity of the receiving media); (2) establishing 'appropriate' individual discharge standards, limiting the quantity and quality of any disposals; (3) banning particularly polluting substances; (4) introducing other forms of legal regulation, for instance, on the location of production, the design of plant and equipment, product type and so forth; (5) paying polluters a subsidy to allow them to install abatement technologies; and (6) requiring all polluters to use collective treatment facilities.

The theoretical case for unit pricing

Until recently most economists favoured the pricing solution. It is the logical extension of the analysis of pollution as an externality problem. If a *rational* producer was required to pay all the social costs caused by each unit of waste discharged, then waste would be withheld until the treatment or reduction costs equalled the social damage cost price. In Figure 7.1 this situation is reached at point Z, and the producer would reduce the waste load by OZ units, but would pay the pollution costs for units ZY. Even if prices cannot actually be based on damage costs, the same approach could be taken. The damage curve is replaced by an ambient air or a stream standard, which then determines the absorptive capacity available for allocation in each time period. This available capacity is then distributed between waste dischargers according to their willingness to pay.

By and large, economists have treated the use of non-price measures to influence waste discharge behaviour as anathema to the achievement of efficiency in the allocation of available quality between users. A whole series of studies supporting the use of the price mechanism could be cited (for example, Beckerman, 1972b; Baumol and Oates, 1975; Anderson *et al.*, 1977), the most striking feature about which is the lack of empirically and objectively derived evidence to support the conclusions.

Numerous arguments have been put forward favouring the pricing solution and rejecting the other means of reducing waste loads. First, it is claimed that only charges exert continuous pressure on the polluter to improve disposal technologies. Standards or discharge consent conditions merely encourage firms to reach that standard, and other legal regulations, such as controls over the design of plant and equipment, fossilize production methods according to currently available technologies, so doing nothing to promote innovation. In fact technological change could be inhibited if firms have to go through complex and costly regulatory procedures to obtain permission to use 'non-standard' production methods or pollution abatement measures. Although it is possible that properly set and enforced standards, particularly ones which are progressively tightened over time in line with new technical possibilities, could provide some innovative incentives, in practice it is often unlikely. Certainly, the way standards are normally established in Britain means that they tend to reflect currently available and installed technologies rather than exerting pressure on companies to invest in innovation (Rothwell and Gardiner, 1983). However, it is debatable whether any implementable charging scheme would produce better results.

The second pro-pricing argument is that charges leave firms free to choose the least-cost method of reducing the waste load. As has already been seen, raw material, product, process and output changes could all act to reduce the quantity of residuals generated, while treatment and recycling could then be employed to lower the discharge of any remaining residuals. Firms would choose the combination of these measures which was most cost effective bearing in mind their particular production circumstances. Other control measures, it is argued, emphasize post-generation treatment of the waste rather than curbing the quantity actually produced. In fact there is no reason why standard setting should deprive firms of their freedom of choice, although it is true that the way regulations and subsidies have been employed in practice does tend to favour treatment. For example, the most common air quality regulations involve the addition of devices to remove elements from car exhausts or stack gases. Similarly, subsidies are normally only paid on capital equipment bought to treat wastes, but are not given to allow producers to make process or product changes. In the United States, for instance, firms can obtain 48 per cent relief of corporation income tax and up to 100 per cent direct subsidies in 'depressed areas', for the purchase of treatment equipment, but can get no help to employ other waste-reducing methods. However, there is nothing inherent in these alternative control techniques which makes the bias towards capital intensive waste treatment inevitable. It is quite possible, for example, to subsidize process changes, as is in fact done by the Seine–Normandie Basin Authority, in France, which allocates 30 per cent of its total subsidy payments to such changes (see p. 287).

The third reason for favouring prices is closely related to the second. Charging systems allow producers the flexibility to discharge different quantities of waste bearing in mind the varying costs of treatment or waste reduction that each faces. Standards, on the other hand, ignore differential abatement costs and penalize producers in old or cramped factories, or those faced with considerable technical barriers to compliance. As Figure 7.5 shows, a uniform effluent standard would impose high-cost penalties on firm A. Whereas firm B could achieve the required waste reduction relatively cheaply, at a cost of Oa, firm A would incur unit costs of Ob. Theoretically an effluent charge scheme could produce the same total reduction in waste discharges; both firms would pay the same unit residual charge, but it would be economic for firm B to curb its disposals by OY, while firm A would choose to make only an OX reduction. It is, therefore, claimed that the price mechanism serves to minimize the overall costs of achieving the required

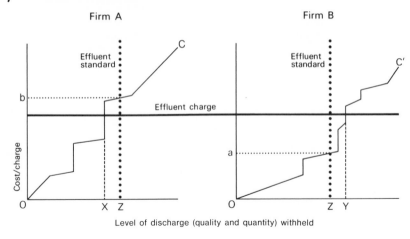

Figure 7.5   The comparative effects of pollution standards and taxes
Source: Rees, 1977, p. 317

quality objectives and to produce an efficient allocation of assimilative capacity between potential dischargers.

The price mechanism has a fourth supposed advantage, in that it is the only system which puts the full costs of pollution control on to the producers of the residuals. A firm is no longer able to pass on part of its legitimate production expenses – the cost of waste disposal – to other consumers of environmental resources. All other control mechanisms involve society bearing the costs of any remaining pollution, unless there is a total ban on *all* waste disposals which exceed the pollution threshold. Subsidy payments clearly mean that part of a firm's waste removal expenses are paid by the taxpayer rather than by the consumers of that firm's goods or services. Moreover, none of the non-price forms of regulation produces any funds to pay the often considerable costs involved in establishing and enforcing the pollution control system itself (Sandbach, 1982).

Theoretically an efficient allocation of all resources in the national economy can only be achieved if polluters pay the full social costs involved in their production of waste. Until this happens goods responsible for high waste loads will continue to be underpriced and consumed in too large quantities. In other words, consumers will respond to false cost–price signals and will not switch their patterns of demand to favour products involving low environmental damage costs. It would be equally inefficient if regulation went too far and required firms to pay *more* than the full social costs imposed by their waste disposal, as may be illustrated by reference to the US Water (Pollution Control) Amendment 1972.

This amendment required that the discharge of pollutants into navigable waters be eliminated by 1985. In addition to the technical problems involved in changing all the industrial and domestic systems which rely on waterborne waste removal, the economic costs would be enormous. Moreover, the achievement of water purity could simply mean major increases in air pollution or in the level of solid wastes dumped on land (Kneese and Schultze, 1975).

The problems involved in the Pareto efficiency approach have already been discussed, but three specific difficulties must be mentioned here. First, full implementation of the 'polluter pays' principle *could* result in a regressive redistribution of real income if highly polluting but essential goods, such as fuel and power or food produced using high levels of chemical fertilizers and pesticides, represent a higher proportion of the income of relatively poor families. Second, the requirement that firms bear all the costs *could* reduce their profitability, in which case they may reduce their output, export sales or employment levels. All of these responses could impose considerable economic and social costs on the economy, or on particular groups within it. And finally, some forms of pollution damage could be regarded as a consumer rather than a producer creation. If consumers change their demands for aesthetic environmental services or choose to buy houses or engage in recreation near existing waste disposers, their decisions in a sense produce the damage. This will not be a popular interpretation of events but is nevertheless a valid one. These three issues mean that it is extremely debatable whether it is *always* socially correct to adhere to a full 'polluter pays' strategy.

The fifth and final of the main pro-pricing arguments rests on the claim that it is the least costly form of control since it requires less information and is self-administering. Other control systems are regarded as inflexible, expensive and cumbersome to administer (Anderson *et al.*, 1977). In practice, this is a highly dubious claim. Both standards and charges require roughly the same amount of information on the production techniques used and the possible abatement options open to firms (Brown, 1973; Storey and Walker, 1975; Walker and Storey, 1977). Both also need a discharge measurement system and a police force to ensure that firms are not by-passing the monitoring devices (Wenner, 1978). In fact, in many cases, a charging policy would be more expensive to administer, simply because it necessitates the calculation of bills and the collection of the payments (Harrison and Sewell, 1980).

In recent years even the theoretical basis of the pro-charging arguments and the rejection of alternative control mechanisms has been questioned. Brown (1973) has, for instance, shown that subsidies used to help firms achieve the required reduction in waste loads do not interfere with the achievement of an efficient level of water or air quality if used (as they normally are) in conjunction with a discharge standard system. And clearly subsidies can have important political and economic advantages in getting agreement to implement pollution control regulations. Both Brown (1973) and Storey and Walker (1975) have also demonstrated that pricing schemes are not unequivocally more allocatively efficient than standard-setting systems which are based on the collection of *a priori* information on firms' abatement costs. Although some theoretical economists have clung to the conceptually satisfying optimal-pricing approach, those concerned with developing implementable pollution control strategies have increasingly come to recognize that charges are not a universal panacea. As Schelling points out,

> most economists ... are not veterans of legislatures or administrative agencies. They have not always done the empirical task of measuring what actual difference it might make to use prices instead of direct controls, and most of them have not devised in sufficient detail for implementation the schemes that their general reasoning leads them to admire and sometimes to advocate (Schelling, 1983, p. x)

There will be cases where some form of pricing system could be the most cost-effective method of achieving a particular environmental quality objective but there will be many situations where other management techniques will prove to be more appropriate.

The practical problems of pricing

The applicability of pricing solutions will depend on three main factors: (1) the ease with which prices can be established to encapsulate effectively the particular pollution problem; (2) the way firms respond to charges in practice; and (3) the consequences of their response for product prices, real incomes, regional growth, employment and so forth.

ESTABLISHING AN APPROPRIATE PRICE SCHEDULE

The practical difficulties involved in capturing the essence of a pollution problem into a single price schedule are not trivial. There are literally hundreds of potentially polluting substances: which, then, should be measured for the purpose of establishing the charge? In practice, an implementable price schedule can usually only be based on one or two components, which are readily identifiable and measurable, although Hungary uses thirty-one different substances in its effluent tax schemes (Johnson and Brown, 1976). Those pollutants left outside the charge structure may, therefore, have to be directly controlled. It is in fact unusual for pricing to be used alone, rather it is seen as a revenue-raising supplement to regulation.

At a minimum all charge schedules have to include both a quality and a quantity dimension; unit volume charges alone would simply encourage producers to concentrate their effluent, whereas quality parameters alone would encourage predischarge dilution. In some circumstances the system would also need a timing component to avoid highly polluting bulk discharges, or to encourage disposal at times when the available regenerative capacity of the receiving media is at its highest. Furthermore, it may be necessary to devise area-specific price schedules; if different quality objectives are set for particular airsheds or stretches of river, or if producers respond differentially to price, then variable charges may be needed to ensure that the control objectives are met. However, politically it may be extremely difficult to implement a charging system in which prices vary markedly depending on the location of the producer.

It is never just a question of devising a price schedule which is meaningful in terms of the physical problem under consideration, but also of constructing a system which is easy to understand and gains a maximum acceptance among the parties concerned (OECD, 1980a). Pricing is likely to be most cost effective when the pollution problem is substance-specific and involves relatively few readily identifiable sources. For example, Nichols (1983) argues that benzene, listed in 1977 as a hazardous air pollutant by the US Environmental Protection Agency, under section 112 of the Clean Air Act, could be most efficiently controlled by plant-specific charges. Similarly, it would not be difficult to devise and implement charges on the emission of SO_2 or NO_x from electricity-generating stations, but whether these would result in the hoped-for response is another matter. However, where the industrial processes are complex, where multiple pollutants are present and when many pollution sources are involved a pollution tax system is less likely to be appropriate (Martindale, 1976).

THE RESPONSE TO PRICING

In all the economic debate over 'polluter pays' strategies little attention has been paid to the way firms respond, in practice, to any set of prices. The assumption has been that producers are 'economic men', will react in a prescribed rational way to any charges and will attempt to minimize their own private costs. A number of studies sponsored by Resources for the Future have indicated that industrial waste-water discharges are potentially highly price-elastic; Löf and Kneese (1967) on the sugar beet industry, Vaughan and Russell (1973) on iron and steel and Russell (1973) on petroleum refining provide just three examples of this work. They all assume that the existence of possible savings means that firms will respond to a properly calculated and implemented charging system. Empirical evidence showing that prices may have little observable impact on discharge levels usually have been explained away by claims that the prices were obviously too low. However, recent research on industrial responses to the trade effluent charges established in Britain for discharges to sewers suggests that there are more complex explanations (Webb and Woodfield, 1979; Rees, 1981b).

Inevitably firms can only react rationally to a price system if they understand it. They need to be able to appreciate how the charges actually affect them and how significantly different levels of payment could arise if they altered the strength/volume composition of the effluent. This problem does not occur when the price only has one dimension – people readily appreciate the costs they incur when they fail to return bottles on which a deposit has been paid. But as has already been seen, most pollution charges need to include various components; the more complex the system, the less likely it is that polluters will clearly understand its implications. In the UK, where the charging structures for trade effluent were relatively straightforward,[7] it was found that between 25 and 30 per cent of all firms were unable to react rationally to the price signals, simply because it was not clear to them how they could affect the total payments. This was so despite the fact that the charges had been in operation for four years and that the pollution control agencies had widely publicized and explained the scheme.

Another aspect of this problem of understanding arose over the firms' perception of their entitlement to discharge. A number of companies took the view that substantial payments gave them the right to discharge what they wished. In one regional water authority (RWA)[8] this attitude had in fact become an accepted part of policy. Consent conditions were not imposed on volume or on 'normal' pollutants, which the sewage works was designed to treat. The argument was that as long as the charges reflected the costs of treatment the RWA was there to provide a service to industry, not to force them to engage in waste abatement investment. However, this argument becomes problematic in the longer run, when treatment plant capacity has to be extended, since the trade effluent charges do not reflect the marginal costs of capacity increments.

The reverse of this lack of understanding occurred in a few firms, who failed to respond because they understood the system too well! Since the charges were based on the cost of treatment at already constructed sewage works, it was realized that if the response was too marked the works would be left operating significantly below capacity. The authority would, therefore, have to increase unit charges in order to cover the high fixed costs. Firms which contributed a large proportion of the total effluent going to a particular sewage works therefore correctly saw themselves in a 'no-win' situation. It was rational for them to avoid making private waste abatement investments when they would, in the end, have to contribute to the costs of existing public capital.

A further response-inhibiting element was the fact that a significant proportion of firms had highly imperfect information about treatment methods and costs, and about the potential for product, process or input changes which could reduce the volume or strength of the generated wastes. There was a clear tendency for those not already engaged in some form of treatment or recycling to overestimate the costs and difficulties involved. Moreover, it was clear that in a number of industry groups producers looked to one particular firm for research leadership, and did not attempt to innovate abatement technologies themselves.

Another form of information constraint arises due to the division of responsibility within a firm. Except in very small concerns, the person responsible for waste disposal was not in charge of paying the bills. Therefore, unless the payments were markedly out of line with inflation or became a significant operating cost item, the firm simply paid the sum requested. The waste engineer was rarely challenged to rethink established disposal practices.

The final and in some ways most important limiting factor was the imperfection of the capital market. Managers of branch plants virtually all had highly constrained capital budgets. Above a very low ceiling all investment proposals had to be referred to head office, whereas operating expenditures did not come under the same close scrutiny, unless dramatically out of line with previous years. Most managers tended to prefer to minimize referral to head office; therefore, investments in abatement technologies were rarely contemplated and the charges were simply paid. Investment was further constrained since most companies insisted on a short two- to three-year payback period; only rarely would any waste control investments achieve payback in less than six years. Smaller owner-managed firms were also inhibited by lack of capital, particularly when interest charges were high. Many preferred, or were forced, to continue paying the effluent charges out of revenue rather than incur debts by investing in treatment facilities. This result has been supported by a recent study of the UK sugar-processing and metal-plating industries, which found that firms curbed their expenditure on pollution control equipment because interest rates were too high and many firms were already at their credit limits for financing day-to-day activities (Rothwell and Gardiner, 1983).

Although these response-inhibiting factors emerged from relatively small samples of firms, there is no reason to believe that they are not widely applicable. The implication is that, at least in the short run, prices alone may well fail to provide sufficient incentive for waste reduction and thus environmental quality objectives will not be met. It is certainly true that we lack enough information to ensure that any particular price level will produce the expected response. Without doubt, it will be necessary to go through several price iterations before the system actually achieves the quality objectives. Such price variations will make it exceptionally difficult for firms to make consistent abatement decisions (Storey and Elliott, 1977; Walker and Storey, 1977). However, if price is regarded in a less purist and more practical fashion, charging could be a valuable adjunct to regulation. At a minimum it would allow pollution control agencies to fund a wider range of abatement strategies. These could include the enforcement of standards, the provision of a technical advisory service and the payment of abatement subsidies or easy-term loans to firms facing steep abatement cost curves or lacking the required financial capital.

THE CONSEQUENCES OF 'POLLUTER PAYS' STRATEGIES

The task of tracing the economic and distributional consequences of pollution-charging schemes is by no means easy, but it is essential if we are to separate bluff from reality. Industrial and commercial interests have consistently claimed that charges would raise production costs, increase price inflation, reduce industrial competitiveness, and so on. Although the Confederation of British Industry has argued that a pollution tax would be more expensive to a discharger than would a standards/enforcement system (Martindale, 1976), it is by no means clear that this is always the case. While it is true that firms would have to pay for the pollution they continued to create, a key element in the charging approach is that it allows firms the flexibility to institute the most cost-effective control mechanisms. Moreover, since it allows firms to choose whether to curb disposals or pay the charge, it could cut abatement costs for those industries faced by steep waste reduction cost curves. A more cynical interpretation of industrial opposition to charges is that they are less easy to evade than standards, which are only costly to firms when strictly enforced (see Chapter 9).

From elementary economic theory it would be expected that the impact of pollution taxes on prices and industrial output will vary markedly depending on the competitive structure of firms and on the price elasticity of consumer demand. The charges would act to increase production costs, thus shifting a firm's supply curve from S_1 to S_2 in Figure 7.6. If the demand for the firm's product was inelastic (D_1), then the bulk of the pollution charges could simply be passed on to consumers as price rises (P_1 to P_3). As has already been seen, public monopoly industries, or utilities regulated by public agency, would have considerable scope for passing on the charges and would have little incentive to reduce their waste costs by instituting abatement measures. On the other hand, where consumers were more price responsive (D_2), product prices would rise less sharply (P_1 to P_2), but the firms concerned would see a marked fall in their sales ($Q_1 - Q_2$). The production levels of perfectly competitive concerns would be particularly affected since they, by definition, are faced by completely elastic demand curves. To sell any output at all they would have to absorb all the pollution abatement costs, unless, that is, every producer within the same industry (domestic and foreign) was subject to the same supply cost increases.

Since very few countries have actually introduced charges which are high enough to act as abatement incentives (p. 285), empirical evidence on the impact of pricing is extremely restricted. Most data are available in the context of charges for disposals of effluent to sewers and this suggests that some small firms,

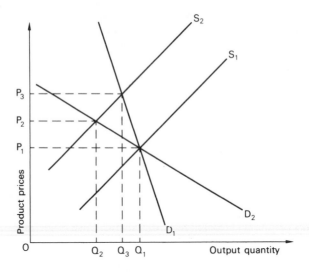

S_1	Supply curve with no charge for, or control over, waste disposal
S_2	Supply curve with effluent charges and controls
D_1	Inelastic demand curve
D_2	More elastic demand curve
P_1 P_2 P_3	Product prices
Q_1 Q_2 Q_3	Output levels

Figure 7.6 The effect of pollution control costs on the quantity and price of goods produced
Source: Rees, 1977, p. 319

particularly in sectors of the economy where domestic production is already marginally economic *vis-à-vis* foreign competition, have found pollution control costs the last straw. The Yorkshire wool textile industry appears to provide a case where firm closure and merger occurred after the imposition in 1975 of new higher-level trade effluent charges. But it is extremely difficult to say that the charges were the cause since the firms concerned were already in considerable economic difficulties and would have been unlikely to survive the economic recession of the late 1970s and early 1980s.

The effects of pollution charges will also vary considerably from industry to industry, depending upon the potential for recycling and by-product recovery. Installation of water filters or air scrubbers can allow the recovery of valuable materials which are then available for in-house reuse or for sale. Moreover, in the water case, the installation of recycling systems can significantly reduce both water supply and energy costs. In the sugar-refining and confectionery industries considerable cost savings can be made by collecting and renovating sucrose wastes; while in industries using high-value metals relatively simple water filtration techniques can allow the recovery and reuse of metal fines. It should be noted, however, that the profitability of by-product collection for sale on the open market must be expected to fall as more firms engage in the activity. In addition, material recovery may have undesirable output and employment consequences for those sectors of the economy producing new raw materials.

Alternative economic incentives

PERMIT AUCTIONS

The discussion so far has concentrated only on one device which can transmit economic signals to polluters; namely, a unit price or charge. This is the method most widely used, in practice, although various other economic instruments have been proposed in the theoretical literature (Dales, 1968; OECD, 1975; Common, 1977). One possibility is that a regulating agency *auctions* pollution permits, up to the limit set by the established quality objectives. Such a system avoids the problem of lack of knowledge concerning the polluters' response to price and ensures that the target emission levels are met.

Unless auctions are held frequently, or producers can resell the rights acquired in the auction, the system could act to fossilize existing patterns of waste production by curbing the incentive of those holding rights to innovate new abatement technologies and by preventing the entry of new firms or urban developments into the area. It seems likely that larger firms would attempt, and be able, to acquire and hold on to rights far in excess of their current disposal requirements. These could then act as a security blanket against the risk that future expansion plans or production changes might be restricted by the lack of discharge rights. Certainly, in England and Wales there was considerable evidence, collected during the early 1970s, which suggested that manufacturers and farmers held on to unutilized rights to *abstract* water supplies privately from streams and aquifers despite the fact that they were charged on the quantity of water they were licensed to take (Rees, 1970). Such charges were regarded as acceptable payments to reduce risk and uncertainty. There is no reason to expect that this behaviour would be modified if long-term pollution rights were acquired by auction.

While short-term (monthly or annual) rights issues may overcome the flexibility problems, they would deny firms the security needed to plan effectively over time their production and pollution abatement strategies. Clearly, enormous economic and social problems would result if plant closures occurred following the failure of firms to acquire disposal rights in an auction round. The whole auction system would inevitably favour the larger firms, which could afford to outbid less affluent companies, irrespective of the real value of the disposal rights in terms of the abatement costs (including closure) at individual plants. This feature alone makes it unlikely that an efficient allocation of available absorptive capacity would occur. Moreover, the possibility that firms might collude to agree on bids cannot be ignored (Schelling, 1983).

MARKETABLE RIGHTS AND PERMITS

A variant of the auction is the *conversion* of *existing rights into marketable, transferable commodities.* For many environmental resources exclusive usage rights have evolved over time, owing more to historical accident and tradition than to any objective assessment of requirements. In Britain, for instance, both water abstraction and effluent disposal licences were allocated on the basis of historical patterns of use (see p. 291), and the same is also true of water right allocations in the United States. More recently the granting of consents to emit wastes into the airsheds created under the US Clean Air Act 1970 was based on traditional pollution sources and abatement practices:

> Where existing sources together are within the required or implied level of total emissions they have been permitted to continue their individual emissions at traditional levels ... while new firms or enlargements of existing firms must be accommodated within whatever room remains for further emissions within the established limits. Once the 'excess' capacity is used up, there is no room for further growth and no room for new firms that might produce more and emit less than existing firms. (ibid., p. 39)

In all these cases the traditional rights act to freeze and protect past, possibly inefficient, usage patterns and penalize new developments.

The proposal is that such established rights should be converted into ownership rights that can be traded, so allowing new or expanding firms to buy disposal capacity and creating a monetary incentive for established concerns to adopt conservation or pollution abatement measures (Liroff, 1979). This idea is currently being considered for Californian water rights and it may be effective in allowing a better utilization of local air capacity under the US airshed control system (Repetto, 1983).

Somewhere between marketable rights and unit pricing is the sale of pollution *permits.* To illustrate how such a measure could operate consider the case of a large urban centre, where vehicle emissions need to be strictly controlled on particular days when the absorptive capacity of the air is naturally restricted.

Instead of arbitrarily controlling vehicle use according to their registration numbers (as occurs in Tokyo), an alternative would be to sell daily travel permits up to a set limit on a 'first come, first served' basis. In principle, this differs little from the sale of parking permits.

FINES AND COMPLIANCE BRIBES

A further potential economic incentive measure is the imposition of pollution fines. Firms or individuals are set performance standards and failure to comply results in automatic financial penalties. Schelling (1983) discusses this option in the context of the fleet-mileage standard established for passenger cars produced in the United States. Each year vehicle manufacturers are set a miles per gallon performance target which on average their cars must meet; by 1985 the average was 27.5 miles per gallon.[9] If the set figure is not reached, penalties will be incurred. This procedure was primarily conceived of as an energy conservation measure, but it could also serve to reduce environmental pollution.

Finally, the use of *compliance bribes* must be mentioned. Although bribes or subsidies are often seen as the reverse of pollution taxes and charges, in some situations it is difficult to dissociate the two. For example, deposits on returnable bottles are a form of pollution charge, which in effect impose a fine for failure to return. However, if they encourage small children to scour the neighbourhood for unreturned bottles then they are acting as clean-up bribes. The most commonly proposed version of bribes is that firms should be given rebates on their pollution charges if they achieve specific abatement levels. The bribe obviously becomes a subsidy if rebates exceed initial payments. Alternatively, firms could pay a deposit or bond, which is then refunded if some set environmental quality target is met or if a satisfactory disposal method is used (Bohm, 1981). A form of this system already operates in the United Kingdom to encourage mineral operators to restore worked land; sand and gravel operators pay a bond which is forfeited if restoration does not occur. The UK House of Lords Select Committee on Science and Technology (1981) has recently recommended that similar bonds should be required from solid waste disposal site operators, to ensure that they institute practices to minimize run-off pollution damage and other environmental nuisances.

None of these economic incentive systems will be universally applicable, but there is scope to employ them to supplement current regulatory approaches.

The operation of pricing systems in practice

Although one will search in vain for an economically pure pollution pricing system, charges are now widely used and are attracting growing interest (OECD, 1980a). Water management is the area yielding the greatest wealth of data on the use of charges in practice, although cases can be found of their application to air quality management, land dereliction, solid waste disposal and noise abatement.

The 'polluter pays' principle is now well established in the rhetoric of West European environmental politics, and a number of EEC countries have interpreted this to mean that *effluent charge* or *user charge*[10] systems should be introduced (OECD, 1976a). Three countries have now implemented fairly comprehensive charging schemes as part of their water management policies. France was the first to adopt effluent charge fees on a nationwide basis under legislation passed in 1964 (OECD, 1976b; Harrison and Sewell, 1980). The water associations responsible for the Ruhr, Lippe and Emscher rivers in Germany have long employed a form of pollution pricing as part of their general water management and allocation system and, in 1981, the use of pollution charges was extended to cover the whole of the country. Similarly, the Netherlands now makes widespread use of both effluent and user charges. Outside these three countries the implementation of price-based schemes for water pollution control is much more patchy. Most OECD countries now charge for sewage disposals and a few regions and municipalities in Canada and the United States have stream discharge taxes (OECD, 1980c).

For the other forms of pollution (air, solid waste and noise) no country has a comprehensive charge policy. The Netherlands, Norway and Japan all impose taxes on SO_2 emissions but not on other air pollutants. Solid waste disposal is characterized by the multiplicity of agencies involved, and not surprisingly there is little consistency in control strategies, even within one country. Some municipal authorities, in the United States, France, Sweden and West Germany for instance, employ user charges for household solid waste (OECD, 1980b). Most commonly these are intended to cover the costs of handling and waste disposal, but evidence from California suggests that they do have an abatement incentive effect (EPA, 1972; Wertz, 1976). In such schemes the tax assessment base varies considerably: Wuppertal (Germany) charges households according to the number of times per year waste contained in standardized containers is removed; Grange sur Bologne (France) and Vimmerby (Sweden) levy charges per disposable bag; and in south Stockholm a computerized invoicing system is used to calculate the exact disposal cost per dwelling (OECD, 1980b). Regional and national governments have also acted to price and regulate particular types of solid waste.

Product charges are commonly levied to cover the cost of collecting and disposing of discarded goods. Germany, for instance, has levied a tax on lubricating oils since 1969, the resulting revenue being redistributed to firms which agree to the collection and non-polluting disposal of such oil. France instituted a similar scheme in 1979, while Norway imposes a high tax on metal beverage containers, in part to promote recycling but also to act as a pollution control measure. A variant of the product charge is the *deposit* system, which has been widely used to encourage the return of bottles and has more recently been applied in Norway and Sweden to car bodies.

Taxes on noise pollution are not common, although a number of countries use economic incentives to curb aircraft noise at airports. In Germany, for instance, rebates on normal airport charges are given for aircraft complying with the noise standards laid down by the International Civil Aviation Authority, and both Japan and France levy special taxes to finance soundproofing around airports or to buy up property too badly affected by noise to be fit for occupation.

THE FRENCH EFFLUENT CHARGE SYSTEM

In 1964 legislation established six autonomous river basin authorities (Agences Financière de Bassin), responsible for formulating a rolling programme of water quality improvements and for implementing a charging scheme (OECD, 1976b). The *agences* are in no sense integrated water management authorities. They neither own nor run any type of supply system or treatment facilities but are solely concerned with technical planning and economic management. Importantly they do not even control the issue of effluent discharge permits (or consents), which is the function of the prefects (local government bodies).

Key features of the charging scheme are that it is used to self-finance the high costs of administering the pollution control system, to directly fund sewerage schemes and collective treatment facilities (including covering part of the operating costs), and to bribe or subsidize individual firms to comply with discharge standards. Initially the charges were seen as a *redistributive* device – any abatement incentive effects were regarded as a bonus. Strictly speaking, then, they were (and still largely are) a revenue-raising mechanism rather than one of pollution control. Although it was intended to increase price levels over time to reach incentive levels, in practice their impact has been eroded by inflation (OECD, 1980a). The charges were designed to collect the financial resources needed to 'catch up' with the problems caused by past neglect of investment in waste abatement, and to do so without drastically affecting industrial growth and urban development.

In the establishment of the tax assessment method and the charges themselves it was accepted that the two essential conditions of simplicity and acceptability must be satisfied. No attempt was made to price a large range of polluting substances. Charges were established only for four types of pollutant (suspended solids, oxidizable matter, soluble salts and toxic materials). A basinwide basic fee per kilogram/day was set for each type of pollutant but a system of simple coefficients or weights was then used to differentiate between polluters at different points in the basin. In some *agences* the view was taken that the concentration of disposal sources created pollution by allowing the absorptive capacity of the watercourse to be exceeded. Therefore, high weights were applied in areas of concentrated industrial and urban development. On the other hand, the Seine–Normandie authority took the opposite view; its prime objective was to protect upstream water quality, therefore, it imposed higher charges (150 per cent of the base rate) in upstream parts of the catchment. Lower rates were justified in the estuary on the grounds that the assimilative capacity was greater and that economies of scale in collective treatment could be achieved.

The favoured weighting system cannot be divorced from the location of powerful economic interest groups within the basins. Within each agency the charging system was in effect negotiated though the Comités de Bassin, which were composed of an equal number of representatives from the water users and the local and regional government authorities (OECD, 1976b). These same committees also decided the assessment base for the taxes. Although firms could opt to be charged on their actual measured discharges – in which case they had to pay the costs of measurement – most firms were given estimated disposal levels, based on the type of processes involved and the type of abatement equipment installed. Municipal sewage treatment plants were likewise assessed, taking into account the size of the served population and the type of plant.

Opinions differ over the effectiveness of the French system. Some have seen it as a promising starting-point, showing that economic incentives have a legitimate role to play as part of a wider pollution control strategy (OECD, 1980a). Others have criticized the narrow range of pollutants used as the charge base and the failure of the price levels to provide any significant abatement incentives (McIntosh, 1978). More recently Harrison and Sewell (1980) have argued that, except in certain specific cases, the quality of the watercourses has hardly improved, and that the whole basin charge system is being undermined by the development of central government *contrats de branche*. These are voluntary agreements reached with particular industrial sectors recognized to be major polluters, such as pulp and paper, sugar beet, wool washing and distilleries. In return for their agreement to reach specific effluent discharge objectives by set dates, the companies are relieved of some of their obligations to pay river basin charges and also receive considerable equipment grants and loans. The *agences* have claimed that central government has been prepared to accept a reduction in water quality standards in order to get the agreements signed.

At both the national and river basin levels the principle that the polluters must be party to the decision-making process has acted to overcome problems of political acceptability. But it has also meant that the control systems have become easy prey to political pressures which limit their effectiveness. Attempts to raise prices to incentive levels have been consistently resisted; industrialists and municipal sewage authorities have sought to manipulate both the assessment base and the weighting coefficients to minimize their own contribution to agency revenues; all efforts to include non-point agricultural sources of pollution have been defeated by the farming lobby; and the payment of grants owes more to political bargaining than to objective assessment of priority investment needs. The French experience offers some support for the views of Majone (1976a, 1976b), Wenner (1978) and Sandbach (1982) all of whom conclude that any enforcement mechanism will have limited effectiveness given the strength of the economic interests seeking to minimize waste disposal costs.

PRICING SYSTEMS AND AIR POLLUTION

In most countries it has simply been assumed that direct regulation is the only appropriate mechanism for dealing with air pollution, an assumption which has led particularly in the United States to the creation of extremely complex regulatory apparatus (see p. 362). Although no one would seriously argue that pricing could replace all forms of regulation, recent studies have suggested that emission charges on specific substances, such as SO_2 or NO_x, could be a cost-effective policy option (EPA, 1974; Baumol and Oates, 1975; OECD, 1980a). Alternatively, in areas where airshed ambient air standards form the basis of control, the possibility is raised that marketable emission rights could serve as an appropriate allocative device. Repetto (1983) points out that the sale of rights is only a very short step from the present so-called 'bubble' policy operated by the

EPA. This was originally introduced to allow regulated establishments to trade off stricter emissions control on some sources within a plant for looser controls on others. It has since been extended to encompass trade-offs between different plants, and firms are now allowed to 'bank' any emission reductions which take them below their disposal limit to offset future discharge needs. As Yandle (1978) argues, this implies that emitters have a property right in their emissions that is transferable over space and time. To date most allowable transfers have, in practice, occurred within one company, and clearly the system favours multiplant operators. But it raises the possibility that new firms or those with high compliance costs could pay other polluters to make offsetting emission reductions.

Despite the potential for economic incentive systems in air quality management, there are few examples of their implementation in practice. The scheme which gets nearest to an emission charge is operated in Japan, where SO_2 taxes are estimated from the sulphur content of fuels and the desulphurized amount of stack gases. However, no direct measurement of emission levels occurs and only major polluting installations are taxed, but these do account for 90 per cent of all SO_2 emissions. As was the case for the French river basin charges, the system was designed as a redistributive measure, with the proceeds being used to compensate those suffering pollution-related damage to their health – i.e. those with chronic bronchitis, asthma and emphysema (Gresser, 1975). The compensation budget is administratively determined, and then the unit SO_2 tax is calculated by dividing the annual budget by the total volume of emissions. This standard unit charge is then weighted to take into account the geographical location of the pollutant source, being highest in areas of urban concentration. As the tax rate has increased markedly over time (from 1.76 yen per cubic metre of SO_2 in 1974 to 42.59 yen in 1977), the system appears to provide abatement incentives.

In both Norway and the Netherlands SO_2 emissions are primarily controlled by standards, but from 1971 and 1972 respectively taxes on fuels have been established as an additional means of pollution control. The Norwegian system is an example of a tax and compliance bribe strategy. A tax is levied on the sulphur content of fuels derived from petroleum and repayments are made to firms carrying out treatment and sulphur recovery. However, both the taxes and bribes have been low; less than 10 per cent of the revenue has actually been refunded and the tax levels have been allowed to fall in real terms as a percentage of the pre-tax oil price from 6 per cent in 1971 to only 1.5 per cent after the 1979 oil price hike. At these levels it provides no abatement incentive.

The Dutch charging system was once again intended as a redistributive, revenue-collecting mechanism, and it provides an interesting example of a 'polluter pays' scheme tempered by social cost considerations. Revenue raised by variable taxes on all fossil fuels are used for four purposes. First, it covers all the costs of implementing and enforcing emission licences and product quality standards. Second, it finances scientific research into abatement technologies and the environmental damage caused by pollution. Third, it contributes to the Air Pollution Fund, which provides compensation for those suffering irrecoverable loss as a result of air pollution. Finally, a proportion of the proceeds provides subsidies to firms faced with high pollution abatement costs and compensates them when output restrictions (or even plant closure) result from the refusal of an emission licence. This last is recognition that the social costs of control can be as important as the social costs of pollution.

CONCLUSIONS ON CHARGES IN PRACTICE

None of the charging schemes implemented in practice even approach the economists' economic efficiency model. In fact they all strongly suggest that governments are less concerned with optimizing the use of environmental resources, *per se*, than with the redistributive consequences of pollution. All the studied schemes were designed to recoup from the polluters some of the costs involved in administering the control system and ameliorating the damage caused. Reliance on regulation alone inevitably places these costs on the affected public and the taxpayer. Economic mechanisms are, therefore, being used not as devices to allocate environmental services between competing users, but to redistribute effective income.

No one pollution control strategy can provide a blanket solution to all environmental quality problems. The most cost-effective method of achieving particular environmental quality objectives will vary from pollutant to pollutant, and from one receiving medium to another. In addition, the political acceptability of the different mechanisms will vary over space and time, reflecting changing notions of distributive equity and the balance of power in the economy. As Kelman (1983) has pointed out, the choice of control method raises ideological or philosophical issues about what kind of society we want to live in. It is interesting to reflect that the industrial lobby, so convinced of the value of market mechanisms and freedom from government interference, has been implacable in its opposition to environmental quality markets, preferring direct regulation! In Chapter 9 it will be argued that one of the major reasons for this seemingly inconsistent preference is that standards can be 'bargained' and manipulated, enforcement can be flexible and regulatory agencies all too often come to operate in the interests of the regulated.

PRICING IN THE MANAGEMENT OF OTHER COMMON PROPERTY RESOURCES: A BRIEF DISCUSSION

Neither the economists' advocacy of pricing as an allocative tool, nor the practitioners' general disregard for such prescriptions are confined to the pollution control case. Rarely have managers of such common property resources as public land, water resources, fisheries or hunting grounds explicitly set out to use the price mechanism as an allocative and demand control device. Direct forms of regulation have been preferred, and where some form of charge has been introduced, it has been viewed primarily as a revenue-generating measure, to allow some contribution to be made to the administrative costs of control. There are basically two types of charge which have been levied by regulatory agencies, *access fees* and *user charges*, the former being by far the more common.

Flat-rate access fees

When licences or permits are issued to regulate levels of hunting, fishing, grazing, water abstraction and timber production, it is widespread practice to charge flat-rate access fees. These must be paid before the permit-holder has any right to use the resource at all, and, if set high enough, they can act to restrict the demand for access. Some potential users will be unable or unwilling to make the pre-entry payment. However, public agencies rarely auction access rights to renewable resources or employ market value criteria to establish the appropriate fee levels. The annual or seasonal charges will be determined adminstratively to meet specific budget requirements; if they then act to reduce demand pressures, that is incidental. Inevitably there are some exceptions to this generalization. In the United States, for example, permits to log timber in national forests are now sold at market rates, broadly comparable to those operating in the private sector. Similarly, fees for hunting licences have recently been dramatically increased as a conservation measure.

Even high flat-rate access fees may do little to prevent overuse or depletion of the resource. They may help limit the number of users but cannot act to control the quantity taken by each of them; the payment remains the same irrespective of whether the licence-holder takes, say, one salmon or 20,000. Therefore, the effective price per unit of the resource is zero. Right-holders have no monetary incentive to conserve and may have every incentive to increase their take, particularly if improved technologies result in decreased unit production costs. In such circumstances any restriction on actual use levels will have to be imposed through the conditions of the licence itself or by other direct-usage controls. For instance, permit-holders with access to a controlled fishery frequently have to abide by catch quotas, gear restrictions and regulations governing the fishing seasons. Licences to abstract water often specify the total allowable take, and may well lay down daily or seasonal maxima. Similarly, logging permits will normally detail the operating conditions under which timber can be cut; these may well require some replanting, forbid clear felling, specify the proportion of trees to be left to facilitate regeneration, and outline the required fire hazard reduction measures.

In the vast majority of cases the access fee payments are purely nominal, set merely to recover the administrative costs of the licensing system and often failing to do even that. Therefore, price levels are generally far too low to remove any excess demand, and the notion that 'ability and willingness to pay' should be the bases for the allocation of usage rights has been implicitly or explicitly rejected. It is in fact a commonly expressed view that it would be quite unethical to use price to curb access to publicly owned land or water resources.[11]

This rejection of pricing implies that the regulatory agencies must adopt alternative allocative criteria and rationing devices if the depletion problems associated with free access are to be tackled. Although something of a generalization, the normally chosen criterion is the protection of established resource users. Regulatory agencies rarely work with a clean slate; existing users have already established some form of access right through law or custom. In Britain, for instance, landowners adjacent to surface water sources or above aquifers had acquired riparian use rights under common law, rights which remain extant in Scotland although they were removed in England and Wales in 1963. Similarly, in the United States 'federal lands often acquire entrenched private users, which are or may be legally "privilege" ... but which politically take on many characteristics of "rights"' (Clawson, 1974, p. 61). Once established, any attempt by a management agency to take away such rights is inevitably met by considerable opposition not only from directly affected economic interest groups, but also from all those who object philosophically to what they see as further state infringement of individual private rights and freedoms. Such opposition in part explains why market value licence fees are so unusual. It would be politically difficult to expropriate someone's rights to water or fish and then demand payment for the privilege of having them back again!

WATER ABSTRACTION LICENCE SYSTEM IN ENGLAND AND WALES

In practice, agencies commonly 'buy' the acceptance of regulation by allocating use licences in the first instance to all established interests, even if this fails to bring about the required reduction in resource use. This can be exemplified by the abstraction licence system introduced in England and Wales under the Water Resources Act 1963. All existing users were entitled to a 'licence of right' for the quantity that they had taken prior to the Act. As no one other than the firms or farmers concerned had much idea of what these quantities were, established abstractors were in effect given a blank cheque to write out a licence for whatever amount they wanted, or felt they could get away with. Not surprisingly, cases arose where the total licence of right claims exceeded the dry-weather flow of the stream or the average rate of aquifer replenishment, much of London, the Colne Valley (a tributary of the Thames, west of London), the Lee Valley and catchments throughout Essex and East Anglia being particularly badly affected. In these circumstances the policy in most areas (Essex being a notable exception) was to refuse any further licences to industrial or agricultural abstractors, irrespective of the use value of the water to existing right-holders or of the additional supply costs imposed on the refused concerns. Established abstractors were protected even when actual consumption fell well below the authorized quantity – or indeed when no supply was taken at all.

It is worth noting that when reasonably accurate consumption data became available in 1969, after monitoring equipment had been installed by most major abstractors, the actual consumption varied between 50 and 70 per cent of authorized throughout south-east England (Rees, 1970). Although revocation of un- or underutilized licences was legally possible under the 1963 Act, most authorities regarded this as an unethical practice, which would negate still further the long-established common law rights of water users. Still less was it felt that any of the licensed quantity actually used could be reallocated if a more productive use for the resource existed elsewhere. The possibility that costly litigation and compensation payments would result from any attempt to rationalize established water use patterns was a further powerful deterrent to action.

In areas where there was sufficient capacity, after the 'licence of right' holders had been catered for, to allow new abstractors to obtain a supply, there was still no move to let the price mechanism determine who should acquire access rights. Rather the rationing procedure of 'first come, first served' was adopted by default, in the absence of any explicit policy decision on an appropriate alternative allocation criterion.

It was, in effect, assumed that there was some 'naturally' fixed limit to the water supplies available for direct industrial and irrigation use. Thames Conservancy, for instance, refused to issue further licences when the already allocated total plus the minimum acceptable stream flow equalled the supply available in the third driest year since records began. Not only is the notion of a minimum acceptable flow a subjective concept, but also there was no objective basis for regarding the third driest year ever known as the natural supply limit. Moreover, the whole policy denied the possibility of increasing available flows if potential abstractors were willing to pay the investment costs involved. Such a possibility was recognized to exist if public supply undertakings required new capacity; in fact it was regarded as impossible to refuse licences to the public undertakings since they had a statutory obligation to meet all domestic requirements. The anomalous situation, therefore, arose that industrial users who had been refused direct abstraction licences could obtain supplies if they were able to pay the much higher prices involved in taking water from the public reticulation system. Not only did this add considerably to the costs of distribution, but also since public supplies had to be treated to potable quality, the water was of an unnecessarily high quality for most industrial uses. From an economic viewpoint the regulation system was highly inefficient, encouraging the retention of outmoded water use technologies, perpetuating low value, even wasteful usage, and possibly denying supplies (or increasing the supply costs) to new or expanding enterprises.

User-charging schemes

It is comparatively unusual for public agencies to employ user-charging systems to regulate access to renewable common property resources, except in the form of entrance fees to recreational or wildlife conservation areas and as payments for water supplies. In the former case charges are often purely nominal, are not designed to restrict demand and rarely cover a fraction of the costs involved in providing and administering the recreational facilities. This applies, for example, to the US national parks where visitor numbers are controlled not by entrance fees but by restrictions on user type and limits on the capacity of car, caravan and tent parks.

The view is often taken that access *should* be 'freely' available to all and that it would be inequitable to allow entrance only to those willing and able to pay. However, it is by no means certain that equity need be served by low or zero charges which fail to cover the supply costs involved. Some commentators have argued that demands for recreational facilities, such as wilderness areas, white-water kayaking streams, yachting or power-boat centres, are 'élitist', coming in the main from the relatively well-off middle class. The interests of the poorest groups in society, who are denied access to such facilities by their location, lack of mobility and the cost of the equipment, may not then be served by allowing provision subsidies from the public purse.

Unit charges for water are commonplace, but by no means universal, wherever public supply authorities have been created to invest in the storage, treatment and distribution systems needed to convert natural flows into a usable product (see p. 224). It is less usual for charges to be levied on private abstractors taking water directly from natural supply sources which occur on, or adjacent to, their own premises, although such systems do operate in France, parts of Germany, England and Wales, Israel, Japan and, somewhat ironically, Hungary (Cunha et al., 1977).

WATER ABSTRACTION CHARGES IN ENGLAND AND WALES

In England and Wales licensed private abstractors became liable, in 1969, for an annual quantity charge based on the total amount they were licensed to take. Only households or farmers drawing water for domestic purposes or for their livestock were entirely exempt from the charges, while spray irrigators were given the concession of paying 50 per cent of their licensed quantity liability, with any further charges being based on actual consumption. This basically meant that irrigators only paid the full levy in dry years when they took all their entitlement. There was little economic justification for this special arrangement, which owed much to the political influence wielded by the farming lobby, since the supply pre-empted by licensed irrigators had to be reserved for their use every year and was not available for reallocation to other stream users. Moreover, in areas where irrigators were concentrated, considerable budgetry problems were created for the regulatory agencies, who could experience revenue shortfalls of at least 20 per cent in wet years.

In designing these licence-charging schemes some attempts have been made to vary the price paid by different types of consumer according to the opportunity costs imposed by their use. 'Consumptive' users, or abstractors taking supplies solely during the summer months, were normally charged much higher rates than consumers returning a large proportion of their intake to the stream courses. In some areas differential charges were also levied depending on the location of, or the supply source used by, the abstractor. In east Suffolk and Norfolk, for instance, those taking water from marsh drains were charged only 20 per cent of the normal surface water charge, while in Essex inland users paid twice as much per unit as those in the coastal area, on the ground that the former affected the supplies available to downstream users. However, in no sense did the schemes conform to the ideal as defined by economic theory.

The possibility of using the price mechanism to ration available supplies until consumers were willing to pay the costs involved in flow augmentation was legally precluded. Charges could only be set to cover costs, to balance the water resources account from year to year. It was, therefore, quite impossible to use price to equate demand and available supplies if, as a result, profits were made. Still less could the price mechanism be used to signal the desirability of supply capacity extensions since this would almost inevitably involve the accumulation of revenue surpluses until demand levels justified investment.

Undoubtedly, when the charging schemes were first introduced, the unit prices were too low to have a measurable effect on demand. For instance, in south-eastern England charges of between 0.1 to 0.4 pence per 4550 l were typical until 1974, which meant that all but the largest industrial users were paying less than £150 per annum. The low price levels were largely a product of the assumption that supplies for direct abstraction were fixed, unless they could 'ride on the back' of extension schemes designed to meet municipal demands. Since little or no capital investment occurred, the revenue required to balance the books was relatively small, confined to not much more than the administrative expenses of the authorities. There was, however, some evidence that the fact of charging itself pushed some abstractors to reduce their licensed entitlement down to the reality of their actual consumption needs. But even this failed to occur in areas where new licences were unobtainable; the licence itself, then, obtained a scarcity value which exceeded the minimal payments incurred through the unit charges. Since 1974 when the multipurpose regional water authorities became responsible for the abstraction licence system, charges have risen and both licence entitlements and actual consumption have fallen quite markedly. But it would be foolish to attribute more than a tiny fraction of this fall to price; the changing structure of industry, the closure of old factory premises and the generally depressed state of the economy have been the more significant factors.

Bribes and subsidies

As was seen in the pollution case, regulatory agencies have often offered compliance bribes or subsidies to persuade individuals to reduce their use of the environment for the disposal of waste. In the same way, once private rights have been established to use other common property resources, so it may be legally, economically or politically necessary to offer financial incentives to restrict demands and to compensate for losses when rights are unilaterally withdrawn. This is particularly likely in countries with rigid constitutions, which lay down the rights and freedoms of individuals, and in societies with a highly developed sense of the importance of private property (Johnson and Brown, 1976). Control problems and the need for compensation most commonly arise for those renewable resources which occur on or utilize land in private ownership (landscape resources, natural habitats, flora and fauna and some water flows all come into this category). In the United States, for instance, attempts to protect wildlife, shorelines, wetland areas and many other resources which involve restricting developments on private land may be regarded as unconstitutional if they entail 'taking without compensation'. Since 1922 it has been held that 'while property be regulated to a certain extent, if regulation goes too far it will be recognized as a taking' (*Pennsylvania Coal Co.* v. *Mahon*, 260 US 393). Subsequent court actions have established that some forms of land. zoning and habitat protection acts are legally acceptable within the 'taking' rule, but the litigation costs involved in reaching this point have been considerable and any new conservation or use regulations inevitably have to be tested in the courts (Rosenblum, 1974; Garner, 1980).

CONSERVATION BRIBES IN THE UK

In Britain the principle that a planning or regulatory agency can limit the development rights of private landowners, without becoming liable for compensation, has long been established as far as urban and industrial developments are concerned. However, any attempts to protect resources, such as particular landscapes or wildlife habitats, or to increase the provision of countryside recreation, which involve imposing restrictions on agricultural or forestry development may well necessitate compensation payments. This anomalous situation arose from the now largely discredited assumption behind the planning legislation of the 1940s that a prosperous agricultural industry was compatible with – and indeed essential to – the preservation of rural landscape resources (Mabey, 1980; Shoard, 1980; Green, 1981). The Scott Report (1942) on *Land Utilisation in Rural Areas* firmly established the doctrines (clung to even today by most farming interests) that 'there is no antagonism between use and beauty', and that 'the cheapest, indeed the only way, of preserving the countryside . . . would be to farm it'. Although more far-sighted analysts, such as Dennison (1942), dissented from these prevailing views, farming and forestry were exempted from development control, and have largely remained so, except for larger farm or forestry buildings. Conservation and recreation provision on privately owned land had to occur through 'co-operation and agreement', not through control.

National Park authorities and other planning agencies had, therefore, to use 'management agreements' in their efforts to preserve particular landscapes or habitats and to ensure public access to them. These were defined in 1973 by the Countryside Commission as 'a formal written agreement between a public authority and an owner of an interest in land . . . who thereby undertakes to manage the land in a specified manner in order to satisfy a particular public need, *usually in return for some form of consideration*' (see Feist, 1978, p. 1; emphasis added). It had, in effect, become accepted that rural landowners were to be treated differently and paid for accepting restrictions on their development and use rights. The National Farmers Union has consistently argued that 'fair' compensation must take the form of an annual sum equivalent to the loss of potential profit, to be renegotiated periodically to take account of inflation (MacEwen and MacEwen, 1982). This would involve a 'bottomless pit' of income redistribution from the general taxpayer to the rural landowners. Even the alternative compensation principle of making a once-and-for-all capital payment equal to the depreciated value of the controlled land would impose an inordinately high financial burden on the planning authorities.

Despite prolonged and acrimonious objections to the Wildlife and Countryside Act 1981, under this legislation 'the farmer is free from all constraints, and has acquired a statutory right to be compensated for losing his grant (paid for agricultural improvements) and the profit he might have made by damaging the environment' (ibid., p. 285). These compensation provisions will prove impossibly expensive since the difference in income between traditional and intensive farming in lowland areas can be over £150–£200 per acre. The cost of protecting just 1800 acres of marshland from conversion into arable land amounts to £100,000 per annum for the next ten years, with no guarantee of protection after that (*ENDS* Report 106, November 1983[12]). In practice, therefore, despite the existence of a plethora of agencies with duties to protect landscapes, wildlife and their habitats, there are neither the control powers nor the financial resources to do so.

RETIREMENT BRIBES IN THE CANADIAN FISHERIES

A somewhat similar form of 'compliance bribe' has been used in the fisheries case. The common practice of giving all established users formal licences when regulation is first introduced does nothing to solve current depletion problems. In these circumstances it is necessary to impose direct physical controls on licensed users and may require the introduction of mechanisms to 'persuade' established users to give up their use rights. A good example of a 'retirement' bribe system is afforded by the 'buy-back' compensation scheme introduced as part of a programme to rationalize the use of the Pacific salmon fishery in Canada. In 1968 a ban was imposed on the entry of additional fishing vessels and on boats which had not fished seriously for about five years, but owners of vessels which accounted for virtually all the catch were given permanent, renewable licences. These licences were transferable to any replacement vessels and the owner even had the right to sell his boat with the licence attached (Copes, 1981). Under these conditions the already considerable problems of resource depletion were left unsolved, and the minimal licence fees could do nothing to reduce the demand for access. Therefore, having given established fishermen a formal right to fish, it became necessary to 'bribe' them to withdraw voluntarily from the fishery.

Owners were encouraged to sell their vessels with the licences attached to an officially established Buy-Back Committee, at a price set at the appraised value of the vessel plus an incentive bonus. The vessels were then auctioned off with the express condition that the new owners would not obtain fishing licences for them. Proceeds from these auctions plus annual licence fees levied on the vessels remaining in the salmon fishery were to provide the funds needed to operate the scheme. However, it quickly became apparent that established fishermen could make more money by selling their vessels with licence on the open market. The incentive bonuses available from the committee were modest, in most part because any moves to increase the licence fees were resisted. It therefore became politically impossible to continue an effective buy-back programme; it was abandoned after operating for less than three years and succeeded in reducing the fleet by only 354 vessels out of a total of 7000 (Mitchell and King, 1984). No one was prepared to pay the costs of compensation, the need for which had been created by the political decision to give established users formal, permanent and transferable access rights.

Despite over fifteen years of regulation and the expenditure of over $ Can. 157 million on artificial breeding and yield enhancement programmes, in 1982 the Pacific salmon fisheries were described as being at a crisis point (Canada, Commission on Pacific Fisheries Policy, 1982). Licensing had cut the size of the fleet, but not the catch taken by each vessel, and fishermen still competed to capture as much as possible of the available fish yield. However, all attempts to implement effective conservation programmes have failed because of strongly entrenched and competing economic interests.

CONCLUSION

Throughout this chapter it has been shown that conventional economic prescriptions for the efficient allocation of available resource flows have severe limitations. In particular, any measures which attempt to put prices on resources, traditionally held in common and freely used, have to confront three major problems.

First, it is a by no means trivial task to actually calculate meaningful price measures. Second, and much more important, the use of 'willingness to pay' as the criterion for allocating resource flows raises crucial equity considerations. As Kapp correctly points out,

> what a person or firm is willing to pay for clean air or recreational facilities or to accept as compensation for tolerating injuries to his health caused by pollution depends upon their income or their *ability* to pay. If incomes are unequally distributed (as they are), and if this inequality of distribution results among other things from unequal exchanges between unequal economic units in dominating and dominated positions (as it does), the resulting ability and willingness to pay are as arbitrary as the price and wage structure of which they are the outcome. (Kapp, 1972, p. 119)

Third, the introduction of realistic prices for goods and services which were previously free or low cost inevitably raises the opposition of those entrenched economic interests which had benefited from being able to pass on to others the social costs of resource degradation and depletion. Although these interests are not always the most affluent members of society (individual fishermen hardly come into this category), they frequently are. It is significant that most resistance to the use of pollution or resource depletion taxes comes from business interests, owners of polluting factories, freezer boats and fish-processing plant, manufacturers or farmers using large quantities of privately abstracted water, and so on.

The dilemma in reconciling the second and third problems is clear. *If the price mechanism is employed this may disadvantage the poor, but if the price mechanism is not used this will certainly advantage the rich!*

NOTES

1   Optimal strategies have been discussed for ground water: Burt, 1967; blue whales: Spence, 1974; migratory birds and nesting sites: Hammack and Brown, 1974; fur seals: Wilen, 1976; and red deer: Beddington *et al.*, 1975. However, the water, fisheries and pollution control cases have dominated the academic literature.

2   There are numerous examples which could be cited here. Improved furnace efficiency to allow the more complete combustion of fuels not only reduces energy inputs (itself a pollution-reducing measure) but also curbs residual emissions. Improved engine or plant design can effect major reductions in noise levels. The use of

low-sulphur oils, metallic ores with small proportions of impurities, scrap metals and recycled paper are all cases where raw material changes cut emissions. While modifications to packaging – the use of lightweight milk bottles, for instance – lead-free petrol and the change from hard to soft detergents are but three cases in which product change can reduce waste generation.

3 There have been some aggregation attempts based on subjective damage ranking; these have particularly been developed within an environmental impact statement framework (see pp. 330–1).

4 For all resources, including the waste assimilative capacity of the environment, there are three basic forms which the natural growth rate of the available stock can take: (1) the growth rate is zero. This applies for stock minerals, such as fossil fuels, and for the capacity of the environment to deal with stock pollutants; (2) the rate is some constant, determined naturally and unaffected by man. Solar, tidal and wind energies came into this group, although clearly the supply of usable power depends on past rates of investment in conversion equipment. It is sometimes assumed that the renewal of water supplies takes this form but, in practice, the replenishment of most aquifer and surface sources is dependent on patterns of water use in the catchment, including any modification to run-off regimes through reservoir construction, changes to vegetation or the natural water-holding capacity of soils; (3) the growth rate is some function of the existing resource population (and is, therefore, dependent on past rates of use) in relation to the maximum carrying (or absorptive) capacity of particular environmental systems.

5 Both the constant price and cost assumptions can be dropped without disturbing the logic of the model, merely adding to its complexity.

6 In the air pollution case this is not strictly true since dispersal has been a popular policy measure: see Frankel, 1974.

7 They are all based on a so-called Mogden formula, which takes into account the volume of the discharge and its quality, measured in terms of BOD or COD, and suspended solids.

$$C = V + \frac{Bt}{Bs} B + \frac{St}{Ss} S$$

where:

C = total charge per unit volume;
V = preliminary treatment and reception charge per unit volume;
Bt = strength of the factory waste in BOD or COD;
Bs = average strength of waste in the region;
B = biological treatment charge per unit volume;
St = suspended solids in factory's waste;
Ss = average solids content in the region's waste;
S = sludge treatment charge per unit volume.

8 Regional water authorities have since 1974 been responsible for all aspects of water resource management in England and Wales, including pollution control. For a brief discussion of the administrative history of the water management system see Chapter 9, pp. 352–4.

9 This mileage is already low by European and Japanese standards, and probably will not act to accelerate the already clear trend towards smaller, more fuel-efficient vehicles.

10 The term 'effluent charge' is used in OECD publications to refer to payments for direct discharges into the environment, whereas 'user charge' is applied when

disposal occurs to sewers. However, to add to the confusion, in Britain, the term 'trade effluent charge' is used for disposal to sewers.

11 It is not entirely clear why it is unethical to adopt price controls over hunting, recreation, fishing or grazing in societies which accept that heat, food, shelter and medical care can be allocated through the price system.

12 *ENDS* is a monthly report on environmental issues, containing short articles, news items and parliamentary questions. It is produced by the Environmental Data Services Ltd., Finsbury Business Centre, 40 Bowling Green Lane, London EC1R ONE.

8   Evaluating conservation and flow augmentation decisions

INTRODUCTION

In Chapter 7 it was assumed that the task of renewable resource management is to allocate existing flows between competing users. However, as was shown, it is normally possible to increase availability either by investment or by conserving supplies now in order to improve future yields. Most non-economists would probably regard the decision to invest in capital facilities to store water, treat effluent or produce usable energy from the tides as a quite distinct conceptual matter from that of conserving a forest or protecting a wildlife habitat. But from an economic perspective all such decisions involve the same conceptual principles. Conservation and investment both require the reduction of current consumption in order to increase potential availability in the future. In other words, costs are incurred now in order to provide future benefits.

Environmental quality and renewable resource issues are treated little differently from the estimation of the optimal use pattern over time for a mineral stock, or indeed for any piece of capital equipment. Munro expresses the conventional economic attitude very clearly when he begins a discussion on the economics of fishing with the statement:

> As is true of all natural resources, fishery resources constitute capital assets from the point of view of society. Similar to man-made capital assets, such as factories and machinery, fishery resources are capable of producing a stream of returns to society through time. (Munro, 1981, p. 129)

The management task is to allocate this stream of returns in order to maximize expected net social benefits. Just as the private firm theoretically should only engage in mineral search and exploitation if the net discounted returns from the investment exceed the costs involved, so a public agency should invest in future renewable resource flows if the benefits exceed the costs (see Chapter 3, p. 71). Moreover, capital and labour should only be expended on flow augmentation and conservation if the expected returns at least equal those prevailing on investments in other sectors of the economy.

Many of the most fundamental methodological criticisms of the entire economic net benefit maximization approach have already been analysed in the earlier discussion of economic efficiency and the minerals sector. It was seen there that it is based on a highly abstract model of the perfectly working competitive market and views the whole resource utilization and conservation question from the present. Discounting procedures used to convert future benefit and cost flows into present values inevitably bias resource usage patterns towards current consumption and away from conservation. Moreover, the use of market prices to determine the benefits and costs clearly loads the evaluation process towards the demands of the already affluent. There is, therefore, nothing in the Pareto efficiency model which necessarily ensures that social equity objectives or long-term environmental quality and stability goals will be achieved. As these undoubtedly crucial issues have already been discussed, attention in this chapter will be focused on two important critiques of the economic optimality approach which are particularly pertinent in the context of environmental resources; first, the appropriateness of the benefit maximization goal; and, second, the deficiencies inherent in techniques designed to measure the costs and benefits of environmental resource use. Rejection of economic efficiency as the management goal, and dissatisfaction with the outcomes from traditional cost–benefit assessments have led to the search for alternative appraisal techniques, the most widely adopted being environmental impact assessment. Its origins and deficiencies will be discussed in the latter part of the chapter. Finally, and by way of conclusion, the question will be addressed of whether *any* form of rational, scientific evaluation can provide solutions to conflicts over the way renewable resources should be used.

THE OUTPUT MAXIMIZATION OBJECTIVE: A CRITIQUE

Authors such as McHarg (1969) have argued that it is ethically indefensible and ecologically unsound to treat the earth's environmental system as just another capital good or commodity. Some economists have also questioned the applicability of the standard welfare maximization paradigm to issues which involve judgements about environmental quality and which concern the long-term sustainability of life support systems. Kapp (1970, p. 844), for example, argued that 'As long as economic theory continues on this methodological path there is no hope for an adequate analysis of environmental disruption and social costs', while Coddington (1970, p. 596) went as far as suggesting that 'the greatest service economists can render to posterity is to remain silent'.

The steady-state concept

Writers approaching the subject of renewable resource use from an ecological perspective have argued that the output maximization approach is incompatible with the limited nature of closed physical systems and call for the introduction of management goals which will allow the long-term survival of society (or indeed of all plant and animal species). For example, Daly (1973, 1976, 1982) has maintained for over a decade that a *steady-state economy* should be established, in which the objective is not to maximize the output of goods and services, but to establish 'the lowest feasible' rate of throughput of matter and energy. Apart from leaving unanswered the key question of what 'the lowest feasible' actually means, the steady-state model raises tremendous practical and ethical problems. It requires a constant population and a constant stock of physical wealth, with the size of these stocks determined by 'the level . . . sufficient for a good life and sustainable for a long future' (Daly, 1982, p. 252). What constitutes a good life? This is never specified, so providing no basis for calculating the desirable population and wealth stocks. As individuals differ enormously over the consumption levels and the types of goods and services they perceive as essential for a reasonable quality of life, whose judgement will be accepted and how will this then be imposed on all?

A further difficulty with the steady-state notion arises over world population numbers. If current levels are already incompatible with 'a good and sustainable life', mechanisms will be needed first to effect the desired population reduction and then to ensure that birth rates are set at replacement levels. Daly advocates that 'the right to reproduce must no longer be treated as a "free good". It should be regarded as a scarce asset, a legal right limited in total amounts' (ibid., p. 258). The device he favours to allocate this scarce asset is a system of birth licences or quotas, issued in the first place on the basis of strict equality and which then can be bought and sold. Such a scheme would be morally repugnant to many and its political feasibility is questionable, to say the least. Another major problem arises over the distribution of the fixed stock of wealth. Daly himself says that as growth in output can no longer be used to alleviate poverty, it becomes absolutely necessary to achieve more fairness in the distribution of income. He suggests that the solution 'is something very simple: a minimum income coupled with a maximum income and a maximum accumulation of wealth, a limited band of inequality necessary for incentives, for rewarding work of varying irksomeness and intensity, yet ruling out extreme inequality' (ibid., p. 259). Such a suggestion may be conceptually very simple, but the institutional and political problems it raises certainly are not.

In Daly's scenario the steady state and the accompanying changes in population and income distribution are to be achieved using existing institutions: 'We have neither the time, nor the leadership, nor the wisdom to wipe out existing institutions and start again with something radically different' (ibid., p. 258). What he means by this is that present market institutions, private property and the price system will be retained, albeit in somewhat modified form. But inevitably massive changes in other social, political and legal institutions would have to occur before anything approaching a steady-state economy could be an implementable reality. Given the lack of precision in defining the throughput objectives and the political impracticality of the steady-state approach, it is hardly surprising that most economists have rejected it as a replacement for the welfare maximization objective.

Sustainable utilization and minimum survival risk

Allen (1980), IUCN (1980), O'Riordan (1983b), Eagles (1984) and many others have advocated that environmental resources should be managed to ensure the long-term sustainable utilization of species and ecosystems, minimize survival risk and generally keep open as many future use options as possible. The various versions of these ideas differ somewhat in emphasis but the underlying theme remains the same. We know too little about the dynamics and capacities of many ecosystems to be certain about the long-run effects of our activities. Therefore, current usage patterns must be changed, exploitative use must be cut down, or even cut out altogether, to minimize the chances of irreversible depletion or harmful feedback effects. The first proponents of risk minimization and sustainability worked from ecological principles; the preservation of species diversity and minimum environmental change were seen as essential if the interdependent life support systems of the globe were to be protected. Inevitably, the most extreme and restrictive demands came from the bio-ethics school of eco-radicals, who took the moral view that the whole of nature has survival rights. These early versions of the sustainability concept have been widely criticized.

Although most analysts would agree that the reduction of survival risk should be one objective in the development of resource management strategies, there is much less support for the idea that it should be paramount, overriding all other goals. Unless risk minimization is a costless activity, it can only occur through the sacrifice of other social welfare objectives. Almost inevitably it would necessitate a major reduction in current levels of resource use, with all the harsh implications that this would entail for the present world's population, and particularly for the poorest sections of the human community already living at or near subsistence levels. If taken to extremes, minimization of the survival risk for future generations will be 'bought' by the failure of millions of people currently alive to survive at all today. The welfare implications of the various ecologically based resource management goals are central to their rejection as an alternative to welfare maximization by the vast majority of economists. Dasgupta, for example, states bluntly that

> Injunctions, such as 'choose programmes so as to maximise the number of future options', are patently silly: they disregard the social costs that would be associated with such plans. (Dasgupta, 1982, p. 193)

Lecomber makes a similar point when he argues

> minimising 'survival' risk could involve a very sharp cut-back in all kinds of activities, including, for example, the use of D.D.T. to control malaria in underdeveloped countries, and the consequence would probably include a marked rise in the current death rate. (Lecomber, 1979, p. 34).

In large measure as a result of these criticisms, the protagonists of sustainability as a management goal have shifted their ground and today they talk not of ecological sustainability but of sustainable utilization. The emphasis is now on the improvement of the real and long-term well-being of people, by ensuring that environmental systems remain as 'a resource bank that will continue to be of use, often in unforeseen ways, for the indefinite future' (Eagles, 1984, p. 3). Such a resource bank would not only provide food and other productive goods, but would also satisfy the aesthetic, inspirational and educational needs of human beings. When expressed in this way, the essential difference between the economists' objective of welfare maximization and the environmentalists' sustainability goal, is that the latter contains the assumption that the indefinite maintenance of ecosystem productivity (or output) *will* maximize human well-being over time. While this assumption may well hold on a global scale, it is less obviously correct when applied to individual species, local 'natural' areas, or landscape features. It certainly is open to doubt that maintaining the sustainability of raised bogs, the sand lizard or the snakeshead fritillary butterfly will always enhance the sum of human well-being, if their survival involves losses in food production. If the achievement of sustainability could occur at zero cost, most analysts would accept it unquestioningly as a management goal; but inevitably it will impose costs at least on some sections of the human community. Its desirability will, therefore, depend upon its distributional consequences.

Incorporating alternative values

Uncertainty and the possibly irreversible effects of environmental resource use undoubtedly pose analytical problems for the conventional welfare maximization approach. However, it is generally argued that the existence of such difficulties emphasizes the need to improve assessment methods, but does not warrant the adoption of new methodological approaches based on different assumed societal objectives. Ideally, attempts to maximize the expected net social benefits from resource use over time would need to include the utility derived from reduced risks, sustainable productivity and a wider range of future options. But these are merely two elements contributing to total human welfare. Their inclusion into the analysis may well result in a modification of the traditional policy prescriptions, and could, under some conditions at least, ensure that economic goals are compatible with the maintenance of renewable resource flows, including environmental quality and the waste assimilative capacity of bio-geochemical cycles (see, for example, Dasgupta, 1982).

It is, however, far easier to say that sustainability of ecological systems and other 'non-material' quality-of-life dimensions of human welfare can be incorporated into the conventional economic approach than it is to do in practice. This takes us to the second basic criticism of the welfare maximization paradigm: namely, the difficulties involved in establishing meaningful measures of welfare and the tendency to focus only on those elements that can be readily translated into money terms.

These difficulties will be considered by looking at cost–benefit analysis (CBA), the most widely used – some would add abused – economic tool for the evaluation of public investment projects and policies. A number of the more basic and general methodological and enumeration problems involved in the use of this technique have in fact already been discussed in the context of private investment decisions (see Chapter 3, p. 71, and Chapter 4, pp. 129–33). This is hardly surprising since cost–benefit is rooted in the ideology of the competitive market. Whereas the accountant in a private concern will concentrate on the internal and purely financial returns on an investment, the public analyst needs to identify and measure the losses and gains in economic welfare which are incurred by *society as a whole* if specific projects are to undertaken or policies adopted (Mishan, 1972). Given the myriad side-effects arising from major public initiatives, the decision-maker needs an analytical technique, which allows the systematic sorting and comprehensive evaluation of the mass of relevant data. Cost–benefit was seen as such a technique.

COST-BENEFIT ANALYSIS

Establishing the appropriate management objective

To assess the desirability of any project or policy it is necessary to know what the objectives are. Most of the analyses undertaken in the 1950s and 1960s – and indeed many current appraisals – assume the aim to be economic efficiency, as defined by the compensation test modification of the Pareto criterion (see pp. 118–20). Critics have attacked such assessments both for their 'single-minded devotion to the paradigm of efficiency' (O'Riordan, 1976) and for their neglect of the way the benefits and costs were distributed within society. Both these criticisms are undoubtedly valid. But it is worth pointing out that it was clearly recognized in the now classic contributions to the development of the techniques (Eckstein, 1958; McKean, 1958; Krutilla and Eckstein, 1958) that governments would have a range of socioeconomic and political objectives. It was acknowledged that other goals, such as regional development, selective improvement in the incomes or living conditions of particular groups within the community, reduction in the variability of agriculture output and the political need to achieve the appearance of 'fairness' in the spatial distribution of government funds, were all of importance in the decision-making process. The fact that in practice the emphasis was on efficiency, particularly in the use of capital, was not solely a reflection of the dominance of the neo-classical paradigm within economics. It also stemmed from the perceived nature of the problems to which cost–benefit analysis was first rigorously applied and to the stress so frequently placed on GNP growth by the political decision-makers.

Although it has much earlier antecedents, the major development of cost–benefit as an analytical tool occurred in response to the burgeoning of expenditure on water resources projects in the United States. The sheer scale of these investments can be illustrated by the fact that they were the largest single item in the federal civil expenditure list, amounting to some $270 million a year (1951), and to this must be added state and local government expenditures. Very low rates of return were generally being achieved on the capital invested. In the case of irrigation projects only between one-quarter and one-third of the total capital costs were typically being recouped (Renshaw, 1957). On purely financial criteria the schemes were loss-making and represented a major drain on the federal and state exchequers. Moreover, the scale of water diversions brought the investing agencies into conflict with downstream water users, including recreational and aesthetic interests, who demanded the maintenance of stream flows. The pro-irrigation lobby claimed that external benefits – from increased rural incomes, greater agricultural productivity and so on – more than justified the continuation of investment, but such claims were unsupported by systematic and comprehensive statistical analysis. Water resource expenditure became a controversial political issue, and the need to maximize the real returns on investment capital became a key political objective of the time.

Similarly, although about a decade later, concern in Australia, over the efficiency with which capital was utilized to subsidize irrigated agriculture, was a major factor behind the Commonwealth government's introduction of cost–

benefit analysis. In 1966 it became a formal requirement that all proposals for new projects, seeking funds from the central Exchequer, must be accompanied by a cost–benefit appraisal. It must be recognized that governments, rightly or wrongly, frequently see growth in GNP as an important – at times the most important – objective in their management of the economy. Where government investment is a significant proportion of total national investment, as it is in Britain, much of continental Europe and throughout the Third World, the returns achieved will have a major impact on the growth performance of the economy as a whole.

This produces particular dilemmas in LDC economies (Pearson and Pryor, 1978). On the one hand, the existence of large subsistence sectors and the common importance of redistributive equity as a policy objective make the net benefit approach difficult to apply and, some would argue, totally inappropriate. But, on the other hand, scarcity of capital, its high opportunity cost and the continued stress placed on economic growth as a societal aim make it vital that positive real returns on capital are achieved. The political need to promote efficiency and GNP growth has become even more pressing in recent years as debt and falling GNP levels have become acute. For instance, in Brazil, one of the most strongly growing economies of the early 1970s, growth had ceased by 1981; GNP actually fell by 2 per cent and the overseas debt reached $80 billion in 1982 (Townroe, 1984). These difficulties have served to re-emphasize economic efficiency as a desired political objective, a move furthered by the conditions set by the international aid agencies and financial institutions, which have curbed programmes and policies producing social and redistributive benefits. In these circumstances it is not surprising that the public decision-makers should place considerable emphasis on an economic criterion, and an associated analytical technique, which aims (or purports) to maximize the value of all goods and services produced in the economy.

THE DISTRIBUTIVE IMPLICATIONS OF OUTPUT MAXIMIZATION

However, while the emphasis on the output maximization goal is understandable, the use of cost–benefit analysis to define optimal investment or conservation strategies has two important implications, which apply to all types of economy but raise particular difficulties in the LDCs. First, what is maximized is output measured in current market terms. Inevitably, therefore, the whole project selection process is skewed away from investments which would benefit those lacking the income to express their demands in the market place, and away from the production of goods and services which traditionally have been excluded from market exchange. A second but closely related implication is that current preferences for consumption and production define the optimal output package. In LDCs, where capital is usually the most scarce factor of production and where poverty and deprivation exert a strong pressure to increase present levels of output, high discount rates are the rule. Therefore, project appraisals are axiomatically biased towards investments which yield high short-term gains. Such projects are not necessarily consistent with long-term output maximization and need not ensure that yields are sustainable over time.

As Pearson and Pryor have pointed out

> the pressure for rapid resource exploitation is perhaps most evident in the forest resource sector, responding to current industrial country market demand, and in the food production sector, in which the population pressure and food needs create increasing pressure on a fragile soil resource base. (Pearson and Pryor, 1978, p. 230)

They clearly show in their model of subsistence agriculture that the strong preference for current output can lead to a deterioration in the productivity of soils and an undermining of long-term yields. The higher the discount rate used in project appraisals, the greater the incentive to mine the soil, and other renewable resources, for immediate output, and the greater the incompatibility between short- and long-term output maximization. In other words, even if it is accepted that economic efficiency is a legitimate political objective, it is by no means clear that economic net benefits will be maximized over time.

The early proponents of cost–benefit were well aware that the use of the technique had major redistributive and intergenerational equity implications. Krutilla and Eckstein (1958), for example, suggested that the redistributive outcomes of each alternative project should be clearly set out. It was then up to the political decision-makers to express value judgements about the acceptability of such outcomes, and to make any trade-offs between equity and total net benefit maximization. However, reservations about the compensation test criterion and the choice of discount rate tended to recede in the practice of cost–benefit analysis, buried under the technical sophistication of the technique itself. As Pearce comments,

> one of the oddities of the recent history of the neoclassical paradigm is that the compensation rule grew in strength and influence through its subtle underpinning of a practical and practised evaluation technique, while at the same time being subjected to what many professional economists would have regarded as devastating methodological criticism in the theoretical literature. (Pearce, 1983, p. 255)

MULTI-OBJECTIVE COST–BENEFIT ANALYSIS

By the beginning of the 1970s attempts were being made to adapt the theory and practice of cost–benefit to incorporate both multiple objectives and distributional effects into the calculations (Dorfman, 1965, Weisbrod, 1968; Howe, 1971; Squire and Van der Tak, 1975). These adaptations were not only a product of academic theoretical debate, but also arose from changing socioeconomic conditions and political circumstances. Three factors were of particular importance. First, the cost–benefit technique was being employed for an ever widening range of projects, including those (such as the delimitation and protection of wilderness areas, flood protection, the Alaska pipeline and airport construction) where non-economic objectives and distributional consequences were of clear importance. Similarly, the increased use of the technique in LDCs required adaptations to take account of the subsistence sector and to include the reduction of wealth disparities as one important policy goal. Second, the rising star of the environmental lobby meant that aesthetic, environmental protection and other 'quality-of-life' objectives achieved much greater political significance. Lastly, but closely related to the second factor, the advanced economies were still enjoying a period of apparent sustained growth and prosperity; further growth, at least as measured in material terms, tended to assume lower relative priority (Inglehart, 1977).

The central problem in multiobjective planning is how to weight or rank the relative importance of each goal. For example, in an analysis of marine fisheries conservation programmes there could be at least five important objectives: (1) ensuring the physical sustainability and ecological diversity of the marine environment; (2) maintaining employment levels among fishing and fish-processing communities in the short and/or longer terms; (3) increasing the traditionally low incomes in such communities; (4) ensuring an efficient stream of returns (or rents); (5) reducing the direct costs of fisheries regulation and of various community support programmes (Mitchell and King, 1984). It is highly unlikely either that any consensus among the interested parties will be achieved on the weight to be given to the alternative aims, or that government agencies will be able to consistently adhere to any one priority ordering. Some analysts have attempted to make alternative, and often conflicting, objectives commensurate by attaching numerical weights to each of them, and then producing an aggregate cost–benefit result (Hill, 1968). Different values have then apparently been reduced to a single value; projects or policies are judged on their aggregate performance over the various objectives. Clearly, the weighting given to each goal will critically affect the results of the analysis. As Streeton (1972, p. 53) has pointed out, the clash of interests between different groups in the economy 'has not disappeared. It has been concealed in the relative values (often highly arbitrary) attached to the objectives'.

The same 'hidden' value problem arises over attempts to take account of distributional effects, by weighting the costs and benefits to specific income or social groups by some 'utility measure'. Normally it is assumed that the marginal utility of a gain or loss would be lower for high-income groups and would increase as income levels fall (Mishan, 1972, p. 22). Inevitably any utility weight system is arbitrary and highly subjective. Weisbrod (1968) has suggested that study of past public projects would yield an implicit set of weights which would broadly conform to the politically acceptable notion of equity. These could be established, made explicit and incorporated into the cost–benefit assessments for future projects. This idea is regarded as preposterous by all those who argue that past decisions are biased towards the most powerful economic interests. Any weighting system based upon them would merely reinforce historic patterns of inequality. Another equally arbitrary system is to derive weights for different income groups from their marginal rates of income tax. (A gain or loss to non-taxpayers could, for example, be rated 1, whereas income changes for those in the 60 per cent tax bracket would only attract a 0.4 weight.) The implicit assumption here is that the tax system is a reflection of a society's true commitment to, and preference for, the equality objective.

All weighting or ranking systems convert political, social and moral choices into pseudo-technical ones. In effect, they allow the analyst to impose his own value judgements on all, unless the political decision-maker or the public play an integral role in the evaluation process (O'Riordan, 1976). Few people would knowingly be prepared to allow economists to set social preferences, despite Turvey's apparent view to the contrary. He states that:

> the value judgments made by economists are, by and large, better than those made by non-economists. . . . The point is simply that those who are experienced in systematic thinking about a problem are usually those who make the best judgments about it. Thus, whatever their theory of aesthetics, most people are prepared to accept the judgment of an art critic about the merits of a painting. (Turvey, 1963b, p. 96)

Few economists would now take such a professionally arrogant view. Some have argued that complex attempts to incorporate multiple objectives and distributive effects in a neat, single net benefit result simply mislead policy-makers or 'lend a spurious authority to purely personal prejudices' (Culyer, 1977, p. 149). Streeton (1972, p. 53) takes the view that 'a planner has a clearer picture by having the issues set out separately rather than being served with single figures that conceal the preferences'. While Nash *et al.* (1975a, 1975b) and Pearce (1977) argue for the introduction of value sensitivity analyses, in which an attempt is made to show how the chosen measure of net social benefit responds to changed value assumptions. The economic analyst is probably in a 'no-win' situation. If non-efficiency goals are neglected the results of the assessment are regarded as misleading and biased but the same criticisms also arise if they are included. On the other hand, if no analysis of the expected effects of public investments takes place, the investing agencies are even more prey to their own professional bias and to pressure from powerful vested interests.

THE SPATIAL SCALE ISSUE

Another somewhat different problem arising in the establishment of management objectives concerns the spatial scale over which the goals should apply. The results from an appraisal of the costs and benefits of requiring the Central Electricity Generating Board to reduce SO_2 emissions from its power stations would clearly be critically dependent on whether the transnational effects of acid rain pollution were included. From an environmental perspective the assessment ideally should encompass all important impacts, irrespective of their location but, in practice, investing or regulatory agencies are rarely concerned with externalities arising outside their areas of jurisdiction.

Putting aside the particularly difficult problems which arise from the depletion of international common property resources, the question of administrative responsibility is an important one at the intranational scale. It is commonplace for the most local tier of government to be responsible for investments in water supply provision, solid and liquid waste disposal, recreation provision, flood protection and so forth. Projects which produce the greatest net returns (or incur the lowest net costs) for residents in the local authority area will not necessarily be desirable if a wider set of interests are taken into account. Flood control schemes, which rely on building up levees or walls, may simply exacerbate problems elsewhere in the river system. Sea defence schemes designed to protect eroding stretches of the coast may result in beach depletion and accelerated cliff retreat farther along the coast in a neighbouring local authority area. And the provision of recreational facilities or wildlife conservation areas may be neglected if only the demands of local residents are considered. Similarly, conservation of one fishery may simply result in greater pressure on, and depletion of, another; or controls over river pollution could transfer the problems to air, land or marine environments. These spatial-scale problems are inevitable, given the interconnected nature of economic and environmental systems,[1] but it is crucial to recognize that cost–benefit results can be critically dependent on the area and environmental media of concern to the decision-making agency.

Identifying the cost–benefit flows: the problem of selection bias

Once the objectives and scale of concern have been determined, the next stage in the appraisal is to identify all the relevant losses and gains associated with the investment project, conservation measure or policy change. Although it is usually a straightforward task to set out the direct or *primary* costs and benefits, problems arise in compiling the list of relevant externalities. In the first place, it goes without saying that as yet unknown side-effects cannot be included; this may be particularly important when environmental changes result, the damage costs of which may not become apparent for many years.

Given the complexity of interrelated physical and human systems, it rarely will be feasible to consider all the known possible spillover costs and benefits. The analyst will tend to be selective, exercising judgement over which effects are relevant, which are significant enough to warrant inclusion and which are too trivial or occur too infrequently to take into account. In some cases, where scientific evidence on the magnitude, frequency and nature of cause–effect relationships conflicts, this will involve making a choice about which evidence to accept or reject. Further choices have to be made when the side-effects are not automatic products of the project itself, but arise because of human responses to it. Judgements will then have to be made about likely human behaviour.

To give one example: when assessing the desirability of a flood protection scheme,[2] should the analyst take into account the possibility that increased floodplain occupation will occur if individuals perceive that the protection measures mean the area is now safe? (White, 1942). Alternatively, should it be assumed that planning authorities will continue to zone the plain, regulating new developments to forms which will involve few damage costs when, and if, a high-magnitude, low-frequency flood exceeds the design capacity of the scheme?

Inevitably the training, experience and personal views of the assessor will influence this selection process, as indeed will the responsibilities and political preoccupations of the organization commissioning the study. It must also be expected that the selected set of relevant costs and benefits will change over time, reflecting changes in societal values and the activity of different interest groups.

Any assessment is likely to prove unacceptable to at least some groups in the community, who feel that their particular interests have been omitted from consideration, so biasing the results of the study. Undoubtedly, most early analyses did suffer from a highly restricted choice of relevant effects, with a clear tendency to concentrate on items which had monetary value and to neglect social and environmental spillovers.

EXAMPLES OF SELECTION BIAS

Cost–benefit studies of transport developments have, for instance, been criticized for their bias towards the losses and gains to transport users and for their lack of attention to the affected public. Sandbach (1980, 1982) argues that the UK Ministry of Transport analyses used for road planning are misleading since they ignore the costs of noise and nuisance from traffic. Similarly, the recent decision to increase the maximum permitted lorry weight was criticized, because, although the extra costs of road maintenance were considered, the effects on roadside buildings and on the water and sewerage pipes beneath the road surface were neglected. The Roskill Commission's study of the proposed sites for the third London Airport, which did attempt to take into account a much wider range of social and environmental costs than was usual at that time, has also been castigated. Self (1970, p. 254) regards the final cost–benefit figures as 'incredible, not only because of the disparate basis of the items included, but because of the important items excluded'.

In the same way, at least until the early 1970s, appraisals of water resource development schemes could easily be censored for their narrow focus, concentrating almost exclusively on the productive output of the projects (be it hydropower, water supplies or increased productivity from drained or irrigated land) and on the direct financial costs of constructing and operating the facilities. The assessments typically neglected several crucial cost elements:

(1) Reservoir construction normally involves the permanent loss of agricultural land, and other land use or development potential; it therefore imposes costs in terms of forgone opportunities and these could be considerable. In Australia, for instance, it remains common practice to restrict access to vast tracts of the catchment around supply reservoirs to prevent pollution and avoid the need for extensive treatment of supplies. The opportunity costs involved in 'sterilizing' these areas are omitted from the cost calculations. As Resources for the Future economists have long pointed out, the loss of future use options could be particularly significant when developments have irreversible effects on unique landscape features or biotic habitats (Krutilla, 1967; Fisher and Krutilla, 1974; Krutilla and Fisher, 1975).

(2) Although the cost to the sponsoring agencies of compensating or rehousing households displaced by the schemes would be part of the assessment calculations, these are only a proportion of the full welfare losses experienced by those forced to leave their homes and land, and by others who suffer as a result of the disruption of established communities.

(3) Large schemes commonly change the local ecology, stream run-off regimes

and drainage conditions. These not only involve aesthetic losses to those that value particular biotic species or habitats, but may also impose material costs on those utilizing land in the catchment. Increased waterlogging, for instance, may result from rises in the water table.

(4) Schemes could also have adverse effects on landscape value. There has been a tendency to assume that reservoirs would act to enhance not detract from amenity, but in cases where the draw-down of water leaves substantial tracts of debris-strewn mud exposed there is some doubt that much enhancement would occur in the summer months when most recreational use is made of the area.

(5) Reservoir projects almost inevitably improve access to the affected areas; this may not only have adverse effects on conservation interests (e.g. the Gordon River project in Tasmania), but may also further disrupt local communities.

It would be highly misleading to suggest that all project appraisal work continues to ignore the less tangible and more difficult to measure social and environmental spillovers. During the 1970s, in line with moves to develop multi-objective assessment techniques, there was a vast body of work, most notably but not exclusively of North American origin, which struggled to incorporate non-material externalities within the conventional analytical framework. It is, of course, still possible to find examples of within-agency appraisals which concentrate on an extremely narrow range of relevant issues; making a token gesture to social, ecological and amenity losses by listing them together under 'other' considerations, seemingly of less importance and set apart from the assessment of the more quantifiable costs and benefits. This is partly a reflection of the jurisdictional responsibilities of specific agencies and is not a problem confined to cost–benefit analysis; it applies equally to all forms of project appraisal. For example, an environmental impact study of the expansion of chemical manufacturing in the Cheshire marshes (UK) omitted consideration of water pollution since this was a regional water authority matter, outside the remit of the local government bodies sponsoring the analysis.

THE 'ADDITIONALITY' PROBLEM

A further problem in the identification of cost–benefit flows concerns the need to establish that they would occur *only* if the investment, policy change, or conservation measures took place, and that such measures were *alone* enough to produce the flow changes. This necessitates knowledge of past trends, and of the often extremely complex set of socioeconomic and environmental variables which can influence the losses and gains under study. The difficulties raised here are best illustrated by examples. To assess the ecological benefits from regulations requiring the retention of hedgerows it would be essential to have reasonable data on the importance of their removal in relation to all the other factors which can affect wildlife populations, such as the natural variation in species numbers, the destruction of other habitats, increased pesticide use and so on.

Similarly, to evaluate the health benefits from improved water supply provision, data are needed on all the environmental conditions which affect health standards. It has been common to assume that the provision of safe water supply sources alone can 'solve' the problems of water-related disease in LDCs. This is rarely so. Improvements in housing conditions, medical care, training in the basic rules of hygiene, more effective sewage disposal methods and the reduced recreational use of polluted streams may all have to occur before the investments in water supplies yield the expected health gains (White *et al.*, 1972; Feacham *et al.*, 1977; Kalbermatten *et al.*, 1980). In other words, the net benefits from supply provision could be grossly overestimated unless the costs of the other necessary measures were included in the assessment. Very similar difficulties arise in identifying the benefits from irrigation schemes in LDCs. Once again it has been found that the water alone is not enough to promote the expected productivity increases and welfare improvements; institutional changes are also necessary to provide credit, technical advice, equipment and mechanisms to allocate supplies between users.

Estimation problems of this type apply not only when cost–benefit analysis is used to assess the desirability of measures pre-implementation, but also to *ex post* audits. It has often been claimed that all the post-1956 reduction in smoke and particulate matter in London's air can be attributed to the smokeless zone regulations introduced under the Clean Air Act 1956. But this grossly inflates the apparent benefits of the legislation as it ignores the fact that the concentrations of these contaminants had been falling steadily since at least the 1920s (Figure 8.1). The declining use of coal for space heating, the conversion of the railways from steam to diesel or electricity, the restructuring of industry, with greater emphasis on assembly and service industries, and the closure of town gas plants and small-scale electricity-generating stations were but a few of the crucial factors contributing to the reduction in pollution levels.

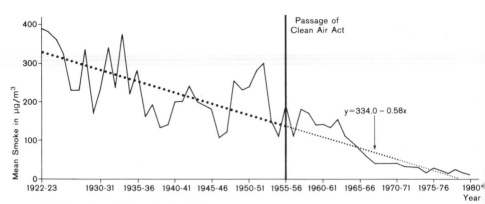

* No Recordings made after December 1980

Figure 8.1   Air pollution trends: average winter smoke levels at Kew, 1921–80
Source: Adapted from Auliciems and Burton, 1973, and updated from Kew records.
Copyright © 1973 by Pergamon Press.

DISTINGUISHING TECHNOLOGICAL FROM PECUNIARY SPILLOVERS

Another major identification problem occurs through the need to differentiate between benefits and costs which are, in the economic jargon, *real technological spillovers* and those which are *pecuniary transfers*. The former represent real losses or gains to society, whereas the latter do not produce any changes in productive possibilities, but involve the transfer of benefits and costs between different groups within the community. When economic efficiency is the management objective, pecuniary spillovers should be ignored, although they may well be highly relevant if the policy aim is to redistribute effective income to selected areas or social groups.

Differentiating between these two spillover types is important if the problem of double counting the costs or benefits is to be avoided. For example, in assessing the benefits of an irrigation project, it would be double counting to include both the increased farm incomes and the increased profits of local shopkeepers who gained the farmers' custom. Actual rules of cost–benefit practice have been far from clear over which spillovers should be considered, and many project appraisals, particularly of water resource developments, have been heavily criticized for double, even triple, counting the benefits, while neglecting to include the full range of costs (Margolis, 1957). Agencies responsible for conducting the analyses all too often have a vested interest in development; the technostructure of irrigation agencies, drainage authorities or forestry departments depends upon continued activity. The no-build option is not therefore a popular one. A good, although now dated, example of the way bias towards construction can be introduced into the assessments is the treatment of project benefits in the so-called *Green Book*.[3] If the extension of irrigated wheat production caused a fall in wheat prices, the pecuniary spillover losses to competing dry-land wheat farmers was not considered as a cost of the irrigation schemes. But on the other hand, the same fall in price was listed as a benefit to secondary activities such as flour milling. In just the same way, whereas increased local wage rates (associated with the labour demands for project construction) were treated as a benefit, the cost of this to non-project employers was omitted (Hirschleifer *et al.*, 1960).

Thus the problems involved in merely identifying which costs and benefits are to be included in the appraisal are considerable. But to them must be added the further major difficulties which arise in establishing the magnitude of the flows over time, and then in translating this diverse set of gains and losses occurring in different time periods into comparable monetary terms.

Calculating the material costs and benefits

Even when the gains and losses are material and have established market values, there are three basic problems involved in their calculation. First, the scale of the cost and benefit flows and the time period over which they occur will depend upon human behaviour. Most cost–benefit analyses have assumed that individuals will respond immediately, and in an economically rational way, to the opportunities afforded by a resource project. It is presupposed, for instance, that farmers benefiting from irrigation or drainage schemes will rapidly change their output patterns to the new profit-maximizing crops or livestock products. Such a notion runs counter to the evidence which shows that the adoption of most forms of innovation is a gradual process (Hägerstrand, 1952, 1967). Some producers will be tied into established practice by their specialized knowledge and equipment; others may lack the capital to make the change; still others will want to wait until the profitability of the new crops and any production or distribution problems have been evaluated; and yet another group will have entrenched lifestyles which they are reluctant to disrupt. Furthermore, producers may have neither the ability nor desire to maximize profits; many will need or prefer to adopt a risk-minimizing strategy to ensure a regular and stable basic income. Any assessment which assumes rational, profit-maximizing behaviour will inflate the total benefits stream, and those assuming instantaneous adoption of innovations will overestimate the output gains in the years immediately after the project comes into operation.

Attempts to evaluate the benefits from conservation or pollution control policies also run into the problem of predicting human response. The gains from any regulations are inevitably a function of the level of compliance. Clearly, the pollution reduction benefits from 'add on' devices to curb exhaust gas emissions are much diminished if a significant number of car owners simply remove them, in the belief that they decrease fuel efficiency. Most appraisals have tended to assume full compliance, despite clear evidence that the compliance record of many forms of regulation is poor (see Chapter 9).

Second, the monetary value of the gains and losses will critically depend upon whether these are measured in opportunity cost or actual price terms. From an economic efficiency viewpoint the former should be employed since it gives the real productive cost to the economy of using a factor of production in the project rather than in the next best alternative use. So, for instance, if labour is unemployed, the opportunity cost of employing people in resource development projects would be zero. This approach meets little favour from resource agencies which have to actually pay market prices for the utilized factors of production. A labour-intensive project could well prove desirable if the wage costs are omitted from the calculations, but it may then fail to yield enough revenue to cover the wages paid in practice. Unless central government is prepared to make good any financial deficits, agencies will continue to calculate cost and benefit flows from their own rather than a total economy perspective.

Third, any form of assessment concerned with future gains and losses is subject to uncertainty, and the problems this raises become more acute the further into the future the analysis is pushed. No one can expect the analyst to be omniscient; changes in consumer tastes, relative factor costs and production technologies may all act over time to alter the cost and benefit streams in ways which could not have been predicted. The presentation of a neat, single net benefit figure tends to give a false sense of certainty, which belies the fact that it is derived from often extremely crude estimates. At best, the appraisal can indicate the most likely outcomes, and ideally it should either employ probability analysis to estimate the probable upper and lower limits to the outcome range or subject the results to sensitivity tests to show how they are affected by possible changes in key output prices or input costs. However, a full cost–benefit study requires a vast amount of quantitative data, which is all too often unavailable or would cost a prohibitive amount to construct or gather.

No projections can be any more accurate than the data on which they are based, and all are critically dependent on the use of appropriate forecasting techniques and on a good understanding of the complex of socioeconomic variables which influence demand levels and factor prices. Even in advanced countries many cost–benefit studies have been, and still are, founded on an extremely flimsy data-base, and employ 'standard' forecasting procedures rather than the methods most appropriate to the circumstances. Whenever the requirement for a cost–benefit study becomes institutionalized, the need to obtain a result tends to become more important than understanding the limitations and implications of the analysis. This is most obviously a difficulty when agencies barely equipped to undertake economic assessments are formally required to submit a cost–benefit analysis with all project proposals. For example, in Britain local authorities must now conduct cost–benefit studies to justify all coastal protection works, but few have the data, expertise or finance to make this a very meaningful exercise.

Placing money values on non-market goods

As has already been seen, the use of money (or market values) has serious implications for distributive equity, but the fact remains that money is the only practicable comparative measure available. Its use does, however, raise considerable, some would say insuperable (Adams, 1974b), problems when the identified gains and losses have no established market price. This clearly applies to a whole range of environmental goods and services – landscape amenity, clean air and so on – which are simply not marketed; and it also occurs when public agencies provide, say, recreational facilities or water supplies at purely nominal or zero unit prices. The need then arises to devise surrogate monetary value measures. Numerous alternative approaches have been suggested (see Pearce, 1978, for a detailed analysis) of which five have been most widely used: (1) estimation of physical damage costs; (2) damage or risk avoidance payments; (3) property and land value change; (4) consumer surplus calculations; and (5) compensation or bribe estimation.

PHYSICAL DAMAGE COSTS

The idea of attempting to value pollution by calculating the physical damage costs is a simple one conceptually but extremely difficult to operationalize in practice.[4] While some forms of damage are amenable to financial assessment, others which involve subjective welfare losses are not (Table 8.1 gives some examples of losses in these two categories). Although a number of cost–benefit studies have attempted to place prices on amenity losses – the Roskill Commission being the classic example – it is now largely accepted practice to leave these so-called 'below the line' items out of direct damage cost assessments (OECD, 1976c). There really is no meaningful way to express in financial terms the aesthetic

Table 8.1 Pollution damage costs

	Damage category					
	Human health	*Fauna*	*Flora*	*Natural resources*	*Materials*	*Climate and weather*
Financial loss	Productivity losses; health care costs including increased research costs to avoid pollution	Lost animal and fish production	Reduced crop production; reduced forest growth; increased aphid predation	Lost production from polluted water or soil; increased treatment costs; reduced flexibility in land use	Reduced life of a material; reduced utility of a material; increased repair costs	Traffic congestion and accident costs due to smogs; reduced agricultural yields and increased lighting costs from decreased sunshine; agricultural losses from shift in world rainfall patterns
Loss of amenity	Risk aversion: cost of suffering; cost of bereavement; cost of limitations imposed upon an individual, his family and his society	Risk aversion: reduced pleasure from fishing and observing wildlife	Risk aversion: reduced pleasure from landscapes and observation of floral species	Risk aversion: decreased recreation benefits	Risk aversion: endurance of soiled or damaged materials; damage to selected aesthetic monuments and objects	Risk aversion: decreased pleasure from reduced visibility

Source: Based on OECD, 1976c.

losses suffered by individuals who know that the Parthenon in Athens has been affected by vehicle emissions, or that the Taj Mahal is slowly being turned brown by industrial air pollution (Gilpin, 1978); still less is it possible to assess what the ruin of these buildings will mean to future generations.

Various studies have attempted to put a cost figure on the material damage imposed by air pollution through the accelerated corrosion and soiling of buildings, paintwork, household fabrics and so on. Most commonly these involve the comparison of cleaning, repair and maintenance costs in polluted and unpolluted areas (Programmes Analysis Unit, 1972; Waddell, 1974) and necessitate a massive data collection effort. Pollution can only be defined in terms of one or two contaminants – most commonly smoke, particulate matter and SO_2 – which raises the possibility that the so-called unpolluted areas are in fact damaged by unmeasured contaminants and, in addition, fails to deal with synergistic effects. Moreover, the approach suffers from the problem, inherent in all cross-sectional studies, of isolating the effects of pollution from the host of other variables which could influence the spatial distribution of material damage (e.g. variations in rainfall, sunshine hours and frost incidence) and of spending on maintenance and repair (e.g. income levels or social attitudes). The PAU study, for example, rather unexpectedly found a negative correlation between household expenditure on cleaning products and air pollution levels in Britain; clearly, the effect of other socioeconomic variables simply swamped that of pollution. Not surprisingly, few analysts have been prepared to present very definite damage estimates; the US study by Waddell, for example, gave a possible air pollution damage range of \$720–\$2900 million per annum.

It is well known that agricultural productivity can be reduced by air pollution: yields of commercial crops can fall or be delayed due to the presence of SO_2; excess amounts of fluoride can create fluorosis in cattle, so reducing milk yields and causing lameness; and it is now even thought that the growth rate of aphids, an important crop pest, is enhanced by exposure to NO_2 and SO_2 (*ENDS* Report 108, 1984, p. 3). However, attempts to quantify these losses with any precision are hampered not only by inadequate knowledge of dose–response relationships under field conditions, but also by uncertainty over the real value of output losses when the products are in surplus or are heavily subsidized. In a sense, from an EEC viewpoint, the opportunity cost of declining milk yields is zero, or in fact negative, if the reduced costs of storage and subsidy payments are taken into account. But the figures look very different if calculated from the perspective of individual farmers. Once again, not unexpectedly, estimates of this form of damage cost vary enormously; work done in Britain in the early 1970s produced figures ranging from £39 million per annum up to £2300 million.

By far the largest body of work on damage cost estimation has focused on health, covering both the increased expenditure on health care and, more controversially, the loss of productive output due to increased morbidity and accelerated mortality. While it has been widely accepted that air, water and land pollution (toxic substances in soils) will tend to have a detrimental effect on health, the precise nature of many cause–effect relationships remains unknown. Epidemiological studies have variously established correlations between high concentrations of atmospheric contaminants and bronchitis, emphysema, heart disease and even the common cold, but part, at least, of this correlation may be explained by the fact that the poor tend to live in the most polluted areas. Work in the United States by Freeman (1972), Berry (1977), Asch and Seneca (1978) suggests that there is an inverse relationship within cities between air pollution and income class, and that overall exposure to pollution is relatively higher in cities with low-income characteristics. In other words, poor housing standards, inadequate diet, heating or medical care, smoking habits and a whole host of environmental conditions differentially affecting the poor may be crucial in explaining variations in disease incidence.

Major difficulties also arise in putting a price on illness or death. One common approach is to calculate the reduction in productive output minus, in the case of death, the saved consumption of the affected individuals. This has been vehemently criticized on moral grounds by those who argue that a human life cannot be treated as a piece of productive machinery. But not withstanding its dubious ethical basis, the inescapable fact is that this type of exercise is very widely employed in insurance assessments and in court decisions on damage claims. The approach is not, of course, without its practical difficulties, one of the most problematic being how to calculate productive output. The pollution-related premature death of old-age pensioners or the unemployed could prove to be a net economic gain since the lost output would be zero, while savings would be made on benefit payments. Similarly, if output is valued in market terms, the death of a housewife would be an economically insignificant matter. Moreover, if income is used as the measure of output, the premature loss of a television quiz-show compère would be much more significant than a farm labourer or water worker.

DAMAGE OR RISK AVOIDANCE PAYMENTS

In order to obtain an admittedly very crude measure of consumer preferences for unmarketed goods attempts have been made to calculate the level of expenditure on *damage or risk avoidance*. Thus household spending on flood insurance, double-glazing to reduce noise damage and hedges or fencing to obscure a source of visual intrusion have all been employed to obtain minimum estimates of the value of pollution control or hazard reduction. Starkie and Johnson (1975) have argued that expenditure on double-glazing represents a minimum valuation of the good peace and quiet; in theory, a household would install insulation if the cost is less than the subjective loss of amenity through noise, and if the amenity loss is less than the cost of moving house. Clearly, this approach has many limitations; some households will not be able to pay the avoidance costs; short-term tenants will be unlikely to incur costs for benefits accruing to subsequent tenants and the landlord; losses outside the double-glazed rooms still occur, and individuals may install double-glazing to increase house values, provide added protection from burglary, reduce heat loss or simply because it is fashionable. In the same way, studies which infer the value of flood control from private avoidance expenditure face the difficulties that individuals have highly imperfect knowledge of damage probabilities and may also expect public agencies to provide relief or protection.

PROPERTY AND LAND VALUES

The property and land value approach has attracted a massive literature, largely but not exclusively North American in origin (Pearce, 1978). It is based on the simple idea that the value of a property should reflect its intrinsic qualities and its surrounding environment, as perceived by the purchaser, including such intrusive impacts as noise or air pollution. Hence it should be possible to observe the effects of pollution through reduced property values and conversely the value of environmental improvements, such as tip heap removal or park provision, should be reflected in increased prices.

A variant of this approach, which has somewhat fewer difficulties, can be employed when pollution reduces the flexibility in land use or when it results in a total loss of all development value. For example, housebuilding may have to be restricted on land contaminated with toxic substances or affected by mining subsidence, or alternatively a cordon sanitaire may be necessary around hazardous or very noisy installations. A crude 'price' can be attached to the pollution loss by comparing the value of the land in its currently restricted use with its undamaged use value. All calculations based on land or house prices inevitably suffer from the problems that property markets are highly imperfect and when used to direct policy decisions have regressive effects on the distribution of effective welfare. The 'cost' of pollution, mining subsidence or the removal of housing in the high noise zone alongside an urban motorway will apparently be less in low-income, low-property-value areas. This carries with it the danger that a disproportionate number of such disamenities will be directed towards the already disadvantaged (see Chapter 9).

Studies using property price variations as a surrogate for the value of amenities or disamenities have been of two types, time-trend analyses tracing the impact of an environmental change, and cross-sectional studies of areas differentially affected by pollution or amenity provision. By and large, the former have produced the more convincing results. There is little doubt that major price increments do occur when new recreational sites (parks, gardens or lakes) are provided or when areas are designated as conservation areas, national parks or green belts (Byers, 1970; Eagles, 1984). It has proved more difficult to assess the impact of many new sources of disamenity, primarily because these normally also bring benefits; new roads improve accessibility and new factories, power stations or airports create employment. A number of studies have, therefore, found no significant change in property values, but it cannot be assumed from this that the value or cost of the disamenity is zero (Pearce, 1978). The results of cross-sectional studies are even more difficult to evaluate since spatial variations in the demand for, and the price of, similar types of property are products of a vast range of socioeconomic variables; differences in accessibility, service provision or prevailing fashions may simply swamp any amenity/disamenity effects (Sharp and Jennings, 1976). There is certainly some evidence that property prices are negatively correlated with increases in air pollutant indices, but then these indices are also correlated with income levels; it therefore becomes exceptionally difficult to sort out cause/effect relationships.

At best the property value approach may be able to provide a *minimum* estimate of noise and other forms of pollution damage. Many will continue to suffer disamenity because they cannot afford 'undamaged' property; others in council housing or in controlled rent properties have little option but to accept the disamenity; while still others will be unable to afford the costs of moving to less damaged areas. Since those in higher-income groups are more mobile, it is not unexpected that levels of price depreciation are greatest for high-value properties. There is, therefore, a clear danger that unduly small values will be attached to amenity losses in the less mobile, working-class sections of the community (Self, 1970; Sandbach, 1980).

CONSUMER SURPLUS

The notion of consumer surplus is critical in the measurement of social benefits; it can simply be defined as a maximum sum of money a consumer would be willing to pay for a given amount of a good, less the amount actually paid (Mishan, 1972). In Figure 8.2 the demand curve DD represents the willingness of an individual to pay for different quantities of water. If the supply was unmetered and a fixed annual rate was levied irrespective of the level of consumption, then the unit price would be zero, OA units of water would be taken and the total consumer surplus would be equal to the area of the triangle OAB. However, if the same consumer decided to install a meter and was then charged a price (OP) for each unit of supply taken, consumption would fall to OQ and the consumer surplus would be reduced; it would now be equal to the triangle PRB. Once a

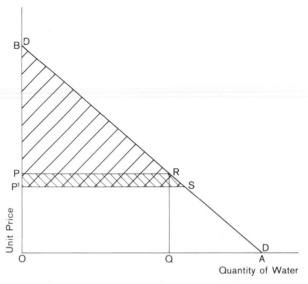

Figure 8.2   The consumer surplus concept

unit-pricing system is in operation, any measures which result in a fall in price produce an increase in consumer surplus. A fall from P to P^1 would, for instance, increase the surplus by the hatched area PP^1RS.

This idea has been widely applied to assess the value of public good provision. Increases in consumer surplus through the reduction in travel time and cost, *and* through the additional number of journeys made in response to the reduced cost of travel, are an integral (often key) part of cost–benefit studies on motorways, rapid-transit systems and airport sites (Self, 1975). A much criticized element in such studies is the way values are imputed for savings in travel time; the arbitrary and highly subjective values placed on time can act to sway the results of the assessment towards development.

Another well-known application of the concept has been to estimate the benefits derived from recreational visits to parks, water sites, bird reserves and so forth (Smith and Kavanagh, 1969; Newton, 1972). According to the Clawson (1959) model, a demand curve for recreation could be constructed by estimating the travel costs incurred in reaching specific sites. Referring back to Figure 8.2, OB represents the costs of those travelling farthest, whereas OA would be the 'price' paid by someone living next to the site. Assuming that *all* the welfare from the recreational experience occurred at the site and *none* on the journey, and that those paying less than OB were obtaining a consumer welfare surplus, a value could be placed on the recreational resource (Knetsch, 1974). This approach has been heavily criticized on three grounds: the assumption that the journey itself has no recreational value, the whole notion of linking the welfare derived from an experience to the cost of getting to it and the arbitrary value attributed to travel time (Mansfield, 1969; Flegg, 1976).

COMPENSATION PAYMENTS

The final common method used to establish the cost of disamenities, including risk, is to attempt to find how much people would need in compensation or bribes to make up for their loss. This can be done by sample surveys which ask households hypothetical questions such as 'what is the minimum sum you would accept to reconcile yourself to the increase in aircraft noise to which you are, and in the future will be, subjected?' Not only will the results inevitably depend upon the wealth of those interviewed – £5000 might seem an inordinately large figure to someone on a low income, with no savings and no capital assets, but would seem a minor amount to others – but also as Self (1975) has pointed out, the subjective evaluations made in a survey situation are unlikely to bear much relation to those actually made under real market conditions. An alternative, but equally problematic, technique is to impute acceptable compensation levels from past human behaviour. For example, the premium paid on wage rates to attract labour into high-risk jobs has been taken as a crude measure of the cost of risk, or rather the income individuals are prepared to forgo to avoid risk. Alternatively, since the principle of compensation is widely accepted in most societies, it might be possible to use court awards, insurance settlements, or the levels of compensation actually paid by private and public agencies to suggest the value placed on a whole range of disamenities (Puschak and Burton, 1983).

Concluding remarks on cost–benefit studies

It must be accepted that there is no objective method of establishing the costs and benefits of projects or policies. Subjectivity is introduced in setting the assessment objectives, listing the relevant losses and gains, calculating their physical magnitude and time of occurrence and, above all, in translating these into monetary terms. Still further subjective judgements are made when choosing an appropriate discount rate to convert money costs incurred and revenues received in different time periods into constant time values. As was discussed in Chapter 4, high rates of discount have crucial implications for intergenerational equity; but, on the other hand, the use of low rates for long-life projects make it possible for virtually any development to appear beneficial. There is little doubt that cost–benefit and related monetary assessment techniques have been greatly misused. By the judicial choice of relevant losses and gains and the selective use of evidence on the value of each of these, it is possible for the analyst to bias the study to achieve answers acceptable to his agency or political masters. But it is far easier to criticize cost–benefit analysis than it is to provide alternative methods of assessment; all assessment tools are equally prone to analyst bias and to misuse by those employing them to justify actions desired for other reasons.

The use of money values in economic assessments is undoubtedly regressive; it is obviously true that prices are not determined by individuals with equal power to maximize their own preferences (Sandbach, 1980). However, there is no other common unit of account, no other easy way of identifying the trade-offs which inevitably arise in all spheres of human activity. It is certainly not rational to vehemently criticize appraisals attempting to incorporate extra market phenomena for 'measuring the immeasurable' and, at the same time, berate the analyst for omitting to value environmental goods and amenity losses. The alternative to monetary assessment is to leave choices solely to administrators, politicians and vocal interest groups. As Pearce (1976, p. 108) has pointed out, 'if money values are not put on these [environmental and social] items, or, rather, if the attempt is not made, it is easy to imagine that when environmental lobbies are not powerful ... the situation could revert to one where environmental problems are simply overlooked'. Without attempts at assessment, the whole decision process could be even more biased towards the powerful economic interests favouring development over conservation and material prosperity over amenity.

ENVIRONMENTAL IMPACT ASSESSMENT

The National Environmental Policy Act and the origins of the environmental impact statement

The development of environmental impact assessment in its current form was largely a product of the rising political salience of the US environmental lobby during the 1960s. It was indisputable that conventional cost–benefit and related evaluatory exercises had downgraded, or indeed entirely neglected, environmental values in the assessment of policies, investment projects and expenditure programmes. Given the political climate of the day, it became necessary to give some formal recognition to the demands of the environmentalists; this came in 1969 with the passage of the National Environmental Policy Act (NEPA). Under this legislation 'major federal actions significantly affecting the quality of the human environment' had to be accompanied by an environmental impact statement (EIS), which detailed 'to the fullest extent possible':

(1) the environmental impact of the proposed action;
(2) any adverse environmental effects which cannot be avoided should the proposal be implemented;
(3) alternatives to the proposed action;
(4) the relationship between local and short-term uses of man's environment and the maintenance and enhancement of long-term productivity;
(5) any irreversible and irretrievable commitments of resources which would be involved in the proposed action should it be implemented (NEPA, section 102 2c).

According to the preamble of the Act, such statements were required to ensure that the federal government met its

> continuing responsibility . . . to use *all practicable means, consistent with other essential considerations of national policy*, to fulfil five key objectives:
> to act as trustee of the environment for succeeding generations;
> to ensure for all Americans safe, healthful, productive, and aesthetically and culturally pleasing surroundings;
> to attain *the widest range of beneficial uses of the environment* without degradation, risk to health or safety, or any other undesirable or un-intended consequences;
> to preserve important historic, cultural and natural aspects of our national heritage, and maintain, *whenever possible*, an environment which supports diversity, and variety of individual choice;
> to achieve *a balance* between population and resource use which will permit *high standards of living* and a wide sharing of life's amenities;
> to enhance the quality of renewable resources and approach the maximum attainable recycling of depletable resources (ibid., section 101(b); em-phasis added).

As with most legislation, the wording of NEPA was extremely general and immediately raised several important issues of interpretation (see Chapter 9 for a more detailed discussion of the role of policy interpretation, implementation and enforcement). In the first place, although the preamble to the Act was strong on high-minded rhetoric, it did nothing to specify what weight environmental policy objectives would have among all 'other essential considerations of national policy'. Throughout it was clear that the Act did not – nor was it designed to – reorder the country's conventional economic and social goals. As Schnaiberg (1980, p. 317) points out, 'euphoria about NEPA's potential role in reshaping state support for the treadmill of production was short-lived'. Although environ-mental quality and diversity were given statutory recognition as important public policy objectives, the caveats surrounding their achievement left little doubt that economic development was not to be sacrificed in any material way to environmental aspirations. The five environmental goals were only to be pursued whenever possible, where practicable and if consistent with economic growth and the maintenance of high living standards. Political tensions would still arise in the numerous situations where conflicts occurred between the claims of environmental and economic interest groups.

The executive agencies, which NEPA was ostensibly designed to control, were left to determine the practicability of meeting the environmental objectives. They were bound by law to consider the impacts of their activities, as revealed by EIS requirements which they themselves prepared, but how much weight was accorded to these effects was largely a matter of administrative discretion. Inevitably this discretion was a formidable force for maintaining the status quo; agencies strongly biased to developmental goals could take the view that the economic, technical, employment, or national security advantages of their proposals overrode the revealed environmental disbenefits. Although environmental pressure groups attempted to use NEPA to push agencies into altering the substantive direction of their policies and practices, court rulings have clearly established that judicial decision cannot overturn the considered judgement of the executive. This emerges from the well-known *Calvert Cliff* v. *AEC* case (1971) (Culhane, 1974) and from *Natural Resources Defence Council* v. *Morton* (1971), where it was held that:

> The Court [cannot] in any way substitute its judgement for that of the Executive agency involved unless the decision of the agency is found to be arbitrary, capricious, or an abuse of discretion, in which case the Court could require the agency to reconsider its decision. (quoted in O'Riordan, 1976, p. 287)

Although there are cases where individual projects have been modified, and a few examples of schemes being abandoned, as a result of an unfavourable EIS (Sandbach, 1980), these at best represent a marginal shift towards environmentalist demands. There is little evidence that the basic priorities of agencies and the developmental thrust of their policies have been altered by NEPA (Greis, 1973; Culhane, 1974; Friesema and Culhane, 1976).

The National Environmental Policy Act merely added a new procedure which had to be undertaken before formal decisions were made, it did not significantly alter the decision system *per se*. The credence given to environmental claims may have been enhanced by improved information and pressure groups were given new opportunities to express their views, but the relative weight given to environmental quality over the other possibly incompatible objectives of public policy is still determined by bureaucratic choice and the power of entrenched interests (see Chapter 9).

It was highly optimistic to expect NEPA, or any similar piece of legislation, to radically reform decision-making practices to produce a rational balance between economic and environmental policy objectives. Just as cost–benefit analyses could be employed to support decisions predetermined by other considerations, so too it was possible for agencies to observe the form of the EIS requirements without building environmental criteria into the substance of their evaluatory procedures (Fairfax, 1978). As Friesema and Culhane argue,

> The expectation that NEPA will cause federal agencies to produce scientific, holistic, optimizing, evaluating, mitigating, and co-ordinating policy seems to be the latest manifestation of the rational decision-making perspective on bureaucratic behavior. . . . [However], public administration behavior is not scientific management; it is politics. (Friesema and Culhane, 1976, p. 340)

When it came to defining the form of the impact statements, their scope and the federal activities which warranted environmental assessment, NEPA was similarly unspecific. No detailed procedures were laid down; the range of relevant effects was not made clear; no criteria were established to distinguish 'actions significantly affecting' the environment from those too minor to justify invoking the EIS process; and the level of detail required in the statements was not determined. The phrase that agencies must provide information 'to the greatest possible extent', immediately raised the question of whether the cost of data collection could act as a limit on the coverage of the studies. In these circumstances considerable scope was left for administrative discretion. Agencies prepared their own EIS manuals, issued their own guidelines interpreting the legislative intent, made internal decisions about the range of relevant effects and the level of detail with which they were assessed, decided which of their actions would justify an EIS and determined what range of alternatives to the proposed action would be evaluated. For instance, according to Wathern (1976), the Federal Power Commission drew an arbitrary dividing-line between hydroelectric schemes of above or below 2000 hp capacity; only the former were regarded as significant enough to warrant environmental assessment. Similarly, agencies have typically only considered a very narrow range of alternative actions, normally merely discussing other potential sites for the proposed development (other dams, roadlines, or power station locations); rarely did they include radical departures from conventional practice as feasible alternative options. Inevitably the extent of intra-agency discretion over the content of their analyses was a further factor biasing the whole process towards the maintenance of the status quo.

However, the executive authorities were not given complete freedom to interpret the requirements of the legislation. A theoretically independent Council on Environmental Quality was appointed to assess the performance of the agencies and to review draft EIS requirements. Over time it has issued a whole series of guidelines; these attempt to clarify and reinterpret the scope of the legislation in the light of implementation experience and emerging environmental or social concerns and are also designed to ensure that agencies follow acceptable (but not uniform) procedures. For example, although NEPA itself did not require agencies to consider those socioeconomic effects of their actions which were not environmental in a physical sense, the CEQ now recommends that EISs should encompass an extremely broad range of impacts, including 'ecological (such as the effects on natural resources and on the components, structures, and functioning of affected ecosystems), economic, social or health, whether direct, indirect, or cumulative' (US Council on Environmental Quality, 1978).

But it appears unlikely that the CEQ has played more than a marginal role in changing the evaluatory practices of the executive. As Sax (1970) and many subsequent analysts have pointed out, the Council had only advisory powers. It could not force agencies to adopt the recommendations and had not the manpower to undertake in-depth reviews of the mass of EISs presented to it. Moreover, it was in effect a branch of government and, as such, was subject to the same sort of political pressures as were the executive agencies themselves.

A more significant constraint on the discretion of the federal agencies was the process of EIS review and the potential this gave for environmental pressure groups to use the courts to challenge the way the legislative intent has been interpreted and implemented. All draft EISs have to be circulated to other federal agencies and made available to the public for comment. A minimum period of ninety days must be allowed for this participation stage and then a final EIS is prepared, which notionally takes account of the received comments. This final statement must then be lodged with the CEQ for at least thirty days before the proposed project can be undertaken; during this period anyone not satisfied with the EIS can institute court proceedings.

In the vast majority of cases few comments have been submitted by other federal agencies; even authorities with an environmental remit, such as the Environmental Protection Agency, have been heavily criticized for the inadequacy of their review and comment procedures (US National Academy of Sciences, 1977a, 1977b). However, environmental interest groups have presented systematic critiques of a great number of assessments and have used the courts to challenge conventional agency practice and to obtain a public platform for their views. But it should be noted that even in the United States where pressure groups have been extremely active and where the courts have a traditionally important constitutional role, the bulk of projects go through the whole NEPA process unscathed (Schnaiberg, 1980). In part this arises because the sheer volume of assessments makes it impracticable to scrutinize every study in depth, and in part because the sponsoring agencies have become adept at EIS report writing. They have learned to avoid, as far as possible, contentious issues and areas, have been careful to conform to the letter if not the spirit of the legislation and have employed the assessment process to defuse potential conflicts (Fairfax, 1978). It nevertheless is undoubtedly true that court rulings, and the possibility of court cases, have influenced the scope of EIS requirements, have pushed agencies to provide fuller statements and have widened considerably the range of activities which are now deemed to have a significant environmental effect (Anderson, 1973; Meyers, 1976; Sandbach, 1980). Judicial review can, however, only ensure that the executive has adhered to the procedures required by law, it cannot force change in public policy priorities (Wandesforde-Smith, 1980a).

The spread of environmental impact assessment

From its beginnings as a federal measure the EIS requirement has been widely adopted by most of the US states and has since been introduced in many western advanced countries[5] and in some LDCs (Wandesforde-Smith 1980a, 1980b; Clark et al., 1980). The exact form of the required assessment, the types of developments covered, the point at which it is formally incorporated into the planning, pollution control or resource development processes, together with the arrangements made for public scrutiny, vary considerably between countries, and in federal systems even within a country. It was inevitable that this should be the case given the very different political, judicial and administrative systems in which EIA had to operate.

Most governments reacted with alarm to the prospect of hundreds of court cases and the attendant decision-making delays, litigation costs and manpower expenses. As a result, it has been normal for post-NEPA legislation to be much more explicit about the types of activity requiring an EIS, restricting its use to the assessment of specific projects and not to the evaluation of policy changes or broad-scale development plans and programmes. Furthermore, EIA has been employed very much as a supplement to established development planning or pollution control procedures; environmental interest groups were to be consulted but the evaluation of the statements and the weighting given to the environmental effects was regarded as a matter for 'expert' managerial judgement. The emphasis was thus placed on the technique of EIA itself as an aid to increasing the rationality of planning (Clifford, 1978). In other words, the political debate over the scope of EIA occurred before the legislation was enacted, not subsequently in the courts, and it was clear that the major directions of public policy would continue to be framed through existing institutions.

In no country which has enacted legislation to require the preparation of EISs does this necessarily signal a shift in policy priorities away from material growth to concern for the quality of life, or ensure state action to protect environmental quality. In the wave of enthusiasm for impact assessment which followed NEPA it was often overlooked that an EIS was merely a method of presenting data. This information would ideally be a comprehensive and systematic appraisal of the effects of alternative development projects and strategies, which could be used to inform the decision process. But it cannot resolve the conflicts of interest which inevitably arise over all significant developments. The importance attached to particular forms of environmental, economic and social change will continue to depend upon which interest groups have access to the effective policy-making process (see Chapter 9).

The problems of assessment

Literally hundreds of environmental impact assessment techniques have now been devised, many of which may be methodologically ingenious but of little practical relevance (Bisset, 1978; Clark et al., 1978). These have been extensively reviewed in the literature (O'Riordan and Hey, 1976; Clark et al., 1980), and it is not the intention here to outline the possible alternative procedures or to debate their respective merits. Rather attention will be focused on the basic and inherent problems involved in all types of environmental analysis. It has to be stressed that the task of identifying, quantifying and comparing the myriad different environmental changes associated with all forms of development is immensely complex and inevitably involves considerable subjectivity. The analytical difficulties and the need for value judgements mean that EIAs can be used to obfuscate issues and that the results can be manipulated to conform to the interests of developers (private and public) and of influential pressure groups (Bisset, 1978). Just as cost–benefit appraisals cannot produce single, axiomatically correct solutions, so the results of EIAs will vary with the training and ideological perspective of the analyst.

The methods of assessment fall into three broad functional divisions or analytical stages: impact identification, evaluation and comparison – the first two stages providing the essential building-blocks of the third.

IMPACT IDENTIFICATION

Techniques of identification aim to present the decision-maker with an inventory of effects in some convenient form (checklists, matrices, linear graphs or networks, or overlay maps). Even this most basic and seemingly simple task is fraught with difficulties since it presupposes a knowledge of cause–effect relationships, which is all too often lacking. Clearly, the analyst cannot identify types of impact as yet unknown, and judgements will have to be made about the veracity of conflicting scientific evidence. Subjectivity is introduced into the identification process through the need for selectivity. Given the complex interrelationships within and between natural and human systems, some spatial and temporal cut-off points must be chosen to keep the assessment within bounds. Similarly, judgements will have to be made in disregarding those effects thought to be too trivial or unlikely to warrant consideration. Furthermore, the assessor will need to make assumptions about the technologies which will be available and employed to ameliorate the effects of development. In other words, the problems of impact identification closely parallel those involved in setting out the relevant cost and benefit flows within a cost–benefit analysis.

IMPACT EVALUATION

Although techniques which stop at the identification stage are widely used and have the advantage of minimizing subjectivity and the degree of assessor bias, they are limited by their failure to evaluate the significance of each identified effect. Impact evaluation attempts to do this by using some form of judgemental scaling to give the decision-maker some information on the magnitude, scale and potential seriousness of the different impacts. The obvious difficulty here is that there is no common unit of account, no agreed criteria on which the effect scales (or scores) can be based. Even when the scores are derived from physical measures of environmental change, they cannot fail to reflect the subjective judgement of the analyst; for example, if the complete loss of some biotic species is given the greatest effect score, say 10, what is the appropriate score if only one-half of the population is lost? Still greater problems are encountered when the evaluation of seriousness must explicitly take account of human aesthetic judgements, as it must when damage to landscape is one of the identified effects.

Inevitably any system which attempts to put a value on an effect – be it a price or an impact ranking – will not meet the approval of everyone; it has to be accepted that people work to different value systems and no amount of technical sophistication in the assessment procedures can circumvent that fact.

IMPACT COMPARISON

The impact comparison stage in EIA involves still more subjectivity. As its name implies, it involves comparing the disparate effects of development proposals, to arrive at some 'best' or 'balanced' solution. The most simplistic of such techniques merely add up the scores reached during the impact evaluation stage to find the project which, in aggregate, is least damaging. Clearly, this involves the assumption that a 10 scored by species loss is equal to a 10 given to all other effects. Alternatively, the different impacts can be weighted in terms of their assumed importance, which immediately raises the question of who does the weighting – the politician, the expert, or the public? Whenever such weighting procedures become buried within the technical evaluation process, there is a clear danger that issues which are essentially normative and political are removed from public debate, the trade-offs involved being made according to the value systems of the analyst. On the other hand, if the weights are set through political bargaining and public consultation, then the 'balanced' solutions will tend to be biased towards the most powerful and vocal interest groups.

It is not suggested here that environmental impact analysis is useless. All efforts to improve the level of environmental information, promote a better understanding of cause–effect relationships and increase our awareness of the costs of conventional development strategies help shift the balance of public and, more important, administrative opinion towards a more sensitive use of environmental resources. However, it gives a far too inflated idea of the importance of EIA to claim that it is 'potentially the most exciting and challenging device for measuring and balancing incommensurables that has yet appeared' (O'Riordan, 1976, p. 199). Incommensurables are just that; no techniques of rational assessment can balance away conflicts which arise from the incompatible objectives of different interest groups.

PARTICIPATORY ENVIRONMENTAL NEGOTIATION: THE WAY FORWARD?

Scientific rationality and political legitimacy

Cost–benefit analysis, environmental impact assessment and similar evaluatory techniques are only tools to inform the decision process. They are all products of the 'scientific' approach to planning, which is predicated on the notion that better administrative systems, more data, improved data handling facilities and more rigorous appraisal methodologies will yield balanced, rational and efficient decisions. In this search for rationality, the 'experts' in government agencies or the courts were meant to exercise their professional judgements, insulated from, and untainted by, the political process; they were to be detached, neutral arbitrators of the public interest. However, it has become increasingly clear that the public (or at least vocal elements within it) was not prepared to rely on experts to assess the competing claims over the use of natural resources.

Conflict did not simply go away because the responsible authorities were required to employ particular evaluation techniques, take account of a wider set of variables, and have regard for the views of affected parties. In fact conflict was often exacerbated. The greater amounts of information generated during the assessment process made the trade-offs more explicit; it was easier to see what would be gained and lost by a policy change or a development programme (Susskind, 1982). The scope for subjectivity, inherent in cost–benefit analysis or environmental evaluation techniques, meant that it was relatively simple for interest groups to challenge decisions that did not please them on the grounds that the assessment was 'defective'. And the judicial or quasi-judicial mechanisms usually adopted to review the evidence pushed the affected parties into adversorial positions, presenting their cases in extreme terms in the battle for victory (Harter, 1982). Attempts to give more scientific credibility to the land-use planning and pollution control systems thus did nothing to enhance the political legitimacy of the decision process. Rather the reverse, the public had learnt to be increasingly sceptical about the neutrality of expert decision-makers.

It has already been argued that disputes over the use of renewable resources are basically about who gets what and when. Such distributional conflicts could not be 'depoliticized' by pretending that they could be settled by rational, value-free scientific assessment. As Carpenter and Kennedy (1980, p. 67) point out, 'efforts to solve environmental problems in terms of purely technical criteria often cause more conflicts than they resolve. Ways to incorporate personal concerns and relationship problems into the development of a conflict management strategy' had to be found. A considerable body of opinion has long held the view that confidence will only be restored in the environmental planning system if the public participate in the decision process. Without participatory democracy, decisions would not be seen to be fair and just and their legitimacy would continue to be challenged.

Public participation

The participation idea assumed the status of a planning fetish during the late 1960s, and in most of the advanced western democracies land-use planning and environmental legislation introduced some measure of public consultation. However, experience of its practice soon revealed that it would not provide any general panacea. The costs and difficulties encountered in ensuring effective involvement by all sections of the community were formidable, and the selective participation by vocal, powerful and well-organized interest groups had major equity implications. Moreover the *forms* of participation normally employed tended to increase not diminish conflict.

Nowhere was this clearer than in the United States. The National Environmental Policy Act, and other environmental legislation enacted at the same period, allowed interest groups to receive information, present their views, and dispute the evidence presented by developers or regulatory agencies, but did not permit them to participate in the final decision. In other words, the participation fell into Arnstein's (1969) tokenism category and did not confer any decision-making power on the public. As interested parties exercised their rights of challenge, so the courts were beseiged with environmental suits; some decisions were delayed for years and the demand arose for new conflict resolution procedures. What emerged from this demand were the concepts of conflict management and environmental mediation. Instead of costly, cumbersome and protracted adversorial confrontation, resource-use conflicts were to be resolved by negotiation and collaboration. This was to be achieved by extending the level of public involvement into true participation at all stages of the decision process, from the definition of the issues to the final decision.

Environmental mediation

The mediation idea was a simple one, at least on paper, and already had a well-established track record, particularly in the fields of labour and race relations. All the various parties in a dispute were to be brought together on a voluntary basis in face to face negotiations 'to thrash out a consensus on the policy to be followed' (Harter, 1982, p. 80). These negotiations were to be facilitated and orchestrated by trained and neutral mediators, but the mediator would have no authority to impose a settlement (Cormick, 1980). Ideally, negotiation would lead to accommodation and reconciliation. The parties involved would gain a better understanding of their respective needs and concerns; collaborative analysis of the problems would generate a wider and more creative range of alternative solutions; and, above all, consensus and legitimate decisions would emerge. Even the most fervent proponents of mediation acknowledge that such ideal outcomes will emerge in only a limited range of situations, but 'at the very least, it is worth a try' (Harter, 1982, p. 84).

Extensive experience of the operation of environmental mediation has now been gained, mostly, but not exclusively, in North America (Bingham, 1981; Haussman, 1981; RESOLVE, 1982 to date[6]; Talbot, 1983). Predictably the results of the various mediation efforts have been mixed. Some have undoubtedly led to the acceptable resolution of long-running controversial disputes. Others have made a promising beginning at conflict avoidance by bringing polarized interest groups together in a dialogue over possible policy directions, alternative regulatory strategies, and over project siting and design. Still others have merely produced stalemate or the refusal of a key interest group to actually adhere to a compromise agreement. The variable response in minor part reflected the differential skills of the mediator, but more crucially it was a function of the nature of the dispute and of the interested parties.

As Cormick (1980) (the Director of the Office of Environmental Mediation) has pointed out, there are four major and related prerequisites to effective mediation:

(1) There must be recognition by all parties of the *need* to negotiate.

"To facilitate the negotiations, all participants have agreed to refrain absolutely from any further disclosure of what may be taking place on the other side of the conference-room door."

Figure 8.3   The environmental mediation process?
Drawing by Ed Fisher; © 1982 The New Yorker Magazine, Inc.

(2) Each of the parties must have *sufficient power* or influence to bargain effectively and stop one group from taking unilateral action.

(3) The negotiators for each party must have *commitment* to the compromise agreements. This not only means that they themselves must be prepared to adhere to the final decision but that they must be able to carry with them the interest constituency which they represent.

(4) There must be some *sense of urgency* – a general recognition that some decision must be made in the near future.

Other commentators have added that successful consensus outcomes are most likely when the dispute issues are relatively well-defined, occur over fairly discrete spatial areas and involve only a limited number of different interest groups.

THE LIMITATIONS OF MEDIATION

Inevitably these conditions place severe limits on the range of environmental conflicts which mediation can successfully resolve. Quite apart from the practical problems involved in organizing effective negotiation when conflicts involve a widely diffused set of issues and interested parties, there is the more crucial question of the distribution of decision-making power. Only those who take a pluralistic view of the political system would argue that power is dispersed over the public at large, in which case there would be many conflict situations where all parties would have adequate negotiating strength. However, those working from élitist or radical perspectives would claim that in few (if any) disputes is effective power spread equally enough to allow Cormick's second prerequisite to be satisfied. In addition, many political scientists would argue that the real holders of power in society exercise it by ensuring that issues which are central to their objectives never reach the political agenda; in other words they do not become subjects for dispute and therefore do not necessitate mediation.

In practice, environmental mediation has proved most useful in site-specific disputes, *when* environmental pressure groups have the power to delay projects by court action, can generate enough media attention to embarrass the developer or the regulatory authority, or have some economic sanctions (such as withdrawal of labour or embargoes on the developer's product) to employ as bargaining cards. Environmental mediation has also been employed by planning authorities to develop land-use plans at various spatial scales, and by agencies charged with conservation or pollution regulation to explore alternative policy strategies. However, as will be shown in the next chapter, reaching agreement over the formulation of plans and policies is one matter, quite another is whether the agreed outcomes actually emerge from implementation practice.

A further critical limitation on the widespread use of mediation is that if it is effective, and the outcomes are actually adhered to, then it restricts the discretion of executive authorities and of democratically elected legislatures. For this reason alone it is likely to be greeted with hostility by professional bureaucracies, who currently have considerable autonomy and can exert a marked influence on the direction of effective policy. Not only would their freedom to react to changing socioeconomic and political circumstances be severely curtailed, but also their ability to achieve their formal mandated duties and internally established organizational objectives could be limited. Moreover there is no guarantee that the outcomes of separate mediations would be consistent, either with each other or with the political aspirations of legislators. This could create severe problems if the results of negotiations at one level of government were seen to infringe the democratic rights of other government tiers.

One final problem with the whole mediation concept which deserves mention here lies in what it could imply for distributive equity. First, when used as a conflict avoidance measure it can and has been 'used consciously and unconsciously to limit the meaningful, power-based participation of non-establishment parties in the decision-making process' (Cormick, 1980, p. 29). And second, when used to resolve manifest conflicts the equity of the procedure rests on the assumption that *all* affected interests are identified, form into clear constituencies, and have recognizable and truly representative leaders. There is a clear danger that some sections of the public will be excluded and that as a result the compromise solutions will merely redistribute the undesirable effects of resource use on to such groups.

These four fundamental and closely related limitations on effective mediation – the distribution of power, implementation practice, administrative discretion and distributive equity – form the basic subject matter of the next chapter.

NOTES

1   It is worth pointing out that these difficulties apply equally to other evaluation techniques, such as environmental impact assessment (see pp. 329–31).
2   This is in fact part of a much wider problem; when assessing the likely results of any project or policy change, assumptions will have to be made about human responses and individuals may well fail to act in the prescribed rational way assumed in the 'economic man' postulate.
3   This is a manual of recommended practices in the appraisal of river basin projects, published by the US government and devised by the Federal Inter-Agency River Basin Committee, 1950, 1958.
4   The damage cost approach is widely used in the management of natural hazards (see Penning-Rowsell and Chatterton, 1977, for a discussion of the flood alleviation case).
5   In Britain there is, as yet, no formal EIA requirement, although planning authorities have the discretion to make assessments, and a form of EIS is usually presented at public inquiries into major developments.
6   RESOLVE is a quarterly newsletter on environmental dispute resolution. It contains numerous reports on mediation cases.

9 The policy and practice of renewable resource management

THE NON-RATIONAL POLICY PROCESS: AN INTRODUCTION

Conventional theoretical discussions of the resource management process have characterized it as a rational sequential system, with a clear hierarchy of stages (Figure 9.1). The first crucial step is policy formulation. It seems only logical to decide what goals are to be achieved before attempting to devise administrative structures and regulatory techniques appropriate to the task. Once the policy goals have been established, the rational decision-maker analyses all the possible organizational arrangements, evaluates the available range of regulatory tools, investigates all the consequences of different implementation strategies and only then decides on the management system. Throughout, the search is for the optimal means of achieving specific ends, and in *ex post* evaluations operational success is measured by the extent to which outcomes conform to the policy goals.

While few would claim that actual decision-making processes conform to this theoretically optimal model, there is a strong body of opinion that suggests the resource management system *ought* to do so. The whole economic approach is strongly geared to 'rationality'; even analysts who drop the assumption that economic efficiency is the correct and only policy goal still start from the premiss that specific goals exist against which programmes and projects can be tested. Recognition that governments have multiple and often conflicting policy objectives merely increases analytical complexity but does not stop the search for the 'best' outcomes. Economists are not, of course, the only professional group to adopt an ordered rational approach as their behavioural ideal; physical scientists, architects and planners all tend to have a sequential ends–means view of their functions. The notional planning process in Britain – with structure planning establishing the broad objectives for a region, local plans constructed to conform to these objectives and then the whole package implemented by public investment and controls over private development – is a classic illustration of the influence of rationalist thinking.

Throughout the renewable resource sector the rational decision model has played an important role in government attempts to improve the quality of management systems (Richardson and Jordan, 1979). The use of cost–benefit or cost-effective techniques, the introduction of environmental impact assessments, programme planned budgeting and corporate management exercises, along with attempts to reorganize administrative systems to allow the efficient integration of

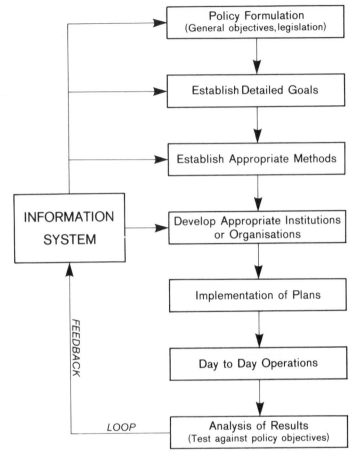

Figure 9.1   The idealized policy-making and implementation process

resource uses, are all products of the rational, ideal model of the management process.

It is often assumed that the distinct management stages mirror a hierarchy of decision-making organizations; policy being determined by the top or central tier of government and handed down to local government, or to various executive agencies, for implementation. As was seen in Chapter 5, most national governments do not have policy statements on stock resource use which are explicit and consistent enough to direct operators in the public and private sectors. This is equally the case for the renewables.

The notion that Parliaments and other legislative assemblies establish policy goals and resolve any conflict of values or disagreements over objectives has little basis in fact. It is true that legislation creates executive bodies with specific duties and lays down very general objectives, such as the maintenance of environmental quality or public health standards, the provision of adequate water supplies or the conservation of wildlife and the natural beauty of the countryside. But the real meaning of policy can only be established by considering the way the executive interprets its duties, implements and enforces specific pieces of legislation, and affords priorities to resource objectives *vis-à-vis* all other societal goals.

Neat hierarchical conceptualizations of the management process present highly misleading pictures of the meaning of policy, its loci of formulation, and of the whole nature of decision systems (Jenkins, 1978; Levitt, 1980; McGrew and Wilson, 1982). Throughout any discussion of the practice of management there is a need to distinguish the formal expressions of policy from the policies as implied by outcomes, and the ostensible decision processes from the hidden decision agendas and the covert influences on choice (Bachrach and Baratz, 1963; Lukes, 1974).

Once the idea of a rationally staged management process is discarded, analysis becomes much more complex. Policy is dynamic and is formed by actions (including the maintenance of the status quo) at all levels in the decision hierarchy from the central legislature down to the individual resource user. This means that there is no standing policy target against which the effectiveness of administrative structures, regulatory techniques or outcomes can be judged. In effect, analysts either have to adopt their own management objectives (economic efficiency, maximization of physical outputs, preservation, environmental stability, distributive equity and so forth) as the assessment criteria *or* have to make the simplistic assumption that specific policy ends can be identified from legislation, statutory duties and stated management plans. To break into the complex, and still only partially understood, process of management the latter approach will be taken here as a starting-point; in which case the key question appears to be how far are the identified policy ends met in practice? Later the nature of the key question will be changed to consider the extent to which alternative decision-models can help explain the practice of management and policy formulation.

THE IMPLEMENTATION OF FORMAL POLICY

It is now well recognized that the way policy statements are interpreted, implemented and then enforced is critical. As Anderson *et al.* (1977, p. vii) have pointed out, 'legislative goals and program impacts are fundamentally altered by the course which implementation takes'. Inevitably this course will be affected by *ex-post* changes in political, economic and social circumstances, but it can also be substantially *pre-conditioned* by three key factors: the degree of responsibility delegated to executive agencies and the amount of discretion allowed to them; the character of such agencies; and the conventional methods employed to augment resource supplies and regulate use.

It must be expected that over time effective policy will shift direction and will be implemented with varying speeds and levels of rigour in response to changing socioeconomic conditions and to altered power relations between different interest groups within an economy. Pollution or land-use planning controls may be eased to meet employment or economic growth objectives; investment in resource augmentation, conservation or pollution abatement programmes may be delayed as an anti-inflation measure; the vigour with which energy conservation or research into renewable energies are pursued may vary with political events affecting the security and price of fuels; and a whole range of controls over renewable resource use may be relaxed under pressure from powerful economic interests.

Change from the centre

In some cases such changes are introduced from the centre; departmental circulars can alter the 'advice' given to lower-tier agencies on the way legislation should be interpreted or enforced, and ministerial orders can amend or suspend regulations to meet specific needs. Noise limits around Heathrow Airport, for instance, were waived to accommodate Concorde, while sections of the UK Clean Air Acts of 1956 and 1968 have been suspended periodically to alleviate problems caused by temporary shortages of smokeless fuel. Moreover, central government can affect policy shifts in a much less explicit way through controls over the level, cost and allocation of investment funds, the imposition of spending or borrowing limits, restrictions on price or local tax increases and reductions in agency staffing levels. In this process changes in the *relative* financial, staffing and political positions of agencies may be as important as the absolute level of resources at their command. As was seen in earlier chapters, governments have various policy objectives which frequently conflict and these are juggled to reflect political and economic priorities. In this juggling process the formal expression of policy may remain unaltered but its effective nature changes.

THE CONTROL OF POLLUTION ACT EXAMPLE

The implementation in the United Kingdom of the Control of Pollution Act 1974 (COPA) affords an excellent example of the way apparent legislative intentions can be significantly modified by implementation practice. In fact the potential for an effective policy shift was explicitly incorporated into the legislation itself, by the agreement that its provisions should lie dormant until activated by commencement orders and amplified by detailed regulations. The rationale for this was that 'the uncertain economic climate' necessitated a gradual implementation process. So, as Levitt comments,

> an important feature of the implementation of the legislation was determined at this stage . . . namely that the policy covering public expenditure was a greater priority than the policy dealing with pollution control, and that the rate of progress would be determined by central government. (Levitt, 1980, pp. 33–4).

Commencement orders for parts III and IV of the Act, concerning noise and air pollution, were made relatively quickly and theoretically came into force on 1 January 1976, although in practice effective implementation of many of the sections was delayed a further twelve months or so until the necessary regulations were actually issued (UK Department of the Environment, 1978). However, for these parts of the Act it was largely a question of giving discretionary powers to executive bodies or of replacing extant legislation. Also important was the fact that they required minimal public expenditure. Part III on noise, for example, to a considerable extent merely replaced provisions in the Noise Abatement Act 1960, except for giving local authorities the power (but not the duty) to create noise abatement zones. Similarly, part IV, dealing with atmospheric pollution, adds relatively minor control powers to those already available under the Public Health and Clean Air Acts. The only potentially important new power was the provision that local authorities *could* monitor industrial emissions and publicize their findings *after* consultations with local interests and *subject to the power of the Secretary of State to prescribe how, and to what extent, they may seek and publish information.* In practice this power, once again only discretionary, was so hedged with provisos that it is difficult to employ.

Parts I (waste disposal on land) and II (water pollution) have both been involved in a ten-year saga of delays in activation. County councils (England) and district councils (Scotland and Wales) were given several new duties connected with the disposal of waste on land from domestic, commercial and industrial sources, including hazardous and toxic waste products. Each was required to survey the volume of waste generated within their areas and to evaluate the adequacy of local disposal facilities. In addition, they were empowered to license land-fill sites and treatment facilities and required to produce waste disposal plans. Sections setting out these duties technically came into force in mid-1976 but, as will be shown later, this means relatively little in terms of improved disposal since most local authorities have not actually produced, let alone implemented, their disposal plans. Other sections of part I remain unactivated, including an important requirement obliging waste disposal authorities to make arrangements for the disposal of waste which 'becomes situated'[1] in their areas, and to collect and dispose of certain difficult (often toxic) controlled wastes.[2]

Still less progress has been made with the highly controversial part II of the Act. This extends the discharge licensing system already operating for inland rivers to coastal waters, estuaries and groundwater; requires the regional water authorities (RWAs) to maintain a public register of dischargers giving details of their compliance record; and makes it possible for members of the public to prosecute the polluters and the control authorities for failure to comply with licence standards. Not surprisingly, industrial interests have compaigned vigorously against activation. The CBI regarded the act as a 'busybody's charter' and has opposed in particular the clauses providing for greater public involvement and freedom of information (*ENDS* Report 103, August 1983, 106, November 1983; Pearce, 1982, 1984). Moreover, implementation had major implications for public expenditure since inadequate sewage treatment facilities were – and still are – a major cause of river and coastal pollution.

The Jeger Report, *Taken for Granted* (1970), clearly exposed the legacy of neglect which the RWAs were to inherit from local authorities when they took over responsibility for sewage treatment in 1974. In a by no means atypical description of conditions, the Yorkshire Regional Water Authority found that the

Huddersfield works 'had to be seen to be believed'. Toxic industrial waste, untreatable with the installed technology, was destroying the works capability of dealing with normal sewage and effluent. The Severn–Trent authority reported that 64 per cent of all treated sewage in their area failed to conform to the required consent conditions, while in the Thames area 50 per cent was found to be unsatisfactory. This story of non-compliance was repeated throughout the country (Tinker, 1975; Porter, 1978; Parker and Penning-Rowsell, 1980). Massive capital expenditure was, therefore, required to bring inland plant up to standard. Further sums would be needed to provide treatment and improved outfall sewers in coastal areas if bacteriological counts on popular bathing beaches were to be reduced in line with EEC directives. Not only was such expenditure opposed by local ratepayers, but it would have been incompatible with national anti-inflation measures and public spending limits. Powerful public and private economic interests, therefore, combined to delay implementation.

In 1974 it had been planned to phase-in part II by the end of 1976, but a year later it was announced that there would be an indefinite postponement. Three years elapsed before it was announced that implementation would be completed in 1979. However, the general election of that year brought a new government and an apparent need to re-examine the financial implications of the provisions. Only in 1982 did the whole question emerge from review, with the announcement in February that the sections would be implemented with the 'maximum use of transitional provisions' between 1983 and 1986. In all probability the sole reason for this move was to ensure that the United Kingdom was formally (if not in substance) meeting its obligations under several EEC directives on water quality (Haigh, 1984).

The reality of policy became only too clear in August 1982, when a Department of the Environment consultative document made a farce out of the legislative intent by indicating that all discharges not already subject to controls under existing legislation would be granted either exemption orders or deemed consents, so allowing a continuation of discharges at present quality levels (*ENDS* Report 92, September 1982). In August 1983 the implementation of part II officially began but, as expected from the consultative document, the first (and at the time of writing the only) provision was the order exempting all currently uncontrolled discharges from the new controls, except those which require authorization under EEC directives; these include discharges from firms using mercury, cadmium, arsenic, dieldrin and titanium dioxide and from sewage works affecting areas covered by the 1976 bathing water and the 1979 shellfish waters directives. But all the discharges which have not been granted exemption will be eligible for an 'authorization' or 'deemed consent'! In this way, the EEC requirement that they must come under control has been formally fulfilled without doing anything to actually reduce the pollutant loads of potentially dangerous substances. In these circumstances Mrs Thatcher's enthusiastic claim made before COPA was passed that it was 'likely to have a greater, more lasting impact on the quality of life in many parts of Britain than most other measures' appears somewhat hollow (Pearce, 1984, p. 10).

Delegation of responsibility

The divergence between paper policy statements and policy in practice is not, of course, solely caused by shifts in central government objectives. It can in major part arise from decisions (or non-decisions) made lower down the hierarchy of executive agencies.

Whenever policy or plan-making is a delegated responsibility, as it often is, considerable implementation delays can occur because the agencies take years to produce their statements. In the meantime, it is 'business as usual' irrespective of the legislative intent. One example will suffice.[3]

As has just been seen, under part I of COPA local authorities were required to survey their areas and produce waste disposal plans. This was regarded as an essential prerequisite for the forward provision of safe disposal facilities, the reduction in dangers from inadequate land-fill sites and, in particular, the improvement of disposal arrangements for hazardous wastes. However, in March 1984 Lord Bellwin, the government's environment spokesman in the House of Lords, revealed that only nine of England's forty-six county councils had fully completed plans, although a further seven were with the Secretary of State who was considering objections from other counties. Twenty-three of the counties had not yet even produced draft documents to issue for public comment and important high waste-producing areas such as Manchester, West Yorkshire and Lancashire were among those without plans (Figure 9.2). In Scotland and Wales, where the lowest tier of government, the district councils, are the disposal authorities, the situation was even worse (but see note[4]): only three out of fifty-six Scottish districts had issued drafts for public consultation and nothing at all had emerged from any Welsh authority (*House of Lords Written Answers*, 15 March 1984, cols 966–8).

To some extent this lack of progress reflects the squeeze on local government spending and, more recently, the moves to abolish the metropolitan counties. But it is also a product of the conflicts of interest which inevitably arise over the siting of unsavoury and potentially hazardous facilities. Some authorities are reluctant to plan the development of sites because they fear that they will be used to dispose of waste generated outside their areas (few councils wish to find a massive site, such as Pitsea, in Essex, on their doorstep). Others have genuine difficulties in finding sites with suitable geological and hydrological conditions, and still others fear the political controversy that will almost inevitably be generated by any disposal plan (Levitt, 1980).

Policy can be effectively changed by executive authorities even when they are required to enforce highly specific legislation which, for example, seeks to bar the use or disposal of particular pollutants or lays down exact environmental quality standards. Such explicit legislation is somewhat unusual in Britain but it occurs widely in other jurisdictions; Ogus cites the examples of water and air quality standards in Japan and the atmospheric quality limits issued under the American Clean Air legislation (see Richardson *et al.*, 1982). Total enforcement is, in practice, unattainable, and the level of actual enforcement will largely be left to the discretion of the responsible agency.

Figure 9.2 Hazardous waste plans: a picture of non- and partial compliance with COPA, 1974

In some cases the legislation may well require measures which are technologically unfeasible. A classic example here was the requirement in the UK Railway Act 1845 that 'engines consume their own smoke' and a more recent illustration is afforded by the US Clean Water Act 1972 referred to earlier. More commonly the technology to permit enforcement exists but the economic, social or political side-effects prove unacceptable; old factories may, for instance, have to be entirely rebuilt or close down completely. In addition, the task of enforcement may be beyond the financial and manpower resources of the appointed agency. Even without allowing for what Richardson *et al.* (1982) call 'improper and/or irrelevant' factors which influence individual enforcement decisions, it is easy to see reasons why the executive may not follow the policies implied by specific legislation. In some cases this may mean turning a blind eye when minor or occasional infringements occur, but in others it may result in the effective mothballing of the legislation.

One good illustration of the latter is the UK Asbestos Industry Regulations of 1931, the history of which has been summarized by Sandbach (1982). The regulations required firms to prevent the escape of *all* asbestos dust into the air inhaled by the workforce, either by the use of exhaust ventilation or the provision of breathing apparatus and protective clothing. This total ban proved unworkable and unenforceable. The crux of the matter was that the cost of attempting to adhere to the no-dust requirement would have put many producers out of business and the Factory Inspectorate, responsible for enforcement, in effect made the policy decision that financial and employment interests outweighed the health risks involved in permitting unlawful operations (Jenkins, 1978). However, it would be naïve to blame the Inspectorate for its interpretation of political priorities; it was too inadequately staffed and funded to maintain close scrutiny over all premises within its purview, and the effect of prosecuting offenders was limited when minimal fines were the result. A successful prosecution in 1964 of the Bermondsey factory owned by Central Asbestos Ltd produced a derisory fine of £170 with 50p costs (Sandbach, 1982, p. 148). It is significant that in 1969 the legislation moved more in line with reality when new regulations introduced dust standards based on what was attainable by the most diligent factories.

Executive agencies have even greater effective policy-making powers when they are given general delegated responsibilities, rather than being required to enforce specific measures or perform tightly defined duties. In Britain, as in many other countries, the principle of delegation is, 'not so much well understood . . . but quite simply taken for granted' (Haigh, 1984, p. 10). Agencies not only have considerable flexibility to interpret what their responsibilities mean, but can develop their own strategies to meet them, set their own implementation timescales and decide their own enforcement practices. As a result, what emerges as practice may appear far removed from the apparent policy intent of the legislature. Numerous examples could be taken to illustrate this point: Carson (1971) has shown the way the UK Factory Inspectorate effectively makes new policy through the interpretation of its duties and its enforcement practice; Walker and Storper (1978) have analysed the non-enforcement of the US Clean

Air Act; Richardson *et al.* (1982) and Hawkins (1983) have assessed the role of discretion and enforcement in water pollution control in England and Wales; and the MacEwens (1982) have clearly shown that national parks policy can be influenced by the priorities and practices of the management agencies.

THE IMPORTANCE OF AGENCY CHARACTER

The common delegation of responsibility means that the character of the executive authorities can be a key variable in determining effective policy (see p. 349). Although very much a generalization, public agencies charged with the development and production of specific renewable resource goods have typically interpreted their functions in technological provision-fix terms. Water supply undertakings, land drainage boards, forestry authorities, irrigation corps and coastal protection agencies tend not to see the political and allocative nature of their activities. Specific physical needs are identified and performance is measured using technical or output criteria (Hirschleifer *et al.*, 1960; Parker and Penning-Rowsell, 1980). The technostructures of such bodies are supported by projects: any reduction in output activity threatens jobs and promotion opportunities and tends to reduce the power and influence of the bureaucracy.

On the other hand, rather different interpretations of responsibilities tend to occur either when provision of renewable resource services conflicts with developmental interests (inside or outside the agency) or when such services are seen as peripheral to the main functions of the management authority. In both these situations non-provision or inadequate provision are the typical results. A classic illustration of this concerns the so-called 'amenity clause' in the 1968 UK Countryside Act. It imposes a duty towards conservation on 'every Minister, government department and public body . . . in the exercise of their functions relating to land under any enactment'; they must '*have regard to the desirability* of conserving the natural beauty and amenity of the countryside'. As the MacEwens (1982, p. 24) have pointed out, this clause is 'no more than a verbal genuflection', of little practical importance in changing the main developmental thrust of the public bodies.

A rather similar case has occurred over the protection of rivers from water pollution. Legislation sets the regional water authorities in England and Wales two basic, very general objectives: to 'maintain and *where practicably possible* improve' river water quality, and to make a water quality plan. Most RWAs have responded by setting themselves noble but ultimately meaningless long-term objectives such as the 'restoration and protection of the Region's river water quality' (North West Regional Water Authority, 1977). Such phrases cannot be interpreted without the specification of quality parameters and without stating who or what the protection is for. As has already been seen, the quality needed to protect all species of aquatic life is not identical to that required to protect potable water standards or aesthetic and recreational interests. However, such long-range aspirations cannot be regarded as policy – the real priorities emerge much more clearly when the short-term aims are considered. In the North West Regional Water Authority (ibid., p. 39) these are summarized in the policy statement as 'first to prevent deterioration of the present situation and second, as far as capital is available and local needs exist, to improve river water quality'.

More recently, in 1983, the authority unveiled a twenty-five-year plan to accelerate the clean up of rivers, estuaries and beaches in the region, which is acknowledged to have the greatest length of seriously polluted watercourses in England and Wales (National Water Council, 1981). But this would cost some £3700 million, not including the major additional abatement expenses incurred by industry; already the RWA is warning that the plan is unlikely to be fulfilled unless it receives financial assistance (*ENDS* Report 104, September 1983). In short, improved water quality may be seen as a symbolic policy objective, and could even be merely a device designed to obtain funds from others to reduce local sewage and effluent treatment costs.

THE DUAL STATE HYPOTHESIS

To an extent the differences between agencies in the interpretation of their responsibilities may be explained by appealing to the dual state hypothesis (Saunders, 1981) and its theoretical antecedents. The distinction between the productive functions of the state (social investment) and allocative functions (social consumption) is useful conceptually and aids the understanding of different decision-making modes (Friedland *et al.*, 1977). It is argued that the former, which basically provide essential inputs into productive enterprise, have tended to become the responsibility of regional or national levels of government. As such, the decision process (mode of interest mediation) has been insulated from 'representational' inputs within technocratic organizations, but has remained open to influence by major capitalist interests through 'corporate mediation'.[5] In the words of Friedland *et al.*,

> Freed ... from partisan and popular constraints ... agencies develop external constituencies among those economic groups that have a keen interest in public policies that influence the parameters of economic growth. ... The ideology of technical planning and professionalism with which these agencies cloak themselves not only legitimates their insulation, but it also discourages any attempts at popular intervention, for it argues that what is being done is not political but technical. (Friedland *et al.*, 1977, p. 458)

On the other hand, it is asserted that social consumption policies are characteristically the responsibility of local government and are, therefore, subject to 'competitive political struggles waged at the local level' (Saunders, 1981, p. 260).

No one could doubt that resource *development* functions have been centralized to a considerable extent, but the simple delineations suggested by the dual state hypothesis do not do justice to the complexity which characterizes the administrative arrangements for most renewable resources. Numerous examples can be cited where functions which are wholly or in large measure related to social consumption are the responsibility of the higher tiers of government. In strongly centralized countries, such as France, Finland and Israel, local government often plays a minimal role in renewable resource provision, allocation or protection.

There are also cases such as air quality control where all tiers of government have some responsibilities, and where the functional division of powers between them rarely follows the neat delineation into those providing forms of social investment and those concerned with social consumption (see pp. 362–71 for a discussion of the situation in the United States and Britain).

Further complexities arise when an agency responsible for a single resource provides productive inputs and social services. In England and Wales, for example, the protection of river water quality, water supply provision and sewage treatment (all of which serve social investment and consumption functions), land drainage (investment) and water-based recreation (consumption) are all the responsibility of regional technocratic bodies. The public have few points of access to, and a very limited impact on, the decision-making processes within such agencies.

It could be argued that incorporation of both sets of functions within one body, isolated from the demands of non-corporated interests, serves to reduce the 'tension' between the requirements of capital accumulation and social needs. Conflicts of interest are not, therefore, mediated by locating the different functions and decision-making modes of the state at different levels of government, but become buried by the mysticism which surrounds the technical expert. Although as much of a generalization as the dual state hypothesis itself, there has been a tendency for *all* substantive aspects of environmental resource management to migrate away from local control. The widespread establishment of Environmental Protection Agencies is one manifestation of this trend. It would be naïve to attribute all such moves to the state's role as a protector of capital; in part they also serve to meet (or some would say diffuse) the demands of environmental groups. Once established, central- and regional-level agencies are undoubtedly subject to corporatist pressures. But this should not obscure the fact that the agencies develop an internal, professionally dominated, logic which critically affects the way they interpret their functions, and by no means all professional groups support the expansion of private sector production and its profitability.

DISCRETIONARY POWERS

The delegation of policy-making functions to executive authorities is still more marked when they are not given clear responsibilities, but discretionary powers to take specific measures, with no requirement that these are actually used. Once again this is an exceptionally common strategy in most countries and does have considerable advantages (at least in theory) in allowing flexibility of response to meet spatial variations in the need for intervention and the preferences of different community groups.

Discretionary powers achieve nothing if the agency chooses to ignore them or has neither the financial nor manpower resources to employ them. With one or two notable exceptions, Newcastle upon Tyne for instance, few local authorities in the United Kingdom have used their new powers to create noise abatement zones in order to make a positive contribution to the reduction of neighbourhood noise. Three factors in particular explain the reluctance of many authorities to embark on the process at all. First, if zones are to be created they must be monitored and policed, but no new resources have been allocated for this. Second, within the zones reductions in noise levels can only be required where this appears 'practicable at reasonable cost'. This in itself raises potential legal difficulties over the meaning of the phrase, and, furthermore, if firms are prosecuted for exceeding the required levels they can use as a defence the argument that they were using the 'best practicable means' of abatement. And finally, there are also political considerations; zone introduction is invariably opposed by those economic interests affected by increased abatement costs. Where zones have been established it is by no means clear that they have always been designated in areas of greatest 'need', as measured either in terms of noise levels or the number of affected individuals, or that they are much more than a cosmetic exercise, designated but unmonitored and uncontrolled. It is a relatively painless exercise to establish a zone in an already quiet area, with perhaps one or two potential high-noise sources, but quite another matter to embark on the task in high-density areas of mixed commercial, industrial and housing developments.

POLICY AS PRACTICE

The fact that so much legislative activity takes the form of delegating duties or powers and giving implementation and enforcement discretion to executive authorities, means that three related factors crucially influence the way overt public policy intentions are translated by practice: (1) the character of such authorities; (2) the forms of intervention they employ; and (3) their internal decision-making processes. Administrative character is used here merely as shorthand for the jurisdictional responsibilities of agencies – expressed spatially and functionally – their size and range of professional expertise and their internal administrative divisions. Likewise the term 'form of intervention' is used as a catch-all to include the whole range of policy instruments which could be employed (consultative mechanisms, legal regulation, economic instruments, codes of practice, supply augmentation technologies, and so forth; see Levitt, 1980). The same apparent policy on, say, pollution control would change its effective nature if it were to be implemented by local government authorities, a centralized regulatory agency, a multifunctional body which has to 'internalize externalities', or by the adherence of the polluters to 'gentlemen's agreements'. In just the same way, the mechanisms used to implement policy may affect both the level of enforcement and its distributive outcomes. The forms of intervention employed and the character of administrative systems are closely interrelated; particular types of agency habitually employ specific mechanisms, and the policy tools perceived to be appropriate can influence the areal and functional jurisdiction of the authority, its professional competence and its internal structure.

The role of 'administrative character'

In Chapter 6 the notion was discussed that problems of renewable resource misuse and depletion are products of the incomplete ownership and control rights which are so characteristic of common property resources. From such an analytical perspective, rational management necessitates the removal of 'free' access rights and the 'internalization of externalities' through private expropriation or, more usually, by state intervention. The state would need to adopt one of three strategies: (1) take all ownership and usage rights and manage the resource directly; (2) take full ownership rights but allocate usage rights up to some 'natural' limit; or (3) establish a public agency with sufficient control powers to curb private users.

NATURAL ENVIRONMENTAL REGIONS

Assuming that the objective of the management exercise is to optimize the resource *per se*, it is common to encounter the idea that 'natural' (physically determined) environmental divisions should set the appropriate jurisdictional limits for public authorities. The argument is that interdependencies within the ecosystem necessitate a holistic, integrated approach, with agencies capable of managing all uses and users of a single resource within specific environmental regions. Only then would it be possible to implement rational resource development and allocation programmes to maximize welfare returns and minimize use conflict (Fox and Craine, 1962; Cunha *et al.*, 1977). Such notions do have considerable appeal and have had a significant influence on administrative arrangements in some countries, particularly in the creation of water management bodies. There is little doubt, for instance, that more cost-effective flood control measures are feasible when the responsible body can control land-use and run-off regimes in the whole catchment. Likewise pollution problems tend to be exacerbated when sewage authorities can minimize their removal costs by passing them downstream into neighbouring jurisdictions.

But the natural region approach is not without its practical and conceptual problems (Coate and Bonner, 1975). For many renewables it is by no means clear what the 'natural' environmental unit is. At one level of analysis the global ecosystem is one interconnected system of interdependent cycles, and it is always a somewhat arbitrary decision to break into the chain of relationships to define an areal and functional unit. Areal delimitation is perhaps simplest in the case of surface water; the resource is confined to distinct channels or bodies, and the catchment represents a well recognized and clearly demarcated physical unit. But even here difficulties arise over where to draw the boundary between land-based and coastal systems. Should the catchment authority control the estuaries and coastal areas affected by river water discharge, or should a coast-based authority manage the coastal zone as an integrated whole? Furthermore, although ground and surface water systems are interconnected, ground water 'regions' do not always coincide with the surface catchments. Therefore, it is not always clear which region should be taken as the management unit. Additional difficulties arise when distinct physical units fail to provide meaningful administrative divisions in terms of the distribution of resource users. Human decisions create dependencies between catchments which are not there naturally. Interbasin transfers occur when demands exceed the capacity of specific catchments or when settlements are developed on watersheds, drawing supplies from one catchment and discharging waste water to the other; Birmingham's (England) position between the Severn and Trent catchments is a good example of this. In such circumstances the appropriate management unit can no longer be defined in purely physical terms but must recognize the spatial distribution of human settlements. Similarly, there are clearly some catchments which are far too large to provide practicable administrative divisions.

When renewables such as air, coastal zones, marine fisheries or migratory birds are the subject of concern, the delimitation of natural regions is even more problematic. Although 'airsheds' have been recognized, in the United States for instance, these are in no sense physical entities; rather they are functional regions defined by the distribution of pollution sources and an administratively determined set of the affected public. For all forms of flora and fauna which depend on land, water and air for their survival the question arises whether management of the resource can be distinct from the management of the complete habitat. Agencies charged with protecting birds could legitimately claim that agricultural land management must come under their jurisdiction, while forestry boards could argue that they need to control industrial air pollution.

INTERDEPENDENCIES AND MEDIA INTEGRATION

Another, but closely related, difficulty arises when there are several different sets of interdependency relationships. Which, then, should determine the functional responsibilities of agencies? In the pollution control case, for example, the laws of thermodynamics determine that unless residuals are recycled and completely reused, waste products must go somewhere in the environmental system. Therefore, it can be argued that one body should control all disposal media in order to be able to develop the least environmentally damaging disposal options. The UK Royal Commission on Environmental Pollution (1976) used this argument when recommending the creation of a unified pollution inspectorate, which would control all forms of pollution arising from particular technological processes. While recognizing that pollution can be transferred from one media to another by modifications to production and treatment processes, it is not clear that this relationship between land, water and air is more significant than the need to manage water as a multipurpose resource, or the need to integrate waste disposal on land with the rest of the land-use planning system. Given the complex interrelationships which exist between *all* physical, economic and social systems, the fact that a particular link exists cannot in itself justify integrated management; judgements have to be made about the relative importance of different types of linkage and essentially arbitrary functional divisions made between organizations.

As there is no necessary coincidence between 'natural' land, water and air regions, the media integration arguments conflict with the demands that all uses of a single resource must come under the jurisdiction of one management agency. Moreover, the media integration approach can be used to justify very different scales of pollution control agencies. The Royal Commission, by concentrating on waste-producing processes, which could occur anywhere in the country, saw the need for a national body, staffed by 'expert' engineers and industrial chemists capable of dealing with the technological problems of control. However, MacNeill (1971) employed the same media integration arguments, but this time from the perspective of the public affected by concentrations of polluting activities, to advocate a local management scale, with each urban area treated as an interdependent ecological system.

When the resource is a multipurpose one, the rational management approach requires that one agency takes responsibility for all forms of use. But merely putting the different management functions under one roof neither guarantees co-ordination nor removes conflicts of interest – they simply occur within rather than between organizations. As a result, allocation decisions tend to become less open to scrutiny, and, depending on the internal structure of the authority, its professional dominance and its openness to particular interest groups, may consistently favour one or two functions over the others. Although a generalization, in agencies dominated by 'output' professions (engineers, foresters, and so on) duties which involve conservation, aesthetics and recreation tend to have a low status and become subordinate to what are perceived to be their main responsibilities. A related difficulty in multipurpose authorities is the so-called 'poacher turned gamekeeper' problem, where to fulfil one function the agency must control its own operations. The regional water authorities in England and Wales, for instance, are responsible for river pollution control and yet are major polluters through their sewage disposal function; while in Wales and Scotland the district councils must control waste disposal on land but are themselves the chief users of land-fill sites. In such situations there is always the danger that pressure to minimize the costs of disposal will result in a relaxation of quality standards.

RESOURCE PRODUCTIVITY OR DEMOCRATIC PARTICIPATION?

The final and, in many ways, the most fundamental difficulty with the environmental integration approach to management units lies in the assumption that the policy objective is to maximize the productivity of the resource, measured either in physical output or economic efficiency terms. It is deeply rooted in the rationalist technocentric ideology, which views pollution control and other resource management issues as physical problems, requiring expert scientific attention and amenable to objective analysis and 'correct' solutions. Throughout the essentially political and distributional character of the problems is denied, and effective policy formulation is entrusted to supposedly neutral, professionally competent bodies[6] (Nelkin, 1977). Almost inevitably these are large-scale organizations, regional or national in extent, and increasingly remote from democratic forms of control.

The administrative history of water management in England and Wales provides a classic illustration of the way the search for organizational efficiency produces a divorce between resource managers and the general public that they are meant to serve. Before 1945, water supply and sewage disposal were essentially local government services, allied to the protection of public health, while both the quality and availability of ground and surface water resources were uncontrolled, except through common law. This situation undoubtedly resulted in: reduced standards of service; the loss of integration and scale economies; inefficient piecemeal development of supply sources; and steadily worsening problems of river pollution and groundwater depletion.

Recognition of these deficiencies set in train a gradual process of administrative change (Parker and Penning-Rowsell, 1980). The common law rights to abstract supplies and discharge wastes were removed; the Minister of Health was given the power to require the amalgamation of neighbouring supply undertakings; and authorities responsible for co-ordinating water management at the river basin level were established. River Boards were created in 1948, with responsibility for land drainage, fisheries, navigation and, after 1951, river water quality. But a more significant step towards integration was taken in 1963 with the creation of twenty-nine River Authorities, nominally controlling all water-users within their areas, including local supply undertakings. Just ten years later the Water Act 1973 swept away over 1400 separate public bodies responsible for some aspect of water management and created in their stead ten multipurpose agencies, the Regional Water Authorities (Figure 9.3).[7]

At first, the RWAs preserved the pretence, if not the reality, of democratic representative control since a majority of authority members were delegates from local government. The effectiveness of such non-expert members in controlling the technocratic bureaucracies of the authorities was always dubious and, in 1983, even the pretence of democratic accountability vanished when elected members were replaced by small management boards appointed by central government. Industrial and agricultural interests are well represented on such boards, which can meet in closed session free from all public scrutiny.

It is not the intention to imply here that the management of water resources would have been any 'better' left to local, democratically elected and possibly more accountable agencies. In fact many of the financial problems currently faced by the RWAs are the historical legacy of local self-interest and decades of neglect of unglamorous, non-vote-catching expenditure on sewage treatment and the repair of water reticulation and sewerage systems. It is estimated that sums of £15,000–£30,000 million (at 1978 prices) are required to replace old, leaky, corroded mains and sewers (National Water Council, 1978).

What is suggested, however, is that administrative units appropriate from a 'rational' resource management viewpoint tend to be incompatible with meaningful public involvement in decision-making. Analysts who see renewable resource issues from a public participation perspective reject the 'nanny knows best' approach to planning, stressing instead the need for management units with a high degree of political accountability and created at spatial scales which facilitate public involvement in establishing policy objectives and implementation procedures. There is no way that catchment-based authorities, which invariably cut across recognized political divisions, can effectively meet the public access criterion. And this is true of any region designed to take into account the major interrelationships between elements within the physical system. In summary, then, there is no one axiomatically correct structure of management agencies. There will always be difficulties in reconciling the needs for integration and a

Figure 9.3   Regional water authorities in England and Wales

high input of technical expertise with public accountability and public determination of policy priorities.

ESTABLISHING MANAGEMENT UNITS IN PRACTICE

There are some examples of wholesale administrative reorganization, the creation of the RWAs is one such case, but normally the development of management authorities has been a much more *ad hoc*, incremental affair. It is relatively unusual for governments to approach the question of organizational structure from a holistic rational assessment of policy needs, the characteristics of particular resources and the nature of the demands placed upon them. Rather they react to specific problems. As dissatisfaction with existing administrations has grown, and the perceived need for further controls or the demand for additional resource services has emerged before the public eye, so a plethora of semi-autonomous agencies, government departments, co-ordinating commit-tees and advisory commissions have been established to deal with them (or to give at least the appearance of action). Alternatively, for administrative ease and to minimize political conflict, new duties have been tagged on to existing authorities, or the jurisdictional boundaries between them have been adjusted. Typically, then, management structures have evolved rather than been purposefully created. Inevitably they vary significantly from country to country, reflecting among other things differences in government style, constitutional arrange-ments, legal systems and the historic development of resource concerns.

Generalizing greatly, it is possible to identify five different types of functional body which have been developed over time in most advanced countries:

(1) *Basic collective consumption services* – commonly the first resource services to come within the public domain were those closely related to health standards (domestic water supply, sewerage and refuse collection). Traditionally these were (and in many countries still are) viewed as the legitimate function of local government.

(2) *Resource development agencies* – particularly since the beginning of the twentieth century government bodies have been created to produce specific resource commodities (irrigation water, hydroelectric power, land drainage and forestry). Administratively these take three basic forms: (a) project-specific public corporations (e.g. the Tennessee Valley Authority, in the United States, and the Snowy River Authority, in Australia) – these are modelled on private corporations and have a high degree of autonomy; (b) government utilities or bureaux (e.g. Bureau of Reclamation, in the United States, the Ontario Hydroelectric Power Commission, in Canada, the Rivers and Water Supply Commission, in Victoria, Australia, and the Forestry Commission, in the United Kingdom) – these report to government but again have a large amount of autonomy; (c) government departments (e.g. the Engineering and Water Supply Department, South Australia, and public works departments in many local or provincial administrations).

(3) *Land-use regulation and planning authorities* – these fall into two categories: semi-autonomous and resource-specific, such as national parks, wilderness area or wetland management boards; and general, where renewable resource regulation and environmental quality management are integrated within the overall planning functions of all tiers of government.

(4) *Pollution control and conservation agencies* – once again these are of two types: resource- or problem-specific (environmental protection agencies, river purification boards, hazardous waste inspectorates, product safety agencies, land and historic buildings conservation councils); and general, where pollution control is viewed as part of the environmental health or planning functions of local and regional governments.

(5) *Hybrid or multipurpose authorities* – some of these are the products of the search for 'rational' integrated management but most have evolved as bodies created for other purposes and have gradually accumulated functions. To

give one example: in Australia the Melbourne and Metropolitan Board of Works was originally established to provide collective consumption services throughout an urban area which had long outgrown its local administrative boundaries. It rapidly took on all the characteristics of a resource development utility, viewing its functions in technological terms and becoming increasingly divorced from local democratic control and the policy priorities of the public it was created to serve. Both its powerful entrenched position and the absence of other authorities with jurisdiction over the whole built-up area combined to make it appear the only appropriate land-use planning agency; it was, therefore, charged in 1949 with the duty of devising the first metropolitan plan (Logan and Ogilvy, 1981).

Commonly, administrative change has served to enlarge the cast of players, creating new agencies and responsibilities, while retaining the bulk of the old ones. Once formed, organizations have proved remarkably durable (Kaufman, 1975). Dissatisfaction with them has rarely resulted in their total abolition, rather new, higher-tier authorities are created as controls, or advisory and co-ordinating committees are provided to improve performance. As Perlman (1976, p. 76) puts it: 'Bureaux are piled on bureaux and the bureaucracy grows on. From the resulting mountain it is soon impossible to unearth the molehill that started it all.'

Consequently, the whole process of administrative improvement is often self-defeating, producing fragmented organizational structures, the diffusion of responsibility and leaving considerable scope for individuals and agencies to pursue ends which have never been explicitly considered by the legislature (Bowman, 1979; Cawson, 1977). It should, however, be stressed that in two senses change in administrative systems tends to have only a marginal impact on policy outcomes. First, governments work within the prevailing political and economic system; the basic institutions – legal, governmental, social and economic – remain largely unaltered, so providing a powerful inbuilt bias to conservatism (Sharkansky, 1970). Second, change in jurisdictional boundaries and duties normally leaves the pool of staff substantially intact, so perpetuating conventional attitudes and modes of behaviour. Even when wholesale reorganization takes place, the 'ring fence' approach (restricting the jobs to those displaced) to recruitment for the new agencies is a major force keeping real change under considerable control. This was very much the pattern when the RWAs were established in England and Wales.

The role of 'intervention form'

The forms of intervention employed by resource agencies can be subdivided into three broad categories: techniques of resource provision; measures to regulate or influence user behaviour; and instruments to inform and control the policy-making and implementation practices of the executive. This last set will be considered later in the chapter, as their use and effectiveness cannot be viewed in isolation from the political decision-making environment.

TECHNOLOGICAL BIAS IN RESOURCE PROVISION

Techniques of resource provision are relevant for all authorities responsible for basic resource services and commodities, as well as for agencies charged with protecting the public from resource hazards, such as floods or coastal erosion. They could also be employed by pollution control and conservation authorities, although as was seen in Chapter 7, these have traditionally restricted their activities to curbing the actions of private users rather than engaging in flow augmentation.[8] The rational model of management demands that all possible alternative methods of achieving policy goals, or of solving specific problems, should be evaluated. But research has shown consistently that the range of provision techniques actually employed by resource agencies comprise only a small subset of the total possible options.

Work by White (1942), Kates (1962), Burton et al. (1978) and many of their followers has clearly demonstrated that managers perceive a very restricted range of adjustments to floods and other hazard events. The duty to minimize flood losses has been translated into the need to regulate rivers, and the methods then perceived to be appropriate are the construction of holding dams or protective embankments, the removal of natural flow obstructions, channel straightening and canalization. Non-engineering methods of flow regulation, such as increasing the tree cover in catchments to reduce run-off rates, are rarely included in the traditional package of perceived techniques. Similarly, in North America at least, there was considerable neglect of options which allowed floods to occur but reduced their damaging effects (land zoning, changing cropping patterns, redesigning buildings to minimize ground-floor usage, the provision of temporary barriers such as sandbags or shutters, and so on). In Britain, where a more comprehensive land-use planning system had been established, land zoning was a considered option within urban areas but the other damage-reducing measures have played a minor role in official thinking.

Appraisals of the water supply industry in most parts of the developed world likewise have concluded that the conventional package of provision measures contains only a limited range of options (Hirschleifer et al., 1960; Holcomb Research Institute, 1976; Rees, 1976, 1982). Authorities have typically seen it as their duty to meet all exogenously determined demands, and have sought to operate with considerable supply safety margins.[9] Neither the use of economic efficiency measures to define appropriate provision levels or safety standards, nor the use of demand management techniques, have traditionally played a significant role in water resource planning; although, in recent years in the United Kingdom at least, pressure from central government to reduce spending and meet rate of return on investment targets, has pushed the industry towards more economic (or accounting) performance criteria. Similarly, in parts of the United States, the cost of supply augmentation schemes and conflict over the allocation of available supplies has increased the popularity of demand management strategies.

Within the technological provision-fix options most attention has been focused on new supply augmentation schemes; little consideration has been given to reducing the need for 'new' water by making more efficient use of existing supplies or by reclaiming and reusing waste-water flows. One important potential method of increasing the effective yield from existing capacity is to reduce the major losses which are still occurring from the distribution system. In Britain what is euphemistically known as 'unaccounted for' water takes on average 30 per cent of total supplies, while in parts of Scotland it appears to approach 50 per cent. High loss levels have also been recorded in North America and Australia. Although, for at least forty years, calls have been made to increase expenditure on pipeline maintenance and leakage detection in order to postpone the need for major supply extensions, these have had relatively little impact. The panel investigating the 1949 water crisis in New York City, for instance, found that an expansion of the leakage detection and repair programme was likely to yield 50 per cent of the supply which would become available through the next large-scale dam project (the Cannonsville scheme) at a cost, per million gallons, of well under 1 per cent of the Cannonsville costs; and yet the recommended programme of waste detection and elimination was never adopted (Hirschleifer *et al.*, 1960).

This story has now been repeated many times; pipeline maintenance and leakage control still remain at the low-status end of the supply and distribution function and nowhere are they seen as fully fledged supply augmentation options. In Hirschleifer's view this 'is a reflection of the "monument syndrome". Commemorative bronze plaques can be prominently displayed on a dam but not on a repaired leak' (ibid., p. 366). While this is far too simplistic an explanation, it does contain an element of truth (Pearce, 1982; Rees, 1982).

Opportunities to increase the efficiency in use of existing capacity also exist by reducing the quantity of potable, often expensively treated, water currently being used for garden watering, industrial processing and toilet flushing, all of which could be quite adequately served from lower-quality sources (Wijntjes, 1974). It would be possible to reduce the non-essential use of high-quality water by developing dual quality systems. Although there are a few dual supply systems in operation – in Hong Kong, for instance – they are rarely incorporated as an option in the routine evaluation of capacity extension schemes (Baumann and Dworkin, 1975; Rees, 1981b).

The potential for reusing water has similarly been neglected. Reuse could occur either within the consumer's property or at the municipal level through waste-water renovation. Despite the successful operation of a 'white water/grey water' scheme in Sweden, whereby storage tanks are installed in new houses to allow used bath water to be recycled for toilet flushing, it is rare for such conservation technologies to be considered elsewhere. In the same way, although the potential for municipal waste-water renovation was officially recognized by the federal government in the United States over a decade ago, examples of its implementation remain rarities (US National Water Commission, 1973). It is claimed that the quality of treated waste water would be significantly higher than the tap water presently available in many communities, but managerial resistance to reuse remains high (Holcomb Research Institute, 1976). The most common reason for rejecting waste-water renovation as a supply option is the assumption that the public would reject it, but remarkably little study of consumer attitudes has ever been undertaken (Johnson, 1971; Baumann and Kasperson, 1974). As it is, consumers have unknowingly accepted a form of reuse, since the practice of using the rivers as the supply transfer medium inevitably involves downstream users consuming the waste-water flows from upstream parts of the catchment.

Water supply and flood control engineers are not, of course, the only professional groups to suffer from 'technological tunnel vision'; assessments of forest management (Steele, 1972), the control of soil erosion, salinity and desertification (Warren and Maizels, 1977) and coastal erosion (Clark, 1978) have all recorded a tendency for management to perceive a severely restricted range of provision options. No single explanation of this bias towards techno-logical provision-based solutions is likely to be found. In part it results from the historic evolution of practice and the professional training of managers (see p. 346), and in part it reflects the aggrandisement aims of bureaucracies (p. 373); and it may also arise from the tendency for most of these agencies to be concerned with social investment policies that contribute to private sector profitability. In other words, there is a strong alliance between the professional interest in construction and the private interest in expanding production.

The narrowness of option range may well have the effect of increasing supply costs in developed nations and inevitably it produces a complex pattern of cross-subsidy flows to those with most to gain from the construction bias. Water consumers demanding supplies during peak periods, the occupants of flood-plains, and farmers owning land amenable to drainage improvements are all effectively subsidized by others. But as long as provision keeps broadly in line with requirements, the technology-fix strategies do not produce acute shortages of the resource commodity or service itself. However, when the same accepted 'good practices' are transferred into the less affluent nations, then acute short-ages of capital prevent more than a fraction of the population receiving the products of the standard provision technologies (Koeningsburger et al., 1971).

FORMS OF REGULATION

In Chapter 7 it was argued that agencies charged with controlling pollution and reducing resource depletion have shown a clear bias towards what Levitt (1980) has called 'written instruments' of regulatory control, with a comparative neglect of both economic instruments to influence user behaviour and measures to increase the effective yield of environmental systems. Standing in marked contrast to the supply-oriented policies of the developmental agencies, the regulatory approach is negative; fixed natural limits are perceived and, nominally at least, users must be controlled to operate within such limits. The seeds of failure are sown immediately. Shortages (of assimilative capacity, access or supplies) are inevitable if controls are rigidly enforced and no attempts are made either to use price incentives to choke off demand, or to increase environmental capacity. On the other hand, less strict enforcement leaves pollution and resource depletion as problems warranting attention.

Since the level of enforcement is largely a matter of administrative discretion, the way officials perceive the importance of particular pollution or conservation problems and the weight they give to environmental issues *vis-à-vis* other economic, social and political problems must both be critical factors affecting enforcement practice. One interesting finding of a recent international study of environmental attitudes strongly suggests that public officials consistently regard pollution and depletion problems less seriously than do the public at large, and give them low priority in relation to other policy objectives (Milbrath, 1975; Cotgrove, 1982) (see Table 9.1). This immediately implies that there is some inbuilt bias in the regulatory system against strict enforcement when this conflicts with economic development goals.

Written regulatory instruments can be grouped broadly into three classes:

(a) *'Open' expressions of law* (Acts of Parliament, local government by-laws, orders, rules and regulations published by statutory authorities and, of importance now in Europe, EEC Directives).
(b) *Licence conditions, standards, or requirements* (e.g. that 'best practicable means' of pollution abatement are used); these all have a legal status but are

Table 9.1 Environmental attitudes

(a) *Percentage giving very urgent ranking to environmental issues*

	Environ-mentalists	Trade union officials	Indus-trialists	Public officials	General public
Noise	42.2	54.1	30.7	38.7	39.2
Air pollution	62.8	66.1	26.4	33.6	67.0
Water pollution	66.1	69.7	51.4	41.6	75.7
Overpopulation	65.9	35.5	38.1	29.0	52.9
Solid waste disposal	55.5	47.1	40.3	21.5	50.2
Toxic waste disposal	75.2	82.7	59.0	50.0	80.5
Nuclear waste	84.3	82.8	58.2	43.6	81.1
Townscape	82.2	65.3	53.3	54.0	67.2
Depletion of resources	90.3	77.1	65.2	62.5	80.7
Energy	87.3	74.3	73.0	57.9	78.1

(b) *Relative importance of objectives for government action*

	Environ-mentalists	Trade union officials	Indus-trialists	Public officials	General public
Welfare	4	2	4	4	2
Law and order	5	3	2	3	3
Economy	2	1	1	1	1
Energy	1	4	3	5	4
Environment	3	5	6	6	5
Foreign affairs	6	6	5	2	6

Source: Cotgrove, 1982, pp. 16–17.

enforceable only by the control agencies, and in Britain are commonly only known to them and the regulated enterprise.

(c) *Voluntary agreements* (EEC Resolutions and Recommendations, advice in government circulars, codes of practice, informal management agreements); these vary greatly in practical effect; some border on written instructions with known penalties for non-compliance, others are little more than statements of 'gentlemanly' behaviour.[10]

The relative importance of these three regulatory measures varies enormously from country to country, with a distinction between societies which, according to O'Riordan (1976), adopt either consensus or adversary approaches to decision-making. In adversorial countries (the United States, Japan, West Germany, for example) the control procedures are 'open'; legal regulation and judicial mechanisms play a key role in the management process. On the other hand, the consensus approach, found in Britain, the Commonwealth countries, Sweden and France, relies much more on consultation, compromise and co-operation between the regulators and the regulated (Lundqvist, 1973a, 1973b). Negotiated licences or standards and voluntary agreements, therefore, play a much more prominent part in management. While there is certainly a noticeable difference in regulatory style in these two sets of countries, any attempt to characterize entire management systems is bound to be rough and ready. Judicial approaches are utilized widely in consensus societies, and corporatist strategies undoubtedly operate behind the open regulatory façade in adversorial societies.

Moreover, it can be argued that the style of government and the particular regulatory tools employed have only a limited impact in terms of reduced pollution or resource depletion, although they can affect both the costs of control and the distribution of the costs and benefits between interest groups. The fact of direct regulation, in itself, implies that the control agencies must develop a relationship with the regulated in order to ensure their co-operation in the whole control process. In consensus systems it is explicitly recognized that trade-offs will have to occur between desirable environmental improvements and the socioeconomic costs involved. From the outset negotiation and compromise are employed as modes of interest mediation; the economic interests of the regulated are considered throughout the bargaining process which fixes the direction of policy and its application to individual firms. In some cases, such as Sweden, the bargaining is reasonably open to public scrutiny (Lundqvist, 1973a; Richardson, 1979) while in others, such as Britain, the public is not only excluded from the process itself but is left in virtual ignorance about the nature of the resulting compromises. An adversorial system, where controls are unilaterally imposed and judicially enforced, does not remove the need for trade-offs between interest groups; negotiation and compromise will still occur, only the bargaining mechanisms change somewhat.

The fact that *all* regulatory authorities (in all types of society) have to maintain close links with the regulated has led to the suggestion that over time they tend to be 'captured' by the interests they are meant to control, to the detriment of the environmental quality or conservation policy objectives, which led to their creation in the first place. This seems particularly likely when the agency is organized as a technical unit, regionally or nationally administered, and divorced from contact with the public it theoretically is designed to serve. The need for trade-offs and the likelihood of capture both suggest that the substantive outcomes of resource management and regulation will not differ markedly between the adversarial and consensus styles of government, as the following case examples of the control of industrial air pollution in the United States and the United Kingdom will serve to illustrate.

INDUSTRIAL AIR POLLUTION

Control in an adversorial system: the United States

The United States usually is taken as an archetype adversarial system, with considerable freedom of information and open to pluralistic pressures from the many environmental interest groups. However, it is doubtful whether the resulting pollution control policy is any more effective, efficient or equitable than it is in much more conciliatory, closed systems. The recent history of industrial air pollution control provides an interesting example of the way in which a regulatory system can become almost impossibly complex, with little pay-off in terms of pollution reduction, and prey to manipulation by powerful vested interests.

Until the late 1960s the federal government had little authority over industrial sources of air pollution; the states and local government were the standard-setting and enforcement authorities. As a result, controls were patchy, and in many areas authorities were reluctant to adopt control standards which, it was thought, would affect adversely existing firms or would deter new industrial developments. In the well-established regulatory tradition the solution was seen to be a new administrative tier, giving greater central direction 'to insure that air pollution problems will in the future, be controlled in a systematic way' (US Department of Health, Education, and Welfare, 1969). The Air Quality Act 1967 empowered the Department of Health, Education, and Welfare to take individual polluters to court if the local control agencies failed to do so, designate air quality control regions, develop maximum permitted concentration standards for important pollutants and specify recommended control technologies. But the states retained the power to set individual emission standards and to enforce them. Just three years later the Clean Air Act Amendments were deemed necessary 'to provide for a more effective program to improve the quality of the Nation's air' (Public Law 91 - 1783, December 1970).

The Environmental Protection Agency was required to set uniform national primary and secondary ambient standards for all 'criteria' pollutants.[11] These in effect dictate the overall goals of the control policy. Primary standards were meant to be the concentration levels which would safeguard the health of even the most sensitive groups in the population with an adequate margin of safety, while secondary standards should protect 'public welfare'. However, in the absence of good data on dose–response relationships, even the primary standards were matters of judgement (see p. 319). Uniform national standards set for individual contaminants, regardless of topography, climate or settlement patterns, could, at best, only be loosely related to individual health conditions. Moreover, the whole ambient standard-setting approach assumes that a 'safe', known and fixed concentration threshold exists; this is simply not the case. Not only do safe concentration levels vary markedly between individuals, but also for many pollutants the effects of exposure over long periods of time to even very low concentrations is not known with any degree of certainty. For example, the US National Commission on Air Quality (1981, p. 3.1–3) has stated that 'for pollutants that cause or are suspected of causing cancer, it is currently assumed that any level of exposure may be harmful'. In such circumstances the requirement for adequate margins of safety would seem to imply zero ambient standards, an unrealistic economic and technical proposition.

A further difficulty with even the primary standards lies in the definition of public health. Is the concern only with premature deaths or increasingly serious morbidity rates, or does it include minor throat irritations and smarting eyes? Under the law all health risks, however insignificant, appear to be treated equally (Ferris and Speizer, 1981). If defining public health is difficult, defining public welfare is virtually impossible. The term could be used to justify the strictest standards but, in practice, the EPA has 'solved' the problem by making the secondary and primary standards identical, except for particulate matter.

In view of the lack of precise health data there is ample scope to interpret the legislation to produce very different environmental quality outcomes, and few commentators doubt that the national standards were the result of bargaining and compromise. The EPA was under pressure from the extremely active environmental lobby and from states already operating stringent standards to impose low maximum concentrations. However, also highly influential was the National Industrial Pollution Control Council, established by President Nixon to ensure that industry was properly consulted on pollution control policy at the highest level of government (Steck, 1975). It was composed of representatives from major industrial corporations and trade associations, and according to Lundqvist (1973a), it reviewed EPA's proposals for standards before these were made available to the public. Yet another source of pressure were state and local authorities in the older industrialized parts of the country, who were also consulted pre-promulgation of the standards. These, by and large, were opposed to a strict interpretation of the legislation since this would inevitably make their task of meeting the standards much more onerous and would affect industrial concerns within their areas of jurisdiction. In the end the national standards were 'set at an intermediate level without consideration of the propagated margin of safety' (Bach, 1972, p. 105).

Responsibility for controlling individual emissions to achieve these nationally determined standards was split between the EPA and the states. Each state had to submit an implementation plan which described in detail its regulatory strategy to bring all airshed areas into compliance with the standards by 1982 or 1987, depending on the particular 'criteria' pollutant. All plans must go through both state and federal administrative processes, including full public consultation, and any revision, however minor, has to run the same administrative gauntlet. As Crandall (1983, p. 11) states: 'the bureaucratic tangle created by such a process in the name of public access is a potent force for maintaining the regulatory status quo'. In any airshed not already attaining the standards, *existing* polluters were to be brought under greater control, with the notion of 'reasonably available technology' being used to establish the new emission standards. Details of these stricter controls must be incorporated within the state plan to convince the EPA that 'reasonable progress toward attainment' would result. However, although the agency could disapprove plans which did not provide adequate control standards, it has no effective means of actually compelling a state to enforce a plan (ibid.).

While individual emission standards for established polluters are a state matter, all new sources are required to meet national performance standards, established by the EPA and applicable everywhere in the country irrespective of local conditions. These are based on the 'best system of emission reduction which . . . has been adequately demonstrated' (BACT), except in non-attainment airsheds where yet another criterion, 'the lowest achievable emission rate' (LAER), is the basis of standard setting – in practice, there is little difference between the two criteria. Not only was the workload required to establish these different performance standards immense, but also there was considerable confusion over the meaning of a new source. Does it apply only to entirely new factories? Or can it include the installation of a new or modified piece of equipment into existing plant? If so, does it then mean that even a minor inplant change can bring the whole factory under the stricter new source standards? The EPA attempted to solve this dilemma by allowing modifications, providing that the total emissions from the factory did not increase as a result, but this was overruled in the courts on the ground that it would allow firms to avoid installing the best pollution control technology in non-attainment areas (*ASARCO* v. *EPA*, 578 F.2d 319, D.C. Cir 1978). This still unresolved confusion, and the risk that any change will make the firm liable to the stricter national standards, is clearly a powerful force for inertia.

From the outset Congress biased the entire control system in favour of established industrial concerns by allowing them either to continue existing emission practices in areas meeting the ambient standards or requiring them to employ only 'reasonably available technology' in non-attainment areas. Crandall has argued, for example, that in the steel industry incremental control costs for new works exceed $2000 per tonne of suspended particulate matter abated – 'for many installations the cost of these new source controls is so high that the replacement of older facilities is seriously discouraged' (ibid., p. 40). Similarly, Math Tech (1979) has shown that the annual total control costs for nitrogen oxides in the Chicago airshed would increase from $44 million under the 'reasonable' technology criterion to $254 million under BACT. A number of commentators (Pashigian, 1982; Crandall, 1983) have suggested that this bias has little to do with environmental objectives, but arises from the powerful lobby which supports any measures which could restrict the outmigration of firms from the older industrial areas of the north and east and increase production costs in the rapidly developing 'sun belt' states.

As was seen earlier, pollution control policies in effect are determined by enforcement practices and enforcement necessitates monitoring. However, data on actual ambient standards 'are seriously deficient because EPA has not succeeded in establishing and maintaining a thorough monitoring network. Monitors are operated by state and local governments . . . and . . . have not been operated consistently over time or across geographical jurisdictions' (Crandall, 1983, p. 26). In 1977 the EPA reported that only 524 ozone, 456 carbon monoxide, 933 nitrogen dioxide and 1355 sulphur dioxide monitors were providing valid annual data in the whole of the country. Since these had to cover 247 separate airsheds, the number of observations in each was clearly too limited to make any meaningful statements about overall achievement levels. Even greater deficiencies occur in monitoring individual emissions. Only 5 per cent of all major pollution sources were subject to continuous stack tests, 38 per cent were monitored by occasional site inspection (often with advance warning) and the rest were subject to 'voluntary certification', which means polluters test their own premises and submit unaudited reports that they were complying with all relevant standards (US Council on Environmental Quality, 1980). It would be a supreme act of faith to conclude that such a monitoring system can reveal much about actual compliance levels.

Compliance levels are also dependent on the ability of control agencies to impose significant penalties on firms found to be contravening their performance standards. However, although the public has the right to bring industrialists and the EPA to court for non-compliance, until 1977 the agency itself 'lacked the ability to levy substantial civil penalties . . . polluters who faced major outlays for control had a strong incentive to delay compliance or even to postpone it indefinitely' (Crandall, 1983, p. 99). While the courts have imposed criminal penalties in some circumstances, enforcement officers in the United States, as in other countries, have been reluctant to use criminal sanctions in the vast majority of cases. In particular, it is extremely difficult politically to bring proceedings against industries known to be suffering financial problems, in which case heavy penalties could result in plant closure and local unemployment. Both the EPA and the state enforcement agencies have, in practice, exercised considerable discretion in exempting firms from their performance standards. For example, many firms in the steel industry have been granted exemptions and only 13 per cent of integrated steel mills were in compliance with their standards in 1980. Since 1977 the EPA has been allowed to levy delayed compliance fees, but the complexity of the procedures[12] invites legal challenge and, in any case, such fees do nothing to solve the problem of firms claiming to be unable to afford either significant penalties or the costs of compliance: 'It seems unlikely that the penalty program will have much effect. The program is so complicated that it merely adds to the backlog of legal challenges with which future administrators must deal' (ibid., p. 106).

From admittedly patchy data it has been shown that the rate of decline in the ambient concentrations of some 'criteria' pollutants was actually faster before the federal control system was instituted; SO_2 concentrations, for instance, appear to have fallen by 11.3 per cent per annum on average between 1964 and 1971, and by only 4.6 per cent from 1972 to 1980. Similarly, particulate matter declined 2.3 per cent per annum between 1960 and 1971, but only by 0.6 per cent thereafter. Given the oil crisis and the slower rate of economic growth after 1973, it would perhaps be expected that pollution levels should have declined more rapidly in the later time period than in the previous decade, irrespective of control policy. However, there are two possible reasons why this did not occur. First, some states were in fact implementing more stringent quality standards than those introduced under the federal system, and although they had the option to retain their more strict requirements, in practice they came under considerable pressure from local economic interests to conform to the national standards. Second, in any period when fears over fuel scarcity and economic growth rates come to dominate political debate, industrial lobby groups have stronger leverage, and changes in enforcement and compliance levels are allowed to occur while maintaining the paper policy standards.

The EPA has long recognized that sections of the 1970 legislation were unworkable. States where existing sources of pollution – even controlled by 'reasonable' standards – were exceeding the national ambient standards, had to deny permission for all new industrial developments, including modifications to established plant. If strictly enforced, this would inevitably have major repercussions on local economies, particularly in the older industrial and most polluted parts of the country. This led the agency to tentatively introduce the so-called offset and bubble policies (see p. 288), which were given limited legal status by the Clean Air Act Amendments 1977 and are still being tested for their precise meaning in the courts. Although these changes are significant as a step towards marketable pollution rights, the 1977 legislation included two amendments which had a more immediate impact.

First, all airsheds already complying with national ambient air standards became subject to a prevention of significant deterioration rule. Pollution from new sources was only allowed to increase by a small fixed amount each year, irrespective of its resulting effect on ambient standards. The allowed increments were particularly small in class 1 areas, which comprised the national parks and wilderness areas. On paper the motive was to stop the deterioration of air quality in clean areas, to avoid producing what Bach (1972) has called 'a nation of equal pollutees', all enjoying the standards of the lowest common denominator. However, it seems more likely that the real motive force was economic interests. The strongest supporters of the amendment were those in the densely populated non-achievement areas of the north and east; the desire to reduce the outmigration of industry from these areas and provide additional barriers to development in the sun belt appeared to be the real policy objective (Pashigian, 1982; Crandall, 1983). Economic interests were also behind the second important amendment. In the case of fossil-fuel-fired stationary sources, performance standards gave way to a specified minimum percentage reduction in emissions from the best available technology. This was basically designed to prevent power utilities in the western states from using low-sulphur coal and so minimizing their expenditure on pollution control technology. An unholy alliance between environmentalists and eastern coal producers combined to ensure that full scrubbing equipment had to be installed in all plant, a measure which it has been estimated will add 11–12 per cent to electricity prices in the south-west (Crandall, 1983).

It is difficult to avoid concluding from this case example that the major effect of the regulatory process has been to develop a massive, cumbersome and expensive bureaucratic machine, supposedly open to public comment but increasingly hidden behind a mesh of procedural complexity and prey to manipulation by economic interests.

Control in a consensus system: the United Kingdom

On paper the British regulatory system stands in marked contrast to that of the United States. It is largely closed to public scrutiny and is based on the premiss that goodwill and co-operation rather than coercion and prosecution are the best means of achieving environmental improvement. Control responsibilities are delegated in part to two national level inspectorates: the Industrial Air Pollution Inspectorate in England and Wales (it is now part of the Health and Safety Executive, but formerly and still popularly known as the Alkali Inspectorate), and the Industrial Pollution Inspectorate in Scotland. These bodies work under the Alkali Acts to control the most highly polluting industrial processes, which have been 'scheduled' by the Secretary of State. Today over sixty processes, used in over 4000 separate operations in some 2500 plants, come under their jurisdiction. Any unscheduled industrial processes, along with domestic and commercial sources of smoke, grit and dust, are however the responsibility of local government. District councils exercise their powers under quite separate legislation, the Clean Air and Public Health Acts, and more indirectly through their planning and development control functions.

The division of responsibilities between national and local bodies owes more to historic accident than to any rational assessment of a desirable regulatory structure.[13] It means that control within one plant can be split between two agencies working at quite different jurisdictional scales, employing officers with significantly different professional skills and subject to very different political pressures.

The first obvious difference between the forms of regulation used in the United Kingdom and the United States is that ambient air standards have traditionally played no role in the British control process. The regulation of individual emissions to prevent 'the escape of noxious or offensive gases' is an end in itself, rather than a means of achieving particular air quality objectives. Ambient standards have been rejected consistently on the grounds that they are impracticable, too rigid and would not allow account to be taken of varying local physical and economic conditions. They also would reduce considerably the discretion of the regulatory agencies and their freedom to negotiate emission standards. Attempts by county councils to incorporate air quality objectives into the structure planning process were rejected by central government, although some authorities, the Greater London Council, for example, have issued quality guidelines. Even the recommendation made by the UK Royal Commission on Environmental Pollution (1976) that national guidelines, with no statutory force, should be issued has not been implemented.

The only exception to this general lack of ambient standards is of very recent origin and has come through an EEC Directive on smoke and SO_2. 'Limit values', intended to protect human health and general environmental amenity, should have been met by April 1983 and must be met by 1993. There is little evidence that this Directive will make any significant difference to pollution control practice in Britain; compliance is to be achieved using existing agencies and under current legislation. The nature of the government's real intentions and commitment to air pollution control is quite clear. Local authorities have been requested to:

> order their priorities *within the general restraint on public expenditure* so as to complete any necessary extension of smoke control by 1983. Where this is not possible authorities should aim to complete any necessary programme as soon as possible after that date and at the latest by 1993. (DOE Circular 11/81, quoted in Haigh, 1984, p. 177; emphasis added)

This request has to be seen not only in the context of the limits imposed on local government spending, but also of reduced central government expenditure on clean air grants. In 1977/8 these totalled £2.59 million but in 1982/3 were down to an estimated £1.3 million; since these figures are in money terms, the real reduction in expenditure, taking inflation into account, is much more marked (*ENDS* Report 97, 1983, p. 19). It remains to be seen what will happen if local authorities fail to find the money to enable the EEC Directive to be met.

As already seen, US legislation requires established polluters to employ 'reasonably available' and new firms to use the 'best available' control technologies. In Britain the same criterion, the 'best practicable means' (BPM) of control, is applied to all firms. This imprecise term, first incorporated in the Alkali Act 1874, clearly gives the regulatory authorities considerable discretion to interpret the required level of pollution abatement. In defining 'practicable' technologies, 'regard' must be given 'to local conditions and circumstances, to the current state of technical knowledge and to the financial implications' (Control of Pollution Act 1974). But how far this regard must go and what weight should be given to the three factors remain matters of discretion. The actual BPM required for processes within particular firms and the emission standards that this implies are notionally negotiated on a case by case basis and are not available for public scrutiny. In practice, however, there is considerable uniformity in the standards for similar types of firm, irrespective of their location. As one chief inspector put it, 'It is to the trade's advantage to have uniformity of application of control measures and it would be unjust to give one works a commercial advantage over another' (Ireland, 1971).

The Inspectorate publishes, after discussions with representatives from the relevant industries, 'Notes on best practical means', which describe the desirable abatement technologies, methods of operation, monitoring requirements and a 'presumptive limit' for emissions. These notes and presumptive limits apply nationally to the scheduled processes within particular industry groups, but they are only guidelines and have no legal force in themselves. It cannot be assumed that the standards imposed on an individual firm will necessarily be the same as the presumptive limits, although in many cases they will be set at the limits in force *when the particular plant was constructed* (Frankel, 1974). Although presumptive limits are changed periodically, normally every ten to fifteen years, the fact that once a plant is operating, it is usually allowed to continue without significant modification for its economic life means that response to improved abatement technologies tends to be extremely slow.

Throughout the negotiations over BPM the essence of the Inspectorate's approach 'lies not in standing back from industry, but on the contrary in being intimately involved with it' (Royal Commission on Environmental Pollution, 1976). The philosophy behind the approach comes out clearly in the way a chief inspector described the Alkali Inspectorate's role:

> We look on our job as educating industry, persuading it, cajoling it. We achieve far more this way. The Americans take a big stick and threaten 'solve your problem'. We say to industry 'Look, lads, we've got a problem.' In this way we've got industry well and truly tamed. (Quoted in Bugler, 1972, p. 11)

Many critics have, however, argued that in reality it is industry which has the Inspectorate 'well and truly tamed', with far too much attention being paid to the financial interests of the firms and too little to the views of the affected public (Frankel, 1974; Sandbach, 1982). The controversy over the Rio Tinto Zinc smelter on Anglesey is a much-quoted case where public concern over pollution levels appears to have been accorded a very low priority. Standards of control given at the public inquiry prior to approval of the plant were promptly relaxed during its construction. The chief inspector apparently dismissed objections to the relaxation with the words:

> We do not accept that the estimates submitted by the Company at the public inquiry were binding in any way. . . . The important point . . . was that the Company should meet requirements of the Alkali Inspectorate . . . it soon became obvious that we had to change our original thoughts on prevention and dispersion *in order to keep the project viable.* . . . Industry cannot be handicapped by rigid rules. (West and Foot, 1975, p. 212; emphasis added)

The emphasis in the whole control process on co-operation rather than confrontation has meant that traditionally few firms were ever prosecuted for infringing their consent standards; many discovered infractions were never reported and, of those that were, only a small proportion resulted in court proceedings. Between 1920 and 1966, when both the Inspectorate and environmental issues were not the subject of much public or political attention, there were only two prosecutions (Frankel, 1974). Although, as Table 9.2 shows, the number of prosecutions has risen over the last few years, they are still small in relation to the number of controlled works. It should be pointed out that the recorded infractions are in fact lower today than they were in 1954, even though

Table 9.2   Alkali Inspectorate's record of infractions and prosecutions

Year	Number of scheduled works	Infractions	Successful prosecutions	Prosecutions as % of infractions
1970	1615	25	2	8
1971	1870	38	2	8
1972	2166	58	3	5
1973	2154	59	4	9
1974	2144	57	2	4
1975	2131	70	2	3
1976	2090	66	8	12
1977	2073	91	8	9
1978	2031	100	13	13
1979	1959	84	6	7
1980	1968	80	10	12
1981	1914	69	17	25
1982	1870	77	20	26

Source: Alkali Inspectorate (now Health and Safety Executive), annual reports.

the number of plants involved has quadrupled. This does not imply a major improvement in the compliance record of firms, rather it is a reflection of the vastly increased workload of individual inspectors. Today it seems unlikely that more than a fraction of total infringements are ever discovered. The Alkali Inspectorate, when at full complement, has only thirty-six fieldstaff to cover the whole of England and Wales; some of these have to travel over 200 km from their base to reach plants under their jurisdiction. Inevitably most monitoring is done by the firms themselves, with the inspectors making occasional spot checks often by appointment.

Since 1974 the Inspectorate has had the power to serve prohibition notices on firms where emissions represent a serious risk to public health, and improvement notices requiring firms to adopt the relevant BPM. Neither of these have been widely used, and are unlikely to be in the near future in view of the results of the recent ruling concerning the Phurnacite smokeless fuel plant at Aberaman, South Wales. The plant, run by a subsidiary of the National Coal Board, has been dubbed 'Britain's dirtiest factory'. In the Inspectorate's view the works had long been operating outside 'best practicable means' and, in part as a response to widespread public concern, an improvement notice was served on National Smokeless Fuels. However, the firm appealed against the notice largely on cost grounds, and an Industrial Tribunal upheld the appeal; the Inspectorate has no legal grounds on which to seek a reversal of this decision (*ENDS* Report 93, p. 3, and 96, p. 5). This case seems to make it quite clear that economic interests are dominant in establishing the realities of pollution control policy.

Undoubtedly, the British control system has the advantages of being flexible and cheap. Not only are the costs of administration relatively minor compared with those in the United States, but also there is little expenditure on court cases. In addition, the economic costs to industry of meeting the regulations appear to be much lower, with little difference in the outcomes *vis-à-vis* the reduction of pollution. However, the élitist and technocratic stance of the Inspectorates and their continued reluctance to involve the public in the bargaining process has produced much hostility and suspicion. The political nature of control decisions is ignored. Rather the whole process is viewed as a neutral technical matter. Calls for greater freedom of information have been dismissed as 'a waste of expert professional time', a 'distraction' from the 'highly technical job' which the inspectors 'are employed to do' (Ireland, 1977, p. 8). However, no technical exercise can be neutral – all decisions on pollution control standards inevitably affect the distribution of real income and welfare between different groups within society.

DECISION-MAKING BEHAVIOUR

In view of the amount of discretion given to public resource management agencies, the way they reach decisions and the factors which influence them are crucial determinants of 'policy as practice'. There is now an enormous body of work developing and justifying numerous models of decision behaviour.[14] This is no place to enter the debate on their relative heuristic value which has raged in the political science literature for over two decades. Rather the view will be taken that no one model can provide a single true explanation applicable to all decisions, made by all individuals, in all time periods, or even within one management agency. And certainly a single model cannot provide a general description of behaviour in the multiplicity of organizations involved in the renewable resource sector.

Three distinct types of model – procedural rationality, organizational process and political bargaining (Allison, 1971; Hall, 1980; McGrew and Wilson, 1982) – can be identified, all of which offer some partial insights into the processes involved, the factors influencing choice and the likely implications. All suggest that the search for substantive rationality, implicit in attempts to devise integrated management structures and objective tools of policy and project analysis, are likely to have a limited practical effect.

Procedural rationality

Following largely on the work of H. A. Simon (1947, 1955) and Lindblom (1959), various models of *bounded* or *procedural* rationality and of *incremental* decision-making have been put forward.[15] Although there has been much debate over the relative merits of Simon's bounded rationality and Lindblom's incrementalism, they primarily diverge over what the management system *ought* to be, and are remarkably similar in their description of existing practices (Richardson and Jordan, 1979; Smith and May, 1980; Carley, 1981). It is their descriptive similarities which are of interest here. First, they both stress that decision-makers can only be rational within the bounds set by their skills, knowledge and habitual modes of thought. Second, management goals are set subjectively, being determined by an individual's value system, range of experience and knowledge. Moreover, these goals are not static. In Simon's formulation if normal practice fails to meet a goal then expectations are lowered; whereas Lindblom sees the decision-maker 'muddling through' solutions, redefining the goals along the way. Third, only a narrow range of problem solutions, regulatory tools or operating procedures are ever evaluated, these once again being determined by the individual's training, areas of interest and conventional modes of operation. Fourth, no effort is made to find the 'best' solution; rather a 'satisfactory' solution will be accepted and this may well involve ignoring any possible consequences which occur outside the individual's, or the agency's, sphere of interest. Fifth, under conditions of uncertainty, decision-makers tend to be risk-averse and will resort to conventional or habit choices where possible, so following given professional codes of conduct, established rules-of-thumb or normal agency practice. And, finally, in the Lindblom formulation, the 'science of muddling through' involves avoiding conflict, seeking agreement between groups and using compromise.

There is now a considerable body of evidence suggesting that the behavioural descriptions contained in the Simon–Lindblom models are relevant to at least some renewable resource agencies. The dominance of engineers and other physical scientists has tended to mean that management goals have been expressed through physical criteria, only a limited range of intervention techniques have been employed and that standard procedures or 'codes of practice' have come to dominate agency thinking. Such management biases are rarely confined to the agencies themselves. Since officials also provide advice to higher administrative tiers and legislators, the same professional attitudes are instrumental in defining the problems to be solved and in devising the appropriate administrative arrangements. When resource problems are defined physically (shortage of water, the need for coastal protection, or increased timber production), technology provides the obvious solutions and it appears rational to create 'expert' agencies, with spatial and functional boundaries determined by the resource rather than the public being served. In the same way, if environmental quality is viewed as a pollution control problem, then once again treatment technologies rather than planning strategies become the accepted management tools. Furthermore, professional perceptions of the problems, and of appropriate levels of service, also help frame the attitudes of the general public. In the water supply case, for example, consumers in most developed countries have been taught to expect a fully piped service, with water of a uniformly high quality, available in virtually limitless quantities at all times and for all purposes. Present per capita consumptions have come to be regarded as a basic necessity and attempts to curb usage resisted. In this way, the professional bias is reinforced by public expectations.

Bureaucratic decision-making

Whereas incrementalism and procedural rationality attempt to describe individual behaviour, organizational theorists have suggested that the organizational process itself fundamentally changes the nature of the decisions which emerge from agencies. Three major factors are used to explain why this should be so.

First, once individuals become part of a bureaucracy they acquire goals or interests distinct from those of their professional independent selves and quite separate from those of their political masters or the general public (Downs, 1967). These are of two types. One set of goals is concerned with maintaining or enhancing the organization as a whole, including increasing its size or the budget (Perlman, 1976), scoring points over other bureaucracies, ensuring its long-term survival and developing its influence, prestige and indispensability (Downs, 1967). The other set concerns the individual's need to enhance or protect his position within the organization; this set ensures all allegiance to the bureaucratic goals and includes avoiding conflict with superiors, minimizing responsibility for risky decisions, finding evidence to support the 'agency line', and so forth. As Downs puts it, 'bureaucratic officials, like all other agents in society, are significantly – though not solely – motivated by their own self interests' (ibid. p. 2).

Second, bureaucracies endeavour to retain a monopoly over information and then utilize this to ensure that their own interests are protected. By the judicial selection of evidence, agencies can help form public opinion and manipulate decisions by legislative bodies, commissions of inquiry and ministers. And third, organizations are coalitions of interest groups; internal horse-trading and compromise rather than the rational evaluation of evidence will characterize final decisions.

There is certainly some evidence suggesting that renewable resource agencies exhibit the traits claimed by analysts of bureaucracies. Some have undoubtedly been extremely successful empire builders; the Corps of Engineers and the Environmental Protection Agency are just two US authorities which have been put into this category. Others have clearly engaged in interbureaucracy warfare to maintain their power and range of responsibilities.

One classic example of the way in which bureaucratic infighting can thwart apparent legislative intent is the successful operation by established agencies to emasculate the Environmental Protection Authority in Victoria, Australia. It began life as a 1970 election pledge to create an independent authority able to draft protection programmes for all environmental media, license all waste dischargers, and with sweeping enforcement powers. The Act which established the authority gave it, on paper, considerable power to control the operation of other state bodies. It could, for instance, ban the issue of building permits and so effectively prevent land subdivision in environmentally sensitive areas. Likewise, it could refuse licences for sewage discharge into rivers and coastal waters, thus forcing the Melbourne Board of Works and local authorities to improve their long-neglected treatment facilities. Moreover, powers traditionally held by other state bodies and by local government were transferred to the new authority. Moves to contain the EPA, however, began even before the

Act was passed; despite statements in the Legislative Council that it would be independent of any ministry, reporting directly to the relevant ministers, this never happened. First, it was placed under the Department of State Development, and then in 1972 it was moved into the low-status Conservation Ministry, a body with very limited powers to conserve anything since it had no control over the Forests Commission, the Agriculture and Mines Departments, or the Rivers and Water Supply Commission.

Less than two years after its formation, the EPA chairman was complaining that staff were not being recruited; whole sections, including the library and the accounts office, were moved without consultation from the EPA to the ministry; and that underfunding was preventing the authority from fulfilling its responsibilities (in 1972–3 it received only 60 per cent of its budget estimate, and in 1973–4 it managed only 55 per cent). In 1974 the complaining chairman was sacked, so ending all pretence of independence: 'It had become prey to the empire-building tendencies of other government agencies, blighted by miserly funding, and cowed into acting out a role for public political consumption' (Russ and Tanner, 1978, p. 17).

It is also undoubtedly valid to suggest that many resource agencies have achieved and used their considerable monopoly over information to pursue their conventional operating practices, with few effective checks on their activities. Various methods have been used in an attempt to curb agency independence. They fall into three broad, but interrelated, categories: requirements to undertake economic, environmental, public participation or corporate planning exercises; some form of public, judicial or parliamentary examination; and democratic control through elected governing boards or councils. None of these mechanisms are particularly effective ways to regulate a professionally dominated bureaucracy, with firmly entrenched goals and working practices.

During the earlier discussion of cost–benefit analysis it was argued that the technique could be, and indeed clearly had been, employed to legitimize decisions already made on other grounds. Numerous commentators have suggested that environmental impact analyses and public participation or mediation exercises have likewise been manipulated to justify past project choices, rather than used to seek advice for improving projects (Ophuls, 1977; Fairfax, 1978; King, 1978; Schnaiberg, 1980). The techniques are thus 'captured' to serve the dominant developmental interests of the agencies (Culhane, 1974; Friesema and Culhane, 1976).

Some renewable resource authorities and the professional bodies representing their employees have apparently welcomed analytical or participatory exercises, which on paper at least should curb their independence. All such requirements can justify staff recruitment and increased budgets, create the appearance of efficiency, environmental concern and openness to public views, act to diffuse political demands, and yet need have minimal effect on outcomes. The use by the much-criticized US Corps of Engineers of public consultation procedures has, for example, been seen as part of a defensive posture to reduce public and political hostility to its operations and thus ensure its long-term survival. More recently the support given to the environmental mediation concept by the US Council on

Environmental Quality and other environmental agencies threatened by the Reagan Administration could be interpreted as a role-justifying exercise. In other cases it has been claimed that agencies employ such exercises to 'mobilize allies from a diverse . . . constituency to ensure renewal of their legislative mandate and funding'[16] (Friedland *et al.*, 1977, p. 458), and to 'legitimize state intervention' (Cawson, 1978, p. 348).

The effectiveness of having democratically elected members on the governing bodies is almost inevitably limited when the agency task is defined in technical terms (Weber, 1947). Politicians, with little or no knowledge of operating technologies and the range of intervention measures which could be employed, have largely to accept the expert advice given them. In the water supply case, for example, alternative supply methods and demand reduction techniques have rarely been offered to council members as management options; traditional modes of operation have, therefore, simply been accepted as the only feasible methods (Rees, 1975). The reality of the situation is clearly revealed in a statement made by a director of one of the English regional water authorities; board meetings were described as 'merely exercises, the outcomes of which are foregone conclusions. In practice, the members have to accept the officer's recommendations on all technical matters and the function of meetings is to endorse decisions already made at the officer level' (personal communication, November 1977).

It is doubtful whether non-expert elected members fare much better in other technically oriented resource management authorities. Of significance is the fact that even at local government level, environmental pressure groups have sought much greater contact with officers rather than with councillors (Darke and Walker, 1977). As Lowe and Goyder (1983) point out, this is in part a reflection of the increasing complexity of planning procedures which has shifted authority away from elected members towards the chief planning officers and their staff. These issues will be considered in more detail in the next section which considers power, influence and the role of the public in the policy-making process.

Political bargaining processes

A large group of decision models employ many of the ideas contained in both the procedural rationality and organizational process models, but the viewpoint differs in that decisions are explicitly analysed in their political context. Decision-making is viewed in terms of conflicts of interest and bargaining power. Policy and practice are not seen as the product of individual or organizational choice processes, but as the outcomes of a political struggle between interest groups within society. In other words, the fact that executive agencies have delegated responsibilities and considerable discretion does not, in itself, give them the power and freedom to pursue their own goals and determine the direction of policy. They can only operate within the constraints set by the real holders of power in society.

Until recently there was little meeting of minds between analysts engaged in theoretical debates over the locus of real power. *Pluralists* have argued that the decision process in twentieth-century democratic societies is an open one, with myriad different interests competing for advantage, and with no one group achieving a dominant position in the longer term (Dahl, 1961). On each issue various interest groups will attempt to gain public support, will form temporary alliances with other interests, and their relative success will depend on political and economic circumstances, prevailing social values and on the resources they are able to mobilize. The outcomes of conflict are thus unpredictable and policy must, in the end, be based on consensus. Any attempt by a minority vested interest to dominate the decision process to its own advantage will be thwarted by the majority through the checks built into the democratic system. Power is, therefore, dispersed; held, in effect, by the 'public' at large. Policy is determined by public preferences, and management agencies must work in response to shifting social values and goals. Legislators and administrators are rarely seen as leaders or formers of public opinion, rather they operate under pressure from exogenously determined public demands (Ashby, 1976, 1978a).

Conversely, élitists of various persuasions have argued that 'establishment' groups can bias the whole policy formulation and implementation process towards their own vested interests. Interests do not compete on equal terms; some groups consistently have more resources, including money, access to decision-makers, bargaining skills, information and links with the media. They are, therefore, better placed to pressure administrators, engage in 'pork barrel' politics, manipulate legislatures and mould public opinion. More radical analysts go one stage further and contend that real power is held by only one élite, the capital-owning class. Policy outcomes are, therefore, largely predetermined, with capital always succeeding in the struggle with other interest groups. Public service and regulatory agencies are seen to operate in support of private capital, by reducing social conflict, providing unprofitable but essential goods and services, safeguarding the health and productivity of the workforce, and so on. This does not mean that they always act in the short-term interests of capital-owners, but that they operate to maintain a social system which is conducive to capital formation and in which the economic developmental interests of capital dominate (Poulantzas, 1973; Habermas, 1976a, 1976b; Macpherson, 1978).

There is clearly an enormous ideological rift between these different perspectives on power in society, but they do have in common the view that decisions are the results of political activity. Within-agency decision-making is not, therefore, a 'neutral' activity, governed in some way by the physical characteristics of the resource or by the objectively determined 'needs' of the public. Nor is it an activity designed to fulfil the goals of the management authorities or of the individuals within them. When viewed from this political perspective, the key question changes from *how* resource management decisions are made to *who* has the power and influence to make the effective policy choices.

POWER, INFLUENCE AND THE ROLE OF THE PUBLIC

Signs of pluralism

As was argued earlier (p. 182), no one body of theory can be expected to cover all situations at all periods of time, and certainly evidence can be selected from the management of renewable resources which appears to support pluralistic, élitist and radical interpretations of events. Particularly when the concern is with environmental quality and amenity resources, the system appears to have all the hallmarks of pluralistic competition. There are indeed 'congeries of hundreds of small special interest groups, representing different, if sometimes overlapping, constituencies, competing to influence decisions salient to them' (Polsby, 1963, p. 118). Moreover, these groups are able to use a 'multitude of techniques' to inform public opinion and 'to influence some officials somewhere in the political system in order to obtain at least some of their goals' (Dahl, 1967, p. 386). Most especially in open adversorial societies, such as the United States, environmental interest groups are able to take advantage of generally good access to information, a reasonably sympathetic press and the many points at which public participation is built into the decision-making procedures, to attempt to influence the direction of policy.

It is difficult to explain the rise of the environmental movement in the 1960s solely in terms of manipulation by established élites (Lowe and Goyder, 1983); certainly, vocal pressure groups stimulated public interest but they also fed on the more deep-rooted and widely felt concern over the nature of society (Andrews, 1980; Buttel, 1980; Cotgrove, 1982). By the beginning of the 1960s environmental quality could no longer be regarded as a minority interest, and particularly in the United States there appeared to be a widespread consensus that cleaning up the environment was in everyone's interest. It is doubtful whether environmental pressure groups would have had the impact they did without this groundswell of public support.

Government was clearly responsive to demands for more controls over resource use; a plethora of legislation (NEPA 1969, Clean Air Act 1970, Water Pollution Control Amendments 1972, The Noise Control Act 1972 and dozens of others) rapidly extended layers of regulation around the activities of private industry and public developmental agencies. It is not really meaningful to regard this response as solely a matter of the state operating in support of capital, either to ensure the productivity of labour, or to moderate acute social conflicts threatening the stability of the entire capitalist system. As has already been shown, the US regulatory system was cumbersome and highly costly to developmental interests. If the sole concern of the state was to divert conflict to protect capital, one might have expected the development of a more cost-effective policy which minimized the burden of compliance costs on industry and which did not penalize new investments.

Even in Britain, with its generally much more paternalistic and closed decision system, environmental interest groups were able to generate a climate of opinion to which policy-makers felt they had to respond. Richardson (1977) cites the public outcries over the illegal dumping of toxic waste and the demolition of particular historic buildings as evidence of pluralism at work, while it seems clear that the disruption of motorway inquiries in the mid-1970s created such difficulties and delays in the construction programme that the government had to reappraise its road-planning procedures (Tyme, 1978; Levin, 1979). More recently, the decisions to ban lead in petrol, curb seal culling, restrict the straw-burning activities of farmers and take Billingham off the list of potential nuclear waste stores all provide examples of the ways in which environmental groups can mobilize public opinion and exert an influence on policy, especially if the media are receptive to the issues.

Moreover, the very existence of vocal pressure groups, which are able to command media attention and wage public compaigns against developments, policies or the failure of regulatory agencies, in itself can play a role in changing the attitudes and behaviour of decision-makers. Few private companies or public agencies willingly get themselves embroiled in lengthy and expensive disputes. Certainly, one of the unwritten goals of most state bureaucracies is to minimize public and political 'flack', while private corporations are well aware of the financial costs involved when planned investment is delayed by protracted battles to obtain planning permissions and by lengthy court proceedings (Elkington, 1980). In addition, large private companies in particular tend to be very sensitive about their public image and have no desire to be labelled as 'polluters' or 'despoilers' of the environment. Considerable steps may then be taken to anticipate and avoid amenity protests. Some of these steps involve 'conditioning' public and political opinion (the well-known television commercial in Britain, depicting a major oil company as the saviour of the countryside and environmental quality, provides just one example). But other steps have meant genuine efforts to avoid environmentally sensitive sites, minimize the external costs of development and reach a compromise with interested groups.

Politicians, at both local and national level, are also not insensitive to pressure exerted through the media, public participation exercises and the electoral system, particularly when demands are imbued with a strong moral flavour – safeguarding public health, preserving the unique character of the countryside, protecting our cultural heritage, ensuring the integrity of the community, and so forth. This has been evident in the way established political parties in continental Europe have responded to the emergence of the so-called 'green parties', by incorporating environmental demands within their manifestos and by introducing new legal and institutional safeguards to protect the quality of the environment.

Many élitist and radical analysts have argued that the legislative gains made by environmental groups were at best temporary and at worst merely an illusion. Developments were delayed but not halted, controls were imposed but not implemented, cosmetic changes were made to decision-making procedures without altering their substance; and throughout, the dominant élites maintained their power and the status quo. In other words, the political system may have had the appearance of pluralism but, in reality, democratic procedures and public participation were 'hollow rituals' or 'theatre' behind which the real holders of power and influence continued to make the crucial decisions.

Although it is clear that restrictions on development and the enforcement of pollution control regulations have been eased as unemployment and inflation have gained greater political salience, this is not necessarily antithetical to the pluralist perspective. Indeed it would be expected that some countermovement would occur as other groups felt the costs of the new controls and sought in their turn to influence public opinion and the decision-makers (Dunlap and Dillman, 1976; Buttel, 1980). Pluralism is based on the notion of 'balance' between competing interests. If environmentalists were a minority, out of line with the values of society at large, then the same democratic processes which allowed them to make an impact on policy would also act to reduce their influence and return the system to the 'centre'. Milbrath (1963) has argued that there is a 'natural balancing factor', in which any vigorous push in one direction almost automatically stimulates an opponent, or a coalition of opponents, to push in the opposite direction.

Proponents of the natural history theory of the rise and fall of social movements have also suggested that the waning influence of environmental interests was inevitable, since all movements go through a natural progression or issue-attention cycle; initial enthusiasms and popular support declines as new pre-occupations claim the attention of the public and the press (Downs, 1972). Moreover, changing circumstances, due to the energy crisis, economic recession and rising levels of unemployment, would in themselves act to tip the balance of power and influence towards developmental interests. In fact it could be argued that in view of the undoubted importance of employment and material prosperity to the mass of people, the environmental interest groups have been remark-ably successful in keeping pollution abatement, nature conservation and improvements in the quality of life widely accepted as legitimate social policy goals.

However, while the decision systems, for some resources at least, may show pluralistic tendencies, it is difficult to interpret more than a fraction of environ-mental and renewable resource policy as the product of open consensual politics. In the first place, although Dahl (1967) and other prominent proponents of the pluralistic case clearly acknowledge that not all individuals and interest groups have equal resources and access to the decision-system, they argue that such inequalities are not cumulative and, therefore, that policy outcomes do not show systematic bias towards particular interests. As Newton (1982, p. 236) has pointed out, such views run counter to a great deal of social science research which suggests very strongly that resources are distributed with cumulative inequality: 'those with more money often have more time to give to politics, have more political skills, fill more political positions, have more information, more con-fidence, more effective organizations to defend their interests, and so on.' Therefore, even when resource use issues are subject to open public debate and democratic procedures, particular interests or élites should be able to bias the system to their advantage. A further factor limiting the general applicability of the pluralist perspective is the closed nature of decision-making in many resource management agencies.

Local environmental élites

DEFLECTED DEVELOPMENT AND REGRESSIVE WELFARE REDISTRIBUTION

There seems little doubt that at *a local scale* vocal and active pressure groups have been able to effect a redistribution of welfare by deflecting unwanted activities from, or attracting desirable forms of investment to, specific areas (Healy, 1976; Lowe and Goyder, 1983). It is now well recognized that the membership, and perhaps even more important, the leadership of most amenity groups are predominantly middle class; by and large, they seek to protect or further enhance areas which already have the most favoured environments. Although members would claim that they are acting in the wider public good to defend important aspects of the country's natural and cultural heritage, at the local level it is extremely difficult to dissociate any disinterested commitment to environmental quality from the natural desire of individuals to protect their own 'positional goods' (Pahl, 1965; Allison, 1975; Hirsch, 1977). There are some examples of working-class pressure groups but it is generally true that manual workers are much less likely to join, and certainly to organize, lobbies to protect their own localities and interests.

Low-income areas tend, therefore, to be much less well defended, and this reinforces the already considerable economic incentives for polluting activities to gravitate to the so-called 'soft areas', where damage (measured in money cost terms) and compensation payments are lower. Goodman (1972) and many others have argued that this has certainly been the case with motorway developments, while Lowe and Goyder (1983, p. 100) see a danger that 'certain areas, inhabited by the poor and the deprived, and already suffering from environmental degradation and dereliction, come to be regarded as environmental sinks where all sorts of non-conforming and noxious land uses can be sited without provoking effective opposition'.

It is important to note that in the vast majority of disputes over the location of economic activities, local environmental interests have not questioned the need for the development; in other words, they have not challenged any dominant societal values or materialist goals.[17] The conflict is not, therefore, between protection and development, but between different groups of citizens, and inevitably some sections of the community are better placed to ensure that they receive the benefits from economic growth, without bearing a significant proportion of the costs (Gregory, 1976).

The bias in the system, however, goes far beyond the unequal ability of different community groups to defend their own areas from unwelcome activities. Analysts have also shown that the designation of urban conservation areas, protected 'heritage' villages, 'areas of outstanding natural beauty', green belts and so on, has been subject to political manoeuvring. Gamston's (1975) study of York, for instance, revealed that the boundaries of conservation areas around particular clusters of historic buildings were drawn not on any 'objective' assessment of the architectural and historic value of property, but under pressure from lobbyists intent on enhancing the price and desirability of their own homes. Similar pressures have operated throughout Britain, transforming legislation designed to preserve areas of special historic importance into a weapon for defending smart residential areas (Barker, 1976), and the same sort of processes have been widely observed elsewhere in Europe and to some extent also in the United States and Australia (Stretton, 1976; Castells, 1977; Skoog, 1983; Goodey and Gold, 1984).

In the countryside, green belts, first envisaged as girdles to contain urban sprawl, have become, largely under pressure from local amenity interests, devices to defend extensive tracts of land from all forms of development (Munton, 1983). In Surrey, for example, the bulk of the rural area is now under one form of protective designation or another (Connell, 1971, 1972; Anderson, 1981). These are then employed in the struggle to deflect unwanted activities, such as sand and gravel extraction, solid waste disposal sites and large-scale public or low-income private housing projects.

A whole series of studies (Connell, 1978; Newby *et al.*, 1978; Buller and Lowe, 1982; Lowe and Goyder, 1983) have concluded that amenity groups demanding conservation and environmental protection have tended to act against the interests of the poorer groups in society. They have served to restrict employment opportunities, reduce housing provision and curb the development of a whole range of public and private services. Moreover, since protective designations have tended to increase the perceived attractiveness of areas and reduce their apparent vulnerability to development pressures, property prices tend to be much higher than in the rest of the countryside (Standing Conference of Rural Community Councils, 1979; Shucksmith, 1981). This not only brings considerable unearned capital gains to established residents, but also prices the relatively low-paid rural working class out of the property market. In addition, the expenditure on 'environmental tarting-up' – tree planting, the burying of service cables, use of appropriate building materials and so forth – has opportunity costs; it possibly reduces the availability of funds for services valued more highly by the less affluent and can act to force up the cost of housing, transport and other essential infrastructure services (Ferris, 1972; Gregory, 1976).

Ironically the well-meant introduction of measures designed to increase public participation in land-use planning decisions has served to reinforce the power and influence of middle-class pressure groups (Lowe, 1977). As Goodey and Gold (1984, p. 436) have forcibly put it, 'participation is a purchasable commodity and most citizens still have to make do with "experiments", revolutionary theft, or the environment achieved by those with the purchasing power'.

At the local level in Britain, active environmental groups have virtually become a surrogate for wider public opinion (Percival, 1972; Gamston, 1975; Barker, 1976). This in part arises from both the costs involved in, and the generally low levels of response obtained from, more broadly based participation exercises – few people fill in postal questionnaires, visit exhibitions of plans or development schemes, or write in to object to advertised planning applications which could affect them (Fagence, 1977).[18]

It also stems from the way many environmental groups have cultivated their non-partisan, responsible, expert and generally helpful image (county branches of the Council for the Protection of Rural England, county trusts for nature conservation and local civic trusts have typically adopted this stance). Over time they have tended to build up a mutual support system with professional planners, who often share their values and aspirations; they work with, rather than confront, the local planning authorities. As a result, they achieve an 'established' status, part of the 'insider' network of contacts which are consulted at the plan formulation stage and which are given prior warning of planning applications and council agendas (Buller and Lowe, 1982; Lowe and Goyder, 1983). In return they tend not to 'rock the boat': 'fighting cases means publicity. Publicity means conflict, and conflict can mean loss of contact and credibility' (Allison, 1975, p. 121). There are, of course, groups that stand outside this cosy consensual arrangement even in Britain, and are forced to adopt the confrontational tactics which are more characteristic of the US environmental movement (Cotgrove, 1982). However, at the local level such confrontational groups have tended to be ephemeral, created to fight specific proposals and dying once that battle has been won or lost. In general, if they survived, they did so only by broadening their concerns, establishing their expertise and political legitimacy and developing a good working relationship with planning departments.

Environmental élites and national policy

Although most established local environmental groups do not seek a direct confrontation with economic interests, their success in achieving a proliferation of protective designations, and in challenging a wide range of development activities, inevitably brings them into conflict with an opposed set of élites – industrialists, builders, property companies, commercial interests and the trade unions.[19] In areas where local authority representatives are drawn disproportionately from local businessmen and trade union leaders amenity interests may have only a marginal influence on the direction of policy (Morris and Newton, 1971; Saunders, 1980). But where, as in the commuter counties of south-eastern England, a significant proportion of the politically active members of a community are dependent on external sources of employment, income and wealth, then protectionist interests can have an apparently marked impact on local plans, amenity designations and the severity with which development controls are implemented and enforced.

However, even in such areas it has to be recognized that amenity groups can only be effective if local government has real power to determine policy. But in two important senses local autonomy is constrained. First, it can only operate within the framework set by the social, economic and political structures of society as a whole (Dunleavy, 1980). And, second, in most countries the land-use planning systems have mechanisms built into them to allow central government to intervene to bring local decisions into line with national policy.

In Britain, for example, developers refused planning permission, or in dispute over development conditions, have a right of appeal to central government. Ministerial 'call in' powers effectively remove all major and contentious development decisions from local determination. Furthermore, exclusions made under the General Development Order leave such major economic interests as agriculture and forestry largely free from local planning controls. Most local plans are subject to ministerial approval and local authorities are expected to heed the 'advice' issued in departmental circulars. Moreover, central pressure is exerted more covertly through controls over local government finance and through the general management of the national economy.

Some commentators have maintained that central departments consistently utilize their power to support pro-development interests (see p. 385), and certainly, since the late 1970s, there is clear evidence that local government is under considerable pressure to relax planning constraints on housing construc-tion and industrial activity. The Secretary of State for the Environment has issued an explicit warning that planning policy must be more closely geared to the government's main tasks of restoring industrial competitiveness and creating new job opportunities. The housebuilding industry must not be 'strangled' by an 'overzealous' use of planning controls, and councils must make adequate provision for new industrial developments (Mr Patrick Jenkins, Association of District Councils Conference, 1 July 1983). Such warnings are a clear indication that any appeals against local planning decisions will be given sympathetic consideration, and they have been reinforced by departmental circulars advising that planning permission should not be refused on the ground that land scheduled for development is available elsewhere (*ENDS* Report 102, 1983, pp. 3–4). Predictably, but somewhat ironically, the strongest opposition to these moves has come from the Conservative green belt and shire county councils, who have been able to utilize their symbiotic relationship with amenity interests to mobilize public and parliamentary opinion behind their stand.

To look at the broader clash between amenity and development interests it is necessary briefly to consider the role of conservation groups in influencing the direction of national policy. In all the then industrializing societies, the late nineteenth century saw the development of a variety of groups espousing the need to preserve the cultural and natural heritage, to shift society away from its overriding pursuit of economic 'progress' and to protect the public from the effects of market forces and private greed (Buttel, 1980; Lowe and Goyder, 1983). These early groups were unashamedly élitest and generally illiberal in their support for traditional forms of social order and the hierarchical division of society (Cotgrove, 1982). They drew their support from a small group of influential intellectuals and from the upper echelons of society who, in Britain at least, regarded trade and industry as base activities and who used their personal standing and patronage to press for change.

Since then the social base of environmental concern has clearly been pro-gressively widened, although there are still left-wing commentators who argue that it remains an élitist movement antithetical to the material needs of the poor. Much recent research suggests that support for environmental protection is broadly based, although the leadership of amenity groups remains predominantly professional and middle class. Despite the commonly held view that popular support for conservation and pollution control, so evident in the 1960s, would crumble before the economic realities of recession and unemployment, this has not been the case. Mitchell (1978) has shown that in the United States 52 per cent of those surveyed thought the government was spending too little on the environment, and 53 per cent supported greater control over pollution regardless of cost. The results of a MORI poll in Britain, carried out in January 1983, similarly found that 58 per cent were prepared to support an increase in income tax to pay for resource conservation measures, and 53 per cent supported tax increases to fund wildlife and pollution protection measures. Even more recently a much wider study, commissioned by the EEC, reports that 60 per cent of the sampled public (10,000 people in the ten member states) regard environmental protection as more important than price control, and 59 per cent gave priority to protection even if it meant restricting economic growth. Although the proportions giving greater priority to conservation and pollution control fell somewhat in areas with high levels of unemployment, even there a majority saw higher prices and reduced growth as acceptable costs of environmental improvements (*ENDS Report* 109, 1984).

All surveys of this type suffer from the problem that verbal expressions of support for something which has acquired the status of a moral good, or a tenet of faith, may have little bearing on actual behaviour when real choices have to be made between material possessions and environmental quality. But even bearing in mind these problems, it is difficult to dismiss environmental groups as totally unrepresentative of wider public opinion, and merely populated by the effete middle classes intent on protecting their privileged position. The key question, however, is whether, even with public support, the environmental interest groups have sufficient power and influence to have any material impact on the direction of policy.

Most analysts have concluded that environmental groups have less influence with governments than do the major economic interests. In a British context Lowe and Goyder (1983, pp. 179–80) conclude that 'they have fewer political resources and lack powerful sanctions . . . they are not of central importance to the effective performance of government, the economy or various sectors of production'. But at the same time, it is possible to see the steadily increasing panoply of legislation, defending elements in the cultural and natural environment, as a visible expression of the achievements of the environmental movement. The beginnings of protection for historic buildings, air pollution control, the development of national parks, nature reserves and indeed the entire land-use planning system, can all be traced back in Britain to the ideas and activities of the Victorian reform groups, while acts such as NEPA can be regarded as testaments to the strength of the environmental lobby in the United States during the 1960s. It would appear, therefore, that environmental groups can sow the seeds of change, act to shift public values and, by maintaining pressure on decision-makers for considerable periods of time, can eventually achieve some of their aims. On the other hand, there is widespread agreement that environmental élites acting *alone* lack the power to overcome the forces of inertia in order to engender policy change. There is, however, no consensus over what else is required before an environmental idea bears fruit as legislative action or as a change in management practice.

PLURALISM OR STRUCTURALISM?

One group of analysts takes a pluralistic perspective and argues that environmental interests will only succeed in changing policy when the time for an idea is right, in the sense that there is a groundswell of public opinion in its favour. Ashby (1978b), when discussing the UK Clean Air legislation of 1956, talked in terms of it being the eventual outcome of a 'glacial movement of public opinion'; a movement influenced by publicity from the smoke abatement lobbies, the 1952 London smog, the increased availability of smokeless fuels and the 'fashionability' of central heating. Public support was, therefore, the necessary condition of change and the force determining its timing. However, even if this interpretation of events is accepted, it is clear that the public at large had no input into the crucial decisions about the organizational structure of control and the regulatory form. Rather these were predicated in part by the precedence set by past legislation and established control agencies, and in part by the advocacy of the National Smoke Abatement Society. The influence of this lobby can most clearly be seen in the introduction of smokeless zones, a concept which had been pushed for some fifty years and which was only one among a set of mechanisms potentially capable of achieving the smoke reduction objective.

The idea that public support is the key force behind policy change is strongly disputed by the more radical interpreters of events; in fact both the general public and environmental élites are regarded as largely irrelevant to the overall direction of policy. From a structuralist perspective the political debate is largely a charade and the actors party to it have little significance. Rather, effective policy is determined by economic interests, which the apparatus of the state is designed to support. Sandbach (1980, p. 128), for example, argues that the 'environmental lobby has been deceived into the belief that the state is an impartial mediator in a pluralist society', whereas 'the state has increasingly become the servant of private enterprise'. Similarly, in the United States, analysts such as Goodman (1972) and Barnet (1980) have concluded that the entire economic and land-use planning systems are subordinate to corporate interests.[20]

From this perspective environmental groups are only able to win specific visible battles in four circumstances: where the proposed policy change serves the interests of capital, or a significant segment of it; where concessions are necessary to safeguard the productivity of the workforce or to diffuse potentially destructive conflict; where no significant costs to development would actually result; and where the control system is loosely defined and administered by sympathetic or manipulable agencies, in which case industry could in effect pursue its own policy irrespective of legislation, plans or other control procedures.

Under a structuralist interpretation of events, the UK Clean Air Act can no longer be explained in terms of any gradual change in public opinion but by 'economic factors involving the development of alternative fuels to coal' (Sandbach, 1982). Gas undertakings had a strong economic interest in developing cheap and efficient appliances for burning by-product coke. There was a well-established trend for commercial and the more affluent domestic consumers to convert from coal; and many changes in the location and structure of industrial activity, the greatly improved efficiency of coal-burning technologies, and the substitution of gas, electricity and to some extent fuel oil, particularly in firms still located in urban centres, all combined to minimize the economic impact of the Act on industry. Moreover, the discretion allowed to local authorities in implementing smokeless zones and the many 'loopholes' in the legislation enabled firms, in effect, to pursue their own fuel policies.

The newly released Cabinet papers from the years preceding the Act lend some credence to both Ashby's pluralist interpretation and Sandbach's structuralism. There was certainly no great enthusiasm among ministers for smoke control; Harold Macmillan (then Prime Minister), for instance, regarded smogs as natural phenomena. But they were embarrassed by the furore in the media and in Parliament, particularly when figures on the premature deaths caused by the 1952 London smog were released. To satisfy the need to be seen to be doing something the Cabinet then employed the classic delaying mechanism used by all bureaucracies. It appointed a Committee (Beaver Committee, 1954) to consider and advise on the matter, seemingly in the hope that by the time it reported public interest in smoke control would have dissipated with the memory of the smog. However, this was not to be. In 1956 a private member's Bill on smoke abatement was put before the House. The government could neither afford to publicly oppose it or to lose control over the details of the legislation. It, therefore, introduced its own Bill. In a sense the Cabinet was pushed by democratic procedures into the legislation, but it is clear that the political concern was with the appearance of action and not with the implementation of strong pollution control measures. The discretion given to the implementation and enforcement agencies, the grant system, which meant that the central Exchequer paid only 30 per cent of the direct costs of conversion from coal and none of the indirect expenditure, and the exemptions built into the legislation all combined to ensure that implementation would, at best, be slow and would probably merely follow behind the well-established decline in smoke pollution.

THE HIDDEN POLICY AGENDA

The discussion so far has concentrated on visible conflicts and on those areas of resource policy which are relatively open to public debate. In theory, within democratic societies public resource management authorities are accountable to one or other tier of the legislature. Virtually all aspects of their plans and practices could become the subject of scrutiny. The media and environmental interest groups also have the freedom to challenge decisions, generate public concern and attempt to get politicians to raise issues in the relevant legislative forum. But in practice, the vast majority of effective policy decisions remain uncontentious, subject to minimal scrutiny and beyond public ken. In Britain, for instance, forestry policy, solid and even hazardous waste disposal, industrial air pollution control, coastal protection and water management practices all, at best, receive sporadic attention and are usually left to the closed decision systems operating within the relevant executive authority. The existence of areas of policy where there is little open public debate raises major problems for the pluralist interpretation of the political bargaining process. Some insights into the nature of policy-making in such circumstances can be gained by considering two related notions which have featured prominently in debates within the recent political science literature, the concepts of the *non-decision* and *corporatism*.

Non-decisions and corporatist influences

Although the work of Bachrach and Baratz has not gone unchallenged, two short theoretical papers (1962, 1963), introducing the notion of a 'non-decision', have influenced thinking on decision-making processes out of all proportion to their length (Lukes, 1974; Parry and Morriss, 1974; Jenkins, 1978). The term non-decision is by no means an easy one to define clearly. It has been used to refer to a whole set of acts supporting the *mobilization of bias*, whereby established practices, values and institutional procedures operate systematically and consistently to bias outcomes to the benefit of certain persons and groups. In a later work Bachrach and Baratz (1971) made it clear that they were not only including situations where no decisions were taken or indeed were necessary, but also those where conscious choices were made to do nothing, to thwart demands for change, to hide relevant information and generally to restrict public access to the decision process. A non-decision, under this formulation, becomes

> A decision that results in the suppressing or thwarting of a latent or manifest challenge to the values or interests of the decision-maker. To be more explicit, non-decision making is a means by which demands for change in the existing allocation of benefits and privileges in a community can be suffocated before they are even voiced; or kept covert, or killed before they gain access to the relevant decision-arena; or, failing all these things, maimed or destroyed in the decision-implementing stage of the policy process. (ibid., p. 44)

This is not the place to rehearse the now considerable methodological debate surrounding the concept (Wolfinger, 1971; Bradshaw, 1976). Rather attention will be focused on five broad bodies of evidence which lend credence to the general tenure of the ideas within the non-decision concept.

First, there is now much evidence which suggests that governments and administrators can act, and have acted, to direct debate into safe political areas, and to divert pressure groups from the centre of government where the major decisions are made about the direction of the economy and the allocation of resources. It is significant that in their survey of the links between natural environmental groups and central government departments in Britain Lowe and Goyder (1983) found that the key developmental departments were generally uninformative and unreceptive to the environmentalist viewpoint. The Ministry of Agriculture and the Departments of Trade, Industry, Energy and Transport all came into the unreceptive category, as did the Central Electricity Generating Board and the Forestry Commission.

Pressure from environmental groups has been deflected on to such quasi-autonomous agencies as the Countryside Commission, the Nature Conservancy Council, the British Waterways Board, the Historic Buildings Council and the Sports Council, all bodies which 'have small budgets, little power and limited policy-making initiative, and they are politically marginal' (ibid., p. 67). Interest groups can safely be involved in discussions about grants for home insulation, but their impact on the direction of the fuel economy can only be minimal if they are not party to decisions on the investment practices and pricing policies of the energy industries. Similarly, commissions, inquiries or advisory committees may be allowed to comment on design details or the location of specific developments, but their effect on the substance of policy can only be significant if their terms of reference allow them effectively to challenge the need for the development *per se* (see Sandbach, 1980, on the motorway inquiry case). It can be argued that moves by central government to promote public participation or facilitate environmental mediation at local level, simply act to divert environmental pressure away from such fundamental policies as industrial growth, transport, energy, agriculture and housing and into internecine struggles between local communities (Lowe and Goyder, 1983).

Second, active and potentially politically embarrassing groups have been 'institutionalized', co-opted into a phoney consultative status, which then reduces the group's freedom to openly challenge policy. This feature has already been noted in the earlier discussion on local pressure groups (see pp. 381–2), but it is equally evident at the national scale. Even a group such as Friends of the Earth, which began life using the tactics of confrontation, has been drawn on to government committees and into consultation with officials. As a result, much greater care has been needed 'in the timing and content of FoE's publicity to avoid embarrassing and antagonising those officials involved' and the group 'now eschews any illegal or disruptive activities' (ibid., p. 132). Bugler (1981) has argued that this amounts to co-option by government and leads to a loss of their campaigning momentum. The famous returnable bottle campaign, which commanded much media attention with events such as the return to Schweppes of thousands of throw-away containers, certainly ground to a halt when FoE became embroiled in the long-drawn-out and ultimately fruitless machinations of the Waste Management Advisory Council.

Third, the internal decision processes of the technocentric resource development and regulation agencies lend further credence to Bachrach and Baratz's thesis that interests challenging established policies and practices are likely to be thwarted. As was seen earlier (p. 374), the professional dominance within some authorities, and the tendency for bureaucracies to retain their monopoly over information, make it exceptionally difficult to curb agency independence. Evaluatory techniques are subject to 'capture', while public scrutiny and democratic control procedures require a level of technical knowledge and expertise which is all too rarely present. Moreover, since these agencies tend to be large-scale and accountable only to the highest tier of government, there are few points in the decision system where the public at large or 'outsider' interest groups have the opportunity to scrutinize and challenge the policy direction.

It is at this point that the notion of corporatism becomes relevant. Officials within public agencies do not work in isolation; they consult specific interest groups, provide inputs to and take the products of the private sector and are influenced by their colleagues within the same profession. All three of these links have led analysts to conclude that agencies effectively closed to the public are open to key economic interests, with whom they develop reciprocally interdependent relationships. Thus the UK Ministry of Agriculture has developed a symbiotic relationship with a major 'client', the National Farmers Union (Self and Storing, 1962). While the Confederation of British Industry has very close links with all government departments concerned with trade, economic development and employment, it is also now consulted as a matter of course when pollution control, conservation or planning policies threaten to impinge on business activities. In just the same way, the road haulage lobby has powerful friends within the Department of Transport (Hamer, 1974; Painter, 1980) and the construction and property development industries are well represented in both national and local bureaucracies (Hood, 1973; Saunders, 1980; Dunleavy, 1980).

A somewhat different pattern of corporate relations with state agencies occurs when one professional group is employed by both private and public sector concerns. This may have three consequences. First, solutions adopted in response to demands in one sector may be generalized to the other. Second, professionals working for the private sector give advice as consultants to public authorities which secures 'a better capital return for the (private) corporation than would otherwise have been the case' (the influence of consultant architects being the classic illustration here). And, third, professional interpenetration of the two sectors 'can come to constitute a key channel of influence by which the sectional interests of corporations distorts public policy' (Dunleavy, 1980, p. 115). Architects are not, of course, the only professional group involved in this type of linkage and civil engineers provide another classic example as indeed do economists and accountants. In all cases where corporate interests have developed a mutually co-operative relationship with public officials, it takes a very determined environmental group, backed by considerable media pressure and obvious public support, to challenge the established consensus of views.

Fourth, there are cases where regulatory authorities have apparently not acted to meet known pollution or resource depletion problems because they were aware that any control measures would affect a powerful economic interest in the community. The issue simply fails to reach the policy-making agenda. In his now much-quoted study on air pollution control in US cities, Crenson (1971) seeks to explain why Gary, a city with generally poor air quality standards, should have waited until 1962 to introduce a control ordinance, whereas in other cities (in particular, East Chicago) the whole air quality issue had been publicly debated and control measures introduced in the late 1940s. He argues that pollution was suppressed as a political issue by the economic power of US Steel, the dominant industrial employer in the city. The company took no direct action to keep pollution off the decision agenda, rather it acted like a 'benign, pliable and passive giant' (ibid., p. 60), maintaining a strategic neutrality and influencing events through its reputation for power. Even when the city was eventually forced to introduce a control ordinance (largely under pressure from the state and federal governments), the company was apparently able to affect the content of the ordinance without taking any overt or even covert action.

Too little empirical evidence exists to say how far Crenson's conclusions apply to other areas where the community is critically dependent on one employer and, therefore, always feels constrained by the firm's ultimate right to curtail its investment. Blowers (1982) finds some supporting evidence in his study of the Bedfordshire brick industry. He argues that pollution from the brickworks in Marston Vale, owned by the London Brick Co., was for long suppressed as a political issue, but in this instance the company took steps to ensure that the matter was kept out of the public eye. Tenant farmers had to waive all rights for damages caused by pollution as a condition of their tenancy of company-owned farms, and financial settlements with other farmers were often reached out of court. These moves clearly had an economic motive but they also decreased the possibility of damaging publicity. When the issue did eventually emerge into the open, at a time when planning permission was being sought for a new works, the company still exercised considerable influence 'through access to politicians, manipulation of evidence, and, ultimately the threat of investment withdrawal' (ibid., p. 18).

The *fifth* area where evidence lends support to the non-decision concept is basically an extension of the fourth. But it also serves to illustrate the critical barrier which all environmental groups face in their attempts to shift policy away from development and consumption to amenity and conservation – namely, the still dominant assumption that economic growth is the basic and legitimate objective of society. Instead of employing the non-decision notion to explain why issues fail to reach the political agenda, it can be used to explain why once plans and legislation have been enacted, these are then imperfectly implemented and enforced.

As was seen earlier in the chapter, some formal policy-making appears to have little more than symbolic value (see pp. 339–47). When the organizations chosen for enforcement (their discretionary powers, financial resources, areas of jurisdiction and conventional practices) and the methods of control are considered in detail, then the real thrust of policy emerges. At best, some official policy statements can be seen as pious hopes or long-term aspirations; at worst, they can only be interpreted as a token gesture, designed to diffuse political conflict, without making any real change in the status quo. The constraints imposed on the implementation of the spirit of such legislation as the UK Control of Pollution Act (1974) and parts of the Wildlife and Countryside Act (1981) serve to draw attention to the strength of powerful economic interests in determining the reality of policy. In both cases environmental improvement and conservation were clearly subordinate to general public expenditure policy and the economic management of the economy. The common use in Britain of enforcement by negotiation inevitably ensures that economic interests are safeguarded throughout the enforcement process. But as shown in the US industrial air pollution example, these same interests are adept at finding mechanisms of expression even under an imposed standards and confrontational regime.

CONCLUSION

The debate over the way the substance of environmental policy is formulated has been characterized by an enormous diversity of views. There is, however, a growing realization that single, universally applicable explanations are inappropriate, revealing more about the ideology of the analyst than the reality of the policy process. It is comparatively easy to abstract from real-world complexity the pieces of evidence required to support a particular model of the socioeconomic and political system. Without doubt, it is valid to argue that environmental interests have only been able to tinker at the margins of policy formulation and enforcement practice, and have had a relatively minor impact on the substance of policy. The underlying policy direction is still towards exploitive resource development and material growth. In an important sense this relative powerlessness of environmentalists (or any other groups which see existing arrangements as antithetical to their interests) is inevitable given the momentum of established political, social, legal and economic institutions. New legislation, the reorganization of resource management agencies, efforts to redirect investments, the introduction of extra redistributive measures, and so forth, only ever affect part of the entrenched institutional base and thus can only have marginal impact on the direction of the economy. However, such small shifts can act incrementally over time to produce quite profound changes in the underlying institutional structure. In all advanced capitalist economies the development of social welfare planning, resource management and pollution control systems has gradually produced a new framework within which the different interest groups must operate. While economic interests may still predominate, few would now suggest that material goals must be pursued to the exclusion of environmental and social objectives.

Superficially, at least, the pattern of incremental policy change has all the hallmarks of pluralism: the system 'muddles through' with a whole series of minor adjustments to practice and to policy objectives in response to emerging problems and conflict situations. It could also be argued that the continued dominance of economic development as the motive force behind policy is merely a reflection of the prevailing material values of the mass of the population. If values shift, as recent opinion surveys suggest they may be doing, so too will the direction of policy. However, values are not exogenous variables, but are derived in large measure from entrenched social, economic and political institutions. Even ignoring the role of 'élites' in manipulating opinions and demands for goods and services, it has to be recognized that 'the central values of industrial society are deeply embedded in most of us through upbringing and have become institutionalized in the social structure' (Cotgrove, 1982, p. 120). Moreover, it is difficult to sustain the pluralist argument that value shifts among the public at large is the relevant, *direct* force behind policy change, not least because the public *per se* has relatively few points of access to the decision process.

Where Ashby's notion of 'glacial movements in public opinion' could have an indirect influence on policy change is through the way it serves to alter the perspectives and attitudes of key bureaucrats, industrialists, professionals and politicians. In much of the literature on the nature of decision-making there has been a tendency to depersonalize the actors; people vanish behind generic titles: industry, capital, bureaucracy, the state, labour, and so forth. But the individuals concerned are all part of the public and, as such, are not immune from the forces influencing wider societal values. For example, it would be valid to argue that the improvements made to river water quality in Britain are as much the product of the 'voluntary' acceptance by many industrialists of the legitimacy of pollution control, as a policy goal, as they are of the relatively weak enforcement system.

The attention paid in pluralistic interpretations to value shifts begs the question of how these shifts come about. At one level of analysis they are clearly responses to the emerging problems created by the process of economic development itself. As industrialization, urbanization, agrarian change and resource exploitation proceed, so political, economic and social systems, including values and aspirations, will adapt to ameliorate what are perceived to be the most significant effects.

But it is impossible to regard the pattern of cause–response events as neutral. What problems are perceived to be critical, and the nature of the response, cannot be understood without reference to the established structure of society and to the power and influence of the different interest groups. Elites, including the owners of capital, environmentalists and professionals all compete to bring their version of reality to the centre of the political stage. However, to explain policy change solely in terms of the unequal struggle between interest élites, glosses over the fact that such élites do not emerge from a vacuum. They are products of existing social, political and economic structures. Structuralist interpretations must, therefore, play a role in understanding the direction of effective policy. This is not to argue for the validity of explanations which reduce all the actors in the decision-making process to ciphers, playing out a predetermined role according to their economic function within the capitalist system. As Lukes (1977, p. 29) has put it, 'any standpoint or methodology which . . . [is] a one-sided consideration of agents without (internal and external) structural limits, or structures without agents, or which does not address the problem of their interrelations, will be unsatisfactory'.

NOTES

1   This simply means waste that has not been generated in the local authority area but has been stored or dumped there; until the section is implemented the local council is not obliged to arrange and pay for disposal.
2   The Deposit of Poisonous Waste Act 1972, now superseded by COPA, required those removing or disposing of toxic or dangerous substances to notify the waste disposal authority at least three days before doing so. The 'notifiable' or controlled wastes are defined negatively to include all toxic or hazardous substances not specifically excluded by regulation. This definition procedure is a recipe for confusion, leaving the question of what is a toxic or hazardous waste open to interpretation (Haigh, 1984).
3   Another well-known example is the very slow development of smokeless zones for the black areas identified in the 1956 UK Clean Air Act.

4　Between March and August 1984, as Figure 9.2 shows, the situation improved slightly. Three Welsh authorities have now produced plans, and eight Scottish districts have some form of plan.

5　Corporatist theorists are a broad church; basically what is meant here is that the state and capital interests are reciprocally interdependent, each performing tasks which the other requires, thus decisions are underpinned by a basic consensus.

6　This process is by no means confined to the renewable resource field, and much has been written about the trend towards managerial solutions in many spheres of urban, economic and welfare service planning: see Cawson, 1978.

7　For political reasons twenty-nine private supply companies were retained as 'agents' of the RWAs.

8　There are, of course, exceptions; fish conservators have developed hatcheries, and some attempts have been made to increase the capacity of the environment to absorb pollutants.

9　In Britain it is standard practice to guard against the 1 in 100 year drought, while in parts of Australia even higher safety margins are common. Sydney, New South Wales, aims to cover *peak* daily use in the event of the worst eight years of drought ever known occurring consecutively, plus one further year's safety allowance, taking the worst twelve drought months ever recorded to make up that year.

10　The notion that British farmers would abide by a voluntary agreement to avoid irreparable damage to important wildlife habitats and sites of special scientific interest before the full notification system, created by the Wildlife and Countryside Act 1981, could come into operation is a clear example of this last type of agreement. It has merely shown that some farmers are not 'gentlemen' (*New Scientist*, 22 March 1984, p. 10)!

11　These were regarded as the most generally significant contaminants and now include particulates, carbon monoxide, sulphur oxides, nitrogen dioxide, hydrocarbons, oxidants and lead.

12　According to Crandall (1983), firms must obtain estimates of the cost of the equipment required for compliance, and then work through a fifty-six equation system, manipulating over seventy variables, to obtain the precise value of the delayed compliance penalty.

13　Ashby and Anderson, 1981, provide a detailed study of the history of the Clean Air movement in Britain, while Frankel, 1974, is a useful study of the Alkali Inspectorate.

14　The reader, *Decision-Making, Approaches and Analysis*, McGrew and Wilson, 1982, provides an excellent and up-to-date overview of the literature.

15　Both are based on rational behaviour, but diverge from substantive or comprehensively rational models in two important respects. The latter assume that goals are objectively determined and are in themselves rational (e.g. economic efficiency, profit maximization), and that individuals will evaluate *all* alternative methods before forming a strategy to achieve the goal. Both Simon and Lindblom argue that goals are subjective, determined by individual value systems, and that only a very limited subset of all possible methods will ever be evaluated.

16　Lowe and Goyder, 1983, p. 155, have argued that the UK Nature Conservancy acted in this manner; in 1952 the director-general 'fully realised that the Conservancy was a weak and vulnerable agency', he therefore sought 'to build up a strong constituency for official conservation policies'.

17　There are some notable exceptions to this, the anti-motorway and anti-nuclear lobbies being the most obvious examples. Similarly, some groups opposed the Belvoir coalfield development on 'need' grounds: see Manners, 1981b.

18 These low response rates are often taken as reflecting lack of interest, but some are unable to respond to these forms of participation exercise and many more are cynical that much notice is ever taken of their views: see Cotgrove, 1982.

19 Although there are isolated cases where trade unions have challenged the need for development *per se* – the short-lived 'green ban' movement in Australia being one example (Roddewig, 1978) – by and large, they have acted in favour of development interests. Unless, that is, a particular economic activity threatens the security of their own membership – the coalminers' union's opposition to nuclear power can be viewed in this light.

20 This is not a view overtly shared by the corporate interests themselves as the previous quoted statements by Tavoulareas serve to show (see p. 133).

10 Muddling through, social revolution or ecocatastrophe?

> Of course, everywhere ... there are the politicians and the priests, the ayatollahs and the economists, who will try to explain that reality is what they say it is. Never trust them; trust only the novelists. (Malcolm Bradbury, *'Rates of Exchange'*, 1983, p. 8)

No book on resource utilization and resource policy can avoid being concerned with the future. The central debates over scarcity, depletion, environmental quality and distributive equity are essentially about future patterns of resource development and welfare allocation, while any assessment of policy must perforce be forward-looking, focusing on potential courses of action. However, consideration of future resource use trends and policy directions is one thing; futurology, science fiction and visions of Utopia are quite another. No attempt will be made here to predict the future – a task which has already generated a vast amount of paper (Jahoda and Freeman, 1978), great heat but little light and one probably much better left to the novelist. Nor will this chapter be a proselytizing exercise. It will not seek to advocate what *ought* to happen to fulfil a particular Utopian dream of a better society.

The whole subject of desirable resource development paths, environmental futures and global welfare redistribution, and the institutional arrangements necessary for their achievement, is one which has attracted much rhetoric, numerous starry-eyed prescriptions and a welter of general exhortations to do good. There is nothing wrong with idealism and Utopian visions, they are after all the major force behind the human desire to change conditions, to 'shape history' (Mannheim, 1966; Cotgrove, 1982). But notions of Utopia differ enormously; the pastoral version of heaven so often proposed by environmentalists will be anathema to many. As Pearson and Pryor (1978, p. 347) point out, 'to assert a harmony [of interests] based on a global ecological unity is a little pious and a little naïve'. Moreover, it is an enormous step from stating a desirable future to actually defining an implementable policy programme to achieve it; certainly, there is little political relevance in such high-minded exhortations as

> we must individually and collectively seize the opportunities of the present situation to end the era of exploitation and enter a new age of humanitarian concern and cooperative endeavour with a driving desire to re-establish the old values of comfortable frugality and cheerful sharing. (O'Riordan, 1976, p. 310)

Rather than embarking on predictive alchemy or on a grand master-plan for a

New Jerusalem on earth, the aims of this chapter are much more modest and pragmatic. Attention will be confined to an attempt to distinguish, on the basis of evidence already presented in the book, the false from the real future resource concerns. It must be stressed once again that such an attempt is bound to be coloured by judgement, by the way in which different interpretations, or meanings, can be derived from the same set of facts; there is no absolute, objective reality.

SOME FALSE ISSUES

Physical resource scarcity as a barrier to continued economic development in advanced nations

The scarcity fears which erupted during the late 1960s and early 1970s were merely the latest manifestation of a recurrent concern that shortages of essential mineral and energy inputs would threaten the economic base of the 'modern' growth process. Apocalyptic visions of the imminent collapse of industrial civilization, crushed against the fixed limits of the physical system, have now receded once again. But there is still a widespread public perception that serious and damaging shortages of essential raw materials will occur; some 59 per cent of the US public appear to believe that severe oil scarcity will arise by 1989, while 37–52 per cent of the general public in Britain, Australia, Germany and the United States think it likely that major and disruptive material shortages will occur (Milbrath, 1983). It is argued that such fears have little basis in reality. Public perceptions have in part been formed by the memory of the 1973 and 1979 oil crises, but they have also been fed by propaganda from two opposed sets of interests. On the one hand, environmental and social groups, demanding a new 'non-material' policy direction, have used scarcity to justify the view that 'the industrial way of life with its ethos of expansion . . . is not sustainable' (Goldsmith *et al.*, 1972, p. 15). On the other hand, the spectres of shortages, breadlines and 'a general lowering of living standards' have been raised by a variety of economic interests, which stand to gain from increased exploration activity, reduced environmental and planning restrictions, higher mineral prices, increased investment in nuclear energy, and so forth.

The view that physical scarcity is a false issue is based on three interrelated features of the resource development system. First, natural resources are products of the human mind; their limits are not physical, but are set by human demands, institutions, imagination and ingenuity. Second, the process of technological change is deeply entrenched, and there is little evidence of a slackening of the innovation needed to redefine *those elements in the resource base which are essential to maintain the growth of monopoly capital.*[1] Third, and most important, the economic system in advanced nations (whether mixed, capitalist or planned) has inherent adaptive mechanisms to combat shortages of specific resource products *when* these are needed to sustain the process of growth and capital accumulation. The potential for substitution, in all its forms, recycling, conservation, the development of new supply materials and shifts in the mix of productive output makes the resource development process highly dynamic. It is the fact that all these adaptive mechanisms act in combination which makes the system so robust. The argument that 'the increasing efficiency of extraction processes, which offset the decline in ore grades (e.g. copper) in the first half of the twentieth century, cannot be expected to improve indefinitely' (Sandbach, 1980, p. 209) misses the point that 'new' supplies of particular minerals are not essential to the continuation of growth. Very few minerals have no substitutes for their economically significant end-uses. Moreover, as Sandbach himself later points out, growth in the advanced countries need not (and already increasingly is not) dependent on resource-based manufacturing industry, but on the export of services. It would be foolish to pretend that adaptations can occur without problems (or without considerable pain for many), but physical shortages of essential material inputs in not likely to be one of them. The economic growth machine may not be efficient or equitable, may not allow full employment, or be sensitive to the environment, but it has shown a remarkable capacity to sustain the flow of inputs necessary to ensure its continuation.

Geopolitically created scarcity as a barrier to growth and a threat to the security of advanced nations

Exponents of the geopolitical barrier arguments are a curiously polyglot group, with an unholy convergence of views between western politicians, defence interests and indigenous resource producers, and some Marxist commentators (Gedicks, 1977). All argue that the long history of indigenous resource exploitation in the advanced countries and the uneven distribution of proven reserves makes the north increasingly dependent on cheap resource imports from the south. This, coupled with the rise of nationalism in the LDCs and their demands for a more egalitarian distribution of global wealth, leads to the possibility of major supply disruptions and cost increases, which could produce a dramatic shift in resource power and affect the 'dynamic nature of capitalism'. However, there the accord ends; in one camp such possibilities are seen as a threat (US National Commission on Materials Policy, 1973; Bergsten, 1974), while in the other they are a cause of celebration.

Undoubtedly, as the actions of OPEC clearly show, geopolitically induced scarcities could produce major perturbations in the economies of the capitalist countries, which then reverberate around the whole interrelated global system. But there is little evidence of a significant and general power shift from the developed countries of the north. The notions that LDC producers can 'hold the consumer nations to ransom' or 'employ their commodity power to create a new economic and social order' depend upon the assumption that growth in the advanced capitalist states is dependent on mineral imports from the south. In large measure this assumption is invalid.

The developed nations are the chief mineral producers and the chief source of their own collective mineral consumption (pp. 79–93), a feature which considerably weakens the cards held by the LDCs. Moreover, as was shown in Chapter 4, even for the relatively small group of minerals where the north is import-dependent to a substantial degree, there are major limits on the effective exercise of commodity power. Aggressive supply restrictions and price rises can only have a significant impact when: the demand for the mineral is price-inelastic; the mineral has end-uses which are essential to the industrial base of the importing countries; there are no close substitutes for the mineral in these end-uses; and there are no conditional reserves in the consumer states which can attain resource value if prices rise. Among the non-fuel minerals there are none where these conditions hold. At most, 'hostile' producer actions, or political upheaval in production centres, could result in short-term disruptions, but the impact of these is minimized by stockpiling. Only in the oil case were the underlying economic conditions favourable for the achievement of resource power and, on present trends, this appears to have been a relatively short-lived phenomenon. The dramatic decline in OPEC's contribution to world oil supplies, the falling importance of oil in the energy mix and the dependence of the OPEC producers on the economic health of the advanced western nations, all make it increasingly unlikely that planned disruptions to supplies will create significant energy shortage problems.

This does not mean, of course, that a major political upheaval in the Middle East could not still produce tumult in the world oil markets, but the economic significance of such events to the advanced nations must decline as the Gulf's contribution to world energy supplies falls. It could be argued that the chief losers from OPEC's actions (and from any future constraints on supplies) are Third World nations, who can never hope to outbid the already industrialized states in restricted supply conditions.

Just as the mineral development system contains adaptive mechanisms to combat the appearance of physical scarcity, so too it has proved capable of adapting to geopolitically induced shortages. Even before the 1973 oil shock, the major mineral multinationals were responding to political risk by redirecting their patterns of investment. The shift in exploration and source development expenditures to 'safe' areas, technological innovation to allow the commercial exploitation of unconventional supply sources and the diversification of investments, both spatially and over a product range, have all served to minimize company, and thereby the north's, vulnerability to geopolitical shortages.

In the same way, mineral consumers have instituted their own defensive measures, including improvements in use efficiency, expenditure on conservation and recycling and investment in alternative supply sources. Furthermore, advanced nation governments have not just sat back and accepted what they regard as threats to their country's economic well-being and security. They have not only sought to reduce the impact of supply disruptions and price rises by reducing import dependence, but have also used their financial and political power to undermine 'hostile' producer governments.

It is this powerful convergence of apparent interests between the multinational producer companies, advanced nation consumers and their governments which stacks the cards so heavily against any significant power shift from the north to LDC mineral producers. The Third World is heavily dependent on the advanced nations for their export markets, capital and technology. Unless this dependence is broken, it is difficult to see that the resource-exporting states have the means to 'hold the north to ransom' or to 'break capitalist hegemony'.

Environmental and planning controls as a barrier to resource and industrial development

It is undoubtedly true that the operation of environmental interest groups and the introduction of planning and pollution control measures have been instrumental in delaying the development of indigenous resource supply projects and the construction of transport and processing facilities. In most advanced western countries examples can be found where nuclear power programmes, open-cast mineral operations, oil and gas exploitation, mineral smelting and refining, forestry projects and water supply extension schemes have been delayed for years by determined opposition. There are also cases where specific projects have been turned down by planning authorities, or where companies have abandoned their attempts to obtain development consents. However, with the exception of nuclear power programmes, there is little evidence to suggest that environmental pressures have reduced the overall *scale* of investment in resource production. Indeed it is significant that the late 1960s and 1970s, when the influence of environmental interests was at its height, was a period in which investment in mineral search and supply source development was switched towards the advanced countries. This strongly suggests that the economic penalties incurred by the mining companies in negotiating their way through the planning procedures, and in meeting pollution abatement or reclamation conditions, were a relatively minor influence on their investment strategies.

Where several alternative supply or processing sites are economically viable, environmental pressure groups have been able to shift the location of unwelcome activities on to less well-defended areas. In all countries there are some regions prepared to accept local environmental degradation in order to attract the employment and economic development advantages which mineral projects are thought to bring. Clearly, companies as part of their assessment of alternative sites investigate the strength of environmental opposition and adjust the spatial distribution of their investment plans accordingly. They also include the anticipated delays in obtaining planning consents in their rolling investment programmes. In the relatively small number of cases where development permission is withheld firms do not normally abandon their planned investment, but successfully search for alternative locations elsewhere in the country; few have been pushed to seek 'pollution havens' overseas (Gladwin, 1977).

Where major resource development opportunities are site-specific, and are highly attractive economically, the environmental opposition has little chance of stopping exploitation, although concessions over the siting of plant, the introduction of pollution control measures or the programme of reclamation may well be gained. The forces favouring development are too strong for the no-production option to be the realistic outcome of the planning process: the major resource companies have good access to government; in fact – particularly in Europe – many are branches of government; resources are regarded as a vital input into the economic growth process; all national governments place a premium on indigenous sources of supply for balance-of-payments and security reasons; and a significant proportion of the influential public in many affected areas welcome the employment and potential spillover effects (through the development of service and processing industry) which resource exploitation can bring. In these circumstances it is difficult to see that the imposition of environmental and planning controls presents any significant barrier to continued investment in resource exploitation.

Similarly, it seems extremely unlikely that conservation measures or pollution controls will have any material effect on the level of economic activity. There are two basic and interrelated reasons for this view. First, as was argued in Chapter 9, the process of effective policy formulation prevents all but marginal and slow adjustments to established practice. It is unusual to encounter sweeping changes in the formal expression of policy, which impose instant and major additional pollution abatement expenditure on to significant sectors of the economy. The economic, social and political consequences of such changes are simply too great for most governments to contemplate. Where legislation is perceived to be necessary to deal with a specific 'crisis' or to diffuse conflict, producers are given time to adjust their production technologies. Established producers are protected by so-called 'grandfather' clauses in the legislation, and by staged compliance timetables or, more usually, adjustment time is given informally through the implementation process. Delegation of responsibility and the discretion given to enforcement agencies is critical here. In all countries, even those with confrontational systems, enforcement practice operates sympathetically to economic interests. It would be rare for any enforcement agency to attempt (even if they had the effective power to do so) to close down a firm for non-compliance and bear the responsibility for the unemployment and local economic repercussions of the closure.

This does not mean that conservation and pollution control measures will not be introduced, but that their introduction will occur at a pace compatible with the technological and economic capability of the industrial system. The threat of enforced controls generates the search for viable adjustments in process technologies, raw material inputs and the product mix. Once this search has produced the means of control, then compliance can be required without affecting the entrenched growth process. It is this potential for adjustment to bring production practice more in line with the demands for environmental quality that is the second basic reason for arguing that conservation and pollution controls will not have any material effect on the level of economic activity. The form of activity will undoubtedly change but the scale *need* not.

By no means all forms of growth pose major environmental problems, and less damaging technologies, when introduced as part of the normal process of technical and economic change, are not necessarily more expensive than established production methods. In addition, some producers will gain economically from conservation and pollution control measures. Some will benefit from reduced input costs; for example, improvements in river water quality can reduce supply costs, and the collection of residuals pre-discharge can provide low-cost

WHY?

Environmental experts agree that acid rain is caused by rain, snow, fog, or dry particles that contain solutions of Sulphuric or Nitric acid.

Q. I am not aware of this problem in my immediate area so why should I worry?

A. Acid rain is being blown by winds everywhere and it is no longer just a regional problem. Damage to paint on cars by acid rain is a growing national and international problem.

Q. What happens if I don't do anything about this?

A. One of the concerns of the experts is that most people do not notice the damage from acid rain until there is discolouring on the bonnet and roof. This is the first stage of damage.

Q. What is the best way to prevent this damage ?

A. Use your car wash at least once a week no matter what the weather because it's your best insurance policy against damage from acid rain or from rusting.

Q. Why should I take the word of the car wash operator? After all, he has a special interest.

A. Don't take just his word for it – not only are there many scientific reports under way but you must have read articles like those in The Times reporting acid rain in the U.K. being "six times as acidic as vinegar".

SO REMEMBER ... **WASH-IT-HERE**

ACID RAIN

SAVE YOUR CAR

WASH-IT-HERE

Q. What is acid rain and why should I be concerned about it?

Figure 10.1   An ingenious method of reducing the damage from acid rain

recycled materials. Others will see an increased demand for their products; this most obviously applies to manufacturers of abatement technologies but, as Figure 10.1 shows, businessmen can display considerable ingenuity in their attempts to make a profit from the amelioration of pollution! Clearly, none of the potential adjustments will occur automatically; the inertia in the system is considerable and only continued pressure will push incremental change in a less environmentally damaging direction. However, given the strength of entrenched economic interests, it is extremely dubious whether environmentalists will succeed in switching the system from the pursuit of some form of growth.

THE REAL ISSUES

The real resource problems are in large measure the corollary of the false issues. It has been argued that when powerful economic interests are directly affected by scarcity, depletion or conflict, then the economic and political system has adaptive mechanisms and can act to submerge or diffuse opposition in order to ensure the continued existence of the processes of growth and capital accumulation. It follows, therefore, that problem resolution is unlikely in cases where the only solutions are directly antithetical to dominant economic interests. In addition, it is not possible to be sanguine about those forms of resource scarcity, depletion and degradation that are largely irrelevant to such interests.

International resource trade and distributive equity

The question of creating a New International Economic Order has attracted an enormous literature since it emerged as an issue for political debate in the early 1970s. Although the notion that market forces will eventually act to reduce spatial inequalities has become fashionable once again, the evidence from the resources sector lends little credence to this view. Mineral exploitation and the export trade has clearly provided LDC producers with much-needed investment capital. But typically it has not led to self-sustainable growth or to the spread of development through the national economy, nor has it acted to narrow the income gap between rich and poor nations. Undoubtedly, in a number of Third World countries economic mismanagement, the activities of powerful indigenous élites and political conflict have squandered the growth opportunities afforded by resource exports. It would be naïve and simplistic to blame all LDCs' ills on the capitalist trade system in general, and the multinational corporations in particular. However, there are features in the international exchange system which act to perpetuate, indeed exacerbate, spatial inequalities.

The whole trend in the economic development process is towards the production of increasingly complex processed goods. This means that the prices of basic primary commodities must fall in relative terms as a proportion of the price of the final goods. Therefore, unless Third World states can break out of their role as crude mineral exporters, their contribution to the total value added in production must fall and with it their relative incomes. Attempts to raise export prices and to increase the share of resource rents going to producer states cannot, in themselves, act to overcome this underlying characteristic of resource trade; although, if successful, the resulting additional capital could be used to generate other forms of development. There are, however, severe constraints on the ability of most producers to increase real price and rent levels. The adjustment mechanisms which protect the mineral corporations and consumers from physical and geopolitical shortages also serve to place a limit on the aspirations of exporting states.

The development of processing and related service industries is clearly important if LDC producers are to retain a significant proportion of the growth and income generated by their resources. It is, however, neither in the interests of the international mining corporations nor the consumer nations to allow such production shifts. The economic advantages to the companies of asset diversification, when added to consumer government interests in discouraging the import of processed minerals for balance-of-payments, security and employment reasons, are powerful forces acting against the redistribution of processing industry. Such forces become even more potent when the LDCs are politically unstable, are prone to make frequent changes in their tax and tariff regimes and have a history of asset expropriation. From 1960 to 1976, of the 1447 nationalizations which took place throughout the world all but 200 occurred in developing countries (United Nations, 1978); it comes, therefore, as little surprise to learn that the multinationals are reluctant to sink more fixed capital in mining centres than is necessary to maintain their supplies of the crude mineral. Although indigenous capital and funds borrowed through the international banking system could be (and have been) used to develop the processing sector, the productivity of such investments is dependent upon market outlets; these are limited by low internal effective demand in most LDCs and by considerable barriers to trade in processed goods.

There seems little possibility, therefore, that trade in resources can act to redress global inequalities, unless that is, strong international institutions are created with the power to enforce a new world economic order. To date there is little evidence to support Tinbergen's (1976) optimistic thesis that it is only a matter of time before international institutions evolve, as they have done at the national scale, to plan and co-ordinate economic development, and to pursue social welfare objectives. Falk (1980, p. 87) may be right in claiming that 'there is now a virtual consensus that the reform of international society requires some significant institutional build up at the global scale'. But is there much real demand for a reform of international society from those with the power to bring it about? Certainly, there is room for considerable doubt if the *Wall Street Journal* reflects influential opinion; in its 'A word to the Third World' (17 July 1975, p. 19) the message is clear: 'Don't expect the US to serve you up prosperity and don't think you can get it through extortion . . . if the Third World countries want to be rich like us, they might try doing a few things our way.'

Renewable resource scarcity: the LDC perspective

Flow resources, such as water, firewood and soil productivity, need not be scarce in any absolute physical sense. The unutilized biological capacity of the land and sea is immense, and for all practical purposes there is a physically unlimited recyclable supply of water. However, this resource potential is irrelevant if human institutions (economic, social and political) are incapable of tapping it and allocating the product to those in need. It is abundantly clear that the millions affected by critical food, water and fuel shortages can expect little from technical aid packages or the flood of well-meant words written on their plight; still less do they stand to gain from yet another international conference of experts or politicians purporting to search for a better understanding of the issues. The 'green revolution' has not provided a miracle answer to food shortages; indeed it has exacerbated the problems of the most disadvantaged groups, making them even more marginal to their national economies. It is now admitted that the ambitious UN Desertification Programme has failed to stop the process of declining productive capacity along the desert margins. And the products of the much-publicized Water Decade have not reached a fraction of those suffering from meagre and poor-quality supplies.

Baseline scarcity problems in most LDCs are rooted in the established socioeconomic structures, which deprive the poorest groups of effective demand and often of any significant political influence. But it would be naïve to believe that the reordering of social relations can provide the complete answer. It may be a necessary condition but it cannot be a sufficient condition. It has not saved China from losing an estimated 30 per cent of its arable land in the past two decades through soil erosion (Smil, 1984), nor has it solved the problem of deforestation, which leaves an estimated 500 million people suffering from fuel shortages for three to five months of the year (Rigdon, 1983). The argument, expounded by Schumpeter (1950), Sherman (1972), Stretton (1976), Schnaiberg (1980) and dozens of others, that only socialist planned economies can prevent ecological degradation and institute egalitarian policies for the distribution of scarce resources may be correct, but there is no automatic link between a change in the political order of things and a solution to renewable resource scarcity problems. Evidence from established socialist states is incompatible with Rothman's Utopian view that:

> A socialist society, unlike a capitalist society, starts from social requirements based on the demands of the population. Members of such a society will claim as a legal and political right a healthy environment. (Rothman, 1972, p. 33)

It is not just a question of reordering society to respond to the demands of the population, but of deciding which demands have priority over what timescale.

The solutions to this type of resource scarcity problem are immensely complex. Undoubtedly, it will necessitate a massive redistribution of real income, both inter- and intranationally, and, in addition, it will require a restructuring of the development priorities of the affected nations. Less stress will have to be laid on short-term economic gain and the expansion of the industrial base, and much more attention paid to increasing the long-term productivity of the rural sector. It is extremely doubtful whether many countries will surmount the formidable political and institutional barriers to action, or whether many governments will have the power to confront the powerful vested interests which would lose most from such sea-changes. Nor can much credence be given to the widely held view that the poor will eventually rise up and take by force what they are denied by the established political system. Desperately poor and hungry people rarely lead revolutionary movements; they are degraded by their conditions into apathy and fatalism.

Scarcity of renewable resources: an advanced nation perspective

It is not possible to say that renewable resources are scarce, or are likely to be scarce, in developed nations in any objective sense. Scarcity is a perceptual matter. From an eco-revolutionary perspective there are already critical scarcity problems since environmental change is an indisputable fact and the 'rights' of non-human species are clearly not being respected. To those who place no, or negligible, value on blue whales, natterjack toads, Scandinavian lakes or German forests their disappearance or degradation does not constitute a scarcity problem. The renewable resource problems in advanced nations basically boil down to conflicts over the package of available environmental goods and services and the way these products are allocated between different groups in society. It, of course, trivializes the whole debate over environmental futures to talk in terms of individual species or landscapes but the fact remains that, at the grassroots level, the issues are normally expressed as crude trade-offs: Arctic alpines v. water supplies, dragon-flies v. houses, wetland habitats v. food production or the aquatic status of Scandinavian lakes v. increased electricity charges. Given that many environmental goods and services have no established price or value, underprovision and overutilization are inherent characteristics of the market system of exchange. Moreover, democratic processes of representation, parti-cipation and influence can in no way ensure that political decision systems will produce an equitable allocation of non-market environmental services. However, there is nothing in a centrally planned socialist economy, or in a reversion to small-scale community life, which necessarily resolves conflict between indi-viduals demanding different products from the resource base. Utopian societies cannot conjure up consensus between those who want to respect the biorights of a wild duck and those who prefer to shoot and eat it!

Despite pseudo-scientific predictions of the imminent collapse of global support systems, the likelihood of total failure of the bio-geochemical cycles appears remote. Change in the environment is, however, inevitable. The crucial question is not whether life will continue, but what type of society and environ-ment will human beings have to live in. As Mann Borgese (1980, p. 193) says, 'history will fumble along its own way'. Spatial and social inequalities will not disappear; Malthusian limits will continue to make life 'nasty, brutish and short' for millions; environmental élites in the advanced world will go on pushing the economic growth process in ways which provide the environmental quality goods they favour most; and the conspicuous patterns of material and 'post-material' consumption of the wealthy will continue to stand in obscene contrast to the conditions of the poor in the Third World. Social movements will come and go; but those looking to LDC resource power or the environmental movement to produce the 'post-industrial' revolution seem doomed to a long wait. Signs are there that a significant proportion of the population in advanced countries are less committed to materialism; but the forces of inertia are immense, deeply en-trenched in systems of value, and in socioeconomic and political structures.

Machiavelli in *The Prince* got to the heart of the matter in 1513; nothing has changed to alter the basic nature of human institutions or the human mentality since he wrote:

> There is nothing more difficult to carry out, nor more doubtful of success, nor more dangerous to handle, than to initiate a new order of things. For the reformer has enemies in all who profit by the old order, and only lukewarm defenders in all those who would profit by the new order. The luke-warmness arises partly from fear of their adversaries who have law in their favour; and partly from the incredulity of mankind, who do not truly believe in anything new until they have had actual experience of it.

NOTE

1   This is not to argue that technology-fix can provide the answer for resource scarcities which do not impinge significantly on advanced nation capital interests (e.g. rural water shortages, scarcity of firewood and the depletion of soil fertility in the LDCs).

References

Abrams, M. (1974) 'Changing values', *Encounter*, October, 29–38.

Adams, J. G. U. (1974a) 'Obsolete economics', *Ecologist*, 4, 280–9.

Adams, J. G. U. (1974b) '. . . and how much for your grandmother?', *Environment and Planning*, 6, 619–26.

Agarwal, A. (1983) 'The poverty of nature: environment, development, science and technology', *IDRC Report*, 12, 4–6.

Ahmed, J. (1976) 'Environmental aspects of international income distribution', in Walter, I. (ed.) *Studies in International Environmental Economics*, New York, Wiley, 225–40.

Allen, G. C. (1961) *The Structure of Industry in Britain*, London, Longman.

Allen, R. (1980) *How to Save the World: Strategy for World Conservation*, London, Kogan Page.

Allison, G. T. (1971) *Essence of Decision: Explaining the Cuban Missile Crisis*, Boston, Mass., Little, Brown.

Allison, L. (1975) *Environmental Planning: A Political and Philosophical Analysis*, London, Allen & Unwin.

American Bureau of Mining Statistics (annual) *Non-Ferrous Metal Data*, New York, ABMS.

Amin, S. (1976) *Unequal Development: An Essay on the Social Formations of Peripheral Capitalism*, New York, Monthly Review Press.

Amin, S. (1977) *Imperialism and Unequal Development*, Hassocks, Harvester Press.

Amin, S. (1979) 'NIEO: how to put Third World surpluses to effective use', *Third World Quarterly*, 1, (1), January, 65–72.

Anders, G., Gramm, W. P., Maurice, S. C. and Smithson, C. W. (1980) *The Economics of Mineral Extraction*, New York, Praeger.

Anderson, F. (1973) *NEPA in the Courts: A Legal Analysis of the National Environmental Policy Act*, Baltimore, Md, Johns Hopkins University Press.

Anderson, F. R., Kneese, A. V., Reed, P. D., Stevenson, R. B. and Taylor, S. (1977) *Environmental Improvement through Economic Incentives*, Baltimore, Md, Resources for the Future/Johns Hopkins University Press.

Anderson, M. (1981) 'Planning policies and development control in the Sussex Downs', *Town Planning Review*, 52, 5–25.

Andrews, R. N. L. (1980) 'Class politics or democratic reform; environmentalism and American political institutions', *Natural Resources Journal*, 20, 221–42.

Arad, R. W., Arad, U. B., McCulloch, R., Pinera, J. and Hollick, A. L. (1979) *Sharing Global Resources*, 1980s Project/Council on Foreign Relations, New York, McGraw-Hill.

d'Arge, R. C. (1972) 'Economic growth and the natural environment', in Kneese, A. V. and Bower, B. T. (eds) *Environmental Quality Analysis*, Baltimore, Md, Resources for the Future/Johns Hopkins University Press, 11–34.

Arnstein, S. R. (1969) 'A ladder of citizen participation', *Journal of the American Institute of Planners*, 25, 216–24.

Arrow, K. J. (1971) *Essays in the Theory of Risk-Bearing*, Chicago, Markham.

Arrow, K. J. and Lind, R. (1970) 'Uncertainty and the evaluation of public investment decisions', *American Economic Review*, 60 (3), 364–78.

Asch, P. and Seneca, J. (1978) 'Some evidence on the distribution of air quality', *Land Economics*, 54, 278–97.

Ashby, E. (1976) 'Protection of the environment: the human dimension', *Proceedings of the Royal Society of Medicine*, 69, 721–30.

Ashby, E. (1978a) *Reconciling Man with the Environment*, Oxford, Oxford University Press.

Ashby, E. (1978b) *Engineers and Politics: A Case History*, 22nd Graham Clark Lecture, London, Council of Engineering Institutions.

Ashby, E. and Anderson, M. (1981) *The Politics of Clean Air*, Oxford, Oxford University Press.

Atwood, G. (1979) 'The strip-mining of western coal', in *Readings from Scientific American: Energy and Environment*, with introductions by Singer, S. F., San Francisco, Calif., W. H. Freeman, 155–63.

Auliciems, A. and Burton, I. (1973) 'Trends in smoke concentrations before and after the Clean Air Act of 1956', *Atmospheric Environment*, 7, 1063–70.

Australian Government, Bureau of Statistics (1981) *Year Book of the Commonwealth of Australia: 1981*, Canberra, ABS.

Auty, R. M. (1983) 'Multinational corporations, the product–life cycle and product strategy: the oil majors' response to heightened risk', *Geoforum*, 14(1), 1–13.

Ayres, R. U. (1972) 'A materials–process–product model', in Kneese, A. V. and Bower, B. T. (eds) *Environmental Quality Analysis, Theory and Method in the Social Sciences*, Baltimore, Md, Johns Hopkins University Press, 35–68.

Ayres, R. U. and Kneese, A. V. (1969) 'Production, consumption and externalities', *American Economic Review*, 59(3), 282–97.

Bach, W. (1972) *Atmospheric Pollution*, Problems in Geography series, New York, McGraw-Hill.

Bachrach, P. and Baratz, M. S. (1962) 'The two faces of power', *American Political Science Review*, 56, 947–52.

Bachrach, P. and Baratz, M. S. (1963) 'Decisions and non-decisions: an analytical framework', *American Political Science Review*, 57, 641–51.

Bachrach, P. and Baratz, M. S. (1971) *Power and Poverty: Theory and Practice*, Oxford, Oxford University Press.

Bain, J. S. (1954) 'Economies of scale, concentration and the condition of entry in 20 manufacturing industries', *American Economic Review*, 44, 15–39.

Balbus, I. D. (1971) 'The concept of interest in pluralist and Marxian analysis', *Politics and Society*, 1(2), 151–78.

Barde, J., Brown, G. M. Jr, and Buchot, P. F. T. (1979) 'Water pollution control policies are getting results', *Ambio*, 8(4), 152–9.

Barker, A. (1976) 'Local amenity societies – a survey and outline report', in *The Local Amenity Movement*, London, Civic Trust, 21–31.

Barnet, R. J. (1979) 'Multinationals and development', in Jegen, M. E. and Wilber, C. K. (eds) *Growth with Equity*, New York, Paulist Press, 149–62.

Barnet, R. J. (1980) *The Lean Years: Politics in the Age of Scarcity*, New York, Simon & Schuster.

Barnett, H. J. and Morse, C. (1963) *Scarcity and Growth: The Economics of Natural Resource Availability*, Baltimore, Md, Johns Hopkins University Press.

Barnett, H. J., Van Muiswinkel, G. M., Shechter, M. and Myers, J. G. (1984) 'Global trends in non-fuel minerals', in Simon, J. L. and Kahn, H. (eds) *The Resourceful Earth*, Oxford, Blackwell, 155–63.

Barratt-Brown, M. (1976) 'The crisis of capitalism and commodity production', in Barratt-Brown, M., Emerson, T. and Stoneman, C. (eds) *Resources and the Environment: A Socialist Perspective*, Nottingham, Spokesman, 5–9.

Bartlett, R. V. (1980) *The Reserve Mining Controversy*, Bloomington, Ind., and London, Indiana University Press.

Bauer, P. T. (1972) *Dissent on Development*, London, Weidenfeld & Nicolson.

Baum, W. C. (1958) *The French Economy and the State*, Rand Corporation Research Studies, Princeton, NJ, Princeton University Press.

Baumann, D. D. and Dworkin, D. (1975) *Planning for Water Reuse*, Washington, DC, US Army Corps of Engineers/Institute of Water Resources.

Baumann, D. D. and Kasperson, R. E. (1974) 'Public acceptance of renovated waste water: myth and reality', *Water Resources Research*, 10(4), 667–74.

Baumol, W. J. and Oates, W. E. (1975) *The Theory of Environmental Policy: Externalities, Public Outlays and the Quality of Life*, Englewood Cliffs, NJ, Prentice-Hall.

Beaver Committee (1954) *Report of the Committee on Air Pollution*, Cmd 1322, London, HMSO.

Beckerman, W. (1972a) 'Environmental policy and the challenge to economic theory', in Sachs, I. (ed.) *Political Economy of Environment: Problems of Method*, Paris, École Pratique des Hautes Études/Mouton, 103–12.

Beckerman, W. (1972b) 'Economists, scientists and environmental catastrophe', *Oxford Economic Papers*, n.s., 24, 3 November, 327–44.

Beckerman, W. (1974) *In Defence of Economic Growth*, London, Jonathan Cape.

Beddington, J. R., Watts, C. M. K. and Wright, W. D. C. (1975) 'Optimal cropping of self-reproducible natural resources', *Econometrica*, 43, 789–802.

Behrman, J. N. (1974) *Toward a New International Economic Order*, Atlantic Papers No. 3, Paris, Atlantic Institute of International Affairs.

Berger, E. L. (1974) *Unions, Parties and Political Development: A Study of Mineworkers in Zambia*, New Haven, Conn., Yale University Press.

Bergsten, C. F. (1974) 'The threat is real', *Foreign Policy*, 14, 84–90.

Berry, B. J. (1977) *The Social Burdens of Environmental Pollution*, Cambridge, Mass., Ballinger.

Bhagwati, J. N. (ed.) (1977) *The New International Economic Order: The North–South Debate*, Cambridge, Mass., MIT Press.

Bienefeld, M. and Godfrey, M. (eds) (1982) *The Struggle for Development*, Chichester, Wiley.

Bingham, G. (1981) *Environmental Conflict Resolution: An Annotated Bibliography*, Washington, DC, The Conservation Foundation.

Bisset, R. (1978) 'Quantification, decision-making and environmental impact assessment in the United Kingdom', *Journal of Environmental Management*, 7, 43–58.

Bisset, R. (1983) 'A critical survey of methods for environmental impact assessment', in O'Riordan, T. and Turner, R. K. (eds) *An Annotated Reader in Environmental Planning and Management*, Oxford, Pergamon, 168–86.

Blowers, A. (1982) 'The triumph of material interests – geography, pollution and the environment', paper delivered to Institute of British Geographers' Conference, Southampton, January.

Bohm, P. (1981) *Deposit-Refund Systems*, Baltimore, Md, Resources for the Future/Johns Hopkins University Press.

Bosson, R. and Varon, B. (1977) *The Mining Industry in the Developing Countries*, New York, Oxford University Press/World Bank.

Boulding, K. E. (1966) 'The economics of the coming spaceship earth', in Jarrett, H. (ed.) *Environmental Quality in a Growing Economy*, Baltimore, Md, Johns Hopkins University Press.

Bowman, M. (1979) *Australian Approaches to Environmental Management: The Response of State Planning*, Hobart, Environmental Law Reform Group.

Bradshaw, A. (1976) 'A critique of Steven Lukes' "Power: a radical view"', *Sociology*, 10, 121–8.

Brandt Commission (1980) *North–South: A Programme for Survival*, London, Pan Books.

British Geological Survey (1984) *World Mineral Statistics: 1978–82*, Natural Environmental Research Council, London, HMSO.

British Petroleum (1979) *Oil Crisis . . . Again*, London, BP.

Bronfenbrenner, M. (1982) 'The Japanese development model re-examined: why concern ourselves with Japan?', in Bienefeld, M. and Godfrey, M. (eds) *The Struggle for Development*, Chichester, Wiley.

Brookings Institution (1975) *Trade in Primary Commodities: Conflict or Cooperation?*, tripartite report by fifteen economists from Japan, the European Community and North America, Washington, DC, Brookings Institution.

Brown, G. M. (1973) 'The efficiency of subsidies and standards for managing water quality', circulated paper.

Brown, L. R. (1975) 'The multinational corporation: economic colossus of modern times', *Horizon USA*, 9, 8–12.

Brown, W. M. (1981) 'Can OPEC survive the glut', *Fortune*, 30 November, 89–90.

Bugler, J. (1972) *Polluting Britain*, Harmondsworth, Penguin.

Bugler, J. (1981) 'Friends of the Earth is 10 years old', *New Scientist*, 30 April, 294–7.

Buller, H. and Lowe, P. D. (1982) 'Politics and class in rural preservation', in Moseley, M. (ed.) *Power, Planning and People in Rural East Anglia*, Norwich, Centre of East Anglia Studies, 21–41.

Burenstam-Linder, S. (1982) 'How to avoid a New International Economic Disorder', *World Economy*, 5, 275–84.

Burt, O. R. (1967) 'Temporal allocation of ground water', *Water Resources Research*, 3, 45–56.

Burton, I., Kates, R. W. and White, G. F. (1978) *The Environment as Hazard*, New York, Oxford University Press.

Burton, I. and Pushchak, R. (1984) 'The status and prospects of risk assessment', *Geoforum*, 15(3), 463–75.

Butlin, J. A. (1981) *Economics of Environmental and Natural Resources Policy*, London, Longman.

Buttel, F. H. (1980) 'The environmental movement: historical roots and current trends', in Humphrey, C. R. and Buttel, F. H. (eds) *Environment, Energy and Society*, Belmont, Calif., Wadsworth.

Byers, W. M. (1970) *An Economic Impact Study of Olympic and Mt Rainier National Parks, Washington*, Washington, DC, National Park Service.

Canada, Commission on Pacific Fisheries Policy (1982) *Turning the Tide: A New Policy for Canada's Pacific Fisheries – Final Report*, Ottawa, Supply and Services.

Cardoso, F. H. (1972) 'Dependency and development in Latin America', *New Left Review*, 74, 83–95.

Carley, M. (1981) *Rational Techniques in Policy Analysis*, London, Heinemann Educational.

Carpenter, S. L. and Kennedy, W. J. D. (1980) 'Environmental conflict management', *Environmental Professional*, 2(1), 67–74.

Carson, R. (1962) *Silent Spring*, London, Hamilton.

Carson, W. G. (1971) 'White-collar crime and enforcement of factory legislation', in Carson, W. G. and Wiles, P. (eds) *The Sociology of Crime and Delinquency in Britain*, London, Martin Robertson, 192–206.

Castells, M. (1977) *The Urban Question: A Marxist Approach*, London, Edward Arnold.

Cawson, A. (1977) *Environmental Planning and the Politics of Corporatism*, Working Papers in Urban and Regional Studies, No. 7, Brighton, University of Sussex.

Cawson, A. (1978) 'Pluralism, corporatism and the role of the state', *Government and Opposition*, 13(2), 178–98.

Chisholm, A. (1972) *Philosophers of the Earth: Conversations with Ecologists*, London, Sidgwick & Jackson.

Chisholm, M. (1966) *Geography and Economics*, Bell's Advanced Economic Geographies, London, Bell.

Ciriacy-Wantrup, S. V. (1938) 'Social conservation in European farm management', *Journal of Farm Economics*, 20(3), 86–101.

Ciriacy-Wantrup, S. V. (1952) *Resource Conservation Economics and Policies*, Berkeley, Calif., University of California Press.

Clark, B. D., Chapman, K., Bisset, R. and Wathern, P. (1978) *Environmental Impact Assessment in the USA: A Critical Review*, Research Report 26, London, Department of the Environment/Department of Transport.

Clark, B. D., Bisset, R. and Wathern, P. (1980) *Environmental Impact Assessment, a Bibliography with Abstracts*, London, Mansell; and New York, Bowker.

Clark, C. W. (1976) *Mathematical Bioeconomics*, New York, Wiley.

Clark, M. J. (1978) 'Geomorphology in coastal zone management', *Geography*, 63, 273–82.

Clawson, M. (1959) *Methods of Measuring the Demand for and the Value of Outdoor Recreation*, Washington, DC, Resources for the Future.

Clawson, M. (1974) 'Comment on A. C. Fisher and J. V. Krutilla, "Managing the public lands: assignment of property rights and valuation of resources"', in Haefele, E. T. (ed.) *The Governance of Common Property Resources*, Baltimore, Md, Johns Hopkins University Press.

Clifford, S. (1978) 'EIA: some unanswered questions', *Built Environment*, 4, 152–60.

Clower, R. W., Dalton, G., Horwitz, M. and Walters, A. (1966) *Growth without Development: An Economic Survey of Liberia*, Evanston, Ill., Northwestern University Press.

Coase, R. H. (1960) 'The problem of social cost', *Journal of Law and Economics*, 3, 1–44.

Coate, L. E. and Bonner, P. A. (1975) *Regional Environmental Management*, London, Wiley.

Coates, B. E., Johnston, R. J. and Knox, P. L. (1977) *Geography and Inequality*, Oxford, Oxford University Press.

Cobbe, J. H. (1979) *Governments and Mining Companies in Developing Countries*, Westview Special Studies in Social, Political and Economic Development, Boulder, Colo., Westview Press.

Coddington, A. (1970) 'The economics of ecology', *New Society*, 9 April, 595–7.

Cohen, S. D. (1978) 'Changes in the international economy – old realities and new myths', *Journal of World Trade Law*, 12(4), July, 273–88.

Common, M. S. (1977) 'A note on the uses of taxes to control pollution', *Scandinavian Journal of Economics*, 79, 347–9.

Commoner, B. (1972a) 'The environmental cost of economic growth', in Schurr, S. (ed.) *Energy, Economic Growth and the Environment*, Baltimore, Md, Johns Hopkins University Press, 30–66.

Commoner, B. (1972b) *The Closing Circle: Man, Nature and Technology*, New York, Knopf.

Connell, J. (1971) 'Green belt county', *New Society*, 25 February.

Connell, J. (1972) 'Amenity societies: the preservation of central Surrey', *Town and Country Planning*, 40, 63–81.

Connell, J. (1978) *The End of Tradition*, London, Routledge & Kegan Paul.

Coombes, D. (1971) *State Enterprise*, London, Allen & Unwin.

Cooper, R. (1977) 'The oceans as a source of revenue', in Bhagwati, L. N. (ed.) *The New International Economic Order*, Cambridge, Mass., MIT Press.

Cooper, R. N. and Lawrence, R. Z. (1975) 'The 1972–75 commodity boom', *Brookings Papers on Economic Activity*, 3, 671–723.

Copes, P. (1981) 'Rational resource management and institutional constraints: the case of the fishery', in Butlin, J. A. (ed.) *Economics and Resources Policy*, London, Longman, 113–28.

Cormick, G. W. (1980) 'The "theory" and practice of environmental mediation', *Environmental Professional*, 2(1), 24–33.

Cotgrove, S. (1976) 'Environmentalism and Utopia', *Sociological Review*, 24, 23–42.

Cotgrove, S. (1982) *Catastrophe or Cornucopia?*, Chichester, Wiley.

Cotgrove, S. and Duff, A. (1980) 'Environmentalism, middle-class radicalism and politics', *Sociological Review*, 28, 333–51.

Crandall, R. W. (1983) *Controlling Industrial Pollution: The Economics and Politics of Clean Air*, Studies in the Regulation of Economic Activity, Washington, DC, Brookings Institution.

Crenson, M. (1971) *The Unpolitics of Air Pollution: A Study of Non-Decision Making in Cities*, Baltimore, Md, Johns Hopkins University Press.

Crowson, P. C. F. (1977) *Non-Fuel Minerals and Foreign Policy*, London, Royal Institute of International Affairs.

Crowson, P. C. F. (1981) 'Reversing the declining investment in metals exploration', *Metals and Materials*, March, 49–53.

Culhane, P. J. (1974) 'Federal agency organizational change in response to environmentalism', *Humboldt Journal of Social Relations*, 2(1), 31–44.

Culyer, A. J. (1977) 'The quality of life and the limits to cost–benefit analysis', in Wingo, L. and Evans, A. (eds) *Public Economics and the Quality of Life*, Baltimore, Md, Johns Hopkins University Press, 141–53.

Cunha, L. V., Figueiredo, V. L., Correia, M. L. and Gonçalves, A. S. (1977) *Management and Law for Water Resources*, Fort Collins, Colo., Water Resources Publications.

Dahl, R. A. (1961) *Who Governs? Democracy and Power in an American City*, New Haven, Conn., Yale University Press.

Dahl, R. A. (1967) *Pluralist Democracy in the United States*, Chicago, Rand McNally.

Dales, J. H. (1968) *Pollution, Property and Prices*, Toronto, University of Toronto Press.

Daly, H. E. (1973) *Towards a Steady State Economy*, San Francisco, Calif., W. H. Freeman.

Daly, H. E. (1976) 'The steady state economy', in Wilson, K. D. (ed.) *Prospects for Growth*, New York, Praeger, 263–81.

Daly, H. E. (1982) 'The steady-state economy: what, why and how', in Birrell, R. (ed.) *Quarry Australia?* Melbourne, Oxford University Press, 251–60.

Darke, R. and Walker, R. (eds) (1977) *Local Government and the Public*, London, Leonard Hill.

Dasgupta, B. (1977) 'India's green revolution', *Economic and Political Weekly*, 12, 241–60.

Dasgupta, P. (1982) *The Control of Resources*, Oxford, Blackwell.

Dasgupta, P. and Heal, G. (1979) *Economic Theory and Exhaustible Resources*, Cambridge, James Nisbet/Cambridge University Press.

Davidson, J. and MacEwen, A. (1983) 'The livable city', pt 2 in *The Conservation and Development Programme for the UK: A Response to the World Conservation Strategy*, London, Kogan Page.

Davis, B. W. (1979) *Politics of Development: The Struggle for South-West Tasmania*, Hobart, University of Tasmania.

Davis, B. W. (1980) 'Problems of Tasmanian economic development: perceptions and reality', paper presented at Three Nations Conference, Development and Under-development in Canada, Australia and New Zealand, University of Canterbury, Christchurch, NZ, 16–20 November.

Davis, R. (1969) 'English foreign trade 1660–1700', in Minchinton, W. E. (ed.) *The Growth of English Overseas Trade in the 17th and 18th Centuries*, London, Methuen, 78–98, 99–120.

Davis, R., Wilen, J. E. and Jergovic, R. (1983) 'Oil and gas royalty recovery policy on federal and Indian lands', *Natural Resources Journal*, 23, April, 391–401.

Deese, D. A. and Nye, J. S. (eds) (1981) *Energy and Security*, Cambridge, Mass., Ballinger.

Dennison, S. R. (1942) 'A dissenting report', in Scott, Mr Justice (chairman) *Report of the Committee on Land Utilization in Rural Areas*, Cmnd 6378, London, HMSO.

Devaux Charbonne, J. (1964) 'The role of the state in French oil exploration', in Hedberg, H. *et al.* (eds) *The Role of National Government in the Exploration of Mineral Resources*, Ocean City, NJ, Littoral Press, 111–24.

Dickens, P. and Lloyd, P. E. (1981) *Modern Western Society*, London, Harper & Row.

Dolman, A. J. (ed.) (1980) *Global Planning and Resource Management: Toward International Decision Making in a Divided World*, Foundation Reshaping the International Order, New York, Pergamon.

Donald, J. R. (1966) *The Cape Breton Coal Problem*, Ottawa, Department of Energy, Mines and Resources.

Dorfman, R. (ed.) (1965) *Measuring the Benefit of Government Investments*, Washington, DC, Brookings Institution; and London, Allen & Unwin, 1968.

Dorfman, R. (1977) 'Incidence of costs and benefits of environmental programs', *American Economic Review, Papers and Proceedings*, 67, 331–40.

Downs, A. (1967) *Inside Bureaucracy*, Boston, Mass., Little, Brown.

Downs, A. (1972) 'Up and down with ecology – the issue attention cycle', *Public Interest*, 28, 38–50.

Dunlap, R. E. and Dillman, D. A. (1976) 'Decline in public support for environmental protection: evidence from a 1970–1974 panel study', *Rural Sociology*, 41(3), 382–90.

Dunleavy, P. (1980) *Urban Political Analysis: The Politics of Collective Consumption*, London, Macmillan.

Eagles, P. F. J. (1984) *The Planning and Management of Environmentally Sensitive Areas*, Themes in Resource Management Series, New York, Longman.

Eckert, R. D. (1979) *The Enclosure of Ocean Resources*, Stanford, Calif., Hoover Institution.

Eckstein, O. (1958) *Water Resource Development: The Economics of Project Evaluation*, Cambridge, Mass., Harvard University Press.

Ehrlich, P. R. (1970a) *The Population Bomb*, New York, Ballantine Books.

Ehrlich, P. R. (1970b) 'Famine 1975: fact or fallacy?', in Helfrich, H. W. Jr (ed.) *Agenda for Survival: The Environmental Crisis*, New Haven, Conn., Yale University Press, 47–64.

Ehrlich, P. R. and Ehrlich, A. H. (1970) *Population, Resources, Environment: Issues in Human Ecology*, San Francisco, Calif., W. H. Freeman.

EIU (Economists Intelligence Unit) (1984) *North/South Countertrade* Special Report No. 174, London, The Economist Publications Ltd.

Elkington, J. (1980) *The Ecology of Tomorrow's World-Industry's Environment*, London, Associated Business Press.

Engler, R. (1961) *The Politics of Oil*, New York, Macmillan.

Environmental Protection Agency (EPA) (1972) *Comprehensive Studies of Solid Waste Management*, Final Report, SER No. 72–3, Berkeley, Calif., US Environmental Protection Agency, University of California.

EPA (1974) *Cost Effectiveness of a Uniform National Sulfur Emission Tax*, Washington, DC, Office of Air Programs, US Environmental Protection Agency, February.

Estall, R. C. and Buchanan, R. O. (1980) *Industrial Activity and Economic Geography*, 4th rev., edn, London, Hutchinson.

Evely, R. and Little, M. D. (1960) *Concentration in British Industry: An Empirical Study of Industrial Production 1935–51*, Cambridge, Cambridge University Press.

Exxon (1978) 'Exploration in developing countries', paper presented at Energy Committee Seminar, Aspen Institute for Humanistic Studies, Boulder, Colo., 16–20 July.

Fagence, M. (1977) *Citizen Participation in Planning*, Oxford, Pergamon.

Fairfax, S. K. (1978) 'A disaster in the environmental movement', *Science*, 199, 17 February, 743–8.

Faith, N. (1972) *The Infiltrators: The European Business Invasion of America*, New York, Dutton.

Falk, R. A. (1980) 'The institutional dimension of a New International Order', in Dolman, A. J. (ed.) *Global Planning and Resource Management*, Oxford, Pergamon, 87–102.

Feacham, R., McGarry, M. and Mara, D. (eds) (1977) *Water, Wastes and Health in Hot Climates*, London, Wiley.

Feder, E. (1976) 'McNamara's little Green Revolution: World Bank scheme for the self-liquidation of Third World peasantry', *Economic and Political Weekly*, 11, 532–41.

Feist, M. J. (1978) *A Study of Management Agreements*, CCP 114, Cheltenham, Countryside Commission.

Ferris, B. G. and Speizer, F. E. (1981) 'Criteria for establishing standards for air pollutants', *The Business Roundtable Air Quality Project*, Vol. 1, New York, Business Roundtable.

Ferris, J. (1972) *Participation in Urban Planning: The Barnsbury Case*, London, Bell.

Fisher, A. C. (1981) *Resource and Environmental Economics*, Cambridge Surveys of Economic Literature, Cambridge, Cambridge University Press.

Fisher, A. C. and Krutilla, J. V. (1974) *Valuing Long Run Ecological Consequences and Irreversibilities*, RFF Reprint Paper No. 117, Washington, DC, Resources for the Future.

Flegg, A. (1976) 'Methodological problems in estimating recreational demand functions and evaluating recreational benefits', *Regional Studies*, 10(3), 353–62.

Fleischman, P. (1969) 'Conservation, the biological fallacy', *Landscape*, 18, 23–7.

Forrester, J. W. (1970) *World Dynamics*, Cambridge, Mass., Wright-Allen Press.

Fox, I. K. and Craine, L. E. (1962) 'Organisational arrangements for water development', *Natural Resources Journal*, 2, 1–44.

Frank, A. G. (1967) *Capitalism and Underdevelopment in Latin America: Historical Studies of Chile and Peru*, New York, Monthly Review Press.

Frank, A. G. (1978) *Dependent Accumulation and Underdevelopment*, London, Macmillan.

Frank, A. G. and Diaz, G. (1974) 'Los ladrónes quieren indemnización' in *Carta abierta en al aniversario del golpe militar en Chile*, Madrid, Corazon (Alberto).

Frankel, M. (1974) 'The Alkali Inspectorate: the control of industrial air pollution', *Social Audit*, 1(4), Spring, supplement, 1–48.

Freeman, A. M. (1972) 'The distribution of environmental quality', in Kneese, A. V. and Bower, B. T. (eds) *Environmental Quality Analysis*, Baltimore, Md, Resources for the Future/Johns Hopkins University Press, 243–80.

Freyman, A. J. (1974) 'Mineral resources and economic growth', *Finance and Development*, 11(1), March, 20–3, 34.

Fried, E. R. (1976) 'International trade in raw materials: myths and realities', *Science*, 191, 641–6.

Friedland, R., Piven, F. F. and Alford, R. R. (1977) 'Political conflict, urban structure and the fiscal crisis', *International Journal of Urban and Regional Research*, 1(3), 447–71.

Friedman, M. (1962) *Price Theory*, Chicago, Aldine.

Friesema, H. P. and Culhane, P. J. (1976) 'Social impacts, politics and the environmental impact statement', *Natural Resources Journal*, 16, 339–56.

Gamston, D. (1975) *The Designation of Conservation Areas*, York, Institute of Advanced Architectural Studies, University of York.

Gardner, R. N., Okita, S. and Udink, B. J. (1977) 'A turning point in North–South economic relations' in *Trilateral Commission Task Force Report*, New York, New York University Press, 57–74.

Garnaut, R. and Clunies Ross, A. (1983) *Taxation on Mineral Rents*, Oxford, Clarendon Press.

Garner, J. F. (1980): 'Land use planning in the light of environmental protection', in Bothe, M. (co-ordinator) *Trends in Environmental Policy and Law*, Berlin, Erich Schmidt Verlag, 155–68.

Garvey, G. (1972) *Energy, Ecology and Economy: A Framework for Environmental Policy*, New York, Norton.

Gedicks, A. (1977) 'Raw materials: the Achilles' heel of American Imperialism?', *Insurgent Sociologist*, 7, 31–3.

Gerasimov, I. P. (1983) 'Land resources of the world; their use and reserves: definition of land quality and agricultural potential by soil survey maps', *Geoforum*, 14(4), 427–39.

Gillis, M. (1982) 'Evolution of natural resource taxation in developing countries', *Natural Resources Journal*, 22, July, 619–48.

Gilpin, A. (1978) *Air Pollution*, 2nd edn, St Lucia, University of Queensland Press.

Girvan, N. (1970) 'Multinational corporations and dependent underdevelopment in mineral export economies', *Social and Economic Studies*, 19(4), December, 490–526.

Girvan, N. (1973) 'Development and dependence economics in the Caribbean and Latin America, *Social and Economic Studies*, 22(1), 1–33.

Girvan, N. (1974) 'Las multinacionales del cobre in Chile', in Ffrench-Davis, R. and Tironi, E. (eds) *El Cobre en el Desarrollo Nacional*, Santiago, Centro de Estudios de Planificación National.

Girvan, N. (1976) *Corporate Imperialism: Conflict and Expropriation, Transnational Corporations and Economic Nationalism in the Third World*, White Plains, NY, M. E. Sharpe.

Gladwin, T. (1977) *Environment, Planning and the Multinational Corporation*, Contemporary Studies in Economic and Financial Analysis, Vol. 8, Greenwich, Conn., JAI Press.

Glaeser, M. G. (1957) *Public Utilities in American Capitalism*, New York, Macmillan.

Goldsmith, E., Allen, R., Allaby, M., Davoll, J. and Lawrence, S. (1972) 'Blueprint for survival', *Ecologist*, 2; reprinted, Harmondsworth, Penguin.

Goldstein, W. (1983) 'Can OPEC survive 1984?', *Energy Policy*, September, 196–203.

Goodey, B. and Gold, J. R. (1984) 'Some qualitative aspects of the urban environment in developed countries', *Geoforum*, 15(3), 433–45.

Goodman, R. (1972) *After the Planners*, Harmondsworth, Penguin.

Gordon, H. S. (1954) 'The economic theory of a common property resource – the fishery', *Journal of Political Economy*, 62, 124–42.

Graham, D. and Herrick, D. C. (1973) 'World dynamics', IEEE, *Transactions on Automatic Control*, August, 415–16.

Green, B. (1981) *Countryside Conservation*, Resource Management series, Vol. 3, London, Allen & Unwin.

Gregory, R. (1976) 'The voluntary amenity movement', in MacEwen, M. (ed.), *Future Landscapes*, London, Chatto & Windus.

Greis, P. T. (1973) 'The environmental impact statement: a small step instead of a giant leap', *Urban Lawyer*, 5, 264–303.

Gresser, J. (1975) 'The Japanese law for the compensation of pollution-related health damage: an introductory assessment', *Environmental Law Reporter*, December, 50229–51.

Habermas, J. (1976a) 'Systematically distorted communication' and 'Problems of legitimation in late capitalism', in Connerton, P. (ed.) *Critical Sociology*, Harmondsworth, Penguin, 348–87.

Habermas, J. (1976b) *Legitimation Crisis*, London, Heinemann.

Hägerstrand, T. (1952) *The Propagation of Innovation Waves*, Lund Studies in Geography, series B4, Lund, Lund University Press.

Hägerstrand, T. (1967) *Innovation Diffusion as a Spatial Process*, Chicago, University of Chicago Press.

Haigh, N. (1984) *EEC Environmental Policy and Britain: An Essay and a Handbook*, London, Environmental Data Services.

Hall, P. (1980) *Great Planning Disasters*, London, Weidenfeld & Nicolson.

Hamer, M. (1974) *Wheels within Wheels: A Study of the Road Lobby*, London, Friends of the Earth.

Hammack, J. and Brown, G. M. (1974) *Waterfowl and Wetlands: Toward Bio-Economic Analysis*, Baltimore, Md, Johns Hopkins University Press.

Harberger, A. (1955) 'The taxation of mineral industries', *Federal Tax Policy for Economic Growth and Stability*, 84th Congress, 1st session, Washington, GPO, November.

Hardin, G. (1968) 'The tragedy of the commons', *Science*, 162, 1243–8.

Hardoy, J. E. and Satterthwaite, D. (1984) 'Third World cities and the environment of poverty', *Geoforum*, 15(3), 307–33.

Hare, F. K. (1984) 'Changing climate and human response: the impact of recent events on Climatology', *Geoforum*, 15(3), 383–94.

Harns, J. and Davis, B. (1981) 'The fifth fuel: energy conservation', *Lloyds Bank Review*, April, 22–35.

Harrison, P. and Sewell, W. R. D. (1980) 'Water pollution control by agreement: the French system of contracts', *Natural Resources Journal*, 20(4), 765–8.

Harrison, R. (1978) 'The offshore mineral resources agreement in the maritime provinces', *Dalhousie Law Journal*, IV(2), 245–76.

Harter, P. J. (1982) 'Negotiating regulations: a cure for the malaise', *Environmental Impact Assessment Review*, 3(1), 75–91.

Hartshorn, J. E. (1962) *Oil Companies and Governments: An Account of the International Oil Industry and its Political Environment*, London, Faber.

Haussman, F. C. (1981) *Environmental Mediation: A Canadian Perspective*, Ottawa, Ontario, Environment Canada.

Haveman, R. H. (1977) 'The economic evaluation of long-run uncertainties', *Futures*, 9, 365–74.

Haveman, R. H. and Margolis, J. (1970) *Public Expenditures and Policy Analysis*, Chicago, Markham.

Hawkins, K. O. (1983) *Environment and Enforcement. Regulation and the Social Definition of Pollution*, Oxford, Clarendon Press.

Heal, G. (1975) 'Economic aspects of natural resource depletion', in Pearce, D. W. (ed.) *The Economics of Natural Resource Depletion*, London, Macmillan, ch. 8, 118–39.

Healy, R. G. (1976) *Land Use and the States*, Baltimore, Md, Johns Hopkins University Press.

Hedberg, B. (1981) 'Large scale underground mining – an alternative to open cast mining', *Mining Magazine*, September, 177–83.

Hedberg, H., Bonini, W. E. and Kalliokoski, J. (eds) (1964) *The Role of National Government in the Exploration for Mineral Resources*, Ocean City, NJ, Littoral Press.

Heilleiner, G. K. (1973) 'Manufactured exports from less developed countries and multinational firms', *Economic Journal*, 83(329), 21–47.

Helmers, F. L. C. H. (1979) *Project Planning and Income Distribution*, London, Martinus Nijhoff.

Henning, D. H. (1974) *Environmental Policy and Administration*, Environmental Science series, New York, Elsevier.

Hicks, J. R. (1939) 'The foundations of welfare economics', *Economic Journal*, 49, 696–712.

Higgins, R. (1978) *The Seventh Enemy: The Human Factor in the Global Crisis*, London, Hodder & Stoughton.

Hill, M. (1968) 'A goals achievement matrix for evaluating alternative plans', *Journal of the American Institute of Planners*, 39, 19–29.

Hirsch, F. (1977) *Social Limits to Growth*, London, Routledge & Kegan Paul.

Hirschleifer, J., De Haven, J. P. and Milliman, J. W. (1960) *Water Supply: Economics, Technology and Policy*, Chicago, University of Chicago Press.

Hirschman, A. O. (1971) *A Bias for Hope: Essays on Development and Latin America*, New Haven, Conn., Yale University Press.

Hodson, H. V. (1972) *The Diseconomics of Growth*, New York, Ballantine Books.

Holcomb Research Institute (1976) *Planning Alternatives for Muncipal Water Systems*, background monograph for conference, French Lick, Indiana, 10–14 October.

Holdgate, M. W. (1979) *A Perspective of Environmental Pollution*, Cambridge, Cambridge University Press.

Holdgate, M. W., Kassas, M. and White, G. F. (1982) *The World Environment: 1972–82*, Dublin, Tycooly International Publishing.

Holt, S. V. (1975) 'Marine fisheries and world food supplies', in Steele, F. and Bourne, A. (eds) *Man/Food Equation*, New York, Academic Press, 77–96.

Hood, C. (1973) 'The rise and rise of the British quango', *New Society*, 16, August, 386–8.

Howe, C. W. (1971) *Benefit Cost Analysis for Water System Planning*, Washington, DC, American Geophysical Union.

Hubbert, M. K. (1969) 'Energy resources', in National Academy of Sciences *Resources and Man*, San Francisco, Calif., W. H. Freeman, 157–242.

Hubbert, M. K. (1974) *US Energy Resources, a Review as of 1972*, Report prepared for the Senate Committee on Interior and Insular Affairs, No. 93–40, Washington, DC, GPO.

Inglehart, R. (1977) *The Silent Revolution: Changing Values and Political Styles among Western Publics*, Princeton, NJ, Princeton University Press.

Institut Français du Pétrole (1978) Executive summaries, in *World Energy Resources 1985–2020*, World Energy Conference Conservation Commission Report, Guildford, IPC Science & Technology Press.

Ireland, F. E. (1971) 'Control of special industrial emissions in Britain', *Proceedings of the Second International Clean Air Congress*, London and New York, Academic Press, 1189–92.

Ireland, F. E. (1977) 'Reflections of an alkali inspector', *Clean Air*, 7(25), Summer, 4–9.

Issawi, C. P. and Yeganeh, M. (1962) *The Economics of Middle Eastern Oil*, New York, Praeger.

IUCN (International Union for the Conservation of Nature) (1980) *World Conservation Strategy*, 1196 Gland, Switzerland, IUCN.

Jacks, G. V. and Whyte, R. O. (1955) *The Rape of the Earth: A World Survey of Soil Erosion*, London, Faber.

Jahoda, M. and Freeman, C. (eds) (1978) *World Futures: The Great Debate*, Oxford, Martin Robertson.

Jeger Report (Ministry of Housing and Local Government) (1970) *Taken for Granted*, Report of the Working Party on Sewage Disposal, London, HMSO.

Jenkins, W. I. (1978) *Policy Analysis: A Political and Organisational Perspective*, London, Martin Robertson.

Johnson, H. G. (1975) 'Man and his environment', in *On Economics and Society*, Chicago, University of Chicago Press, 317–39.

Johnson, J. F. (1971) *Renovated Waste Water: An Alternative Supply of Municipal Water Supply in the United States*, Research Paper No. 135, Chicago, Department of Geography, University of Chicago.

Johnson, R. W. and Brown, G. M. (1976) *Cleaning Up Europe's Waters*, New York, Praeger.

Johnson, S. P. (1983) *The Pollution Control Policy of the European Communities*, London, Graham & Trotman.

Jubak, J. (1982) 'EPA starves the states', *Environmental Action*, 13(9), 20–2.

Juster, K. (1977) 'Foreign policy-making during the oil crisis', *Japan Interpreter*, XI, Winter, 293–312.

Kahn, H., Brown, W. and Martel, L. (1976) *The Next 200 Years*, New York, Morrow.

Kalbermatten, J. M., Julius, D. S. and Gumerson, C. G. (1980) *Appropriate Technology for Water Supply and Sanitation: A Summary of Technical and Economic Options*, Washington, DC, World Bank.

Kaldor, N. (1939) 'Welfare propositions and interpersonal comparisons of utility', *Economic Journal*, 49, 549–60.

Kapp, K. W. (1970) 'Environmental disruption and social costs: a challenge to economics', *Kyklos*, 23(4), 833–48.

Kapp, K. W. (1972) 'Social costs, neo-classical economics, environmental planning: a reply', in Sachs, I. (ed.) *Political Economy of Environment: Problems of Method*, Paris, École Pratique des Hautes Études/Mouton, 113–24.

Kates, R. W. (1962) *Hazard and Choice Perception in Flood Plain Management*, Research Paper No. 78, Chicago, Department of Geography, University of Chicago.

Kaufman, H. (1975) *Are Government Organizations Immortal?*, Washington, DC, Brookings Institution.

Kay, J. A. and Mirrlees, J. A. (1975) 'The desirability of natural resource depletion', in Pearce, D. W. (ed.) *The Economics of Natural Resource Depletion*, London, Macmillan, 140–76.

Kellogg, W. W. and Schware, R. (1981) *Climatic Change and Society: Consequences of Increasing Atmospheric Carbon Dioxide*, Boulder, Colo., Aspen Institute for Humanistic Studies/Westview Press.

Kellogg, W. W. and Schware, R. (1982) 'Society, science and climatic change', *Foreign Affairs*, Summer, 1076–109.

Kelman, S. J. (1983) 'Economic incentives and environmental policy: politics, ideology and philosophy, in Schelling, T. C. (ed.) *Incentives for Environmental Protection*, Cambridge, Mass., MIT Press, 291–331.

Kincaid, J. (1983) 'The contest of body and soul: resource scarcity in western political theory', in Welch S. and Miewald, R. (eds) *Scarce Natural Resources: The Challenge to Public Policymaking*, Sage Yearbooks in Politics and Public Policy, Vol. 2, Beverly Hills, Calif., Sage, 25–46.

King, W. (1978) 'Documents indicate Corps misled Congress on major southern canal', *New York Times*, 26 November.

Kitamura, H. (1982) 'Rationale and relevance of the new international economic order', *The Developing Economies*, X-VIII(4), Tokyo, Institute of Developing Economies, 341–54.

Klass, M. W., Burrows, J. C. and Beggs, S. (1980) *International Mineral Cartels and Embargoes: Policy and Implications for the US*, New York, Praeger.

Kneese, A. V. (1964) *The Economics of Regional Water Quality*, Baltimore, Md, Johns Hopkins University Press.

Kneese, A. V. and Bower, B. T. (1968) *Managing Water Quality: Economics, Technology and Institutions*, Baltimore, Md, Johns Hopkins University Press.

Kneese, A. V. and Schultze, C. L. (1975) *Pollution, Prices and Public Policy*, Washington, DC, Brookings Institution.

Knetsch, J. (1974) *Outdoor Recreation and Water Resources Planning*, Washington, DC, American Geophysical Union.

Koeningsburger, O., Bernstein, B., Foot, M., Rees, J. A., Roberts, M., Tyler, M. and Wylie, J. (1971) *Infrastructure Problems of the Cities of Developing Countries*, New York, Ford Foundation.

Krutilla, J. V. (1967) 'Conservation reconsidered', *American Economic Review*, 67, 777–86.

Krutilla, J. V. and Eckstein, O. (1959) *Multiple Purpose River Development*, Baltimore, Md, Resources for the Future/Johns Hopkins University Press.

Krutilla, J. V. and Fisher, A. (1975) *The Economics of Natural Environments*, Baltimore, Md, Resources for the Future/Johns Hopkins University Press.

Labys, W. C. (1980) *Market Structure, Bargaining Power, and Resource Price Formation*, Lexington, Mass., D. C. Heath (Lexington Books).

Lanning, G. and Mueller, M. (1979) *Africa Undermined: Mining Companies and the Underdevelopment of Africa*, Harmondsworth, Penguin.

Layton, E. T. (1977) 'Conditions of technological development', in Spiegel-Rosing, I. and Price, D. de S. (eds) *Science, Technology, and Society*, London, Sage, 197–222.

Lecomber, R. (1979) *The Economics of Natural Resources*, London, Macmillan.

Lee, T. and Yao, C.-L. (1970) 'Abundance of chemical elements in the earth's crust and its major tectonic units', *International Geology Review*, July, 778–86.

Levin, P. (1979) 'Highway inquiries', *Public Administration*, 57, 21–49.

Levitt, R. (1980) *Implementing Public Policy*, London, Croom Helm.

Lewis, W. A. (1955) *The Theory of Economic Growth*, London, Allen & Unwin.

Lichtblau, J. H. and Frank, H. J. (1978) *The Outlook for World Oil into the 21st Century with Emphasis on the Period to 1990*, Palo Alto, Calif., Electric Power Institute.

Liebenow, J. G. (1969) *Liberia: The Evolution of Privilege*, Ithaca, NY, Cornell University Press.

Lindblom, C. E. (1959) 'The science of "muddling through"', *Public Administration Review*, 19, 79–99.

Liroff, R. A. (1979) *Air Pollution Offsets: Trading, Selling and Banking*, Washington, DC, Conservation Foundation.

Lister, L. (1960) *Europe's Coal and Steel Community: An Experiment in Economic Union*, New York, Twentieth Century Fund.

Little, I. M. D. and Mirrlees, J. A. (1969) *Manual of Industrial Project Analysis in Developing Countries. Vol. 2, Social Cost–Benefit Analysis*, Paris, OECD.

Little, I. M. D. and Mirrlees, J. A. (1974) *Project Appraisal and Planning for Developing Countries*, London, Heinemann.

Little, I. M. D., Scitovsky, T. and Scott, M. (1970) *Industry and Trade in Some Developing Countries: A Comparative Study*, Oxford, Oxford University Press.

Löf, G. O. G. and Kneese, A. V. (1967) *The Economics of Water Utilization in the Beet Sugar Industry*, Washington, DC, Resources for the Future.

Logan, T. and Ogilvy, E. (1981) 'The statutory planning framework', in Troy, P. N. (ed.) *Equity in the City*, Sydney, Allen & Unwin, 172–94.

Lovell, C. H. (1983) 'Intergovernmental "deregulation": readings from the first Reagan years', *Environment and Planning C: Government and Policy*, 1, 273–84.

Lovelock, J. E. (1979) *Gaia: A New Look at Life on Earth*, Oxford, Oxford University Press.

Lowe, P. D. (1977) 'Amenity and equity: a review of local environmental pressure groups in Britain', *Environment and Planning*, A, 9, 39–58.

Lowe, P. D. and Goyder, J. (1983) *Environmental Groups in Politics*, Resource Management series, Vol. 6, London, Allen & Unwin.

Lukes, S. (1974) *Power: A Radical View*, London, Macmillan.

Lukes, S. (1977) *Essays in Social Theory*, London, Macmillan.

Lundqvist, L. J. (1973a) 'Environmental policies in Canada, Sweden and the United States: a comparative overview', paper given at Special Session on Comparative Public Policy of the Committee on Political Sociology, IPSA Ninth World Conference, Montreal, September.

Lundqvist, L. J. (1973b) 'Environmental policy and administration in a unitary state: Sweden', in Caldwell, L. K. (ed.) *Organization and Administration of Environmental Programmes*, New York, United Nations, 126–48.

Mabey, R. (1980) *The Common Ground*, London, NCC/Hutchinson.

Mabogunje, A. L. (1984) 'The poor shall inherit the earth: issues of environmental quality and Third World development', *Geoforum*, 15 (3), 295–306.

McDonald, S. L. (1961) 'Percentage depletion and the allocation of resources: the case of oil and gas', *National Tax Journal*, December, 323–36.

McDonald, S. L. (1967) 'Percentage depletion, expensing of intangibles and petroleum conservation', in Gaffney, M. (ed.) *Extractive Resources and Taxation*, Madison, Wis., University of Wisconsin Press, 269–88.

MacEwen, A. and MacEwen, M. (1982) *National Parks: Conservation or Cosmetics?* Resource Management series, Vol. 5, London, Allen & Unwin.

McGrew, A. G. and Wilson, M. J. (eds) (1982) *Decision-Making, Approaches and Analysis*, Manchester, Manchester University Press/Open University.

McHarg, I. L. (1969) *Design with Nature*, New York, Natural History Press.

MacInerney, J. (1981) 'Natural resource economics: the basic analytical principles', in Bultin, J. A. (ed.) *Economics of Environmental and Natural Resources Policy*, London, Longman, ch. 3, 30–58.

McIntosh, P. (1978) 'Water pollution, charging systems and the EEC', *Water*, 23, November, 2–6.

McKean, R. (1958) *Efficiency in Government through Systems Analysis*, New York, Wiley.

MacNeill, J. W. (1971) *Environmental Management*, constitutional study prepared for the Government of Canada, Ottawa, Information Canada.

Macpherson, C. B. (1978) 'Do we need a theory of the state?', *European Journal of Sociology*, XVIII (2), 223–44.

Majone, G. (1976a) 'Standard setting and the theory of institutional choice: the case of pollution control', *Policy and Politics*, 4, 35–51.

Majone, G. (1976b) 'Choice among policy instruments for pollution control', *Policy Analysis*, 2, 589–613.

Malthus, R. T. (1798, reprinted 1969) 'An essay on the principle of population', in Hardin, G. (ed.) *Population, Evolution and Birth Control*, San Francisco, Calif., W. H. Freeman, 4–17.

Mann Borgese, E. (1980) 'Expanding the common heritage', in Dolman, A. J. (ed.) *Global Planning and Resources Management*, Oxford, Pergamon, 181–94.

Manners, G. (1971) *The Changing World Market for Iron Ore, 1950–1980: An Economic Geography*, Baltimore, Md, Johns Hopkins University Press.

Manners, G. (1977) 'Three issues of minerals policy', *Journal of the Royal Society of Arts*, 125, 386–401.

Manners, G. (1979) 'The geography of mineral supply: the mainsprings of future uncertainties', *Geoforum*, 10 (3), 323–32.

Manners, G. (1981a) 'Our planet's resources', *Geographical Journal*, 147, pt 1, 1–22.

Manners, G. (1981b) *Coal in Britain: An Uncertain Future*, Resource Management series, Vol. 4, London, Allen & Unwin.

Mannheim, K. (1966) *Ideology and Utopia*, London, Routledge & Kegan Paul.

Mansfield, N. W. (1969) 'Recreation trip generation', *Journal of Transport Economics and Policy*, 3, 1–13.

Margolis, J. (1957) 'Secondary benefits, external economies and the justification of public investment', *Review of Economics and Statistics*, 39, August, 284–91.

Marsh, A. (1981) 'Environmental issues in contemporary European politics', in Goodman, G. T. (ed.) *The European Transition from Oil*, London, Academic Press, 121–54.

Martindale, R. (1976) 'How should industry view pollution charges?', *CBI Review*, 21, 11–20.

Martindale, R. (1979) 'Charging for direct discharges', *Chemistry and Industry*, 17 March, 195–8.

Marwell, G. (1970) 'Who is worried about the environment?', *Bulletin of Peace Proposals*, 2, 187.

Maslow, A. H. (1954) *Motivation and Personality*, New York, Harper & Row.

Math Tech (1979) *The Effect of New Source Pollution Control Requirements on Industrial Investment Decisions*, report prepared for EPA, Arlington, Va, Math Tech, January.

Meacher, M. (1976) 'Global resources, growth and political agency', in Barratt-Brown, M., Emerson, T. and Stoneman, C. (eds) *Resources and the Environment: A Socialist Perspective*, Nottingham, Spokesman, 42–7.

Meadows, D. H., Meadows, D. L., Randers, J. and Behrens III, W. (1972) *The Limits to Growth*, New York, Universe Books.

Meadows, D. L. (1974) *Dynamics of Growth in a Finite World*, Cambridge, Mass., Wright-Allen Press.

Meadows, D. L. and Meadows, D. H. (eds) (1973) *Towards Global Equilibrium: Collected Papers*, Cambridge, Mass., Wright-Allen Press.

Metal Bulletin (annual) *Metal Bulletin Handbook*, Vol. 11, Worcester Park, Metal Bulletin.

Meyer, R. A. (1975) 'Monopoly pricing and capacity choice under uncertainty', *American Economic Review*, 64 (3), June, 326–37.

Meyers, S. (1976) 'US experience with national environmental impact assessment', in O'Riordan, T. and Hey, R. D. (eds) *Environmental Impact Assessment*, Farnborough, Saxon House, 45–55.

Mezger, D. (1980) *Copper in the World Economy*, London, Heinemann.

Miewald, R. and Welch, S. (1983) 'Natural resources scarcity: an introduction', in Welch, S. and Miewald, R. (eds) *Scarce Natural Resources: The Challenge to Public Policymaking*, Beverly Hills, Calif., Sage, 9–22.

Mikdashi, Z. (1974) *The International Politics of Natural Resources*, Ithaca, NY, Cornell University Press.

Mikesell, R. F. (ed.) (1971) *Foreign Investment in the Petroleum and Mineral Industries: Case Studies on Investor–Host Relations*, Baltimore, Md, Resources for the Future/Johns Hopkins University Press.

Mikesell, R. F. (1979) *The World Copper Industry: Structure and Economic Analysis*, Baltimore, Md, Resources for the Future/Johns Hopkins University Press.

Mikesell, R. F. (1983) *Foreign Investment in Mining Projects*, Cambridge, Mass., Oelgeschlager, Gunn & Hain.

Milbrath, L. W. (1963) *The Washington Lobbyists*, Chicago, Rand McNally.

Milbrath, L. W. (1975) *Environmental Beliefs: A Tale of Two Countries*, Buffalo, State University of New York.

Milbrath, L. W. (1983) 'Images of scarcity in four nations', in Welch, S. and Miewald, R. (eds) *Scarce Natural Resources: The Challenge to Public Policymaking*, Beverly Hills, Calif., Sage, 105–24.

Miller, C. and Wood, C. (1983) *Planning and Pollution*, Oxford, Oxford University Press.

Milliband, R. (1973) *The State in Capitalist Society*, London, Quartet Books.

Mining Annual Review (annual) London, Mining Journal.

Mishan, E. J. (1967) *The Costs of Economic Growth*, Harmondsworth, Penguin.

Mishan, E. J. (1972) *Elements of Cost–Benefit Analysis*, London, Allen & Unwin.

Mitchell, B. and King, P. (1984) 'Resource conflict, policy change and practice in Canadian fisheries management', *Geoforum*, 15 (3), 419–32.

Mitchell, R. C. (1978) 'The public speaks again: a new environmental survey', *Resources for the Future*, 60, 1–6.

Moran, T. H. (1975) *Multinational Corporations and the Politics of Dependence: Copper in Chile*, Princeton, NJ, Princeton University Press.

Morris, D. S. and Newton, K. (1971) 'The social composition of a city council: Birmingham, 1925–66', *Social and Economic Administration*, 5, 29–33.

Mosher, L. (1981) 'Environmentalists sue to put an end to regulatory massive resistance', *National Journal*, 13(6), 256–9.

Mosher, L. (1982) 'Reagan's environmental federalism – are the states up to the challenge', *National Journal*, 14(5), 184–8.

Muldoon, R. D. (1983) 'Rethinking the ground rules for an open world economy', *Foreign Affairs*, Summer, 1078–98.

Munro, G. R. (1981) 'The economics of fishing: an introduction', in Butlin, J. A. (ed.) *Economics and Resources Policy*, London, Longman, 129–40.

Munton, R. (1983) *London's Green Belt: Containment in Practice*, London, Allen & Unwin.

Myrdal, G. (1957) *Economic Theory and Underdeveloped Regions*, London, Duckworth.

Nash, C., Pearce, D. W. and Stanley, J. (1975a) 'Criteria for evaluating project evaluation techniques', *Journal of the American Institute of Planners*, 41(2), 83–9.

Nash, C., Stanley, J. and Pearce, D. W. (1975b) 'An evaluation of cost–benefit analysis criteria', *Scottish Journal of Political Economy*, 22(2), 121–34.

National Water Council, (1978) *Water Industry Review 1978*, London, NWC.

National Water Council, (1981) *River Quality: The 1980 Survey and Future Outlook*, London, NWC.

Nelkin, D. (1977) *Technological Decisions and Democracy*, London, Sage.

Newby, H. Bell, C., Rose, D. and Saunders, P. R. (1978) *Property, Paternalism and Power*, London, Hutchinson.

Newton, K. (1982) 'The theory of pluralist democracy', in McGrew, A. C. and Wilson, M. J. (eds) *Decision Making: Approaches and Analysis*, Manchester, Manchester University Press, 231–45.

Newton, T. (1972) *Cost–Benefit Analysis in Administration*, London, Allen & Unwin.

Nichols, A. L. (1983) 'Case study 2, the regulation of airborne benzene', in Schelling, T. C. (ed.) *Incentives for Environmental Protection*, Cambridge, Mass., MIT Press.

Nicholson, E. M. (1970) *The Environmental Revolution*, London, Hodder & Stoughton.

Nobbs, C. and Pearce, D. W. (1976) 'The economics of stock pollutants: the example of cadmium', *International Journal of Environmental Studies*, 8(4), 245–55.

Nordhaus, W. D. (1973) 'World dynamics: measurement without data', *Economic Journal*, 83, December, 1156–83.

Nordhaus, W. D. (1974) 'Resources as a constraint on growth', *American Economic Review*, 64, 22–6.

North West Regional Water Authority (1977) *Annual Report and Accounts*, Warrington, NWRWA.

Nurkse, R. (1953) *Problems of Capital Formation in Underdeveloped Countries*, Oxford, Blackwell.

Nye, J. S. (1981) 'Japan', in Deese, D. A. and Nye, J. S. (eds) *Energy and Security*, Cambridge, Mass., Ballinger, 211–27.

Odell, P. R. (1970) *Oil and World Power*, Harmondsworth, Penguin; 2nd rev. edn, 1983.

Odell, P. R. (1977) 'Optimal development of the North Sea's oil fields – a summary', *Energy Policy*, 5(4), December, 282–3.

Odell, P. R. and Rosing, K. E. (1977) 'Optimal development of the North Sea's oil fields – the reply', *Energy Policy*, 5(4), December, 295–306.

Odell, P. R. and Rosing, K. E. (1980) *The Future of Oil. A Simulation Study of the Inter-Relationships of Resources, Reserves and Use 1980–2080*, London, Kogan Page.

Odell, P. R. and Rosing, K. E. (1983) *The Future of Oil*, 2nd rev. edn, London, Kogan Page; New York, Nichols.

Odum, H. E. (1971) *Environment, Power and Society*, New York, Wiley.

Ophuls, W. (1977) *Ecology and the Politics of Scarcity: Prologue to a Political Theory of the Steady State*, San Francisco, Calif., W. H. Freeman.

Organization for Economic Co-operation and Development (OECD) (1975) *The Polluter Pays Principle: Definition, Analysis, Implementation*, Paris, OECD.

OECD (1976a) *Pollution Charges: An Assessment*, Paris, OECD.

OECD (1976b) *Water Management in France*, Paris, OECD.

OECD (1976c) *Economic Measurement of Environmental Damage*, Paris, OECD.

OECD (1977) *Water Management Policies and Instruments*, Paris, OECD.

OECD (1980a) *Pollution Charges in Practice*, Paris, OECD.

OECD (1980b) *The Contribution of Economic Instruments to Solid Waste Management*, Paris, OECD.

OECD (1980c) *Water Management in Industrialized River Basins*, Paris, OECD.

O'Riordan, T. (1976) *Environmentalism*, London, Pion.

O'Riordan, T. (1977) 'Environmental ideologies', *Environment and Planning*, 9(1), 3–14.

O'Riordan, T. (1983a) 'Environmental issues', in *Progress in Human Geography*, London, Edward Arnold, Vol. 7(3), 403–13.

O'Riordan, T. (1983b) 'Putting trust in the countryside', Part 3, *The Conservation and Development Programme for the UK*, London, Kogan Page, 171–259.

O'Riordan, T. and Hey, R. D. (1976) *Environmental Impact Assessment*, Farnborough, Saxon House.

O'Riordan, T. and Turner, R. K. (1983) *An Annotated Reader in Environmental Planning and Management*, Urban and Regional Planning series, Vol. 30, Oxford, Pergamon.

O'Toole, R. P. and Walton, A. L. (1982) 'Intergenerational equity as it relates to conservation and coal extraction standards', *Natural Resources Journal*, 22(1), January, 53–69.

Paddock, W. and Paddock, P. (1967) *Famine – 1975! America's Decision: Who Will Survive?*, Boston, Mass., Little, Brown.

Page, T. (1981) 'Economics of a throwaway society; the one-way economy', in Butlin, J. A. (ed.) *Economics of Environmental and Natural Resources Policy*, London, Longman, 74–87.

Pahl, R. E. (1965) *Urbs in Rure: The Metropolitan Fringe in Hertfordshire*, Geographical Papers No. 2, London, London School of Economics.

Painter, M. (1980) 'Whitehall and roads: a case study of sectoral politics', *Policy and Politics*, 8, 163–86.

Parker, D. J. and Penning-Rowsell, E. C. (1980) *Water Planning in Britain*, Resource Management series, Vol. 1, London, Allen & Unwin.

Parry, G. and Morriss, P. (1974) 'When is a decision not a decision?' in Crewe, I. (ed.) *British Political Sociology Yearbook. Vol. 1, Elites in Western Democracy*, London, Croom Helm.

Pashigian, B. P. (1982) *Environmental Regulation: Whose Self-Interests Are Being Protected?*, Chicago, Graduate School of Business, University of Chicago.

Pearce, D. W. (1976) *Environmental Economics*, London, Longman.

Pearce, D. W. (1977) 'Justifiable government intervention in preserving the quality of life', in Wingo, L. and Evans, A. (eds), *Public Economics and the Quality of Life*, Baltimore, Md, Resources for the Future/Johns Hopkins University Press, 125–40.

Pearce, D. W. (ed.) (1978) *Valuation of Social Cost*, London, Allen & Unwin.

Pearce, D. W. (1980) 'The social incidence of environmental costs and benefits', in O'Riordan, T. and Turner, R. K. (eds) *Progress in Resource Management and Environmental Planning*, Vol. 2, Chichester, Wiley, 63–87.

Pearce, D. W. (1983) 'Are environmental problems a challenge to economic science?', in O'Riordan, T. and Turner, R. K. (eds) *An Annotated Reader in Environmental Planning and Management*, Oxford, Pergamon, 253–64.

Pearce, D. W. and Walter, I. (1977) *Resource Conservation: The Social and Economic Dimensions of Recycling*, New York, New York University Press/Longman.

Pearce, F. (1982) *Watershed: The Water Crisis in Britain*, London, Junction Books.

Pearce, F. (1984) 'The great drain robbery', *New Scientist*, 15 March, 10–16.

Pearse, P. H. (1972) 'Rationalization of Canada's west coast salmon fishery', in *Economic Aspects of Fish Production*, Paris, Organization for Economic Co-operation and Development, 172–202.

Pearson, C. and Pryor, A. (1978) *Environment: North and South – an Economic Interpretation*, New York, Wiley.

Pedlar, K. (1979) *The Quest for Gaia*, London, Granada.

Penning-Rowsell, E. C. and Chatterton, J. B. (1977) *The Benefits of Flood Alleviation: A Manual of Assessment Techniques*, Farnborough, Saxon House.

Penrose, E. T. (1968) *The Large International in Developing Countries*, London, Allen & Unwin.

Percival, A. (1972) *The Amenity Society Movement: Success or Failure?*, London, Civic Trust.

Perlman, M. (1976) 'The economic theory of bureaucracy', in Tullock, G. (ed.) *The Vote Motive*, London, Institute of Economic Affairs, 70–9.

Perloff, H. S., Dunn, E. S., Lampard, E. E. and Muth, R. F. (1960) *Regions, Resources and Economic Growth*, Baltimore, Md, Johns Hopkins University Press.

Perloff, H. S. and Wingo, L. (1960) 'Natural resource endowment and regional economic growth', RFF Reprint 24, Washington, DC, RFF. Reprinted in Burton, I. and Kates, R. W. (1969) *Readings in Resource Management and Conservation*, Chicago, University of Chicago Press, 427–42.

Pickens, D. K. (1981) 'Westward expansion and the end of American exceptionalism: Summer, Turner, Webb', *Western Historical Quarterly*, 12, October, 409–18.

Pigou, A. C. (1932) *The Economics of Welfare*, 4th edn, London, Macmillan.

Plamanetz, J. (1954) 'Interests', *Political Studies*, 2, 3–17.

Polsby, N. W. (1963) *Community Power and Political Theory*, New Haven, Conn., Yale University Press; 2nd edn, 1980.

Porter, E. A. (1978) *Water Management in England and Wales*, Cambridge, Cambridge University Press.

Poulantzas, N. (1973) *Political Power and Social Classes*, London, New Left Books.

Prain, Sir R. (1975) *Copper: The Anatomy of an Industry*, London, Mining Journal.

Prebish, R. (1961) 'Economic development or monetary stability: the false dilemma', *Economic Bulletin for Latin America*, VI(1), 1–25.

Price, E. T. (1955) 'Values and concepts in conservation', *Annals of the Association of American Geographers*, XLV(1), March, 65–84.

Programmes Analysis Unit (1972) *An Economic and Technical Appraisal of Air Quality in the United Kingdon*, London, HMSO.

Puschak, R. and Burton, I. (1983) 'Risk and prior compensation in siting low-level nuclear waste facilities: dealing with the NIMBY syndrome', *Plan Canada*, 23(3), 68–79.

Raggatt, H. G. (1964) 'Australia: the participation of the Australian government in exploration for mineral resources', in Hedburg, H. *et al.* (eds) *The Role of National Government in the Exploration for Mineral Resources*, Ocean City, NJ, Littoral Press, 61–79.

Ramsey, F. P. (1928) 'A mathematical theory of saving', *Economic Journal*, 38, December 554–9.

Randell, A. (1975) 'Growth, resources, and environment: some conceptual issues', *American Journal of Agriculture Economics*, 57(5), 803–9.

Rees, J. A. (1970) 'Industrial water abstractions and the 1963 charging schemes', report to Water Resources Board, Reading, WRB, mimeo.

Rees, J. A. (1975) *The North-West Tasmanian Regional Water Scheme: Optimal Development and Financial Implications*, Canberra, Department of Urban and Regional Development.

Rees, J. A. (1976) 'Rethinking our approach to water supply provision', *Geography*, 61(4), 232–45.

Rees, J. A. (1977) 'The economics of environmental management', *Geography*, 62(4), 311–24.

Rees, J. A. (1981a) 'Urban water and sewerage services', in Troy, P. N. (ed.) *Equity in the City*, Sydney, Allen & Unwin, 85–103.

Rees, J. A. (1981b) 'Irrelevant economics: the water pricing and pollution charging debate', *Geoforum*, 12(3), 211–25.

Rees, J. A. (1982) 'Profligacy and scarcity: an analysis of water management in Australia', *Geoforum*, 13(4), 289–300.

Rees, J. A. and Rees, R. (1972) 'Water demand forecasts and planning margins in south-east England', *Regional Studies*, 6, 37–48.

Renshaw, E. F. (1957) *Toward Responsible Government*, Chicago, Idyia Press.

Repetto, R. (1983) 'Air quality under the Clean Air Act', in Schelling, T. C. (ed.) *Incentives for Environmental Protection*, Cambridge, Mass., MIT Press, 221–90.

RESOLVE (quarterly) newsletter on environmental dispute resolution, Washington, DC, The Conservation Foundation.

Ricardo, D. (1817, reprinted 1962) *Principles of Political Economy and Taxation*, London, Dent.

Richardson, G., with Ogus, A. and Burrows, P. (1982) *Policing Pollution: A Study of Regulation and Enforcement*, Oxford, Clarendon Press.

Richardson, H. W. (1969) *Regional Economics: Location Theory, Urban and Regional Change*, London, Weidenfeld & Nicolson.

Richardson, J. A. and Scott, L. C. (1983) 'Resource location patterns and state severance taxes: some empirical evidence', *Natural Resources Journal*, 23, April, 352–64.

Richardson, J. J. (1977) 'The environmental issue and the public', in *Decision Making in Britain: Pollution and Environment*, D203V, Milton Keynes, Open University.

Richardson, J. J. (1979) 'Agency behaviour: the case of pollution control in Sweden', *Public Administration*, 57, 471–82.

Richardson, J. J. and Jordan, A. G. (1979) *Governing under Pressure. The Policy Process in a Post-Parliamentary Democracy*, Oxford, Martin Robertson.

Ridker, R. G. (ed.) (1972) *Population, Resources and the Environment*, Washington, DC, Government Printing Office.

Ridker, R. G. and Watson, W. D. (1980) *To Choose a Future. Resource and Environmental Consequences of Alternative Growth Paths*, Baltimore, Md, Resources for the Future/ Johns Hopkins University Press.

Rigdon, S. (1983) 'Resource policy in communist states', in Welch, S. and Miewald, R. (eds) *Scarce Natural Resources: The Challenge to Public Policy*, Beverly Hills, Calif., Sage, 65–84.

Roberts, P. W. and Shaw, T. (1982) *Mineral Resources in Regional and Strategic Planning*, Aldershot, Gower.

Robinson, J. (1981) *Economic Philosophy*, Harmondsworth, Penguin.

Robson, W. A. (ed.) (1937) *Public Enterprise*, London, Heinemann.

Roddewig, R. J. (1978) *Green Bans*, Sydney, Hale & Iremonger.

Rosenberg, N. (1976) *Perspectives on Technology*, Cambridge, Cambridge University Press.

Rosenblum, V. G. (1974) 'The continuing role of courts in allocating common property resources', in Haffele, E. T. (ed.) *The Governance of Common Property Resources*, Baltimore, Md, Resources for the Future/Johns Hopkins University Press.

Rosing, K. E. and Odell, P. R. (1983) *The Future of Oil: A Re-Evaluation*, Paper 83–1a, Centre for International Energy Studies, Erasmus University, Rotterdam, Eurices.

Ross, T. D. (1985) 'The status and strategies of the international oil corporations', LSE, International Resources Programme 1984–85, typescript.

Rothman, H. (1972) *Murderous Providence: A Study of Pollution in Industrial Societies*, London, Rupert Hart-Davis.

Rothwell, R. and Gardiner, P. (1983) *The Impact of Environmental Regulations on Technological Change Processes in the UK Sugar Processing and Metal Plating Industries*, SPRU, Brighton, University of Sussex.

Russ, P. and Tanner, L. (1978) *The Politics of Pollution*, Melbourne, Visa.

Russell, C. S. (1973) *Residuals Management in Industry: A Case Study of Petroleum Refining*, Baltimore, Md, Resources for the Future/Johns Hopkins University Press.

Sachs, I. (1972) 'Approaches to a political economy of environment', in *Political Economy of Environment, Problems of Method*, papers presented at the Symposium held at the Maison des Sciences de l'Homme, Paris 5–8 July, 1971, Paris, École Pratique des Hautes Études/Mouton, 125–37.

Sampson, A. (1975) *The Seven Sisters*, London, Coronet.

Sandbach, F. (1980) *Environment, Ideology and Policy*, Oxford, Blackwell.

Sandbach, F. (1982) *Principles of Pollution Control*, Themes in Resource Management, London and New York, Longman.

Saunders, P. R. (1976) *The Estimation of Pollution Damage*, Manchester, Manchester University Press.

Saunders, P. R. (1980) *Urban Politics: A Sociological Interpretation*, Harmondsworth, Penguin.

Saunders, P. R. (1981) *Social Theory and the Urban Question*, London, Hutchinson.

Sawhill, J. C. (1981) 'Foreword', in Deese, D. A. and Nye, J. S. (eds) *Energy and Security*, Cambridge, Mass., Ballinger, xv–xvi.

Sax, J. (1970) *Defending the Environment: A Strategy for Citizens Action*, New York, Knopf.

Schaefer, M. B. (1957) 'Some consideration of population dynamics and economics in relation to the marine fisheries', *Journal of the Fisheries Research Board of Canada*, 14, 669–81.

Schaeffer, F. A. (1970) *Pollution and the Death of Man: The Christian View of Ecology*, Wheaton, Ill., Tyndale Press.

Schelling, T. C. (ed.) (1983) *Incentives for Environmental Protection*, Regulation of Economic Activity series, Cambridge, Mass., MIT Press.

Schervish, P. G. (1979) 'Employment problems in a global perspective', Jegen, M. E. and Wilber, C. K. (eds) *Growth with Equity*, New York, Paulist Press, 97–123.

Schnaiberg, A. (1980) *The Environment: From Surplus to Scarcity*, New York, Oxford University Press.

Schumacher, E. F. (1973) *Small Is Beautiful: Economics as if People Really Mattered*, New York, Harper Torch Books.

Schumpeter, J. A. (1950) *Capitalism, Socialism and Democracy*, 3rd edn, New York, Harper.

Schwing, R. C. and Albers, W. (eds) (1980) *Societal Risk Assessment: How Safe is Safe Enough?*, New York, Plenum Press.

Schwob, M. (1964) 'Pre-investment activities of the United Nations in the mineral field', in Hedberg, H. *et al.* (eds) *The Role of National Government in the Exploration for Mineral Resources*, Ocean City, NJ, Littoral Press, 185–93.

Scitovsky, T. (1976) *The Joyless Economy: An Inquiry into Human Satisfaction and Consumer Dissatisfaction*, New York, Oxford University Press.

Scott, A. D. (1955a) *Natural Resources: The Economics of Conservation*, Canadian Studies in Economics No. 3, Toronto, Canadian Social Science Research Council.

Scott, A. D. (1955b) 'The fishery: The objectives of sole ownership', *Journal of Political Economy*, 63, 116–24.

Scott, A. D. (1975) *Natural Resources Revenues. A Test of Federalism*, Vancouver, University of British Columbia Press.

Scott, Mr Justice (chairman) (1942) *Report of the Committee on Land Utilization in Rural Areas*, Cmnd 6378, London, HMSO.

Self, P. (1970) 'Nonsense on stilts: the futility of Roskill', *Political Quarterly*, 41, 249–60.

Self, P. (1975) *Econocrats and the Policy Process. The Politics and Philosophy of Cost–Benefit Analysis*, London, Macmillan.

Self, P. and Storing, H. (1962) *The State and the Farmer*, London, Allen & Unwin.

Sharkansky, I. (1970) *The Routines of Politics*, New York, Van Nostrand Reinhold.

Sharp, C. and Jennings, T. (1976) *Transport and the Environment*, Leicester, Leicester University Press.

Sherman, H. (1972) *Radical Political Economy: Capitalism and Socialism from a Marxist–Humanist Perspective*, New York, Basic Books.

Shoard, M. (1980) *The Theft of the Countryside*, London, Temple Smith.

Shucksmith, M. (1981) *No Homes for Locals*, Aldershot, Gower.

Simon, H. A. (1947) *Administrative Behaviour*, New York, Macmillan.

Simon, H. A. (1955) 'A behavioural model of rational choice', *Quarterly Journal of Economics*, 69, February, 99–118.

Simon, J. L. (1977) *The Economics of Population Growth*, Princeton, NJ, Princeton University Press.

Simon, J. L. (1981) *The Ultimate Resource*, Princeton, NJ, Princeton University Press.

Simonis, U. E. (1984) Preventive Environmental Policy: Concept and Data Requirements, Discussion Paper 84–12, International Institute for Environment and Society, Berlin, IIUG.

Singer, S. F. and Stamas, S. (1982) 'An end to OPEC', *Foreign Policy*, 45, Winter, 115–25.

Skoog, B. (1983) *Immigrants and Cultural Development in European Towns*, Strasburg, Council for Cultural Co-operation.

Smil, V. (1984) *The Bad Earth, Environmental Degradation in China*, New York, M. E. Sharpe; and London, Zed Press.

Smith, D. N. and Wells, L. T., Jr (1975) *Negotiating Third-World Mineral Agreements*, Cambridge, Mass., Ballinger.

Smith, G. and May, D. (1980) 'The artificial debate between rationalist and incrementalist models of decision making', *Policy and Politics*, 8(2), 147–61.

Smith, P. J. (ed.) (1975) *The Politics of Physical Resources*, Harmondsworth, Open University/Penguin.

Smith, R. J. and Kavanagh, N. J. (1969) 'The measurement of benefits of trout fishing', *Journal of Leisure Research*, 4, 316–22.

Snyder, E. E. (1971) *Please Stop Killing Me*, New York, Signet, New American Library.

Spence, A. M. (1974) 'Blue whales and applied control theory', in Gottinger, H. W. (ed.) *Systems Approaches and Environmental Problems*, Göttingen, Vanderhoeck and Ruprecht.

Squire, L. and Van der Tak, H. (1975) *Economic Analysis of Projects*, Baltimore, Md, Johns Hopkins University Press.

Standing Conference of Rural Community Councils (1979) *Whose Countryside?*, London, National Council for Social Service.

Stankey, G. H. and Lime, D. W. (1973) *Recreational Carrying Capacity: An Annotated Bibliography*, Ogden, Utah, Intermountain Forest and Range Experiment Station.

Starkie, D. and Johnson, D. (1975) *The Economic Value of Peace and Quiet*, London, D. C. Heath.

Steck, H. J. (1975) 'Private influence on environmental policy: the case of the National Industrial Pollution Control Council', *Environmental Law*, 5, 241–81.

Steele, R. C. (ed.) (1972) *Lowland Forestry and Wildlife Conservation*, Monks Wood, Monks Wood Experimental Station.

Stewart, F. (1977) *Technology and Underdevelopment*, London, Macmillan.

Stillman, P. G. (1982) 'The tragedy of the commons: a re-analysis', in O'Riordan, T. and

Turner, R. K. (eds) *An Annotated Reader in Environmental Planning and Management*, Oxford, Pergamon, 299–303.

Stocking, G. W. (1954) *Basing Point Pricing and Regional Development*, Chapel Hill, NC, University of North Carolina Press.

Storey, D. J. and Elliott, D. J. (1977) 'An effluent charging scheme for the River Tees', *Chemistry and Industry*, May, 335–8.

Storey, D. J. and Walker, M. (1975) *An Evaluation of Alternative Systems for Controlling Direct Discharges to Estuaries and Tidal Waters*, Tees Industrial Discharge Study Workshop Paper No. 3, University of Newcastle upon Tyne.

Streeton, P. (1961) *Economic Integration*, Leyden, A. W. Sythoff.

Streeton, P. (1972) 'Cost–benefit and other problems of method', in Sachs, I. (ed.) *Political Economy of Environment: Problems of Method*, Paris, Ecole Pratique des Hautes Etudes/Mouton, 47–59.

Streeton, P. (1979) 'Transnational corporations and basic needs', in Jegen, M. and Wilber, C. K. (eds) *Growth with Equity*, New York, Paulist Press, 163–74.

Stretton, H. (1976) *Capitalism, Socialism and the Environment*, Cambridge, Cambridge University Press.

Styrikovich, M. A. (1977) 'The long range energy perspective', *Natural Resources Forum*, 1(3), April, 252–3.

Sunkel, O. (1972) 'Big business and "dependencia": a Latin American view', *Foreign Affairs*, 50(3), April, 517–31.

Susskind, L. (1982) 'Restoring the credibility and enhancing the usefulness of the EIA process', *Environmental Impact Assessment Review*, 3(1), 6–7.

Sutcliffe, B. (1972) 'Imperialism and industrialisation of the Third World', in Owen, R. and Sutcliffe, B. (eds) *Studies in the Theory of Imperialism*, London, Longman, 171–92.

Talbot, A. (1983) *Settling Things: Six Case Studies in Environmental Mediation*, Washington, DC, The Conservation Foundation.

Tanzer, M. (1969) *The Political Economy of International Oil and the Underdeveloped Countries*, Boston, Mass., Beacon Press.

Tanzer, M. (1980) *The Race for Resources. Continuing Struggles over Minerals and Fuels*, New York and London, Monthly Review Press.

Tavoulareas, W. and Kaysen, C. (1977) *A Debate on a Time to Choose*, Cambridge, Mass., Ballinger.

Thoman, R. S. and Conkling, E. C. (1967) *Geography of International Trade*, Foundations of Economic Geography series, Englewood Cliffs, NJ, Prentice-Hall.

Tilton, J. E. (1977) *The Future of Nonfuel Minerals*, Washington, DC, Brookings Institution.

Tinbergen, J. (co-ordinator) (1976) *Reshaping the International Order: A Report to the Club of Rome*, New York, E. P. Dutton.

Tinker, J. (1975) 'River pollution: the Midland dirty dozen', in Porteus *et al.* (eds) *Pollution: The Professionals and the Public*, Milton Keynes, Open University, 108–17.

Tivy, J. and O'Hare, G. (1981) *Human Impact on the Ecosystem*, Edinburgh, Oliver & Boyd.

Townroe, P. M. (1984) 'The changing economic environment for spatial policies in the Third World', *Geoforum*, 15(3), 335–47.

Tsuru, S. (1972) 'In place of GNP', in Sachs, I. (ed.) *Political Economy of Environment*, Paris, École Pratique des Hautes Études/Mouton, 11–26.

Tuan, Y.-F. (1974) *Topophilia: A Study of Environmental Perception, Attitudes and Values*, Englewood Cliffs, NJ, Prentice-Hall.

Tucker, R. (1975) 'Oil: the issue of American intervention', *Commentary*, 59, January, 21–31.

Turvey, R. (1963a) 'On divergence between social and private cost', *Economica*, 30, 309–13.

Turvey, R. (1963b) 'Present value versus internal rate of return: an essay on the theory of third best', *Economic Journal*, 73, 93–8.

Tyme, J. (1978) *Motorways versus Democracy*, London, Macmillan.

UK Department of the Environment (1978) *Pollution Control in Britain: How it Works*, 2nd edn, Pollution Paper No. 9, London, HMSO.

UK Government (1961) *Financial and Economic Obligations of Nationalized Industries*, Cmnd 1337, London, HMSO.

UK Government (1967) *Financial and Economic Obligations of Nationalized Industries*, Cmnd 3437, London, HMSO.

UK Government (Secretary of State for Energy) (1978) *Energy Policy: A Consultative Document*, Cmnd 7101, London, HMSO.

UK House of Lords, Select Committee on Science and Technology (1981) *Hazardous Waste Disposal*, vol. 1, London, HMSO.

UK Royal Commission on Environmental Pollution, (1976) *Air Pollution Control: An Integrated Approach*, Fifth Report, Cmd 6371, London, HMSO.

United Nations (1978) *Transnational Corporations in World Development*, New York, UN, 20 March.

United Nations Conference on Trade and Development (UNCTAD) (1982a) *Handbook of International Trade and Development Statistics, 1981 Supplement*, New York, UNCTAD.

UNCTAD (1982b) *Trade and Development Report*, New York, UNCTAD.

United Nations Economic Commission for Europe (1978) *Coal: 1985 and Beyond*, Oxford, Pergamon.

US Bureau of Mines (1974) *Recovery of Secondary Copper and Zinc in the United States*, Information Circular 8622, Washington, DC, US Department of the Interior.

US Congress (1974) *Outlook for Prices and Supplies of Industrial Raw Materials*, Hearings before the Subcommittee on Economic Growth of the Joint Economic Committee 93–2, Washington, DC, Government Printing Office.

US Council on Environmental Quality (1978) *Environmental Quality 1978*, Paper 25244, Council on Environmental Quality, Washington, DC, Government Printing Office.

US Council on Environmental Quality (1980) *Environmental Quality*, 1980 Annual Report, Washington, DC, Government Printing Office.

US Department of Health, Education, and Welfare (1969) *Guidelines for the Development of Air Quality Standards and Implementation Plans*, Washington, DC, NAPCA.

US Department of the Interior (annual) *Minerals Yearbook. Vol. 3, Area Reports International*, Bureau of Mines, Washington, DC, Government Printing Office.

US National Academy of Sciences (1975) *Mineral Resources and the Environment*, Committee on Mineral Resources and Environment, Washington, DC, NAS, February.

US National Academy of Sciences (1977a) *Decision-Making in the Environmental Protection Agency*, Report of the Environmental Studies Board, Commission on Natural Resources, Washington, DC, NAS/NRC.

US National Academy of Sciences (1977b) *Research and Development in the Environmental Protection Agency*, Report of the Research Assessment Committee, Commission on Natural Resources, Washington, DC, NAS/NRC.

US National Academy of Sciences (1978) *Technological Innovation and Forces for Change in the Mineral Industry*, Committee on Mineral Technology, Board on Mineral and Energy Resources, Commission on Natural Resources, Washington, DC, NAS.

US National Commission on Air Quality (1981) *To Breathe Clean Air*, Washington, DC, Government Printing Office.

US National Commission on Materials Policy (1973) *Material Needs and the Environment. Today and Tomorrow*, Final Report, Washington, DC, Government Printing Office.

US National Water Commission (1973) *Water Policies for the Future*, Washington, DC, Government Printing Office.

US President's Science Advisory Committee (1967) *World Food Problem Reports*, Pr 35.8:Sc 2/F73, Washington, DC, Government Printing Office.

Van Rensburg, W. C. J. and Bambrick, S. C. (1978) *The Economics of the World's Mineral Industries*, Johannesburg, McGraw-Hill.

Vaughan, W. J. and Russell, C. S. (1973) 'A residuals management model for the integrated iron and steel industry', paper presented at American Iron and Steel Institute Conference, Dekalb, Ill., April.

Vogt. D. U. (1983) *US Government International Barter*, Congressional Research Service, Library of Congress, Washington, DC.

Waddell, T. E. (1974) *The Economic Damages of Air Pollution*, Washington, DC, US Environmental Protection Agency.

Walker, M. and Storey, D. J. (1977) 'The "standards and price" approach to pollution control: problems of iteration', *Scandinavian Journal of Economics*, 79(1), 99–109.

Walker, R. and Storper, M. (1978) 'Erosion of the Clean Air Act of 1970: a study of the failure of government regulational planning', *Environmental Affairs*, 7, 189–257.

Wall, C. G., Wilson, D. C. and Jones, W. (1977) 'Optimal development of the North Sea's oil fields – the criticisms', *Energy Policy*, 5(4), December, 284–94.

Wandesforde-Smith, G. (1980a) 'Environmental impact assessment in Europe', in O'Riordan, T. and Turner, R. K. (eds) *Progress in Resource Management and Environmental Planning*, Vol. 2, Chichester, Wiley, 205–37.

Wandesforde-Smith, G. (1980b) 'Environmental impact assessment', in Bothe, M. (co-ordinator) *Trends in Environmental Policy and Law*, Berlin, Erich Schmidt Verlag, 101–30.

Ward, B. (1979) *Progress for a small planet*, London, Temple Smith.

Ward, B. and Dubos, R. (1972) *Only One Earth*, Harmondsworth, Penguin.

Warman, H. R. (1972) 'The future of oil', *Geographical Journal*, 138, pt 3, September, 287–97.

Warren, A. and Maizels, J. K. (1977) 'Ecological change and desertification', in *Desertification: Its Causes and Consequences*, UN Conference on Desertification, Oxford, Pergamon, 169–260.

Warren, K. (1966) 'Steel pricing and public policy', *Urban Studies*, 3(3), November, 185–99.

Warren, K. (1973) *Mineral Resources*, Problems in Modern Geography series, Newton Abbot, David & Charles.

Wathern, P. (1976) 'The role of impact statements in environmental planning in Britain', *International Journal of Environmental Studies*, 9, 165–8.

Webb, M. G. and Ricketts, M. J. (1980) *The Economics of Energy*, London, Macmillan.

Webb, M. G. and Woodfield, R. (1979) *Standards and Charges in the Control of Trade Effluent Discharges to Public Sewers*, Discussion Paper 43, Institute of Social and Economic Research, Department of Economics, University of York.

Weber, M. (1947) *The Theory of Social and Economic Organization*, New York, Macmillan.

Weisbrod, B. (1968) 'Income redistribution effects and benefit–cost analysis', in Chase, S. (ed.) *Problems in Public Expenditure Analysis*, Washington, DC, Brookings Institution.

Weisbrod, B. (1978) *Distributional Effects of Collective Goods: A Survey Approach*, Madison, Wis., University of Wisconsin Press.

Wenner, L. M. (1978) 'Pollution control: implementation alternatives', *Policy Analysis*, 4(1), 47–65.

Wertz, K. L. (1976) 'Economic factors influencing household production of refuse', *Journal of Environmental Economics and Management*, 2(4), 263–72.

West, R. and Foot, P. (1975) 'Anglesey: aluminium and oil', in Smith, P. J. (ed.) *The Politics of Physical Resources*, Harmondsworth, Penguin, 202–32.

White, G. F. (1942) *Human Adjustment to Floods: A Geographical Approach to the Flood Problem in the United States*, Research Paper 29, Department of Geography, University of Chicago.

White, G. F., Bradley, D. J. and White, A. U. (1972) *Drawers of Water: Domestic Water Use in East Africa*, Chicago, University of Chicago Press.

Whyte, A. V. and Burton, I. (1982) 'Perception of risks in Canada', in Burton, I., Foule, C. D. and McCullough, R. A. (eds) *Living with Risk: Environmental Risk Management in Canada*, Institute for Environmental Studies, University of Toronto, 39–69.

Wijntjes, I. W. C. (1974) 'Waste water and undue consumption in the Netherlands', in *Proceedings of Symposium on Waste Control*, London, Institution of Water Engineers.

Wilen, J. E. (1976) 'Common property resources and the dynamics of over-exploitation: the case of the North Pacific fur seal', Resources Paper No. 3, Research Programme on Natural Resource Utilization, Vancouver, University of British Columbia, September.

Williamson, J. G. (1965) 'Regional income inequality and the process of national development: a description of the patterns', *Economic Development and Cultural Change*, 13, 3–84.

Wilson, C. (ed.) (1970) *Man's Impact on the Global Environment: Assessments and Recommendations for Action*, Cambridge, Mass., MIT Press.

Wilson, L. O. (1981) 'Water: wins and losses', *State Government*, November, 4–6.

Wise, D. and Ross, T. B. (1964) *The Invisible Government*, New York, Random House.

Wolfinger, R. (1971) 'Nondecisions and the study of local politics', *American Political Science Review*, 65(4), December 1063–80.

Woodwell, G. M. (1978) 'The carbon dioxide question', Scientific American, 238 (1), January, 39–44.

Yandle, B. (1978) 'The emerging market in air pollution rights', *Regulation*, July–August, 21–9.

Young, O. R. (1980) *Resource Regimes: Natural Resources and Social Institutions*, Berkeley, Calif., University of California Press.

Young, O. R. (1981) *Natural Resources and the State: The Political Economy of Resource Management*, Berkeley, Calif., University of California Press.

Zimmermann, E. W. (1951) *World Resources and Industries*, rev. edn, New York, Harper.

Zysman, I. and Cohen, S. S. (1983) 'Double or nothing: open trade and competitive industry', *Foreign Affairs*, Summer, 1113–39.

Author index

Subject index

absorptive capacity, 15, 27–8, 267–70, 273
acid rain, 253, 401
additionality problem, 313, 314
adversorial system, 361–7
Africa, 248; climatic conditions, 233, 235
agency: administrative role, 349; bias, 387;
    bureaucratic infighting, 373; character,
    346; decision-making behaviour, 371,
    373; discretionary powers, 348;
    enforcement, 359; intervention, 356;
    management bias, 372; procedural
    rationality, 373; regulatory control, 359,
    361
agriculture: and environmental change,
    52–4; land availability, 26
airport noise, 286
Alaska, oil, 190, 196, 210, 308
Alberta (Canada), oil, 156, 204
Alcoa, 75, 109, 110
Algeria, 95t.
allocative efficiency, see efficiency economic
alternative values, 246, 254–6, 305
aluminium, see bauxite
ambient air standards, 367, 368
amenity value, 50
Anaconda, 76, 102, 108, 218
Anglo-American Corporation, 74, 138
antimony, 91
aquifers, see groundwater resources
Argentina, 217
artificial fertilizers, 236, 277
ASARCO v. EPA, 578; F.2d 319; D.C. Cir
    1978, 364
asbestos, 33t., 88, 345
assimilative capacity, see absorptive capacity
atmospheric change, 15, 233–5
Australia: aboriginal lands, 49; Agriculture
    and Mines Department, 374; bauxite, 96,
    97t., 167t., 170, 171, 207; coal, 104, 155,
    207, 216; Conservation Ministry, 2;
    Department of State Development, 374;
    Engineering and Water Supply
    Commission, 355, 374; Environmental
    Protection Authority, 373, 374; Forests
    Commission, 374; Gordon River, 248,

313; Green Ban Movement, 394n.; iron
ore, 100; irrigated agriculture subsidies,
306; labour conditions, 104; Melbourne
and Metropolitan Board of Works, 356,
373; mineral search, 57, 58, 61, 62, 67;
policy, taxation, 194; prices/pricing, 160,
168, 201; reservoirs, 342; Rivers and
Water Supply Commission, 355, 374;
Snowy River Authority, 14; Tasmania
Hydroelectric Commission, 248;
unaccounted water, 358
availability measures: renewable resources,
    25–8; stock resources, 15–25

Bahrain, 95t., 100
BASF, 210
basing-point system, see CIF pricing
bauxite: alumina, aluminium, 17t., 38, 43,
    94ff., 113, 127, 128 (consumption, 2, 78,
    79, 82f., 101; non-bauxite ores, 37, 66,
    75); costs and prices, 128, 145, 164, 188;
    countertrade, 192; market structure, 43,
    109, 122, 127, 140, 145, 167t., 170;
    production, 33t., 88, 93, 96, 97t.;
    resources and reserves, 31, 32f., 33t., 35;
    security concerns, 166; substitution,
    difficulty of, 167t.
Belgium, 220, 222n.
Best Practicable Means (BPM), 368–70
biodegradable wastes, 28, 268–9
bio-geochemical cycles, 3, 50, 405
biological capacity, 25
Biological Oxygen Demand (BOD), 262,
    299
biological simplification, 3, 14, 25, 27, 233,
    405
blue whales, 298n.
Bolivia, 95, 95t., 187, 188, 191, 201, 217
Botswana: coal, 58, 105
Brazil, 63, 100, 170, 218, 307
British National Oil Corporation (BNOC),
    208ff., 216
British Petroleum (BP), 33, 75, 113, 114t.,
    159, 161, 164
British Steel Corp. (BSC), 112, 114